Politics, Self, and Society

POLITICS, SELF, AND SOCIETY

A Theme and Variations

HEINZ EULAU

HARVARD UNIVERSITY PRESS
Cambridge, Massachusetts
London, England   1986

LIBRARY OF CONGRESS CATALOGING-IN-PUBLICATION DATA

Eulau, Heinz, 1915–
  Politics, self, and society.

  Bibliography: p.
  Includes index.
  1. Political science.   2. Political science—Research.
I. Title.
JA74.E883   1986   320   85-17585
ISBN 0-674-68760-4 (alk. paper)

For the next generation

Lauren and Paul
Peter and Kendra

Preface

THERE IS no simple way to describe and give a single name to the *program* of research begun about thirty years ago and represented in this book. By program I mean a set of more or less interdependent intellectual concerns and scientific puzzles embedded over the decades in a variety of empirical, and I hope theory-driven, research *projects*. While the particular projects were diverse, though mainly dealing with the political behavior of citizens in the mass and of legislative elites at the state and local levels of government, they all turned, in one way or another, on the relationship between the individual person and society in its many manifestations. How to deal with this relationship contextually and developmentally as it appears in politics is the pervasive theme of the program that emerged from the several research projects in which I was and still am involved.

A program is not a plan. It need not be something clearly and self-consciously "laid out" from the beginning. The operative condition for its emergence is invariably a particular project. And a project is usually stimulated by contemporary enthusiasms in the wider research community and by momentary opportunities—funding and personnel resources, availability of data, occasions for scholarly presentation and publication. Insofar as there is a latent program, however, it is likely to be carried over, expanded, revised, and refined from one project to the next. The particular projects, then, though topically diverse, in fact constitute a fundamentally thematic program of research.

As a whole the program that, in retrospect, seems to have guided the several research projects is not identifiable as an integrated theory or as a consistent methodology. This is the reason why it cannot be easily named. A program of research, as I understand it, is always in some stage or phase of development because it is necessarily defined by the intellectual puzzles encountered in research projects and does not have some immanent purpose or goal that can be clearly stated at the outset. Moreover, an evolving program itself tends to be contextually defined. The program to which the chapters in this book attest evolved in the context of what has been variously called the behavioral "revolution" (Truman, 1955), "mood" (Dahl, 1961b), "persuasion" (Eulau, 1963a), "movement" (Easton, 1965b), and even "renaissance" (Eulau, 1969b)—a hodgepodge of theoretical and methodological approaches to the study of politics. The catholicity, eclecticism, and open-endedness of this context left individual investigators ample room to chart their own courses. Latter-day attempts to characterize "behavioralism" as a concerted ideology or monolithic movement, especially one married to philosophical positivism, have largely failed to demonstrate any essence.

Efforts of one sort or another at systematic theorizing, methodological rigor, and empirical verification there were; but the new dispensation in the study of politics was accompanied, at least in the cases of its leading practitioners, by a healthy dose of sheer imagination that defied paradigmatic closure. And much as there tended to be an emphasis on continuity, cumulation, replication, extension, and revision—what Martin Landau once called "due process of inquiry"—the behavioral enterprise in its diverse manifestations was above all guided by scientific puzzles whose solution required imagination rather than iteration and reiteration.

The puzzles that in my own case came to shape and dominate the research program would center on the problem of how to deal in theory and method with the relationship between self and society as it unfolds in and through politics. Some of these puzzles are expressed, if all too succinctly, in the titles of the book's parts and chapters, although they cut across the projects subsumed under a given title. It cannot be otherwise for, as Max Weber (1946b, p. 136) once put it, "ideas occur to us when they please, not when it pleases us." It is also by no means clear which of the puzzles are major and which minor. That is the reason why "A Theme and Variations" appears as the book's subtitle.

I have become indebted through the years to many colleagues and students with whom I collaborated; to several institutions with which I was or am affiliated; to both private and public foundations that funded my research; to editors and publishers who were always helpful; and last, but not least, to Cleo, who, skilled though she is in the ways of therapeutic psychiatry, could cure my compulsive involvement in political science only at the edges, for which I am nonetheless grateful. I must also thank here the anonymous referee for Harvard University Press whose judicious comments made me aware of the theme's many variations. I hope that in the Credits I have given their due to all of those whose help and support I enjoyed. If not, only my poor memory can be blamed.

Contents

Introduction   1

I. OF INDIVIDUAL AND GROUP   17

1. The Behavioral Persuasion in Politics   19
2. Units and Levels of Analysis   76
3. Closing the Micro-Macro Gap   92
4. Multilevel Methods and Comparative Analysis   107

II. OF STRUCTURE AND LINKAGE   127

5. Class and Party as Interactive Role Systems   129
6. Conflict and the Network of Legislative Roles   179
7. Law and Politics: Professional Convergence   205
8. Polarity in Representational Federalism   222

III. OF CONTEXT AND CONFIGURATION   239

9. Configurative Analysis: Some Philosophical
   Underpinnings   241
10. The Informal Organization of Small Decision-Making
    Groups   258
11. Political Matrix and Political Representation   277
12. Life Space and Social Networks as Political Contexts   300

IV. OF EMERGENCE AND DEVELOPMENT   325

13. Developmental Analysis and Constructs   327
14. Policy Maps and Policy Outcomes: A Developmental
    Analysis   340

15. A Quasi-Longitudinal, Quasi-Experimental Design for
      Comparative Policy Analysis   367
16. Representation as an Emergent: A Situational Analysis   392

V. OF CHOICE AND DECISION   415

17. Logics of Rationality in Unanimous Decision Making   417
18. Decisional Models in Political Contexts   439
19. Components of Representational Responsiveness   452
20. Skill Revolution and Consultative Commonwealth   470

     Notes   503
     References   534
     Credits   557
     Index   561

Politics, Self, and Society

Introduction

POLITICS is neither "who gets what, when, how" (Lasswell, 1936) nor "the authoritative allocation of values for a society" (Easton, 1953). Whatever politics is about, I do not think that it can be so conveniently captured by one-tailed definitions that, like Lasswell's, point toward the individual person or, like Easton's, toward the social whole. This is not to say that by defining politics as they do, Lasswell is revealed as a methodological individualist or Easton as a methodological holist. On the contrary, both are eminently sensitive to the dualism of self and society, of individual and group, of part and whole that, paradoxically, their definitions seem to suggest but also obscure. How to cope with this dualism, in its "false" and "true" formulations, is the major theme in my own research program and its various projects.

I have never found it necessary to define "politics" in my research. In fact, when I tried or used the definitions of others, I did not find any one definition particularly useful. In various chapters of this book I suggest what politics means to me—ruling and obeying, persuading and resisting, promising and disappointing, coercing and freeing, compromising and claiming, deceiving and unmasking, negotiating and bargaining, neglecting and representing, fearing and fighting, and so on and so forth. As all of these behaviors and others go on, simultaneously in varying degrees, it seems to me that politics can be thought of as a "field," *gestalt,* or configuration of tendencies-in-tension, often opposed to but also attracting each other like the poles of a magnetic field.

An analogy can be deceptive but may also be useful. If one thinks of politics as a "field of action," it appears as a continuum of political actors—at one pole the individual person with needs, preferences, demands, expectations, attitudes, and identifications; at the other pole the social whole in its manifold manifestations, from the small group like the nuclear family to giant organizations like the modern nation-state or the transnational business corporation. Politics, therefore, as a field of action is always characterized by individualistic and collectivistic tendencies that make it an enormously complex set of social events and processes that cannot be harnessed by definitions centered in either one or the other pole of the self-and-society continuum. Self and society are inextricably intertwined in political life.

As a false formulation, the dualism of individual and society was the hallmark of nineteenth-century social thought. There was said to be an "inevitable conflict" between the individual and society, and social philosophers came down on one or the other side of the presumed conflict—"collectivists" (ironically both conservatives and socialists) generally asserting the primacy of "community" or "social class" to which the individual is or should be subservient; and "individualists" (again ironically both liberals and anarchists) affirming the primacy of the individual person whose worth and dignity are or should be the goals of organized society. The theme, as in Herbert Spencer's *The Man versus the State* (1884), appeared in many disguises in political theory and social science. On the academic front, the dualism gave rise to and seemed to justify the development of specialized disciplines—anthropology dealing with "whole" societies, sociology with social institutions, and psychology with the individual person. Economics, ironically, while making individualistic assumptions about human behavior, dealt in impersonal aggregates like markets, regulated by supply, demand, and prices, or in large-scale processes like production, consumption, and trade. The new late-nineteenth-century political science stressed governmental constitutions and institutions, remaining rooted in the traditional disciplines of law, history, and ethics.

When, after World War II, for reasons that need not be detailed here,[1] an interdisciplinary enthusiasm came to engulf the social sciences, political science was especially receptive.[2] Having for so long been concerned with institutions, the interdisciplinary orientation in political science meant primarily the discovery of the individual, as citizen in the mass or member of an elite, as a unit of observation and analysis.[3] But, inadvertently, the methodological individualism accompanying this discovery threatened to revive the false dualism of individual and society. Behavioralists, reducing all collective phenomena to the individual person, or trying to do so, tended to throw out the baby with the bathwater: by denying the "reality" of collective phenomena like groups or organizations, they widened the gap between individual and society as an intellectual problem when attention once more turned to the description and explanation of collectivities and their actions. As Donald E. Stokes (1966, p. 1) later commented, "It is in a way remarkable that the antithesis between institutions and behavior should ever have seemed plausible to political scientists. Perhaps it never did to the keenest observers."

It was in the intellectual environment of the controversy between behavioralists and institutionalists that I first came to tackle the dualism of individual and society in empirical research. In 1952 and 1956 the national election studies conducted by the Survey Research Center, University of Michigan, included a series of rather unusual questions about social class in the United States.[4] Given the opportunity to use the data stemming from these and other questions, I found that there was no adequate microanalytic theory to guide the explanation and interpretation of the individual-level data in social class terms—except, perhaps, a rather "soft" ego psychology, on the one hand, and a rather "hard" social-deterministic sociology, on the other hand.[5] But I also found that political scientists and sociologists had long speculated, in rather global language, about the relationship between the American class structure and the American two-party system, with at times contradictory, at times indeterminate, conclusions. The task of my research (perhaps I should say puzzle, for there was no ready-at-hand solution) was to make the bits and pieces of the individual-level survey data germane to the received macroanalytic wisdom about the relationship between social classes and the parties in American politics, in turn to bring macroanalytic discourse to bear on the analysis and interpretation of the data, and to do so with concepts that might be helpful in closing what I sensed to be the "micro-macro gap" (Chapter 5).

The concept of "social role" seemed especially appropriate for this purpose, for it intrinsically refers to the relationship between "self and other" that makes an individual into a "social" being (a *persona*) and links him or her, through an intricate set of multiple and reciprocal relations, to society and the "world" (*mundus*). The various meanings and uses of the concept need not be explicated here, for that is done in Chapters 1, 5, and 6 as well as elsewhere in this book. Suffice it to say that today, with the power of hindsight, the notion of class and party as "role systems" that are interactive by virtue of individuals taking relevant roles in both strikes me as a somewhat tortured exercise in conceptualization. The same idea could have been expressed in simpler formulation. At the time, however, it seemed to be at least one way to cope with the problem of closing the micro-macro gap, at least in theoretical discourse. The analysis probably did also not escape what later came to be recognized as the "individualistic fallacy" (Scheuch, 1969), but it seemed to be helpful in shedding at least some empirical light, if only by way of inference, on the issue of political cleavage and consensus in American society.

The class-and-party project was a "secondary analysis," as the data were used for a theoretical purpose for which they were not intended. Although I continue to think of role as absolutely necessary in all social and political analysis that seeks to come to grips with the problem of the relationship between self and society at either the microlevel or macrolevel of analysis, I would not now use the concept of "system" in this connection. But in the 1950s this concept was in the intellectual air of the social sciences, largely stimulated by the pervasive influence of the interdisciplinarily oriented sociologist Talcott Parsons (1951; also Parsons and Shils, 1951). As with so many other concepts in the social sciences, "system" faded away in the 1970s, is more often than not used loosely and metaphorically, and does not seem particularly useful in an era in which causal models of political phenomena increasingly stress their nonrecursive, reciprocal, and developmental character.

An opportunity to formulate a research project in role terms directly was given in 1955 by a collaborative and comparative study of four American state legislatures sponsored by the Committee on Political Behavior of the Social Science Research Council. While my collaborators and I from the outset of the project self-consciously rejected what we considered the false dualism between political behavior and institution, we yet faced a number of theoretical and methodological puzzles, especially how the individual-level data collected by way of interviews with legislators could be brought to bear on an understanding of the legislature as an institution. Rejecting the behavior-versus-institution dualism was one thing; to show how an institution like the legislature can be described and explained in behavioral terms—as structured pattern of behavior—was another. Moreover, we were interested in clarifying the linkage of the institution to other ("external") collectivities like interest groups and electoral constituencies.[6] And there was a need for theoretical formulations that would make genuine comparison across partly similar, partly different "legislative systems" possible (Eulau, 1962c).

Despite its macroanalytic formulations, the great bulk of the analysis presented in *The Legislative System* (Wahlke et al., 1962) remained at the level of the individual. What was being compared across the four states were individual legislators and not four legislative bodies or eight legislative houses as institutional units (see Chapter 4). Only in the final section of the study (Chapter 6) was the attempt made, by way of rather stylized aggregational procedures and measures, to delineate the eight chambers as institutionalized role structures. This was done for the purpose of showing the effect of these structures on the legislature as an institution designed to crystallize, clarify, and resolve societywide political conflicts. It was in this connection that I first used the concept of "network" rather than system, though it was used not to trace connections between and among individual actors but rather to specify the links between legislators' self-defined roles that would permit one to speak of the total set of links as a role *structure*.

The value of role as a variable is not in its predictive capacity as an *explanans* of individual political behavior but in its uses as a tool in the morphology of institutions. It is important to point this out because role analysis is sometimes said to "fail" as an avenue to prediction. This is an inappropriate charge. Insofar as roles are identified in responses to interview questions, they are better treated as indicators of what premises may underlie a person's behavior or what cultural understandings a person may have of a given role. They cannot possibly be used to predict a specific act: they are not "causes" of the act, though they can give the act meaning. And insofar as roles are inferred from actual behavior, logic requires that they not be used to predict that behavior. Critics of role analysis who think in causal terms may have been confused by the fact that, when the class-and-party and legislative studies were done, much of the analytic discourse was in functional rather than structural terms. Like the concept of system, "function" was in the intellectual air of the social sciences and especially in the study of comparative politics. Causal analysis as it is now understood and practiced was still beyond the horizon.

This is quite apparent in the attempt made to explain an empirically observed lack of difference in the attitudes, perceptions, and roles of state legislators who are lawyers, on the one hand, and who have other private occupations, on the other hand. As reported in Chapter 7, the findings were puzzling because it had been assumed that lawyers would bring to their legislative position some attributes unique to their profession and would therefore differ from legislators who are not lawyers. Yet, in general, the research findings showed this not to be the case. How could it be explained? The individual-level data seemed to point to a convergence of law and politics as professions in that politicians perform many societal functions traditionally performed by lawyers, but lawyers also seem to perform functions associated with various roles of the politician. This macroanalytic and functional explanation, however, also implied the emergence of a structural isomorphism between the two professions that, at the microanalytic level, constrains the attitudes, perceptions, and roles taken by lawyer and nonlawyer legislators. The developmental convergence hypothesis seemed to fit the facts at both the microlevel and macrolevel of analysis and seemed helpful in overcoming the dualism between self (private occupation) and society (public profession).

These and related experiences in research attempts to make individual-level data relevant to the more traditional institutional and organizational interests of political science came together, if only in a very tentative way, in *The Behavioral Persuasion in Politics* (1963; here abridged as Chapter 1). The book has struck some readers as a somewhat didactic introduction to the interdisciplinary orientation in the study of political behavior, as it was meant to be, but also, for this very reason, seems to have been misinterpreted at times as a "to a certain extent 'official' representation of the behavioralistic standpoint" (Falter, 1982, p. 44).[7] In fact, rather than being anything "official" (because there was no "office" to be held in the kaleidoscopic enterprise of behavioral studies), I had characterized the book as a "personal document."[8]

Writing *The Behavioral Persuasion* sensitized me further to what increasingly came to be called the "level-of-analysis problem." The problem had been poignantly articulated by J. David Singer (1961, p. 77) when he wrote that "we have roamed up and down the ladder of organizational complexity with remarkable abandon, focusing upon the total system, international organizations, regions, coalitions, extra-national associations, nations, domestic pressure groups, social classes, elites, and individuals as the needs of the moment required." My essay raised but hardly answered some questions concerning units and levels of analysis. Rather than being a "behavioral manifesto," as it has also been called, the essay distinguished between empirical and theoretical units of analysis, challenged the reductionist bias of radical behavioralism, and thus served to jettison an overly individualistic view of political behavior.[9] Moreover, it seemed to me that the individual person should be treated, from the beginning, as a "social self," as being defined in his or her individuality by the presence of another individual, that is, as a role taker; and it also seemed to me that groups, from the dyad to the nation-state, can and should be used as units of analysis in their own right, as "units of action." The papers here included as Chapters 2, 3, and 4, originally published in 1969, 1971, and 1977, respectively, are elaborations of the theme and its variations.

The puzzling questions concerning units and levels of analysis had not been systematically addressed in empirical research on politics at the time when *The Behavioral Persuasion* was written, though in sociology the work of the "Columbia School," led by Paul F. Lazarsfeld, had made significant contributions, as is acknowledged in many chapters of this book. Three questions in particular required answers. First, while role analysis made more realistic assumptions, it seemed to me, about interpersonal relationships and political behavior than the emerging "rational choice" approaches derived from economics, could these be directly observed and measured by way of survey research? They were observed and measured in small-group experimental research long practiced in social psychology, and this work was brought to the attention of political scientists by Sidney Verba (1961); but with a few exceptions (for instance, Barber, 1966), political scientists, being real-world oriented, eschewed laboratory experimentation. Second, if groups of all sizes are "real" units of action with "laws of composition" of their own not replicable at the microlevel of observation and analysis, could individual-level data be so combined with group-level information that research could proceed at the level of the group and make the group as well as the individuals composing it the *explananda*? And third, was there a principle of thinking that could be helpful in rejecting the false dualism between self and society or individual and group, yet also be helpful in explaining the emergence of new group-level phenomena (such as unanimity in voting situations or professional convergence of law and politics) out of the existence of true but not necessarily contradictory opposites?

A project on the politics of city councils, begun at about the time when *The Behavioral Persuasion* was written, came to address the first question (among others, of course). The institution of the city council, being a small legislative body, recommended itself as a research site because in survey research one has to rely on the observations of the members of a group about their own and others' behavior. Reliable and verifiable observations about interpersonal relations are possible only in small groups. Moreover, one needs a fairly large number of groups if one wishes to avoid the inferential hazards of the case study. The council project interview schedule included a battery of sociometric questions that, as shown in Chapter 10, permitted us to develop a typology of "decisional structures." These structures could then be used to explain other group properties of the councils as well as the behavior of individual members of the council.[10]

Once the group had been constructed (or, rather, reconstructed) from the individual-level sociometric and other observations, it was possible to address the second question about combining data from different levels of social complexity. It seemed viable, indeed, to aggregate other individual-level data in one way or another, depending on the hypothesized group properties involved, as well as attribute to the group certain features of its environment, such as the city's demographic or policy-developmental characteristics. This allowed us to conduct analysis exclusively at the group level, making over eighty councils rather than their several hundred members the "object units" of comparison. *Labyrinths of Democracy: Adaptations, Linkages, Representation, and Policies in Urban Politics* (Eulau and Prewitt, 1973) was the capstone of the project.

The third question, concerning false dualistic formulations in political theory, was raised in connection with an essay on polarity in representational federalism (Chapter 8). Federalism as a mode of territorial organization has been traditionally concerned with the relationship between parts and whole, and a dualistic interpretation had been at least one prominent theme in its analysis until, in the mid-1960s, Morton Grodzins (1966) proposed what he called the "marble cake" model of federalism, as against the level-related notion of "layer cake." In fact, he rejected the notion that a federal structure (at least in the American situation) represented a "level problem" at all. But one must not confuse the descriptive use of the concept of level with its analytic use. In the analytic perspective, federal structures do involve a level problem because the puzzle of parts and whole remains. At issue is whether this dualism creates "contradictions" that cannot exist side by side but must be resolved, as the Hegelian solution has it, by thesis as one side of the dualism and antithesis as the other side, ultimately giving rise to a synthesis that is altogether new and has nothing in common with either side of the original dualism.

The Hegelian dialectic, now largely in the custody of Marxists, has always seemed to me a kind of miracle approach to social phenomena. I have never been able to understand why, in the real world, *logically* contradictory opposites cannot coexist in continuing tension, for the real world is not a matter of logic but of empirics and pragmatics. I found a suggestive lead in the work of the "rationalist" but also quite pragmatic philosopher Morris Cohen, who had formulated a "principle of polarity" (Eulau, 1963b). The prime exemplar of a true dualism that need not go away for logical reasons is, as I suggested earlier, the poles of a magnetic field that are held together by mutual attraction even as they pull in opposite directions. The polarity principle, Cohen suggested, is applicable to human behavior and organization. It points to the possibility that a dualism, like that between self and society or between part and whole, is not necessarily a "contradiction." It assumes a "field" in which seemingly opposed forces, like the "interests" of the individual and those of society (or any group to which the individual belongs), can coexist precisely because the tension between them, as in politics, is an immanent feature of their existence.

Many of the concerns connected with the theme of self and society and the level-of-analysis problem had been anticipated and articulated by Harold D. Lasswell, in my view the only true immortal among twentieth-century political scientists. Two essays in this book (Chapters 9 and 13) attest to Lasswell's influence on my own work. This is not to say that I was not influenced by other social theorists who, in one way or another, tried to cope with the problem of the relationship between self and society and the analytic problems it creates—notably the philosopher George Herbert Mead, whose work steered me to role analysis; the social psychologist Kurt Lewin, whose topological "field theory" I found attractive; the German sociologist Georg Simmel, whose studies of dyads are really the foundation of social network analysis; the sociologist Talcott Parsons, whose theory of "social action" impressed me even before I really understood it;

or the sociologist Everett C. Hughes, whose down-to-earth investigations on "men and their work" always reminded me of staying close to the empirical evidence. All of these social scientists rejected the individual-*versus*-society dualism and had a comprehensive vision of the relationship between self and society, even though their vocabularies differed a great deal. But Mead's notion of the "generalized other," Lewin's concept of "life space," Parsons' "pattern variables," Hughes's "career perspective," Cohen's "polarity principle," and, last but not least, Lasswell's concept of "configuration" all point to the same thing.

Just what is meant by "configurational analysis" is difficult to grasp and the mode of analysis involved seems elusive. As Chapters 9 and 13 suggest, the dominant concern of configurational analysis is with a set of intellectual puzzles that stem from the evident coexistence of opposites—individual *and* society, elite *and* mass, part *and* whole, fact *and* value, uniqueness *and* regularity, existence *and* emergence, and so on. Lasswell saw these opposites as intrinsically interdependent, as when he spoke of the state as a "manifold of events" or of past, present, and future as constituting a single perspective. A configuration of phenomena arises out of the interplay of current context *and* simultaneous development, and it involves both interlevel relationships among diverse units of political action as well as multiple and reciprocal causation. As a result of my long association with Lasswell and immersion in his terminology, many of his concepts, sometimes reformulated to make them operational and serviceable, found their way into my own empirical work.

Among other things, the configurative analysis of human or social behavior postulates that the most significant factor in the environment of a person is another person, and that the most significant factor in the environment of a group is another group. The data transformation strategy used in the council project, while capable of constructing group properties out of its members' behaviors, cannot really observe, except in its sociometric components, how a group may *emerge* out of interpersonal interactions. The notion of being able actually to trace interpersonal relations beyond the dyad by way of network analysis had been present in my thinking, I noted earlier, in the effort to construct a legislature as a network of roles, but this had been an analytic and somewhat metaphorical rather than observational enterprise. The desirability of social network analysis as a means of studying a person's interpersonal environment and the social *context* created by these interactions had also suggested itself in the theoretical essay on "representational federalism" (Chapter 8), but to carry out such a project requires considerable resources for collecting appropriate data.

Social network analysis, in a generic sense, is concerned with the structure of interactions or communications among individual persons of a particular role type (family members, friends, neighbors, work associates, political leaders, and so on) but also among individuals playing different roles. As a technique it may of course also be used in the study of intergroup relations. Many methods are associated with network analysis, ranging from the anthropological field investigator's own observations or informant knowledge of who interacts with whom to rigorous mathematical techniques. More recently network analysis has been introduced into empirical survey research on the mass public by way of snowball sampling of respondents. Network analysis thus is attractive because it contributes to correcting the overindividualized view of social and political behavior as a form of economic behavior promoted by rational choice theory.

I came to pursue network analysis in two projects, both initiated in the late 1970s. One, still incomplete, is in fact a field study of "representational federalism" in a local community in which I am engaged in collaboration with James H. Kuklinski. In barest outline, this is a study of citizen participation and representation in the local and national domains of the federal system as seen or experienced generally and in a variety of policy situations. The study's theoretical unit of analysis is the ego-centered or ego-anchored social network as it penetrates into social groups and the political order. The objective is to understand representation at different levels of the federal system not merely as a one-to-one relationship between the citizen and a single representative or representative body, but as a web or network of both direct and indirect relations. A two-stage snowball sample interview strategy served the purpose of collecting the data. Although the project's field phase has been completed, no results were available for inclusion in this book (for further description of the project, see Eulau, 1984b).

A second project in the network mode was made possible by the inclusion of a set of relevant questions in the September wave of the 1980 National Election Study (Chapter 12). Unfortunately a national probability sample survey cannot determine whether and to what extent sociometric choices are reciprocated. Nevertheless, by examining the respondents' "life space"— the places where they spend most of their waking hours, on the one hand, and their ego-centered social networks in the residential neighborhood, on the other hand—the study could make the important distinction between a social *environment* and a social *context*. In contrast to environment, context emerges out of a person's social interactions. The study concludes that while the neighborhood seems to be of minor importance as a political environment, social relations among particular neighbors make for an interpersonal context that has an impact on political behavior.

More often than not, political behavior research is cross-sectional, cutting into the sequence of time at some moment in time, rather than historical or longitudinal. Of course, in the early years of behavioral research in political science there was no history to study because no time-series data were available. Panel studies, involving interviews with the same respondents, are costly and difficult to conduct, though a few have been done in electoral research and studies of political socialization (for instance, Jennings and Niemi, 1981). Yet it is obvious that all social phenomena are developmental, each present moment in time being linked to some past and some future. What Lasswell called "developmental constructs" (Chapter 13) are stylized images of past, present, and future whose formulation is not simply a matter of extrapolation from trends or tendencies. How the notions of emergence and development could be fruitfully applied in cross-sectional research was a question raised in several of the projects, if only in part successfully answered in analysis.

Public policy, a macrophenomenon, is almost by definition an emergent and ever-changing outcome of political processes at both the macrolevel *and* microlevel of social complexity. Its scientific study in the developmental perspective is relatively rare, and this despite the popularity of "policy studies" from the middle 1960s on. My own stance toward most of these studies has been critical. This is not the place to expound my critical view of the "new public policy," which, I once wrote, "is the old public administration in a refurbished wardrobe."[11] What continues to bother me most is that most policy analysis, as practiced, ignores Lasswell's (1951c, p. 8) long-ago injunction that "the basic emphasis of the policy approach is [should be] upon the fundamental problems of man in society, rather than on the topical issues of the moment."

The city council project applied developmental notions of policy and sought to observe policy as an emergent at both the macro- and microlevels of analysis. The study reported in Chapter 14 was in part stimulated by my critical reaction to a mode of policy research announcing results that seemed rather incredible. In the first place, some investigators had found that what they called policies, as measured by governmental budget data, correlated only with economic, not with political, variables. Rather than blaming their rather crude political—mostly structural—data and mode of analysis, they concluded that politics seemed to have little to do with public policy. This struck me as rather absurd. We therefore designed questions in the council project's survey that would yield data giving insight into what we called decision makers' "policy maps"—the configuration of problem perceptions, issue positions, and images of the future they brought into the political process. Second, it seemed to me that the prevailing correlational procedures in analyzing budget data were too itemistic to capture the notion of policy as a developmental phenomenon. By observing the ebb and flow of budget allocations in broad areas of policy over a ten-year period, we created, at the macrolevel, comprehensive "developmental policy profiles" for the cities that, the analysis demonstrated, were not unrelated to the decision makers' policy maps, whether observed at the individual or group levels.

In a follow-up study (Chapter 15) I set out to test the validity of the policy development model by a variety of procedures—a quasi-longitudinal analysis that made temporal assumptions about the developmental stage of the city as an environment, though measurement was made at only one point in time (stage in urbanization); a quasi-experimental analysis that would permit comparison across the hypothetical time periods; a causal analysis of the relationship between policy development, urbanization, and different constellations of council policy maps; and analysis of the policy maps themselves by way of examination of distributions at the margins, certain "conjunctive patterns" in the policy map's components, correlational procedures, and finally some alternative predictive models. It seemed to me that confronting the data in a multimethodological manner of this sort is more interesting and conducive to theorizing than feeding dozens of perhaps relevant and often irrelevant variables into a mindless regression analysis, especially if the data are not measured and calibrated in terms of the same values (like dollars in economic analysis) that can be meaningfully interpreted.

How to use both individual and group data in a configurative, that is, both contextual and developmental, manner was the methodological challenge in a study that made use of data collected in the famous research on political representation in Congress by Miller and Stokes (Chapter 16). For this purpose a rich portfolio of data was available: data stemming from interviews with a longitudinal panel of citizens interviewed in 1956, 1958, and 1960; data from interviews with congressmen in 1958, at the midpoint of the panel; and congressional roll-call votes in the intervening Congresses. These unusual data sets permitted us to examine, by way of what we called a "situational analysis," the emergence or nonemergence of representation as a collective phenomenon—a possibility suggested by the political theorist Hanna F. Pitkin (1967).[12] In this study a typology of "representational situations"—called pervasive, conflictual, dissonant, and blocked—was constructed from the individual-level data, and turnover analysis at the macrolevel was used to validate the procedure and observe the effect of the representational situations on changes in congressmen's perceptions of their constituencies' policy preferences at two "moments" in time.

All of these studies were made in terms of group-level or macropolitical constructs—some static like the analyses of decision making or representational structures in Chapters 10 and 11; some dynamic, made possible partly by the availability of time-series data, partly by assumptions about stages of development, like the "policy studies" in Chapters 14 and 15, or the analysis of representational situations in Chapter 16. All involved modes of data transformation of individual attributes into the collective properties of groups—most of them action units capable of making collective decisions—or, as in Chapter 16, aggregates. All depended for information on both "objective" data and the testimony of the actors involved about interpersonal relations or group behavior. All of the studies are, therefore, "problematic" in that they depend on the plausibility of assumptions made about the relationship between self and society or individual person and group. Nevertheless, I believe that some progress was made in understanding just what transpires when individuals meet; form groups, networks, or aggregates; and, as groups or as individuals in networks or aggregates, make political decisions and public policy.

How decisions are made in and by groups that are action units like legislative bodies rather than aggregates of such units, like electorates, and how outcomes of decision making come about should vary with institutional arrangements and norms. In the years when I did most of the work represented in this book, the decision-making process at the group level was of particular interest to analysts of administrative or hierarchical organizations who were inspired by the ideas of Herbert A. Simon (1957c). As my own research was on legislatures, the question arose whether organizational decision-making theory is germane in these quite different institutional settings. In general I came to feel that it is not, though increasing bureaucratization of legislatures may make it so (Cooper, 1977; Cooper and Mackenzie, 1981; Hedlund, 1984). Organizational analysts assume, I suggest in Chapter 18, that organizations have goals or purposes independent of those of their members. An organizational decision is a kind of event or series of events, then, that intervenes and mediates between available means and well-defined ends. This organizational model is analytically attractive because it allows for rationality in the decision-making process. But it has always seemed to me that a truly legislative body is not an organization as specified by the model. Legislatures are action units with rules and norms to conduct their business, but the "business" itself does not have goals or purposes in the sense in which these are treated in organizational theory. Only the legislature's individual members have goals and purposes. Insofar as legislatures are autonomous, it is their peculiar "function" to identify and reconcile the divergent goals of their members, of those whom the members represent, and of other "interested parties" (the executive establishment, interest groups, and so on), as well as to make these divergent goals palatable as societal goals. Rather than being givens, therefore, the goals and purposes expressed in legislation are "discovered" in the course of the representational processes that are at the core of the legislature's operations as a collective decision-making body.

While I only hint at this problem and, in doing so, express some doubt as to the utility of rational choice theory in understanding, *at their own level,* complex political decision-making institutions like legislatures, I respect the importance of relevant inquiry if it can be made empirically operational. Indeed, in recent years it has seemed to me that this whole matter can best be investigated at the intervening structural level of legislative committees (Eulau, 1984a; Eulau and McCluggage, 1984), and I think that the work of an institutionally inclined choice theorist like Kenneth A. Shepsle (1978) is in this connection enormously important.

My own sole outing into rationality as a behavioral assumption in the study of legislative decision making came in an attempt to explain the common yet puzzling phenomenon of unanimity in situations in which conflictual outcomes should be expected but none occur. What evidence there was for how and why this collective phenomenon comes about suggested that it does so in many disguises. On the one hand, it seems to depend on the ways in which individual and group interests or utilities are rationally articulated—whether in a specific or diffuse manner; on the other hand, it also seems to depend on the mode of how decisions are handled—whether in a consensual, political, or ministerial style. It appeared that, in the intersections of these cognitive-motivational and behavioral patterns, six quite different forms of unanimity may be latent in decision-making situations: when articulation of individual interest is specific but of group interest is diffuse, the (perhaps paradoxical) result occurs that unanimity is what I called false, projected, and injunctive, depending on the mode of decision handling. The result seems to be paradoxical because in these situations individual rationality is presumably dominant. But when individual interest is diffuse and group interest is specific in articulation (and when, presumably, individual rationality is minimal), the resultant form of unanimity is what I called ancestral, bargained, and functional, again depending on the mode of decision handling. Karl Mannheim (1948) had distinguished between functional (means oriented) and substantial (ends oriented) rationality, but that other modes of "rationality" may be involved in unanimous decision making was something of a surprise. The evidence I gave for the six types of unanimity was only by way of exemplars and had no viability as proof. But the types suggested that there are also different modes of rationality—satisfying, procedural, and maximizing—as well as of prerationality, counterrationality, and irrationality.

That rationality in citizens' political choices may vary with the level of complexity at which the object or target of choice is assessed appeared in a puzzle usually credited to Richard F. Fenno. "On the evidence," he observed in a celebrated essay (1975, p. 278), "we seem to approve of our legislators a good deal more than we do our legislature. And therein hangs something of a puzzle. If our congressmen are so good, how can our Congress be so bad? If it is the individuals that make up the institution, why should there be such a disparity in our judgments?" Fenno himself, in the down-to-earth manner of his political ethnography, gave some reasons for the existence of the puzzle he had identified. The "puzzle of representation" dealt with in Chapter 19 does not refer to exactly the same puzzle that Fenno had in mind but is related to it. Some aspects of representation, interpreted as responsiveness, may be individual-level properties of the legislature, like "service responsiveness"; others may be group-level properties, like "policy responsiveness"; and others may be in between, like "allocation responsiveness."

Modern rationality as a mode of authoritative decision making at the societal level, as against what Max Weber identified as the charismatic and traditional modes, is increasingly in the custody of the professions. Chapter 20 shows the influence of Weber's prognosis of societal rationalization and bureaucratization but more the influence of Lasswell's substantive and methodological suggestions.[13] The essay originated in my preparations for a research project on the professions and politics with a number of doctoral candidates for whom I sought to define a common frame of reference. Research, it had become clear to me, in order to avoid the charge of triviality, can best proceed in the framework of a "developmental construct"—like the construct of the "consultative commonwealth" proposed here—that will orient particular inquiries and give them meaningful direction because a developmental construct, in contrast to a scientific theory, explicitly incorporates the nonscientific end values of research. The construct of the consultative commonwealth was also intended to counter the view of those who, largely by way of simple extrapolation of current trends, envisaged contemporary society as inevitably moving toward bureaucratic and possibly autocratic control by the engineers (Veblen, 1921), managers (Burnham, 1941), technologists (Ellul, 1967), and other highly skilled professionals.[14] While I concede the political influence that the skilled professions already have and are even more likely to have in the future, I noted countervailing tendencies, both internal and external to the professions themselves (as the polarity principle would lead one to expect). Rather than seeing the strength of the professions in their "power," a concept I like to eschew whenever possible because of its ambiguity, I see it in their tendency to make "consultation" a new mode of political interaction and behavior. At the same time, however, the construct of the consultative commonwealth posits that other modes of politics—democratic, representational, pluralistic, and bureaucratic—will for the time being and in the foreseeable future continue to shape societal governance. The professions are of course particularly interesting "institutions" in the micro-macro perspective because their "members," much more than the members of other institutions or organizations, are eminently sensitive to all of those with whom they interact—their clients, their colleagues, the groups they serve, and, above all, the profession itself as a segment of the larger society whose interests the profession "represents."

Diverse as the projects reported on in the chapters of this book may appear to be, then, they are held together by the common thread of the theoretical, methodological, and substantive issues that arise out of the self-and-society dualism with its many variations and possible fallacies. As a whole they constitute a research program, only dimly perceived at the outset but increasingly self-conscious as the years went by. I conclude with two of my favorite quotations from two of my favorite social scientists whose work is very much unlike my own. "If you want to understand what a science is," the anthropologist Clifford Geertz (1973, p. 5) once wrote, "you should look in the first instance not at its theories or its findings, and certainly not at what its apologists say about it; you should look at what the practitioners of it do." And there is the observation of the sociologist Everett C. Hughes (1958, p. 63) that "subjectively, a career is the moving perspective in which the person sees his life as a whole and interprets the meaning of his various attributes, actions, and the things which happen to him. This perspective is not absolutely fixed either as to points of view, direction, or destination."

ONE

Of Individual

and Group

The Behavioral Persuasion

in Politics

THE ROOT is man. I do not think it is possible to say anything meaningful about the governance of man without talking about the political behavior of man—his acts, goals, drives, feelings, beliefs, commitments, and values. Man has built nations and empires, created customs and institutions, invented symbols and constitutions, made wars, revolutions, and peace. Politics is the study of why man finds it necessary or desirable to build government, of how he adapts government to his changing needs or demands, of how and why he decides on public policies. Politics is concerned with the conditions and consequences of human action.

A study of politics that leaves man out of its equations is a rather barren politics. Yet such is the propensity of man that he can consider his own creations without measuring them by himself. Political science has studied political ideas, values, customs, symbols, institutions, processes, and policies without reference to their creators for a long time, but the cost has been high. I do not want to belabor this point. I mention it only because the simple question I want to ask—Why do people behave politically as they do?—seems to have explosive consequences for the study of politics.

Just what *is* political behavior? I have been asked the question many times, by students as well as by colleagues, in and out of political science. Is it a field of study, a method, or an approach? If it is a field, it must have content and boundaries. If it is a method, it must have rules. If it is an approach, it must have direction. I cannot say that it is one or the other. It is none of them alone, and it is not all of them together.

The difficulty begins with definitions. If taken seriously, definitions commit and constrain. They orient their user and reveal his orientation. They are embedded in his concepts and his theorizing, are a source of sense, but also of nonsense. So it is with "political behavior." For some years now, I have asked my students to define politics. Politics, they tell me, has something to do with government, power, policy, influence, decision making, conflict, or even "authoritative allocation of values." I cannot but marvel at such ingenuity. But when I ask just what people *do* when they *act* in ways to which these concepts presumably refer, there is a perplexing silence.

I wonder why this is so. Evidently we are the victims of our own sophistication. However, this is not the case when I ask what people do when they practice religion. The students will tell me that a man is religious when he prays, attends mass, sings hymns, listens to sermons, immerses himself in baptismal water, senses the presence of divine guidance, abides by the Ten Commandments, or believes in immortality. And there is no trouble with economics: man produces, buys, sells, exchanges, invests, speculates, consumes, and so on. Not so with politics. When I suggest that what makes man's behavior political is that he rules and obeys, persuades and compromises, promises and bargains, coerces and represents, fights and fears, my students are baffled.

Certainly these verbs do not define politics. But they do refer to those of man's acts that are at the core of what we study when we talk about politics. And there are many more. If human behavior is the root of politics, these verbs are more useful in studying political things than are nouns like authority, power, conflict, allocation, or government. It seems to me that behavior comes first: ruling before government, obeying before authority, voting before decision, demanding before value, fearing before sanction, coercing before power, persuading before influence, fighting before conflict, believing before ideology.

But such is the enterprise, whether we call it politics, political study, or political science, that we must define first and then sense, rather than sense first and then define. As we define politics, so we behave politically, for our definitions of politics are themselves evidence of political behavior. They determine, at least in part, what we observe and how we explain it. It would be silly to deny that man in politics, being a defining animal, has various definitions of politics. I am merely pleading that in seeking, clarifying, or refining our definitions of politics, we turn to what men do as they behave politically and why they do it.

The behavioral persuasion in politics is concerned with what man does politically and the meanings he attaches to his behavior. Politics asks about ancient traditions and grandiose designs, about complex systems and intricate processes, about fearful atrocities and superb achievements. But as an eminent physicist once remarked, it is a subject "more difficult than physics." The physical scientist seems to have one great advantage over the political scientist: whatever meanings he may give his objects of study, they do not talk back to him. Atoms, neutrons, or electrons do not care how they are defined; political actors do mind. This is precisely why a political science that ignores man is necessarily a very incomplete science of politics.

However, the fact that men give meanings to their behavior need not be a handicap. On the contrary, what men say about themselves and others represents an infinitely rich source of information about behavior. And the meanings that people give to politics are appropriate data for scientific analysis because people behave in terms of these meanings. These meanings do not provide the scientific observer with the kind of definitions he needs in order to proceed with his investigation. He must develop his own. But, whatever definition of politics the political scientist adopts, it cannot be altogether arbitrary. It must itself be "meaningful" in terms of the meanings that men give to their political behavior. The meanings that political actors, consciously or unconsciously, attribute to their own behavior are of interest to the political scientist because they provide a partial explanation of the motives for that behavior.

A rigorous approach to definitions alone will not spur progress in the study of politics. In fact it might well stifle in infancy a new approach that requires not definitional rigor so much as new categories and concepts with which to explore new terrain. In returning to the behavior of man as the root of politics, the behavioral persuasion has opened up new possibilities in the study of politics. If this has created more problems than it has solved, including those of definition, it is more of a challenge than a defeat.

The return to the behavior of man as the root of politics is a new beginning. For in dealing with the conditions and consequences of man's political conduct, the behavioral persuasion represents an attempt, by modern modes of analysis, to fulfill the quest for political knowledge begun by the classical political theorists. The behavioral persuasion in politics, as I understand it, is a return to the bases of man's political experience in which the great theorists of the past found nurture and sustenance. What makes the so-called classic theories great are their sometimes explicit, sometimes implicit assumptions about human nature in politics. The theoretical constructions of the polity found in the classics are "peopled systems," model communities based on some notion of how men behave politically as they do and why, in addition to frequently being prescriptions for how men ought to behave in the polity and what the polity should look like.

It may seem startling that the behavioral persuasion is a continuation of the classical tradition of political inquiry. On the face of things, the discontinuities between the ancient and the modern approaches seem more significant than the continuities. Modern modes of thought, criteria of validation, and methods of investigation are so radically different that the link between classical political theory and the behavioral persuasion would seem to be rather tenuous. A good deal depends on what one means by continuity. If one means continued textual exegesis of the classics as if they were sacred writings, the behavioral persuasion does, in fact, make a radical break with political theory. But if by continuity one means, as I think one should, the application of modes of thought and techniques of inquiry appropriate to one's own time to the political problems of the time, then the behavioral persuasion is a direct and genuine descendant of the classical tradition. The classical theorists, from Plato to Mill and beyond, in building their models of the polity, sought to bring to political inquiry the best conceptual and technical tools at their disposal. The modern political scientists who adapt the new theories, methods, and techniques of behavioral science to political analysis are in the tradition of the classical political theorists.

It is the function of science to understand and interpret the world, not to change it. A science of politics that deserves its name must build from the bottom up by asking simple questions that can, in principle, be answered; it cannot be built from the top down by asking questions that, one has reason to suspect, cannot be answered at all, at least not by the methods of science. An empirical discipline is built by the slow, modest, and piecemeal cumulation of relevant theories and data. The great issues of politics, such as the conditions and consequences of freedom, justice, or authority, are admittedly significant topics, but they are topics compounded with a strong dose of metaphysical discourse. I do not think that they are beyond the reach of behavioral investigation, but before they can be tackled, the groundwork must be laid.

In returning to man as the root of politics, the behavioral persuasion reveals itself as a "radical" orientation in the study of politics. What the behavioral persuasion challenges in the traditional study of politics, if it challenges anything, is the comfortable assumption that theory is the same thing as knowledge. But theory is only a tool. If it is a tool, like all tools it tends periodically to wear out and need replacement. The behavioral persuasion in politics is both theoretical and empirical in direction. Its radicalism stems from the conviction that a proposition may be worn out when, on being tested, it can be disproved.

Behavioral Approaches

The behavioral persuasion in politics has more than one approach, and there are many voices that speak in its name. But they all have in common a commitment to the study of man as the root of things political or, to put it more technically, to the individual person as the empirical unit of analysis.

Therefore I think it is legitimate to speak of "the behavioral persuasion in politics." However, these voices do not necessarily speak in harmony. Behavioral researchers on politics differ among themselves in many respects: in their conception of the nature of knowledge and its relation to reality; in their formulation of the theoretical propositions guiding their investigations; in the choice of strategies and tactics of research; in their selection of problems and research sites; and, finally, in their appraisal of their own role in relation to the world of politics they are studying. It seems preferable, therefore, to speak of behavioral approaches when it comes to technical matters.

UNITS OF ANALYSIS

The political behavior of the individual person is the central and crucial empirical datum of behavioral approaches to politics. This does not mean that research is restricted to the individual person as the theoretical focus of investigation. Indeed, most behavioral researchers are not concerned with the individual political actor as such. A small group, an organization, a community, an elite, a mass movement, or a nation may be the focus of behavioral inquiry; and events, structures, functions, processes, or relations may serve as categories of behavioral analysis.

This does not imply that behavioral investigations dealing with units other than the individual actor "reduce" them to the level of the person. We mean different things when we say that an individual behaves in certain ways and that a nation behaves in certain ways. To speak of a nation's behavior in the conduct of its foreign relations is, quite clearly, to engage in metaphorical license, just as we do when we speak of the behavior of stars, storms, or stocks. The use of metaphors for the purpose of analogical thinking is feasible and even necessary, but it can be dangerous because it may make for a good deal of distortion. It is only too easy to speak of a group's or nation's behavior *as if* it were identical with that of the individual person. Consequently, inferences drawn from such practice are likely to be false.

The political behaviorist concentrates on the behavior of individuals whose interactions and transactions make up collective behavior, even if he is concerned with describing and explaining the actions of groups, organizations, or other large collectivities. Groups, organizations, or nations have no independent status apart from the conduct of the individuals who are related by behaving toward each other in certain ways. This does not mean that groups, organizations, or other formations are not "real" and meaningful units with structural properties and functions of their own. They certainly are. In fact, the great bulk of problems interesting the political scientist concerns the actions of such groups. But, from the behavioral perspective, these collectivities exist and behave the way they do only insofar as the people composing them act in certain ways.

In choosing the individual as his empirical unit of analysis, the political behaviorist does not deny the reality of institutions. He merely asserts that institutions do not and cannot exist physically apart from the persons who inhabit them. The political behaviorist is likely to stress this point because institutional and behavioral analyses have, at times, been treated as if they were opposed to each other. They are not. Political institutions are never more or less different from the patterns of behavior of the people who create them or the regularities of their actions. If this be so, institutions can and must be analyzed in terms of the behavior of their molecular units, the individuals whose relations to each other and behavior toward each other are more or less rigidly structured. We speak of "the opinion of a court," "the decision of a bureau," or "the action of a legislature" only because speaking in "institutional language" brings the great complexity of political life into a manageable perspective. Behind the opinions, decisions, or actions of institutions are human beings who decide, who have opinions, and who act.

Political institutions are behavior systems or systems of action. Just as they cannot exist apart from the persons whose behavior brings them into existence, so political behavior cannot exist apart from the network of interpersonal relations that we call political institutions. Presumably, political behavior has much in common with other types of social behavior, but the adjective "political" warns us that the behavior in question represents a special case. The difference is in the institutional setting of the behavior.

An attempt is sometimes made to define what seems to be political in behavior by identifying some special characteristic assumed to be inherent in behavior. For instance, interpersonal behavior constituting relations of "power" or "conflict" have been singled out as the characteristic features of *political* behavior. But power or conflict relations, though admittedly frequent in politics, are not exclusively political aspects of interpersonal actions. We can speak meaningfully of "economic power" or "racial conflict" without attributing peculiarly political characteristics to them. Otherwise almost all behavior could be called political and the term would lose whatever discriminatory meaning it may have. This does not mean that power or conflict cannot serve as useful organizing concepts. But I doubt that they are useful in specifying the context of political behavior.

Political seems to be a residual rather than a generic term. This makes it futile to search for characteristic features of political behavior apart from an institutional or situational environment that shapes and patterns certain types of interpersonal relations. Political behavior is invariably "electoral behavior," "administrative behavior," "judicial behavior," and so on. Or it is behavior relevant to the making of public policies, training the young in the norms of a group or society, recruiting people into political institutions, and so on. There may be great similarities in the behavior of legislators, bureaucrats, judges, party leaders, and statesmen, or of agitators and revolutionaries, or of voters and nonvoters. But our concern is with those characteristics of behavior that we expect to occur because the behavior is relevant to the institutional political order of which it is a part. For this reason, political behavior is not a separate field of investigation. It would be meaningless to treat political behavior apart from situational conditions in the political order. Institutions differ in the structure of relations between individuals and the functions they perform in the political order. Interinstitutional analysis of political behavior can reveal, therefore, significant similarities or differences in political relations, between groups as much as between individuals. This type of analysis does not take politics out of behavior. On the contrary, it makes possible the behavioral analysis of institutions.

The relationship between institution and behavior is necessarily complementary. Institutional arrangements, norms, or functions express behavioral patterns that have been stabilized through the passage of time. In turn, current behavior is necessarily circumscribed and directed by the past patterns we call institutions. If the student of political behavior ignores the institutional sphere of politics, he imposes a severe handicap on his research. He sometimes does so because institutional parameters are so taken for granted that their consequences for current political behavior seem minimal. A great deal of political behavior can be accounted for most economically by viewing it as a result of institutional prescriptions. To take a very simple and obvious case, electoral behavior is certainly influenced by the institutionalized characteristics of the party system or the representational system. Decision-making behavior in a legislative body differs from decision-making behavior in a bureaucratic setting. Behavior involving authority relationships is likely to be different in differently structured formal institutions: let us say, in a police department or a social welfare agency. No political behaviorist would be so foolish as to ignore the institutional environment in which behavior occurs, even though his main focus of attention is the individual actor rather than the institution.

LEVELS OF ANALYSIS

The behavioral persuasion in politics is not readily contained by the conventional, academic subject-matter boundaries. Its interdisciplinary orientation stems, at least initially, from the very simple assumption that man's political behavior is only one aspect of his total behavior, and by no means a very important aspect. This does not mean that we can know about political behavior only if we know about all aspects of human behavior. Just what aspects of political and other behavior are to be related in a particular investigation depend on the problem at hand and the theoretical scheme for solving it. Being interdisciplinary means selecting from what is known about man those of his behavioral characteristics investigated by different behavioral sciences that seem to be especially relevant to the solution of political problems.

If one were to rank the reasons for the interdisciplinary orientation of the behavioral persuasion in politics, the borderline character of political behavior problems would have to be given high priority. The kind of problems that the political behaviorist formulates cannot be solved without recourse to the concepts and theories of the several behavioral sciences. Problems have a way of spilling over disciplinary boundaries. Attempts to solve them in terms of a single discipline's concerns are likely to be partial and unsatisfactory. For instance, elections cannot be studied fruitfully on the assumption that the voter is a rationally calculating, self-interested political man. But one need not assume the opposite and deny the rational interests of the voter as a family man, a wage earner, or a church member. The question of how and why the voter decides as he does cannot be answered by abstracting his behavior in the voting booth from his total experience. His loyalties to family or class, his identifications with group or party, his career demands and expectations, his cultural milieu, and even his personality may have to be taken into account. The interdisciplinary orientation prevents neglect of the wider context in which political behavior takes place. It calls attention to the possible effects of social, cultural, and personal factors that, on the face of things, are not political as such.

This formulation may give the impression that what is political in behavior can somehow be separated out of what is social, cultural, and personal. Actually, what we call social, cultural, and personal pervades all behavior, including political behavior. Only for the purpose of inquiry do we think of what is social but not political, cultural but not political, or personal but not political as analytically distinct. It is more appropriate, therefore, to speak of levels of analysis—the social, cultural, and personal levels—on which political behavior may be examined. A configurative analysis of political behavior cannot ignore any one of these levels, although a problem may be more effectively treated on one level than on another.

The study of political behavior is concerned with the acts, attitudes, preferences, and expectations of man in political contexts. But there is little reason to assume that his behavior in politics is basically different from his behavior in other contexts. People who do not participate in the social life of their community or in voluntary associations are also likely to be politically apathetic. The problem of the union leader seeking a maximum of concessions at the bargaining table does not seem to differ significantly from the problem of the legislator seeking a maximum of advantages for his district.

Similarities in behavior sensitize the observer to critical differences, once institutional contexts are varied. For instance, superficially viewed, the behavior of a bureaucrat in a public agency appears to be very similar to the behavior of his opposite number in a private organization. Much bureaucratic behavior can be explained in terms of generic characteristics that stem from structural similarities of different institutional settings. But there are differences of a personal or social nature that cannot be ignored. A bureaucrat working for a public agency may be quite differently motivated and have different career expectations than the bureaucrat working for a private firm, with determinable consequences for the organization of which each is a member. Or the fact that the public bureaucrat's actions are more likely to be scrutinized by legislators than the private bureaucrat's actions by stockholders may have behavioral consequences that only interdisciplinary inquiry, with a focus on different institutions, can harness.

An interdisciplinary orientation has value quite apart from its usefulness in a particular research situation. It points to the level of analysis on which research may be conducted most fruitfully. It saves the researcher from formulating particularistic hypotheses where generic ones may be more appropriate. It suggests to him the feasibility of controlling different institutional contexts in order to identify similar behavioral patterns, or of controlling behavioral patterns in order to examine their effects in different contexts.

Even if political problems and patterns of political behavior were totally different from problems and behavioral patterns in other contexts, theoretical formulations concerning human behavior are unlikely to coexist in splendid isolation. Theory found useful in one context will sooner or later fertilize investigations in other contexts. A theory's viability is best judged by its range of interdisciplinary applicability. If it contributes to the explanation of behavior in many different settings, political as well as nonpolitical, the knowledge gained will be the more significant. A theory that explains more rather than less variance is preferable. For this reason, the behavioral researcher in politics is forever on the lookout for theoretical models developed in the other social sciences. If they apply to his own problems, he can be all the more certain that his work deals with a significant problem.

How far one should go along interdisciplinary routes depends largely on the particular research problem. Many problems in politics can be dealt with without recourse to theoretical propositions or empirical findings of other disciplines. A politician's attitudes toward constituents are likely to vary with the degree of competition in the district where he stands for election. The more competitive his district, the more likely it is that he will be accessible to conflicting interest groups, that he will seek to mediate political conflicts in terms of his appraisal of the relative strength of competing groups, and that he will try to explain his conduct in a way that will antagonize as few groups as possible. It would be most uneconomical and, in fact, expendable to seek an explanation of such behavior on the level of the politician's personality. It would contribute little, if anything, to the problem of why politicians from competitive areas behave differently from politicians in noncompetitive areas.

On the other hand, one might pose this problem: are men who seek public office in a competitive political environment different in their personalities from those who seek office in a noncompetitive arena? In other words, does competition attract a different manner of man than noncompetition? Just what is it that makes some men cherish and others avoid political battle? Answers to these questions would require the investigation of political attitudes in terms of personality.

The behavioral persuasion in politics has been especially criticized in this connection and charged with "reductionism": that is, that an interdisciplinary orientation inevitably reduces the political to the social, cultural, or personal; that the political is taken out of political behavior. I believe that it is not reduction but rather expansion of political relevance that marks the behavioral approaches. Just what *is* political in behavior cannot be determined by criteria of immanence. If it can be shown that explanation of things political is possible, if not necessary, on different levels of analysis, including that of personality, the product of inquiry is not the result of reduction but rather of expansion of the political arena.

THEORY AND RESEARCH

The goal is the explanation of why people behave politically as they do, and why, as a result, political processes and systems function as they do. There are many methods of explanation. Whatever they are, they require theorizing activity.

What behavioral researchers do when they theorize—by which I mean, very tentatively, when they seek explanations of why people behave politically as they do—differs a good deal from one to the other. At one pole, some would probably say that they are not theorizing at all but only describing what they see. They deceive themselves, for what they see depends on how they see it, and how they see it depends on images in their minds. These images may be very diffuse and hardly deserve being called theories. But they orient the observer, innocent as he may be of what he is doing and though he may be protesting his theoretical innocence. His work will not get him very far because, paradoxically, his very attempt at *only* describing what he sees is suspect. Did he really see all that could have been seen? What did he leave out? How did he order what he saw? Did this really follow that? On the whole, the overwhelming number of modern behavioral practitioners no longer plead theoretical innocence. More often than not, they seek to make explicit the assumptions and ways of thought that guide their work. This is what I have called theorizing activity, though it does not necessarily entail theory.

At the other pole are the builders of logically consistent, deductive models of political systems, perhaps theories in the sense that "formal truth" is the distinctive content of the theorizing activity in which model builders are engaged. There are not many practitioners of the behavioral persuasion in politics who believe that this is the right time for constructing logically closed, deductive pictures of the political process. I have a great deal of admiration for these efforts, but I must confess to some doubt, not because I question the practicality of formal models or their suggestiveness in research, but because I suspect they are not as theoretically pure as their creators insist. At least I cannot avoid the impression that behind the most formal models there lurk quite explicit images of empirical reality. In other words, just as pure empiricism has theoretical components, so pure theory has empirical components.

In my opinion, this is not a drawback. Out of this duality stems the conviction that, in the present stage of development, theory and research are necessarily interdependent, that theoretical questions must be stated in operational terms for the purpose of fruitful empirical research, and that, in turn, empirical findings should be brought to bear on the theoretical formulation of political problems. This does not deny the possibility of a high road to theorizing about political behavior and a low road. But I am not sure, if there are two roads, which is high and which is low, and I have a hunch that there are many roads in between that are more immediately viable. This is why it seems most feasible to attack the problems of political behavior research on as broad a theoretical front as possible. Whatever the weight given to one or another, it seems quite clear that if the condition of mutual interdependence between theory and research is to be achieved, some theorizing activity must precede empirical work if the latter is to be theoretically relevant, just as empirical considerations must enter theoretical efforts if hypotheses are to be tested by research.

Admittedly, theorizing must be sufficiently independent of operations to give it room in which to breathe. But it cannot be altogether separate from empirical research. One might argue, as some have, that the condition of interdependence is met, and that a theory's operational utility can be appraised, if it can be tested *in principle* by reference to empirical data. This may be a necessary condition, but it is not a sufficient one. I cannot see how one can *know* in principle whether theoretical propositions are testable. For theory is not the same thing as knowledge. Whatever the plausibility or validity of theoretical speculations, they are not truths, full, partial, or probable. Theory is not knowledge but a tool on the road to knowledge, just as facts are not knowledge but only the raw materials to be molded, through theorizing activity, into statements acceptable as probably true, or at least not false, because they have been tested in the process of empirical research. It is the theoretician's responsibility not only to assert that his propositions can be tested, but to suggest *how* they can be tested. But not even this makes his propositions empirical, though it may make them empirically relevant.

Commitment to the interdependence of theory and research and to solving the problem of the relationship between special political and general behavioral theory has some interesting consequences for the development of political theory. The behavioral persuasion, in attending to both theory and empirical research, may bring the definitional game that has been played so long in the study of politics to some conclusion. However one defines politics, as the process of allocating values authoritatively, as a competitive struggle for power, as collective decision making for the community, and so on, each definition includes more or less well articulated premises, postulates, or assumptions about politics. One function of behavioral theorizing, certainly, is to lay bare these premises. Another is to clarify the empirical referents of concepts, definitions, and propositions. The notion that politics is an allocative process, for instance, assumes that resources are scarce and may be used in alternative ways. It further assumes that the goals are multiple and that, therefore, choices must be made among them. This definition also implies that political actors will disagree over what ends are preferable, as well as over how resources are to be allocated in order to achieve agreed-on ends.

It is evident that we are dealing here not simply with a primitive definition of politics, but with a model of the political process borrowed from economics. On closer inspection, it also appears that the model makes assumptions about human rationality and about the behavior of rational human beings. And rational behavior is assumed to maximize preferred returns on the investment of resources.

In subjecting the model to empirical testing, behavioral research alone can give the theorist some feeling as to what concept or definition is operationally useful and what is not. The specification of the empirical data needed to test a model may reveal which of rival definitions are serviceable and which are expendable. It may show which definitions are empirically, and possibly theoretically, necessary for each other. For instance, I have found in some of my own work on legislative behavior and institutions that a definition of politics as allocation is insufficient unless it is implemented by some definition of politics as conflictual behavior.

Moving simultaneously along both theoretical and empirical paths quickly sensitizes the investigator to what definitions, concepts, or even theories are expendable. For instance, it seems that power, long accepted as the central organizing concept of politics, is rapidly losing ground from the point of view of its operational, if not analytical, utility. Paradoxically, it is losing ground not because it is abused, as it has been by some theoreticians in the past, but because it is used. For as it is used in empirical research, it proves increasingly useless. In recent years there has been much research interest in community power structures and in power relations in legislative bodies. We now have a large body of research findings as to how, presumably, decisions are made in villages, cities, and metropolitan areas, as well as in legislatures. The more research there is, the more elusive the concept of power shows itself to be.

Theorizing depends on the problem to be solved. Some problems are more complex than others, and more may be known about simpler ones. Political behavior involved in the conduct of foreign policies in the international arena is probably more complex than behavior in the domestic legislative process, and the latter is likely to be more complex than a person's behavior in the voting booth. How complexity is handled depends, in turn, on the model used in the analysis of empirical data. Although a simple model is preferable to a complicated one, it is also likely to be empirically more exclusive. On the other hand, an elaborate model or conceptual scheme may make the problem technically unmanageable. Just as the analysis of only two variables that are theoretically linked in rather simple propositions may not explain very much, a comprehensive scheme of a potentially all-inclusive range may defy the practicalities of research. The most feasible alternative is to deal with modest propositions that require simultaneous manipulation of only a few variables, but to do so in a larger conceptual system that, although it cannot be tested directly, serves the very useful purpose of guiding an investigation and giving it theoretical significance.

Considerations of this kind have some further consequences for the development of behavioral theory in connection with problems of varying degrees of complexity. The more complex the empirical problem with which the research is dealing, the more difficult access to relevant behavioral data is likely to be, and the more need there will be for theoretical exploration on high levels of generality. On the other hand, the less complex the empirical problem, the easier the collection of relevant data and the less incentive to theorize. Therefore theoretical formulations will be very specific and of relatively low generality. This makes plausible the theoretical unevenness of behavioral research in different, substantive areas of political science. In recent years the behavioral persuasion has generated a considerable body of theoretical work of high generality in the study of international politics, but it has so far produced little *hard* empirical research. On the other hand, empirical studies of electoral behavior are abundant, but this research has been limited to testing very modest propositions of low theoretical generality, and no comprehensive theory of the electoral process has as yet been formulated.

It does not seem very fruitful to specify what a behavioral science of politics might look like "in the end" because science is an ongoing endeavor that has no end. In general, the behavioral persuasion tries to develop rigorous research designs and to apply precise methods of analysis to political behavior problems. In its methodological orientation it is concerned with problems of experimental or post facto design, reliability of instruments, criteria of validation, and other features of scientific procedure. Its function, as I see it, is to produce reliable propositions about politics by reducing error, which involves the invention of appropriate tactics of research, and by measuring error that remains through the application of relevant statistical techniques. As limited as the present success of the behavioral scientific enterprise in politics may be, the alternatives are even less satisfactory.

The discriminating feature of the behavioral persuasion in politics is, above all, its sensitivity to error in its observations of politics and its suspicion of a priori formulated, universal "truths." It proceeds in terms of contingencies and probabilities, rather than in terms of certainties and verities. It represents an attitude of mind, a persuasion as I have called it, that takes nothing for granted and accepts as valid only the results of its inquiries when it would be unreasonable to assume that they can be explained solely by the operation of chance. This is a difficult standard to live by, perhaps more difficult in politics than in other fields of human action. For in politics as in physics and metaphysics, man looks for certainty but must settle for probability.

The Social Matrix

Not all of man's manifold social relations are politically relevant, but enough are to suggest that we pay attention to the social matrix of political behavior. Otherwise political description and explanation may be readily distorted or seriously misinterpreted. A person deeply involved in politics may be dealt with exclusively from the political point of view, or a person who is not involved very much may be treated as if he were totally alienated from the political arena. The elite and mass models of contemporary political society come close to making assumptions of this kind about political behavior. Neither image is likely to do justice to political reality. Political man, unlike some other models of man, is not an abstraction but is socially related to other men in a variety of ways that make him a total human being.

The analysis of political behavior can best proceed, therefore, by locating man as a political actor in the social matrix of interpersonal relations. The notion of a matrix implies that human behavior, including political action, consists of interactions and transactions that orient people toward each other, making them mutually responsive. I find the concept of "role" most useful to capture these relations, but it is the web of all of man's interpersonal relations, the social matrix, that gives behavior, including political behavior, its characteristic structure.

It is convenient to think of this structure in terms of a vertical and a horizontal dimension. The vertical dimension consists of man's group relations and can be analyzed in terms of the concept of "group" broadly interpreted to include all interpersonal collectivities. The horizontal dimension consists of those differentiating strata that define the upper and lower limits of either interpersonal or intergroup contacts. Role, group, and strata, then, will serve as conceptual building blocks of the social matrix.

ROLE AS A BASIC UNIT

In its simplest form, political behavior, like all social behavior, involves a relationship between at least two human beings. It is impossible to conceive of political behavior on the part of a person that does not have direct, indirect, or symbolic consequences for another person. The most suitable concept for analyzing a relationship between at least two actors and for determining the political relevance of the behavior characteristic of the relationship is "role," for we are interested not in all of a person's behavior but only in that aspect which is relevant to a political relationship.

The concept of role is familiar to most people. We speak of the father's role, and the teacher's role, the minister's role, the judge's role, and so on. What we mean in all of these instances is that a person is identified by his role and that, in interpersonal relations activating the role, he behaves, will behave, or should behave in certain ways. In looking at man's social behavior or judging it, we do so in a frame of reference in which his role is critical. If we do not know a person's role, his behavior appears to be enigmatic. But a child ringing a doorbell is unlikely to be mistaken for a political "doorbell ringer." Political behavior, then, is always conduct in the performance of a political role.

Role can be used as a conceptual tool on all three levels of behavioral analysis: the social, the cultural, and the personal. It is a concept generic to all the social sciences. On the social level, it invites inquiry into the structure of the interaction, connection, or bond that constitutes a relationship. On the cultural level, it calls attention to the norms, expectations, rights, and duties that sanction the maintenance of the relationship and attendant behavioral patterns. And on the personal level, it alerts research to the idiosyncratic definitions of the role held by different actors in the relationship. Role is clearly a concept consistent with the analytic objective of the behavioral sciences. It lays bare the *inter*relatedness and *inter*dependence of people.

On the social level, many of the most immediate interactions can be analyzed in terms of polar roles: husband implies wife; student implies teacher; priest implies communicant; leader implies follower; representative implies constituent, and so on. The behavior of one actor in the relationship is meaningful only insofar as it affects the behavior of the other actor or is in response to the other's behavior. Whatever other acts a representative may perform, for instance, only those in the performance of his constituent relationships are of immediate interest in political behavior analysis. I say of immediate interest because, in actuality, no single relationship is isolated from other social relationships in which the partners to the focal relationship are likely to be involved.

Many relationships are not structured by unipolar roles alone. In most cases a role is at the core of several other roles, making for a network of roles that can be very complex. A legislator is "colleague" to his fellow legislators, "representative" to his constituents, "friend" (or "enemy") to lobbyists, "follower" to his party leaders, "informant" to the press, and so on. Whatever role is taken, simultaneously or seriatim, what emerges is a very intricate structure of relations in which one role is implicated in several other roles.

Some roles are more directly related to each other than are other roles. For instance, the roles of husband and father or legislator and representative are intimately connected. Other roles may be less so. The existence and degree of their mutual implication are always subject to empirical determination. The legislator's role as a lawmaker is less likely to be related to his role as a parent than it is to his occupational role as, say, an insurance agent. This does not mean that the parent role is altogether irrelevant in his legislative behavior. A legislator with children attending public schools is probably more interested in school problems than a legislator who is a bachelor.

On the cultural level, role refers to those expectations of a normative sort that actors in a relationship entertain concerning each other's behavior. These are the rights and duties that give both form and content to the relationship. A relationship can be maintained only as long as the participants are in agreement as to what each actor must or must not do in the performance of his role. If there is disagreement over what kind of behavior should be expected, the relationship is likely to disintegrate.

Expectations that define roles and give direction to the behavior of actors in a role relationship are cultural in two ways. People do not continuously define and redefine their mutual relations and expectations. If a relationship had to be defined anew with each interaction, or if expectations had to be elaborated with every new encounter, stable social life would be impossible. In fact, most of the crucial role relationships are well defined. They are well defined because expectations are widely shared and transmitted through time. There is, then, a broad cultural consensus as to what the rights and duties pertaining to social roles are, and there is consensus on the sanctions available to participants in a relationship if behavior should violate agreed-on norms.

Precisely because role expectations may be widely shared and relatively permanent, they give stability to the relationship. Role relationships thus make for stable patterns of behavior and minimize what would otherwise have to be considered arbitrary behavior. Understanding a role means that we know how a person should behave and what he should do in the performance of a role. This includes knowledge of probable sanctions and thus makes accurate prediction in social relations possible. The ability to predict another's behavior, always, of course, within the limits set by expectations and on the assumption that the behavior will agree with the role, permits the partners in a role relationship to shape their own conduct in anticipation of the other's reactions.

Role analysis aids in discriminating between norms for behavior and actual performance of a role. It may be argued that the best way to identify a man's role is to see how he actually behaves. A role, it would seem, is best reconstructed from performance. But this procedure, apparently so objective, ignores an important aspect of behavior, its meaning. The same bit of action may have different meanings for different actors (and, of course, different observers). Meanings are important in politics because politics is eminently concerned with the consequences of behavior. These consequences require evaluation. Roles as normative expectations of an actor himself concerning his conduct or of others provide meaningful criteria of evaluation that would otherwise remain quite arbitrary. For this reason, the distinction between the normative and behavioral components of a role is analytically and empirically necessary.

Even if there is a wide consensus on roles, there is always a good deal of variation in their performance. This may simply be due to the fact that a role is defined not only by others' expectations but also by an actor's own conception of his role. Admittedly no self-conception of a role can be completely different from the conceptions of others in the role relationship. In spite of differences in behavior, most conduct is recognized for what it is because roles can be identified. But although we may see ourselves as others see us and take appropriate roles, roles are never taken in identically similar ways. The explanation may be that two actors taking the same role may have somewhat different self-conceptions of the role because the others to whom they react are different actors.

Actors do bring idiosyncratic perceptions of the interpersonal situation, attitudes, and motivations to a role. Role analysis does not preclude, but may require, investigation of role conceptions from the point of view of the actor's personality. An actor's capacity to take certain roles is predicated on the possession of certain personality characteristics. Just what these are is a subtle problem of theory and research. I shall come back to it later on.

Role conflict may stem from various conditions, but two are noteworthy. These may actually be divergent expectations of a person's behavior. A city councilman may expect the city manager to guide and direct the council's legislative business, while another councilman may expect him to abstain from policy recommendations. Or there may be disagreement between others' expectations and an actor's own conceptions of his role. Moreover, the demands made from one role to another may be so intense that behavior in the performance of various roles cannot satisfy role requirements. For example, involvement in the life of the Senate may so absorb a member's time that he cannot meet his obligations as a representative of his state. In all of these cases, role conflict is likely to have dysfunctional consequences of either a social or a personal sort. On the social level, certain functionally necessary roles may not be taken. For instance, conflicting expectations concerning the democratic politician's role may deprive a group of strong leadership. On the personal level, role conflict may so disorganize behavior that it becomes highly erratic, irregular, and even irrational.

Study of how role conflict is avoided or resolved suggests a number of possibilities. I shall only list them. First, some roles are more pervasive than others and conflict is resolved in their favor. Second, some roles are more clearly defined than others, which again aids the resolution of conflict in their favor. Third, some roles are more institutionalized than others, leaving the actor relatively little choice. Finally, roles are more or less segmentalized so that, depending on circumstances, even potentially conflicting roles can be taken.

THE VERTICAL DIMENSION—GROUPS

One might argue that "group" is an expendable concept. The argument would be that group is a loose, connotative term, impossible or at least difficult to define operationally, and what cannot be defined does not exist. What exists in reality is not a group but a pattern of interaction among people. Therefore the concept of group is useless because it cannot tell us anything significant about reality.

The argument is fallacious. We cannot deny that, for certain purposes, individuals interacting with each other cannot be treated as empirically joint units, that is, as groups. And as a group, people can be treated analytically as interacting with other groups, even though, in reality, individuals rather than groups are involved in concrete relationships. Otherwise one could not speak meaningfully of intergroup, intergovernmental, or international relations.

However, along with the vagueness of the concept, there is a problem in the enormous variety of groups that may be politically relevant. This does not represent an insuperable obstacle to the use of the concept. For it is possible to reduce the great number of concrete groups to manageable analytic proportions. Once we distinguish between group as a concrete structure and an analytic one, group, given its proper label, may prove useful. If concrete groups—family, neighborhood, party, organization, or whatever—are thought of as analytic structures such as primary or secondary groups, in-groups or out-groups, formal or informal groups, reference or membership groups, two very practical results may be noted. First, retention of the concept of group with analytic labels attached reduces empirical complexity; and second, it permits generic considerations about diverse, concrete groups that would otherwise be difficult to entertain.

Attaching analytic labels to a concept is not the same thing as defining it. It has an orienting function. It saves us from claiming too much or too little for analysis of political behavior in group terms. It does not say that all political behavior is group behavior, as some extreme group theorists would have it; nor does it suggest the opposite, that group analysis of political behavior is a dead end, as some antigroup theorists claim. It seems to me that a model of politics that ignores group altogether risks incompleteness.

But are role analysis and group analysis not mutually exclusive? The answer is no. There is no intrinsic conflict between analysis of political behavior in terms of either role or group. Whether one wishes to employ one or the other concept is largely a question of the problem to be analyzed, a matter of theoretical preference or research strategy. For some purposes it is certainly sufficient and economical to think of political behavior almost exclusively in group terms. For instance, voting behavior can be and has been analyzed in this way. Group analysis of electoral behavior does not exhaust what one may want to know but, depending on the problem one poses, it may be superior to either role analysis or some other type of treatment. On the other hand, the study of legislative behavior is not likely to get very far without a more refined analysis of the roles that each legislator can take as the member of a legislative group. While his membership as such can tell us something about his legislative behavior in general, it is not likely to tell us very much.

The very vagueness of the concept of group forces the investigator to discriminate initially among the types of relationship in which he is interested. Clearly the relevance of a group in a person's political behavior is likely to vary with the character of the interaction. Of critical importance are the size of the group, its permanence, the degree of intimacy or formality in intragroup relations, the degree to which members identify with each other or with group symbols (solidarity), the extent to which attributes or attitudes are shared (homogeneity), the group's tasks and the degree of specialization among the members, the formal system of coordination of individual activities, and so on. Depending on specification of these group properties, we can characterize groups as primary or secondary groups, associations, organizations, communities, factions, cliques, parties, and so on. Whatever the classification, political behavior is likely to vary with the type of group in which the individual is involved.

Group properties probably account not only for stability in political behavior but also for change. That the children from a Republican family may become Democrats, that friends who are no longer members of the same social circle may part political ways, that people long politically apathetic may be activated by group influences, and so on are empirical phenomena well enough known. Changes in political behavior may be due to a person's shifting from one group setting into another, since new patterns of political behavior often follow new group affiliations or identifications.

It would be folly to rely exclusively on knowledge of a person's group

affiliations to predict his behavior. While the group is a factor to be reck-
oned with, it is only one factor. If the individual's behavior itself is viewed
as a component of the group, we can avoid the rather mechanistic notion
of group influence on behavior. Instead of thinking in one-directional terms—
the group's influence *on* or *over* the individual—we can view the relationship between group and individual as reciprocal or transactional. Indeed,
people may use political opinions or behavior to gain entry into a group,
to find new friends, to make themselves at home in a new community.
This may involve conscious or unconscious behavior, and it may or may
not involve changes of belief.

The group has at its disposal powerful sanctions in the form of positive
commandments or negative injunctions to enforce conformity to group
values, attitudes, and expectations. But we cannot assume that the individual is simply the victim of forces he cannot resist and influence in turn.

Groups range from the most casual and informal small groups to highly
institutionalized and coercive organizations. If one adds the degree of
political relevance that a group may have for an individual's behavior, the
task of research appears formidable. Moreover, and paradoxically, groups
one might least expect to have political relevance are likely to be sources
of lasting identifications, demands, and expectations in the political order.
The pervasiveness of group-anchored aspects of political behavior has been
demonstrated by research on such varied subjects as the family as an agency
of political socialization, on peer groups as reservoirs of political recruitment, on neighborhoods as foci of political involvement, on communities
as carriers of political values, on organizations as molders of political opinion, on nations as recipients of political loyalties, and so on.

Not the least important factor in determining the character of the
individual-group relationship is the simultaneity of groups in the individual's social environment. Multiple group membership or overlapping
group membership facilitates or impedes social integration on levels above
and beyond the group itself. Multiple group membership interests us not
only because of its consequences for individual political behavior but also
for the whole network of intergroup relations that constitutes the vertical
dimension of the social matrix.

Of more immediate interest in the analysis of political behavior is the
possibility that an individual's relationship to one group somehow affects
his relationship to another group. If the attitudes, values, or goals of the
groups are harmonious, the individual's political behavior is surely affected
in ways different from a situation in which they clash. In this case, the
individual is likely to be subject to "cross-pressures." This is an unfortunate
term because, once more, it connotes a kind of individual helplessness vis-
à-vis the group. But whatever the expression, one individual-group rela-

tionship always seems to implicate another. The notion of cross-pressure suggests the need to disentangle often complex patterns of social and political relationships.

The possibility that group interests and loyalties may be at odds is also an important source of role conflict. Conflicts engendered by cross-pressures become most evident in critical situations where choices must be made and where latent contradictions, arising out of multiple group memberships not normally experienced, make behavior erratic. For instance, on an issue like censorship of a particular book or movie, a man's religious affiliation and commitment might well come into conflict with his membership in or identification with an organization devoted to civil liberties. Of course, many roles stemming from relationships with different groups need not conflict. And even if they do conflict, men may be only vaguely aware of the contradictions. It is not the fact of multiple group relationships, but its possible dysfunctional consequences for role taking in situations where political decisions must be made, that is of special interest from the behavioral point of view.

A group's significance to a person is a psychological problem. If every person brings into the group relationship certain predispositions and attitudes, group analysis cannot be limited to group structure, processes, and goals, but must accommodate these individual psychological variables. Groups are objects of human experience making for different orientations. Perception of the group's relevance to an individual's personal needs and goals or one group's greater attractiveness as compared with other groups, and so on are factors that, in turn, affect the relations among groups as collective actors.

A person's goals, values, attitudes, and opinions may be derived from and shaped by identifications, perceptions, and comparisons that are not immediately traceable to his group memberships, but for which the existence of groups constitutes an environment of reference. The more generalized concepts of "reference group" and "reference group behavior" are potent explanatory tools of political analysis.

The orientations characteristic of reference group behavior may be affective, as in identification; cognitive, as in definitions of a situation; or evaluative, as in comparative judgment. Identification with a political party, a reform movement, or a persecuted minority may lead to a wide range of political action not explicable in terms of either a person's roles or group affiliations; yet the existence of groups in the individual's symbolic environment may be critical. Likewise an individual may explain political situations to himself by referring to the attitudes or opinions of groups he values. The reference group becomes a source of perceptions and standards, definitional or normative, that affect political behavior. Finally, reference groups can serve the individual as a frame of comparison for evaluating himself and others. Comparing his own circumstances with those of others, a city resident who pays high tax rates may move into an unincorporated suburban neighborhood with low tax rates. These distinctions between affective, cognitive, or evaluative reference group functions are, of course, only analytic. In reality, reference groups may serve all three functions simultaneously.

In a political world removed from one's own direct experience, what one perceives as real or significant is likely to vary from one group context to another. Groups provide the individual with those definitions of the situation without which behavior, in politics as elsewhere, would be highly arbitrary. Seeing one's own political opinions and values shared by others will validate political reality. This is probably true of the person only occasionally concerned with politics, and even more so of the person continuously involved—the politician, the party worker, the legislator, the judge, the bureaucrat, and so on. Group "belongingness" or reference group orientations not only reinforce a person's political perceptions and beliefs, but they also tend to shield him from political experiences that he might find unpleasant. It is a common observation that we read only what we wish to read, or that we avoid contact with people with whom we might disagree.

THE HORIZONTAL DIMENSION—STRATA

In politics and out, people do not interact with each other beyond an identifiable range of relationships. Even within a group, if it is large enough, some members rarely meet or have direct contact with other members. This is partly due to different persons performing functionally differentiated roles that do not require direct relations. In part, the roles are differently evaluated and interaction between the incumbents of such roles is not considered desirable. Or, if interaction does occur, what the incumbents of functionally differentiated and differently evaluated roles should or should not do—their rights and obligations—is more or less strictly regulated, for example, in a military organization or a feudalistic social formation. But even in as intimate and small a group as the nuclear family, the parents (and sometimes even the husband vis-à-vis his wife) and children are set off from each other in clearly discernible ways. Similarly in the huge group formations we usually call societies, certain individuals or groups are differentiated from others, thus creating a system of relationships that would in all likelihood not exist if functional or valuational differentiation were absent.

Just as the concept of group alerts one to the vertical pattern of social relations, so the concept of stratum calls attention to the horizontal levels of the social matrix within which individual and group relations take place. The notion that political behavior and social relations are generally stratified is, of course, one of the oldest, most central, and persistent organizing ideas of political and social thought. Built around it one finds numerous and diverse concepts, such as formulations of caste, class, or status—in short, formulations of social structure as the horizontal dimension of the social matrix. The concept of stratum seems to me analytically and empirically more serviceable because it is valuationally neutral and does not commit the analyst of political behavior to a particular theory that might seek to account for the sources of stratification and its effects on political behavior and the whole system of relations in which people are involved.

To think of social or political relations, whether interindividual or intergroup, as stratified means that behavior is bounded by upper and lower limits beyond which it does not extend. In general, status refers to interindividual and class or intergroup differentiation, although these concepts have no stable and unambiguous empirical referents on which observers might agree. The distinction between status and class as a distinction between individual and group referents seems to be useful in looking at a functionally very complex matrix such as that of the United States. Here incumbents of high-status positions in groups of relatively low-class character may yet interact with their opposites in groups of high-class character. For instance, labor union leaders interact with industrial managers more often than with their own rank and file. The example suggests the utility of the concept of stratum. Evidently a new stratum—the "higher servants" of labor, business, or government—that is neither a status group nor a class in the conventional uses of these terms, has emerged as a result of such differentiation and collaboration.

Whether one thinks in terms of status or class, then, the limits imposed on behavior, including political behavior, by a person's or group's location in a stratum of the social matrix may be more or less rigid or flexible, depending largely on the total number of horizontal levels that can be identified. Within any horizontal order, whether characterized in terms of class or status, individuals or groups in neighboring strata are more likely to come into contact with each other than individuals or groups in widely separated strata. In a highly stratified system with many levels of status differentiation, there is little contact between incumbents of status positions that are removed from each other by more than two or three steps. On the other hand, in a small entrepreneur-manager type of system with few intervening levels, the boss is in continuous contact with all employees, even if they occupy different status positions.

The same is likely to be the case in the larger social order characterized by classes. In the United States as a whole, classes are difficult to identify, although most observers speak of a middle class and a working class, or of white-collar and blue-collar classes. Due to lack of sharp differentiation, there is a great deal of interaction across these class lines and class is less likely to be a critical factor in political behavior than in societies with more highly stratified social orders. Where class stratification produces many levels, there is more interaction within than between classes and political behavior takes on a more pervasive class character.

The determination of any system of stratification is an empirical question guided by theoretical speculations about relevant criteria of differentiation. The notion of stratification is grounded in the assumption that patterns of behavior in the performance of social roles, within or without particular groups to which people belong, are socially evaluated. This assumption is shared by most theorists concerned with stratification, though they disagree on the criteria of evaluation, the character of the ensuing horizontal structure, the rigidity or permeability of strata boundaries, and, last but not least, the problem of *whose* evaluations should supply relevant criteria of stratification.

In general, two approaches to stratification pervade the bulky body of writings on the topic. For better or worse, they are called objective and subjective approaches. According to the objectivists, the existence of status or class strata and the order of stratification—what is high and what is low—are immanent in the social order and quite independent of the feelings, attitudes, or perceptions that people may have concerning them. It is the task of the observer, using whatever objective indices his theoretical propositions suggest, to stratify a population. He may do so, as Marx did, by locating a person in terms of his position vis-à-vis the relations of production or, as some modern social scientists do, by applying such criteria as income, education, or occupation. Although people objectively located in a stratum are assumed to share a "consciousness of kind," certain "interests," or other subjective feelings, these aspects are considered dependent variables that cannot be used in ascertaining the system of stratification.

The subjectivists, on the other hand, start with the assumption that precisely because social evaluation accompanies every functionally differentiated relationship, those in the horizontal order are themselves best qualified to supply criteria of stratification. Again the criteria are thought to be immanent. The observer is only supposed to find out just how people appraise either their own or others' location in the social order. Various methods have been used to discover the subjective meanings that people give to their class or status, but they need not concern us here. Whatever method is chosen, the critical issue is the utility of the notion of stratification as a handle for analyzing political behavior in the social matrix.

Stratification is only one of the many variables in terms of which differences in political behavior may be explained. Any hypothesis that seeks to explain a particular pattern of political conduct is always circumscribed by several other variables. As stratification involves some valuation, a group's set of values is always necessarily relevant. On the societal level, class systems in two nations may appear to be very similar from a structural perspective, yet the valuational meanings given to both class and politics may be quite different. As a result, political behavior related to stratification in the two nations may differ a great deal. For instance, practices regarding recruitment into the political elite may vary. Civil servants might be largely recruited from the upper social stratum in one system; in another, they might be recruited from the lower strata. In the first system, public service might be looked on as an obligation; in the second, as a sinecure to be exploited for personal advantage.

For reasons such as these, hypotheses about the consequences of stratification for political behavior are unlikely to be universally valid. The general proposition that stratification and political behavior are significantly related is probably viable only to the extent that analysis is contextual. Just what particular patterns of political behavior will be found in any social matrix analyzed in terms of stratification cannot be predicted from the structural characteristics of the matrix alone.

Insofar as politics is purposive activity through which a group—whether a national society at one end of the matrix or the nuclear family at the other end—engages in collective decision making, it is generally considered to have the attributes of self-consciousness as a group and interest. Both of these are very vague concepts. But we assume that, whatever the particular system of stratification, the existence of strata makes for self-consciousness and the specification of interests. The notion that a stratum, whether a class or status group, develops consciousness of kind stems from the observation that it is a necessary correlate of interaction. People in constant contact with each other but cut off from others are likely to see themselves as being the same and to see the world around them in similar perspective. They are also likely to view their interests in similar ways and they will behave in politically like ways to advance these interests. Out of speculations such as these Marx built his theory of class consciousness, class interest, and class conflict. But whether stratification makes, in fact, for consciousness of kind and common interests and, therefore, for similar patterns of political behavior, cannot be taken for granted. It must always be subjected to empirical testing.

Much in the relationship between stratification and political behavior depends on the extent to which a given social order is open or closed, that is, the extent to which it permits or prohibits, facilitates or impedes social mobility. The rigidity or flexibility of a stratification system is a function of many factors, ranging from material conditions to customary practices and ideological perspectives. The relatively high degree of social mobility in the United States for both individuals and groups has impeded the development of class consciousness, at least in the Marxian sense, and made politics relatively free of class considerations, but only relatively so when compared with societies where stratification is more rigid and pervasive. This is only another way of saying that, compared with other systems, stratification is less relevant in the Uited States in explaining variance in political behavior.

It does not mean that class is irrelevant in American politics. A great deal of research on voting behavior, pressure politics, community politics, and recruitment practices shows that stratification may have more to do with politics than the American ideology of mobility and equality led earlier observers to suspect. On the other hand, the same studies show that it is relatively easy for individuals or groups in American society to identify with the values and symbols of the elite, even if they cannot actually change their place in the order of things. Such identification across strata boundaries makes for limited awareness of class interests in a collective sense, with obvious consequences for political behavior.

The Cultural Context

Like the air we breathe, culture, however defined, is so close, so natural, so much a part of what we are that we are not aware of it. We notice it only when we move from one culture into another. The most important aspect of culture is that its existence is predicated on the existence of another culture. One culture always constitutes the environment for another. Only awareness of different cultures sensitizes us to the culture in which we live, act, think, feel, and judge. Otherwise we are culture bound— we do not know who we are nor why.

Culture is all pervasive. It permeates, without our awareness, every aspect of our daily living. Political behavior is no exception. We cannot fully understand it unless we treat it culturally and locate it in the wider cultural context. This enables us to see how our own political behavior is similar to or different from political behavior in another culture.

The difficulty of analyzing political behavior in terms of culture is that our language and language-related modes of thought, themselves products of culture, stand in the way. We say that culture *is* this or that, or that it *does* this or that; but culture is not a thing nor can it act. It does not exist outside or apart from behavior as something that can be identified independently of behavior or the results thereof, regardless of whether these results are symbolic or material. Culture is a mental construct abstracted from the behavior of people and their works.

When looking at political behavior in cultural terms, we are still observing the same behavior that we observe when we use social terms. It is not the behavior involved that is different but our observational standpoint. We are simply moving to another level of analysis. Just as the notion of social matrix and related concepts are useful in viewing politics in social terms, so the notion of cultural context and related concepts call our attention to the cultural environment of politics and to politics as a cultural phenomenon itself.

CULTURAL PATTERNS

We speak of culture patterns when we observe similarities in the behavior of people in the same culture that are relevant to diverse, functional aspects of social action. Although their religious, economic, military, or political practices serve quite different functions in a group's[1] existence, the patterns of behavior involved may be very similar. For instance, authoritarian patterns of behavior may be characteristic of different functional areas of a group's life: child rearing, religious practices, economic organization, or political decision making. If we observe similar patterns that are pervasive and stable through time (or, if they change, do so gradually), we can assume that they are not due to chance.

Suppose we ask why so many people in the United States are relatively uninvolved in politics? The question invites us to compare political behavior in this country with political behavior elsewhere. But we need not necessarily make such a comparison in order to look at American political behavior in cultural terms. It impresses us that political interest and involvement rise rapidly as an election approaches but fall off even more rapidly thereafter. Moreover, the interest seems to be more like a spectator's than an active participant's. The idea of spectator interest makes us look for other functional areas where spectatorship seems to be the typical response pattern.

It has often been suggested that American politics has the characteristics of a game. Indeed, a perceptive journalist once called it "the great American game." The analogy itself is a cultural artifact, and our language supports it. Like baseball or any other game, politics is "played." It is played by "rules of the game" that must be observed, and professionals play the best game. Admiration for a job well done and emphasis on winning are part of the general behavioral pattern. We cheer the victor, forget the loser. The game, in sports as in politics, is partly for entertainment. The spectator pattern of American mass behavior, mirrored in the language of sport, is a pervasive feature of the culture. (Notice, too, that we "watch" the stock market and "play" it.)

To avoid any misunderstanding, I am not saying that all behavior within a group that shares a culture is characterized by identical patterns. It is not. The concept of culture merely suggests that viewing behavior as a whole may help in explaining particular items of behavior. Moreover, there are enormous difficulties in employing cultural analysis as we move from relatively small, functionally undifferentiated simple groups, such as preliterate societies or even an adolescent urban gang, to complex, functionally highly differentiated modern collectivities.

Although some sweeping and ingenious characterizations have been made of American culture in all its heterogeneity, they are little more than impressionistic. But this is not an argument against the use of the concept of culture in modern settings. In the first place, if discontinuities in behavioral patterns outweigh the continuities, this is itself a cultural datum to be taken into account in the analysis of political behavior in a complex, cultural context. And second, the very useful concept of subculture is predicated on the assumption of the existence of a common culture. This common culture may prove to be empirically elusive, leading to the kind of impressionistic analysis that has been made of American culture, but its existence must be assumed nevertheless.

The culture concept puts the accent on wholeness, which guards us against taking behavior in a functional arena—be it sports, religion, the economy, or the polity—out of its cultural context. The failures of attempts to transfer political institutions from one culture to another are well known. In these cases, behavioral patterns could not adjust or be adjusted to externally imposed arrangements. Similarly, within a group it is risky to view political institutions and processes outside of the cultural context in which they are embedded. *How* individuals behave in functionally different areas of activity is likely to be more continuous than *what* they do.

The pervasiveness of cultural patterns from one functional area of life to another, from politics to economics, from economics to crime, from crime to sports, and so on, suggests that cultural analysis may be particularly useful in understanding public policies and the manipulative aspects of political behavior. All too often, social problems in the real world, graft and corruption, apathy and resistance to reform, social justice and peace, and so on, are seen as if they were soluble only on the political level of action. Cultural analysis suggests that these problems may be deeply rooted in a group's total way of life, and that their solution requires more than treating them by political means.

We speak of cultural patterns of behavior when they are widely shared, rather than social or personal patterns. The degree to which they must be shared before we can say that they are is an interesting question. I have never encountered a very satisfactory answer. More critical in appraising the cultural factor in political behavior is the degree of stability in the patterns. This stability of behavioral patterns is probably the most telling evidence of the working of culture in politics. Moreover, the rate of change that can be observed in behavioral patterns is itself a cultural phenomenon. The rate of change may reach a point where it is hardly permissible to speak of patterns of behavior at all. What this point is, I cannot say. In any case, increasing randomness in behavior suggests cultural crisis and possibly cultural transformation. From this point of view, political institutions are cultural products par excellence. For by definition, an institution is a set of widely shared, regularized patterns of behavior that are fairly stable through time. Institutions are, of course, only the most overt aspects of cultural patterns in political behavior. Covert patterns are equally crucial components of a political culture.

In general, then, we can speak of cultural patterns in political behavior if the patterns are similar to other patterns in a group's way of life, if they are widely shared and change only slowly. How these patterns have come about and how they are transmitted are questions of considerable interest to the cultural analyst of political behavior. The most plausible hypothesis is that they are the cumulative results of learning, and that they are transmitted from generation to generation in the process of socialization. The patterns are a group's adaptations to the environment in which it lives, and they change as new generations are forced to adapt to changing environmental conditions, including cultural changes in the environment of other cultures. The more cultural contact there is, the more cultural patterns are likely to change.

CULTURAL ORIENTATIONS

Cultural analysis of political behavior cannot be limited to objective observation of patterns. It is concerned with the meanings that people give to these patterns, regardless of whether they are formally institutionalized or not, including the functions that they see as being served by politics. Such analysis is impossible unless the individual person, as bearer of cultural meanings, is the unit of analysis.

The meanings people give to their behavior may be highly conscious, subsconscious, or unconscious. They may be so sacred they forbid articulation, or they may be highly secular and profane. Whether they are one or the other or in between is likely to depend on a culture group's exposure to other cultures. The more isolated a group, the more ingrained and traditional its behavioral patterns are likely to be and the more unconscious the meanings given these patterns. At the other extreme, groups in close cultural contact are likely to be highly conscious of the meanings they attribute to their own behavioral patterns and those of their cultural neighbors. Homogeneous groups take their patterns for granted; heterogeneous groups are forever in search of meanings that give their behavior symbolic significance.

Behavioral analysis of politics cannot afford to ignore the meanings that people give their own behavior because these meanings have consequences for their own political actions and those of others. Meanings are the organizing principles of behavior through which people make themselves at home in the world and orient themselves to action, including political action. If, like behavioral patterns, meanings are widely shared and relatively stable, it is possible to construct a group's cultural self-image. How people orient themselves to the groups to which they belong and those to which they do not belong gives meaning to their behavior. Indeed *social* behavior is impossible without the existence of widely shared, stable, and agreed-on meanings that serve as a frame of reference in conduct. Meaning, figuratively speaking, is the glue that binds people together in groups and divides them from others.

In general, cultural analysis of political behavior can easily discriminate between various types of meanings in terms of a group's orientations to political action. Some of these orientations are cognitive. These are a group's perceptions of reality in terms of which it defines its environment. Such perceptions can range from highly scientific and sophisticated concepts at one extreme to the most superstitious and irrational notions about reality at the other, from scientific knowledge to the most primitive beliefs. How people behave in politics, how they make those collective decisions that guarantee their survival as a group, is powerfully influenced by their image of the world they live in.

Differences in image from one culture to another are potent determinants of political conduct. Whether the environment is seen as friendly or hostile, whether expectations about the future are optimistic or fatalistic, whether group demands are pathologically exaggerated or minimized, orientations of this sort are critical frames of reference for political behavior. The belief that man can shape his world through his own efforts will lead to a different kind of political action than the view of man at the mercy of forces over which he has no control. A culture group whose time perspective is in the past may find it difficult to cope with the present, just as a group whose perspective is largely in the present may be unable to plan wisely for the future.

Orientations to political action are also affective. Here we deal with those widely shared emotional responses to which we give names like loyalty or morale. These emotions may be positive or negative, and they may be directed in different degrees toward different objects.

Whether man relates himself to others in terms of what is conventionally called love or hate, trust or fear, is likely to have significant consequences for his political behavior. The degree to which one or another of these orientations is shared and accentuated in a given culture makes an enormous difference in politics. It will produce notions about other political actors, whether individuals or groups, as friends or enemies, as objects of identification or withdrawal. Whether politics is experienced as a life-and-death struggle for existence, as a competitive though friendly game, or as a cooperative enterprise for mutual aid is likely to be a function of widespread affective components in the culture.

Finally, orientations to political action are normative. Included here are the evaluative standards by which judgments are made about political behavior, the ethical rules that guide behavior, as well as the goals considered worthy of attainment. Some of these orientations may be actually operative ideals whose observance is not in doubt. Others may be ideal standards that differ from what people actually do when they guide or evaluate their own and others' conduct. In politics, the degree of agreement on ideal patterns of conduct is probably an important stabilizing and legitimizing factor in actual behavior. Conflict between ideal patterns and operative ideals becomes a central source of political tensions that call for solutions.

Just as meanings are implicit in patterns of political behavior and transmitted by the members of a group, so are cognitive, affective, and normative orientations. Insofar as meanings and orientations constitute a more or less coherent and integrated set of symbolic expressions, they come to be accepted as self-evident systems of belief.

By belief I mean the nonlogical, prerational components of the total cultural ideology. Belief in this sense is not rooted in reasoning and direct observation, and it is highly resistant to disproof. Belief can be given up only in exchange for another belief. Beliefs are the self-evident propositions that everybody knows to be true without need for further proof. Putting these propositions in doubt arouses hostility, causes pressure for conformity, or leads to excommunication in rigid cultural contexts. From the cultural point of view, the analytical problem is not whether beliefs can, in fact, be tested by the methods of social science or at least dissected by the criteria of logic. Cultural orientations to action differ in the degree to which their components can or cannot meet the requirements of proof or logic. Rather the point is that propositions of this order are believed because they are widely shared, relatively stable, and successively transmitted and, in turn, give direction to social and political action.

Belief systems are characteristic of even highly sophisticated and secularized cultures. That one's own form of government is far superior to any other; that only a particular economic system can guarantee a high standard of living; that war is rooted in human nature and cannot be prevented; that one group is out to destroy another—these are some of the beliefs more or less widely shared at one time or another, even in cultures that take pride in rational conduct. Often these beliefs have only symbolic functions with few consequences for actual political action. But under certain conditions—for instance, in crisis situations when the group's survival is at stake—beliefs have an important effect on the political order.

Analysis of political culture is not concerned, then, with the truth of beliefs but with the functions they perform. Precisely because beliefs are grounded in emotion rather than logic and because they are experienced as certainties rather than probabilities, orientations to political action grounded in a total system of belief that defies disproof have a strong influence on political cohesion. Belief systems serve to give people a sense of mutual identification, to protect them against doubts and the dangers, real or imaginary, of an environment that must be controlled. For this reason, threats to belief systems arouse the most passionate and violent types of reaction. They are considered as equally necessary to the survival of the individual as of the group. There is generally a discrepancy between the degree of sacredness with which belief systems are invested and the realistic functions that the systems and their component orientations may perform as integrating or disorganizing elements in the total cultural configuration of political behavior.

POLITICAL CULTURE

The concept of a political culture is something of a paradox. I have argued that cultural analysis cannot successfully focus on a particular functional area of a group's total way of life without simultaneously focusing on other areas. Yet the concept of political culture seems to limit our attention to those patterns of behavior and those orientations that, presumably, characterize only one aspect of a group's existence. Such a self-imposed setting of boundaries would seem to make it impossible to specify and measure the salience of politics within the larger culture and the consequences of different political patterns and orientations on the culture as a whole.

But cultural analysis, like all scientific inquiry, always involves a process of theoretical abstraction and empirical isolation. The concept of political culture does not deny that the political culture is embedded in a larger culture. In short, it must be interpreted to refer to a subculture, and it is only for convenience' sake that we do not speak of political subculture (as we should) or political sub-subculture (as we might). A subculture, the notion suggests, shares certain patterns and orientations with the larger culture from which it is analytically (but certainly not empirically) set off by other patterns that are *relatively* unique to itself. There may even be a conflict of patterns between the political subculture and the more general culture. For instance, the hierarchical patterns of military behavior may conflict with egalitarian patterns in the general culture. Indeed, observable tensions in the American military establishment may be traced to conflict between the military subculture and the general culture. Sacred orientations in the political culture, like its fetishes, may conflict with the generally secularized views of the culture as a whole.

Cultural analysis of political behavior seems more viable in a group (using the term in its most generic sense to refer to an institution, a local community, a social class, a religious order, a geographical region, an age group, and so on) than in the larger societal contexts where it is usually employed. In fact, within the United States, for instance, fruitful subcultural analyses of political behavior have been made in groups as diverse as the Senate, a small village community, a slum area of a metropolitan city, the military establishment, a democratic trade union, an old-age movement, a Japanese relocation center, and many other political groups or settings. Although all of these groups share the larger culture, each exhibits its own patterns of behavior, including political ones. And there are subcultures within subcultures as there are groups within groups. Even the smallest social unit—the nuclear family, the clique, the work team, the committee—has its own culture. In most respects a dual cultural function is performed in these groups: the group transmits not only its own peculiar way of thinking and doing things but also serves as a kind of conveyor for transmitting the more general cultural patterns.

The existence of political subcultures in particular political situations, whether formally institutionalized or not, is always an empirical question. It cannot be prejudged. But the notion of subculture as the more general concept of culture alerts the analyst of political behavior to the possibility that otherwise nonexplicable variances in political action may stem from subcultural differences. In a country like the United States with its high degree of social intercourse and mobility, both vertically in the group order and horizontally in the stratification order, there is a great deal of cultural homogeneity among subcultures. Differences in political behavior due to subcultural differences may be difficult to observe. But on close scrutiny, subcultural political contrasts will not escape the behavioral microscope. Indeed, any empirical construct of the American political culture will have to be built on minute, subcultural analyses of political behavior.

Political culture, then, refers to the patterns that can be inferred from the political behavior of groups as well as the beliefs, guiding principles, purposes, and values that the individuals in a group, whatever its size, hold in common. Each individual, of course, has his own conception of the political culture that influences what he does or does not do politically. For this reason, cultural analysis alone, just as social analysis alone, does not exhaust what is to be discovered about political behavior. Full analysis must also take account of the personal basis of political conduct.

In this sense, political culture refers to the consensus of numerous individuals, but a consensus that need not be precisely duplicated in any one person. Most people within a group are likely to have some experience with many of the same patterns, although all may not be exposed to all the prevailing patterns. In the study of political behavior within a single culture, widely shared patterns can, therefore, be considered as constants, providing a base line for examining particular individual responses to particular political situations. On the other hand, in cross-cultural analysis of political behavior, differences in observed patterns and orientations are critical variables for studying responses in functionally similar political situations. In either case, cultural analysis permits the investigator to transcend the boundaries of his own culture.

The Personal Basis

The analysis of political behavior should be exhausted once man's social relations and cultural milieu have been accounted for. There would seem to be no room for looking at it on a personal basis. Indeed, even if one knew nothing about a man's personality, a great deal of his political behavior could be satisfactorily explained in social or cultural terms alone. But throughout the history of political speculation from the Greeks to the present, there has always been the realization, however vague or mistaken in detail, that a politics which does not consider human nature can only be a very partial politics.

But to say that a man's personality has something to do with his political behavior is not saying very much. It only states an assumption: that what kind of personality a man brings to politics makes a difference. More relevant are these questions: when is it feasible and worthwhile to study political behavior from the point of view of personality? what can personality study contribute to the analysis of political behavior? These questions make the assumption that differences in political behavior are due to personality differences somewhat problematical. Personality may or may not make a difference.

Personality, like culture, is an abstraction from behavior, not something independent of behavior. It is not directly accessible to empirical observation. Rather it is abstracted from and constructed out of the very patterns of behavior and feeling, past and present, that it is intended to explain and interpret. In speaking of the effect of personality on political behavior or of the relationship between them, we are once more using conceptual shorthand. I prefer to speak of the personal basis of political behavior because it suggests a distinction between those aspects of political behavior that are personal and those that are social or cultural. It is the relationship between the personal aspects, on the one hand, and the social or cultural aspects, on the other, that is the heart of the matter.

OPINIONS AND ATTITUDES

Political behavior research can be conducted on a broad front. At one end, there is the biographical study of outstanding individuals, statesmen, warlords, revolutionaries, and so on. At the other end, the emotional reactions of whole nations, especially in times of crisis, or the aspirations and behavior patterns of mass movements are of intrinsic interest. Between these extremes, the political behavior of small groups (families, committees, juries), of politically attentive publics (politicians, opinion leaders, journal readers), of demographic aggregates (small businessmen, senior citizens, women), of organized collectivities (labor unions, farm organizations, utilities), or of institutionalized groups (legislatures, bureaucracies, military formations) is a matter of inquiry.

The greater the number of individuals involved in a political system, the less sense it makes to seek full data concerning the personal basis of political behavior. It clearly is impossible to subject an adequate random sample of a national population or of a large group like an army to the same kind of intensive personality study that is possible in the case of individual political biography. This need not mean that survey analysis of the political behavior of large groups or aggregates, even of national societies, cannot benefit from theoretical formulations of personality. But in general, the kinds of problems that interest the political scientist, involving not only individuals as individuals but also more or less complex collectivities, though possibly psychological in formulation, do not readily lend themselves to analysis as problems of personality.

It is difficult to use concepts referring to the personal basis without becoming entangled, wittingly or not, in some particular theory of personality. Almost every relevant psychological concept is invariably tied to some particular school of psychology or given different meanings by different schools. However personality is defined, in studying the personal basis we may deal with unconscious motivations and thought processes, including fantasies; with more or less visible reaction patterns (mechanisms of defense or cognitive dissonance); or with attitudes, perceptions, and preferences, rational or not, that can be more readily verbalized and discovered.

Analysis of political behavior in its personal aspects need not proceed from a theoretically consistent and integrated conception of personality. It may select those aspects that seem relevant to the problem and fit the population to be investigated to them. Research tools, as they are dictated by the size of the sample, and conceptual tools, as they are dictated by the problem at hand, are likely to influence each other. Formulations of political behavior in a large sample survey, which involves relatively short interviews with a population of considerable heterogeneity, must be necessarily limited to inquiry in terms of rather superficial perceptual or attitudinal questions. That these attitudes or perceptions may be anchored in interpersonal relations rather than the personality is beside the point. They may reveal some personal meanings that the individual gives his political activity. One may wish to interpret scaled responses to a handful of questionnaire items as indicative of an authoritarian *personality,* an anomic *character,* a tough-minded *attitude,* or simply a *feeling* of efficacy. The pattern of an individual's responses may be suggestive, though it may or may not be evidence of personality in politics.

On the other hand, if one's research deals with a single individual or a few people, the personal basis of political behavior can be fruitfully explored through a prolonged interview of the Freudian tradition or, where interviewing is impossible, by exhaustive analysis of documentary data. In these cases political behavior analysis will employ the intricate set of concepts from one or another theory of personality. This will undoubtedly yield a rich harvest of knowledge about the relationship between personality and politics. For instance, the interpretation of Hitler as a hysterical-paranoid personality may be set against the background of social and economic conditions in Germany and the emotional state of the German masses, providing insight into the dynamics of large political systems under certain conditions of stress and strain.

Somewhere between survey analysis and depth analysis, efforts are made to combine intensive, though not prolonged, interviews with projective tests, standardized personality inventories, and other procedures. These techniques are well suited to inquiry into political behavior because they are more widely applicable than deep analysis, yet more thorough than survey research can afford to be.

Depending on the strategy employed, then, different conceptual aspects of personality can be selected for investigation of the personal basis of political behavior without commitment to some overarching conception of personality in politics. A comprehensive model of political man may be more of an obstacle than an aid.

The study of attitudes and perceptions is more immediately useful in discovering how political behavior affects large-scale political processes and systems than the kind of intensive inquiry that seeks explanation in terms of unconscious drives or other adaptive mechanisms of the psyche. Knowledge of how man perceives himself as a political actor, how he interprets the world of politics, how he values what he sees, and how he acts politically in pursuit of personal values can tell us a great deal about his political behavior.

Overt behavior, including opinions, can be revealing in several respects. Most obviously, perhaps it can tell us something about government and politics as objects of perceptions and attitudes. Does the world of politics enter a man's perceptual field at all? Is the legislator aware of the interest groups in his environment? Are political campaign issues important to the voter? Once we establish perceptual relevance, we may investigate affective components of political attitudes. Does the legislator feel that pressure groups are helpful or harmful? Does the voter consider government as benign or evil, political candidates as attractive or not, political issues as urgent or not? Answers to these simple questions can tell us a great deal about a person's ability to differentiate, the values in terms of which he appraises reality, and his time perspectives. If not all pressure groups are perceived as powerful, which ones are and which ones not? What degree of influence is attributed to these groups? What criteria of judgment are applied? It is likely that the values involved in political judgments or the perceptions of urgency that reveal the political time perspective constitute a more or less permanent syndrome of political predispositions.

While different levels of the personal basis of political behavior are probably interrelated, one need not assume a one-to-one correspondence. A great many varieties of behavior or opinion may be rooted in common personality characteristics at the deep level of analysis, but the political behavior of diverse personalities may be identical. For instance, distrust of authority may express itself in unconventionnal political opinions or radical behavior *or* in compulsive demands for a just and powerful leader. Deep-felt dependency needs may underlie an ideology that glorifies obedience or one that insists on freedom. For this reason, we should always take care in interpreting opinions and attitudes, even if they seem to constitute a consistent pattern that suggests a personality syndrome.

VALUES AND PERSONALITY

Most psychological theories of personality consider typical mental states, drives, or mechanisms—whatever the nomenclature—as the most basic determinants of behavior. They consider perceptions, attitudes, or values as more or less peripheral layers of personality. Values can serve as central organizing principles in studying the personal basis of political behavior. Presumably a person's values are sufficiently structured to constitute a value system; and if they do, the value system may well be the most stable component of political behavior.

To conduct this type of analysis, it is necessary to differentiate as sharply as possible between the personal and the cultural components in an individual's scheme of values. The culturally transmitted set of values is validated by being widely shared, though we can only discover it through studying the values of individuals. On the other hand, the value system of an individual, though transmitted culturally, should be more or less identifiable as unique in his political behavior. Unless the distinction is made, political behavior analysis is likely to be trapped in what I would call the fallacy of cultural correlation: that is, the error of inferring a personal value from a cultural value system.

Whatever the degree of political involvment, culture determines significant aspects of an individual's personality. It does this not only in the form of role expectations and other behavior norms, as well as perceptual cues that orient the individual to his social and material environment, but also in the form of values. The individual internalizes these values in the course of socialization. They thus become aspects of his personality. Personalities in a given culture group can probably be characterized in terms of values held in common because the socialization process itself is culturally patterned. But as there are also discontinuities in a culture, and as socialization practices vary a great deal from subculture to subculture, values are transmitted and internalized in varying combinations and degrees of intensity, depending on an individual's peculiar circumstances. A personal value system, then, is not simply a replica of a cultural value system. Otherwise it would be impossible to account, on the personal basis, for the great variety in political behavior within the same culture.

This may be illustrated by the possibly different consequences in different value contexts of primary identification as part of the socialization process. Identification seems to have two main types of consequences for political behavior: submissiveness to or rebelliousness against authority. However, a culture's value system will emphasize these possible types of response differently. In a culture that highly values authority as a set of expectations defining adult relationships, it is likely that the process of identification in the nuclear family will tend to polarize the alternatives of submission and rebellion toward more extreme solutions. On the other hand, in a culture that places relatively low value on authority, the working out of child-parent identification is less likely to have extreme solutions. In turn, because the individual repeats the patterns experienced in different stages of growth, primary identification and resultant solutions tend to reinforce cultural values. But as normality in behavior is defined culturally rather than personally, individuals do not necessarily experience a system of authority relations, whatever its shape, as either especially indulgent or deprivational.

As a result, authority relations in some political systems engender a great deal of submissiveness or assertiveness without negatively affecting the system's stability, while in other systems, comparatively lax authority relations also fail to affect adversely political stability. It seems that in either case, differential evaluations of authority are sufficiently internalized to become strong organizing principles at the personal basis of political behavior. For instance, if giving or withholding affection in childhood has differential consequences for behavior in maturity, empirical analysis has yet to determine just how affective orientations experienced early in life are interpreted in the cultural context. Discipline has different meanings in different cultures and subcultures. In a culture where severe disciplining is not only widely practiced but also approved, its consequences are likely to be different from those in a culture where stern discipline is restricted and disapproved. But just what these consequences are can never be left to deductive inference; they must be empirically verified.

For this reason we should distrust attempts at characterological interpretations of whole nations in terms of some pervasive set of personality attributes inferred from the nature of socialization. Although "national character" is a widely used term, it is not a meaningful empirical concept. Many of the constructions of national character that have been made are largely intuitive and often based on casual observations, literary statements, or case analyses of limited scope. If they are based on large opinion or attitude surveys, the surveys may tell us something about the distribution of attributes in a population, but we should be even more suspicious of inferences about a hypothetical, if not mythical, national character. I doubt that a given political structure, let us say democracy, is predicated on the existence of a democratic character, whatever that may mean. Of course, psychologically healthy people are preferable to unhealthy people in any system. But definitions of mental health are difficult to come by. Equating mental health with democratic predispositions only symptomizes cultural myopia, pleasant and self-congratulatory as it may be.

ROLE AND PERSONALITY

We can think of role as that aspect of personality that refers to an individual's social identity. If this is so, research on political behavior must deal with the agreement between political roles as aspects of personality and other aspects. One may approach this problem from either end of the relationship. A psychologist, I would think, would be interested in learning how harmony or conflict among several concurrent role requirements affects the degree to which the personality is capable of modifying itself in response to particular role requirements. He would want to know how the relationship between role and other aspects of personality varies with the special characteristics of the individual. He would try to discover the degree to which a role is central or peripheral to a person's private needs and demands.

On the other hand, if role is the starting point of analysis, somewhat different concerns come into focus. No assumption need be made about the direction of the relationship—whether other aspects of personality shape role or are shaped by it. Nor is it necessary to assume either a zero or a one-to-one relationship. The degree of congruence between role and other aspects of personality is likely to vary a good deal.

The complexity of a political system is one cause of this. The more complex a system, the greater the number and variety of political roles. The sheer number of available roles and their heterogeneity are likely to reduce congruence between role and requisite personality characteristics. In a democracy like the United States, there are millions of citizens who participate in public decision making by voting in elections. Hundreds of thousands engage in other forms of political activity. Thousands of others fill a great range of elective and appointive offices, in government or political organizations. People with quite different personality characteristics can function effectively in this sort of political system with its great variety of political roles. Only in the upper tiers of the political structure are personality characteristics more likely to be relevant in recruiting personnel for particular roles and in shaping the performance of these roles.

Congruence is also likely to vary with the degree to which roles and role performance are institutionalized, standardized, and routinized. The more a role is institutionalized and role performance is secured through institutionalized sanctions, the less likely will behavior require the mobilization of energies rooted in the personality. Personality variables have no elbow room in which to function. This does not mean that certain personality types are not more suited than others for filling highly standardized roles. But it is probably the role that limits behavior rather than the particular personality that is attracted to the role.

We should not oversimplify the problem of congruence. For instance, the definition of bureaucratic roles is highly standardized, and the performance of bureaucratic roles depends on stable, disciplined behavior and adherence to prescribed rules. The kind of conduct that is expected is ensured by appropriate attitudes that are transmitted, learned, and reinforced through institutional training. Now it is quite likely that the bureaucratic organization attracts personalities with predispositions more or less well suited to the kind of behavior that is expected and, in fact, rather severely enforced. It is probable, therefore, that although bureaucratic role performance may not be dependent on personality, recruitment into the bureaucratic role will be facilitated by appropriate predispositions.

Congruence of role and personality is likely to vary, too, with the range of available behavior alternatives. In the American two-party system, for example, the citizen can vote or abstain from voting. If he votes, he can vote a straight ticket, split his ticket, or perhaps vote for a third party. In general, his behavior alternatives are quite restricted. We can explain performance of the citizen role more economically in social or cultural than in personal terms. That John Smith votes Republican because all of his friends are Republicans or because he sees his interests better served by the Republican party is probably sufficient explanation of his behavior. On the other hand, if we should find that John Smith votes Republican although all of his friends are Democrats, or that he votes as he does although his interests would be better served, even in his own opinion, by the Democrats, analysis of his political behavior on the personality level may supply a missing link in explanation. In short, analysis of political behavior in terms of personality seems advantageous if we are confronted with deviant conduct—deviant in a statistical, not a pathological, sense.

There are other situations in which the relationship between role and personality may be accentuated and where relatively high congruence has significant consequences for the functioning of a political system.

High congruence may occur in connection with largely voluntaristic roles, that is, roles that are not solidly institutionalized. In Western democracies, for instance, the roles of rebel, hermit, or prophet are less likely to be taken in response to others' expectations (although this element is ever-present by definition of role) than in response to strong motivations at the level of personality. In an institutional setting like a legislature, this category might include the role of maverick. Individuals with appropriate personality predispositions will take and shape these roles. In their case, then, analysis of the personal basis of political behavior in personality terms may be very rewarding.

Personality may also be the decisive factor in role taking and performance where a person is exposed to conflicting expectations. How role conflict of one sort or another is resolved can be analyzed in social or cultural terms alone, of course. But it may also be a function of personality predispositions. For instance, withdrawal from political participation can be due to the neutralizing effect of cross-pressures, an explanation on the social level of analysis. But it can also be due to anxieties occasioned by the conflict that are associated with similar experiences in the formative stages of personality development.

Role and personality may approximate a high degree of congruence in perceptually ambiguous situations in which the actions, expectations, and sanctions of others in a role relationship are blurred, for whatever reason. If no stable points of behavioral reference are available and no directional cues are forthcoming, the actor, unable to cope with ambiguity in any other way, will define his role for himself by falling back on personal values and experiences that may or may not be objectively relevant in orienting himself to others. While this behavior functions to resolve personal strains brought about by the ambiguous situation, it tends to make for a great deal of projective thinking, stereotypic responses, and irrationality.

Finally, roles allowing for a high degree of discretion in performance may be highly congruent with other personality characteristics. The king who cannot do wrong, the authoritarian or charismatic leader, and similar roles are almost by definition predicated on the expectation that there shall be no expectations. In the absence of institutional sanctions, personality has much leeway to shape the role in socially and culturally unpredictable ways. Of course, there are limits to what incumbents of such roles can do. Autocrats have been toppled from power and prophets have lost their glamour. But the limits set to behavior in these roles are sufficiently vague to allow the actor to shape his social environment in line with his personality needs and predispositions more than is usually the case.

These examples of relatively high congruence between role and personality might give the incorrect impression that analysis of political behavior is confined only to them. The examples are exceptions to support the general proposition that in complex political systems it is difficult to postulate theoretically or discover empirically personality attributes that are invariably and inevitably linked to particular roles. On the other hand, it does not follow that recruitment into or performance of certain roles cannot at times entail the possession of appropriate personality characteristics. I am merely arguing that behavior in the performance of culturally validated roles, on the one hand, and behavior in response to personality predispositions, on the other, is sufficiently plastic to prohibit any kind of dogmatic assertion about the relationship between them.

The relationship between role and other aspects of personality is not easy to determine empirically because the behavior involved is elusive. Take, for example, what is sometimes called policy planning. As conduct in the performance of a specific role, policy planning requires the appraisal of many alternatives and even greater numbers of consequences flowing from these alternatives under conditions of more or less uncertainty. In terms of personality, an actor in an uncertain situation must be able to tolerate ambiguity. Persons given to undue anxiety, whatever its source in their life histories, are probably unable to live up to the expectations and demands made on the policy planner as a role type.

It is equally difficult to make a distinction between the function of personality in role recruitment and role performance. In some cases, such as that of the organizer as against the administrator, the roles are clear enough to make discovery of suitable personality characteristics relatively easy. Whatever they are, the personality features necessary for organizing are probably quite different from those necessary for administering. Indeed, in these cases high congruence between personality and role is deliberately cultivated in the selection of personnel. It may be difficult to find a single person who possesses the personality attributes deemed desirable to fill both roles simultaneously.

One final example suggests how subtle the problem is. Leadership is sometimes equated with dominance as a personality trait. It is fairly safe to say that a dependent or withdrawing person is unsuited for the role. But leadership does not necessarily require dominance at the personal basis of behavior. Congruence between the role and other aspects of personality is likely to be incomplete as well as variable, because performance of leadership takes place in response to social situations and cultural norms that may be quite independent of personality needs. Indeed, if complete congruence between the leader role and dominance as a personality trait were to occur, it would in all probability have disastrous consequences for political behavior and the political system, whatever its ideological complexion. The resultant tensions between the demands of personality and social or cultural requirements for behavior would make any sort of political system unmanageable. Just as Hitler's hysterical and paranoid personality came ultimately into conflict with the realistic requirements of the system that he had created in his own image and doomed it, so a totally involved democratic citizenry, involved in the sense of being compulsively committed to participation in all decision making, would probably doom a democratic polity. It is, therefore, neither necessary nor correct to interpret all political roles as more or less power oriented in a psychological sense, or to expect, depending on the degree of power actually associated with a role, that only persons with the appropriate increment of power orientation in their personalities can fit into corresponding political roles.

Behavioral Dilemmas

The behavioral persuasion in politics is difficult to live by. Behavioral practitioners make exacting scientific demands on themselves. They encounter great practical obstacles; the dilemmas of behavioral inquiry are perplexing and often frustrating, and the increments to political knowledge that any single piece of research may make are very modest. My purpose here is to highlight some of the difficulties and dilemmas that make behavioral research in politics a venturesome enterprise, just as the prospects of solution represent the continuing challenge of the behavioral persuasion.

OBSERVATIONAL DILEMMAS

Behavior is a series of acts through which man moves in time and space. It is a datum of observation, but a datum that does not constitute a self-evident fact. Instead it is a fact that is given meaning by the observer in the very process of observation. Otherwise observation itself would be meaningless. And if observation had no meaning, it would not occur. Observation is itself a form of behavior that involves giving certain types of meaning to the object of observation, depending on who the observer is. This is true of the mother who observes her baby, of the tourist who observes a new landscape, of the astronomer who observes the movement of the stars, and of the political scientist who observes the action of a legislature or the behavior of voters.

Observation is as much giving meaning to the behavior that is observed as being engaged in meaningful behavior. The observer necessarily observes himself in the act of observing others. The extent of his success determines, at least in part, his success in observing others. This double aspect of observation makes it a scientific challenge.

Error in observation means that the observed act or behavioral pattern has been given false meaning. We say that the observed behavior has been misinterpreted. Whether the misinterpretation is willful or not, the false meaning is due to the behavior of the observer. The sources of error in observation—giving false meaning to the object of observation—are manifold. Their discovery has been a matter of interest to the philosopher, the theologian, the psychoanalyst, and the scientist. Whatever the approach to the discovery of error, there is agreement that the reduction of error involves changes in the behavior of the observer, not of the observed. If the history of humanity is a history of errors, as some believe, the history of science is a continuing effort to reduce errors in observation.

The problem of reducing error in the behavioral sciences is compounded by the complexity of human behavior. The smallest observable unit of behavior, the act, is inordinately complex, even if treated as a biological or neurological phenomenon alone. How much more complex is the series of acts that constitutes the behavior of the human organism as a whole! And this complexity is compounded when we come to deal with man's behavior in his social relations. The observer's task would almost seem hopeless if it were not for one significant aspect of human behavior: the fact that man himself gives meaning to his multiple actions. Of course, a man may err in the meanings he gives to his own behavior. There may be quite a discrepancy between what he is doing and what he thinks he is doing. But it seems quite clear that the human dilemma need not be the observer's dilemma. The observer has one advantage over the observed: he can check and, in fact, must check his own meanings against those that the observed gives his own behavior. In this respect, then, the behavioral approach in politics has a decided advantage over those that describe and analyze actions without considering what these actions mean to the actors.

But this creates another problem. If our observations of political behavior are to meet the test of intersubjective agreement between observer and observed, the meanings given to behavior by the observer and those given by the observed must be captured in a single structure of meanings that is internally consistent. This does not mean that their *language* must be alike. On the contrary, the scientific observer must use a language that is sufficiently abstract to contain the language of the observed. But clearly the meanings, though expressed in different languages, must be consistent.

Neglect of this two-way flow of meanings can seriously damage the reliability of behavioral research. Though it is now generally recognized that research must attend to latent as well as manifest meanings of political behavior, little progress has been made as yet in publicly defining the observational standpoint and the meanings of the investigator. I am thinking of something more than an explicit statement of the observer's theoretical framework and its scientific meaning-content, or even a clear statement of his goal values or policy preferences. What I have in mind is those often preconscious or unconscious meanings that may affect his observational stance. For even though two observers may work with the same formal-theoretical frame of reference or with the same goal values, they may still make different observations. I am not demanding that every behavioral researcher should expose himself to intensive psychoanalysis. I am only suggesting that sustained self-observation on the observer's part as he relates himself to the observed will considerably reduce what I feel to be a very genuine dilemma of political behavior research.

An empirical science is built by the slow, modest, and piecemeal cumulation of theory, methods, and data. The importance of a study, no matter how big or small, must be judged in the total context of relevant research. The dilemma of behavioral research in politics is not scarcity of studies but absence of a cumulative body of theory within which new studies can be accommodated and digested so that as research proceeds, one can speak of an expansion of knowledge.

An abundance of studies does not make for cumulative knowledge. Studies may be inventoried and codified, but even if they are reinterpreted in terms of some comprehensive, theoretical schema, codification is no substitute for cumulation. Reinterpretation may do violence to the original intent of a study, and the dilemma of cumulative knowledge is confounded. On the other hand, the prescription that all research on a given substantive problem should be undertaken within the same theoretical framework is a counsel of perfection that is quite unrealistic in the present stage of development in political behavior research. There are too many competing theoretical approaches that are plausible and possible, and it will take a good deal more empirical work before any one theoretical orientation can be expected to seize the field. A theory's success is not legislated. It is proved or disproved by research.

It is difficult to disprove a hypothesis in political research. To be acceptable, it would seem to require much more replication—the independent empirical testing of theoretically derived propositions—than is practiced at present. Without a great number of retests, it is impossible to assess the reliability of proof or disproof; there is much professional prejudice against repeat performances. So-called originality rather than replication receives the kudos of the men of learning. It is difficult to find financial support for replicative studies. This is only part of the dilemma. The difficulty of maintaining sufficient controls over external conditions is more important in the long run. If conditions vary, changes in hypothesized relationships cannot be observed and measured. Replication seems worthwhile only if the analysis proceeds from hypotheses about the constancy of relationships among variables under like conditions.

Again, I am not proposing perfection. I am merely hinting at perfection to pinpoint a dilemma. Conditions in political life are rarely alike, but this is no reason for despair. It is probably enough if conditions are sufficiently similar to make replication worthwhile. If undertaken properly, comparative analysis serves in many respects as a substitute for more rigorous replication that is possible in laboratory experiments.

I do not believe experimental replication is impossible in political behavior research, and I disagree with those who say that a rigorous science of politics is beyond our reach because human beings cannot be manipulated to suit the experimental needs of the researcher. Experimentation in political behavior research will do more than facilitate replication and cumulation. It will also make available new data that can only be guessed at now.

The availability of behavioral data is itself facilitated by new methodological and technical advances. The study of elections and electoral behavior was limited for a long time to the use of aggregate voting records alone. It was the systematic interview survey and probability sampling that brought the study of elections, which are surely critical democratic institutions, to the point where genuine explanation of variances in behavior became possible. We now take the probability sample survey so for granted that we easily forget the lack of behavioral knowledge about elections only a few years ago.

At the same time, behavioral research must be modest in appraising its data. Much unnecessary argument follows the lack of candor about limitations in the new kinds of data that are being made available. In view of the difficulties with direct observational techniques when it comes to the study of large groups, behavioral research must rely, of necessity, on opinions, perceptions, and verbal reports of behavior. The behavioral persuasion in politics cannot claim more for these data than what they are. For instance, sometimes research seeks to discover the influence attributed to certain individuals in a group, organization, or community on people or decisions. These data cannot be taken as evidence that these individuals are actually influential in general or in particular situations. Statements about influence or power based on measures of attribution are always inferential, and this should be admitted frankly. On the other hand, I cannot accept the argument that influence attribution is altogether meaningless, and that it should be tested independently in some objective, factual sense. It seems to me that if such independent testing of influence were possible, the discovery of influence attribution would be unnecessary in the first place. The point is, of course, that apart from case studies it is very difficult, if not impossible, to discover influence or power as real, generic phenomena.

Moreover, perceptions may have consequences for observable behavior all their own, whether factually true or not. If I perceive another person as influential, I may well behave toward him as if he were in fact influential. If I find out that he is not, or less so than I expected, I will have "misbehaved," again with identifiable consequences for the political relationship involved. I will have to change my perception. Undoubtedly, attributions of influence are based on just such experiences and, for that reason too, constitute "definitions of the situation" that have a very real existence of their own and, therefore, are proper objects of behavioral investigaton. Even a situation that is misperceived may be real in its consequences.

Perceptions may or may not correspond to reality, but as the determination of reality is elusive, they may have to serve as substitutes. They simply should not be made as statements about reality. The methodological problem is not the degree of correspondence between perception and reality. The problem is rather to decide just what degree of intersubjective agreement among informants or observers should be accepted as constituting sufficient evidence for making inferential statements about reality. This is very much like agreeing on what constitutes an acceptable level of confidence in probability statistics. No injection of metaphysics is needed to cope with the problem of the relationship between perceptions and reality.

MACRO-MICRO DILEMMAS

The great issues of politics, war and peace, freedom and justice, order and revolution, and so on require as much minute investigation as more modest problems. Political science is necessarily concerned with these issues. It has been in the tradition of the discipline to cope with them in molar rather than molecular fashion. As a result, there has been a misunderstanding between those interested in the great issues and those who settle for solving simpler problems. I do not believe that the broad perspective characteristic of large-scale policy studies is at odds with the microscopic inquiries of the behavioral persuasion. Indeed, linking different levels of analysis, the levels of individual or small-group behavior and the global levels of institution, community, or nation, constitutes a major unsolved item on the methodological agenda of the behavioral persuasion, and a challenging one.

The solution of the macro-micro problem is far from clear. The problem is, first of all, a theoretical one. Concepts of sufficiently high and abstract generality are needed to accommodate the multitude of levels on which political discourse can be conducted within a single theoretical schema. The theory must also be satisfactorily operational to permit empirical research on the level of the individual political actor. Recently schemata centering on concepts like decision making and conflict have made progress along these lines. But not surprisingly, empirical research has been conducted in connection with issues where access to behavioral data is relatively easy.

Concentration of empirical research attention on areas where behavioral data are accessible makes sense if one respects the methodological difficulties of behavioral analysis on macroanalytical levels. If this has given the impression that behavioral investigation is possible only in areas where data are easy to come by, the impression is understandable but false. Because the problem of linking the macrolevel and microlevel of analysis is not simply theoretical but methodological, it would be sheer folly, at this stage of development, to seek solutions in areas where data are difficult to gather.

The macro-micro problem can be visualized as a dilemma of diverse, though continuous, observational standpoints. From this perspective, the distinction between macrounits and microunits of analysis becomes relative. Small units like the individual or the small group, and large units like the organization or the nation-state, can be treated not as polar but as continuous variables. If this is so, all units, small or large, should be subject to ordering on a single continuum. Research can cut into this continuum anywhere along the line. In fact, this is what traditional analysis has largely done in concentrating on institutions as units of analysis. From the observational standpoint of a political system conceived as a macrounit, institutions appear as relatively small units. On the other hand, from the standpoint of individual behavior, an institution, even one as small as a committee, looms as a fairly large unit. A nation-state is a macrounit if looked at from below, and a microunit if looked on from above (the standpoint of a regional system or the global community of states).

As I have already suggested, such research is predicated on the availability of sufficiently general and abstract concepts that permit theoretical and operational linkages between and among different levels of analysis. Role analysis or system analysis, alone or in combination, is well suited to this task. For example, if *position* is taken as the basic microunit of any behavioral system, act and position can be linked, and with them the macrounit called institution and the microunit called individual, by virtue of the *role* that an actor (the microunit) takes in the performance of acts that are relevant to the position he occupies in an institution (the macrounit). Put somewhat differently, the macrounit institution now appears as a role system that can be analyzed on the microlevel of the individual actor.

The problem is not one of immanent conflict between individual and group, or between group and state, as it is sometimes made out to be in normative political doctrine. Rather, from whatever point on the macro-micro continuum one proceeds, the task of research is to build, by patiently linking one unit with another, the total chain of interrelations that link individual to individual, individual to group, group to group, group to organization, organization to organization, and so on until one gives the entire network continuous order. The use of behavioral data in political analysis depends quite clearly on some theoretical construct of the total system in which the individual actor is the basic empirical unit. I am not speaking of conceptual linkage alone, but of operational linkage. The availability of the great issues to behavioral analysis is clearly contingent on the solution of the macro-micro dilemma.

The problem of using both discrete and aggregate data in behavioral analysis is closely related. What may be true of aggregates need not be true of the individuals who compose them. The use of aggregated data conceals much of the variance in the behavior of individual political actors that the use of discrete data reveals. This does not mean that statements based on aggregated data cannot be trusted and accepted. Aggregate data are often the only kind of behavioral information available for the purpose of making statements about groups or large collectivities. But we should not make this necessity into a virtue. If we want to make behavioral statements about large systems, we still have the problem that aggregate data are evidently not sufficient. On the other hand, even if individual data are available and are combined to permit statements about units larger than the individual, such aggregation may still do violence to findings about individual behavior. It has the advantage of showing how great the variance is that aggregate or broad institutional language conceals. But just what we mean empirically when we speak of a group's loyalty, a party's cohesion, or an organization's morale remains unanswered. Do we speak about a group property that is independent of the behavior of any one individual belonging to a group, party, or organization? Or are we really speaking only about the aggregated characteristics of individuals? The extent to which certain problems of politics can be subjected to behavioral analysis depends on answers to these questions.

DYNAMIC DILEMMAS

By all odds, the most troublesome of methodological dilemmas in the study of political behavior is the analysis of change through time. Most behavioral research in politics is cross-sectional, dealing with individuals, samples, or institutionalized groups at one point in time. Treatment of political change has been left largely to the historians of institutions, with the result that historical and institutional study in political science are often considered identical. This is unfortunate because, from the perspective of a science of politics rather than a history of politics, the analysis of change through time has as its goal not historical reconstruction but the discovery of causal relationships. Emphasis on change as a series of conspicuous, successive events often leads to spurious causal interpretation.

Behavioral study relies on talk, and dead men do not talk. Of course, it is possible to analyze changes in past behavioral patterns, or at least their symbolic expressions, by applying content analysis where documentary evidence is available. But this type of work is enormously time-consuming, and unless one is interested in historical patterns for purposes other than their own sake, the scientific yield is not likely to be rewarding. As a result, behavioral analysis of politics has been largely ahistoric (though not antihistoric). The defense, or better, the rationalization, has been that, in any case, the task of behavioral research is to establish functional rather than causal relations between variables. This is a rather disingenuous avoidance of the causal challenge.

There is nothing intrinsically ahistoric in the behavioral persuasion in politics. In fact, as cross-sectional studies accumulate—for instance, in the voting field—it becomes increasingly possible to study change and infer causation from the presence or absence of correlations. Comparison and correlation of cross-sectional studies made at different points in time are subject, of course, to the same limitations that characterize trend analyses of aggregate data. They permit identification of net changes in the behavior of the cross-sections, but they do not allow analysis of internal changes in the behavior of individual persons. The behavioral changes characteristic of individuals may be compensatory in the cross-section as in the aggregate; that is, changes in one direction may be offset by changes in the other. But the marginal results may indicate no, or little, change. Moreover, if there is too brief a period for which cross-sectional data are available, the time series constructed from the cross-sections is likely to reflect a sequence of unique events and again makes for spurious inferences about causation. However, in the absence of genuinely longitudinal information, comparison and correlation of cross-sectional data are still more reliable than global historical-institutional analysis based on spectacular occurrences. The analysis of cross-sections through time and through comparison is, of course, possible only if the data collected in different periods are genuinely comparable.

Longitudinal treatment of behavioral data may range from a minute-to-minute account of the behavior of a single individual to the use of aggregate data where the unit of analysis is a well-delimited territory. These are the extremes. At the present time, however, longitudinal analysis of political behavior at the individual level has been applied most successfully through the panel method. In this method, a panel of the same respondents is interviewed at different points in time. This makes it possible to observe changes in behavior that might otherwise be ascribed to intervening events like an election or a crisis. We can then ask respondents about these events directly and identify the sequence of cause and effect. Repeated interviewing of the same respondents is expensive, and for this reason alone the panel method has not been used as widely as it might. It has been used most often in before- and after-election studies, that is, over a relatively short period of time. But there is no reason to suppose that, given sufficient resources, it could not be used in the study of political behavior over a number of years.

Apart from cost, the main difficulty with the panel method of longitudinal analysis involves sampling. In order to investigate a sample over an extended period of time, the characteristics of the population-to-be—that is, the population concerning which statements are to be made—must be specified. Loss of subjects, or dropout, and changes in the attributes of the respondents in the course of the study, such as age or economic status, make this specification of the population-to-be extremely difficult. It is probably for this reason that panel studies have been short-range, involving from two to four interview waves. This avoids technical difficulties stemming from changes in both interviewers and respondents. Other difficulties that will adversely influence spontaneity in answers to the same questions are "sample bias," arising out of differences in the characteristics of those willing to be interviewed several times and those unwilling; and "reinterview bias," that is, undue self-consciousness on respondents' part about being interviewed repeatedly.

Even in the face of these problems, the panel method is the most promising technique for studying political behavior through time. Its application belies the contention that the behavioral persuasion in politics is necessarily antihistorical. It certainly is the most dependable technique for studying the process of cause and effect, for it permits description of the direction, degree, and character of change.

This suggests a subtle interplay between techniques of developmental analysis, logistic requirements of research, and theoretical formulations. If cross-sectional analyses are framed in terms of models that are ahistorical, such as structural-functional or input-output formulations, adoption of these theoretical models has, in turn, tended to limit behavioral studies to cross-sectional techniques. On the other hand, theoretical models of change through time are rarely satisfied by cross-sectional surveys taken at different points in time. But the expensiveness of longitudinal research and other tactical difficulties have militated against much theoretical concern with political change at the level of the individual person.

Developmental analysis is perhaps the most exciting approach to the study of political change through time. Using this approach, the researcher deals with political behavior in the present by studying cross-sections in terms of whatever theoretical behavior model he may choose, but he does so against the background of both historical reconstructions and trend analyses, as well as against the foreground of whatever images he may build for the future. These are developmental constructs that emphasize the "from where, to where" sequence of actual and hypothetical events. Moreover, developmental analysis seems well suited to bridge the empirical world of the political scientist and the normative world of the policy planner.

The Goal Is Man

The goal is man. This is the ultimate justification for pursuing the behavioral persuasion in politics, as it is of any other human enterprise. Like art for art's sake, science for the sake of science has never made sense to me. This, of course, is a statement of value, and as such it cannot be scientifically demonstrated to be either true or false. In this regard, then, my understanding of the behavioral persuasion in politics rests on a premise that may be accepted or rejected but that cannot be proved or disproved.

But to say that the scientific study of man in politics has man as its goal is not saying very much, for men disagree on the nature of man in politics. Which is the man in whose service the behavioral persuasion finds its reason for existence? Is he a democratic man? A just man? A power seeking man? Is he a man who must be controlled because he is brutish and nasty? Or is he a man who must be liberated from the shackles of oppression to live a dignified life? These are philosophical questions better left to the philosophers. Whatever answer one chooses, there is likely to be a corresponding predicament. The most we can say is that different men have different conceptions of man and, as a result, give different meanings to what they do and why they do it.

I do not believe that the philosophical predicament need be a scientific predicament. Whatever philosophical views different scientists may hold about man and the reality of man, they need not interfere with their work in the laboratory or in the field. For there the validity of theoretical propositions about human behavior, from whatever philosophical position derived, is a matter of intersubjective agreement, not absolutist assertion, and the reliability of observations is a function of measures that are intersubjectively agreed on as well. The very existence of any scientific enterprise is predicated on intersubjectively consensual rather than subjectively philosophical notions about man, reality, or universe.

Is the man in whose service scientists do their work a mere phantom then? Clearly not. For if "man" does not exist, there are many men, acting men, valuing men, goal-seeking men, and among them the scientist himself. If this is so, and if science is justified by its services to men, is it possible for science to be value free, unconcerned with the values men cherish and the goals they seek? Can a science that seeks to maximize whatever particular values particular men prefer be neutral in a world of men who disagree? The issue has been debated for decades, with little agreement.

This should not be a source of despair. It does not mean that a science of man is impossible because behavioral scientists cannot agree on the relationship between empirical methods and their normative implications. Indeed, I believe that the very multiplicity of human goals and values makes the scientific enterprise, including the behavioral persuasion in politics, the challenge that it is. For it is because of the seeming multiplicity of values which men hold that behavioral science cannot and must not avoid dealing with the preferences, values, and goals of men. It doe not follow that science cannot investigate preferences, values, or policy objectives because it cannot tell us what goal is best or what action is just. I do not believe that these things are any more inscrutable than more mundane matters of political behavior.

While ethics is a legitimate pursuit in its own right, it does not have a copyright on propositions of value. Logicians have long occupied themselves with the problem of consistency in the order of values. Behavioral scientists, in politics and out, might be able to contribute something as well. This something, I daresay, is nothing less than inquiry into the problem of the universality of values, a universality that any ethical philosopher must *assume* if he wishes his propositions of how men should conduct themselves to be accepted. I do not believe for a moment that the ethical philosopher engages in his search for what is wise, right, or just for its own sake any more than the scientist does his work for the sake of science.

In seeking to discover empirically whether and what universal values are held by men anywhere, the behavioral scientist proceeds from the same assumption as the ethical philosopher. Whatever success may accompany his search, it seems to me that he is in a better position than the ethical philosopher to pass judgment, not, of course, in his role as scientist, but in his role as moralist. As long as there is talk about man's inhumanity to man, the behavioral scientist cannot escape the task of determining what is human and what is not. But unlike the ethical philosopher he can say, "I have been there."

The question of whether a value-free science of politics is possible must not be confused with the question of whether a value-free science is desirable. The former is a problem of fact that, in the end, can be answered only through empirical research into the nature of science as a form of human activity. The latter is a problem of value that will remain open as long as scientists themselves give different answers. I think it will remain an open question for generations to come.

If a value-free science of politics is possible, it can be put to the service of good as well as evil, of freedom as well as slavery, of life as well as death. In this respect a science of politics only shares the supreme dilemma of all the sciences, natural and behavioral. It would be most presumptuous to assume that political science has at its disposal a knowledge of good and evil, of justice and injustice, of right and wrong. But I believe that the position that a value-free science of politics is undesirable makes just that presumption.

It does not follow that a value-free science of politics is undesirable because it may be difficult to achieve. Values may creep into investigations of politics at almost any stage of the research process, from the selection of the problem to the interpretation of the findings. I do not believe that any clarification of the researcher's value biases will make his study any more scientific. I find it rather strange that some behavioral scientists, in politics and elsewhere, feel that if they only lay bare possible value biases, their research will gain in scientific stature. In that case, so the argument goes, any scientific appraisal of the research can discount the value bias and determine the degree of objectivity that has been reached. This argument strikes me as curious, because if the scientist is cognizant of his biases, it would seem to be up to him rather than to his critics to control them. If, on the other hand, he persists in proceeding with his scientific work though he knows it is biased, I can only conclude that he must find his practice desirable. He says, in fact, that he cannot eliminate his biases and that, therefore, he might as well live with them.

This stance should not be mistaken for the approach to the problem of values and scientific research on politics called policy science. The policy science approach does not assume that a value-free scientific study of politics is impossible because men pursue values through politics. Indeed, it sharply distinguishes between propositions of fact that are believed to be subject to scientific-empirical inquiry and propositions of value for which empirical science has yet no answer. But it does not deny that scientific research on propositions of fact cannot serve policy objectives; indeed, it asserts that political science, as all science, should be put to the service of whatever goals men pursue in politics.

In seeking to place the scientific study of politics at the disposal of the search for policy objectives, policy science need not violate the canons of scientific method. In fact, it is genuinely sensitive to the tensions and the subtle balance that exist between fact and value. Rather than confuse the two realms, it keeps them apart. If it did not make the sharp differentiation, we would soon have a "democratic political science," a "communist political science," an "anarchist political science," a "Catholic political science," and so on. Curiously enough, this absurdity is not altogether a fantasy. It is the inevitable outcome of the position that if only values are clarified, scientific research can move on its merry way.

It is more than likely that as long as men seek to impose their own values on other men, scientists will have to face the question of whether to place their services at the disposal of the combatants. Their answer will undoubtedly depend on the values they cherish as individuals with a moral conscience, but it will also depend on the institutional structure in which they are involved. The decision to serve group, class, nation, church, or world community, as one sees these collectivities, is always a matter of personal ethics. But whatever the choice, the scientific way of life is always dangerous. Even if the scientist sees his work as being in the service of goals that he himself cherishes, there is nothing in his science that prevents its being used for ends of which he disapproves. In this sense, at least, science is value free. I do not think the scientist can escape this dilemma of having his work misused without giving up his calling. Only if he places himself at the service of those whose values he disagrees with does he commit intellectual treason.

Units and Levels

of Analysis

POLITICAL INQUIRY is concerned with the actions of and relations between units of greatly varying size and complexity, ranging from individual persons or small groups to large organizations, associations, and inclusive territorial collectives like nation-states. Political science has been singularly free of controversies over the "reality" of groups or collectives in the social process that from time to time have raged in the other social sciences. That collectives as well as individuals are real and can be effective units of political decision or action has always seemed self-evident and common-sensical to political scientists. The institutional tradition of political analysis takes for granted the primary reality of decision-making collectives—nations, governments, parliaments, agencies, courts, parties, interest groups, and so on.

But, in avoiding the nominalist denial of the group as real and the nominalist view of the group as nothing more than "an assemblage of individuals" (Malinowski, 1939, p. 938), institutional analysis has failed to pay more attention to the manifold of interindividual actions and relationships that make the group what it is.[1] By treating the group as a "whole" or global entity rather than as *also* a set of interacting persons, institutional analysis has not done justice to the internal complexity of the group, its multiple properties, and the multiphasic nature of group behavior.

This approach has changed in recent years. Political scientists now study, both intensively and extensively, the behavior of individuals as members either of organized and institutionalized collectives such as legislatures, or of decision-making aggregates such as electorates. The focus on individual political behavior has increased the range and reach of political research. But as yet it has not contributed as much as we might hope to the analysis of the behavior of collectives and especially of very large collectives (which are as real as individual human actors). As a result, the scientific study of collective phenomena in politics has not achieved the precision and rigor now standard in the analysis of individual political behavior. In the study of international politics where nations are the action units, or in the study of comparative politics where subnational collectives such as parties or parliaments are the action units, research relies either on inferences from the unit's distributive, integral, or contextual properties (Merritt and Rokkan, 1966; Singer, 1968) or on impressionistic accounts of the unit's behavior (Banks and Textor, 1963).

The long-standing reluctance in political science to take its methodological problems seriously led to much conceptual and analytical confusion. Rather than coping methodologically with the problems arising from the fact that political science must deal with both individual and collective actors, the issues were thought soluble by some sort of compromise between behavioral and institutional analysis.[2] A textbook of the late fifties, when the controversy between behavioralists and institutionalists occasioned discomfort among those who had a foot in both camps, was subtitled *An Institutional and Behavioral Approach* (Leiserson, 1958). Though this work juxtaposed behavioral and institutional statements, it did not come to grips with the methodological problems stemming from the *simultaneity* of individual and collective action.

Let me explicate what I mean when I speak of the simultaneity of individual and collective action. When, after discussion, a committee makes a decision, two sets of decision are in fact made simultaneously. Each member of the committee makes a decision about the merits of a proposal and votes one way or another. As each member votes, the group's decision emerges simultaneously as a collective product. It is not that the individuals decide and vote first, and then the group decides. The group's decision is simultaneous with each individual member's decision as votes are being combined into the collective decision. Institutional analysis would be satisfied with knowing the outcome of the decision process, with the decision as an emergent property of the group. It might speculate about how the group decision came about; but having no information on the behavior of the individuals in the group, it can only rely on inference.

The methodological problem of "moving" from the level of individual behavior to the level of collective behavior has also not been coped with in the research that has an institutional setting but focuses on the behavior of individuals. These studies deal with the behavior of individuals *in* collectives but not with the behavior *of* collectives. For instance, in their study of four state legislatures John C. Wahlke and his associates (1962) treat the attitudes, perceptions, orientations, and norms *of* individual legislators and compare the distributions of individual responses *in* the legislatures rather than the structures or behavior patterns *of* the four legislatures as collectives. Similarly, Almond and Verba (1963) in their five-nation study of citizen behavior compare the distributions of individual characteristics *in* five nations rather than five nations as collective actors. This is not to minimize the importance of this type of research. Treating individuals *in* groups is a proper task of political science. But it is not the same as dealing with groups as behavioral units in collective decision making and action.

The reluctance of students of individual behavior to be concerned with the behavior of the units to which individuals invariably belong is understandable. In part the reluctance is a negative reaction to the often rather sweeping statements made by institutionalists. But there are other reasons as well. In particular, there are some familiar fallacies of logical inquiry that are to be avoided. Because these fallacies point up some problems involved in the relationship between individual and collective actors, I shall briefly discuss them.

The Fallacy of Reasoning by Analogy

Because two units are structurally, functionally, or behaviorally homologous—that is, there is a real identity or near-identity between them—it does not follow that we can treat them as analogues and assume that statements about one are as good as statements about the other. Because a legislative subcommittee may have properties very similar to the properties of the whole committee, it is erroneous to believe that explanation of subcommittee behavior can be simply applied to committee behavior. The error is aggravated by the assumption that the smaller unit may be a "replica" of the larger unit, in a sampling sense, just as a "representative sample" is a numerically smaller replica of a population universe. To illustrate, let us listen carefully to Robert A. Dahl's (1961a) justification for studying the politics of New Haven. He studied New Haven, he informs us, because it lay conveniently at hand, but he also made this guarded comment: "Though no city can claim to represent cities in general, and though certainly none can claim to display the full range of characteristics found in a national political system, New Haven is *in many respects typical* of other cities in the United States" (p. v; emphasis added).

The issue Dahl here raises is one of New Haven's representativeness in a sampling sense. I have no quarrel with the statement as a matter of logic. Whether New Haven is "typical" of other cities is a soluble empirical question. But, Dahl continues, New Haven is also atypical in certain respects that he finds advantageous to his purposes. One of these is: "Because, unlike most American cities, it has had a highly competitive two-party system for over a century, it *offers analogies* with national politics that few other cities could provide" (ibid.; emphasis added).

In this sentence Dahl implies that because New Haven has a property—a competitive two-party system just as the nation has such a system—it is feasible to reason *from* the case of New Haven *to* the nation as a whole. In the following paragraph Dahl further justifies the choice of New Haven as a research site:

If the disadvantages and limitations of studying one city are self-evident, the overwhelming and, I hope, compensating advantage is that the enterprise is reduced to manageable proportions. Many problems that are almost unyielding over a larger area can be relatively easily disposed of on this smaller canvas. It is not, perhaps, wholly accidental that the two political theorists who did the most to develop a descriptive political science were Aristotle and Machiavelli, who, though separated by eighteen centuries, both witnessed politics on the smaller, more human scale of the city-state. Nonetheless, I had better make clear at once that explanations presented in this study are tested only against the evidence furnished in the political system of New Haven. (Pp. v–vi)

As his caveats indicate, Dahl is much too sophisticated an investigator to be insensitive to the methodological problems involved in reasoning by analogy. But he nonetheless leaves the impression that his study of New Haven politics tells us something about national politics. And I am not sure what Dahl means when he tells us that Aristotle and Machiavelli witnessed politics "on the smaller, more human scale of the city-state." Applied to the New Haven situation, it means that Dahl is dealing with three types of unit—the good citizens of New Haven, New Haven itself, and the nation. Perhaps political science would be better off if it could free itself of notions of politics developed in the small city-state units of Aristotle's and Machiavelli's (and now Dahl's) worlds.

The Fallacy of Reasoning by Inference

This fallacy of reasoning by inference takes two forms (Cohen and Nagel, 1934, p. 377). First, there is the "fallacy of composition," which is probably more widespread than one might suspect. It involves inference from the properties of subunits to the properties of the unit they compose. For instance, the fact that the members of a collective are "unstable" in their behavior patterns does not permit the conclusion that the group is "unstable." The word "unstable" does not mean the same thing on the two levels of analysis—that of the individual member and that of the group. Applied to the individual, it refers to a personality trait; applied to the group, it refers to the structure of relationships obtaining in the group.

One cannot explain or predict the group's structure or behavior from knowledge of its individual parts.

The converse error is the "fallacy of division." Because of the nature of the data with which social scientists are often dealing, it is better known today as the "ecological fallacy."[3] It is most frequently encountered with units whose distributive properties are known but whose subunits cannot be singly identified. The fallacy of division involves inference from the properties of a whole to the properties of its parts. For instance, we may say that the Supreme Court is a "just" body, but this statement does not mean that all judges are just. The administrative inertia that may be characteristic of a bureaucracy does not prove that every bureaucrat in the organization is inert.

The same fallacies arise at other levels of analysis. The committees of a legislature may be well integrated, yet the legislature itself may be poorly integrated. To make inferences about integration from the larger to the smaller unit, or from the smaller to the larger, is fallacious. In fact, it may be that high integration of "lower-level" units (such as families, cliques, tribes, cities, regions, and so on) impedes the integration of "higher-level" units. And the integration of a large unit is no guarantee that its component parts are also similarly integrated.

These fallacies should not be confused with what I think are two viable analytic operations that involve relationships between smaller and larger units. Both create methodological problems of their own, but both are either theoretically or empirically soluble. There is, first, the question of "linkages" between larger and smaller units, regardless of whether the smaller units are parts of or independent of the larger units.[4] Role analysis and reference group theory are propitious approaches to the linkage problems (Biddle and Thomas, 1966; Hyman and Singer, 1968). There is, second, the question of "impact," either of the larger on the smaller unit or of the smaller on the larger unit. The contemporary work on "structural effects" and "breakage effects" seeks to deal with relevant methodological issues (Blau, 1960; Davis, 1961a). I do not propose to pursue these issues here. For my interest is in the problem of simultaneity—the problem arising from the fact that a larger unit and its smaller subunits are simultaneously involved in political action. The larger unit cannot act unless its constituent subunits also act, but the latter cannot act without implicating the larger unit in the action.

Although the individuals *in* a group and the group as a whole make decisions simultaneously, in the real world of politics where institutionalized groups make decisions and take action, it is the group as a whole and not its individual members that, under given decision rules, is the *effective* decision maker. The city council, not the individual city councilman, commits the city to a course of action; the Senate of the United States, not Senator Jones, ratifies treaties.

It follows that we may want to say something about the behavior of the group rather than the behavior of its component parts. In that case, the behavior of the individual members may get in our way. This is particularly so if we want to compare the behavior of many groups—say, all the city councils in a metropolitan area, all the committees of the Congress, or all the nations in the world. Yet it is difficult if not impossible to observe the behavior of the group without observing the behavior of the individuals in the group. How can we go about our business of making statements about group behavior without either talking about the individuals in the group or using analogical and inferential reasoning?

The answer lies, I think, in bringing all of a unit's properties, whether residing in the group as a whole or in its parts, on to the same level of analysis. But what does it mean to "bring properties on to the same level of analysis"? Let me give some examples. For instance, the group's decision rules—its constitution—are integral properties of the group. By an integral property is meant an attribute of the unit as a whole that under no circumstance is an attribute of a subunit. The decision rules are of the group and not of the individuals composing the group. We can find out what the rules are by asking questions of the members, or by reading the rule book, or by observing the group. Plurality voting, majority voting, extraordinary majority voting, or unanimous voting may be required by the rules. The rules as an integral property can tell us a good deal about the behavior of the group as a whole. We need not investigate the individuals in the group to say something about the group's behavior.

But now take the case of a five-member group that has majority rule. This information tells us that there must at least be three members in the majority on every vote. But the rule itself cannot tell us whether a *particular group* has or has not a three-member majority or majority faction. If by inspection of recorded vote divisions we can determine that over many issues there always seems to be the same majority of three and the same minority of two, we are no longer observing the group as a whole but are examining two subunits whose patterned relationship to each other makes for one structural property of the entire group. What we are actually doing is this: we reduce the group to two subunits and then reconstruct it by saying that it has a bipolar structure. The factions are the subunits out of which the group property "bipolarity" is being constructed. In other words, we have brought a relational property initially characteristic of the subunits unto the unit level as a structural property.

But now let us assume that although we know that the group splits along majority and minority lines, we do not know the composition of the two factions. In that case we cannot really say that the group has a bipolar structure. If we did, we would commit the compositional fallacy. The group may, in fact, have a nonpolar structure; that is, different individuals may compose the majority and minority in any *particular vote.* Put differently, the composition of the minority and majority is so unstable that one can hardly speak of factions. Rather than being bipolarized, the group is fragmented. The group's subunits are not factions but individuals or possibly cliques. At this point we must look at the relationships that obtain among all of the group's individual members. If we find no stable relationships among the individuals—that is, if their individual voting patterns appear random rather than regular—we employ the irregular individual voting to characterize the whole group as fragmented or having a nonpolar structure.

We might also discover that whenever three-to-two voting splits occur in the group, it is always the same two individuals in the majority and the same two in the minority, while a fifth member "swings" back and forth. How can we characterize the group in which this behavior occurs? Our subunits are now two dyads, but what gives the group its characteristic property is the presence of a "pivotal" individual as another subunit. The pivotal voter's erratic behavior becomes, at the group level of analysis, a property that characterizes the group as a whole.

All of these examples suggest that if we are to discover a group's relational or structural properties, we must reduce the group to the relevant subunits—factions, dyads, or individuals—that compose the group. But having reduced the group to subunits, we must reconstruct it from the data gathered about the behavior of the subunits.

The procedures I have tried to illustrate by various examples differ significantly from the methods of analogy and inference. Reducing larger units to smaller ones in order to discover group properties "at a lower level" and constructing larger units out of smaller ones to permit comparative or correlational analysis "at a higher level" are operations quite different from making inferences from individual to collective phenomena or from collective to individual phenomena. These operations clearly involve a great deal of methodological contrivance. I shall try here to present them more formally and systematically.

OBJECT UNITS AND SUBJECT UNITS

The level-of-analysis problem stems from two requirements. First, diverse units can be compared only at the same level of analysis and the properties of diverse units can be correlated only at the same level. And second, a unit's properties may have to be derived from other units at other levels because they are not available at the unit's own level. Only the unit's integral and possibly some of its emergent properties are directly observable. All other properties must be constructed or imputed to the unit as contextual properties. I shall first clarify what is meant by "unit of analysis" and "level of analysis."

Let us distinguish between an "object unit" and a "subject unit" of analysis.

By *object unit* I mean the unit whose behavior is to be explained. The unit whose behavior is to be explained is given by the *research problem.* If we want to explain how voters make up their minds in an election, individual persons are the object units, or simply objects, of analysis. If the Supreme Court's pattern of decisions in a set of cases is to be explained, the Court is the object unit of analysis. If our research problem is to compare the concentration or distribution of power in local communities, our object units are communities. If we are interested in the actions of nation-states in an international crisis, our object units of analysis are nations.

By *subject unit* is meant the unit whose behavior is observed in order to explain the behavior of an object unit. The notion of subject unit is more difficult to explicate than the concept of object unit. It is perhaps best understood in the sense the experimental psychologist uses the word "subject." His subject is the person he brings into the laboratory in order to observe his behavior. But the notion of the person as subject can be extended to collectives. A group, a committee, a party, a state, and so on can be treated as subject units if their behavior is observed.

The distinction between object unit and subject unit is purely conceptual. But because the distinction is conceptual, in empirical reality *an object unit can be the subject unit.* For instance, for the clinical psychologist the individual person is both the object to be explained and the subject to be observed (Hilgard and Lerner, 1951).

The conception of the individual person as object and subject of analysis is simple enough. More complex is the notion that a collective, too, may be both object and subject of analysis. A group as a group is more difficult to observe than is an individual person as a person. It involves technical problems of analysis that are by no means easy to solve. But if they can be solved, considering a collective both object and subject of analysis is viable.

The conception of a unit, be it an individual person or a group of varying size, as both object and subject of analysis serves to clarify what is meant by *level of analysis.* For if we say that a unit is both object and subject, we are in effect saying that the behavior of the unit is to be both observed and explained *at its own level.*

By itself the conception of observing a unit's behavior at its own level is nothing more than a linguistic convention of little practical use. It is simply a shorthand expression. But it is of formal logical use. For it implies, in a logical sense, the possibility of *observing* the unit *at another level,* while *explaining* it *at its own level.* In other words, if our object unit is a group, the notion of level of analysis suggests that it may be observed at its own or at another level. The conception does not tell us automatically at which level the group is to be observed—at a "lower level" in terms of properties inherent in its subunits, which then become the subject of analysis; at its own level; or at a "higher level," say the level of intergroup relations.

The crucial methodological question then is what subject units are to be chosen as foci of observation in order to explain the behavior of the object unit. David Singer (1961, p. 77) has rightly complained that choice of level is often "ostensibly a mere matter of methodological or conceptual convenience." Speaking of his own discipline of international relations, he writes: "We have, in our texts and elsewhere, roamed up and down the ladder of organizational complexity with remarkable abandon, focusing upon the total system, international organizations, regions, coalitions, extranational associations, nations, domestic pressure groups, social classes, elites, and individuals as the needs of the moment required" (ibid., p. 78).

Singer's distress is not exaggerated. If choice of level is a mere matter of convenience, it can lead only to analytic confusion. But, it seems to me, the issue is not "moving up and down" from one level of analysis to another, but failure to distinguish between object and subject units of analysis. If this distinction is not made, it is certainly never clear just which unit's behavior is to be explained and which unit's behavior is to be observed. As I have suggested already, moving from one level, the level of the object unit, to another level, where a subject unit is observed, may be necessary if the object unit cannot be fully observed at its own level—that is, if it cannot also serve as the subject of analysis. But such movement to another level cannot be a matter of methodological convenience. If we were limited to observing a unit only at its own level, political science would be deprived of a powerful mode of analysis.

MULTILEVEL ANALYSIS

Are there limits on the observer's freedom to move from one level of analysis to another? In answering this question, let me emphasize that the language employed in talk about levels of analysis is clearly metaphorical. If I continue in this vein, it is because metaphors can be useful. My concern is whether there is an upper and a lower limit in the hierarchy of levels beyond which one cannot move, no matter how theoretically desirable it might be to do so.

My answer is that there are limits, practical limits, just as a house has a roof and a basement floor. Much as I might want to, I cannot move beyond the roof or below the basement floor. I can possibly build another story on top of the roof, or I can dig a second basement. But while endless building up and digging down is speculatively conceivable, in practice it is not. Sooner or later my house will collapse under the weight of new stories, or I will hit rock bottom as I try to dig new levels below.

In the language of the philosophy of science, what is involved in the choice of levels of analysis is *reduction* and *construction*. I am concerned with reduction and construction as procedures of analysis and not as philosophical issues. Reduction and the strategy of reductionism have been topics of hot controversy in the past. Reductionism as an approach holds that it is desirable, if not necessary, to explain larger units in terms of the smallest units or elements into which they can be decomposed. The assumption underlying reductionism is that events occurring at a "simpler" level of a unit's organization are also more "fundamental" (Nagel, 1961, pp. 345–358, 541–544). I cannot get particularly excited about this philosophical aspect of reduction, because it seems to me it is a metamethodological issue that is not per se soluble, for three reasons.

First, level of analysis—that is, the choice of a subject unit—is determined by the observer's theoretical standpoint and not by methodological considerations. I see no absolute virtue in reducing an object unit to its "ultimate" subject units. How far one wishes to reduce an object depends on one's theory.

Second, the object unit may have properties that cannot be reduced. Because an object unit cannot be reduced, it does not follow that it cannot be scientifically investigated.

Third, reduction may not be feasible on practical grounds, because although the object unit may be reducible in theory, relevant subject units may simply not be available. For instance, ecological units characterized by aggregate data cannot be reduced to individuals as units.

It was perhaps inevitable that in response to radical reductionism some analysts would insist on observing object units as "wholes."[5] But in my opinion the position that objects can be understood *only* as wholes is as metamethodological as the pure reductionist formula. Intuitively, I will admit, we see wholes before we see parts—the tree before the branches, the branches before the leaves. But when it comes to empirical operations, the advice of the holist is easier given than carried out. Except for their integral properties, the properties of wholes are not easily observable. They must often be constructed out of subject units that are parts of the whole.

Again, whether one wishes to treat object units as wholes or construct them out of component subject elements is not a matter of methodological virtue but of theoretical relevance, again for three reasons.

First, what from one theoretical standpoint may appear to be a part may from another standpoint appear to be a whole. Some students of political behavior have been criticized for being concerned "only" with the individual political actor and for not using their knowledge of individual behavior in saying something about the "larger" political system (although it is rarely made clear just what "system" the critic has in mind). This position seems to me ill founded. If one wants to study individual political behavior and has good theoretical grounds for doing so, he cannot be criticized for not doing what he does not want to do. In fact, by choosing the individual actor as both object and subject of analysis, he may treat him as a whole very much as the holist would have it. He would be mistaken to hold that only individual political behavior "matters" and that other units do not matter. But I am not aware of anyone who takes this position.

Second, whether a unit is to be treated as a whole, either directly in terms of its integral properties or indirectly through construction from subunit properties, depends on whether it is a collective actor. Whether or not it is a collective actor depends on whether the unit is a genuinely "behavioral system" or an artifact of aggregation. No one will deny that the Supreme Court, or the U.S. Senate, or the Corps of Engineers are not collective actors. Collective actors are of intrinsic scientific interest just as individual actors are, and statements about them as units describe some behavioral reality. By way of contrast, aggregates are artificial wholes. An electoral unit like a precinct does not act as a whole. Precincts may be treated *as if* they were wholes. For instance, they are treated as wholes in correlational analysis because other subject unit data are not available. If they were, correlational analysis would be based on individual data precisely because the precinct is not a collective actor. Similarly, an aggregate of foreign-born in a population is not a collective actor. Foreign-born citizens may combine into an ethnic association that becomes a collective actor and may be studied at the level of the individuals composing it.

Third, as in the case of reduction, there are practical limits to construction. At some point construction may have to cease if the edifice is not to look absurd. I sometimes sense an absurdity when I read the more imaginary constructions of theoretical-system builders whose edifices defy our powers of empirical observation and construction. More often than not the systems erected in theory become reified as if they corresponded to something "real" in the real world of politics.

I am not denying that philosophical issues are involved in the procedures of reduction and construction. But it seems to me that in addition to theoretical considerations the choice of level of analysis should be guided by practical exigencies and not by counsels of methodological perfection. There are simple practical reasons for following the strategy of reduction in some research situations and for following the strategy of construction in others. Stokes (1966, pp. 5–6) has suggested that analytic reduction of institutional phenomena of politics to the level of the individual has at least these advantages: (1) it allows us to generalize the phenomenon under review; (2) it increases our power to predict or explain variations of gross phenomena; and (3) it permits observations at a lower level of analysis, which may be more generous in a sampling sense. This attitude makes good sense if the object unit is in fact reducible and if there are good theoretical reasons for doing so. But once we have reduced an object unit and observed its properties at a lower level of analysis, it is desirable to reconstruct the object unit, especially if it also contains nonreducible properties and is besides a significant collective actor in the political arena.

The notion of levels of analysis does not preclude treatment of the object unit on more than one level other than its own. Several subject units may be inspected at different levels, some higher and some lower than the object unit level. We may want to explain the behavior of the subcommittees of the House Appropriations Committee. We have, minimally, three options that stem from the subcommittees' location in the hierarchy of levels.

First, we can deal with the subcommittees at their own level of analysis, that is, we can treat them as both objects and subjects of analysis. We might correlate such integral properties of the subcommittees as their size, their jurisdiction, their budget estimates, their partisan division, and so on.

Second, we can deal with the subcommittees at the level of the individual members who sit on them. We can identify the proportion of liberals and conservatives on each subcommittee and characterize each subcommittee accordingly. We can ascertain each subcommittee's median tenure. We can determine each member's attitudes on budget cutting and construct the subcommittee's collective orientation in this respect. The subcommittees are still our objects of analysis, but our subject units are now examined at the lower level of the subcommittee's individual members.

Third, we can move to the higher level of the whole Appropriations Committee. We may impute certain characteristics of the whole committee, such as its goals or norms, to the subcommittees. We might wish to compare Appropriations subcommittees with Agriculture subcommittees, and so on. Again, the subcommittees remain the object units of analysis, but they are now attributed contextual properties characteristic of the larger committee of which they are parts.

This example of a three-level analysis is not fanciful. It formalizes in part the mode of analysis pursued by Richard F. Fenno (1966, pp. 127–190) in his study of congressional appropriations politics. Fenno's work is an outstanding case study of how moving up and down from one level of analysis to another can enrich our understanding of the political process. Fenno uses levels of analysis to good effect in dealing with questions of linkage and impact.

I shall follow the notion of multiple levels of analysis by way of an illustrative diagram. The matrix columns in Figure 2.1 refer to the object units of analysis—the units whose behavior is to be explained. Seven object units, all conceivably real decision makers, ranging from an indivdual actor to the large collective actor called "government," are introduced. The matrix rows refer to the corresponding subject units of analysis—the units whose behavior is being observed. Level of analysis is defined by the intersections of the columns and rows. The shaded cells represent the levels where object unit and subject unit are the same, where the unit is observed and explained at its own level. Reductive and constructive operations are indicated by the vertical arrows. Arrows pointing downward suggest the possibility of reduction. Arrows pointing upward suggest the possibility of construction. The cells to the right of the shaded diagonal cells represent the conditions under which a subject unit provides the context the object unit is located in. The horizontal arrow denotes that some of the subject unit's properties may be imputed to the object unit as the latter's own

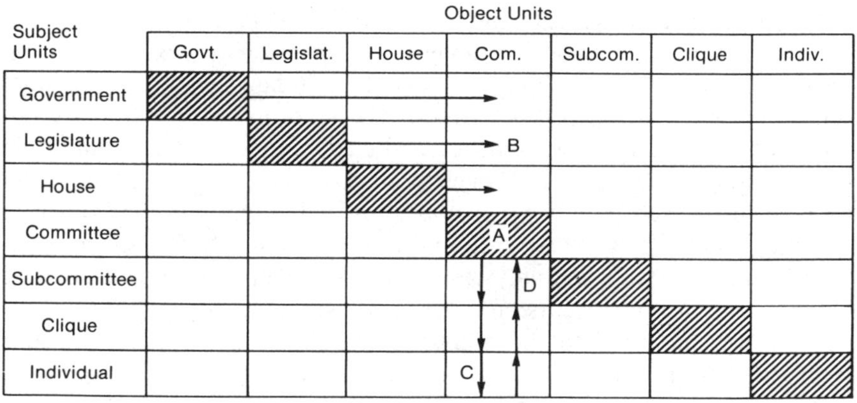

Key: A   Shaded cell: unit analyzed at own level
       B   Horizontal arrow: unit property imputed from context
       C   Vertical arrow down: unit properties reduced to lower level
       D   Vertical arrow up: unit properties constructed from lower level unit

Figure 2.1   Units and levels of analysis

contextual properties. The smaller the object unit, the greater the number of subject units that may provide relevant contextual properties.

Let me take the case of the committee as the object unit. We can observe and explain the committee at its own level in terms of its integral properties. We can reduce the committee to three types of subject unit: subcommittees, cliques, and individuals. We can ascertain characteristic properties of these subject units and reconstruct the committee by appropriate procedures. For instance, from study of individual roles we can construct the committee's role structure. From study of cliques and interpersonal relations we can construct the committee's degree of integration. From study of subcommittee functions we can ascertain the committee's division of labor.

Analysis may of course proceed on several levels at once. Individuals take roles in networks of interpersonal relations that are a property of the whole. Cliques function within and across subcommittees, and as they do they constitute the interpersonal networks within which individual roles are taken. The organized complexity of a unit such as a committee makes for simultaneous actions, reactions, interactions, and transactions of the different subject actors who, for one theoretical reason or another, are selected to serve as foci of observation.

The contextual properties that may be imputed to the committee have their origin in the subject units that constitute the committee's environment. The committee is located in a house, the house in a legislature, and the legislature in the government. Characteristics of these subject units— whether the government is partisan or nonpartisan, whether the legislature is urban or rural, whether the house is apportioned or not—may be imputed to the object unit as contextual properties.

Reduction, construction, and imputation make possible comparison and correlation of unit properties that otherwise could not be compared or correlated. We cannot correlate the properties of individuals and the properties of a group. Either the properties of individuals must be constructed into group properties, if the object unit is the group, or group properties must be reduced to individual properties, if the object unit is the individual. Similarly, we cannot correlate the properties of an object unit, say, a city council, with the properties of the city environment, say, whether it is urban or rural. But we can impute a characteristic of the environment to the council as a contextual property and speak of "urban councils" or "rural councils." We can then correlate the imputed contextual property with some other council property at the same level of analysis.

Throughout this discussion I have avoided using the concepts of *micro* and *macro,* chiefly because I believe that they are not particularly useful in dealing with the problems of levels of analysis. And they may actually confuse the issues involved. Their use is least harmful, but also not very informative, if micro is simply applied to individual political behavior and macro to all collective political behavior. If usage is so restricted, the terms themselves add nothing to our understanding.[6]

Yet if it is not fashionable the micro-macro terminology is prestigious, largely because it is used in economics, the most "advanced" in explanatory or predictive power of the social sciences. I am not impressed by this reason for using the terms, but their usage in economics may be instructive. Economists speak of "microeconomics" if the unit of analysis to be explained is not further reducible *according to economic theory*. Consumers (individuals) and firms (collectives), for instance, are treated by economic theory as nonreducible units. By "macroeconomics" economists refer to units that in practice are reducible but which for theoretical reasons are treated as wholes, such as gross national product, national income, and so on. This usage is very close to one I prefer, for I have insisted throughout that level of analysis is a matter of theoretical determination. In any case, economists do not restrict the term "micro" to individuals alone but apply it to any unit that is theoretically not reducible.

The economist, it appears, has no trouble with identifying a unit as either micro or macro because he maintains a rather fixed theoretical standpoint. This is not the case in political science. Precisely because much analysis in political science is concerned with the linkage between different types of units and with the impact of one unit on another, the observer's theoretical standpoint may change as he seeks to explain the behavior of different object units. As a result, what is micro and what is macro also changes with changing theoretical standpoints. Moreover, we are dealing in politics with a great variety of actors whose unit properties are both nonreducible and reducible, depending on the theoretical standpoint of the observer.

Rather than thinking of micro and macro in dichotomous terms, the political scientist is better off if he thinks of a "micro-macro continuum." What in this continuum is micro and what is macro depends on the point on the micro-macro scale where the observer "dips in," where he fixes his object unit of analysis. If his object unit is the legislative committee and his subject units are the subcommittees or individuals composing the committee, his procedure is microanalysis. If his object unit is still the committee but his subject units are the committee itself or those units that constitute the committee's environment from which derive its contextual properties (the house or the legislature in which the committee is located), his procedure is macroanalysis.

If we envisage, as in Figure 2.2, a micro-macro continuum and fix the observer's standpoint, it is apparent that as he moves toward the *micro*

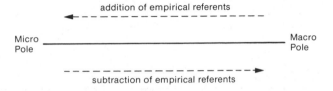

Figure 2.2   The micro-macro continuum

pole, he *adds* empirical referents to his analysis. And as he moves toward the *macro pole,* he *subtracts* empirical referents. In other words, it is not the absolute size of a unit that makes it micro or macro. A nation of millions and the Supreme Court composed of nine justices differ enormously in size. Both may be thought of as subjects of microanalysis if they are decomposed through reductive procedures, that is, through the addition of empirical referents. Or both may be subjected to macroanalysis by treatment in terms of their own integral properties or contextual properties.

Let me give another example. There are 50 state legislatures in the United States. We can deal with these 50 legislatures as both objects and subjects of macroanalysis. But we can also reduce them by moving to the micro pole of the continuum. If we were to select legislative chambers as subjects, 99 units would be available for analysis (as Nebraska has only one house). If we were to concentrate on party delegations, the number of subject units would increase to perhaps 198 (on the assumption that there are two delegations per chamber or four per legislature). If committees were to serve as subject units, data on perhaps more than 2,000 units would serve our analysis. If individual legislators were chosen as subjects, we would have several thousand cases available for analysis.

Many of the arguments in political science about "triviality" and "significance" have probably something to do with the observer's movement toward or away from the poles of the micro-macro continuum. The analyst who moves toward the micro pole adds empirical data that make for greater validity and reliability, but he possibly sacrifices significance; the analyst who moves toward the macro pole deprives himself of data, loses in validity and reliability, but possibly gains in significance. I am not convinced by this argument, however. It seems to me that the critical issue is the level-of-analysis problem, regardless of the judgments of validity, reliability, or significance. And this problem, I have suggested, consists in manipulating data in such a way that the properties of various subject units, whatever their level, can be made to serve analysis of an object unit at that unit's own level.

3

Closing the

Micro-Macro Gap

PROPOSITIONS in political science typically consist of elements whose referents are collective actors. Take, for instance, the proposition that nations with multiparty systems experience more cabinet instability than nations with two-party systems. The truth or falsity of this proposition is not at issue. At issue is the nature of the elements in the proposition and their empirical referents. In this example, the object units of analysis—the "things" whose behavior is to be explained—are nations, and their behavior is to be explained in terms of the relationship between two variables: first, "party system," and second, "cabinet stability."

What is actually to be compared, then, is not "national behavior" but the relationship between two properties or variables of nations. To make the comparison and test the relationship expressed in the proposition, "party system"—a property of the nation—has to be reduced to another set of units, namely, parties: what we observe and count is the distribution of parties in the nation. Although the proposition may have given the impression that "party system" is some global or integral property of the nation, it is in fact a distributive-structural property. Similarly, cabinet instability as a property of the unit nation has to be reduced to the comings and goings of individual ministers over time. Thus cabinet stability or instability is measured by ascertaining, through summation, the turnover rate of the men who come and go, the length of their stay in office, and so on.

In fact, then, the only way in which the original hypothesis can be rigorously tested is by reducing the object unit "nation" to some component smaller unit—in the case of the property "cabinet instability," to individual persons. Only after we have reduced the unit "nation" to "parties" and "ministers" can we construct the properties of the larger units in which we are interested and compare them in order to test the hypothesis that multiparty system and cabinet instability are related.

I have chosen an example that is simple and obvious because its simplicity and obviousness disguise the profound methodological problem that is involved. Obviously one must count parties and minister turnovers to determine the nature of a "party system" or "cabinet stability." But what is involved is not only a process of reduction but also of construction. The whole is constructed out of its parts.

Yet, I would argue, we have not self-consciously faced the issue of reduction. For if reduction is a viable procedure, there is no reason to stop short, as in the earlier example, with units like parties. For these units are also "large" and in turn decomposable. Rather, once the reductionist route is taken, there is no reason for not taking it all the way—that is, reducing macrophenomena like nations, parties, or cabinets, to their smallest analytic and empirical units. Yet, few students of comparative national politics have taken the leap from the nation as the object unit of analysis to the individual as the subject unit of analysis. This, it seems to me, is the main reason for the relative lack of rigor in the testing of propositions about national behavior.

Political science has produced very sophisticated propositions about the relationships of properties of political units—stability, legitimacy, authority, integration, development, power, and so on. But these propositions are not tested rigorously over many units because relevant data have not been generated. Although aggregate statistics have served as empirical indicators of social-structural (independent) variables and other quantifiable data as decisional-output (dependent) variables, valid and reliable indicators of political process variables are difficult to come by in the study of large collectivities (Merritt and Rokkan, 1966; Dogan and Rokkan, 1969). When such indicators were generated, the data were highly suspect (Banks and Textor, 1963). In other words, the issue of reduction—the problem of reducing macrophenomena to the level of individual behavior and using data collected from or about individuals to construct the properties of collective units of action—has not been solved.

When reduction has been made, as in *The Legislative System* (Wahlke et al., 1962) or other studies using survey research, analysis has proceeded on the level of the individual, and statements about the behavior of collective actors were in the nature of inferences from individual behavior. These inferences—involving the "individualistic" or "compositional" fallacy—are dangerous and possibly misleading. Reduction, it appears, is only a first step, and though it is necessary to generate data that can be rigorously treated, it is not sufficient to test propositions about the behavior of units that are larger than the individual actor. Another step is required: the whole must be reconstructed from the parts. If construction does not occur, it is possible only to test propositions about the behavior of individuals *in* larger units, but not about the behavior *of* larger units. Yet most propositions of politics are not propositions about individuals but about collective actors—on the very good assumption that collective units are, in fact, *real* political actors.

Let me develop the theme in a different way. Insofar as political research has been "behavioral," in the sense that it is based on the individual person as the unit of analysis, it has dealt with the behavior of individuals in collectivities and not with the behavior of collectivities. What is found are similarities or differences in the behavior of individual members of collectivities like nations, bureaucracies, or legislatures. This is easy enough. More difficult is the identification of the factors that make for these similarities or differences. Explanation is sought in extraneous social-structural or speculative "cultural" conditions that are introduced post hoc and not part of the data set itself. What is involved is a shift in level of analysis: concepts or indicators of concepts that refer to macrophenomena are used to explain individual behavior. Or, as the case may be, individual behavior is used to explain macrophenomena by way of inference.

If the empirical unit of analysis is the individual, research on large units must come to grips with two further problems: first, as already mentioned, the problem of how units on different levels of analysis are "linked" and second, how a unit on one level of analysis has an "impact" on (causes) the behavior of a unit on another level. Both are important problems of analysis, but I shall not deal with them here. For my concern is with the testing of propositions about the behavior of collectivities *in their own right.* For these propositions can only be tested at these units' *own* level and cannot be tested at the level of subunits or individual members. Such testing cannot rely on inferences from subunit or member behavior but involves the construction of unit properties out of their behavior.

One consequence of dealing with the problem of reduction and construction has been the false distinction between "behavioral" and "structural" variables. But what is involved is a level-of-analysis problem, and, if it is a problem, some solution must be sought. In fact, of course, structural variables are behavioral variables writ "large." And if they are of this nature, I see no reason why the properties of large units should not be constructed out of data gathered at the lowest feasible level of analysis. Data at this level can be manipulated in more or less elegant ways—as frequency distributions, proportions, rates, and other parametric measures. And they can forcefully bring to our attention the fact that the global ("structural" or "functional") language common at the macrolevel disguises much of the variance in the behavior of collective actors that occurs at the microlevel of individual behavior. Unless the properties of collective actors are obtained through reduction and construction, analysis of large units will inevitably remain literary, discursive, and speculative.

I shall, from this point on, ignore the issue of reduction. There is much controversy in this matter between "reductionists" and "holists"—those who believe that scientific advance is predicated on reduction and those who hold that in social relations there are units which, because they act as wholes, should be treated as wholes and, therefore, must not or cannot be reduced to parts. I shall ignore this controversy because I am sympathetic to both sides. I believe that, as is the case with many dualisms, the whole-part dualism is a pseudoproblem that has no empirical merit (see Chapter 9). Instead, I suggest a pragmatic guideline that does not require commitment to either an intransigent reductionist or holistic position. The guideline is simple: *reduce if you can and if it makes theoretical sense; do not reduce if you cannot and when it makes no sense.* In other words, use as a starting point the data that are available or the data that can be generated, regardless of the level on which the analysis is to be conducted. But in conducting the analysis, keep in mind that it can only be conducted on one level of analysis. In other words, keep in mind that correlation is possible only between units on the same level of organizational complexity. If, however, data are available from units at other levels, they must be *transformed* to make them manipulable at the level of the units whose behavior is to be compared and explained.

In general, data are available at three levels of analysis. First, at the unit's own level; that is, we have direct knowledge about some property of the unit; for instance, we know a nation's size, boundaries, or formal constitution. Second, at the level of subunits or members; for instance, we may have knowledge of the opinions, attitudes, or expectations of a legislature's members. And third, at the level of the unit's environment; for instance, we may have information about the character of a party organization's surroundings—whether it is located in a large or small city, in a densely populated slum area or a sparsely populated suburb, in a region with many natural resources or with few natural resources, and so on. If this is the case, the methodological problem is how such data from different levels can be made manageable at the level of the units whose behavior is to be compared and explained.

The Nature of Unit Properties

In order to tackle the problem of data transformation (that is, bringing data from different levels onto the unit's own level), let us assume for a moment that transformation is in fact possible. If it is possible, we must have a clear picture of the properties of the units to be treated.

Comparison involves relationships among unit properties at their own level of complexity or comparison of interlevel relationships (as when we wish to compare the impact that leaders have on groups). Thus clarification is all the more necessary for two reasons: first, properties of collective actors and properties of their members must not be confused and false inferences must not be made from one level of analysis to another; and second, the data base of the properties to be compared must be unambiguous; for different unit properties can be ascertained on different levels and can be constructed by different transformation techniques. Put differently, conceptual clarification of unit properties is necessary because it affects the practical operations performed on data gathered on different levels of organizational complexity. It affects *what* data are transformed, *how* the data are transformed, and *why* the transformed data are interpreted as they are.

There has been some attention to this in the sociological literature; however, as is so often the case in the social sciences, the nomenclature has not been identical. In general, variables identified at the unit's own level are called its global, integral, or syntality properties; variables stemming from subunits or members and transformed into unit variables are called population, aggregative, or analytical properties; and variables characterizing the environment and transformed into unit variables are called structural or contextual properties.[1] For reasons that will become clear later on, I shall suggest two other properties that are called "relational" and "structural" properties. Table 3.1 presents these properties, with the nomenclature used by other scholars and by Eulau-Prewitt.

Because I think that methodological matters are best discussed in the context of empirical research, I shall draw on my current research for illustrations. Thus I must briefly refer to the units with which I am concerned. I am interested in the behavior of small legislative councils because I believe that they are important decision-making units in democratic politics. But more important, I am interested in these groups because I believe that the methodological problems of social science can best be tackled in research arenas in which data are available and can be fruitfully manipulated. But, as has been argued, the distinction between what is to be considered "large" or "small" is a matter of observational standpoint. While the legislative groups with which I am dealing are "small" from the perspective of national parliaments or assemblies, they are "large" from the perspective of the members who compose them. And national assemblies are "small" from the perspective of the nation that they serve. Both relatively large or small legislative groups have in common the represent-

Table 3.1 Nomenclature of Unit Properties

Property is constructed from information about—	Nomenclature of—	
	Sociologists	Eulau-Prewitt
Unit itself	Integral Global Syntality	Integral
Members (subunits)	Population Aggregative Analytical	Distributive
		Relational
		Structural
Environment	Contextual Structural	Contextual

ative function: whether large or small, they are in fact acting *for* even larger units or aggregates.

Research on small legislative groups of from five to nine members has a number of methodological advantages. First, the smaller the group, the easier is it to observe the interaction. Second, as the methodological problem is that of reduction and construction, the choice of small, formal groups facilitates both the identification of the group's members and the collection of the same kinds of data from or about each member. Third, in small, face-to-face groups the information from each individual can be used in two ways: (1) as "respondent" data—that is, as information about the respondent himself; and (2) as "informant" data about either other individuals in the group or the group as a whole. Fourth, informant data collected from individuals in a small, face-to-face group are probably more reliable than data collected in a large group: there can be a strong presumption that the respondent as informant in fact describes reality, and the information given by one can easily be checked for reliability against the information given by another member of the group. Finally, the number of small legislative groups is large: while there are only one Congress and fifty state legislatures, there are hundreds of committees. In our research we happen to deal with eighty-two city councils. These still are not enough cases for more than bivariate analysis, although, if linear assumptions are met, it is enough for at least some multivariate comparisons.

INTEGRAL PROPERTIES

A group's integral properties are attributes or characterizations that pertain only to the group as a whole. They are properties that cannot be decomposed or reduced to properties of its members. They are, in short, properties that can be conceived as "belonging" only to the group as a whole and not to its parts.

Integral properties are of various kinds. Some of them are descriptive attributes, such as a group's "age" (longevity or period of existence as distinguished from the "median age" of its members, which, we shall see, is a distributive property); its "wealth" (the amount of money in its treasury as distinguished from the individual wealth of its members); its language (as distinguished from dialects or idioms of subgroups or individual members); its size (number of members) or "boundaries" (which may be territorial in the case of a unit that occupies space, as a city or nation, or which may be functional, as when there is a formal division of labor between two governmental agencies).

A second set of integral properties is a group's organizational attributes—such as its "constitution" or "laws." Included here are such aspects of a group as its criteria for membership, the procedures by which members are inducted or officers chosen, the conditions of continued membership, the specification of positions, and so on. These properties are usually enumerated in documents that are themselves, in a literal sense, properties of the group. These documents may be adopted by the group under given decision rules—say, majority voting—which are also integral properties.

The third kind of integral property is a group's "external relations." For instance, the number or kinds of links that exist between the council as a whole and organizations in the community are integral to the group as a whole. The relationship may be one of domination, subordination, or equality—modes of relationship that define a group property. Similarly, such terms as "authority," "legitimacy," or "officiality" refer to integral properties of governmental units that set them off from other groups and that depend for validation on external support of the group as a whole.

A final set of integral properties relates to the group's action or performance as a whole, notably its decisions and policies. Although concepts like decision or policy are difficult to define, they refer to empirical indicators such as legislative statutes, court opinions, or fiscal expenditures. Such outputs are properties of the group and not properties of its members. Knowing the group's decisions or policies is independent of knowing any one member's policy views. As integral properties, decisions, policies, and other outputs arise or emerge out of member interactions, but they are different from the properties that individual members may possess.

The fact that a group has integral properties does not mean, of course, that it cannot be reduced with respect to others, such as distributive, relational or structural properties. But it is important to point out that such constructed or reconstructed properties, though inevitable or necessary, are not sufficient to make the unit "whole." For instance, interaction—a relational property—defines a group, but unless the "interaction set" observed is also characterized by integral properties, it can hardly be conceived as a group that is itself capable of action.

DISTRIBUTIVE PROPERTIES

A group is composed of subunits or members with their own integral and nondivisible properties. For instance, all members of a group are individually characterized by age, race, income, or educational achievement. Each member has these attributes quite independent of any other member or of the group to which he belongs. Hence it is possible to ascertain these attributes from each member without having information about the group as a whole or about his relationships with other members.

At the level of the group, these properties of members can be conceived of as distributive properties. Because a group can be decomposed or reduced to its individual members with respect to members' own integral properties, these properties of the members can be transformed into properties of the unit. Put differently, because members' own integral properties are attributes of *all* group members, they constitute distributive properties of the group. They are "spread" throughout the group or distributed among the group.

Distributions have the quality of being subject to mathematical computations. A group's distributive property is, therefore, always a property upon which some mathematical or statistical operation has been performed. For instance, we can speak of a group's "median age"—as when we say that it is a "young group" or an "old group." We can speak of a group's "racial composition"—as when we say that it is "all white," "all black," or "racially mixed." Or we can characterize a group as "highly educated" or "poorly educated." These characterizations of the group are possible because member properties can be transformed into group properties through some kind of computation.

Age, race, income, and education are not the only attributes of members that can be transformed into distributive properties of the group. It is possible to discover members' individual attitudes, perceptions, beliefs, orientations, identifications, demands, expectations, values, or other "psychological" characteristics and treat them at the group level as distributive properties of a collective. Although these characteristics of the members may not be unrelated to their membership in the group—in the sense that "group belongingness" may influence the attitudes or perceptions, and so on, that members hold—it is possible to characterize the group in terms of the distribution of such member characteristics. For instance, a group may be said to be "like minded" in a matter of policy if a specified proportion—a bare majority, or a two-thirds majority, or a larger percentage—"share" the "same" view. Or a group's reaction to an external event may be treated as a distributive property if member reactions have been ascertained and transformed.

In short, a group's distributive properties are the result of reducing the group to subunits or members and then constructing group properties out of member characteristics through some kind of mathematical manipulation.

RELATIONAL PROPERTIES

A group is, by definition, a set of members who interact with each other and who stand in specifiable relationships to each other. It is this quality that distinguishes a unit that is a group from a unit that is an "aggregate." While a unit that is an aggregate—say, a population in a given census tract or voting precinct, or all persons in a population of a certain occupation or ethnic background—may be characterized by distributive properties, it does not possess what we shall term "relational properties." Relational properties are group characteristics that arise out of interactions between and relationships among members of a social unit.

The building blocks of relational properties are the relationships that occur among group members as a result of interaction. In other words, relational properties are constructs that characterize the group or unit as a whole, but they are not derived either from member characteristics or from the unit's integral properties. A group's relational properties can be ascertained only through observations of interactions or relations existing *among* members, or from information about such relationships. For instance, if all of a group's members are found to be tied to each other by strong bonds of friendship—they consider each other friends, they get along well with each other, they frequently see each other in the pursuit of common interests—the group as a whole seems to be characterized by a property that we may call "cohesion." On the other hand, if the interactions are characterized by disagreements, competition for status, mutual disregard, and so on, the relational property of the group may be called "tension." Similarly, if members in their interactions disagree on issues but engage in interpersonal practices or strategies that involve compromise, bargaining, or other forms of exchange, then the group as a whole may be characterized in these terms.

There are also "informal" organizational characteristics that are best thought of as relational properties. For instance, what are called "group norms" or sometimes "rules of the game"—conventional or traditional "ways of doing things"—are relational properties. These kinds of property are not so much attributes as emergents from group interactions. They are difficult to observe, as is evident in the vagueness of some of the concepts that refer to them, such as culture, ethos, style, or atmosphere. A city council's "ethos," for instance, is more than the aggregation of its members' individual orientations to action. One may have to rely on members' interpretations of how the council as a whole copes with its decision-making tasks, but one cannot predict its "ethos" from the values that individual members may hold. If we say that a council's ethos is "political" or "pragmatic" or "paternal," we refer to a relational property of the group.

Relational properties, then, are distinguished from integral properties in that they are minimally reducible to dyadic relationships, that is, to interactions between two members. They are distinguished from distributive properties in that they are not arithmetic products of individual member characteristics but of intermember relationships. However, relational properties as such cannot tell us anything specific about particular patterns of interaction that may occur in the group. Such patterns, we shall suggest, represent "structural properties." In other words, relational properties are undifferentiated qualities that characterize the group as a whole. This is not to say that these qualities cannot be measured. Metrics such as the Rice "index of cohesion" or the Proctor-Loomis "index of expansiveness" are sociometric devices to summarize a group's relational properties.

STRUCTURAL PROPERTIES

If both the interactions and relationships existing in a group assume forms or patterns in which the positions of members vis-à-vis each other can be ascertained, we speak of "structural properties." For instance, if there is an identifiable "leader" who occupies a position of primacy in a group, the resulting relationship is a structural property of the group.

More precisely, a group is not simply a set of interacting members, but the interactions tend to be uniform and regular, constituting structures of more or less stability. These structures can take many forms. For instance, the group's status system or stratification may resemble a pyramid, a diamond, or a flat box. Or its communication net may resemble a line, a fork, or a wheel. In other words, structures are aspects of behavioral patterns or relationships that can be divorced from time yet, of course, are also subject to change through time. A structure is, in this sense, a snapshot of the unit's behavioral processes. It "catches" the positions and statuses occupied by the members of the group. These positions and statuses define the flow of transactions and interactions in the group as a whole.

If the patterns are lasting and become formally recognized, they may become, over time, characteristics of the unit that appear to be quite independent of the members and their behavior, as when we speak of the group's "organizational chart." The chart is, of course, only a symbol that stands for or represents the unit's structure: having a chart (or charter that specifies positions, relationships among positions, and forms of prescribed behavior) is a defining characteristic of a group that has become "institutionalized." There may also exist "informal" structures that are more flexible and subject to change as particular members move into and out of positions or statuses and redefine their mutual relationships. This informal organization of the group is a structural property that may or may not be congruent with its formal organization or constitution.

The tendency to reify concepts, especially if the concepts refer to relatively stable social phenomena such as the behavioral patterns and interactions in a group, leads to confusion in the use of the notion of "structure." For instance, such institutionalized groups as the family, the factory, or the government are often referred to as "structures." But structures are not "things" as stones are things; they are qualities or properties of things, like the roundness or flatness of a stone. If we denote a thing by its properties, we confuse the thing with its properties. Structure cannot refer to a thing like a group but only to some property of the group.

By structural properties, then, we refer to specifiable linkages and organizational patterns among group members, so that we can speak of a group's decision-making structure or status system. We may also observe patterned relationships between subgroups and the group as a whole. For instance, there may be a high rate of interaction between some group members but not others, making for two different sets of members, with comparatively little interaction between the members of each set. "Cliquishness," as the phenomenon may be called, is a *relational* property of the group. But if one clique is noted to dominate the other more or less regularly, a *structural* property has been identified, and the group as a whole may be called "clique dominated."

Structural properties are emergents. This is not to say that such structural properties like the status order, the net of communication, or the leadership structure are any less "real" than distributive or integral properties. They only differ in the ways in which they must be ascertained, usually involving more complex modes of data transformation than is the case with other properties.

CONTEXTUAL PROPERTIES

Contextual properties are induced from a group's environmental characteristics. The context or environment may be another "higher-level" unit—such as a committee in a legislature, a legislature in a government, or a government in a nation—or it may be what we conventionally think of as environment—say, an "urban environment" as against a "rural environment," or a "lower-class environment" as against a "middle-class environment." Contextual properties, then, are generated by a group's inclusion or location within a higher level of social organization. In other words, any group below the level of a hypothetical "superunit" can be described contextually. A contextual property has the same value for all groups or group members located in the same environment. For instance, a city council, all of its committees, and all of its members have the property "rurality" to the same degree if the council is located in a "rural city."

Contextual properties, then, are induced from a group's context or environment. The data transformation procedure involved is simple and straightforward; it does not require particular new ways of constructing the relevant indicators. Nor is there any prejudgment that the context has an impact on the group. It may or may not have. This is a matter for empirical verification.

Contextual properties may themselves be distributive, structural, or integral properties of the context or environment. For instance, a city council may be located in a city with a city charter (an integral property), a "power elite" (a structural property), and a heterogeneous population (a distributive property). It partakes of these various properties of the city that constitute its environment. However, one must not mistake such contextual properties with the unit's properties that are generated at its own level or stem from lower-level units. For instance, being located in a working-class suburb does not mean that a council is composed only or necessarily of working-class men. It may well have the distributive property "middle class."

Contextual properties may serve as independent or control variables. For instance, in the proposition that "urban councils are more likely to allocate substantial funds for planning than do rural councils," the contextual property serves as the independent variable in a bivariate analysis. On the other hand, in the proposition that "strong leadership in a council and unanimity in decision making are more likely to be related in working-class than in middle-class cities," the contextual property "class character of city" serves as a control variable in a multivariate analysis. What contextual properties one wishes to attribute to a group depends, of course, on the theoretical objective one has in mind.

The Transformation of Unit Data

Conceptually, we have seen, unit or group properties can be classified as follows: (1) properties that are immanent in the unit and that cannot be reduced to a lower level of organizational complexity—integral properties; (2) properties that are member properties and, because they are distributed throughout the group, belong to the group—distributive properties; (3) properties that arise out of the interactions and relationships among group members—relational properties; (4) properties that represent statistical or behavioral patterns among the group's distributive or relational properties—structural properties; and (5) properties that describe the unit's physical or social environment and are attributed to the unit—contextual properties. These distinctions are important for theoretical and analytic reasons, but they are especially important for methodological reasons. The different "natures" of unit properties clearly call for different methodological assumptions and procedures.

If, as is the case with distributive, relational, and structural properties, reduction of the unit to subunits or members is possible, there is in principle no reason for not pursuing it as far as possible. For instance, a state legislature can be decomposed into houses, the houses into committees, the committees into subcommittees, and the subcommittees into members; or the houses can be decomposed into party delegations, the delegations into regional subdelegations, the subdelegations into cliques, and the cliques into members. All of these units have their own properties on their own level of organizational complexity. They cannot, therefore, be manipulated at will but are subject to the limitations imposed on a given unit by the nature of its properties.

It may be, of course, that data on subunits or members are not available. For instance, if the unit of interest is a voting precinct, one can describe its distributive properties and possibly some structural properties, but one cannot reduce the unit and then work with aggregate or global indicators of its behavior. In particular, one can say nothing about its relational properties that can only be constructed out of data from or about relationships among individual members. Similarly, while in principle data about integral or contextual properties should be directly available, they may in fact not be available. In that case, although these properties cannot be derived from data about subunits or members, it may be possible to construct them from member information. For instance, group norms are integral properties; yet it may be impossible to apprehend them directly. Thus it may be necessary to construct them from indirect information that group members can give. On the other hand, direct data about a unit's environment may not be available. Hence contextual properties may have to be constructed out of information given by group members. One may wish to know, for instance, whether a city council is located in a community characterized by an active group life. Ideally, one might wish to go into the community and determine, through observation or survey research, whether private associations are active, how many are active, or whether the members of these associations are active within the group. But if, as in the city council research, one deals with many units and direct information is not available because of limited research resources, it may be necessary to rely on well-placed informants for relevant data.

If, as may be necessary, a group's members not only serve as respondents but also as informants, the information they give may be of varying reliability. For instance, informant data concerning the city council's norms or external relations are probably more reliable than informant data about contextual properties, such as whether the citizenry is well organized, interested, or active in local affairs. This is simply due to the fact that the individual councilman as informant is in a better position to observe his colleagues than the public at large. There is, of course, a standard justification for accepting an actor's information concerning his environment as reliable data: an environment constitutes a contextual property to the extent that it is perceived; that is, it is the actor's "definition of the situation" that constitutes the socially effective reality. While it is in principle possible to appraise such perceptions of the environment by juxtaposing them with "objective" data of the context if they are available, they may in fact not be available. In that case, one must rely on correlations between the constructs of the context that are derived from informant data and other directly observable contextual properties to support one's acceptance of the former as valid and reliable.

In the study of natural-state groups, be they large or small, the survey is a powerful instrument of data collection because it can simultaneously serve as a source of data that permit the construction of distributive, relational, and structural properties once the group has been reduced to its members; and as a source of informant data that permit the construction of integral and contextual properties. The construction of group properties calls for different technical procedures, depending on the nature of the property in question and the kind of data that are available.

Data transformation is a necessary first step in solving what has been called the micro-macro problem. Bringing data collected on different levels of organizational complexity onto a single level of analysis makes it possible to compare comparables and to do so in a more rigorous way than would otherwise be the case. While the procedure is more difficult in larger units, it is applicable in both principle and practice. It is less the technique of transformation and more the lack of data at the level of individual behavior that is the major stumbling block in the way of more rigorous comparative analysis.

4

Multilevel Methods and

Comparative Analysis

CONCERN WITH level-of-analysis problems seems to be rooted in three sources of discomfort with prevailing modes of inquiry. First and probably earliest, there was the discovery that correlations based on aggregate data and correlations based on equivalent individual data produce different values and can be substituted for each other only at considerable risk. This apparent weakness of aggregate analysis led to something of an overreaction in political science. Coming, as it did, at just about the time when advances in survey research projected the individual person as the unit of analysis into the discipline's consciousness, there developed a tendency to neglect aggregate data analysis (but see Ranney, 1962). Although sounder methods for inferring individual correlations from aggregate data were to be soon developed (Goodman, 1959; Shively, 1969), political science, as Price (1968, p. 131) put it, "was to take a fifteen-year detour in which aggregate data were first denounced as leading only to 'fallacy' and then eventually reinstated." Whatever the difficulties, it is now recognized, first, that aggregate data can be used as direct indicators of group properties (see Linz, 1969); second, that ecological or demographic data can be treated as a unit's environmental or contextual properties; and third, that what is at issue is "the relation of the criterion according to which units are grouped, to the types of inferences intended when using the results of aggregated units" (Scheuch, 1969, p. 137n13).

Second, there was the discovery that in the analysis of "whole" systems—notably, nations and societies—the neglect of within-unit variations leaves too much of the between-units variance unexplained (see LaPalombara, 1970). Vallier (1971, p. 215), in what I think is the best critical statement of this genre, points out that observers of "whole" systems aggregate various kinds of data (systematic, experiential, and impressionistic) into some kind of "modal measure" and they submit that as descriptions of the macro-structure . . .

When we get right down to it, then, macro-structural inferences are actually subtle, intuitive aggregations about structural patterns in sub-societal contexts. There is not something "out there" which can be called the "overall structure" of American society, but only a diverse and specialized range of structural arrangements that involve concrete role systems, concrete sequences of problem-solving, and concrete collectivities and their environments.

Although the comparative analysis of large units such as cities, states, or nations now makes ample use of "aggregate statistics" (ecological, demographic, electoral, and budgetary data) and, as a result, makes possible wide and rigorous testing of hypotheses, the uses of such data remain limited for a number of reasons. First, analysis is all too easily guided by the availability of the data rather than by theoretical considerations. Second, there are difficulties in connecting these global indicators to corresponding social and political concepts, making for ambiguity in comparisons that test hypotheses. And third, even if the difficulties of measurement of large units were solved, as Blalock (1970, p. 11) has stated, "when comparisons are being made among units as large as societies, one may very well run out of cases before adequate statistical controls can be made." There is little one can do about this: the fifty states of the United States are fifty units and not more, and one must cope with this number in whatever statistical manner seems most appropriate if it is the between-unit variations in the behavior of the states that are to be explained.

Finally, there was the discovery that analysis carried out exclusively at the level of individuals by way of survey research, in neglecting contextual and environmental factors, cannot come to grips with the consequences of political structures for political action. Regardless of whether these studies are intranational or cross-national, they are deficient for structural analysis. As Blau (1969, p. 51) has pointed out,

with individuals as units of analysis, it is possible to investigate variations in the behavior and attitudes of individuals and how these are related to variations in the social conditions to which these individuals are exposed, but it is not possible to study variations in social structure and their determinants. To do the latter requires that the collectivities whose social structure is under examination be made the units of analysis in order to be able to compare structures with different characteristics and search for related variations in antecedents that may account for the differences.

Not only do structural phenomena such as authority, integration, competition, or centralization elude research that is exclusively anchored in the individual, but such research is sometimes prone to proceed by inference to a level of analysis not calibrated into the research design. While various forms of contextual analysis built on individual distributions serve as correctives, they enrich analysis only in regard to possible independent variables. The dependent variables remain individual-level properties—opinions, attitudes, perceptions, role orientations, and so on. Nevertheless, the possibility of creating contexts out of the aggregation of subunit properties encourages multilevel approaches. These approaches, however, encounter problems of their own.

A first step in solving these problems is to abandon the false dualism between individual behavior and collective action that, I think, still plagues political analysis. Although multilevel analysis is a way to overcome the traditional dualism, the latter's pervasiveness lingers on. "In cross-level explanations," writes Scheuch (1969, p. 134), "our chains of inference are often frightfully long, in spite of the verbal respect that in empirical social science is paid to Robert Merton's notion of 'theories of the middle range.' " Why, one may ask, is it that frightfully long chains of inference are still cultivated? Because, one must answer, theorists do not seem satisfied until they penetrate to "wholes" at either end of the continuum that binds individuals and societies. In this respect the psychoanalysts who seek to understand the "whole" individual and the sociologists who seek to understand "total" societies are brothers under the skin (see Klausner, 1967; Weinstein and Platt, 1973).

Yet most social scientists do their work in the interstices of the individual-society continuum, and most of them settle for less than the study of "wholes." Needed, evidently, are not just theories of the middle range but also research approaches of the middle range. Intervening between the individual and society are many other units of varying complexity whose properties are relevant to political analysis not only at their own level but also at other levels. This realization brings pressure on even the most convinced reductionist to make his work germane to the concerns of the holist; and it brings pressure on the holist to pay attention to the findings of the reductionist as these may impinge on the construction of wholes.

The Problem in Brief

The "units" of *political* analysis, in contrast to the units of sociological and psychological analysis, are *decision or action units* rather than geographic areas or categoric aggregates. These units are *invariably* individual actors, but they may also be collective actors—dyads, triads, committees, agencies, organizations, associations, governments, and polities. A unit composed of individuals is an action unit or "collective actor" when it has, as an integral or global property, a decision rule or set of rules, formal or informal, that enables the individuals in the unit to act in common and commit the unit as a whole or other units to a course of action. Moreover, a unit of action is not only composed of individuals but may also be composed of groups, as when a committee is composed of subcommittees. Just as the unit, so the subunit is characterized by a decision rule or set of rules.

This is not to say that "having a decision rule enabling the unit to act" is the unit's only integral property or that there are no other properties in terms of which its behavior can be analyzed. But it is inconceivable that there can be a collective unit of action that does not have, minimally, a rule that makes action possible—either action that commits the unit's "members" or action that commits some other unit.

What justifies using collectivities as units of analysis, then, is that they are indeed "actors" in the political arena. The unreconstructed reductionist may still argue that any unit composed of individuals is not a "real" unit because it obviously cannot act without its component parts, individual persons, behaving in some manner. He is obviously correct. He is also correct in cautioning against the easy personification of social or political units that has often embarrassed political and especially legal theory. But what the reductionist would have considerable difficulty in denying is the fact that social units do have properties that are integral and that are not in any imaginable way replicated or replicable at the level of the individual person.

Action units are not only capable of committing their members and possibly others, but they are also "nested" in each other. Indeed, it is this nesting that makes unit action under the decision rule possible. My favorite example is the modern legislature. Not only is the legislature a unit of action in its own right, but it is composed, on the one hand, of its individual members and, on the other hand, of all the formal and informal groups that play a part in its functioning—committees, subcommittees, caucuses, delegations, study groups, joint committees, houses, and so on. Each of these units constitutes a context or an environment for other units at their own or other levels. I distinguish between "context" and "environment," reserving the former term for the social situation created by units at their own level due to interaction; just as individuals constitute a context for other individuals, so groups create contexts for other groups, states for states, or nations for nations. The meaning of "environment" should be clear if we think of a "higher-order" unit as constituting an environment for a "lower-order" unit: the subcommittee is an environment for both its subcommittees and its individual members; the house is the environment for its committees, subcommittees, individual members, and so on.

Granted, then, that collective units are capable of independent action at their own level but with consequences for other actors, individual or collective, at other levels, it follows that they may, can, or should be studied as *units* at their own level (one might say "in their own right") and not simply as either parts of a larger whole or as aggregates of their components. Yet it would be a very partial analysis if units of action were compared—for comparison is the method indicated—only in terms of their integral properties. Obviously their constituting an environment for other units or being environed by other units makes for a set of social circumstances that are significant for their functioning as action units. The stage is thus set for a brief overview of the methodological problems involved in what will be called "data transformation."

Even if it is agreed just what units are of problematic interest—problematic in the sense that it is *their* behavior, structure, or functioning that is to be explained—it is by no means clear at what *empirical* level of analysis the comparison should be conducted. Scientific bias sometimes suggests analysis at the least-complex level. Frey (1970, p. 289) articulates this position:

the analyst is usually well advised to adopt the strategy of proceeding upward from the "lowest" and least complex level. Ordinarily, this means proceeding from the individual level through levels of ever-increasing complexity. In principle, he does not want to introduce into his explanation any analytic level higher than is needed to provide an acceptable explanation of the variance which concerns him.

If, for instance, behavioral differences among individuals in various nations are washed out or greatly reduced with education held constant, then "national systemic variables may be unnecessary for an adequate explanation of such differences." Frey (1970, p. 290) recognizes that higher-level factors may still have to be considered because the lower-level explanation of variance may be spurious or the lower-level independent variable may merely intervene, but he concludes that "the principle of seeking the lowest level explanation which satisfies the mind is a useful guideline." Przeworski and Teune (1970, p. 68), speaking in the language of regression, put it this way:

When regression coefficients within systems equal zero, then differences can be attributed to a system-level variable, most likely of a setting nature, operating at the level of systems. When regression coefficients within systems differed from zero, we concluded that the difference between the within-systems and ecological regressions stems from the differences of the context. In general the ecological relationship is spurious whenever within-system regressions have the same slope, hence on the basis of the assumption of similar variances, the same fit. There is no need to change the level of analysis.

The point to be made in this connection is not that the strategy of reduction or disaggregation and, for that matter, the strategy of construction or aggregation are beset by the fallacies of the misplaced or wrong level—that is, the danger of false inferences from one level of analysis to another, of which Frey as well as Przeworski and Teune are well aware. Rather, the point to be made is that the choice of the empirical level on which analysis is to be conducted is a substantive rather than a method-ological problem. It is the problematic nature of the unit whose behavior is to be explained that should determine the level of analysis and not methodological bias for or against reduction. It is precisely because political science deals with more or less autonomous collective units, in the legal but also political sense, which through their decisions and actions commit themselves, their members, and other units, that the choice of level of analysis is a matter of substantive appropriateness and not a matter of methodological prejudgment.

Once the level of analysis has been determined, analytic reduction may be feasible, provided there are theoretical reasons for bringing subunit or superunit properties to the level of analysis called for by the research problem. That such transformation is also methodologically advantageous is readily evident. As long as the number of relatively large units of research interest is small—for instance, the five nations studied by Almond and Verba (1963) or the four state legislatures studied by Wahlke and his associates (1962)—within-unit variations at the level of the individual may serve the purpose of comparative analysis, provided the individualistic fallacy is avoided; of course, what is being compared if there is no trans-formation from the subunit to the unit level is the behavior *of* the subunits *in* the larger units and not the behavior of these units.

However, if the number of collective units becomes relatively large, as in the Feierabend and Feierabend (1966) study of aggessive behaviors in some seventy nations or the Eulau and Prewitt (1973) study of eighty-two city councils, and if, moreover, the problem calls for statements about these units and not about their members, the reductionist strategy alone is no longer feasible: it is very difficult, if not impossible, to compare within-unit variations of behavior across a large number of units without aggregation. Analysis of within-unit variations must yield to analysis of between-unit variations. What research strategy calls for, then, is not sim-ply reduction and explanation at the least-complex level within the unit, but transformation of the lower-level or subunit properties into the level of the unit whose behavior is to be explained.

Similarly, as the behavior of the units to be compared takes place in environments consisting of higher-order units, and as the properties of these higher-order units may have an impact apart from or in addition to the contextual effects of lower-order units, they must be calibrated at the level of the object units. Data transformation in this connection involves assignment of the object units to classes of higher-order units. The methodological problem to be addressed concerns the application of multilevel *observation* to single-level *analysis* and the reasons for this approach.

The Micro-Macro Perspective

The accent in micro-macro thinking is on the hyphen, for the hyphen is the bond—it is critical for the type of analysis that is predicated on the transformation of microlevel and macrolevel unit properties. What micro-macro language points to is, of course, the continuity of behavioral and structural phenomena, both vertical and horizontal, in the real world of politics. This continuity and, with it, an awareness of the importance of the level-of-analysis perspective tends to be obscured by the disciplinary division of labor as each specialization concentrates its attention at the level where it encounters its dependent variables. For scholars in international relations, the level of analysis is the nation; for students of comparative government, it is largely institutional structures and processes; for behavioralists, so-called, it is the individual person. Linkages between these levels, if not ignored, may be treated in cavalier fashion (see Singer, 1961, who was among the first to challenge this treatment).

What, then, are the utilities of the micro-macro perspective? There are, of course, several; but if one excludes, on the one hand, the fallacies of inference to which it calls attention and, on the other hand, the advantages it brings to genuine and systematic comparison (with which I shall deal in the next section), one consideration stands out: while sensitizing the observer to the complexity of social and political phenomena, it also gives him a handle on reducing what appears to be chaos to some kind of order where disciplined inquiry has a chance to succeed. It does so by introducing the notion that human action can be observed on different levels of structural complexity.

The concept of level has several uses. One familiar usage refers to "level of generality," especially in the search for functional equivalents in comparative analysis. Referring to the shift in emphasis possible from the content to the structure of belief, Verba (1971, p. 316), for instance, writes that "such a shift in level may enable us to find comparable problems where comparability does not exist at a lower level." There is Parsons' usage (Parsons and Shils, 1951, p. 54) when he speaks of personality, social system, and culture as modes of organization, conceptually abstracted, whose empirical referents "are not on the same plane." More approximate is Frey's (1970, p. 288) usage, but (as I shall point out) he confuses levels and units of analysis:

Levels of analysis are probably most often and perhaps most fruitfully distinguished in terms of the property of inclusion, though there are various dimensions or types of inclusion. The individual is included within the family, the family in the community, the community in the region, the region in the nation, and so on. Structurally embedded levels of this type open up critical possibilities for contextual analysis.

Not levels but units of analysis are "structurally embedded," as Frey himself suggests in his examples—the individual being included in the family, the family in the community, and so on. It is the structural embedding of units that makes it possible to think of levels as *analytic* categories in terms of which units as *concrete* entities can be ordered. Moreover, levels are not distinguished by the relative size, complexity, or structural elaboration of the units, for these are properties of the units and, therefore, cannot serve as characteristics of levels. If level of analysis were determined, for instance, by a unit's size, it would be impossible to compare units of widely varying size, as Dahl and Tufte (1973) have done. It is not the absolute nature of unit properties that defines the level of analysis but rather the standpoint of the observer—literally, the position he occupies in looking at things above or below the place on which he stands.

There are advantages to thinking of the level-of-analysis problem, at least initially, in these terms. As used in economics, "micro" refers to individuals and "macro" to aggregates, although micro has been extended to the analysis of the firm. Similarly, in sociology micro is used to refer to individuals or small groups and macro to larger collectivities. In political science, Scarrow (1969, p. 32) points out, "it has beome customary . . . to differentiate between *micro* analysis, usually thought of as analysis of the attitudes and behavior of individuals, and *macro* analysis, which focuses upon characteristics of the polity (e.g., the 57 characteristics listed in *A Cross-Polity Survey*)." The complexity of an object unit, then, is not an absolute property but depends on the levels at which it is observed. The greater the number of subject units and their properties that can be harnessed at the object unit's level (and regardless of whether the subject units are subunits or superunits), the more complexity will the object unit's structure assume.

Complexity, then, is a unit property that can be identified and measured only in terms of the unit's location in relationship to its subunits and superunits on the micro-macro continuum. Micro does not ipso facto mean structural simplicity, and macro does not mean complexity. A very small unit, say a governing triumvirate, can be structurally very complex, as it may be situated in a hierarchy of superunits whose properties have an impact on its behavior; but another three-person unit may be structurally simple if its range of entailment on other levels is limited. It is the number of levels on which the investigation is conducted that defines complexity. A very large unit may be treated "simply" by attention only to properties at its own level. The virtue of the multilevel strategy is that it enriches the explanatory power of analysis. As Scheuch (1969, p. 143) has put it, "a research design becomes more powerful when it provides for direct measurement of phenomena on different levels."

The utility of the micro-macro frame of reference consists principally in sensitizing the analyst to the interdependence of units at different levels. And because units at different levels are not independent, they cannot be substituted for inference from one level to another. As Lazarsfeld and Menzel (1965, p. 424) point out, "one can speak of 'collectives' only when their 'members' are also being referred to, and of 'members' only when their 'collectives' are also involved. Furthermore, there must be a multiplicity of members if the term 'collective' is to be meaningful. It is perhaps less obvious . . . that there must also be a multiplicity of collectives." The micro-macro perspective extends this entailment of units to all levels, so that the distinction between individual and collective units appears as only a special case of the more generic frame of reference that conceives of superunits, units, and subunits. From the standpoint taken at the level of a superunit or macrounit, the properties of a subunit are "individual" (in an extension of Lazarsfeld and Menzel's sense) or micro; from the standpoint taken at the level of a subunit or microunit, the properties of a superunit are "collective" (again in Lazarsfeld and Menzel's sense) or macro. A group, then, whatever its absolute size, can be thought of as a microunit or a macrounit, depending again on the observer's standpoint. It is only convention that one conceives of a person's "social class" as an individual attribute, for it is in fact an attribute assigned to the person from the position he or she occupies in a class structure that is a collective property. Vice versa, a collective property may be an aggregate of individual properties, as when one speaks of a legislature's "partisan complexion."

There is nothing intrinsically micro or macro in a unit. It is not unit properties as such or the degree to which they may be present or absent that makes for a unit's identification at one or another level, but it is the degree to which a unit can be partitioned into subunits or the extent to which it is embedded in superunits that makes for its designation as micro or macro. The micro-macro continuum thus calls attention to possibly significant data sources at levels of analysis above or below an object unit's own level. For instance, if the individual is the object unit of analysis, thinking in terms of levels calls attention to the social context created by the interaction of individuals and to multiple external environments. Explanation is oriented toward the macro pole of the micro-macro continuum.

But explanation may also be sought in terms of psychological, physiological, and possibly even chemical-biological elements. In this case, explanation is oriented toward the micro pole of the micro-macro continuum.

If, by way of contrast, the object units are national societies, the macroperspective orients the observer to the international context created by the relations of nations and to the world environment, while the microperspective orients him to a wide range of subunits from individuals to intranational institutions and organizations. How far the investigator wishes to push observation "up and down" the micro-macro continuum depends, of course, on his theory—which subject units he considers relevant or adequate to explain the behavior of the object unit. Whatever the strategy, the micro-macro frame of reference enriches the analytic possibilities of research.

CROSS-LEVEL INFERENCE AND INFERENCE BY COMPARISON

There are two reasons for data transformation: first, to avoid the fallacies of false inference to the wrong level; and second, to facilitate inference by genuine comparison.

Data transformation and inference may be confused. "The central problem," writes Vallier (1971, p. 216), "is to work out rules that will allow us to reach down into society to lower-level units as sources of data—thus allowing us to increase the N—and subsequently to move from those data to *make inferences* about the total society" (emphasis added). Yet, in the very next sentence, he describes this strategy as one of "aggregation": "It means constructing societal level indexes from units lower in the hierarchy of systems than the society." One might think that Vallier is simply careless in speaking of "inference," but he continues:

The problem of validity is extremely obvious, since an attempt is being made to treat lower-order units as a "sample" of societal phenomena. This is not a problem of part to whole. The idea of a part (as used in macro-structural studies) is quite different from a "sample" or a unit that is intended to bear an isomorphic relationship to a higher level of structure . . . Instead of a sample being part of the whole in the structural-functional sense, it is in fact a set of *representative* units of the macro-structure. (Emphasis added)

Now, it is quite appropriate to "reach down into society to lower-level units" for the purpose of *constructing* a societal index that can serve the purpose of comparative analysis across societies; but it is mistaken to treat subunits as a "set of representative units of the macro-structure" or as a "sample" that "is intended to bear an isomorphic relationship to a higher level of structure." In the first place, even if a unit and its subunits were structurally isomorphic, in order to avoid the compositional fallacy a unit measure would have to be constructed. And second, sampling units at their own level, which is legitimate as a basis of inference if proper sampling criteria are met, should not be confused with sampling subunits whose properties can serve inference only at the level of the sampled subunits and not at the level of the unit.

But is it not desirable to compare units in terms of the properties that may be available at the subunit (or, for that matter, superunit) level? Dogan and Rokkan (1969, p. 8) raise this question in connection with what they call a "micro-macro design," as follows:

your dependent variables are the characteristics of the territorial social systems, but you seek your explanatory variables not only at the global/aggregate level (such as geographical configurations, concentration factors, distance factors) but at the level of *individual decisions* . . . In the field of electoral ecology there is a clear need for a continuous shuttle between the "macro" and the "micro" levels. The behavior of the citizens cannot be understood without knowledge of the ecological alternatives set for them by parties, electoral arrangements, and so on, but at least some of these alternatives (such as the maintenance of a party list as an alternative) are, in turn, dependent on the behaviors of individuals.

But how does one compare in an analysis of many units the "continuous shuttle" between levels? If units can be compared only at one level, the shuttle itself would seem to elude analysis. It would seem possible to compare the points of departure or destination at one or another level but not the journey itself. If citizen behavior is to be explained in terms of ecological alternatives—that is, if citizens are the object units of analysis—the microlevel provides the arena of comparison; if, on the other hand, the maintenance of parties or electoral arrangements is to be explained by the behavior of citizens, the macrolevel is the arena of comparison.

There is, then, something deceptively simple in the "micro-macro design" as conceived by Dogan and Rokkan. The design can become operative for comparative analysis only *after* unit properties at different levels have been harnessed at one or another object unit's level by way of data transformation. Or, put differently, the problem of the relations between microunits and macrounits must be resolved *prior* to comparison.

Common sense suggests that comparison is feasible only between units at the same level of analysis and correlation is possible only between unit properties at the same level. But the logic of comparison should not be taken for granted. For, as already suggested, units at different levels of analysis are not truly independent. As the logic of comparison and correlation requires the independence of the units to be compared or of the unit properties to be correlated, the micro-macro frame of reference seems to create a paradox. But it creates a paradox only if one ignores the possibility of data tranformation. One must clearly distinguish between interlevel and intralevel independence: what comparison and correlation require is intralevel but not interlevel independence.

What makes a unit a unit—that is, what makes for its unity—is its possession of a number of integral properties that cannot be disaggregated and that can be observed only at the unit's own level (see Campbell, 1958). One such property is its action: a decision by the Supreme Court is an integral property of the Court and not a property of its individual members. This is not to say that an individual judge cannot have an influence on the outcome of the decision or that group pressure cannot have an impact on the behavior of an individual judge. Interlevel analysis is predicated on the interdependence of actions units; intralevel analysis assumes independence.

Now, precisely because units exist at different levels and are not independent, it follows that an object unit's structure is a property that derives from variations in the behavior of its subunits or superunits, be they individuals or groups. Implicit in this condition is a shift in some property present among subunits or superunits to the level of the object unit. For instance, differences in the social status of individuals become, at the group level, a manifestation of the group's class structure; or the performance of different tasks by subcommittees becomes, at the level of the committee, the property called division of labor.

However, because the level of analysis shifts as a result of the interdependence of units, the relation between unit properties and subunit or superunit properties cannot be isomorphic. For instance, the properties characteristic of the House Appropriations Committee are not properties of the House, for the committee is neither a microreplica nor in any way representative, in a sampling sense, of the House. The Appropriations Committee cannot be a microcosm of the House, even if there were an isomorphism between them in all other respects, because its location in the House is an environmental property it shares with, say, the House Ways and Means Committee but not with the House itself. It is permissible, therefore, to compare the two committees, but it is not permissible to compare either with the House. The two committees are both independent of each other as units at their own level of analysis; they are not independent in interlevel analysis. Units at one level of analysis cannot be substituted for units at another level: one cannot compare a father with his family or New Haven with the United States.

The theme requires some elaboration because of the evidently compelling argument that seemingly isomorphic units and subunits may yet be compared if certain sampling assumptions are made. For instance, is it not permissible to compare, say, committees and subcommittees in the U.S. House if both sets are properly sampled? There are at least two objections. First, even though both sets of committees may have been randomly sampled in a multistage sample design, there is an unknown probability that they—or at least some of them in each set—are not independent of each other in the structural sense. But second, even if the two sets were purposefully selected and independent of each other structurally (that is, the set of subcommittees were selected from a universe of subcommittees not part of the set of committees sampled), the two sets would still not meet the requirements of intralevel comparison, for each set has quite different environments and contexts. While committees share, as already suggested, the common environment of the House, subcommittees are environed not only by the House but also by their respective committees. In turn, subcommittees or committees, in interacting with each other, create contexts that, as properties of the respective units, are not comparable.[1] As this is so, the assumption of structural isomorphism between units and subunits as ground for comparison is not warranted. Comparison is possible only between units at the same level of analysis. Comparison of units requires their independence because if units and subunits (that is, interdependent units) were isomorphic, no new information would be forthcoming in studying them and nothing would be gained from comparing them.

It would also seem that the units to be compared, whatever the level of analysis, must be indivisible. But this is only an analytical or logical requirement that cannot be empirically obtained. Logically, if a unit is divisible into subunits, one wants to disaggregate it, for this will yield more information about the unit. By dividing it, the unit becomes a superunit. The requirement that object units to be compared be indivisible simply means that they must have at least some (integral) properties not possessed by the subunits into which they are in fact divisible. But the analytic indivisibility criterion again suggests why it is not permissible to compare a unit with its subunits.

Comparative analysis across a great variety of units at all levels of analysis is theoretically useful because it permits extensive elaboration of critical subunit properties and of contextual effects. Both types of analysis were pioneered in studies using the individual person as the object unit, but the mode of analysis can be extended to comparison of units other than individuals—provided, of course, that relevant subunit and superunit properties can be transformed to the level where comparison is to be made. Comparative analysis making use of the micro-macro perspective requires that the complexity of within-unit variations be simplified through transformation to get on with the study of between-unit variations.

DATA TRANSFORMATION

Because comparative analysis can be conducted only at an object unit's own level, data transformation is not needed if a unit is described solely in terms of its integral properties. In that case, possibly spurious correlations between two unit properties can be detected by introducing a third property characteristic of the unit at its own level. But description of a unit in terms of its integral properties does not exhaust its explanatory potential. Subunit properties may be relevant not only to the unit's internal variations but also to the between-unit variations of concern in comparative analysis. And a unit is likely to be environed by superunits that, in turn, possess properties of possible relevance to the unit's behavior. The problem of analysis that seeks to avoid fallacies of the wrong level is, in Blalock's (1970, p. 21) words, "just how one translates back and forth between the macro level, where groups are the units of analysis, and the micro level where the focus is on individuals." Przeworski and Teune (1970, p. 28) have stated the problem as follows: "The currently available theoretical and statistical techniques allow us to distinguish spurious correlations between two variables, X and Y, measured as deviations from their respective regressions on a third variable, Z, only when Z is measured at the same level as X and Y." And they continue: "What we need in comparative research, however, are statistical techniques that would allow the control variable to be measured at a level different from the two variables that are tested."

I am unable to say whether it is possible to invent statistical techniques that would make such measurement possible, and I am not convinced that it is necessary. What is necessary and possible is the transformation of unit properties, observed at levels higher and lower than the object unit's own level, to the latter's level.

The transformation of subject unit properties (subunit and superunit properties) into the level of the object unit is basically a translation of multilevel analysis into multivariate analysis at a single level. By harnessing at the object unit's level properties observed at subject unit levels—say, behavioral, perceptual, or attitudinal variables at the level of the individual; relational and contextual variables at the level of interaction among units; or structural variables at any unit's own level—it is possible to conduct partial correlation analysis, multiple regression analysis, path analysis, and so on. Transformation recommends itself, therefore, not just because comparative analysis is possible only at a single level but because it is an economical way to maximize the supply of exploratory variables and to apply sophisticated statistical methods in between-unit comparisons.

Multivariate analysis of transformed data at the object unit's level is by no means "unproblematic" as far as inference is concerned. But the problem is no longer one of inferences from units observed at one level to units not observed at another. Rather, it pertains to the assumptions one makes about the direction of the causal relations between the transformed properties. For instance, if the object unit is treated as a macrounit, is it permissible to use behavioral or structural assumptions about its respective subunits? Or, vice versa, if the object unit is treated as a microunit, is it permissible to bring to bear on its analysis assumptions made about its respective superunits? In principle, it is plausible to make at least some cross-level assumptions. Speaking of making individual-level (psychological) assumptions relevant to macroanalysis, Blalock (1970, p. 27) comments:

In the ideal, I suppose that most social scientists would agree that such assumptions should in fact be explicitly incorporated, and that they should not be overly simplistic. But as a *practical* question, one wonders how this can in fact be achieved without becoming immobilized by questions concerning basic motivations, underlying values, and other issues that would be more properly studied by psychologists.

The issue is acute if in analysis of macrounits, for which aggregate data are available, it is impossible to transform possible indicators of microunit properties because relevant data are not available. Blalock (1970, p. 28) points to the case of "prejudice," which it is impossible to construct as a macrounit property from microindicators, but for which aggregated measures derived from the U.S. Census may be available. In that case, he suggests, "if micro-level analyses would help to clarify or qualify the nature of these [macro] interrelationships, then they would seem appropriate, even though micro variables might not themselves ever appear explicitly in the formal theory that is ultimately developed." Behind this position, as Blalock also points out, is the philosophical assumption "that individual goals, motives, and needs are major causal agents in social systems and that adequate explanation requires that they be taken into account."

There is, then, the question whether collective units can have goals, motives, or needs independent of the persons composing the unit, as well as the question of what assumptions one may make about the goals, motives, or needs of collective units. Although they can be empirically ascertained as macrounit properties, it is yet a question of what they mean, for it is doubtful that their meaning can be independent of some individual-level interpretation. There seem to be three possibilities: first, their meaning is what the individuals composing the unit give them; second, their meaning is what observers give them; and third, their meaning derives from some combination of participant and observer meanings. In these possibilities individual-level meanings of macrolevel "psychological" properties are putatively ascribed to the macrounits.

The individual-to-group and group-to-individual transformation problem involving psychological properties can be generalized to more complex structures. Data transformation is a "problem" because each level of analysis at which a unit can be observed generates its characteristic properties that, nomenclature notwithstanding, require appropriate assumptions to be made about the measures that are used. These assumptions are not critical where the measures, like those of central tendency or rates, convey the same meaning at the unit and subunit levels; assumptions about the nature of properties are critical where measures, as in the case of correlations or standard deviations, apply only to units and not to the subunits composing them. Lazarsfeld and Menzel's (1965, p. 430) example of the "hung jury" has become legendary: this jury is indecisive because it cannot obtain the required unanimity. But "indecisiveness" has a very different meaning at the level of the jury and the individual jurors; it is the very decisiveness of some jurors in opposite directions that makes the jury indecisive.

What is true of correlational measures is even more true of more complex transformational techniques. There is no longer any kind of parallelism between the properties of the subject unit and those constructed at the level of the object unit. Ecological correlations are predicated on the assumption of an equivalence of meanings attached to microproperties and macroproperties, and the aggregation relations are based on the equivalence of meanings. But how is one to interpret a property such as a unit's stability? It may refer to stability of the unit as a whole through time despite changes of and in subunits; it may refer to stability in and among subunits; it may refer to stability in goals or functions; and so on. Although both a unit like a committee and its subunits, subcommittees, can be measured on a relational property like "cohesion," assumptions about cohesion at the subunit level may have to differ from assumptions about cohesion at the unit level. The structural integration of a national society involves assumptions different from those made about the structural integration, say, of metropolitan cities. If structural integration at the level of cities is to serve as a subunit property to be transformed into a property of the nation, the assumptions made about the former cannot be ignored because of assumptions concerning the latter. As Riley (1964, p. 1014) puts it, in speaking of the simpler individual-group relationship, the analyst "may encounter some difficulty in understanding these two different types of data, which, because of the systemic relationship between parts and whole, are interrelated." Before transforming data from one level of analysis to another, therefore, the nature of the properties involved must be understood in terms of the assumptions made about them and their appropriateness to the level at which the analysis is to be conducted. This pertains to both subunit and superunit properties.

Reduction of a unit to subunits as a strategy of transformation—that is, for the subsequent purpose of using subunit properties at the unit level of analysis—does not assume that unit and subunits are necessarily similar in structure or function. The strategy of reduction for the task of transformation differs, then, from the strategy of reduction which assumes that the "problem" to be analyzed is "less complex" at the subunit level (hence more accessible to analysis) and that the unit's behavior can be explained as a special case of a more general pattern of behavior that also occurs at the subunit level.

Stokes (1966) has persuasively argued the advantage of reducing an institution like the presidency to the individual staff members if one wants to know something about the presidency's effectiveness under different patterns of staff organization. Reduction would (1) allow one to generalize the phenomenon under review, (2) yield increased power to predict or explain variation of the gross phenomenon, and (3) make for observations at a lower level of analysis that are more generous in a sampling sense. These are "advantages," but only for some and not other purposes. What reduction makes possible is analysis of *within-unit* variations, which, in turn, makes possible analysis of linkages between unit properties observed at different levels, or analysis of emergence of unit from subunit properties. But because comparison of *between-unit* variations is possible only at one level of analysis, reduction is helpful only if the unit is reconstructed from the subunit properties to which it was reduced.

To make comparisons among many units, one needs measures of the comparison units at their own level. For instance, if Almond and Verba had confronted their individual-level data in, say, fifty rather than five nations, they undoubtedly would have had to construct nation-level measures for meaningful comparison in order to generalize about the relative stability of democratic regimes. In succumbing to the individualistic fallacy on several occasions,[2] they were partly victimized by their research design. They drew a purposive sample of five "democratic" nations to observe, at the subunit level of individuals, internal variations in political behavior. This is legitimate enough as long as between-unit variations are analyzed at the level of reduction. But as they did not have a "control group" of "nondemocratic" nations, the design did not permit falsification of hypotheses even at the microlevel. They could not, therefore, control their individual-level data for spurious correlations possibly due to the intrusion of properties characteristic of "nations" as the significant macrounits, for they did not mobilize for the purpose of cross-national analysis independent indicators of the national environments. Rather, they employed inferential variables concerning the presumed context for individual behavior—that is, contextual macrovariables *inferred* from the distribution of individual-level properties. But such variables, Cartwright (1969, pp. 201–202) points out, "imply some explanatory principles beyond and behind any immediately observable data," yet (like altitude or latitude, for instance) they "do not denote any particular events or processes or entities; rather they refer simply to certain dimensions of an arbitrary framework of reference axes: they are abstract. As defined, abstract variables can be neither causal nor caused." But if the variables assumed to constitute the context are neither causal nor caused, their utility is limited to interpretation, which Almond and Verba did with considerable imagination, rather than to explanation in the sense of empirical proof.

Insofar as Almond and Verba were interested in the explanation of differences between political institutions at the level of the nation, they conducted their analysis at the wrong level. One does not know whether this was their original intent. If it was, they might have used the reductionist strategy of observing within-nation individual behavior as a first step followed, as a second step, by the construction of the relational, structural, and contextual properties needed in the anticipated (or perhaps unanticipated) macroanalysis. Macrolevel properties derived or constructed from the microlevel properties can then be used as "controls" in a multivariate analysis conducted at the microlevel, or they can be correlated with direct indicators of the macrolevel unit properties; and comparative analysis can then proceed at the macrolevel by using constructed (rather than inferred) macrounit properties as controls for variations in context.

Reduction is not enough because in the study of social, as against physical, phenomena the behavior of the units observed at lower levels of analysis may, but need not, affect the behavior of units at the higher level. In the physical sciences, reduction of a unit to its subunits is justified and legitimized by the assumption that changes in the behavior of the microunits—atoms, molecules, elements—do in fact cause changes in the properties of the macrounits. In the social sciences, on the other hand, as Abell (1971, p. 97) points out, "the characteristic latent ontology is a macro one—we try to construe people's behavior in terms of their location in social collectivities. So for the latent causal approach to be effective we require ways of observing and characterizing groups independently of the properties of their individual members. This is, of course, a restatement of the old problem of 'emergence.' "

Fallacies of inference stemming from the multilevel nature of human and social data, on the one hand, and the presence of individual and collective actors, on the other hand, are common and familiar in political research. The problem of multilevel analysis is particularly acute if research calls for comparison and / or correlation as modes of inference, for these modes are possible at only one level of analysis. To avoid false inferences from a unit observed at one level (a subject unit) to a unit to be explained at another level (an object unit), it is necessary to transform data to make them amenable to comparative and/or correlational treatment.

I have reviewed some of the intellectual and theoretical issues and questions that are germane to data transformation from one level to another level of analysis—micro to macro and macro to micro. I have not addressed either technical matters of measurement or sampling problems. The former includes such problems as measurement effects of transformation on the measurement of between-object unit variations, or when and how within-unit measurements affect (influence, bias) the results obtained from the measurement of between-unit variations. The latter involves, among other questions, the problem of generalizability. For there is no guarantee that second-stage and third-stage sampling frames pertaining to subunits or superunits are representative of such units, even if the universe of object units (whose behavior is to be explained) has been properly defined and, through multistage sampling, both object and subject units have been randomly chosen. These and other concerns remain on the agenda of multilevel methodology.

TWO

Of Structure

and Linkage

Class and Party as Interactive

Role Systems

AN ADAGE, now more notorious than famous, and as tantalizing from an ideological as from a scientific point of view, asserts that "a person thinks, politically, as he is socially. Social characteristics determine political preference" (Lazarsfeld, Berelson, and Gaudet, 1948, p. 27). The maxim has, of course, not gone unchallenged. The style set by such analysis, it has been said, "threatens to take the politics out of the study of electoral behavior" and "tends to divert attention from critical elements of the electoral decision." Crucial among these elements are "traditional or habitual partisan attachments" (Key and Munger, 1959, pp. 281–282).

What is said about the relationship between socioeconomic status and voting behavior is, apparently, what Karl Marx said long ago—that a person's position in the class structure determines his political ideas and interests. And what the class formula seems to deny is what most interpreters have always asserted—that American politics is singularly free of socioeconomic determinism. In short, the dictum on social characteristics implied that the element of critical importance in a man's vote is not his political party affiliation or attachment but his preparty class position and related characteristics.

In general, the higher a person's class position, the more likely is he to vote Republican, and the lower his class position, the greater the likelihood of his voting Democratic (Lipset et al., 1954). Only in 1956 did a majority of the American working class indicate a preference for the Republican candidate in the presidential election of that year (Table 5.1).

But the very consistency of earlier findings, which showed that working-class people tended to vote Democratic in greater proportions, in contrast to their dramatic shift in 1956, further crystallizes our problem. In the institutional context of American politics, party preference means voting either the Republican or the Democratic ticket.[1] If it should turn out that

Table 5.1   Voting preferences of middle class and working class, 1952 and 1956, by percent

	Middle class		Working class	
Voting preference	1952 ($N = 389$)	1956 ($N = 417$)	1952 ($N = 811$)	1956 ($N = 892$)
Democratic	30	33	54	37
Republican	69	66	43	58
Other, Don't know, Refused	1	1	3	5
Total	100	100	100	100

the swing of the working-class majority to the Republican candidate in 1956 was only a temporary aberration, the problem of the relationship between class and party becomes even more a matter of theoretical interest. For in that case it may be asked whether the swing was due to the Republican candidate's personal appeal or whether it represented a collective movement, however temporary, of the working class away from the Democratic party. For the latter would, indeed, make it a class phenomenon.[2]

The politics of eighteenth-century America was a politics of social class and economic interests.[3] The struggle of economic interests had been the dominant experience of those who had come to government as public servants. Only a well-constructed Union, James Madison wrote in Number 10 of *The Federalist,* would tend to "break and control the violence of faction." Factions had their most common and durable source in "the various and unequal distribution of property. Those who hold and those who are without property have ever formed distinct interests in society." But unlike the optimistic Marx several decades later, the skeptical Madison concluded that "the *causes* of faction cannot be removed, and that relief is only to be sought in the means of controlling its effects" (Beloff, 1948, pp. 43–44).

For Madison, then, social class—his reference to "distinct interests" does not conceal that meaning—was an intrinsic, and irremovable, structural factor of the political system. And insofar as he clearly perceived the connection between class and party, or faction, as he called it, his analysis has much to commend it. But as he anticipated disastrous consequences for the political system flowing from the relationship, his political theory lost a good deal of the relevance it might otherwise have had for subsequent political analysis. His model was well grounded historically in ancient and modern experience, but it necessarily failed to anticipate the adjustment that was to be made, under democratic conditions that he did not foresee, between class and party in the American political system.

Later observers came to neglect the role of classes in American politics.

This neglect was rooted in a number of sources. First, by its very nature the democratic ideology of equality militated against recognition of class as a vital dimension of the political system. Second, as long as America was predominantly agricultural, major political cleavages were seen to lie chiefly in the unequal rates of growth of different sections, and concern with sectionalism—itself undoubtedly a very real issue—tended to obscure the role of classes in politics. Third, as both the opportunity for and the fact of social mobility tended to reduce the contagion of "class consciousness" on the American scene, the existence of classes and their relation to party division eluded political observation. Finally, the overlap of classes with the more obvious ethnic and religious groupings in the population obstructed a class analysis of party politics. As successive waves of immigration supplied the labor force for the lowest and most menial tasks in an increasingly urbanized society, mass political behavior was more readily described in terms of the Irish or Polish, the Catholic or Jewish, vote than in class terms.

Long-range as well as short-range variations in the political significance of social classes are quite likely to occur. For instance, in a recent study it has been shown that correlation coefficients between occupational status (an index of class) and presidential vote can change markedly from one election to the next. In the 1944 election the relationship could be expressed by a coefficient of .26; in 1948 it rose to .48; in 1952 it dropped to .29; and in 1956 it reached a low of .16.[4]

The degree of "polarization" in class relations as it appears in voting is undoubtedly very significant in telling us something about the state of the political system and the possible relevance of class in the political order. But it does not follow that when the index of correlation is high, class considerations alone influence party preferences, that they influence them to a greater degree than other considerations, or that party preferences are a function of varying class relations.

Furthermore, measurement of the degree of "polarization" between the classes does not automatically define just what meaning one should attach to high, medium, or low associations between the class position of voters and their party preferences. It only tells us that at different times, for reasons that are presumably determinable and worthy of determination, class is more or less involved in political choice. As V. O. Key, Jr. (Key and Munger, 1959, p. 295) has pointed out, factors such as "the differentials in impact of market forces on different groups, the changing structure of political alternatives, the interaction of group memories of past and contemporary events" may at different times bring different social characteristics into "the zone of political relevance."

We can take it for granted, then, that variations in the relationship between class and party occur, making at times party and at other times class the more critical determinant of political behavior, other factors being equal. But the problem at the core of the controversy over social determinism versus partisan determination of the vote is neither the degree of variation between class and party considerations from one election to the next nor the degree of variation in any one election. Given the institutionalization of the two-party system, which leaves the voter no choice but to vote for either one party or the other,[5] and given the admittedly fluid boundaries between classes in a relatively mobile society, then the significant problem is the structure of the relationship between class and party that seems to obtain through time.

The political process, as David Easton (1953, p. 129) has defined it, involves "the authoritative allocation of values for a society." This is a useful definition for an inquiry into the relationship between class and party. The allocation process is authoritative insofar as decisions concerning the distribution of values are widely accepted. An overconcentration of a single social class in one party or the other, or an overemphasis on promoting a single-class interest by one party or the other, would jeopardize acceptance of decisions in the political system. It is probably for this reason that a two-party system generates parties that are not based exclusively on class and not oriented toward the achievement of class values.[6] In an effective two-party system, it has been said, "agreement is necessary both on basic processes and on basic issues" (Dahl and Lindblom, 1953, p. 295).

It is the allocation of values through the political process that MacIver (1947, p. 217) must have had in mind when he wrote that "the party-system is the democratic translation of the class struggle. It postulates national unity beneath the divisions of class. It postulates the rationalization of class interests so that these can make appeal on the grounds of their service or to compatibility with the national interest." If, as we understand MacIver to say, the party system translates conflicting class interests in the process of allocating available values, the function of parties in this respect is paradoxical. On the one hand, the parties are not independent of those potential clashes of interest that derive, as Madison suggested, from the unequal distribution of property (to which we may add the unequal distribution of such other values as are widely cherished and sought, whether social status and prestige, income and educational opportunities, occupational mobility, or possession of political influence). On the other hand, the same parties are the very instrumentalities of governance, designed to balance conflicting class interests, effect compromise between them, and finally integrate them in a broadly consensual framework of public policy.

No society is conceivable without some sort of class structure. The social rationale for this need not concern us here: we simply accept class stratification as given. But what makes a class structure more or less accepted by the members of a society is probably the fact that there also exists more or less wide agreement on the values in terms of which social positions and status rankings are either assigned or achieved. In other words, when there is broad agreement on what a society's members value, the class structure reflecting these values is likely to be widely accepted by people occupying particular positions in the structure.

Only if and when the nationally shared set of values disintegrates, when the values themselves are put in question, or when a society is characterized by anomie does the class system function as a predominantly harmful source of cleavage. This, however, is the exception rather than the rule in democratic-pluralistic systems, although disagreement on values underlying the class structure may serve as a very sensitive barometer of social change. But just as agreement on the rules of the game serves as the integrating element in the struggle of the parties for power, so the agreed-on values supporting the class structure serve as integrating elements in what Riesman (1950, p. 256) has gently called "the conversation of the classes." The classes, like the parties, function simultaneously as catalysts of cleavage *and* consensus.

What keeps the party battle within manageable limits is the integrative function of the class system. Because the class system, as we have seen, is predicated on a differential but agreed-on distribution of values, the parties cannot afford to ignore the existing pattern of allocation and its boundaries. In formulating issues and proposing policy alternatives, political parties necessarily operate within the limits of values institutionalized, if only temporarily, in the class system.

Reciprocally, the two-party system functions as a "brake," so to speak, on class conflicts and their political implications. As, generally speaking, differentiation is by definition a built-in characteristic of class, the existence of classes always represents a potential source of conflict in the political process. But in a two-party system the parties, in order to be successful at the polls, recruit leaders, candidates, and workers as well as followers from all strata in the class structure. Their appeals, policy proposals, and activities will not be directed to one class alone. In other words, a competitive two-party system, by not allowing either party to cater to any one class, tends to blur lines of social cleavage and to make for political dispersion of class interests in the political system.[7] We should therefore expect the structural relationship between class and party in the American political system to be fluid, kaleidoscopic, and diffuse.

In this review and formulation of what I consider to be the "problem" of the relationship between class and party in the two-party democratic political system, I have largely dealt in institutional-theoretical terms. For the purpose of research on the level of the person, however, the concepts of class and party must be translated into concepts that permit simultaneous manipulation of empirical referents found in the behavior (broadly conceived as including acts as well as attitudes and perceptions) of individuals. In other words, what is needed is a conceptual bridge, so to speak, that will allow easy crossing from the realm of discourse concerning class to that of party, as well as from the level of macroanalysis to the level of microanalysis.

Both class and party, while quite dissimilar structures on the concrete-empirical level, can be thought of as role systems on the analytical-theoretical level.[8] As role systems they are predicated on the empirical reality of role orientations and expectations. This formulation allows us, then, to treat class and party as phenomena of the same empirical order for the purpose of research. What links class and party empirically is the *possibility* that individuals may simultaneously take roles in class and party systems as they also take voter (or nonvoter) roles in the larger political system. Whether such roles are taken in fact is, of course, a matter for empirical inquiry. Only if class and party roles do interrelate in influencing voting behavior can one meaningfully speak of a relationship between class and party in the political system and examine the structure of the relationship between them.

Party as Role System

The notion of the party as a role system directs attention to a constituent element in the system, namely, role. Instead of asking "what persons . . . are to be included within the 'party' contesting for power" (Key, 1952, p. 220), we ask what roles are requisite for the functioning of party. This formulation avoids much of the conventional controversy over the "composition" of parties. Edmund Burke's (1871, vol. 1, p. 151) classic definition of party as "a body of men united, for promoting by their joint endeavors the national interest, upon some particular principle in which they are all agreed," lacks validity in the American context. But equally useless for our purpose is the popular conception, often promoted by party leaders, that the party is made up of "all voters who participate in a party primary or support a party candidate."[9] As Schattschneider (1942, p. 54) has pointed out, "the concept of the parties as a mass association of partisans has no historical basis and has little relation to the facts of party organization." But Schattschneider's (p. 61) recommendation that we abandon "the mental image of the party as an association of all partisans" and "recognize frankly that the party is the property of the organization" ignores the fact that the inner core of party leaders and workers could never succeed in acquiring political power without a reasonably stable following of faithful partisans. What all of the formulations suggest is that a party can be conceived as a system of mutually interdependent roles ranging from that of the professional functionary to one of an occasional supporter.

We can think of the party role system as a set of concentric circles with a hard inner core and a series of proximate circles fanning out until the periphery is reached. Though all "party roles" share one party label or another, the party as a role system, though differentiated, need not be either highly cooperative or solidary. In fact, quite different expectations may be held for those at the center, in the middle, or at the periphery of the system.

At the periphery of any party system are those roles whose determinant expectations are least clear-cut and whose resultant behavior patterns reflect little consistency. While all those who vote for a party's candidates may be thought of in the role of "followers," this is often a temporary and not very pervasive role, partly because it is activated for a limited amount of time, partly because it involves a minimum of acts, and partly because other roles taken in other role systems (such as family, work group, professional association, church, class, and so on) may be more salient in the voting decision. Consequently behavior expected in terms of party role at the periphery of the system may involve little consistency.

In the structure of the party system, therefore, the role of party follower is crucial. Unless the party leadership or party candidates can rely on their expectations concerning the behavior of party followers, their own roles remain in jeopardy. If followers fail to carry out their major assignment—the casting of a ballot on election day—or if they shift too readily from one party to the other, their conduct introduces uncertainty into the system. Of course, there is considerable differentiation in follower roles, and a wide range of expectations is afforded by the roles available at the periphery of the party system. In the American two-party system, these would include not only the Republican or Democratic regular but also such roles as fringe supporter, ticket-splitter, independent, nonvoter, and so on.

Indeed, it is the proliferation of roles at different times that makes the American party system a relatively "open" system. For the temporality of performing in the peripheral roles makes for variability in aggregate voting behavior and injects a highly dynamic quality into the system. On the other hand, the relative stability of the system is made possible by the ability of party leaders and candidates to arrive at reasonably stable expectations concerning the behavior of voters whose party roles at the periphery can be specified.

Class as Role System

Few concepts of social analysis have proved theoretically and empirically more elusive than the concept of "class." An initial difficulty is the bewildering and disconcerting amount of disagreement concerning definitions of class. As a sociologist (Gordon, 1949, p. 265) has pointed out,

> there is no general agreement among sociologists at the present time as to what factor or combination of factors delineates the social class. All concur that the concept of class deals with the horizontal stratification of a population, but whether it is based on economic power, occupation, status feelings, culture differences, or their combination, and to what extent separate group life is indicated by the term, are questions on which there is no substantial agreement.

Perhaps central to these conceptual difficulties is failure to relate class to some theory of social conduct, without which the concept of class must necessarily remain meaningless, as well as failure to specify the purpose to which any particular concept of class is to be put. Only within the theoretical framework of an investigation can one determine which dimension or which complex of variables is most adequate in the development of a concept of class—as, for instance, whether objective or subjective criteria are relevant, or on what level of the society an inquiry into class-related behavior seems to be most fruitful.

Political scientists presumably inquire into the relationship between class and party because they expect to derive from such investigation some insight into the allocation of values through the political process. Among these values "power" is of particular interest, because its distribution affects the allocation of other values.

There is an abundance of evidence that the most important decision makers—with exceptions, of course—are recruited from the more-favored levels in the class structure (Matthews, 1954). Even in voting, which in a democratic society is an important decision-making process, position in the class structure is a significant factor influencing the distribution of power. For nonvoting—that is, nonparticipation in the making of important decisions—increases as possession of such class-related values as occupational skill, wealth, or education decreases.

Of course, the members of a class may, on investigation, be seen to share party preferences in voting, attitudes on party-related issues, or other party-relevant perceptions. And if a relationship between class position and these various aspects of political behavior can be demonstrated to exist, there is a good presumption in favor of the relevance for political behavior of the institutional pattern of relations characterized as "class." However, positive correlations in this regard are at most a necessary, but need not be a sufficient, condition for the reality of a relationship between class and party as determinants of political behavior. For it may be argued that the way in which class is *experienced* by participants in the political process makes a significant difference in their political behavior. As Newcomb (1950, p. 559) has pointed out, to have both objective and subjective information about a person is better than either alone.

Societies vary a great deal, of course, in the degree to which they evaluate social roles, and they differ as well in the extent to which they permit individuals to leave one role for another. A "class," then, may be conceived as a grouping of roles that are more or less equally evaluated. The "members" of a class—that is to say, individuals who take a role in the class system—engage "in practices giving them a similar relation to the shaping and distribution (and enjoyment) of one or more specified values" (Lasswell and Kaplan, 1950, p. 62).

What makes class a role system is, of course, that "consciousness of kind" without which evaluation is impossible. For evaluation requires an awareness of self and other as the basis for comparisons. If, then, the expectation concerning another's behavior is accompanied by an evaluation of the other's position, a class role is seen in a value-oriented frame of reference. Social stratification, as Barber (1957, p. 7) puts it, is "a structure of regularized inequality in which men are ranked higher and lower according to the value accorded their various roles and activities."

The notion that class constitutes a role system is helpful in resolving the controversy over whether or not class is an objective or subjective phenomenon. Roles derive from one's own orientations coupled with others' expectations regarding behavior appropriate to a position in the class structure. These orientations and expectations must necessarily be cognized if they are to give rise to relevant behavior. In other words, some kind of class awareness would seem to be necessary if class roles are to affect political behavior. Only if class, like party, provides a salient frame of reference in which the voter makes his choices or relates himself to politics can it be said that class roles function as premises of political behavior.

But "class awareness" may not only be absent, it may also be false. A person occupying a position in the class structure may see himself as taking a role in a class to which he *objectively* does not belong. This makes the task of investigating the relevance of class roles for their relationship to party roles all the more poignant. For, as Gerth and Mills (1953, p. 340) have discerningly suggested, "if psychological feelings and political outlooks do not correspond to economic and occupational class, we must try to find out why, rather than throw out the economic baby with the psychological bath water, and so fail to understand how either fits into the national tub."

Identification as Role Potential

While many of the measures used in the analyses are interpreted as they were interpreted in the Survey Research Center's (SRC) original studies, some expository liberties had to be taken to relate the data to role formulations. As an example, no direct measure of what we have called "party roles" was available. But the SRC surveys included two indicators that could be considered pertinent.

First, there was a measure of "party identification." Since this measure was clearly interpreted as a perceptual and attitudinal statement of "personal attachment or belonging which an individual feels toward a given political party" (Campbell and Cooper, 1956, p. 16), it is to be considered at most as indicative of a "potential" for role taking in the party system, but not as evidence of such role taking.

While "presidential choice" in the case of voters could possibly be accepted as evidence of actual role taking in the party system, in the case of nonvoters "preference" can at most be taken only as an indicator of "role potential." Moreover, it may be objected that neither voting for a candidate nor preferring a candidate necessarily means voting for or preferring a party. The choice may be a result of the candidate's personal appeal rather than a matter of his party label. Yet, on the level of national politics, a vote or preference for a party's presidential candidate is the only readily available measure of party-connected role behavior.

With regard to a measure of social class, the SRC studies, though utilizing various indicators of socioeconomic status, do not provide a composite index. On the assumption that it is better to have both objective and subjective information about a person than to have either alone, it was necessary to construct an index of social class that would reflect the existence of a national class system.

An index of social class was constructed, built on respondents' occupation, education, and income in the case of the 1952 sample, and on occupation and education alone in the 1956 sample.[10] The terms "middle class" and "working class" (white-collar and blue-collar classes, essentially) were assigned to the dichotomized aggregates for convenience of discourse. While admittedly ambiguous concepts, they are not altogether arbitrary. As we shall see, in response to a question concerning their own class, about 95 percent of all respondents had no difficulty in accepting the terms "middle class" or "working class" as properly descriptive of their class position. It is interesting to note that the final dichotomy yielded the same proportions in both years—68 percent "working-class" and 32 percent "middle-class" respondents.

Another measure of class, subjective in character, available from the

SRC studies was a person's "class identification." In 1952 respondents were asked this question: "There's quite a bit of talk these days about different social classes. If you were asked to use one of these four names for *your* social class, which would you say you belonged in—the middle class, lower class, working class, or upper class?"

In 1956 this question was broken up into two questions, the first designed to determine respondents' "awareness" of class, the second to determine their identification. The first question read: "There's quite a bit of talk these days about different social classes. Most people say they belong either to the middle class or to the working class. Do you ever think of yourself as being in one of these classes?" This question was followed by another: "Which class? Would you say that you are about an average (middle or working class) person or that you are in the upper part of the (middle or working) class?"[11]

Class analysis in terms of class identification is most frequently associated with the work of Richard Centers. Centers (1949, p. 27) defines classes as "psycho-social groupings, something that is essentially subjective in character, dependent upon class consciousness (i.e. a feeling of group membership), and class lines of cleavage [which] may or may not conform to what seem to social scientists to be logical lines of cleavage in the objective or stratification sense."

Despite criticisms, the class identification measure was used in the following analysis for want of another index of "subjective" class, but only after identification with class had been conceptualized somewhat differently from Centers' and others' formulations.

The concept of identification was first introduced into psychology by Sigmund Freud. Later psychologists have elaborated Freud's definition, but more often than not they have failed to incorporate in their redefinitions elements that were vital in Freud's formulation. In Freud's thinking, it is precisely because he wants to be like his father that "the little boy notices that his father stands in his way with his mother." According to Freud (1949, p. 61), identification "is ambivalent from the very first; it can turn into an expression of tenderness as easily as into a wish for someone's removal." And in another connection, speaking of identification in which "the ego sometimes copies the person who is not loved and sometimes the one who is loved," Freud (1949, p. 64) suggests that "in both cases the identification is a partial and extremely limited one and only borrows a single trait from the person who is its object."

It follows that insofar as identification is ambivalent, as in Freud's first case, or partial and limited, as in the second case, it may be the source of consistent as well as inconsistent attitudinal or behavioral patterns. One should expect, therefore, that identification with class may correlate only partially or in varying degree with different components of political behavior.

Although Edward C. Tolman (1951, p. 308), within the forbidding nomenclature of "topological psychology," initially defines identification in conventional terms, his spatial model yields two important insights. First, identification involves not only locomotion or movement *toward* "a region of love and approval," but also—and simultaneously—locomotion *away from* "some other region of valenced activity." Or, as Tolman (1951, p. 310n4) puts it more concretely in connection with group identification, "the actor wants love and approval from the group, and to get them he has to behave in ways similar to those of the group. In so doing he has to locomote away from behaving in other ways which, because of other needs, also have for him positive valences." In other words, identification conceived as movement *from* and *to* social groups may produce conflict in that it involves cross-pressures; and identification will be partial to the extent that in some instances the countervailing forces will be stronger than the forces of identification, so that behavior will be inconsistent.

And second, with its emphasis on movement, Tolman's conception recaptures some of the dynamic quality of the Freudian approach; identification, in short, appears as a process, and as a process it permits us to conceive of the relationship between identification and other attitudinal or behavioral dimensions along a theoretical continuum from zero to full identification.

Our discussion of identification suggests the following conclusions concerning the operational uses to which the concept may be put as an analytical tool in the study of class-related political attitudes or behavior:

1.   Identification refers to a *process of becoming* like someone, rather than the state of being like someone. As a process, identification may be thought of in terms of a continuum from zero to full identification. The polar extremes of this continuum are hypothetical constructs and are unlikely to be found empirically.

2.   Identification involves *simultaneous movement away from and toward* regions of valence. As such it is likely to create conflict, to be partial, and to be limited. Hence it need not effectuate other attitudes or behaviors so that a logically consistent role necessarily emerges as a result of its operation.

To isolate the effect of class identification as a variable, independent of objective class position, respondents were divided into four class groupings:

1.   Those objectively classified as working class and self-identified as working class—working-class consistents, or WW;

2. Those objectively classified as working class but self-identified as middle class—middle-class affiliates, or WM;
3. Those objectively classified as middle class but self-identified as working class—working-class affiliates, or MW;
4. Those objectively classified as middle class and self-identified as middle class—middle-class consistents, or MM.

The distribution of these groupings for the 1952 and 1956 samples is shown in Table 5.2.[12]

In order to measure the operation and effect of class identification, the following instruments will be used in testing hypotheses:

1. The four class groupings evolved from the cross-tabulation of objective and self-identified classes (WW, WM, MW, and MM). Attitudes or behaviors of those objectively classified as working class or middle class, but identifying themselves with the opposite class (WM and MW, or "affiliates"), should differ significantly from those who identify themselves with their objective class (WW and MM, or "consistents"). Such differences would be indicative of the *operation* of class identification as an independent variable.

2. In order to have some descriptive measure of the relative effect of class identification in its varied interaction with other variables, either of an attitudinal or a behavioral sort, a simple "class-identification-effect" (CIE) scoring procedure will be used.

The CIE scores are constructed by subtracting the proportion of "low" respondents on any dependent variable from the proportion of "high" respondents. The score yielded for each class grouping reflects the actual distribution of respondents on particular variables. This permits easier comparison of the class groupings than is possible by inspection of the individual cells in a column and across columns. In other words, the scores for each class grouping (in columns) may be compared, and the *difference*

Table 5.2 Class groupings based on objective classification and self-identification, 1952 and 1956, by percent

| | Objectively classified as— | | | | | |
| | Middle class | | Working class | | Total 1952 | Total 1956 |
Self-identified as—	1952 (N = 366)	1956 (N = 402)	1952 (N = 766)	1956 (N = 856)	1952 (N = 1,132)	1956 (N = 1,258)
Middle class	64	70	24	22	37	37
Working class	36	30	76	78	63	63
Total	100	100	100	100	100	100

in scores between consistents and affiliates may be used as an index of movement of the affiliates from the objective class to which they belong to the objective class with which they identify.

Since it is to be expected that the difference between the CIE scores of the two consistent groupings (WW-MM) is always greater than the difference between the scores of a consistent and an affiliate (WW-WM or MM-MW), the smaller the difference of the differences between the latter combinations and the former (WW-MM), the less partial or limited—or the more complete—can class identification be conceived to be with respect to any indicator of political attitudes or behavior.

3.   Chi square will be used as the measure of significance for determining whether a significant relationship exists between respondents' class position and their political preferences, perceptions, and orientations.. In other words, it will also serve as a rough indicator of whether class or party seems to be the decisive factor. Where $p<.01$, class may be accepted as the factor that seems to circumscribe the frame of reference within which political perceptions or behavior acquire meaning; where $p>.01$, party would seem to be the more relevant factor in shaping this frame of reference.

Class Identification and Party Perspectives

A convenient and useful starting point in a discussion of the perceptual aspects of political behavior is Harold D. Lasswell's concept of "perspective." A perspective is defined as "a pattern of identifications, demands, and expectations." What Lasswell means by this is that certain identifications, demands, and expectations tend to be clustered. But, Lasswell points out, "a perspective need not be a logically unified whole, and indeed seldom is. It may include 'stray' identifications, demands, and expectations, so to speak, as well as integrated interests, faiths, and loyalties" (Lasswell and Kaplan, 1950, p. 25).

Identification with class may be assumed to constitute only one element, though an important one, in the cluster of identifications, demands, and expectations characterized as "political perspective." If by voting for a particular candidate citizens identify with one another, identification refers to the process by which a political "we" comes into existence. Identification with party, for instance—which presumably means that people identify with candidates and leaders under a party label—has been shown to be a highly significant motivational factor in the voting behavior of Americans (Campbell, Gurin, and Miller, 1954, pp. 88–111).

It is on behalf of this collective "we" that those similarly identified make political demands. These demands relate to the shaping and sharing of desirable values. Because demands delimit the political "we," in the sense that they give identification substantive content, they should be significantly related to identification.

Expectations, on the other hand, may be independent—theoretically, at least—of either identifications or demands. They need not be related to identifications because they do not automatically circumscribe the political "we" in identifying terms. Nor need expectations be related to demands because these are statements of value, while expectations are statements of fact, which may be true or false, concerning a future state of affairs.

Since expectations need not be related to demands, nor identifications to expectations, it follows that a perspective need not be a logically consistent attitudinal pattern. Moreover, as Lasswell suggests, "it may even include in varying degrees, conflicting commitments of the ego and the self" (Lasswell and Kaplan, 1950, p. 25). Presumably Lasswell has in mind the possibility that identification is a process which operates selectively; in other words, that identifications may be related in varying degrees to other identifications, demands, and expectations.

Insofar as class identification is politically relevant, one should expect it to be congruent with party identification. For parties rather than classes serve as primary vehicles of political expression. If no relationship at all existed between class identification and party identification, the possibility of conflict arising from different identifications would probably be heightened and would make political behavior inconsistent and unpredictable. It is more likely, however, that people will tend to integrate class and party identifications in order to play reasonably consistent roles in the political system.

If these theoretical speculations are viable, we should expect that, with minor variations, appropriate data would support them in at least two different situations. This was in fact the case in both 1952 and 1956. We are not surprised by the results as such, but we are surprised that the variation between the two years is as small as it is, in view of the fact that in 1956 working-class people dramatically shifted their preferences from the Democratic to the Republican candidate (see Table 5.1). The most noticeable change from 1952 to 1956 is evident in the party identification of the working-class consistents. Nevertheless half of them, as Table 5.3 shows, still clung to a Democratic identification in 1956, and almost one-quarter declared themselves independents.

Apparently, working-class consistents and affiliates found it congenial in both years to identify more with the Democratic party than with the Republican party, in spite of their preference for the Republican candidate. Middle-class consistents, on the other hand, were surprisingly ambiguous

Table 5.3 Class identification and party identification, 1952 and 1956, by percent

Party identification	Working class				Middle Class			
	Working		Middle		Working		Middle	
	1952 (N=557)	1956 (N=625)	1952 (N=185)	1956 (N=187)	1952 (N=130)	1956 (N=118)	1952 (N=235)	1956 (N=279)
Democratic	59	50	39	41	49	48	32	36
Independent	22	24	22	29	28	33	27	26
Republican	19	26	39	30	23	19	41	38
Total	100	100	100	100	100	100	100	100
CIE score	+40	+24	0	+11	+26	+29	−9	−2

Tests for:		χ^2	df	p
WW-WM	1952	33.12	2	<.001
	1956	4.76	2	>.05
MM-MW	1952	12.93	2	<.01
	1956	14.13	2	<.001

in their party identification in 1956. In almost equal proportions they called themselves Republicans or Democrats, while middle-class affiliates decisively identified themselves as Democrats rather than Republicans. Although in both years voters who remained consistent with their objective class and those who deviated from it differed in their party identifications, thereby suggesting that class identification operates as a factor influencing party identification, objective class position still appears to serve as a countervailing, restraining influence. This is most evident in the identifying behavior of the middle-class affiliates in 1956.

Political demands, specifically demands made on government to act or refrain from acting in such matters as unemployment, education, housing, and so on, are expressions of valuation. As valuation of this kind is essentially social in character and determined by the groups to which a person belongs or refers, one might expect that voters identified with one class or another would differ on opposition to or support of government action in the social welfare field. Class identification would be meaningless if those similarly identified did not also share the emotional bonds symbolized by common political demands. As Table 5.4 shows, in both years the affiliates differed in their attitudes from the consistents on the role of government in the welfare field, and identification functioned in the expected direction. Regardless of objective class position, those identifying themselves as working class tended to favor government action.

But some changes that occurred between 1952 and 1956 may be noted. In the first place, a considerably larger proportion of working-class consistents supported an active role of the government in 1956 than in 1952, and a somewhat greater proportion of the middle-class affiliates did likewise. This result is of interest because it throws some light on the dynamics of political demands. Although both groups preferred the Republican standardbearer in the 1956 election, they were evidently—as members of the "objective" working class—less satisfied with the Republican record in the welfare field. In the case of the middle-class affiliates, then, class identification was restrained, so to speak, by their actual location in the class structure, although identification continued to have an independent effect.

Second, about half of both the middle-class consistents and working-class affiliates (as well as of the middle-class affiliates) felt in 1956 that government activity in the welfare field had been "about right"; and among the working-class affiliates, in particular, a somewhat smaller proportion felt that the government "should do more" than had felt so in 1952. In other words, objective class position seemed here, too, to countervail the effect of class identification. Nevertheless, both affiliates, being under cross-pressure arising out of conflict between objective class position and sub-

Table 5.4 Class identification and government activity demands, 1952 and 1956, by percent

Character of demand	Working class				Middle class			
	Working		Middle		Working		Middle	
	1952 (N=528)	1956 (N=533)	1952 (N=173)	1956 (N=168)	1952 (N=123)	1956 (N=111)	1952 (N=230)	1956 (N=257)
Government should do more	31	50	23	31	34	28	24	22
Activity about right	59	38	51	49	46	52	43	54
Government should do less	10	12	26	20	20	20	33	24
Total	100	100	100	100	100	100	100	100
CIE score	+21	+38	−3	+11	+14	+8	−9	−2

Tests for:

		x^2	df	p
WW-WM	1952	36.85	2	<.001
	1956	19.27	2	<.001
MM-MW	1952	8.35	2	<.02
	1956	0.62	2	>.05

jective class identification again occupy a middle location between the consistents.

In addition to demands on specific issues, voters' party preferences in the election of president may be considered valuative judgments that, if integrated as identifications and demands in a political perspective, should be related to class identification. However, here a most striking break in pattern occurred between 1952 and 1956. As Table 5.5 indicates, while in 1952 a great majority of the working-class consistents had preferred the Democratic candidate, in 1956 the majority shifted to the Republican candidate. Class identification continued to have an independent effect on party preference. It is also interesting to note that in 1956 a somewhat larger proportion of the middle-class consistents indicated a Democratic preference than had done so in 1952, while working-class affiliates were somewhat less pro-Democratic in their 1956 preferences than in their 1952 preferences. This tended to reduce the margin of difference between them and the middle-class consistents to a statistically insignificant point.

The data suggest that a political perspective need not be an integrated cluster of identifications and demands: not only class identification but even "objective" class position may have merely a tenuous relationship to party choice (at least as revealed by candidate preference). In other words, the structure of the political system as determined by the relationship between class and party seems to be fluid rather than fixed and to be subject to periodic change as the relations between voter class and party identifications converge or diverge.

It was suggested that identifications and expectations may be independent of each other because expectations, unlike demands, need not delimit any collective political "we." However, it can be argued that while the hypothesis may be adequate on the most general theoretical level, it may be less than adequate in terms of class identification and class-related political expectations. For insofar as expectations may be shaped by objective position in the social structure, and objective class differences may be reinforced by identifications, expectations may also be shaped by identification. On the other hand, differences in expectations between objective classes may be so small that there is no room for meaningful variation in expectations as a result of class identification.

The latter possibility may be illustrated by similar data from the 1952 and 1956 surveys. In 1952, respondents were asked this question: "Some people say there's not much opportunity in America today—that the average man doesn't have much chance to really get ahead. Others say there's plenty of opportunity, and anyone who works hard can go as far as he wants. How do you feel about this?"

One might expect that working-class respondents would be less inclined

Table 5.5 Class identification and party preferences, 1952 and 1956, by percent

Party preference	Working class				Middle class			
	Working		Middle		Working		Middle	
	1952 (N=561)	1956 (N=631)	1952 (N=182)	1956 (N=184)	1952 (N=129)	1956 (N=120)	1952 (N=233)	1956 (N=278)
Democratic	60	41	37	31	43	39	23	31
Republican	40	59	63	69	57	61	77	69
Total	100	100	100	100	100	100	100	100
CIE score	+20	−18	−26	−38	−14	−22	−54	−38

Tests for:

		χ^2	df	p
WW-WM	1952	26.35	1	<.001
	1956	4.00	1	<.05
MM-MW	1952	16.47	1	<.001
	1956	2.62	1	>.05

than members of the middle class to anticipate a rosy future. Yet, as results reported in Table 5.6 show, the differences between the two consistents were small and insignificant and did not give the identification factor any room in which to function independently. It would thus appear that within the American cultural context, the future is seen in such unambiguous and widely shared terms that class position or class identification fails to be important in shaping expectations.

A similar result may be noted in 1956. While the identical question was not asked, a related question that was asked may serve the purpose of comparison. It somewhat particularized the content of the expectation to the respondent's financial situation and limited the time dimension. The question reads: "Now looking ahead and thinking about the next few years, do you expect your financial situation will stay about the way it is now, get better, or get worse?" The results, as Table 5.7 shows, are not very

Table 5.6   Class identification and opportunity expectations, 1952, by percent

Character of expectation	Working class		Middle class	
	Working (N = 565)	Middle (N = 183)	Working (N = 232)	Middle (N = 131)
Yes, opportunity (qualified and not)	86	92	91	93
Pro-con and no opportunity[a]	14	8	9	7
Total	100	100	100	100
CIE score	+72	+84	+82	+86

a. Pro-con and no-opportunity responses have been combined because of the small number of cases in the relevant cells.

Table 5.7   Class identification and financial expectations, 1956, by percent

Character of expectation	Working class		Middle class	
	Working (N = 611)	Middle (N = 185)	Working (N = 114)	Middle (N = 274)
Get better	42	47	53	61
Stay as is	48	47	42	33
	90	94	95	94
Get worse	10	6	5	6
Total	100	100	100	100
CIE score	+80	+88	+90	+88

different from those obtained for opportunity in 1952. If we combine the categories "get better" and "stay as is" as being equivalent to the positive response ("yes, there is opportunity") in 1952, the results are amazingly similar. Like general expectations touching opportunity in 1952, so financial expectations in 1956 do not seem to relate either to objective class differences or to differences in class identification.

However, if financial expectations are appraised in a party-related frame of reference, class position and class identification may then be salient aspects. The same question was asked in 1952 and again in 1956: "Do you think it will make any difference in how you and your family get along financially whether the Democrats or Republicans win? [If it makes a difference, or if not answered]: Well, do you think you will be better off or worse off if the Republicans win the election?" When financial expectations were evaluated in a frame of reference that included class and party, large enough differences appeared between the two consistents to permit class identification to operate as an independent factor. But this was more the case in 1952 than in 1956.

As Table 5.8 shows, statistically significant differences appear between both consistent class groupings and those disaffiliated in terms of class identification. In 1952 the Democratic party was perceived by working-class identifiers, regardless of their objective class position, as the party of prosperity, while middle-class identifiers were somewhat more inclined to associate their well-being with the Republicans; but in 1956 the relationship is less clear. Working-class identifiers, regardless of objective class position, were still somewhat more inclined to see their financial future favored by the Democrats, but the difference between middle-class consistents and working-class affiliates is no longer statistically significant. By 1956 also, middle-class identifiers were more hesitant to associate their financial well-being with a Republican victory. In other words, it would seem that in 1956 financial expectations were not perceived in a party-related frame of reference, and class seemed relevant only in the case of working-class consistents, although less so than it had in 1952.

So far we have analyzed the relationship between class identification and certain attitudinal or perceptual dimensions of political behavior that would seem to constitute a person's political "perspective." But we have not examined the effect of class identification on manifestations of political conduct or on orientations related to conduct, such as political participation, interest, exposure to the mass media, sense of political effectiveness, and so on. While class identification may be related to other identifications or demands, the question whether it has an independent effect on conduct—in the sense that the self-identifier succeeds in taking the role of a person in the class with which he identifies himself, remains unexplored.

Table 5.8 Class identification and financial expectations in party context, 1952 and 1956, by percent

| | Working class | | | | Middle class | | | |
| | Working | | Middle | | Working | | Middle | |
Character of expectation	1952 (N=522)	1956 (N=601)	1952 (N=169)	1956 (N=170)	1952 (N=122)	1956 (N=108)	1952 (N=222)	1956 (N=268)
Better off under								
Democrats	44	27	28	17	32	20	16	16
Makes no difference	45	63	48	67	52	67	50	65
Better off under								
Republicans	11	10	24	16	16	13	34	19
Total	100	100	100	100	100	100	100	100
CIE score	+33	+17	+4	+1	+16	+7	−18	−3

Tests for:

		χ^2	df	p
WW-WM	1952	22.29	2	<.001
	1956	10.71	2	<.01
MM-MW	1952	18.75	2	<.001
	1956	3.10	2	>.05

The literature on identification affords us little guidance. Parsons and Shils, possibly because they are sociologists rather than social psychologists, seem to have sensed the multimodal complexity of the concept of identification. Although they relegated their pregnant observation to a footnote, they distinguish "(1) the internalization of the values but not the role of the model from (2) internalization of his specific role" (Parsons and Shils, 1951, p. 310n4). But they do not follow up this distinction. Stuart M. Stoke (1950, p. 177), in a critical appraisal of the concept, points out that

an emotional identification cannot produce a behavioral manifestation if *capacity* for the behavior is lacking. It also seems reasonable that different degrees of capacity are bound to produce different degrees of behavioral identification, even though effort to identify is held at a constantly high level.

The success of behavioral identification, Stoke (ibid., p. 180) continues, "will be affected by the capacity of the individual to adopt the role."

One should expect, therefore, that self-identification in terms of class ought to be more effective when it involves other identifications or preferences predicated on "internalization of values" than when it involves taking a class-related role in political conduct. In other words, participation in politics as a manifestation of role performance may depend less on class self-identification and more on those objective characteristics that seem to be a prerequisite for a person's capacity to take the role of a member in another class. This does not mean that *only* common characteristics, defined in terms of objective class position, matter in political conduct. But it does suggest that self-identification with class is likely to be less effective in the performance of political roles than are more strictly attitudinal aspects of political behavior.

A number of questions concerning political role behavior or role orientations were asked in both 1952 and 1956. For the two concerning participation and exposure to the mass media, detailed tables are included here; the others are treated in a summary table. Most of the results in both years show significant differences between the two class-consistent and the two class-disaffiliated groupings. However, CIE scores suggest the more limited and partial effect of class identification in its influence on political role behavior and may be accepted as indicative of the importance of capacity in political role performance. This will be most evident when these scores are compared with those obtained on the relationship between class identification and the more attitudinal aspects of political behavior.

Participation in the campaign and the act of voting are the most tangible manifestations of political role behavior on the part of the citizen. While in both years (Table 5.9) differences existed between the consistent groupings and the disaffiliates, in 1956 working-class affiliates did not differ from middle-class consistents to any statistically significant extent. Moreover, the CIE scores indicate that the "pull" of identification, though present, was evidently counteracted by a relative lack of capacity for role performance on a par with identification. This will become more apparent later on when we compare the CIE scores here obtained with those obtained in connection with the more attitudinal measures of political behavior.

Attention to the mass media of communication during an electoral campaign may be considered a form of vicarious political activity. What, then, is the relative effect of class identification and capacity for role behavior in this connection? The results in Table 5.10 show an exposure pattern very similar to that recorded for participation. Although there are, again with the exception of the working-class affiliates–middle-class consistents comparison in 1956, significant differences between the class groupings, the CIE scores are indicative of the relatively limited effect of class identification. In other words, political capacity for class role behavior is limited.

Similar tests, summarized in Table 5.11, were made with regard to what one may call "role orientations" rather than role behavior. While one should not expect perfect results here, one might suppose that CIE scores in this tabulation would lie somewhere between those obtained for role behavior and those obtained for the more strictly attitudinal measures of political behavior. The results tend to confirm this expectation.

In general, the differences between the class-consistent and class-disaffiliated groupings suggest that class identification is not altogether irrelevant in political role orientations. Only a few exceptions may be noted. In both 1952 and 1956 working-class affiliates did not differ significantly from middle-class consistents on the "sense-of-citizen-duty" scale. Apparently, a sense of civic responsibility, learned by a person in the environment of his objective class position, is not lost as a result of identification with the class "lower" in the stratification scheme than the class to which he objectively belongs. On the other hand, for middle-class affiliates—those working-class people identifying with the "higher" class, identification seemed to have some influence on their sense of civic duty in both 1952 and 1956. "Sense of citizen duty," it seems, is a middle-class virtue that one can come by either through being objectively middle class or through identifying with the middle class.

To present an over-all picture of the findings concerning the effect of class identification on political perspectives, on role orientations, and on role behavior, Table 5.12 reports the differences obtained between the CIE scores for the class groupings being compared as well as the differences between these differences and the "ideal" difference of zero for a hypothetical "full" or "complete" identification.

The results tend to support the notion that for class identification to be

Table 5.9 Class identification and political participation, 1952 and 1956, by percent

	Working class				Middle class			
	Working		Middle		Working		Middle	
Level of participation	1952 (N=580)	1956 (N=665)	1952 (N=186)	1956 (N=191)	1952 (N=131)	1956 (N=121)	1952 (N=235)	1956 (N=281)
High	22	22	28	35	30	35	49	46
Medium	47	42	53	45	53	45	43	42
Low	31	36	19	20	17	20	8	12
Total	100	100	100	100	100	100	100	100
CIE score	−9	−14	+9	+15	+13	+15	+41	+34

Tests for:		χ^2	df	p
WW-WM	1952	10.83	2	<.01
	1956	23.16	2	<.001
MM-MW	1952	12.04	2	<.01
	1956	5.28	2	>.05

Table 5.10 Class identification and exposure to mass media, 1952 and 1956, by percent

| | Working class | | | | Middle class | | | |
| | Working | | Middle | | Working | | Middle | |
Level of exposure	1952 (N=580)	1956 (N=665)	1952 (N=186)	1956 (N=191)	1952 (N=131)	1956 (N=121)	1952 (N=235)	1956 (N=281)
High	33	29	48	42	55	59	71	61
Medium	27	58	26	53	23	36	14	35
Low	40	13	26	5	22	5	15	4
Total	100	100	100	100	100	100	100	100
CIE score	−7	+16	+22	+37	+33	+54	+56	+57

Tests for:

		x^2	df	p
WW-WM	1952	17.86	2	<.001
	1956	16.61	2	<.001
MM-MW	1952	10.50	2	<.01
	1956	0.39	2	>.05

Table 5.11 Class identification and political role orientations, 1952 and 1956

Role orientations	Tests for—	1952				1956		
		χ^2	df	p	CIE scores	χ^2	p	CIE scores
Interest	WW-WM	26.81	2	<.001	−6/+29	25.23	<.001	−16/+15
	MM-MW	22.15	2	<.001	+59/+26	10.43	<.01	+27/+6
Care for outcome	WW-WM	8.04	3	<.05	+11/+23	1.79	>.05	+5/+11
	MM-MW	21.28	3	<.001	+46/+21	10.04	<.01	+33/+13
Sense of efficacy	WW-WM	18.31	2	<.001	+4/+18	29.24	<.001	+9/+38
	MM-MW	10.21	2	<.01	+44/+21	18.58	<.001	+67/+40
Sense of citizen duty	WW-WM	22.46	2	<.001	+23/+50	6.56	<.05	+28/+47
	MM-MW	3.06	2	>.05	+62/+51	1.79	>.05	+57/+51

Table 5.12 Differences in class-identification-effect scores

	Differences between WW-MM		Differences between WW-WM		Differences between WW/MM-WW/WM		Differences between MM-MW		Differences between WW/MM-MM/MW	
	1952	1956	1952	1956	1952	1956	1952	1956	1952	1956
Party identification	49	26	40	13	(9)	(13)	35	21	(14)	(5)
Govt. activity demands	30	40	24	27	(6)	(13)	23	10	(7)	(30)
Vote preference	74	20	46	20	(28)	(0)	40	16	(34)	(4)
Interest	65	43	35	31	(30)	(12)	33	21	(32)	(22)
Care for outcome	35	28	12	6	(23)	(22)	25	20	(10)	(8)
Sense of efficacy	48	58	22	29	(26)	(29)	23	27	(25)	(31)
Citizen duty	39	29	27	19	(12)	(10)	11	6	(28)	(23)
Participation	50	48	18	29	(32)	(19)	28	19	(22)	(29)
Media exposure	63	41	29	21	(34)	(20)	23	3	(40)	(38)

effective, capacity must be less nearly equated with political attitudes making for perspectives than with political role orientations and role behaviors. This is quite evident if we inspect the means that can be obtained for the differences between differences among the various measures combined under the three dimensions of political behavior:

Comparison of means for—	Differences in differences between—			
	WW-MM and WW-MW		WW-MM and MM-MW	
	1952	1956	1952	1956
Political perspectives	16.25	7.00	18.00	10.75
Role orientations	22.75	18.25	23.75	21.00
Role behavior	33.00	19.50	31.00	33.50

The analysis of the results through inspection of the means for the differences in CIE scores for the compared class groupings suggests that role manifestations of political behavior differ from political perspectives in degree, and that there is a gradual transition from personal or emotional identification to functional or role behavior. The more a given aspect of political behavior is in performance of role, the greater, apparently, is the need for capacity to effectuate behavior in line with class identification. In other words, Parsons and Shils's types of identification—"internalization of values" and "internalization of role"—rather than representing a dichotomy, may be considered mutually interdependent poles of an identification continuum. Our empirical findings, then, support our theoretical considerations to the effect that both types of identification operate simultaneously but with more or less relevance for particular aspects of political behavior. Identification with class tends to mobilize a person's "role potential" in the political system, but capacity for role performance seems to be more immediately grounded in objective class position.

Finally, we may note that the size of the differences between differences in the CIE scores was smaller in 1956 than in 1952. This is further evidence for the observation that both objective class and class identification were less obviously effective in 1956 in orienting the public to political choice. Yet the structural features of the relationships between objective class and class identification, on the one hand, and the various dimensions of political behavior—such as perspectives, role orientations, and role conduct—remained relatively stable from one election year to the next. In spite of different degrees of "polarization" in class relations with regard to politics, the structure of the relationship remained fluid but similar in the two years.

Awareness of Class and Role Behavior

Identification with class is itself not enough to produce behavior adequate to the performance of class-related political roles. Rather, political conduct seems to depend more on capacity for behavior as determined by the individual's "objective" position in the social stratification scheme.

The *logical* difficulty with identification is that one cannot assume that it creates class. Yet this has been the assumption of those who define class exclusively in subjective terms. As R. H. Tawney (1929, p. 66) has pointed out, "the fact creates the consciousness, not the consciousness the fact. The former may exist without the latter, and a group may be marked by common characteristics, and occupy a distinctive position vis-à-vis other groups, without, except at moments of exceptional tension, being aware that it does so." We must assume, therefore, that it is the fact of class that makes for identification and, similarly, for those expectations that define relevant roles.

But there is also a *psycho*logical difficulty involved in the use of the concept of identification in connection with role behavior. A role, we suggested earlier, implies a relationship between at least two actors—a self and an other. The continued existence of this minimal relationship is predicated on a set of *mutual* expectations that defines the roles. Identification theory cannot account for this two-way character of role. It does not call for the person or group identified with to reciprocate and respond to the identifying actor. The limited effect of class identification on class-relevant political role behavior should, therefore, not occasion surprise. The identifier has no way of knowing whether or not he is fulfilling the polar role in the self-other relationship. There is, in short, no feedback, an essential in social relationships.

George Herbert Mead's (1934) formulations of the "self" may clarify the theoretical problem of the relationship between class and party as role systems. Basic to Mead's social theory is the proposition that "the behavior of an individual can be understood only in terms of the behavior of the whole social group of which he is a member, since his individual acts are involved in larger, social acts which go beyond himself and which implicate the other members of that group" (1934, pp. 6–7). It is just for this reason that "role" is the basic conceptual unit in Mead's thought. For the existence of the "self" is unthinkable except in terms of the "other" toward whom a differentiating relationship is maintained—a relationship that is made specific by this social process, variously referred to as "calling out a generalized other," "participation in the other," or "taking the role of the other." It requires "the appearance of the other in the self, the identification of the other with the self, the reaching of self-consciousness through the other" (1934, p. 253).

Extended to the functioning of the political system, Mead's role-taking model of the social process means essentially this: political conduct implies a pattern of mutual adjustment of demands and expectations. Insistence on demands and expectations beyond what may be called the "zone of acceptance" of parties or classes would tend to make the political system unstable.

Operation of the two-party system depends on the ability of those who take certain roles within a party to anticipate as correctly as possible the demands and expectations of role takers in the other party. Without such role taking, the party system could not function. For the converse—that is to say, projection of one's own party demands on the other—would interfere with a realistic appraisal or definition of the political situation.

Similarly, awareness of class means the ability of role takers in one class to take on the role of the other class. Absence of such awareness would not abolish the fact of class, but it might seriously interfere with a mutually satisfactory adjustment of class demands and expectations. Awareness of one's own class without concomitant ability to take on the role of another class might lead to overdetermination of one's own class interests and to undue demands on the other class—a situation of intense class conflict. Again, inability to take on the role of the other is likely to be detrimental to the continuance of class relations.

It follows that class differences in the awareness of class members with regard to the political behavior of the classes may be considered eufunctional from the point of view of the two-party system. For they would indicate that in the perception of members of the classes the parties offer a real choice in class-relevant terms. On the other hand, persistent and continuous equating of a given class with one party, and the resultant projection of class perspectives on the parties, would introduce a considerable element of rigidity into the two-party system. In that case, party-specific and class-specific frames of reference would overlap, with resultant strains and stresses showing up in the operation of the system. It would not matter that *in fact* the parties are not perfectly divided along class lines of cleavage. It would suffice that their differences are so perceived by the electorate. Relevant to political behavior here is W. I. Thomas' (Volkart, 1951) dictum that "if men define situations as real, they are real in their consequences."

The two-party system would lose its consensus-making function, therefore, if in voter perceptions the parties were too closely identified with particular classes. Of course, if by "class consciousness" in political behavior is meant that a person should vote for one party rather than the other because support of that party would serve his "class interest," then class consciousness does not exist in the United States. But if it can be shown that in people's perceptions of the voting behavior of their own class, and in the voting behavior of the other class, elements relevant to their class positions are present, some kind of "generalized class awareness" may be said to operate in the political situation.

As has been noted, social class played only a minimal role in voter choice in the 1956 presidential election compared with the 1952 election. While in 1952 a significantly greater proportion of the working class than of the middle class voted or preferred the Democratic ticket, in 1956 the difference between the classes had almost disappeared. In fact, majorities in both classes preferred the Republican candidate.

However, to interpret the 1956 results as implying the complete irrelevance of class considerations in voting behavior is as precarious as to overinterpret the existence of a relatively higher relationship between social class and party choice.

Social class can be considered salient as an influence on party choice, regardless of whether the actual relationship between class and party preference is high or low, if:

1. Voters perceive their *own* class as voting for one party rather than the other party;
2. Voters perceiving their *own* class as voting for one party do themselves prefer that party;
3. Voters who see their *own* class as voting for one party then attribute this to considerations of "class interests";
4. Voters in a class perceive the *other* class as voting for one party rather than for the other party;
5. Voters in a class who see the *other* class as voting for one party then attribute this to considerations of "class interests."

The following analysis will be concerned with the stability of the perceived relationships between class and party as they are specified in these conditions.

A first condition for class to be considered salient in voting behavior is that voters perceive their own class as voting for one party rather than for the other. Somewhat different questions concerning interclass and intraclass perceptions were asked in the 1952 and 1956 surveys. However, they seem to tap the same dimensions of class–political party images. The 1952 question reads: "Now I'd like to ask some questions about how you think other people will vote in this election—How about working class (middle class) people—do you think they will vote mostly Republican, mostly Democratic, or do you think they will be about evenly split?" The second part of the 1956 question reads as follows: "Now how about working class (middle class) people—do you think more working class (middle class) people will vote Republican, more will vote Democratic, or do you think they will be about evenly split?"

In order to place subsequent findings in their proper quantitative context, it is essential to note the total distributions of *perceptions* of middle-class and working-class voting behavior, regardless of political party preference. In 1952, as Table 5.13 shows, only small majorities in either class could definitely say whether their own class would vote Democratic or Republican. In 1956 only minorities in either class were definite in their perceptions of the voting behavior of their own class, while majorities were either ambiguous in their perceptions or had no perceptions at all. In other words, class was not perceptually salient for large minorities in either class in 1952, nor for small majorities in 1956. Therefore, although the first of the test conditions was only partially met in both elections, the distributions of responses were sufficiently alike to permit examination of some contingent hypotheses concerning those voters who indicated awareness of class in the voting situation.

The hypothesis to be advanced is that voters who do acknowledge a collective class image tend to perceive their own class as voting for one party rather than for the other. As Table 5.14 shows, this hypothesis tends to be confirmed by the data for both election years. In 1952 more than four-fifths of these class-aware working-class respondents saw their own class as voting Democratic, and almost three-fourths of the class-aware middle-class respondents saw their own class as voting Republican. The same pattern recurs in 1956, although the proportion of working-class respondents perceiving their class as voting Democratic fell from 88 percent in 1952 to 77 percent in 1956.

The maintenance of these perceptual relationships is all the more remarkable because, as we saw earlier (Table 5.1), the actual proportion of working-class people preferring the Republican candidate rose from 43 percent in 1952 to 58 percent in 1956. Yet, while in 1952 both classes not only expressed vote preferences in opposite directions but perceived themselves as doing so, the 1956 results suggest that actual party choice need not be congruent with class perceptions.

In order to explore further the relationship between class and party in voter perceptions, the image of the two parties held by each of the two classes requires analysis in terms of respondents' voting preferences. For it may be that rather than being perceptions of class voting behavior, the results noted in Table 5.14 are merely projections of respondents' own party preferences. In other words, for our hypothesis to be valid, the perceptual image of their own class's voting behavior must not be distorted

Table 5.13 Middle-class and working-class expectations of own class vote, 1952 and 1956, by percent

Own class will vote—	Middle class		Working class	
	1952 (N = 389)	1956 (N = 414)	1952 (N = 811)	1956 (N = 848)
Democratic	15	12	52	37
Republican	40	36	7	11
Split	32	36	25	30
Don't know	13	16	16	22
Total	100	100	100	100

	χ^2	df	p^a
1952	2.64	1	>.05
1956	0.00	1	

a. Test for class differentiation in ability to perceive direction.

Table 5.14 Perception of own class vote of middle class and working class giving party direction, 1952 and 1956, by percent

Own class will vote—	Middle class		Working class	
	1952 (N = 212)	1956 (N = 198)	1952 (N = 481)	1956 (N = 407)
Democratic	27	26	88	77
Republican	73	74	12	23
Total	100	100	100	100

	χ^2	df	p
1952	252.77	1	<.001
1956	149.62	1	<.001

by working-class and middle-class respondents' projection of their actual party choices.

As Table 5.15 shows, this condition was largely met in both 1952 and 1956. In general, even with party preference controlled, the pattern noted in Table 5.13 was maintained in both 1952 and 1956. Some projection of party preferences took place, but it was not sufficient in either year to undermine the positive relationship between respondents' social class positions and their perceptions of how their own class would vote.

The decline in the proportions of both Democratic and Republican working-class respondents who perceived the working-class vote to be

Table 5.15 Perception of own class vote by Republican and Democratic middle class and working class, 1952 and 1956, by percent

	Vote preference							
	Republican				Democratic			
	Middle class		Working class		Middle class		Working class	
Own class will vote—	1952 (N=269)	1956 (N=276)	1952 (N=346)	1956 (N=521)	1952 (N=116)	1956 (N=138)	1952 (N=431)	1956 (N=327)
Democratic	7	5	33	24	32	27	70	58
Republican	52	45	14	16	10	16	3	3
Split and don't know	41	50	53	60	58	57	27	39
Total	100	100	100	100	100	100	100	100

		χ^2	df	p
Democratic perception	1952	33.09	1	<.001
	1956	46.83	1	<.001
Republican perception	1952	112.96	1	<.001
	1956	87.90	1	<.001

Democratic does not disturb the pattern, but it requires interpretation. As Table 5.15 suggests, it seems to have been due less to a concession of the working-class vote by working-class respondents to the Republicans than to a much greater inability of both groups in 1956 to say for which party they expected the working class to vote. In other words, the 1956 findings, like the 1952 results, indicate that in perceiving the voting behavior of their own class, middle-class Democrats excepted, respondents did not too greatly distort the original image of the class-party relationship by projecting their own party preferences.

The similarity of the 1952 and 1956 findings in this respect suggests that Republican working-class and Democratic middle-class respondents were finding themselves in a social environment more divided, probably, than that in which middle-class Republicans and working-class Democrats were located. In both cases the ambiguity of the situation was apparently decisive enough to make for the large percentage of "don't know" and "split" perceptions. However, while in the case of the middle-class Democrats the ambiguity leads to perception of the middle-class vote in a party-related frame of reference, in the case of the working-class Republicans the same inherent ambiguity is not sufficiently strong to prevent perception of the working-class vote in a class-related frame of reference. This is quite un- derstandable in view of the traditional American political folklore that identifies the working class with the Democratic party but does not likewise identify the middle class with the Republican party. It is apparently easy for working-class Republicans to perceive the connection between their class and its traditional Democratic voting tendency. In sum, such projec- tion of party preference as might take place among working-class Repub- licans is immediately corrected by the long-assumed relationship between working class and Democratic party.

The second condition specifies that social class can be considered salient in voting behavior if voters who perceive their own class as voting for a given party themselves prefer that party. The condition derives from the assumption that people who see themselves and those like them in similar ways do so out of a need to feel supported in their political positions and opinions, and that they will tend to behave in terms of the positions or opinions they attribute to the group to which they belong.

Distributions for both years in Table 5.16 show that respondents, re- gardless of whether they were middle class or working class, seeing their own class as voting Democratic themselves preferred the Democratic party, while those seeing their own class as voting Republican preferred the Re- publican party. In both years, then, the data show that although class may be perceptually salient, party preferences are less a function of class po- sition than a function of the party frame of reference in which class vote

perceptions are located. This conclusion is reinforced if the vote preferences of those who perceive their class as about evenly split, or who do
not know how it will vote, are examined. We should expect that these
voters will not themselves differ on party preference.

As Table 5.17 shows, regardless of class position, respondents for whom
class was not perceptually salient tended in greater proportions to prefer
the Republican party, in both 1952 and 1956. The only difference between
the two years is a slight shift of middle-class voters away from, and a
somewhat greater shift of working-class voters toward, the Republican side.
These shifts suggest that those for whom class has perceptual salience, in
the sense that they entertain an expectation concerning the party direction
of their class vote, also tend to display voting preferences in terms of this
salience. On the other hand, those for whom class has little meaning, in
the sense that they have no directional expectations concerning the party
choice of their class, do not seem to be influenced by their class position
in their own voting preferences.

A third condition for class to be salient requires that voters in a given
class who see their own class as voting for one party rather than for the
other differ in their concern with "class interests," which may or may not
color their perceptions. This condition is based on the following premise:
in political behavior, awareness of class may be psychologically meaningful
to those who see their class as voting for one party or the other, and who
actually vote along perceived class lines. But in order to be reasonably
confident about the importance of these perceptions, it seems desirable to
examine their attitudinal contents. Only if those who agree on the party
direction of a given class vote are also found to agree on the reasons given
for their views can it be said that class vote perceptions are politically
significant.

To what extent, then, is class belongingness politically meaningful in
terms of class interest? In order to investigate this question, respondents
were asked why they felt that working-class or middle-class people were
likely to vote Republican or Democratic. Responses to the question were
coded under a number of categories but are reported here according to
two major classifications:

1.   Those clearly "interest oriented"—such responses as that a given
party benefits one class or the other, supports legislation in favor of one
class, or creates conditions advantageous to one class rather than the other;

2.   Those "not interest oriented"—such responses as that a party is
against corruption and promises certain things, or that the time has come
for a change, and so on.

As Table 5.18 shows, in 1952, regardless of class, respondents who perceived their own class as voting Democratic gave "interest-oriented" rea-

Table 5.16 Relationship between party direction of perceived class vote and vote preference, 1952 and 1956, by percent

	Own class will vote—							
	Democratic				Republican			
	Middle class		Working class		Middle class		Working class	
Vote preference	1952 (N=56)	1956 (N=50)	1952 (N=414)	1956 (N=314)	1952 (N=152)	1956 (N=147)	1952 (N=59)	1956 (N=93)
Democratic	67	74	72	60	8	15	18	11
Republican	33	26	28	40	92	85	82	89
Total	100	100	100	100	100	100	100	100

		χ^2	df	p
Democratic perception	1952	0.89	1	>.01
	1956	3.55	1	>.01
Republican perception	1952	6.29	1	>.01
	1956	0.61	1	>.01

Table 5.17 Voting preferences of middle class and working class who did not perceive party direction of own class vote, 1952 and 1956, by percent

	Own class will vote—							
	Split				Don't know			
	Middle class		Working class		Middle class		Working class	
Vote preference	1952 (N=126)	1956 (N=146)	1952 (N=189)	1956 (N=252)	1952 (N=51)	1956 (N=69)	1952 (N=115)	1956 (N=187)
Democratic	40	38	34	28	31	33	49	31
Republican	60	62	66	72	69	67	51	69
Total	100	100	100	100	100	100	100	100

	χ^2	df	p
Split and Don't know 1952	0.67	1	>.01
Split and Don't know 1956	3.48	1	>.01

Table 5.18 Interest orientation of middle class and working class perceiving party direction of own class vote, 1952 and 1956, by percent

	Own class will vote—							
	Democratic				Republican			
	Middle class		Working class		Middle class		Working class	
Interest orientation	1952 (N=58)	1956 (N=51)	1952 (N=421)	1956 (N=332)	1952 (N=154)	1956 (N=148)	1952 (N=60)	1956 (N=94)
Interest oriented	67	55	76	68	32	52	36	72
Not interest oriented	24	43	16	27	51	42	48	25
Don't know	9	2	8	5	17	6	16	3
Total	100	100	100	100	100	100	100	100

		χ^2	df	p
Democratic perception	1952	2.25	1	>.01
	1956	5.40	1	>.01
Republican perception	1952	0.12	1	>.01
	1956	9.43	1	>.01

sons, and, again regardless of class, respondents seeing their class as voting Republican gave "not-interest-oriented" reasons. In other words, the voting behavior of the two classes seemed to have been perceived in a frame of reference that clearly linked class interest to a particular party, and there were no significant differences in this respect between the two classes. The third condition was not met in 1952.

It was also not met in 1956, but with an important change: apparently, after four years of Republican rule under conditions of high prosperity, the Democratic party was no longer considered as *alone* being congenial to both middle-class and working-class interests. The 1956 election was characterized, of course, by the disappearance of those political "style issues"—like communism or corruption—which in 1952 were cited by Republicans in both classes as reasons for their perceptions. In 1956, therefore, majorities of both classes that saw their own class as voting Republican now gave "interest-oriented" reasons to explain why their class would vote that way, while among respondents who saw their own class as voting Democratic the proportions giving "interest-oriented" reasons somewhat declined. Both parties were seen by majorities in either class as serving the interests of both classes. Nevertheless, in 1956, regardless of whether they saw their own class as voting Democratic or Republican, working-class respondents were more likely to give "interest-oriented" reasons than were middle-class respondents.

These results place the class hypothesis in a more comprehensive psychopolitical context. If class alone accounted for the perceptions of people as to how their class would vote, one should expect a significant difference in interest orientation between those middle-class and working-class people who perceived their own class as voting for one party or for the other. But, as Table 5.18 demonstrates, this was not the case. Although both classes perceived themselves as voting in one direction rather than in the other (Tables 5.13 and 5.14), not only did both classes let their party preferences be influenced by their perceptions of the direction of their own class's expected vote (Table 5.16), but the attitudinal content of these perceptions also seemed to derive as much from a party-related frame of reference as from a class-related one.

However, party-related interest orientation only modifies class members' perceptions of how their class will vote. Otherwise one should expect that, regardless of class, "interest-oriented" people would see their own class as voting Democratic, and "not-interest-oriented" people would see theirs as voting Republican. This was not the case. For when class is controlled by interest orientation, class-related rather than party-related attitudes seem to give class vote perceptions their meaning. As Table 5.19 shows, in both 1952 and 1956 class was still significantly related to perception of

Table 5.19 Own class vote perception of interest-oriented and not-interest-oriented middle class and working class, 1952 and 1956, by percent

Own class will vote —	Interest oriented				Not interest oriented			
	Middle class		Working class		Middle class		Working class	
	1952 (N = 88)	1956 (N = 105)	1952 (N = 340)	1956 (N = 294)	1952 (N = 93)	1956 (N = 84)	1952 (N = 95)	1956 (N = 112)
Democratic	44	27	94	77	15	26	69	79
Republican	56	73	6	23	85	74	31	21
Total	100	100	100	100	100	100	100	100

		χ^2	df	p
Interest oriented	1952	130.24	1	<.001
	1956	85.15	1	<.001
Not interest oriented	1952	58.85	1	<.001
	1956	57.31	1	<.001

how a respondent's class was likely to vote. However, it may also be noted that in 1952 a significantly larger percentage of "interest-oriented" working-class respondents than of the "not-interest-oriented" respondents perceived their own class as voting Democratic, while among the middle class the "not-interest-oriented" people saw their class as voting Republican to a significantly greater extent than did the "interest-oriented" people. But in 1956 these differences disappeared.

One may conclude from both the 1952 and 1956 results that, insofar as class is perceptually salient in party choice, the relationship between class and party is not explainable in terms of any definite interest orientation on the part of middle-class or working-class people when they entertain expectations concerning the voting behavior of their own class.

The fourth condition provides that voters in one class perceive the other class, to which they themselves do not belong, as voting for one party rather than for the other party. Shared perceptions of one's own class voting behavior may be symptomatic of some kind of class awareness. But while such perceptual linkage of class and party may tend to create a political "we" or "self," awareness of the self is predicated on awareness of the "not-we," or "other." Class-related political behavior is assumed to be based, therefore, not only on awareness of one's own class but also on awareness of the other class.

How, then, is the other class perceived in terms of its party-related voting behavior? If there is no significant difference between the perceptual image both classes hold of a given class's party choice, then "interclass perception" may be said to be present in the political situation. If, on the other hand, there is a significant difference between the way one class is perceived by another class and the way it perceives itself, interclass perception would seem to be absent.

Tables 5.20 and 5.21 show that in 1952 middle-class respondents saw the working class as voting Democratic, just as working-class respondents themselves had done (see Tables 5.13 and 5.14). But in that year working-class respondents misperceived middle-class voting behavior, seeing the middle class as voting Democratic (while middle-class people themselves had seen their class as voting Republican).

In 1956 middle-class respondents continued to see the working-class vote as Democratic, just as working-class respondents themselves did (and counter to the actual behavior of that class). Evidently, prior to the 1956 election neither middle-class nor working-class respondents had any way to anticipate the change in the working-class vote from its traditional Democratic direction to a Republican direction. The perceptual ambiguity of the situation in which both classes found themselves in 1956 is evident in the increased proportion of respondents who either saw the other class as split

Table 5.20   Interclass perceptions of middle class and working class, 1952 and 1956, by percent

	Middle class		Working class	
Other class will vote—	1952 (N = 389)	1956 (N = 417)	1952 (N = 811)	1956 (N = 892)
Democratic	55	37	24	12
Republican	12	14	19	19
Split	24	32	30	39
Don't know	9	17	27	30
Total	100	100	100	100

	χ^2	df	p^a
1952	64.28	1	<.001
1956	46.85	1	<.001

a. Test for class differentiation in ability to perceive direction of other class vote.

Table 5.21   Interclass perceptions of middle class and working class giving party direction, 1952 and 1956, by percent

	Middle class		Working class	
Other class will vote—	1952 (N = 260)	1956 (N = 214)	1952 (N = 342)	1956 (N = 281)
Democratic	82	73	56	38
Republican	18	27	44	62
Total	100	100	100	100

	χ^2	df	p
1952	46.77	1	<.001
1956	55.09	1	<.001

or could not say how it would vote. However, as Table 5.21 shows, working-class respondents who were able to perceive class voting behavior in 1956 saw the middle class as voting Republican (as the middle class actually did), but they had not seen this in 1952. In both years, then, class estimations of party choice were partially blurred in interclass perceptions.

Our fifth and final condition for class to be salient in party choice stipulates that voters in one class who see the other class as voting for one party rather than for another will attribute such voting behavior to the fact that the "interests" of the other class are served by the party for which it is seen voting. We should expect these outcomes: middle-class respondents who see the working class as voting either Democratic or Republican, and working-class respondents who see the middle-class vote as going one way or the other, should give "interest-oriented" reasons for their perceptions.

As Table 5.22 shows, this condition was not met in 1952. Regardless of whether they were middle class or working class, respondents who saw the "other" class as voting Democratic gave "interest-oriented" reasons for their perception, while those seeing the "other" class vote Republican gave "not-interest-oriented" reasons (although working-class people who saw the middle-class vote going Republican gave reasons that were almost evenly divided). In other words, in 1952, insofar as socioeconomic "interest" was considered by respondents in either class, they saw the interests of the "other" class as better served or—as in the case of working-class people seeing the middle class vote Repubican—at least as well served by the Democrats.

In 1956 the pattern appears to be more complex, similar to the 1952 pattern in some respects but different in others. The interests of the "other" class were no longer seen by respondents in either class as being so completely served by the Democratic party. Working-class respondents who saw the middle class as voting Democratic were even more inclined to attribute the expected behavior to interest orientation. And working-class respondents who saw the middle class as voting Republican were now perfectly divided, suggesting that in working-class perception middle-class interests could at least be as well served by the Republicans as by the Democrats. In this respect, then, the 1952 and 1956 distributions are more or less similar.

But middle-class respondents who in 1952 saw "interest-oriented" reasons for the working class to vote Democratic were much less likely to think that way in 1956. Even more pronounced was the reversal of reasons given by middle-class people who perceived the working class as voting Republican in 1956. While in 1952 some 68 percent had given "not-interest-oriented" reasons for expecting the working class to vote Republican, an almost equal proportion in 1956 (67 percent) gave "interest-oriented" reasons for the same expectation. In other words, in middle-class perceptions in 1956 working-class interests appeared to be as well served by the Republicans as by the Democrats.

If in 1952 interest orientation in voting behavior could be interpreted as deriving from a combination of party-related and class-related frames of reference that favored the Democrats, the 1956 results suggest not a contradictory but rather a supplementary interpretation: in a period of prosperity, such as the 1952–1956 period, each class tends to see the interests of the other as well served by either party. In neither 1952 nor 1956 was

Table 5.22 Interest orientation of middle class and working class perceiving each other as voting either Democratic or Republican, 1952 and 1956, by percent

	Other class will vote—							
	Democratic				Republican			
	Middle class		Working class		Middle class		Working class	
Interest orientation	1952 (N=196)	1956 (N=151)	1952 (N=139)	1956 (N=100)	1952 (N=37)	1956 (N=55)	1952 (N=77)	1956 (N=158)
Interest oriented	77	53	68	79	32	67	48	50
Not interest oriented	23	47	32	21	68	33	52	50
Total	100	100	100	100	100	100	100	100

		χ^2	df	p
Democratic inter-class perception	1952	4.01	1	>.01
	1956	18.17	1	<.001
Republican inter-class perception	1952	2.61	1	>.01
	1956	4.84	1	>.01

the fifth condition fully met: class and party were not perceived in a single frame of reference that would have made class voting for one party or the other a reflection of class interests.

Social class has long been accepted as an important factor in determining party preference in the American political system. But its meaning to class members themselves as they take roles in the party system has been obscure. While it is recognized that the relationship between class and party varies from one election to the next, the perceptual significance of this variation has not been known. Comparison of relevant data for the 1952 and 1956 presidential elections shows that, in general, both class and party serve as sometimes interlocking, sometimes independent frames of reference in which voters arrive at electoral decisions.

Moreover, comparison of the 1952 and 1956 data suggests that if class self-perceptions of party choice, interclass perceptions of party choice, and the "reasons" for these perceptions in terms of "class interest" are taken as minimum conditions for class to be considered salient in voting behavior, these conditions were either met or not met in each year in surprisingly similar fashion—despite the fact that the actual voting behavior of the working class differed considerably in the two elections. In other words, the comparison suggests that perceptual stability may be more constant than actual conduct in politics. This perceptual stability supports the interpretation that the existence of the two classes injects an important element of genuine stability into the political system. On the other hand, the fact that class lines tend to blur in voting behavior perceptions and that class interest orientation is not identified with any one party seems to make for flexibility in the political system. This, in turn, allows voters of both classes to shift from one party to the other. The extent, then, to which class and party are related in voters' attitudes and expectations as they cast their ballots may be crucial in appraising the mutual functions that class and party exercise on the structure of the political system.

Cleavage and Consensus

As agents of cleavage and consensus in the process of value allocation for a society, class and party are critically interdependent properties of political systems. How they are related, and the structure of their relationship, has been our concern. It was an assumption that some understanding of this structure could be had by tests involving relevant attitudes, perceptions, orientations, and expectations of individuals in the voting situation. The subjects of our analyses, selected by way of nationwide area probability surveys, were located in the class system in terms either of "objective" characteristics they shared or of their "subjective" identification with the middle class or the working class. And they were located in the party system in terms of either their party preferences or party identifications. What inferences can be drawn from findings on the microlevel of the person concerning the structure of the relationship between class and party on the macrolevel of a political system?

1.   The relationship between class and party is clearly reflected in the operation of a cluster of indivdual identifications, demands, and expectations we called "political perspective." But this cluster of attitudinal characteristics does not constitute a consistent pattern. The differences observed between the classes are "countervailed" by variations in the relation between class identification, on the one hand, and party-relevant variables on the other—variations from one measure to the next that make "political perspectives" appear kaleidoscopic and diffuse. Expressed in global terms, it would seem that the structure of the relationship between class and party is not monolithic, but that the boundaries between class and party interpenetrate in a flexible and fluid fashion, very much as do geographic boundaries determined by the course of a river.

2.   Differences observed between strictly attitudinal manifestations of political behavior, like those comprising "political perspectives," and orientations more directly appropriate for role taking suggest that class as an independent factor affecting conduct in the party system is limited by an individual's capacity actually to take a given role. This capacity would seem to be dependent on interaction in the social process. In global terms, it would appear that class, in restricting freedom of movement in role taking and role behavior, makes for cleavage in the political system. However, the fact that party roles can be taken independently of class suggests that the propensity of cleavage due to restrictions imposed by the class system is offset by consensual tendencies arising out of the party system and cutting across class lines. Moreover, rather than being dichotomous and opposed, it appears that attitudinal and role-oriented manifestations of political behavior are interdependent poles of a single continuum. Class and party can thus be said to function as mutually limiting elements in the political process.

3.   Analysis of perceptions touching the party preferences expected of the classes as voting aggregates revealed a good deal of variability. Insofar as this perceptual variability can be assumed to reflect social and political reality, it suggests that while clearly interdependent under some conditions, class and party also function independently of each other in shaping the structure of the political system. The conditions making for interdependence seem to have their existential base in the numerical situation of the classes. Precisely because the working class outnumbers the middle class

by approximately two to one, a strictly middle-class party aspiring to power is not feasible in a democratic two-party political system. Indeed, voters behave in terms of both party-relevant as well as class-relevant considerations. Their perceptions partake of a good deal of ambiguity because, we can assume, in political reality on the global level of the political system the class cleavage potential is countervailed by the integrating, consensual function of the parties. On the other hand, party conflict is kept within bounds by the consensual elements in the class system, which is characterized by high mobility and agreement on desirable values.

4.   The replication of largely identical analyses as between the two election years of 1952 and 1956 reveals a surprising degree of stability in attitudes, orientations, and perceptions. While the patterns are not absolutely alike, they are sufficiently similar to suggest that the structure of the relationship between class and party, though fluid and diffuse, is relatively stable through time. In other words, the structure seems to serve as an element of stabilization rather than disruption in the political system. While by no means means inflexible or inert, the structure of the relationship between class and party as reflected in relevant attitudinal and perceptual patterns seems to make for equilibrium in the relations between the two properties of the political system.

Similarly, intra-class and interclass perceptions of expected party preferences were either very similar or not altogether inconsistent as between the two election years. And this in spite of the fact that the actual party preferences of the working class differed considerably between 1952 and 1956. Evidently, perceptions are more stable than actual voting conduct. This would suggest that perceptions, rooted in the existential situation of class and party as properties of the political system, perform an important function in politics, with two apparently conflicting but actually integrative consequences of their own for the operation of the political process:

a.   On the one hand, clear-cut interclass perceptions of party differences in class terms might tend to increase actual class differentiation in political behavior and class cleavage in the political system. For if people define a situation as real, it may be real in its consequences. An acute and perhaps even exaggerated awareness of the political behavior of the other class in class terms might tend to reinforce whatever actual differences do exist. This might lead to viewing party in an exclusively class-oriented frame of reference, and so interfere with the flexibility in voting behavior on which a two-party system is predicated. From this point of view, the perceptual blurring in interclass awareness tends to maintain the flexibility of the political system.

b.   On the other hand, the fact that the parties may be perceived within a class-related frame of reference, as well as the fact that the two parties actually derive varying degrees of support from both classes, suggests that the two-party system is not unrelated to the existence of two large class blocs whose relatively persistent expectations concerning their own behavior and that of the opposite class injects an important element of stability into the political system. In other words, the class system allows the parties to form reasonably stable expectations concerning the behavior of class members and so facilitates the mobilizing activities of the parties. While American parties are not "class parties," the structure of the relationship between class and party is such that cleavage is minimized and consensus is maximized.

6

Conflict and the Network

of Legislative Roles

IN CONTRAST to the burgeoning body of sophisticated theoretical writings about organizational or administrative behavior (see March and Simon, 1958), the legislative process and legislative behavior, and especially the legislature's environment, have been given little theoretical attention. Most of the writing is descriptive of either formal or informal structural arrangements or of functions; or it is concerned with pathological and therapeutic aspects. There has been little concern with analytic theory of the legislative process (Driscoll, 1955).[1]

What theory there is involves a series of inarticulate assumptions centered in the notion, well expressed by Stephen K. Bailey (1950, pp. x, 236), that "legislative policy-making appears to be the result of a confluence of factors streaming from an almost endless number of tributaries." Bailey's "attempt to make a vector analysis of legislative policy-making" is suggestive. The "tributaries" most frequently recognized, and probably correctly so, are parties, pressure groups, constituencies, and administrative agencies. But the vector model implicit in most studies is essentially a one-way street. It assumes that the actions of "outside" forces are the independent or causal factors having direct effect on legislative decisions as dependent variables. Studies along this line are not concerned with how the external factors are themselves related to each other—how these forces are received by legislators and, in turn, related to by them or transformed into legislative results.

More specific theoretical formulation conceives of the legislative process as a struggle among groups in conflict.[2] But most studies using the "group-influence model" seem to be primarily devoted to the group character of political conflict in the legislative setting, not with the place of the legis-

---

Written with John C. Wahlke, William Buchanan, and Leroy C. Ferguson.

lature in the political system.[3] The same is largely true of those studies that focus on party and constituency as influences on the legislature.[4] This does not mean that other assumptions are absent from the many descriptive studies of legislatures. The legislature is variously conceived as a "decision-making mechanism," "a structure of power," or an "equilibrium system," but suggestive as these notions are, they have only rarely been tested in the crucible of empirical research.

Perhaps most valuable in understanding the concrete reality of legislative behavior within the larger political system are the studies that concentrate on particular decisions (see Cohen, 1957). But the notion of the legislature as a decisional system tends to limit the focus of inquiry more than seems appropriate for the purpose of specifying just how legislature and political system are interdependent. In the main limited to case studies, the decisional approach ignores the fact that a good deal of legislative behavior does not involve decision making at all. Much of what happens between legislatures and other institutions or organizations in the political system, and between legislators and their clients, is not a matter of decision processes. The legislature may serve as a channel of executive information, as a tool for maintaining community consensus, or as an investigating agency. The many services legislators perform—the errand-boy function—are not covered by the decision-making scheme. As Roy C. Macridis (1955, p. 66) has remarked, "we may discover that the function we took for granted, i.e., legislation, is only incidental to the other functions that it may perform."

Indeed, the decisional model, at least as borrowed from organizational theory, does not really seem applicable to the legislative process, even if the latter calls for decision making. In organizational theory a decision involves a choice of a preferred project from among a number of clearly specified and numerically limited alternative projects. But in the legislative process it is often by no means clear what the alternatives are. In fact, it is one of the objectives of the legislative process to evolve and identify alternatives, and the whole process is much less rational than the organizational decision-making model assumes. The legislative process is political precisely because the choices facing legislators may be ill defined. In contrast to bureaucratic organizations, the legislature is, by its very nature, compelled to be rooted in conflict. For just this reason the criteria used in appraising administrative behavior—efficiency and effectiveness—seem out of place. If the resolution of conflict is the goal of legislative decision making, an "effective" legislature is one in which the lines of cleavage can be expected to be sharply drawn so that issues may be crystallized and clarified. Of course, cleavage is not absent from other types of governmental institution, such as courts of law or even administrative agencies.

But here division is not formally expected and institutionalized. Even in a court a unanimous opinion is preferred to a close decision. Conflict may characterize informal relations in an administrative organization, but it cannot be formally acknowledged: indeed, "unity of command," fictitious though it may be, is the formally recognized mode of interaction. But in a legislature unanimity, though perhaps present more often than expected, is suspect. Only in "emergencies" is consensus the predicate rather than the goal of legislative decision making.[5]

Among the legislature's purposes and goals, the crystallization and resolution of political conflicts is central, for politics is rooted in conflict. Capacity to facilitate the crystallization and resolution of political conflicts is, therefore, one important criterion of the "functionality" of the legislative structure. Functionality of the formal institutional elements of the modern democratic legislature has not been our research concern. The fact that legislatures continue to exist as vital centers of decision making in democratic political systems may be taken as face-value evidence that, in spite of possible needs for reform, the formal institutional structure remains viable. Our interest here is with the problem of whether the legislative role structure, insofar as we can specify it, is conducive to the task of crystallizing and resolving political conflicts.

Power Structure and Purposive Roles

Analysis of legislative role orientations is one way of studying the power position and the functions of the legislature in different political systems. Role orientations are legislators' own expectations of the kind of behavior they ought to exhibit in the performance of their duties. They may be considered as providing the premises in terms of which legislators make decisions.[6]

His role orientations are probably not unrelated to the legislator's perception of the power pattern of the political system and the kinds of function that the legislature is called on to perform. For instance, in a party-disciplined legislature the individual legislator is unlikely to find much room for independence or inventiveness; the purely routine aspects of his job probably loom large in his legislative role orientations. In a legislature particularly exposed to the pulls and pressures of interest groups, role orientations are likely to derive from the need to arbitrate, compromise, and integrate group conflicts. In a legislature subservient to the whims and wishes of the electorate, the spokesman function is likely to be accentuated in legislative role orientations. In a legislature that enjoys relatively great independence from the executive, legislative role orientations may stress the creative, policy-making aspects of the job. Moreover, legislative role orientations need not occur in pristine singularity. Two and three, or even more, orientations may be held by a legislator.

The complexity of institutionally derived legislative role orientations becomes even more apparent if we place them in a historical perspective. They may be, and probably are, patterned by past as well as current configurations in the power structure of the political system. For like institutions, legislatures are phenomena in time, with memories of their own going beyond the limitations of time. These memories are transmitted by legislators themselves from generation to generation, consciously or unconsciously shaping the perceptions of the present. The past may thus continue to serve as a model for contemporary role orientations.

A legislature is the product of a long and slow growth over centuries, with a veritable maze of rules, procedures, privileges, duties, etiquettes, rituals, and informal understandings and arrangements. Every phase of the lawmaking process—from the introduction of bills through their deliberation in committee and debate on the floor to the final vote—has gradually become circumscribed by appropriate strategies and tactics. The legislator was always expected to master the rules of parliamentary procedure and be familiar with available strategies. Hence the legislator could traditionally orient himself to the job of lawmaking in terms of the parliamentary rules and routines, rather than in terms of legislative functions as they may be shaped by the power situation in the political system. Parliamentary ritual rather than parliamentary goals would absorb his attention. One may call this orientation to the legislative role that of the *ritualist.*

A second orientation is particularly deeply rooted in American political history. It was probably generated by the conflict between the British Crown, acting through the agency of the appointed governor, and the colonial legislatures. In the course of this conflict the legislature came to be viewed as the instrument through which colonial interests could be defended against what were perceived as royal encroachments on colonial rights. It does not matter, in this connection, that the colonists differed among themselves with regard to the proper object of legislative activity— whether the defense of property rights or the natural rights of man were the goals of colonial claims. The crucial point is that the legislature and legislators were expected to be advocates or defenders of popular demands. Wilfred E. Binkley (1947, p. 4) has aptly described the role orientation of the colonial legislator—what we shall call the role orientation of *tribune:* "The assemblyman, chosen by popular election as a representative of his neighborhood . . . set forth to the provincial capital, commissioned, as he believed, to fight the people's battle against the governor."

A third major orientation seems to have originated at a later stage of colonial-executive relations, the stage when the legislature asserted itself as an institution capable of performing independent, policy-making functions. As Alfred De Grazia (1951, p. 70) has summarized this later development, "The Colonial legislatures already conceived of themselves as possessed of a positive legislative capacity removed from the ancient English idea of Parliament as an agency for wresting concessions from the Crown. They had learned well the lessons of the seventeenth century revolutions as well as those to be obtained from the Bill of Rights. Legislatures, they had come to realize, could govern." Once the colonial legislature was expected to be an instrument of governance, rather than an instrument of obstruction, a role orientation more appropriate to the legislature's new function was likely to emerge. We shall call this the orientation of *inventor*. The legislator was now expected to be sensitive to public issues, discover potential solutions, and explore alternatives, both with regard to means as well as to ends. The problems of government were deemed soluble by way of rational deliberation and cogent argument in debate, partly because the issues were relatively simple, not requiring technical, expert knowledge; partly because the range of governmental activity was seen as very limited.

Just as the role orientation of inventor derived from the conception of the legislature as a creative, policy-making institution, a fourth orientation—we shall call it that of *broker*—developed in response to the rise of interest groups and the increasing number of demands made on legislatures by pressure groups. The legislature became, in the course of the nineteenth century, a major integrating force in the pluralism of American political, social, and economic life. This development had been foreshadowed by the struggle of interests in the Constitutional Convention and in early Congresses and state legislatures, and had suggested to the authors of *The Federalist* the balancing function of legislative bodies.

This review of legislative role orientations, whether theoretically derived from the legislature's place in the power structure of the political system or historically reconstructed, has suggested four major types—ritualist, tribune, inventor, and broker. There may be others.

Representational Roles: Style and Focus

The problem of representation is central to all discussions of the functions of legislatures or the behavior of legislators. For it is through the process of representation, presumably, that legislatures are empowered to act for the whole body politic and are legitimized. And because, by virtue of representation, they participate in legislation, the represented accept legislative decisions as authoritative. It would seem, therefore, that legislation and representation are closely related.[7] And if they are related, the functional relevance of representation to legislative behavior needs to be articulated.

But agreement about the meaning of the term "representation" hardly goes beyond a general consensus regarding the context within which it is appropriately used. The history of politcal theory is studded with definitions of representation, usually embedded in ideological assumptions and postulates, which cannot serve the uses of empirical research without conceptual clarification.[8]

A *distinction between focus and style of representation.* A convenient and useful starting point in theoretical clarification is Edmund Burke's theory of representation. For, in following his classic argument, later theorists have literally accepted Burke's formulation and ignored its contextual basis and polemical bias. Burke ingeniously combined two notions that, for analytical purposes, should be kept distinct. In effect, he combined a conception of the focus of representation with a conception of the style of representation. "Parliament," Burke (1949, p. 116) said in a famous passage in 1774,

is not a *congress* of ambassadors from different and hostile interests; which interest each must maintain, as an agent and advocate, against other agents and advocates; but Parliament is a *deliberative* assembly of *one* nation, with *one* interest, that of the whole; where, not local purposes, not local prejudices ought to guide but the general good, resulting from the general reason of the whole.

The sentence indicates that Burke postulated two possible foci of representation: local, necessarily hostile interests, on the one hand; and a national interest, on the other hand. He rejected the former as an improper focus and advocated the latter as the proper focus of the representative's role. But in doing so, he also linked these foci of representation with particular representational styles. If the legislature is concerned with only one interest, that of the whole, and not with compromise among diverse interests, it follows that the representative cannot and must not be bound by instructions, from whatever source, but must be guided by what Burke called "his unbiased opinion, his mature judgment, his enlightened conscience." Moreover, Burke buttressed his argument by emphasizing the deliberative function of the legislature, presumably in contrast to its representational function. Yet if one rejects his notion of the legislature as only a deliberative body whose representational focus is the whole rather than its constituent parts, the logic of Burke's formulation is no longer necessary or relevant.

The generic extension of Burke's special case, broken down into analytic components, suggests that the focal and stylistic dimensions of representation must be kept separate in empirical research. Burke combined them for polemical reasons: he was writing in opposition to the idea of mandatory representation, which had much popular support in the middle of the eighteenth century.[9] But the fact that a representative sees himself as reaching a decision by following his own convictions or judgment does not mean that the content of his decisions is necessarily oriented toward a general interest rather than a particular interest, just as his acceptance of instructions from a clientele group does not necessarily mean that he is oriented toward a special interest rather than the public interest. A representative may base his decisions on his own conscience or judgment, but the cause he promotes may be parochial. Or he may follow instructions, but the mandate may be directed toward the realization of the general welfare.

The distinction between the focal and stylistic dimensions of the representative's role allows us to suggest that representation is concerned not with what decisions should be made, but with how decisions are to be made. Now, it is axiomatic that decisions made in institutional contexts, such as legislatures provide, are made in terms of a set of premises that guide the behavior of decision makers. The notion—explicit in Burke and other traditional formulations—that legislative decisions can be purely rational is not tenable in view of the fact that rationality, while not altogether absent, is invariably bounded by the legislature's institutional environment.[10] One of these boundaries is the representational fabric of the legislature. The representative system provides the legislator with some of the assumptions in terms of which he defines his representational role. The roles he takes, in turn, whether in the focal or stylistic dimensions of representation, provide the premises for decision.

Trustee. The role orientation of trustee finds expression in two major conceptions of how decisions ought to be made. These conceptions may occur severally and jointly. There is, first, a moralistic interpretation. The trustee sees himself as a free agent in that, as a premise of his decision-making behavior, he claims to follow what he considers right or just, his convictions and principles, the dictates of his conscience. Second, the trustee claims that he must fall back on his own principles in making decisions because those from whom he might take cues—constituents, lobbyists, leaders, or colleagues—cannot be trusted. There is also a judgmental conception of the role of trustee. The trustee is not bound by a mandate because his decisions are his own considered judgments based on an assessment of the facts in each decision, his understanding of all the problems and angles involved, his thoughtful appraisal of the sides at issue.

Evidently a great variety of conceptions of representation are involved in the role orientation of the trustee. In particular, it seems that this orientation not only derives from a normative definition of the role of the representative, but that it is also often grounded in interpersonal situations that make it functionally inevitable. The condition that the represented do not have the information necessary to give intelligent instructions, that the representative is unable to discover what his clientele may want, that preferences remain unexpressed, that there is no need for instructions because of an alleged harmony of interest between representative and represented—all of the circumstances may be acknowledged as sources of the role orientation of trustee, at times even forced on the representative against his own predilection for a mandate if that were possible.

Delegate. Just as the trustee role orientation involves a variety of conceptions of representation, so does the orientation of delegate. All delegates are agreed, of course, that they should not use their independent judgment or principled convictions as decision-making premises. But this does not mean that they feel equally committed to follow instructions, from whatever clientele. Some merely say that they try to inform themselves before making decisions by consulting their constituents or others; however, they seem to imply that such consultation has a mandatory effect on their behavior: "I do ask them (that is, constituents) quite often, especially where there's doubt in my mind." Others frankly acknowledge instructions as necessary or desirable premises in decision making: "I do what they want me to do. Being re-elected is the best test"; or, "A majority of the people always gets their way with me." Finally, there is the representative in the delegate role who not only feels that he should follow instructions, but who also believes that he should do so even if these instructions are explicitly counter to his own judgment or principles: "Some things I'm not particularly sold on, but if the people want it, they should have it"; or, "Reflect the thinking of my district even if it is not my own private thinking."

What strikes one in these comments, in contrast to those made by trustees, is the failure to elaborate in greater detail the problem of why the representative should follow instructions in his decision-making behavior. Delegates, it seems, have a simpler, more mechanical conception of the political process and of the function of representation in legislative behavior. Perhaps most noticeable, in contrast to the trustee orientation, is the omission of delegates to raise the question of political responsibility under conditions of strict instructions. Apparently the problem is ignored by the delegate precisely because he rejects the possibility of discretion in his decision making. It is a matter of speculation whether the role orientation of delegate is based on a conscious majoritarian bias that he could elaborate and defend if necessary, or whether it simply reflects lack of political articulation and sophistication. On the other hand, the fact that the delegate seems to have so little doubt about his role suggests that, whatever his reasons and regardless of whether his decisions are really in accord with the views of different groups among his clientele, he is likely to be characterized by a fairly high sense of personal effectiveness in his approach to lawmaking.

Politico. As suggested earlier, the classical dichotomization of the concept of representation in terms of independent judgment and mandate was unlikely to exhaust the empirical possibilities of representational behavior. In particular, it would seem to be possible for a representative to act in line with both criteria. For roles and role orientations need not be mutually exclusive. Depending on circumstances, a representative may hold the role orientation of trustee at one time, and the role orientation of delegate at another time. Or he might even seek to reconcile both orientations in terms of a third. In other words, the representational-role set comprises the extreme orientations of trustee and delegate and a third orientation, the politico, resulting from overlap of these two. Within the orientational range called politico, the trustee and delegate roles may be taken simultaneously, possibly making for role conflict, or they may be taken seriatim, one after another as legislative situations dictate.

Both role orientations—that of trustee and that of delegate—may be held serially, depending on whether the legislator's focus of attention is centered in one clientele or another. For instance, he may see himself as a delegate in matters of local interst, and a trustee in all other matters. Or the legislator may feel that he must follow his party's instructions in political matters, though on others he can be a free agent. And both the trustee and delegate roles may be taken, depending on the character of the issue involved or the legislator's focus of attention. But no attempt is made to reconcile the two orientations. They coexist side by side and may be invoked as political circumstances require. These legislators do not seem to feel that they are facing a situation that makes for conflict of roles, largely because they succeed in avoiding conflict by not attempting to reconcile the two orientations.

On the other hand, some legislators may be more sensitive to the potential conflict to which they may be exposed by the ambiguity of the representational relationship and seek to come to grips with it. These representatives not only are aware of the problem, but, instead of solving it by sometimes taking the trustee role, sometimes the delegate role, they seek to balance simultaneously the instructions or preferences of clienteles against their own judgment.

In general, then, the politico as a representational-role taker differs from both the trustee and the delegate in that he seems to be more sensitive to conflicting alternatives, more flexible in the ways in which he tries to resolve the conflict among alternatives, and less dogmatic in his orientation toward legislative behavior as it is related to his representational role.

Areal Roles: The Geographic Factor

Representation of geographic areas introduces a certain amount of ambiguity into the relationship between representative and represented.[11] Part of this ambiguity involves the widely held expectation, contested by Edmund Burke but shared by many citizens and politicians alike, that the legislator is a spokesman of the presumed "interests" of his district. Implicit in this expectation is the assumption that a geographic unit has interests that are distinct and different from those of other units. This assumption has been challenged on a variety of grounds: that the geographic area as such, as an electoral unit, is artificial; that it cannot and does not generate interests shared by its residents; that it has no unique interests; and so on. Schemes of proportional or vocational representation have been advanced to make possible the representation of allegedly more "natural" interest groupings, such as minority, skill, or economic groups.

Yet the assumption that geographic districts have unique interests that are, or ought to be, taken into consideration when legislative decisions are made, continues to be shared not only by voters, politicians, and others involved in policy making, but also by scientific students of the political process. It underlies many studies that seek to relate legislative roll-call votes to socioeconomic characteristics of electoral districts (Turner, 1951; MacRae, 1958), as well as studies that analyze the socioeconomic composition of legislatures (Hyneman, 1938; Matthews, 1954).

Such an interpretation is most tenuous under modern conditions. Electoral districts tend to be so heterogeneous in population attributes, so pluralistic in the character of their group life, so diverse in the kinds of values and beliefs held, that whatever measures of central tendency are used to classify a district are more likely to conceal than to reveal its real character. The notion that elections are held as a method to discover persons whose attributes and attitudes will somehow mirror those most widely shared by people in their district appears to be of dubious validity. The function of representation in modern political systems is not to make the legislature a mathematically exact copy of the electorate.

But the difficulty of finding an identity between representative and represented does not mean that a legislator's point of reference in making decisions cannot be his district. It may or may not be, and whether it is or not is a matter of empirical determination. We may doubt that what orients a legislator toward his district rather than some other focus of attention is the similarity between his district's characteristics and his own. Or we may assume that a legislator incorporates in himself the characteristics of his district—which, for argument's sake, may be admitted when he comes from a relatively homogeneous area. But it is still an empirical question whether or not the legislator is subjectively concerned with his district and seeks to discover its "interests."

In spite of the considerations just mentioned, state legislators perceive representation of the interests of some geographic area as a proper function of their legislative activities. Responding to our questions about what they thought were the most important things they should do in the legislature and how their constituents felt about it, more than two-thirds in the three states of California, New Jersey, and Ohio spontaneously mentioned either district or state, or both, as clienteles (although in Tennessee almost two-thirds failed to do so). Of those who took cognizance of a geographic unit, some would mention only their district or county, others only the state, and still others would mention district and state as equally important foci of attention. On the basis of their responses, we classified legislators into "district oriented," "state oriented," and "district-state oriented."

Interest Groups and Legislative Roles

The once-prevalent view that "special interest groups," by their very existence, constitute a threat to the general "public interest" has generally given way to a belief that interest groups collectively constitute a legitimate clientele in the formulation of policy.[12] The central problem in representation posed by pressure groups for the modern legislature, therefore, is the problem of relating to each other, and to a public interest espoused by no organized group, the multitudinous particular interests voiced by countless organized groups.

Yet there are surprisingly few theoretical explanations or cumulative and comparative empirical data about this phase of the representative process.[13] The notion that legislative decisions are simple mathematical resultants of "pressures" by lobbyists, parties, and constituents, all impinging on passively reacting legislators, has often been criticized (MacIver, 1947, pp. 220–221; Truman, 1951, pp. 332–333; Odegard, 1958). Much research on pressure politics attempts to explain the actions of supposedly "pressured" legislatures and legislators by looking not at them but at the pressuring groups. Little is said about how or why the legislator is influenced by the supposedly critical characteristics of pressure groups—size of membership, geographic distribution, wealth and resources, extent and character of leadership and organization, strategic position in society, and so on.[14]

Further insight into the character and function of pressure politics requires examination of individual legislators' postures toward pressure groups and their reasons for them—both "reasons" they adduce and correlations between legislators' postures and analytic variables established by analysts. We are concerned here, it should be emphasized, with the functioning of the legislative *institution* and not with unique historical events or outcomes. Similarly, we are concerned with legislators' orientations toward pressure groups as a *generic* class of "significant others," not with their particular individual group affiliations and identifications.

With respect to the bearing of pressure politics on the function of representation, the basic question is, how, and how much, are demands of interest groups considered by a legislature in the course of its decision making? In general some members will accommodate the demands of organized interest groups in the legislative process.[15] Others will resist consideration or accommodation of these demands. Still others, presumably attuned to other persons or factors, will play a neutral or varying and indeterminate role toward such group demands.

It seems obvious that a legislator's reaction to the activities of pressure groups and lobbyists will depend in part on his general evaluation of pressure politics as a mode of political activity in the world he lives in. It likewise seems obvious that legislators' reactions to pressure groups or lobbyists will vary with their different degrees of knowledge or awareness of groups activities. The legislator who knows what the Municipal League is, what it wants, and who speaks for it and when, will react differently to cues from the league than one who never heard of it and does not identify anyone as its spokesman.

Assuming, then, that any given legislator's behavior with respect to pressure groups will depend largely on his general affective orientation toward pressure politics and his awareness of such activity when it occurs around him,[16] one can construct the following very simple typology of legislators' role orientations toward pressure groups:

Facilitators: Have a friendly attitude toward group activity *and* relatively much knowledge about it.

Resisters: Have a hostile attitude toward group activity *and* relatively much knowledge about it.

Neutrals: Have no strong attitude or favor or disfavor with respect to group activity (regardless of their knowledge of it) or have very little knowledge about it (regardless of their friendliness or hostility toward it).

The Network of Roles: An Ideal-Type Construct

The analytical distinction between clientele, representational, and purposive roles is helpful in dissecting the legislator's total role. Actual behavior, however, is a function not of discrete roles but of a system of roles. It is the network of interpenetrating roles that gives structure and coherence to the legislative process. Comparative analysis of the eight chambers of four states included in this study supports the notion that roles are meaningfully related to each other. Moreover, the patterning of observed relations and differences is such that it is possible to develop an ideal-type construct of the total network. Such an ideal-type construct is, of course, an exaggeration of empirical reality, but it can serve two valuable purposes: first, it can demonstrate the logic of the postulated network; and second, it can serve as an independent criterion for comparing the concrete, empirical role systems.

Figure 6.1 presents a diagram of the ideal-type network of legislators' roles suggested by the clustering of role orientations empirically found in the four states and by theoretical considerations. The diagram reflects the observed tendency of certain orientations in one sector to be associated with particular orientations in others. Thus the upper half of the diagram idealizes the following pairs of role orientations: majority–state oriented, majority-facilitator, state oriented–facilitator, facilitator-politico, majority-politico, majority-broker, state oriented–trustee, state oriented–inventor/broker, facilitator-broker, broker-trustee/politico, and inventor-trustee. The lower half idealizes these pairs: minority–district oriented, minority-resister, district oriented–resister, resister-delegate, minority-delegate, minority-inventor/tribune, district oriented–delegate, district oriented tribune, resister-tribune, and tribune-delegate. The diagram thus suggests two essentially reciprocal sets of relationships or dimensions, one represented in the upper, the other in the lower half of the diagram. The neutral and district-state orientations do not associate readily in theory (nor, as we have seen, empirically) with either of these, but, as the diagram shows, stand more or less outside and between them.

Any individual legislator is likely to be located more in one than in another dimension of this network of available roles. Moreover, it is the network as such, rather than simple adoption of one orientation instead of another, that is crucial to the individual's behavior. That is to say, the difference between one role and another in a given subsystem—such as, for instance, the difference between facilitator and resister, or between trustee and delegate—is a function of the total network of roles. In such a network, each role is somehow related to every other role, and the

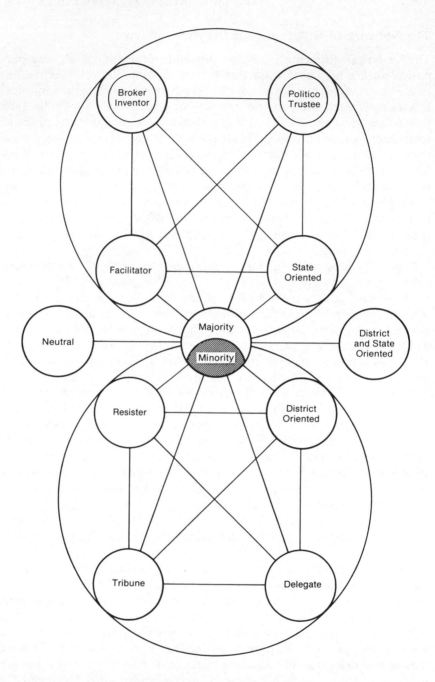

Figure 6.1   Ideal-type network of roles

character and extent of these relations gives any one empirical legislative role system its peculiar character.

We have not attempted to characterize the different patterns or clusterings of role orientation that might be manifested by the individual legislator, in terms of the ideal-type network illustrated in Figure 6.1. We have, instead, sought to characterize the system differences resulting from the various constellations of role orientation found to prevail in the four legislatures. In other words, although the diagram represents the coincidence of particular role orientations for the individual legislator, we are interested in it as a representation of the aggregates of role orientations and role relationships constituting a system of role relationships among legislators in particular legislatures. We wish to use the ideal-type construct of the network of roles to characterize differences among legislative systems.

Legislative Role Structures in Four States

Ideally, it would be desirable to identify and specify the entire matrix of all role combinations in a given legislative system. For instance, just how many members of the majority are also trustees, brokers, facilitators, and state oriented? Does this combination constitute the dominant pattern? What secondary and tertiary patterns exist? Unfortunately, even the largest chamber in this study includes too few cases to isolate empirically the theoretically possible matrix of roles in combination. However, we can construct a partial framework by dealing with the most frequent individual pairs of roles that are taken in a legislative chamber. Each of these "dominant pairs" may or may not be linked because any one role in one pair may also be linked with a third role in another pair.

Table 6.1 presents the dominant (that is, the most frequent) pairs of roles in the two chambers of each state legislature. The base of the proportions is the total number of legislators whose individual roles appeared in the dominant pairs. For instance, of the California House members for whom data were available, 30 percent are district-oriented minority members, 26 percent are majority-neutrals, 27 percent are district-oriented facilitators, and so on.

House role structures. The distributions in Table 6.1 yield some interesting results, but they are difficult to inspect and appraise. There are two ways in which we can simplify the emerging structures—one numerical, the other graphical. First, we can single out the number of times a given role appears in a dominant pair. Table 6.2 presents this alternative. The patterns for each role set are clear. They sensitize us to the significance of

Table 6.1 Proportions of dominant role pairs in the four legislatures

Ohio	N	%	New Jersey	N	%	California	N	%	Tennessee	N	%
						LOWER CHAMBERS					
Ma/Di-St	94	31	Ma/Di-St	38	34	Mi/Di	50	30	Ma/Di	38	42
Ma/Fa	125	32	Ma/Fa	57	28	Ma/Ne	68	26	Ma/Re	87	31
Di-St/Ne	89	19	Di-St/Fa	37	19	Di/Fa	44	27	Di/Re	38	23
Ma/Tr	94	35	Ma/Tr	39	41	Ma/Tr	37	30	Ma/Tr	61	59
St/Tr	75	20	Di-St/Tr	26	23	Di/De	23	30	Di/Tr	31	29
			St/Tr	26	23						
Fa/Tr	92	24	Fa/Tr	39	26	Ne/Tr	32	31	Ne/Tr	59	36
Ma/Br	130	36	Ma/Tri	58	47	Mi/Tri	78	28	Ma/Tri	89	48
Di-St/Br	95	27	Di-St/Tri	37	32	Di/Tri	49	47	Di/Tri	37	49
Fa/Br	125	24	Fa/Tri	57	23	Ne/Tri	68	22	Ne/Tri	87	28
Br/Tr	120	23	In/Tr	55	31	In/Tr	47	19	Tri/Tr	66	41
						SENATES					
Ma/Di-St	18	22	Ma/Di	16	25	Ma/Di	28	25	Ma/Di	8	50
Ma/Di	18	22	Mi/Di	16	25						
Mi/Di	18	22									
Ma/Fa	32	28	Ma/Fa	21	29	Mi/Fa	29	28	Ma/Re	29	38
Di/Fa	19	27	Di-St/Fa	16	31	Di/Ne	24	21	Di/Re	8	38
Ma/Tr	20	50	Ma/Tr	15	33	Ma/Tr	12	33	Ma/Tr	17	76
Di/Tr	13	23	Di/De	13	31	Di-St/Tr	12	34	Di/Tr	5	80
St/Tr	13	23									
Ne/Tr	20	30	Fa/Po	15	27	Fa/Tri	12	50	Re/Tr	17	41
Ma/Br	32	28	Ma/In	21	38	Ma/Tri	35	34	Ma/Tri	31	42
Di/Tri	17	41	Di/Tri	16	44	Di/Tri	28	29	Di/Tri	8	63
						St/Tri	28	29			
Fa/Br	32	22	Fa/Tri	23	38	Ne/Tri	29	28	Re/Tri	29	28
In/Tr	24	25	In/Po	21	19	Br/Tr	17	24	Tri/Tr	18	50
Br/Tr	24	25	Tri/De	21	19	Tri/Po	17	24			

Table 6.2 Number of times a role appears in combination with another in a dominant pair, lower chambers

Role	Ohio	New Jersey	California	Tennessee
Party				
Majority member	4	4	2	4
Minority member	0	0	2	0
Representational				
Trustee .	4	5	3	4
Politico	0	0	0	0
Delegate	0	0	1	0
Purposive				
Inventor	0	0	1	0
Broker	4	0	0	0
Tribune	0	3	3	4
Areal				
State oriented	1	1	0	0
District-state oriented	3	4	0	0
District oriented	0	0	4	4
Pressure group				
Facilitator	3	4	1	0
Neutral	1	0	3	2
Resister	0	0	0	2

particular distributions in the more-complex array of Table 6.1. In the first place, in the New Jersey and Ohio Houses, where "party government" has genuine meaning, the role of majority member appears among the dominant pairs, but the role of minority member does not. In California, where "party control" has little meaning, both the roles of majority and minority member are encountered in the dominant pairs. Tennessee represents a special case: although formally the role of "majority member" alone occurs in the dominant pairs, we know that the "majority" is factionalized and not a majority in the same sense as in the competitive party states. The Tennessee House is actually composed of competing "minorities," and although the role of majority member seems present in the dominant pairs, it cannot be taken in a literal sense.

Second, in the representational-role set, the role of trustee occurs in the dominant pairs almost exclusively, with the single exception of California, where the delegate role appears in one dominant pair. This role of trustee is, as noted earlier, so universal that it is necessarily linked to any cluster in the total network of dominant pairs. In other words, it does not serve as a discriminating factor in a typology of role structures.

Third, in the purposive-role set, the Ohio House role structure differs from the other three lower chamber structures in the pervasiveness of the broker role in dominant pairs, while elsewhere the tribune role is more prominent, suggesting a more "populist" milieu than prevailed in 1957 in the Republican-dominated Ohio House.

Fourth, of the areal-role set, the district role is present in dominant pairs in California and Tennessee, but not in Ohio and New Jersey. In the latter two states, the district-state role occurs in the dominant pairs, as does the state role in one pair, but neither of these two roles is present in the dominant California and Tennessee pairs. The pattern suggests that the areal-role orientations held by legislators may serve as critical discriminating devices in the characterization of legislative role structures.

Finally, the pressure-group-role set seems to perform a similar function. The facilitator role is prominent in Ohio's and New Jersey's dominant pairs, and the neutral role in California. Only in Tennessee does the resister role appear in dominant pairs, and it does so twice, while the facilitator role is altogether absent from dominant pairs.

The frequency of a role's appearance in dominant pairs and the pattern of occurrences from state to state give a first view of what one might expect when the linkages between those roles that constitute the dominant pairs are constructed graphically. The diagrams of the House structures presented in Figure 6.2 can be readily compared with the ideal-type construct (Figure 6.1). This comparison makes it possible to develop an empirical typology of legislative role structures.

The Ohio diagram in Figure 6.2 shows a relatively highly integrated role cluster of what we may call the "majoritarian type." Almost all the ideal-type linkages are present, and where they are not they are replaced by "intermediate" roles in the dominant pairs (such as the district-state role instead of the "pure" state role, or the neutral role instead of the facilitator role). But the linkages in no way penetrate into the reciprocal "minoritarian" cluster of the ideal-type model. Minority members are totally eclipsed as role takers in the dominant structure, as are such minority-linked roles of the ideal-type model as tribunes, resisters, delegates, and district oriented.

In the New Jersey House structure, also, the role of minority members and its ideally associated roles of delegate, resister, and district oriented are missing from the dominant majority-centered cluster. But, in contrast to Ohio, the tribune role of the minority cluster is linked three times to majority-anchored roles, and the reciprocal roles of the purposive-role set, ideally located in the majoritarian cluster, are not among the dominant pairs. With this one exception, then, the New Jersey House role structure is very similar to Ohio's. We can characterize the Ohio House structure

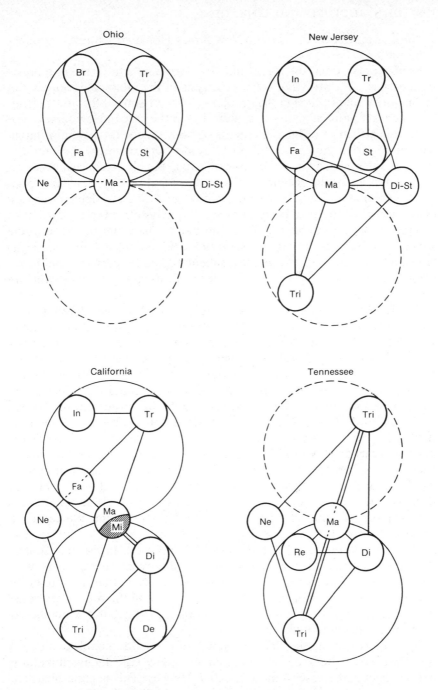

Figure 6.2   Role structures of four lower houses

as "broker-majoritarian" and the New Jersey House structure as "tribune-majoritarian."

By way of contrast, the California House role structure reveals a bipartisan pattern. The structure is not solely, as in the Ohio case, centered in the majority role (although the "majority" has organized the lower chamber), nor is it predominantly so centered as in the case of New Jersey. The California structure includes elements of both the ideal-type majoritarian and minoritarian clusters. And not only do both majority and minority member roles appear in the dominant pairs, but the linkages cut across the boundaries of the reciprocal sets of the ideal-type model. The "populist" component is outstanding; the tribune and district-oriented roles are linked across cluster boundaries, but the majority-related roles of inventor and facilitator each appear in dominant pairs. The California House role structure reflects the strongly "atomistic" orientation of California legislators, and it is indicative of the low salience of party roles as premises for legislative behavior. We may term the California House role structure "populist-bipartisan."

Finally, the Tennessee House role structure is altogether different from the previous types. Though formally "majoritarian," it is in fact minority geared: the tribune and district roles are more pervasive, and, alone among the four chambers, the role of resister appears in at least one dominant pair. At the same time, such majority-anchored roles as inventor or broker in the purposive-role set, facilitator, and state oriented are missing altogether in the Tennessee House structure. Only the trustee, ideally located in the majority cluster, is present. Apparently it is a role that cannot be shed in contemporary empirical reality, even in a system that is so clearly minority geared. These results, we already suggested, are easy to explain, and they confirm that the "majority" in Tennessee is only a pro forma majority. In fact, the "majority" Democrats are divided into competing factions, none of which can permanently control the legislature, and that behave more like minority parties in a multiparty system. We can characterize this structure as "populist-minoritarian."

Senate role structures. Tables 6.1 and 6.3 show that in the four Senates more pairs are tied for dominance, making the overall picture somewhat more complex. But a glance at Figure 6.3 will indicate that, in spite of the greater complexity, the general patterns observed in the role structures of the lower houses are maintained from state to state, but a number of differences may be noted.

In the first place, in the Ohio and New Jersey Senates the role of minority member seems to be somewhat more integrated into the dominant majority pattern than is the case in the respective Houses. This is quite plausible. In the smaller chambers, the minority is more likely to be in closer contact

Table 6.3 Number of times a role appears in combination with another in a dominant pair, Senates

Role	Ohio	New Jersey	California	Tennessee
Party				
Majority member	5	4	3	4
Minority member	1	1	0	1
Representational				
Trustee	6	6	4	4
Politico	0	2	1	0
Delegate	0	2	0	0
Purposive				
Inventor	1	2	0	0
Broker	3	0	1	0
Tribune	1	3	5	4
Areal				
State oriented	1	0	1	0
District-state oriented	1	1	1	0
District oriented	5	4	3	4
Pressure group				
Facilitator	3	4	2	0
Neutral	1	0	2	0
Resister	0	0	0	4

with the majority, it is more likely to be given attention, and it is more likely to play an active role in the legislative process. As a result, ideally minority-centered roles are likely to be more frequently linked to majority-anchored roles. In New Jersey, for instance, we may note the facilitator-tribune combination among the dominant pairs, or in Ohio the facilitator district pair.

Second, we note that in the Ohio and New Jersey Senates the district-oriented role appears in dominant pairs, while this is not the case in the respective Houses. Also, in New Jersey the delegate role and in Ohio the tribune role are paired with some other roles, while this pairing does not occur (with the exception of the tribune in New Jersey) in the lower chambers. These three roles—tribune, delegate, and district oriented—seem to loom as latent premises of their behavior in Senators' self-conceptions of their legislative role in general. Senates have been historically looked on as performing more distinctly "ambassadorial functions" in the representative system. And although now popularly elected just as the members of the "popular" lower houses, the notion that Senates are, in part at least, conclaves of ambassadors from geographically based constituencies may

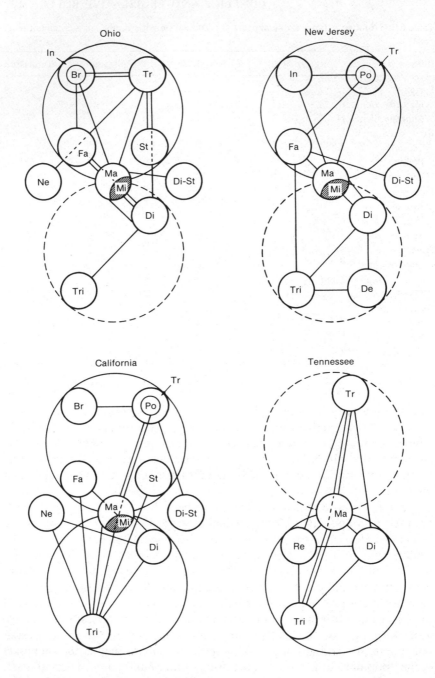

Figure 6.3 Role structures of four senates

linger on in Senators' self-definitions. This, of course, we cannot prove, but as a hypothesis it is congruent with the fact that in the lower houses these "populist" roles are minority centered. Minority members are likely to perceive themselves as "ambassadors"—spokesmen of the "outs"—vis-à-vis the controlling majority with its predominant state orientation.

The "constructions" of legislative chambers as role structures suggest that through the use of nonconventional analytical categories, in our case derived from a role analysis of legislators, we can describe the structure of a legislative chamber, not as it is embodied in rules and bylaws (which are important parameters for behavior), but as it represents a system of action. Are the structures we delineated "functional," then, in being adapted to and, in turn, facilitative of conflict crystallization and resolution?

Political Conflict and Role Structure

Ohio. The Ohio role structure is centered in a strong, well-organized majority that, in the House, eclipses the minority in giving the legislature its characteristic format, although in the Senate the minority-centered roles of tribune and district oriented are joined in the dominant pattern. But the outstanding and distinguishing feature in both Ohio chambers is the presence of the broker in the role structure. Legislators' rankings of types of conflict may be relevant to the emergence of the broker as a dominant role. Although Ohio's legislature is organized as an unequivocal two-party system, in the 1957 session, at least, a variety of conflicts, especially those involving urban-rural cleavage, labor problems, and ideological disagreement, were seen as more important than party conflict. Apparently, majority members, feeling free from conflict with a minority, come to function as brokers among interests whose conflicts are deemed more important than party conflicts. Moreover, as we saw, both Ohio chambers have the lowest mean consensus score in regard to the conflicts deemed important. Again, if this is the case, the brokerage function becomes critical, and the role structure tends to be adapted to the situation as it is perceived. The characterization of the Ohio role structure as "broker-majoritarian" is predicated on its functionality in regard to the kinds of conflict deemed important and the low consensual quality of the legislature. In a system in which highly differentiating conflicts, as those between city and country, business and labor, liberals and conservatives, are considered important, but in which legislators are little agreed, the functions associated with the broker role seem to serve the needs of political integration. The prominence of the broker role in the role structure gives the system its characteristic ability to function effectively in a complex conflict situation.

New Jersey. The role structure of this state's legislative system is similar to Ohio's, but, in contrast to Ohio, party conflict is considered as the most important among all others, and there is strong consensus in this respect. The conflict situation mirrored in legislators' perceptions is strongly focused also on tensions arising out of the minority's control of the governorship. In such direct combat between organized and disciplined sides, decisions are less likely to require the taking of the broker role in the dominant structure. Rather, conflict is centered on those popular mandates that the majority receives in its competition with the minority. And if governmental control is divided between the parties—one controlling the legislature, the other the governorship—the functional requirements of the system seem to incline toward a role structure in which the populist orientation finds expression. The appearance of the tribune role in the dominant New Jersey role structure seems to meet these requirements. Just as in Ohio the solution of the perceived conflicts seems to generate the adaptation of the role structure through emphasis on the broker role, so the solution of the centrally perceived New Jersey conflicts—those between the parties and between the minority governor and the legislative majority—seems to fit into what we have called a role structure of the tribune-majoritarian type.

California. The California role structure, we noted earlier, is not singularly anchored in either majority or minority. Majority and minority roles seem to have little meaning, with the result that the role structure partakes of elements found in both major role clusters of the ideal-type model. Party and gubernatorial conflicts ranked lowest in both chambers, and there was a good deal of crystallization in this respect. Instead, other conflicts—involving regional differentiation, urban-rural cleavage, labor, and ideological difficulties—were judged important. Why, then, does the broker role not emerge as a component of the dominant role structure in California, as it does in Ohio?

An answer to this question is difficult. It may be suggested that the broker role is missing in the California structure because it is linked to the role of majority member. But as party roles are essentially meaningless in the California system, the brokerage function fails to be performed. For this function is predicated on the presence of a fairly stable point of reference—the majority's stand on issues in terms of which the brokerage function must be performed. If this stable point of reference is missing, the brokerage function cannot be readily executed, and there is relatively little need for legislators to take the broker role.

Instead, the populist component dominates in the California role structure. The large number of bills introduced and passed in California, in contrast to the other states, seems to confirm our characterization of the California system as "populist-bipartisan." Unable to select and sift among the huge amount of legislation introduced by legislators in behalf of particular interests, the California role structure is adapted to the demands made on the legislature from "outside" by providing a counterbalance to group pressures in the form of a populist component. It is interesting to note that in California the pressure-group role of neutral rather than that of facilitator appears more often in the dominant pairs. California politics of an earlier period than the one studied here had been notorious for its submissiveness to special interests and group pressures. By 1957, evidently, the role structure had developed in a direction that permitted legislators to offset pressure-group influence by taking roles more responsive to popular demands. Being under cross-pressures from both organized interests and grass-roots influences, California legislators take the role of tribune rather than broker in the purposive-role set and the role of neutral in the pressure-group-role set. Conflicts are resolved by way of negotiation in terms of popular demands rather than by way of brokerage in terms of a majority's stand on issues.

Tennessee. To speak of a "majority" in Tennessee is merely using a figure of speech. In actuality, the effective organized units of the legislature are factions, usually centered in the governor. If anything, therefore, the Tennessee system is a multiminority system par excellence. The dominant role pairs that serve to "build" the legislative role structure converge in the minority-anchored cluster of roles. The structure seems reasonably adapted to the prevailing appraisal of the importance of different conflicts by the legislators themselves. Party conflict is considered of little importance, but conflicts involving the governor are given prominent rank. As a multiminority system in which the governor's faction is only a transient clique, the Tennessee system is strongly populist: urban-rural and labor-business conflicts perceived in the legislative arena reflect popular tensions, and legislators take roles as minority proponents of diverse popular interests. The roles of tribune and district oriented, as well as other minority-centered roles, such as delegate and resister, tend toward what we have termed a "populist-minoritarian" role structure.

The legislature is a human group with a determinate role structure that serves two interdependent functions: (1) to link the legislature as a subsystem with other subsystems of the political system, notably electoral constituencies, parties, pressure groups, and administrative agencies; and (2) to institutionalize and resolve the social, economic, and political conflicts generated as legislative inputs in the various subsystems. We find that American state legislatures, so similar in their formal structures and processes, differ significantly in their adaptations to political reality, depending on the types and importance of conflicts encountered in particular contexts within and among the other political subsystems with which the legislature is linked. The roles taken by legislators in different political contexts (such as the degree of competition between parties or factions, or the relative strength of majority and minority) constitute a role structure of consequence for the performance of legislative tasks, especially the resolution of conflicts, and for the achievement of democratic integration.

7

Law and Politics:

Professional Convergence

PREOCCUPATION with real or alleged dysfunctional consequences of the law-yer's ubiquity in politics has had the effect of orienting research toward analysis of differences rather than of similarities in the behavior of the politician who is a lawyer and the politician who is not. Because the lawyer is more visible in politics than any other private-occupational type, it is easy enough to assume not only that he is different, but that whatever differentiates him from the nonlawyer pervades his conduct in public life and his identifiable effects on the functioning of a political system. "My notion is," writes the sociologist David Gold (1961, p. 84), "that by virtue of training, experience, and perhaps a prior process of selectivity, the lawyer is apt to behave differently *in the political arena* than the nonlaw-yer."

It is, of course, a very conventional sociological assumption—for which there is a good deal of evidence—that a man's total perspective is crucially conditioned by his position in the social structure and notably by the struc-ture of occupations. But many of the data suggest that the standard soci-ological formula may have to be modified. Lawyer-politicians do not differ much from politicians who are not lawyers. Now, most studies of lawyers in politics, discovering only slight differences between lawyers and others, or no differences at all, usually conclude on a somewhat disappointed note. Paradoxically, the conclusion of such a study may sound triumphant: does not the absence of significant differences between lawyers and nonlawyers in politics prove that a man's occupation has little to do with his public decision-making behavior? Does it not prove that he can transcend what-ever narrow viewpoints may be associated with his occupation and rise to the responsibility of a public career by giving disinterested service—dis-

---

Written with John D. Sprague.

interested, that is, in terms of his occupational background and predispositions?

But the function of occupation in politics need not be denied simply because it cannot be directly confirmed by comparing lawyers with nonlawyers and noting the absence of differences between them. In fact, the affinity of law and politics as vocations suggests the need for a theoretical formulation of the problem that, on the one hand, does not reject the general hypothesis that a man's occupation is critical in his political behavior but that, on the other hand, allows for treating the lawyer's role in politics as a special case.

The intellectual problem involved in formulating an empirically viable conception of the lawyer's role in politics stems from the notion, well articulated by Max Weber, that the lawyer is prototypical of the modern professional politician (see Bendix, 1960, p. 436). But this cannot mean that nonlawyers in politics are, as if by automatic exclusion, less able politicians. The conventional search for differences between lawyers and nonlawyers in politics ignores an assumption that must necessarily be made about the political system in which both are involved—namely, that the polity constitutes an autonomous system of role relationships with a culture of its own that makes for attitudes, values, and styles of behavior that are characteristic of the political as contrasted with any other type of social system. Both lawyers and nonlawyers are "socialized" into this political culture, which is sufficiently pervasive to have an impact on political practitioners regardless of what their private occupations are or have been.

However, it does not suffice to argue that the roles imposed on the participants in a political system are so penetrating that all other influences are nullified. This would be equivalent to arguing that individual determinants of political behavior are of no theoretical interest or practical importance because the present situation in which an individual finds himself is inevitably the controlling circumstance. Aside from the drastic nature of such a proposition, its disregard of the existence of *some kind* of intimate relationship between law and politics is precisely what leads us to reject it. In effect, it sidesteps the problem of explanation.

In particular, comparison of lawyers and nonlawyers reveals two empirical phenomena that must be accommodated in a theoretical formulation that can help in accounting for both. On the one hand a review of their political backgrounds and careers indicates that lawyers in politics may well be politicians first, chronologically speaking, whose political orientation precedes their choice of law as a private pursuit and who enter the profession of law in order to promote better their political aspirations. In other words, what Woodrow Wilson said of himself—that he "chose" politics as his profession, but that he "entered" the law as a profession because he thought that entering the one would lead to the other—may well be true of the lawyer-politician generally. There are likely to be exceptions to the rule, of course. But entering the profession of law in order to pursue a career in politics would seem to make sense only, given the far-reaching character of the career choice, if the two professions are somehow accounted for in a single system of explanation.

On the other hand, juxtaposition of some of the roles taken by lawyer- and nonlawyer-legislators in their public clientele relationships, such as those of trustee, tribune, facilitator, broker, inventor, and so on, and the roles taken by lawyers in their private client relationships, such as those of fiduciary, advocate, attorney, counselor, or contact man, suggest their functional equivalence. This functional equivalence, it would seem, goes a long way in accounting for the fact that lawyers and nonlawyers do not differ as they assume legislative roles in terms of which they relate themselves to their legislative tasks, or that they seem to take legislative roles in an arbitrary manner. But functional equivalence is an empirical phenomenon that itself requires theoretical explication.

In order to come to theoretical grips with the problem, consider the notion of "professional convergence." This, it will appear, is a strictly theoretical construct that must not be confused with the affinity or compatibility of law and politics as professions in empirical reality. For it is this affinity that the concept of professional convergence is supposed to explain. Rather, the notion of convergence posits the isomorphism of the two professions: Although they are distinct and structurally independent of each other as professions, law and politics come to exhibit similar forms—a convergence that, it is postulated, would have occurred even if law and politics did not in reality intersect with one another as professions.

For the purpose of explicating the concept of professional convergence, we assume that, were convergence *not* to occur, relevant professional characteristics would be distributed at random among *all* the various professions. To put this positively, professional convergence is present if two professions have common characteristics that are especially relevant to the performance of professional functions, while a third, fourth, or fifth profession does not share these attributes. In the case of law and politics, for instance, there are functionally equivalent roles in terms of which the professions can be analyzed. One task of research, then, is to discover the conditions under which two professions are likely to be convergent.

"Convergence" is a developmental concept. It refers to a tendency or trend of two phenomena to develop similar forms. When speaking of "professional convergence," then, as in the case of law and politics as vocations, we mean that these professions will come to exhibit similar forms as a result of developmental tendencies in response to the society's needs and to the demands that are made by the society on both professions.

Some theoretical assumptions must be made if the concept is to serve the heuristic objective for which it is being formulated. The central assumption is that law and politics, though of different ancestry *as professions,* are isomorphic—that is, similar in structure because of convergent development; and that, because convergence is conceived as a continuous process, the similarity will "grow" as time goes on. Although the terms used here are theoretical, not empirical, convergence can be demonstrated. But at the same time it should be emphasized that an isomorphism is never complete. In other words, it does not cover the whole range of empirically observable phenomena. On the other hand, it is meant to be a "true representation" of the phenomena to be observed. For instance, a map is not a complete representation of the terrain, but a good map is a true representation: it permits the reader to locate himself accurately in the terrain. Because a theoretical construct is necessarily abstract, it refers only to selected aspects of the phenomena that may be observed, and it omits other aspects. A map symbolizes the relations between aspects of the terrain, but it is not in one-to-one correspondence with the terrain. Indeed, if a map (or model) were a "replica" of empirical reality, no new knowledge, even of a descriptive kind, would be forthcoming—for all that might be observed would have been observed already (see Brodbeck, 1959, p. 374).

The assumption of convergence, then, is especially applicable in comparing two phenomena that have properties and relations between these properties that are similar (or better, that are postulated to be similar). But this does not mean that the two phenomena are identical. If they were identical, there could be no discussion of isomorphism. Applied to the present concern, then, law and politics are descriptively distinct. They are not considered, for theoretical purposes, to act directly upon one another. Although law and politics as professions may be structurally isomorphic, no connection between them need be assumed. Because of convergence, however, both exhibit the same set of "logical" relations or "common" properties, so that a single type of conceptualization will fit both.

Although two phenomena may perform similar functions, they need not be structurally isomorphic. This fact is often observed in studies of political functions that are performed by structurally quite different organizations. Political parties in multiparty systems, for instance, perform many of the functions that, in a two-party system, are performed by interest groups, and vice versa. Thus the argument presented here does not rest on the premise that, as a matter of undemonstrable assumption, there *must* be some structural similarities between parties when similar functions are carried out by different structures. From the theoretical point of view, such a relationship must be demonstrated empirically and spelled out in precise detail to be admissible as an explanation.

That professional convergence of law and politics is evident, then, does not mean that law and politics have merged or will merge into a single profession, or that one profession will be absorbed by the other. Nor does it mean that one profession is identical with the other in internal structure, in external relations, or in the functions it performs both internally and externally. Law and politics are quite distinct, each having its own unique ways of socializing an individual into the profession, recruiting him to a particular post and assigning him particular tasks, transmitting professional knowledge and lore, forming and enforcing its norms of proper conduct. The two are distinct with regard to the institutional settings in which each performs its functions, and these functions remain in many respects quite different. This discussion merely postulates that the two professions converge in an isomorphic sense.

To avoid misunderstanding, the argument can be restated briefly. A similarity (not identity) between law and politics as professions can be shown to exist empirically; this similarity can be specified precisely in theoretical terms; and accurate operations can be performed that will allow measurement of the similarity. This is, of course, a very strong set of assumptions. But in the cases where the tasks that the three assumptions specify can be accomplished, it can be said that an isomorphism between law and politics exists. Remember that we have not as yet carried out these tasks in regard to the professions of law and politics, but only made the theoretical problem more precise. It remains to delineate the relationship of the structural isomorphism of the two professions to the developmental concept of professional convergence.

The assumption here is that structural isomorphism is a product of a similar development of the two professions. That is to say, similar development over time has resulted in acquisition of similar properties and similar relationships between properties by the professions of law and politics. This development can be viewed as a process of which the beginning point may not be clear but for which the end point may be precisely stated. The end point is that point at which an isomorphism exists between two professions, in the strong sense that professional membership no longer differentiates any relevant aspect of behavior. This is the point, in the present case of law and politics, where all lawyers (and not just lawyer-politicians) behave precisely as politicians who are not lawyers behave, and the converse.

The fact that the beginning of the development of convergence cannot be clearly specified is of little theoretical importance. It can be assumed that the initial point is one at which law and politics are not closely related and at at which the behavior of lawyers in politics clearly differentiates them from other politicians as much as from other persons with differing occupations or social roles.

The theoretical argument may now be restated. If two professions exhibit similar developments with respect to specified properties characteristic of these professions, they are in the process of converging. If the two professions are in the process of converging, then they will show a structural isomorphism that is dependent, first, on the similarity of the development of the properties deemed relevant and, second, on the opportunity for such development (that is, "time"). If two professions are highly convergent, they will exhibit an isomorphism with properties approximating those of the theoretical end point of the convergence process—that is, professional membership will not differentiate behavior. If law and politics are isomorphs, *and* if this isomorphism approximates the end point of the theoretical convergence process, then it may be expected that lawyers will not differ in their political behavior from other politicians. And this seems to be true.

It is well to keep in mind that convergence may not lead to similarity in all respects. There remain matters, for instance, in which the functions of lawyer as lawyer and of politician as politician do not converge, and in which corresponding roles in fact diverge. This seems to be the case with roles that require specialized expertise and skill in parliamentary leadership. The lawyer who becomes active as a politician, regardless of whether his primary commitment is to law or to politics, still remains a lawyer, so that, when his legislative activity involves specialized problems directly relevant to his private occupation, especially legal or constitutional matters, he differs from the nonlawyer in the roles he takes. He is more likely to name fewer areas of "expertise," and, among those he names, "law" predominates. Moreover, in giving reasons for his expertise, in law or in other fields, the lawyer is more likely than the nonlawyer to refer to his private-professional background and experience. Similarly, as an expert in parliamentary law and procedure, the lawyer as lawyer seems to have an advantage over the nonlawyer-politician in that he is more "available" for roles of legislative leadership. In these two empirical aspects, then, the professions of law and politics seem to be more divergent than convergent, for the moment at least.

One final point must be emphasized before we attempt to suggest some content for the convenient assumptions that have so far been made. The properties and relationships between properties that remain to be specified are properties of the professions as aggregates, independent of the characteristics of any particular individual member of the profession. In other words, any particular person may not in fact participate in the relationships that are asserted to be typical of his profession. For example, it will be suggested that an ethics of service is characteristic of both law and politics as professions. But this does not imply that any particular lawyer or politician accepts such an ethics as his own. Overall, of course, the assertions must be true for a preponderance of those members of the professions that are included in any empirical study.

Conditions of Convergence

In turning to the problem of specifying those properties and relationships that have undergone the process of convergence and now constitute for law and politics elements of a structural isomorphism between the two professions, we shall initially suggest two conditions for convergence in this particular case. First, both law and politics as professions tend to be integrated into the structure of political authority; and, second, both exhibit similar tendencies, within their distinct areas of authority and competence, to perform functions either political in nature or depending on the governmental and political system. These conditions of the political system tend to make for the convergence of the two professions by facilitating the lawyer's adaptability to the political sphere and also the politician's preference for law as a private occupation.

That the politician is integrated into the structure of the political system may seem self-evident today, but it is well to recall that he has not always been an "insider." His integration has been a relatively slow, secular process. This is not the place to recapitulate the growth of representative institutions in the West, but the broad outline may be suggested. The medieval "representative," whether he was found in the English Parliament, the Spanish Cortez, or any other "representative" body, was not regarded as an official of the government. He stood in well-defined relations of more or less dependence to political authority, but he was not himself a direct participant in that authority. His integration into the political system was not direct but was mediated by his membership in the subsidiary estates or corporations whose representative he was vis-à-vis political authority. Only in the course of centuries, as representative assemblies gradually replaced the Crown and its bureaucracy as effective centers of power did the politician become directly responsible for public policy making— that is, integrated into the structure of political authority. But no more need be said about this here, since the integration of the elective public official in the structure of political authority is well beyond doubt in democratic societies.

The lawyer's relation to political authority is somewhat more complex. As Talcott Parsons (1954, p. 374) has pointed out, the legal profession "is in a curiously ambiguous position of dependence and independence with reference to the state. The laws for which it is responsible are official enactments of the state . . . The member of the bar is formally an 'officer of the court,' and for example, disbarment is an act of the political authority." At the same time, Parsons continues, "and at least equally important, the profession is independent of political authority. Even judges, though public officials, are treated as in a special class with special immunities."

The lawyer's ascendancy in politics coincided, in the eighteenth century and again in the nineteenth, with periods of commercial and economic growth—that is, periods of increasing division of labor. While, as a result of this division, both lawyers and politicians came to assume specialized roles, they are in a particularly favorable position to serve as the "go-betweens" of polity and society. Each in his own way, lawyer and politician respond to the requirements of increasing complexity in the social order generally by further developing their specialized roles. And this fosters their increasing integration into the structure of political authority.

Where social organization is relatively simple and collective decision making can be handled without particular skills in mediation, arbitration, negotiation, bargaining, compromising, coordinating, and so on, lawyers and politicians function within a restricted sphere. But, as relations are established between large corporations, trade associations, labor unions, and other collectivities as influential centers of power; as the growth of administrative regulatory agencies with wide discretionary powers makes for inclusion of once-private matters in the public sector; and as the range of legislative concerns gives rise to a vast proliferation of laws politicizing and legalizing once-private relationships, the distinction between private and public aspects of social and political life becomes increasingly ambiguous and, in many cases, altogether irrelevant. As a result, not only do the professions of law and politics converge as their members acquire similar skills, but both professions are increasingly integrated into the political system—in different ways, to be sure, but in sufficiently similar fashion to foster professional convergence. Professional convergence in this sense means that, as the two professions become more integrated into the political system, their members find opportunities that facilitate the actual interchange of institutional positions, careers, and professional roles more than is the case with other occupations.

The integration of the professions of law and politics in the structure of political authority provides a general criterion that permits speaking of a particular structural isomorphism. In order to identify the isomorphism, the sought-for characteristics must relate the work of the lawyer and the politician to the integration of these professions in the structure of political authority.

Law and Politics as Professions

That law is a "profession" in whatever way one wishes to define a profession does not require explicit demonstration. But what of politics as a vocation? Is it not too much to assume that even those who devote all their time to politics are "professionals" in the same sense as that in which lawyers, doctors, or engineers are professionals? The answer is probably that, in empirical reality, it may indeed be too much to assume that politics is a profession like those of law, medicine, or engineering. And politicians are not "professional" in the sense in which the term is conventionally used.

But the interest of this study, it must be reemphasized, is theoretical, not empirical. Isomorphic analysis does not require that two phenomena have all properties in common, although they obviously must have enough in common to permit comparison. Moreover, as isomorphic theorizing seeks to extend the range of empirical observation, it may be fruitful to look at both law and politics from the standpoint of the sociology of professions. It need not be assumed that politics is *in fact* a full-fledged profession in order to deal with it from this standpoint. Indeed, this perspective may suggest the "professional potential" of politics as a vocation and, as a result, serve as a yardstick in prognosticating about the future of politics as a vocation. Such prognostication is not the objective here, though a "developmental construct" of politics as a profession may be useful in appraising current manifestations of what may be a long-range trend.

In dealing with both law and politics in the perspective of the sociology of professions, it is not necessary to introduce all the criteria that might be mustered in defining "profession," but only those which are particularly relevant in explicating the professional convergence of law and politics. Three criteria, then, will be used to assess the professional status of each field—the presumed "independence" of the professional worker in contrast to other occupational types; the more or less explicit articulation of a set of norms that are designed to guide the professional's conduct; and the professional's alleged orientation to "service" rather than to private gain.

PROFESSIONAL INDEPENDENCE

Perhaps more than by anything else, professions are set off from other occupations by the requirement that they be relatively independent of control by laymen who, by definition, do not have the requisite training and skills to judge the work of professionals. Lawyers have, of course, always taken great pride in their independence. The lawyer's independence is assumed to be a necessary condition of his effective performance of the functions that he is called upon to undertake, vis-à-vis both his clients and the institutional structure in which he has, at least traditionally, performed his work—the system of courts. Not the least important criticism periodically made of the legal profession is that it fails to live up to this criterion. As the historian Richard Hofstadter (1955, p. 158) has reported, in the opening decade of the present century, "with the rise of corporate industrialism and finance capitalism, the law, particularly in the urban centers where the most enviable prices were to be had, was becoming a captive profession." The charge of the legal profession's captivity by business and financial interests is still common and often appears in a highly vulgar and biased form (see, for instance, Mills, 1951, pp. 121–129). Such conspiratorial approaches ignore altogether the fact that the lawyer has also become, to use the invidious term, the "captive" of labor unions (Wilensky, 1956) and the government bureaucracy (Blaustein and Porter, 1954, pp. 58–63). Undoubtedly, the meaning of "independence" has changed; but if the lawyer has become an "organization man," it is all the more important to study rather than condemn the profession's relationship to the organizations in which he performs his functions. As Talcott Parsons (1960, p. 219) has pointed out in a comment on the approach of the late sociologist C. Wright Mills, especially with regard to the *control* processes in the business world:

Mills tends to assume that the relation between law and business is an overwhelming one-way relation; lawyers are there to serve the interests of businessmen and essentially have no independent influence. This, I think, is an illusion stemming largely from Mills' preoccupation with a certain kind of power. His implicit reasoning seems to be that since lawyers have less power than businessmen, they do not really count.

Before the legal profession is indicted *in toto,* it is necessary to be more specific about the number of lawyers who may be "captive" and those who presumably are not. In 1958 there were 262,320 lawyers listed in the Martindale-Hubbell census. They were distributed into various categories, as follows:

Private practice	73.0%
Government service	9.0
Salaried in private industry	7.0
Judiciary	3.0
Law school	0.4
Other	7.6
Total	100.0%

These figures do not discriminate between types of private practice. But of the 176,680 practicing lawyers reported on in the Survey of the Legal Profession in the early fifties, almost 68 percent were individual practitioners having neither partners nor associates; 27 percent were partners in law firms; and 5 percent were associates in law firms (Blaustein and Porter, 1954, p. 8).

Clearly it is hazardous to generalize to the legal profession as a whole, especially in a study of lawyers in politics. Nevertheless, in view of the fact that most lawyer-legislators are private practitioners, it can be assumed that they are reasonably independent.

But does the politician meet the standard of independence in such a way that one can meaningfully speak of politics as a profession? The question is admittedly complex, and an answer must necessarily be conditional. In one respect—the institutional—the politician cannot be considered "independent" at all. As an elected public official, he is dependent on the electorate, just as the lawyer is dependent on clients who may or may not come to his office. Of course, some elective officials have, under certain conditions, achieved a great deal of independence from their constituents—partly by virtue of lack of competition for the office they occupy, or partly because their personal stature makes their reelection almost automatic. But this kind of independence is seen more appropriately as an attribute of particular individuals than as an attribute of the political profession.

Yet, as the perennial controversy over the "nature" of representation shows, the politician's status vis-à-vis his nominal "superiors" has always been ambiguous. Should his representative role be that of a "free agent" unbound by a mandate, or that of a "delegate" who must follow instructions from his various clienteles (see Eulau et al., 1959)? Once the distinction between institutional status and political role is made, the politician, though clearly dependent on the electorate for his status as an officeholder, may yet be independent in his relations with his clients. In other words, the politician's client relationship is very much like that of the lawyer, who is "retained" by his client—that is, dependent on the client for employment, yet independent in regard to the roles he may take in the relationship.

Empirical evidence in recent studies about legislator-client relations indicates that the politician's representational style is structurally isomorphic with the lawyer's style. The reasons for this are many, but two may be mentioned. First, unable to give instructions in an ever more complex society, the political client must increasingly depend on the representative for correct decisions on the basis of his own appraisal of the problem at hand. Reciprocally, representatives find it increasingly difficult to consult their clients because electoral districts have grown in size and heterogeneity of population. Under these conditions, the politician tends to become increasingly independent in his client relations. In this sense, then, the politician can meet or approximate the independence criterion set for the professional. And the trend toward increasing independence in politician–client role relations is likely to be accentuated in the future, contributing to the professionalization of politics as a vocation.

PROFESSIONAL ETHICS

Its independence from direct supervision by laymen as well as by political authority places a profession in a position where the improper use of its special skills and competences could easily do enormous social harm. In particular, the exploitation and manipulation of clients for personal gain or advantage would not seem out of the question. In order to protect both the profession's clients and its own reputation and prestige, and to safeguard the profession's position of trust in the community, most professions have developed more or less explicit codes of ethics or appropriate etiquette directed toward the self-regulation of relations with peers, clients, and society in general. The specific norms of conduct of a profession are, therefore, a second criterion by which its "professionalism" can be appraised. Responsible professional behavior can be judged in terms of the professional's adherence to the code of professional ethics.

The distinctive aspect of professional ethics is not the fact that it provides standards of proper conduct; it is the formalization of these standards in the code itself. In general, most codes of professional ethics are not unique but represent the application of generally accepted ethical rules of behavior to the particular spheres of the profession's competence. The lawyer, for instance, is seen as subject to very specific duties to his clients, the public, his professional colleagues, and himself. As a result of such multiple commitments, lawyers may at times experience serious conflicts concerning appropriate conduct. Should the lawyer lie for his client? Should he defend an accused person if he is convinced of the person's guilt? What is and what is not "conflict of interest"? How can the lawyer make himself known without advertising his business? There is disagreement within the legal profession concerning these and other questions of proper professional conduct. But the fact that the matter is discussed, time and again, is enough proof of the profession's sensitivity to the importance of its code of ethics as a safeguard of its professional status.

The politician's status as a professional from this perspective again presents a more difficult problem. For a long time it was assumed that politics was guided by a peculiar code, however informal, that freed the politician from conformity with ordinary ethical standards. But there cannot be permanent conflict between politics and ethics, because a code of professional political ethics, if such were to be written, could not avoid incorporating and applying the principles that belong to social ethics generally. An ethics that did not meet generally accepted standards of behavior would make politics a deviant profession, indeed—a situation that is most unlikely.

Although the condition may derive from public ignorance and from a traditional lack of respect for authority, politics remains a "dirty word" in the United States (Klain, 1955). The history of American politics, if it were to be a very partial history, could be written as the history of corruption. As Hyman and Sheatsley (1951, p. 22) have noted in commenting on the public opinion polls concerning politics as a vocation, many people

took the stand that it was "almost impossible" for a man to go into politics without becoming dishonest. This same reason, incidentally, was advanced by about half of the group who would not like to see their sons enter politics: public service is essentially dishonest and corrupting. Many among those who would favor a political career for their sons explain their attitude by saying that politics is corrupt now and honest men are needed to reform it. Yet, when asked whether or not they are satisfied with the way most office holders in their state are handling their jobs, about half the population indicate satisfaction.

The status of the politician is ambivalent.[1] As William C. Mitchell (1959, p. 696) has pointed out in a perceptive attempt at explanation, the fact that

Americans have tended to regard political offices as not requiring any special training and the fact that political office has been so accessible to the poor and formally uneducated has in turn attracted persons whose performances in office have not always been very exemplary. Thus, a vicious circle developed in which offices with low status attracted less desirable office-holders and their inadequate or corrupt actions further confirmed the low status of public office.

The condition described here is probably no longer valid; and insofar as it was valid, it was so largely on the "lower" levels of politics and mainly in the great urban centers. It does, however, help in explaining the traditional view as it seems to have been historically determined. The fact that there is no code of ethics for politicians would seem to confirm popular apprehensions.

This is not to deny that the development of a voluntary code of ethics for politicians presents difficulties that may be *sui generis*. What is and what is not permissible conduct in politics is likely to be more ambiguous than in other areas of social life precisely because politics, by definition, operates in a twilight zone of behavior where disagreement over acts of omission and commission makes the problem of sanctions in the case of breakage of norms particularly subtle (see Jones, 1962), and where the relationship between means and ends is always a matter of continuing formulation rather than of definitive settlement. But efforts to establish codes of ethics for both the executive and legislative branches of government, often including prohibitions that already have legal sanction, suggest that politics is not immune to this aspect of professionalization (see Leys, 1962).

Perhaps more telling than these formal attempts to bring norms of professional ethical conduct to politics is the discovery that there exist, in fact, numerous informal rules of behavior—often called "rules of the game" and sometimes "folkways"—that are more or less specific concerning what is and what is not proper political behavior. Particularly in legislative bodies, as recent research shows, there can be found many unwritten and even unspoken norms whose influence on conduct must not be underestimated. Moreover, all indications are that these "rules of the game" are viewed as being of great functional value to political success (see Matthews, 1960, pp. 92–117; Wahlke et al., 1962, pp. 141–169). Just why these rules of the political game have not as yet been formalized in a code is an interesting question. It is well to point out, therefore, that, except in the case of a few professions, professional codes of ethics do not antedate 1900, and the great majority of them have been adopted since 1918.[2] It would seem that, even though a professional ethics of politics is underdeveloped, there is enough consensus among the politicians as to what is proper conduct in office to suggest that, from this point of view, politics may partake of more professionalism than is often assumed.

PROFESSIONAL SERVICE

Closely linked to the standard of independence in a profession's definition, and often explicitly incorporated in its code of ethics, is the criterion of public service. In their own judgment as well as in the estimation of the public, the members of a profession are expected to devote themselves to their occupation as a public responsibility that stems from their monopoly of skills that are highly valued because they are so rare. Possession of these skills and ability to render requisite services is considered a public trust; and—contrary to the general view in the case of ordinary occupations—pecuniary acquisition is not looked upon as a professional's legitimate goal.

In spite of deviations from this ideal, a sense of public responsibility has characterized the moral and intellectual tradition of the legal profession. In the Anglo-American context, this tradition can be traced back to the barristers in the Inns of Court in London during the twelfth and thirteenth centuries. Sons of well-to-do parents, these legal ancestors of the modern lawyer, according to Henry S. Drinker (1955, p. 37),

did not have to worry about earning their keep and [they] traditionally looked down on all forms of trade and on the competitive spirit characteristic thereof. They regarded the law in the same way that they did a seat in Parliament—as a form of public service in which the gaining of a livelihood was not an objective. The profession of law hence acquired a certain dignity which it has been the aim of the bar to preserve ever since.

In fact, of course, the ideal is at times violated, and much of the criticism of the lawyer has been directed at his failure to live up to the ideal of service. "His constant need to propagandize himself and his client," writes Otto Kirchheimer (1961, p. 242), "his putting his talents out for hire to an everchanging clientele, and the aleatory character of his success have brought him along with admiration much criticism and contempt." Nevertheless, the conception that he is not only his client's agent but also an "officer of the court"—a public servant—remains an explicit criterion of the lawyer's professional status. Speaking of the legal profession in particular, Talcott Parsons (1954, p. 381) writes:

Its members are trained in and integrated with, a distinctive part of our cultural tradition, having a fiduciary responsibility for its maintenance, development and implementation. They are expected to provide a "service" to the public within limits without regard to immediate self-interest. The lawyer has a position of independent responsibility so that he is neither a servant only of the client though he represents his interest, nor of *any* other group, in the lawyer's case, of public authority.

It is probably accurate to say that the lawyer's participation in public affairs is so widely expected because, *as a lawyer,* he is expected, more than any other professional, to devote himself to public service.

The politician is, of course, a public servant by definition. Although his motives are often distrusted, the politician, as Max Weber (1946, p. 84) suggested, in addition to enjoying the possession of power, is conscious that "his life has meaning in the service of a cause." Whatever his private motives, service is, so to speak, "built in" the role of the politician. His often self-declared devotion to "public service" may be a stereotypic conception of his role, but his very survival as a politician is predicated on his fulfillment of the expectations of a public that sees him as a public servant. What are sometimes called his "errand-boy" functions may not rank high in his own estimation, and he may view them as a nuisance that interferes with his more lofty functions as a decision maker. But, insofar as successful performance of these service functions contributes to his survival as an elected public official, they have come to be regarded as the mark of the political "professional" perhaps more than any other aspect of the politician's complex role.

The politician's orientation to public service would not seem to implicate him as much in professional conduct as the professional with a "private" occupation: the politician's performance of service does not seem to be entirely voluntary. Rather, it would seem to be in response to sanctions that can be expected to be enforced in case of lack of service. In other words, public service in the politician's case does not seem to be a corollary of a professional role but rather a corollary of the institutional position that he happens to occupy. The distinction is more sharp in its abstract conceptualization than it probably is in reality. The lawyer, in serving his client, also serves the public precisely because he does not embrace his client's cause. In this sense, then, the lawyer's public service is as inadvertent as that of the politician, a corollary of his "office" rather than of his professional role. In the politician's case, the order may well be revised: as a public servant he may come to represent, over the long haul or the short, certain special interests whose agent he is in the public arena. But such agency does not seem to detract from the politician's public responsibility unless it leads to forms of conduct that are not tolerable—bribery, corruption, nepotism, and so on—and that are punished by criminal rather than political sanctions.

Convergence and the Future of Law and Politics as Professions

This study has identified three convergent characteristics in law and politics that help to define the structural isomorphism of the two professions—professional independence, a code of ethics, and a norm of public service. Convergence in regard to these properties of the two professions seems to be made possible by their integration in the structure of political authority. This integration of the two professions in the structure of authority must not be confused with their affinity, which refers to the fact that lawyers become politicians or politicians choose law as a vocation. As suggested earlier, two phenomena need not come into physical contact with each other or "interact" in empirical reality in order to be considered convergent. It is sufficient that they have the same, or highly similar, forms. Affinity, on the other hand, refers to the empirically demonstrated or demonstrable fact of a close relationship between two phenomena, such as the affinity of law and politics as vocations. Convergence is the conceptual tool through which the affinity of law and politics may be explained. It may be said that lawyers tend to become politicians more than members of other occupations do, or that politicians tend to choose law rather than another career, *because* law and politics are convergent professions.

The notion of professional convergence makes it possible to explain, then, why studies of lawyers in politics fail to discover significant differences between lawyer- and nonlawyer-politicians in many of the roles that both must take in the public arena. Moreover, even in regard to roles that still differentiate lawyers from others, such as expert and leader roles, it is probable that the professional convergence of law and politics will, in due time, obliterate present differences. The reason for this is quite simple. As occupational groups with private skills and roles similar to those of the lawyer come to be more widely represented in politics—"new" occupations such as real estate, insurance, public relations, union management, and so on—their members will vie successfully with those of the legal profession in filling roles or posts traditionally monopolized by lawyers. For, just as these "new" occupations have come to take on functions in the private sphere long considered the lawyer's specialties, such as preparing deeds or mortgage papers, or dealing with problems arising out of conditional sales or accidents, they are likely to be available for the performance of functions in the public sphere in fields where, until now, the lawyer's skills as a lawyer—such as expertise in legislative investigation, bill drafting, or parliamentary procedure—gave him an advantage.

Convergence, then, has another result as well: the more law and politics converge as professions, the less distinct will be the particular kind of contribution that the lawyer-politician is likely to make to politics as a lawyer. Whether this development will have the effect of displacing the lawyer as the most ubiquitous private-occupational type and of reducing his prominence in positions of leadership is an empirical question that cannot be answered at this time. But one might suggest as a very general hypothesis that the more politics becomes professionalized, the greater is the probability of further convergence. For if the two professions are initially convergent, greater professionalism in politics should mean that the two professions will become more similar structurally—that is, that the political behavior of lawyers and politicians will tend to be identical. If this is so, it would be expected that the affinity of law and politics as vocations would also be accentuated.

8

Polarity in Representational

Federalism

AFTER ALMOST 200 years of experimentation, America's "experiment in federalism" remains experimental. This is surely the conclusion one must reach on viewing the great variety of patterns in federal-state-local relations that in the past decade accompanied the expansion of governmental activity into new fields of public policy. American federalism has involved an ever-changing series of innovations in governmental structures and functions, some successful and some unsuccessful. Success and failure alike have brought forth, from the beginning of the republic, a great many hypotheses to explain the American experiment in federalism. Indeed, because American federalism has been and continues to be multifaceted, it can accommodate many alternative propositions and interpretations.

Whatever the truth or falsity of the hypotheses about the historically specific case of American federalism, it was and still is *the solution of a fundamentally theoretical problem* that distinguishes the American experiment from earlier and later attempts in federalistic organization elsewhere. To what extent the Founding Fathers were aware of having solved, in the Constitution of 1787, not only a practical problem but also a theoretical problem, is difficult to say. But had they not solved the theoretical problem as they were solving the practical problem, the American experiment in federalism might not have proceeded as it did.

The great innovation in political theory implicit in the American Constitution consisted in the theoretical fusion of two basic principles of governmental engineering—the principle of federation and the principle of representation. The two principles were known, though only crudely articulated, as separate principles before being joined in the Constitution. It had been the previous failure of political theory to weld the two principles into a single model of governance that had proved to be of disastrous consequence in earlier federalistic experiments. Any federal arrangement likely to have long-term survival prospects is predicated on representation as a necessary condition. A federated order unable to accommodate in its structure the representation of its constituent parts, whether collectivities or individuals, is *ab origine* doomed to fall apart. This is not to say that representation is the only condition of federal engineering. It is to say that federation without representation is theoretically unthinkable. At issue is, of course, what should be represented and how it should be represented.

My inclination is to believe, by inference from *The Federalist,* that at least its authors were well aware of the theoretical solution of the relationship between federalism and representation implicit in the Constitution of 1787. Not that all of what its authors asserted in this connection was historically correct and theoretically sound. But it is curious that so learned a commentator as Max Beloff altogether missed the theoretical significance of just those papers in *The Federalist* that explicated the great breakthrough in political theory made in this respect in the Constitution. I am referring to papers Numbers 52 to 67, and especially those concerning the House of Representatives. These papers, Beloff (1948, p. xlxxx) wrote in his introduction, "are of interest to the student of the American constitution as revealing the original prognostications of its likely development, *rather than to the student of political theory.*"[1] Rarely, I think, has a commentator so missed the theoretical boat.

A common flaw of most political theory is its post facto nature and low predictive capability. Both representation and federalism as theories emerged only *after* the political phenomena to which they refer had already been institutionalized and, in some cases, declined. What usually stands in the way of recognition, if not prediction, of new political structures is some powerful paradigm, like the Aristotelian conception of the *polis,* or at least a fashionable theoretical perspective. But occasionally constitution-builders can draw on novel ideas that, whatever their existential roots, prove serviceable beyond the moment of their use, especially if they are adaptable to prevailing conditions and practical necessities. The makers of the American federal constitution drew on the contractual and mechanistic metaphors of Hobbes, Locke, Harrington, and Montesquieu, but in their hands—or better, in the bargaining situation in which they worked—these metaphors were translated into viable formulas of governmental engineering. They were, indeed, self-fulfilling prophecies that give *The Federalist,* for instance, an aura of some predictive power. Not that all of its predictions were fulfilled; but enough were to make it, in retrospect, more than a tract for the times. The passage of almost 200 years and altogether unanticipated developments notwithstanding, *The Federalist* as a treatise of political theory remains an amazingly suggestive work.

This is particularly true of its deft and subtle meshing of the principles of federation and representation. While other aspects of theory found in *The Federalist* have been justly celebrated, it is sometimes overlooked that it was the linkage of federalism and representation that in Madison's view constitutes "a republican remedy for the diseases most incident to republican government" (No. 10, p. 48). Much has been made, and probably rightly so, of the great compromise by which the small states were given equal representation in the Senate in exchange for the power of the House to initiate money bills. The compromise avoided what otherwise might have become an insurmountable deadlock in the Philadelphia convention. But, in retrospect, the role of the Senate in the federal-representational scheme of things is less significant than the role of the House of Representatives. Despite the guaranteed equality of the states in the Senate, the "upper house" became a much more nationalized and nationalizing institution than the House. It is in the House that federalism and representation meet.

The vice of sacred documents like the Constitution or of commentaries like *The Federalist* is their ambiguity, which so readily permits revisionist interpretations. But if one assumes that history as an approach to human affairs is inherently revisionist because history as a subject of study is always liable to be reinterpreted, the vice of ambiguity becomes a virtue. It forces the revisionist to clarify assumptions, even though such clarification runs the double risk either of being historically false or of not even being an accurate reflection of current reality. It is idle to speculate, therefore, whether *The Federalist* articulated the doctrine of "dual federalism" read into the Constitution for 150 years or so after its adoption. As Daniel J. Elazar (1962) has shown, that doctrine was not an accurate description of the working of American federalism even in the middle of the nineteenth century because the federal and state governments were already working jointly in fields like banking, railroad construction, and internal improvements.

Any reading of *The Federalist* today is, therefore, necessarily influenced by current conceptions of the evolving structure of national-state-local arrangements. Morton Grodzins (1966) and Elazar (1966) made a persuasive case for viewing the emergent structures of American federalism in terms of such theoretical concepts as partnership, sharing, and cooperation. If their diagnoses and prognoses did not yield a full-fledged contemporary theory of federalism, by which is meant an internally consistent theory that joins the representational and federational principles, it is probably all to the good. For even as they were writing, American federal arrangements were undergoing fast and vast changes in the name of a "creative federalism" whose implications and consequences for the American commonwealth are yet to be theoretically understood.

If anything, the "little chaos" that Grodzins and Elazar found to make for the responsiveness of American federalism had become even more chaotic in the late sixties, raising the question whether the multiplicity of arrangements among federal departments, state agencies, local authorities, and even nongovernmental organizations did not require drastic steps in coordination in order to overcome administrative confusion, bureaucratic jealousies, and jurisdictional conflicts. It is interesting that the emphasis of those seeking an answer is almost exclusively on the administrative aspects of the problem and seems to neglect the issue of representation, which is so intrinsically tied up with the problems of federalism.

James L. Sundquist (1969, p. 31), for instance, enjoins us to view American federal arrangements as a "single system." What recommends the system notion is that it would alert policy makers or administrators to otherwise unanticipated and presumably dysfunctional consequences for some parts of the system as a result of changes in other parts. The system of American federalism, Sundquist admits, "is so complex that it can be altered only piecemeal. Yet the piecemeal changes should be guided by some model . . . The federal system is an intricate web of institutional relationships among levels of government, jurisdictions, agencies, and programs—relationships that comprise a single system, whether or not it is designed as one." It is not useful to dwell on the appropriateness or inappropriateness of the system metaphor, even if the administrative reforms recommended by Sundquist were to make for a system rather than for what he calls a "jumble." For, one suspects, even if the American federal system were guided "according to a consistent set of principles and governing doctrine" (1969, p. 278), it would probably remain multicentered, loose, fluid, or porous—in other words, a system that is not very systemic.

However, this is not the critical point. The point is that the administrative view of federalism ignores the multiple legislative-representational components of American federalism from the houses of Congress down through the state houses to city councils, school boards, and other legislative bodies. Sundquist (1969, p. 278) gives the federal game away, so to speak, when he concludes that the guidance of the federal system "can come from but a single source of authority—the President. It is he who must apply the principles and the doctrine in proposing legislation to the Congress and in directing the execution of the laws." This is clearly a counsel for the demise of federalism in the name of federalism; and perhaps it would be more candid to argue, as Harold J. Laski (1939) did some decades ago, that federalism in America is obsolete.

Before reaching this dismal conclusion, however, it may be desirable to take another theoretical look at federalism as a *political* process. One cannot ignore the political parties that serve as decentralizing institutions, or the universe of pluralistic interests that seek access to government, or the host of constituencies represented in the House of Representatives. I shall not deal here with the role of the parties, so well treated by Grodzins, and the role of cultural and social interests whose importance in the federal scheme of things Elazar has emphasized. Rather, I want to return to *The Federalist*'s treatment of the House of Representatives and the role assigned to it in the federal system.

The Federalist Revisited

The purpose of the exercise is neither conceptual exegesis for its own sake nor some kind of patriotic semanticism. While exegesis is a necessary prerequisite of theory *development,* it all too often degenerates into exegetical competition among commentators as to what some text "really means." This is not the purpose here. And while semantic clarity is important, to call what one likes in politics "federal" or, for that matter, "democratic" serves no good purpose. What makes it difficult to construct the drift of the theoretical argument concerning the relationship between federalism and representation in *The Federalist,* however, is the fact that these papers were written in response to objections to the Constitution. Yet it would be too tedious to review all the objections and answers because they are not germane to the objective. One must therefore be selective.

Four themes concerning the relationship between federation and representation can be derived from *The Federalist* in connection with its discussion of the House of Representatives. I shall briefly and separately outline these themes and then comment on the model that seems to be implicit in them. This procedure omits discussions in *The Federalist* that deal with representation or federation as separate topics.

First, it is unmistakably clear that the House of Representatives is in no way to be dependent on the state governments, but rather on the people in the states, although the states can maximize the representation of their interests in the House by making full use of the number of representatives in the House. The definition of the right of suffrage was written into the Constitution and not left to state discretion because "it would have rendered too dependent on the state governments that branch of the federal government, which ought to be dependent on the people alone" (No. 52, p. 269). Subsequently referring to the constitutional article which provides that "the Congress may at any time by law make or alter such regulations" for elections, a task generally assigned to the state legislatures, *The Federalist* defends the propriety of the provision on the ground that "every government ought to contain in itself the means of its own preservation"

(No. 59, p. 302). If the state legislatures had exclusive power of regulating elections, "every period of making them would be a delicate crisis in the national situation" (ibid., p. 305).

Dependence on the people is, of course, the corollary of the independence of the House from the state legislatures. The House, it is pointed out in connection with a defense of biennial elections, "should have an immediate dependence on, and an intimate sympathy with the people. Frequent elections are unquestionably the only policy by which this dependence and sympathy can be effectually secured" (No. 52, pp. 269–270). Moreover, the people not only elect but also evict their representatives. The House is so constituted "as to support in the members an habitual recollection of their dependence on the people" (No. 57, p. 293).[2]

But this apparently sharp distinction between the House's dependence on the state legislatures and the people is qualified. Elsewhere *The Federalist* suggests that despite the constitutional division, the states will (should?) have an interest in what goes on in the House. Pointing to a "peculiarity in the federal constitution" that in the House "the larger states will have most weight," while in the Senate "the advantage will be in favor of the smaller states," *The Federalist* continues: "From this circumstance it may *with certainty* be *inferred* that the larger states will be strenuous advocates for increasing the number and weight of that part of the legislature, in which their influence predominates" (No. 58, p. 298; emphasis added). It is inferred further that, formal equality of authority between the two houses notwithstanding (except for originating money bills in the House), "it cannot be doubted that the house composed of the greater number, when supported by the more powerful states, and speaking the known and determined sense of a majority of the people, will have no small advantage in a question depending on the comparative firmness of the two houses" (ibid., pp. 298–299).

What is of interest in these passages is not only the manifest inferences made, but also the unspoken premise that, through their popularly elected delegations, the states have a presence in the House as they do in the Senate—in other words, that legislative representation at the national level cuts across the formal division of powers. The House, being rooted in the people, serves as a kind of hyphen between the federal and representational principles of the Constitution. *The Federalist* evidently did not fully accept the notion of "dual federalism" that the general government and the states are "separate and distinct sovereignties, acting separately and independently of each other, within their respective spheres."[3] Rather, especially the larger states are expected to have a very real interest in and influence on the conduct of the House of Representatives, and through the House on national affairs.

A second theme deals with the social composition of the electorate and the consequences of this composition on the federal quality of representation in the House. To refute the objection that the House may consist of representatives "taken from that class of citizens which will have the least sympathy with the mass of the people," *The Federalist* rejects the anticipated evil as ill conceived because "the elective mode of obtaining rulers is the characteristic policy of republican government." The inference evidently to be made is that the House will be a true mirror of the electorate. Who, it is asked, "are to be the electors of the federal representatives?" The answer is one of the classic passages in *The Federalist:*

Not the rich, more than the poor; not the learned, more than the ignorant; not the haughty heirs of distinguished names, more than the humble sons of obscure and unpropitious fortune. The electors are to be the great body of the people of the United States. They are to be the same, who exercise the right in every state of electing the correspondent branch of the legislature of the state. (No. 57, p. 292)

Because the same people vote for "correspondent" branches, another paper continues, "no rational calculation of probabilities would lead us to imagine" that the union would use its power to regulate elections "to promote the election of some favorite class of men in exclusion of others." That it would happen "is altogether inconceivable and incredible." But were it to happen, "it could never be made without causing an immediate revolt of the great body of the people, headed and directed by the state governments." And there is another reason why it will not happen—the pluralistic nature of the union:

There is sufficient diversity in the state of property, in the genius, manners, and habits of the people of the different parts of the union, to occasion a material diversity of disposition in their representatives towards the different ranks and conditions in society. (No. 60, p. 307)

In other words, federalism is promoted by the representational mix that stems from the diversity of the people who elect the members of the House. There is the expectation that "an intimate intercourse under the same government will promote a gradual assimilation of temper and sentiment," but this tendency of federation will not destroy the pattern of diversity in representation. *The Federalist* envisages the interpenetration of polar tendencies—the federal tendency toward "assimilation of temper and sentiment," and the representational tendency toward "material diversity of disposition."

The third theme centers in the consequences for representation of the size of the House, notably that a small number of representatives "will be an unsafe depository of the public interests," and that "they will not possess a proper knowledge of the local circumstances of their numerous constituents" (No. 55, p. 283). The first objection is set aside on the ground that "nothing can be more fallacious than to found our political calculations on arithmetical principles" (a somewhat hypocritical argument given all the other arithmetic in many of the papers). But *The Federalist* is more candid; the familiar fear of "the confusion and intemperance of a multitude" is enough reason to keep the House relatively small: "Had every Athenian citizen been a Socrates; every Athenian assembly would still have been a mob" (ibid., p. 284).

The second objection to a small House is dealt with more seriously. *The Federalist* admits that "it is a sound and important principle that the representative ought to be acquainted with the interests and circumstances of his constituents." But it is emphasized that "this principle can extend no farther than to those circumstances and interests to which the authority and care of the representative relate" (No. 56, p. 288). This restriction seems to involve the definition of "dual federalism" as a limit on the role of the federal representative. But, weaving into consideration that in a *federal* legislature the representatives come from several states, *The Federalist* recognizes the severity of the knowledge problem in a compound polity. The federal representative, precisely because he is a *federal* official, cannot avoid being cognizant of what goes on in the states (and presumably the different constituencies) other than his own:

This information, so far as it may relate to local objects is rendered necessary and difficult, not by a difference of laws and local circumstances within a single state, but of those among different states . . . Whilst a few representatives, therefore, from each state, may bring with them a due knowledge of their own state, *every* representative will have much information to acquire concerning *all* the *other* states. (Ibid., p. 290; emphasis added)

The passage is prescriptive and recommends that the federal representative should have two foci of attention, not only his own state but also all other states in the aggregate. His role is multilateral. Again one notes the effort to combine federational and representational criteria in appraising the place of the House of Representatives in the Constitution.

The fourth and final theme occurs in a passage addressed to the problem of the potential abuse of power by the House. Some of the reasons given for why this should not occur are the familiar ones—the House's limited legislative authority, its dependence on the people, and the separation of powers within the national government. But to these is added another that is less known. The House is unlikely to abuse its power because it "will be moreover watched and controlled by the several collateral legislatures, which other legislative bodies are not" (No. 52, p. 272). The sentence is ambiguous and difficult to interpret, for an interpretation must turn on (1) the meaning of "control," (2) the meaning of "collateral," and (3) some implicit premise as to what "collateral legislatures" can do to each other.

One can rule out the conception of collateral as meaning "secondary" or "subordinate," for the House and the state assemblies are generally treated in *The Federalist* as parallel legislative bodies, each with its own sphere of competence. More suggestive is the notion that collateral means "belonging to the same ancestral stock but not in a direct line of descent." If, in this connection, this be the meaning of *The Federalist's* use of collateral, both the federal House and the state assemblies were thought to be of the same genus though of different species, and one may infer that what makes them belong to the same genus is their representational base in a *shared* electorate. The "control" of the federal House exercised by the "several collateral legislatures" is presumably not direct, for this would violate the federal principle; it is presumably indirect and made possible by the representational principle of collateral legislatures having a common electorate that controls the abuse of power by the representative bodies. It is the interpenetration of federal and representational structures envisaged by *The Federalist* that makes for a particular kind of control that "collateral legislatures" exercise less *over* each other than *on* each other. And this interpretation would be consonant with the general notion of balance and equilibrium that pervades *The Federalist*.

The Contribution of *The Federalist*

If one reads the relevant papers of *The Federalist* with care, what is impressive is their effort to integrate both federal and representational principles into a single model of republican governance. It is not that first the federal aspects of representation and then the representational aspects of federation are treated. Although the emphasis necessarily shifts from one to the other and back again, for it is impossible to speak about everything at once, the argument is clearly predicated on the meshing of the federal and representational principles in a polar rather than dualistic model of government. I shall come back to this later, but here I wish to assess more generally *The Federalist's* contribution to political theory.

What is throughout impressive is *The Federalist's* high level of theoretical self-consciousness in pursuing a variety of themes. Evidence of this self-consciousness is not just the persistent references to actual historical experiences with federation and representation from the ancients down to the American colonists, but the effort to exploit these experiences from a theoretical standpoint. If some of the inferences seem false or labored, it is less the logic of the argument than the fragility of the empirical base from which the inferences are drawn that must be faulted. But given the state of historical scholarship in the eighteenth century, *The Federalist* can hardly be censured on that account. What is of importance is that *The Federalist* was a theoretical treatise that, in suggesting and analyzing the interdependence of the federal and representational principles in the new Constitution, has remained a force of its own in shaping the course of the American experiment in federalism.

Without theoretical explication, political experience must be an unassimilated, almost random experience that cannot serve as a guide to the future. By being devoted to political theorizing, *The Federalist* made possible the transmission of the Founders' political experience and its serviceability in subsequent governmental engineering. It is the merit of theory that, by abstracting from practical experience, it distills what is significant and abandons what is not significant. It therefore makes for comprehension long after the particular and concrete conditions involved in an experience can no longer be readily apprehended, no matter how much insight or empathy may be brought to bear.

Although theory cannot altogether neglect the context of its emergence, the logic of a theory need not be dependent on the context. For instance, if one reads what Number 62 of *The Federalist* has to say about the makeup of the Senate as against what is said about the makeup of the House in the preceding papers, one is impressed by the practical arguments for the composition of the Senate, things in the real world of the American states at the time being what they were. By way of contrast, the arguments concerning the House of Representatives are eminently theoretical—more a matter of logic than, as in the case of the Senate, a matter of prudence. When, in due time, the Senate came to be elected by the vote of the people, it was possible to abandon the prudential stance, so necessary in 1787, and argue the case for the popular election of senators on the logical grounds advanced about the election of the House of Representatives. Without theory, the experience in constructing the House and its application to the Senate may have been lost.

To appreciate the importance of theory in political engineering, one may well compare the American experience with that of the Greeks on whom *The Federalist* drew so much of its own formulation of a "compound republic," as the creation of 1787 is occasionally called. It is pointed out that "the scheme of representation, as a substitute for a meeting of the citizens in person, [was] but imperfectly known to ancient polity," and there is an immediate turn to "more modern times" for "instructive examples" (No. 52, p. 270). *The Federalist* was essentially correct. Although recent scholarship has shown that the Greeks, and later the Romans, did in fact have representative institutions in the modern sense, their theoretical meaning was never understood. If anything, representation seems to have been designed to limit rather than extend citizen participation in government (see Eulau, 1967). This theoretical failure was one reason, though probably not the only one, why the various late Hellenic confederacies could not surmount the structural handicaps inherent in their large size that exceeded the size of the familiar polis. These confederacies did provide for representative assemblies based on population, but in the absence of a theory of representation they were unable to cope with the problem of making collective decisions (see Larsen, 1955). As Carl J. Friedrich (1946, p. 267) pointed out, "the attempts at solving this problem [that is, of governing a large unit] through a federal organization foundered upon the inability of the ancients to work out a representative scheme."

Representation again emerged in the Middle Ages for reasons that need not be spelled out here, except to say that it gave rise to a variety of theories that were known to the framers of the Constitution. Yet, although much of the discussion centered on the problem of the relationship between the whole and its parts, as well as on the problem of the relationship between representative and represented, medieval political theory could not conceive of governance in other than hierarchical terms, with the result that it failed to observe and elaborate the emerging federational character of the Holy Roman Empire. Just as the Greeks had been unable to construct a viable theory of representation that might have undergirded their experiments in federation, so the medieval writers were unable to construct a theory of federalism that might have served in solving the empire's structural problems. What stood in the way was, once more, the Aristotelian conception of the unitary state that, medieval feudalism and corporatism notwithstanding, provided the pervasive paradigm of medieval theory. Ironically, federalism as a working concept for understanding the structure of the empire did not emerge until the second half of the seventeenth century, when disintegration had gone so far as to make the empire little more than a mere shadow of its medieval organization (see Eulau, 1941).

Both the Greek failure to conceive a theory of representation and the medieval failure to conceive a theory of federation had not only practical consequences for contemporary and subsequent governmental engineering, but they pinpoint the achievement of the Founding Fathers in creating a constitutional framework that was built on a federational-representational symbiosis. The symbiosis that was achieved gives added significance to its theoretical statement in *The Federalist*. This does not mean that *The Federalist* fully understood the creation that it justified and defended, or that it accurately anticipated the course of the American experiment in popular self-government through representational federalism. But it suggests that *The Federalist* deserves our close attention as a masterpiece not only of constitutional wisdom but also of empirical theory construction.

The Polarity Principle in American Federalism

The image of the federal order that emerges from *The Federalist*'s four themes focused on representation in the House of Representatives is not one of a dual structure but of a polar structure. Nation and states are opposites that, like the poles of the magnetic field, are yet linked. What links the poles of the federal system is representation of the people—what *The Federalist* refers to as "proportional" representation (as against the "equal" representation of the states in the Senate) (No. 62, p. 316). This formulation was, of course, simplistic and did not anticipate the plural system of representation that has developed in the United States over the last 200 years, notably the emergence of political parties and interest groups as mediating agencies in addition to direct constituency linkages between representatives and represented. But the underlying model is not a structural dualism that presumes the existence of two *kinds* of entities whose interaction is made difficult by some immanent qualitative difference. Rather, the underlying model is one of structural continuity which presumes that poles of the federal structure are yet linked by the workings of a plural system of representation.

The polarity principle is a heuristic tool which assumes that in all determination of empirical reality there are opposing elements or categories. It differs, therefore, from a conception like "system," which also assumes that in the real world different things are more or less connected, but which cannot explain any particular thing. The notion of system can give direction to the scientific effort; it is not helpful in the search for adequate explanation. By way of contrast, by assuming that all determinate effects are necessarily opposed yet mutually entailed, the polarity principle is implicit in the testing of relevant hypotheses. In a bivariate relationship, for instance, one value or "force" is assumed to pull the association in the direction of the hypothesis, while the second value is assumed to pull it in the opposite direction.[4] For this reason, the principle of polarity is a supplement to the principle of causality rather than an alternative mode of explanation: "Not only must every natural event have a cause which determines that it should happen, but the cause must be opposed by some factor which prevents it from producing any greater effect than it actually does" (Cohen, 1949, p. 12).

By calling attention to the basic interdependence of opposites and their mutual entailment, the polarity principle sensitizes the observer to the complexity of seemingly paradoxical facts as well as to the possibility of alternative hypotheses. In contrast to dualistic thinking, the polarity principle aids the analyst in avoiding one-sided and easily false formulations.[5] The notion that the poles of a phenomenon (like magnetism or federalism) are distinct and opposed, yet mutually entailed and inseparable, denies false dichotomies like individual versus society, fact versus value, means versus ends, constancy versus change, form versus content, growth versus decay, unity versus plurality, homogeneity versus heterogeneity, activity versus passivity, simplicity versus complexity, cause versus purpose, organism versus environment, and so on and so forth. If conceived as polar opposites, each category involves the other when applied to a significant phenomenon; each is impossible without the other; there is no action without reaction, no force without resistance, no identity without difference, no individuality without universality, no centralization without decentralization, no division without combination of powers, and so on.

The workings of the polarity principle also differ from the workings of the dialectic in its Hegelian-Marxian version. The dialectic is uncomfortable with the contradictions immanent in a phenomenon and seeks to absorb or transcend them in their unity.[6] The polarity principle accepts as given the coexistence of opposites. In contrast to the dialectic, it stresses the interdependence of the poles in what is a continuous phenomenon; and it does not deny the existence of the poles but calls for their measurement.[7]

Application of the polarity principle to social phenomena has two further advantages over dialectic thinking. First, as Morris Cohen (1933, p. 263) pointed out, polarity thinking implies "wise scepticism about sharp antitheses. Certainty and flexibility may be difficult qualities to bring together, but they are not really logical contradictions." Rather than being real contradictions, many traditional dilemmas involving opposites may only be *difficulties* and, therefore, are soluble. But unless the effort is made to solve them, they remain seeming contradictions: "For a man to cross the water and not get wet was a patent contradiction before the invention of boats" (Cohen, 1933, p. 145; 1949, p. 16).

Moreover, difficulties must be distinguished from *impossibilities* if facile reconciliation of incompatible alternatives is to be avoided. "How to live long without getting old," or "how to eat the cake and have it too," are real impossibilities. Apart from such impossibilities, however, the polar mode of thought is helpful in that it avoids both exaggerating and underestimating difficulties in human affairs. On the one hand, it is a mistake to treat real difficulties as absolute impossibilities; on the other hand, it is a mistake to minimize difficulties by calling them false alternatives. For instance, it is not sufficient to say that unity and diversity are false alternatives and that both are needed. Although unity and diversity are mutually entailed, it may be frequently difficult to have both, at least at the same time. "Social problems are generally difficulties which arise because we do not know how to attain what we want without also having something which we do not want" (Cohen, 1931, p. 399).

American federalism is predicated on the coexistence of localities, states, and nation (and, more recently, also many other jurisdictional units) as mutually entailed entities. The political order envisaged by *The Federalist* is one of polar federalism rather than dual federalism. Polar federalism is predicated on the complementarity of institutions and especially of representational institutions. The model of representational federalism induced from a few passages in *The Federalist* is admittedly amorphous and truncated. *The Federalist*'s concern was only with the relationship between two levels, and what it said directly about the implicit model was cryptic. What is obviously needed is an elaboration of polar federalism in the perspective of representation as the process by which government can be made responsive to the people,[8] its extension to the multilevel structure of present-day American federalism,[9] and, above all, empirical demonstration of its theoretical viability.

There is every reason to believe that the polarity principle can go a long way in explaining the paradoxical fact that as the federal center is strengthened there is yet also a noticeable strengthening of the federal periphery. However, belief is not enough. Research should address itself to the mutual entailment of centralization and decentralization in the federal system. Insofar as the glue that holds the system together is the representation of multiple constituencies—geographic, demographic, social and associational interests, and so on—the linkages involved in representation are of paramount research concern. Yet, perhaps owing to the long-prevailing dualistic conception of the federal structure, there has never been commensurate research. Representation has been studied in isolation at each level of the federal system—national (Miller and Stokes, 1963), state (Wahlke et al., 1962, pp. 267–376), and local (Eulau and Prewitt, 1973, pp. 397–462)—but it has not been studied as a network of linkages among the three levels of American government.

An appropriate research design would select a policy area in which federal, state, and local representatives are significant decision makers. For instance, if the policy area were primary and secondary education, one would want to interview the members of the Education Committee in the U.S. House of Representatives and, perhaps, a random sample of congressmen who are not members of the committee. These respondents would be queried along two main lines: first, about their actual and symbolic relationships with state legislators and school board members in their districts; and second, about their actual and symbolic relationships with educational constituencies and clienteles. As a second step, a sample of state legislators *in* the congressmen's district would be interviewed and asked essentially the same questions. Finally, a sample of school board members *in* the state legislative districts would be selected for parallel interviewing. This procedure would not only yield information about the linkages among representatives at the three levels (which may or may not exist—no one at present knows), but it would also indicate whether the representatives on the three levels share or do not share the same constituents and clienteles (again, no one at present knows).

In addition, the persons or groups named by representatives at each level would in turn provide the anchor points for snowball-sample interviewing of the cross-level constituents and clients, thereby making possible, first, a check on the reciprocity of relations between representatives and represented, and second, the construction of the total sociometric network of representational relationships. Figure 8.1 is a rough approximation of the research design.

The data generated by this investigation would permit an appraisal of the federal representational system in its entirety in a given policy arena. It would presumably show the simultaneous ebb and flow of centralizing and decentralizing tendencies in the federal system as these are mediated by the working of representation. It would show both the equilibrating and disequilibrating forces in the division of authority and functions among the three levels of the federal representational system. If the polarity principle can serve not only as a heuristic but also as an explanatory tool of political analysis, it should be possible both to describe the state of the federal system in a given policy arena and to explain this state of the system in terms of the particular sets of relationships among the representatives and represented who are the significant actors in this policy arena. A more ambitious effort would, of course, want to replicate the analysis in other policy fields. And, again, the polarity principle would not rule out—indeed, it might lead one to discover—the possibility that centralizing trends in one policy arena are contemporary with decentralizing trends in another. Comparative analysis of centralizing and decentralizing tendencies, in different policy fields themselves joined in polar opposition, would maximize our understanding of the enormously complex federal representational system and possibly contribute to an explanation of why centralizing and decentralizing forces serve as change mechanisms in national-state-local relationships.

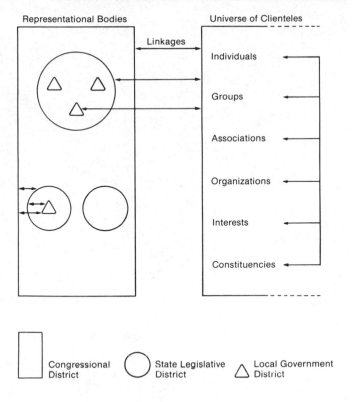

Figure 8.1   Graphic view of the federal representational system
with network of governmental and clientele linkages

It is only if the complexity of the federal system is harnessed in a research design commensurate with this complexity that the theoretical insights of *The Federalist* into the interface between federalism and representation can be extended in line with modern developments in the real world of public affairs and in line with modern developments in political theory and methodology.

THREE

Of Context

and Configuration

9

Configurative Analysis:

Some Philosophical Underpinnings

THERE ARE few ideas in contemporary political science that cannot be found in H. D. Lasswell's early work. Too much emphasis, I think, is often put on his psychoanalytically influenced interest in political personality. It is, of course, an important part of his total work, but it is only one component. Many other current enthusiasms can be found in his early writings. He anticipated the current interest in system theory, in functional analysis, in the study of roles, in the diagnosis of symbolic behavior, in the science of public policy, and in many methodological topics, such as content analysis, participant observation, objectifying interviews, or experimental designs. Careful reading of his work shows that these things are all here, even if, at times, the nomenclature is different.

Although contemporary political science bears the mark of the Lass-wellian influence, Lasswell remains an enigma to many of his professional colleagues. Despite all the words he has written, there seems to be something inscrutable about his ideas that proves elusive. It is my feeling that there has been a failure to understand and appreciate the philosophical underpinnings of his theoretical, methodological, and substantive writings. For this reason, going back to Lasswell's early work may prove to be especially fruitful. For, unlike most of us, he was profoundly concerned with philosophical matters that were the current coin of the realm in his formative years.

The major premises of his approach to politics are well known. His adaptation for the study of political behavior of Freudian propositions about the powerful working of unconscious and often irrational motivations is common knowledge. The sources of his interest in values and public policy, on the other hand, are less clearly understood. One must go back to the *Psychopathology*'s chapter titled "The Politics of Prevention" (Lass-well, 1930) to appreciate Lasswell's strong and lasting commitment to political science as a therapeutic enterprise.[1] But these are only the more obvious premises that fertilized his work. Others are more difficult to identify, for Lasswell's simultaneously curt style and discursive form of presentation do not easily lend themselves to textual exegesis. Moreover, because Lasswell made these philosophical underpinnings his *working* assumptions, he evidently did not feel compelled to explicate them except only occasionally, and then in the barest manner. Much of the failure of political scientists to understand what Lasswell is all about has been due to their failure to concern themselves with the philosophical assumptions of his work beyond its most obvious aspects. And I think that even today few appreciate the philosophical complexity of his thought.

The Individual-Society Dualism

There are some overt clues that are suggestive. In what is still the most significant methodological essay he ever published, "General Framework: Person, Personality, Group, Culture," Lasswell (1948a, p. 195) explicitly states that his terminology "owes something to the Cambridge Logical School, and especially to A. N. Whitehead. The debt is evident in the use of such expressions as 'event' and 'event manifold.' " What interests me is Lasswell's use of the notion of "manifold of events" and the methodological implications of this use for some of the problems of political science as a behavioral science.

As far as I know, Lasswell never discussed Whitehead's cosmology in detail. Useful as he apparently found the British philosopher-scientist's concepts, he did not subscribe to his intricate metaphysics. One can only do violence to Whitehead's thought by seeking to summarize it in a few lines. I shall do so at the risk of enormous simplification, but I hope that this summary will pinpoint Lasswell's indebtedness to Whitehead.

For Whitehead the world is due to a "creative advance of nature"—a process that pervades the whole of nature and produces "events" that never existed before. The world is always incomplete, but it moves toward novelty and further completeness through the workings of something that Whitehead called the "Principle of Concretion." As nature is a purposive process moving toward achievement, indeterminate actualities are transmuted into determinate ones. Actualities and potentialities are the two poles of nature that the process of emergence seeks to link and unify.

It is easy to see why this philosophy of emergence should be attractive to Lasswell. Throughout his work he was preoccupied with actualities and potentialities. But, unlike Whitehead, the potentialities were for Lasswell not teleological properties inherent in nature. Rather, they resided in man as an action-oriented, purposive animal.

In using the concept of "event manifold," Lasswell confronted a central and critical problem of political analysis that still confronts us today. "Implications," he wrote in the last chapter of *Psychopathology and Politics,* titled "The State as a Manifold of Events,"

have continually been drawn in the foregoing pages about the bearing of the intensive study of *individual* personalities upon the *meaning* of the political process as a *whole.* (1930, p. 240)

I am taking the liberty of italicizing three key words in the sentence because they bring out the problem. How can one make meaningful, empirically reliable statements about wholes—that is, human collectivities—on the basis of knowledge about individual behavior? For, Lasswell, continues,

since the psychopathological approach to the individual is the most elaborate procedure yet devised for the study of human personality, it would appear to raise in the most acute form the thorny problem of the relation between research on the individual and research upon society. (Ibid.)

Why did Lasswell see a problem where most other political scientists saw none? The simplest answer is that political scientists saw no problem because they had no problem. They largely ignored individual behavior and concerned themselves only with large-scale institutions and processes. But once the strange fruit of individual behavior had been tasted, the joy was soured by the "thorny problem." Lasswell set out to cut the Gordian knot of the familiar dualism between individual and society:

It may be asserted at the outset that our thinking is vitiated unless we dispose of the fictitious cleavage which is sometimes supposed to separate the study of the "individual" from the study of "society." There is no cleavage; there is but a gradual gradation of reference points. Some events have their locus in but a single individual, and are unsuitable for comparative investigation. Some events are widely distributed among individuals, like breathing, but have no special importance for interpersonal relations.[2] Our starting-point as social scientists is the statement of a distinctive event which is widely spread among human beings who occupy a particular time-space manifold. (Ibid.)

But denying the dualism of individual and society by mere assertion is not enough. Lasswell's denial involved a search for philosophical underpinnings. To follow his search, one must appreciate the fact that philosophy, and notably the philosophy of science, is a search for answers to certain recurring questions. Often these questions are put in the form of dualism. Perhaps best known is the dualism of "soul" and "body" inherited from primitive thought and Greek philosophy, a dualism that still persists, if in diluted form, in the distinction between psychological processes and the processes of the nervous system. In biology the dualism between the "organic" and "inorganic," or in physics the old dualism between "force" and "matter," are other instances from the history of scientific thought. The dualism of individual and society is of the same generic class.

Often a dualism is of such long standing that it becomes part of the cultural heritage, hardened and resistant to resolution precisely because its reality is taken for granted. A dualism, then, assumes the existence of two kinds of entities or processes that are seen as interacting, but the interaction is yet to be explained. Once a dualism "exists," it serves as a powerful stimulus to thought, but it represents a "problem" because the interaction of the two poles of the dualism proves elusive. Moreover, the problem involved may be a pseudoproblem if the dualism is merely a figment of the intellectual imagination. In that case the problem has only subjective significance and is not a soluble scientific problem. If, on the other hand, the dualism has been empirically discovered, as for instance the dualism between consciousness and unconsciousness, the problem is genuinely scientific because, though two kinds of reality may be involved, their relationship is presumably connected in some causal manner that can be investigated and explained.

But a dualism may be the result of both intellectual imagination and empirical inquiry. In this case it is extremely difficult to disentangle its speculative and empirical components. As it is in the nature of a dualism to make for increasing polarization and hardening of the lines between its end terms, the dualism is likely to give rise to antagonistic "schools of thought" that stress the primacy of one pole over the other. Not surprisingly, the history of political and social theory has often been written as a history of conflict between the individual and society.

Decomposing the speculative and empirical components of a dualism has been the achievement of logical positivism in that it distinguished between *statements* that are subject to falsification and those that are not. The specific problem of resolving the question of whether the dualism of individual and society is an empirically viable phenomenon or a pseudophenomenon was facilitated by the scientific theory of "emergent evolution" or the philosophical idea of "emergence" that became prominent in the 1920s and had its most distinguished philosophical exponent in A. N. Whitehead. Although Lasswell never explicitly and directly discussed emergence as a philosophical assumption, his frequent use of the terms "event manifold" and "emergent" indicates his acceptance, if not of the doctrine of emergent evolution, at least of the philosophical notion of emergence. For instance:

If the significant political changes of the past were signalized by revolutionary patterns which rose and spread until they were blocked or superseded by new revolutionary innovations, the future may well follow the same course of development. Hence our "present" would be transition between the latest and the impending world revolutionary emergent. (1935, p. 4)

Lasswell's consistent emphasis on the need for developmental analysis of political processes, from his earliest major writings to his latest, supports this contention (see Chapter 13). Moreover, the topography of his "General Framework" is predicated on a necessary corollary of the assumption of emergence—the conception of discrete levels of organization and analysis.

Because in attacking the problem of the individual-society dualism Lasswell also called for a new form of thinking about social phenomena, it may be useful to review, if only superficially, earlier attempts to cope with the dualism problem in cognition. Materialism—from Thomas Hobbes to the behavioristic psychology of John Watson—eliminated the dualism of mind and matter by reducing everything to a single basic reality, material substance. For Hobbes thinking was but the motion of some unidentified substance in the head; for Watson thinking was simply "subvocal speech." On the other hand, idealists from Bishop Berkeley on sought to abolish the dualism of the physical and the psychical by reducing everything to some fundamental spiritual reality. As a result of these formulations, instead of being resolved, the dualism was aggravated by the arguments and counterarguments of the materialist and idealist warriors. Escape from the materialist-idealist cul-de-sac could be had only if it was possible to occupy a new observational standpoint. Such a new standpoint was also sought by the theory of "emergent evolution."

This aspect of the new philosophy of emergent evolution must have been attractive to Lasswell in his attempt to overcome the dualism of logical and free-associational modes of thinking. The "new position" he came to occupy, and for which he became famous in his own right, was of course his insight that Freudian psychology could serve not only as an instrument of mental therapy, but also as a powerful instrument of thought. In chapter 3 of the *Psychopathology*, Lasswell attacked the prevailing emphasis on logic as the sole mode of thinking about politics:

A totally different technique of thinking is needed to get on with the task of ridding the mind of the distorting results of unseen compulsions . . . Logical thinking is but one of the special methods of using the mind, and cannot itself achieve an adequate inspection of reality because it is unable to achieve self-knowledge without the aid of other forms of thinking. (1930, pp. 31–32)

. . . The mind is a fit instrument of reality testing when both blades are sharpened—those of logic and free-fantasy. (Ibid., p. 37)

Emergence and Levels of Organization

"Emergent evolution" was a philosophical doctrine that was bred by crossing Darwin and Hegel. It implied, therefore, two conceptions—one of *existential* emergence and one of *functional* emergence. These conceptions are by no means opposed to each other. Existential emergence means that in the course of development certain qualities, objects, or events come into existence which did not previously exist, and that knowledge about such novel types of existents—that is, emergents—cannot be derived from knowledge of what previously existed. Functional emergence means that the functioning of different types of existents is irreducible so that no single theory can explain the characteristic functions of all types. These functional discontinuities are due to the existence of "levels of organization," regardless of whether these levels are novel or were always present. If novelty is stressed, the notion of functional emergence, like that of existential emergence, holds that the emergents cannot be explained by propositions that could explain previously existing phenomena; if levels of organization are emphasized, the doctrine holds that explanations of lower-level phenomena cannot be applied to the functioning of higher-level phenomena. But regardless of where the accent is put, the notion of emergence assumes an ultimate pluralism in the propositions that are needed to describe and explain the functioning of different types of phenomena. Both existential and functional emergence assert the nondeducibility of the phenomena with which they are concerned. In the case of existential emergence, this nondeducibility can be called "unpredictability." In the case of functional emergence, it can be called "irreducibility."

I do not know whether Lasswell, had he been explicit, would have preferred the notion of existential emergence or the idea of functional emergence. It does not matter, in any case, because for Lasswell ideas are never rigid formulas whose internal logic is to be respected, but rather suggestive starting points for innovative thinking. In other words, it is not clear whether he viewed emergence as descriptive of an actual process of progressive development in the cosmos whereby the present variety of physical, biological, and social phenomena emerged from a primitive stage characterized by undifferentiated and isolated elements, while the future contains unpredictable novelties; or whether he accepted emergence as a conception of an irreducible hierarchical organization of phenomena or processes and of the existence of properties at "higher" levels of organization that cannot be deduced or predicted from properties characteristic of "lower" levels.[3] My inclination is to believe that he toyed with both conceptions, but did not adopt either in its pristine purity.

The notion of emergence has aided in overcoming many old dualisms. Just as such "nothing but" ways of thinking—pluralism versus monism, determinism versus free will, or materialism versus idealism—could be abandoned by philosophy, so Lasswell could dispose of the logic versus free-fantasy dualism and suggest a compromise. In this new mode of thought it was unnecessary to make a choice between extreme views. What appears to be antithetical is reconciled on a new plane. It represents a position that Lasswell has repeated time and again in his writings when he enjoins us to occupy as many observational standpoints as possible in the analysis of individual, social, and cultural phenomena.

But what of the "thorny problem" of research on individual and society that bothered Lasswell? We can see now that it was linked in his mind to the problem of utilizing appropriate ways of thinking about the phenomena involved. In the *Psychopathology* he had probed deeply into the micro-behavior of individuals, but there remained the problem of how such knowledge could be made relevant to an explanation of the behavior of social entities. Lasswell did not assume, as is sometimes assumed by less-sophisticated students of individual behavior, that societal phenomena can be explained solely by means of a theory concerning their microstructures. Insight into societal behavior at the level of the individual may be a necessary condition for explanation of social phenomena, but it is not a sufficient condition. Lasswell came to identify classes of events in society and culture that could not be explained by theoretical propositions about the behavior of individuals in terms of personality. His concern, clearly, was a theory of classes of events that were unexplained. Similar concerns were at the roots of the doctrine of emergence.

Wholes and Aggregates

Emergence, we have seen, refers to the process by which *new* effects (or processes or events) arise from the operation of antecedent causes (or processes or events). As a result of emergence new *wholes* (or configurations) appear which include or show *novel* properties that are qualitatively different from the sum of the properties of their constituent parts. This is not to say that aggregation of individual properties is not a legitimate operation to describe new wholes. For instance, if we speak of the median age of a group, the property "age" is stated in the form of a summation. But when we speak of a group's cohesion or integration, we do not refer to some arithmetic value, but to something new—an emergent property that cannot be reduced to some characteristic of its individual members. The new phenomenon is a "whole" that cannot be dissected or taken apart like an automobile and then reassembled. We can see better now, I think, what Lasswell meant when he characterized the state as a manifold of events. What he meant was that state behavior cannot be analyzed by disassembling it into parts. In this connection, we must not make too much of Lasswell's use of the term "state," which, at the time, was still the prevailing theoretical concept in political science for what we would call today "political system." A political system can be any political whole whose boundaries are identifiable—the historical "state" as much as a "legislature" or a "party" or a "party system." The important point to keep in mind is that in leading to a conception of the whole, the idea of emergence called attention to the manifold of events that constitutes the whole.

Lasswell articulated the relationship between thinking in terms of emergence and wholes, as follows:

Sound political analysis is nothing less than correct orientation in the continuum which embraces the past, present, and future. Unless the salient features of the all-inclusive whole are discerned, details will be incorrectly located. (1935, p. 4)

. . . The gradual creation of a sense of wholeness, and of assurance in the discovery of interdetail connections within the all-encompassing totality, also requires new methods of formal exposition. (Ibid., p. 16)

Lasswell's words and concepts, as I suggested earlier, sounded strange to his contemporaries in political science (but not to behavioral scientists in other disciplines who recognized his stature earlier, I think, than political scientists did). It is by now abundantly clear that Lasswell was not playing with neologisms for effect, as some of his critics alleged. As his future research and the research of those whom he influenced have amply demonstrated, these were not empty or meaningless words. Yet Lasswell felt compelled to defend himself when he wrote that "our function is not to introduce a new cult but to give a sounder general analysis than has been possible heretofore" (ibid., p. 17). His approach to politics was not a cult because he knew, as his critics did not know, that in utilizing the ideas of emergence and wholeness he was anticipating the course of social scientific inquiry in the next few decades, with its emphasis on *gestalt* thinking, interdisciplinary frames of reference, development, functional categories and procedures, and, last but not least, the distinction between levels of analysis.

To understand the levels-of-analysis "problem," we must keep in mind a distinction between resultant effects and emergent effects. Resultant effects—as in the parallelogram-of-forces model of mechanics—are ana-lyzable in terms of the independent forces or vectors whose confluence can be expressed algebraically or geometrically. In the case of emergent effects, on the other hand, the component "events" interact to produce a new whole in such a way that they are no longer independent of each other. Emergent wholes like "personality," "society," or "culture" are units that are something more than the sum of the items, elements, or traits that constitute them individually. An emergent whole differs, for instance, from the collection and arrangement of pieces of furniture in a room where individual pieces may be introduced or removed without disturbing the basic arrangement. A configuration is an emergent whole, made up of parts, of course; but statements about its "shape" or "pattern" can neither be deduced from knowledge of the properties of its individual parts nor be reduced to the properties of the constituent parts.

If it is correct, then, that in the course of interaction of individual parts new properties appear or emerge that characterize the whole, the behavior of parts and whole must be analyzed on different levels—a macroscopic and a microscopic level. And as behavior on the macrolevel is new and emergent, it requires new descriptive concepts and possibly new empirical propositions that are independent of the concepts and propositions relevant to the microlevel. Confusion of levels has disastrous consequences for scientic explanation and interpretation. If macrolevel explanations are sim-ply extrapolated from observations of behavior on the microlevel, as for instance in the older "national character" studies, the behavior of the whole is likely to be misunderstood and misinterpreted. On the other hand, if the behavior of the whole, say a society, is used to explain the behavior of its component individuals, violence is done to the explanation of the constituent parts. For instance, if it is proper to characterize German so-ciety as "authoritarian," in the political-structural sense on the macrolevel of analysis, it does not follow that the behavior of all Germans or even most Germans is "authoritarian" in some psychological sense on the mi-crolevel of analysis.

The notion that human behavior in its totality can and must be analyzed from the perspective of different analytical levels does not imply empirical discontinuity from one level to the next. On the contrary, as the new macrolevel configuration emerges out of the behavior of the constituent parts that is also observable on the old or microlevel, empirical continuity is implicitly assumed. Macrolevel phenomena, then, are not mere epiphe-nomena or in any sense less "real" than microlevel phenomena. The be-havior involved, whatever the level of analysis, is the same. A group, for instance, is a unit of interacting individuals whose behavior is the same, regardless of whether the analyst occupies a microlevel or macrolevel standpoint of observation. But if the behavior of the individuals is observed from the group or macrolevel perspective, it is possible to identify qualities that are new because they do not exist if any one constituent individual is observed as a single unit. For instance, no analytic operation whatever on the microlevel of the individual enables the analyst to describe a group's "cohesion" or "solidarity." (In other words, an individual's *feeling* of solidarity is a property of the individual, not of the group; "group solidarity" is an analytically distinct property of the whole group.) It is for just this reason that the conception of levels of analysis and the notion of emergence are complementary. Emergence entails the appearance of new levels of organization; the recognition of new levels entails a developmental perspective and the need to disinguish between levels of analysis.

Although he did not directly deal with considerations of this kind, they are clearly implicit in Lasswell's "General Framework." The key concepts that constitute the framework—person, personality, group, culture—refer to different levels of behavioral organization and to different levels of analysis. The "thorny problem" that he had identified in "The State as Manifold of Events"—the relation between research on the individual and on society—was the problem of how one can move empirically from one level to another. The answers he gave are of different degrees of strength and scope. Minimally, there is the issue of frequency: many new patterns that emerge out of individual behavior at the group level of analysis can be analyzed as statistical regularities. Lasswell's early commitment to quantitative analysis did not stem from some compulsion to "count" for the sake of counting. Rather:

What is known as the "quantitative method" provides a valuable discipline for the student of culture because it directs his attention toward the discovery of events which are often enough repeated to raise a strong presumption that a particular sequence does actually exist. These events must be so defined that similar events can be identified by other workers. This necessitates an operational definition of the concept, which is to say, terms must be used to specify the position of the observer in relation to the configuration which it is proposed to describe. (1930, p. 251)

Lasswell was, above all, sensitive to the deficiency of macrolevel explanations. He complained about "the impatience among students of culture with the slow-footed quantitative approach" which

is partly due to the diffuse, implicit nature of the experiences upon which is based the judgment about a subjective event outside one's self, and the resulting bias of the student of culture against exaggerating the significance of items in the pattern. (Ibid.)

This theme is continued in "General Framework" and linked to the theme of configurative analysis:

Although we have defined culture trait and personality trait, we have not defined culture or personality. These terms refer to wholes, and as wholes they include *not only* the traits of which they are composed, but the interrelationships of these traits. (1948, p. 202; italics added)

Lasswell's emphasis on quantification led, as is well known, to his pioneering studies of political elites and symbols whose objective it was to uncover the emergence and shape of the world configuration of values (see Lasswell et al., 1949; Lasswell, 1951a). But his acceptance of the notion of emergent levels as real phenomena that are empirically continuous also implied the further analysis of the causal conditions under which the new phenomena occur and of the immanent conditions that maintain them independently of the component events. Hence his attention turned to the analysis of wholes as developmental as well as equilibrated phenomena. And just as he had encountered opposition to the "slow-footed" method of quantification, so he noted opposition to "systemic" analysis: "To some extent, there has been resistance against this mode of conceiving the task of students of personality and culture" (1948a, p. 208). Not that this resistance was due to a lack of knowledge of the calculus of variations on the part of social scientists. Psychologists, for instance,

have operated with variables, but they have not undertaken to select a list in terms of which they could describe the fluctuations of the whole personality in relation to its environment. The essential point about the "systemic" pattern of analysis is not that it uses variables, but that it chooses a list whose interrelations are studied with regard to fluctuations in the environment. (Ibid., p. 210)

In part, then, the problem was to develop specific categories and modes of observation for systematic analyses of such configurative wholes as personality or culture. Yet, Lasswell pointed out, "science seemed to be growing by the discovery and exploration of new standpoints, and by the discovery of interpart relations independent of explicit modes of describing 'wholeness' " (ibid., p. 211). Organic metaphors and analogies were suspect on political grounds. Here Lasswell once more acknowledges the suggestiveness of the doctrine of emergence: "It is not one of the least distinctive achievements of Whitehead that he lifted the conception of the organic from the battle-scarred phraseology of preceding centuries" (ibid.).

The Contextual Principle

My task is not to review Lasswell's particular substantive formulations. The significant point is that, in "General Framework," he clearly distinguished between levels of organization and raised the issue of the relationship between levels. The methodological issue is, essentially, that of reduction and nonreduction, or of continuity and discontinuity of levels. I do not think that the issue has been in any way resolved. The reductionist standpoint envisages a unified science of human behavior in which all the sciences are integrated in terms of a microlevel theory of behavior. This theory, it is argued, is the only guarantee of scientific knowledge of any phenomenon, on whatever level it is observed, for it alone gives insight into the "inner workings," so to speak, of phenomena. But if levels are seen as discontinuous, analysis on each level presumes the generation of empirical propositions appropriate to that level and not applicable to another. Hence the continued autonomy of the three basic behavioral sciences, each primarily concerned with the study of human behavior from a particular level-relevant perspective—psychology with behavior at the level of the individual person, sociology with behavior at the level of the group (society), and anthropology with behavior at the level of culture. However, as behavior on different levels gives rise to independent empirical phenomena, the study of the interstices between levels makes for the development of intermediate disciplines, such as social psychology, political sociology, or culture and personality, that are in search of principles which can connect macrocharacteristics and microcharacteristics of behavior as parts of total analysis.

If I understand it correctly, the "General Framework" was Lasswell's attempt to come to grips with the problem of interlevel relations. Just what motivated him to deal with the problem was, I suspect, his desire to avoid the reductionist trap into which his preoccupation with individual psychological mechanisms might have led him, as indeed is the case with many psychologists interested in societal phenomena. He was too much of a social and political scientist not to sense that behavior at the level of group or culture followed laws that were quite independent of propositions about microscopic behavior items. Yet, although he resisted reduction, or perhaps because he resisted it, Lasswell recognized problems of interlevel or translevel relationships that must necessarily arise if reduction is not feasible. The amazing thing is, I think, that his essay is as suggestive today as it was almost fifty years ago, for we have made little progress in the solution of the problem. Although the essay was reprinted in a volume devoted to political behavior, its original appearance in *Psychiatry* as well as its unfamiliar vocabulary seem to have deterred political scientists from following up on his suggestions; and this despite the fact that political science occupies an eminently interstitial position between the three basic behavioral sciences. I am confident that in the future, as political scientists must come to terms with the interstitial position of their discipline and hence with the problem of emergent properties in the macrostructures and processes that interest them, they will have to turn to the "General Framework" for guidance and enlightenment.

Careful reading of the essay will also show, I think, that Lasswell was concerned with another problem—namely, whether and how, after the emergence of higher-level phenomena, the behavior of the lower-level units might be changed so that the behavior of these units follows empirical laws not discoverable when there is no "intervention" of the emergent phenomenon. Lasswell must have had this problem in mind when he referred to an observer who

uses the expression "trait of a specified culture" to refer to an act which is expected to appear and which does occur with at least a specified minimum frequency in a given field of observation. Our observer may use the word "conduct" to refer to an act which conforms to a culture trait and the word "behavior" to refer to an act which does not conform. We may note that an act which is behavior in one community may be conduct in another community, but it is also possible that an act may conform to no pattern anywhere. (1948a, p. 200)

In another example a person's "career line" rather than culture is the emergent. The observer

is also interested in placing the act in proper relationship to another dimension of this manifold of events. The act is one of the acts which compose the career line of the actor. Some of the acts are representative of the person under specified conditions. (Ibid.)

In other words, because the behavior of individuals takes place in what Lasswell called "the personality-culture manifold," the behavior should be expected to follow empirical laws that are not operative if it took place independently of such higher-level phenomena as personality or culture. In simpler language, we would say that the cultural content of behavior permeates otherwise nonpatterned acts of behavior. Culture is, of course, the most pervasive emergent in human relations. But on the social level, too, the impact of an emergent phenomenon on its constituent parts can be observed. Recent studies of "structural effects" or "compositional effects" seek to measure the impact of emerging group properties on the behavior of the individuals who constitute the group (see Blau, 1960; Davis, 1961b).

In Lasswell's terminology, the possibility of analyzing behavior on several and diverse levels brings into play what he has sometimes called the "contextual principle," sometimes the "principle of interdetermination." Precisely because certain phenomena, say "value systems" or the "language of politics," can have considerable internal independence so as to constitute distinct levels of organization in society or culture, they may be analyzed on their own level. But they may also be analyzed in terms of development from presumably prior or lower levels to present levels. The traditional procedure of nineteenth-century social science had been to search for single-factor explanations. In rejecting single-factor approaches, Lasswell did not simply substitute a multifactor design. Let us listen carefully:

This standpoint [that is, of interdetermination, as against overdetermination] is sometimes formulated as a principle of "multiple causation." *But more is involved than multiple causes;* there are multiple effects as well, and more important, there are patterns of interaction in which it is impossible to distinguish between cause and effect. (Lasswell and Kaplan, 1950, p. xvii; emphasis added)

Or he may speak of a "principle of situational reference":

Empirical significance requires that the propositions of social science, rather than affirming unqualifiedly universal invariances, state relations between variables assuming different magnitude *in different social contexts*. (Ibid., p. xxi; emphasis added)

Contextual analysis and developmental analysis may go hand in hand. Individuals, Lasswell stated early in "Configurative Analysis,"

may be investigated by special methods to disclose the genetic sequence of personality development and to place the individual career line in relation to the career line of others living in the same epoch. *It is a question solely of expediency and not of principle* whether the total configuration is approached extensively or intensively by the individual observer, since either starting point draws the investigator toward the opposite. (1935, p. 24; emphasis added)

Here, once more, we encounter the impact of thinking in modern terms of emergence with an emphasis on avoiding the mistakes and simplifications of nineteenth-century evolutionary thought. Rather, whatever phenomena are to be observed on whatever level of analysis—political institutions, social structures, cultural patterns, norms of conduct, symbolic systems, and so on—they are to be observed in relation to the total context in a given stage of human development. Just as developmental analysis is predicated on the existence of stages in terms of which the developmental process can be ascertained, so contextual analysis is predicated on the existence of levels in terms of which behavior is given meaning. For meaning changes from level to level.

It is for all of these reasons that the behavioral scientist must at all times be cognizant of the level of analysis that defines for him the frame of reference or observational standpoint from which he generalizes about the phenomena at his focus of attention. What on one level, say that of culture, may appear as a generic value also may, on the social level, appear as a norm of interpersonal conduct; and it may appear, at the level of personality, as a rationalization of hidden motives. The behavior that is observed is the same; what is different is the emergent level—be it culture, society, or personality—that defines the appropriate mode of analysis and guides interpretation. Confusion of levels is to be avoided. A system of values as a cultural phenomenon cannot be analyzed as a set of mechanisms of defense that may be appropriate on the level of personality. Similarly, a group's "interest" is something different from the private agendas that are rooted at the level of personality. Mobilizing all levels of analysis in behalf of understanding or explaining the manifold of events that constitutes any one particular phenomenon, like Lasswell's "state," is a strategy of research, not a confusion of levels of analysis.

The Problem of Prediction

The conception of emergence has certain implications for the problem of scientific prediction in human affairs. If emergent properties at a higher level of organization cannot be deduced with logical rigor from statements about the constituent parts of a whole, prediction is not always possible. But this does not foreclose the making of anticipatory statements that are sometimes more than fortunate guesses. In other words, emergents as altogether novel phenomena are unpredictable only in a strictly logical sense. But this does not necessarily mean that an emergent phenomenon, *on its own level of analysis,* cannot be predicted from determinate conditions for the occurrence of all events, whatever the level. Put differently, emergence is not incompatible with assumptions about causation. It does not involve some acceptance of either indeterminism or teleological principle. An emergent property is not some ontological, immanent aspect of a phenomenon. Rather, one can assume that the probability of its being observed is relative to the state of theoretical knowledge at a given time. An emergent property may lose its emergent status as level-relevant theoretical propositions become available, so that the phenomenon can be explained or predicted on its own level. For instance, a group's cohesion may vary with varying threats to the group's survival. In other words, an emergent phenomenon is always contingent on the total configuration in which the emergent event occurs. The difficulty is that the configuration may be unique and for this reason make prediction hazardous. Note Lasswell's early statement of the predicament:

Now the whole world of "causation" is implicated in any event, and the whole number of significant mechanisms which may be discerned in the "mind at the moment" is infinite. So our hypothetical volume might conclude by accepting the assumption that some events can be brought about by more than chance frequency, subject to the reservation that experimental confirmation is never reliable as to the future. *The critical configurations may never "reappear."* We commonly say that the probability of an event's future repetition is greater if it has been oft repeated in the past. *But there is no means of demonstrating that the future contains analogous configurations to the elapsed.* The probability of the future repetition of an event is "no probability." If events appear to be predictable, this is so because our knowledge of contingencies is limited, and our sequences of similar configurations may still be treated as special instances of "no sequence." The stable is a special case of the unstable, to put the ultimate paradox. (1930, p. 260; emphasis added)

The problem of prediction, then, is not just a matter of logical deduction but of multilevel empirical investigation into the manifold of events that constitutes the context of emergence. Lasswell stated this problem in "Configurative Analysis" as follows:

Now it is impossible to abolish uncertainty by the refinement of retrospective observations, by the accumulation of historical detail, by the application of precision methods to elapsed events; the crucial test of adequate analysis is nothing less than the future verification of the insight into the nature of the master configuration against which details are constructed. Each specific interpretation is subject to redefinition as the structural potentialities of the future become actualized in the past and present of participant observers. The analyst moves between the contemplation of detail and of configuration, knowing that the soundness of the result is an act of creative orientation rather than of automatic projection. The search for precision in the routines of the past must be constantly chastened and given relevance and direction by reference to the task of self-orientation which is the goal of analysis. (1935, p. 17)

In this quotation Lasswell's indebtedness to A. N. Whitehead is most evident. The problem of relating actualities to potentialities is a problem of the creative orientation of the observer. The evidence is overwhelming that Lasswell was fascinated by this problem, and that it was this problem, perhaps more than any other, that led him to his deep interest in what, in later writings, he called the "problem-solving approach." In a magisterial statement addressed to his colleagues in *The Future of Political Science,* he stated his position succinctly:

Any problem-solving approach to human affairs poses five intellectual tasks, which we designate by five terms familiar to political scientists—goal, trend, conditions, projection, and alternative. The first question, relating to goal, raises the traditional problem of clarifying the legitimate aims of a body politic. After goals are provisionally clarified, the historical question arises. In the broadest context, the principal issue is whether the trend of events in America or throughout the world community has been toward or away from the realization of preferred events. The next question goes beyond the simple inventories of change and asks which factors condition one another and determine history. When trend and factor knowledge is at hand, it is possible to project the course of future developments on the preliminary assumption that we do not ourselves influence the future. Finally, what policy alternatives promise to bring all preferred goals to optimal fulfillment? (1963, pp. 1–2)

In its cool simplicity this statement conceals the intellectual labor that went into it over a professional career of forty years. There are still those who accuse Lasswell of braggadocio and empty phrase making. What they miss is Lasswell's profound and lifelong concern with the most subtle philosophical underpinnings of a science of politics and social science in general. While he may have had an image of the complex problems involved early in his career and envisaged in a broad perspective possible solutions, his incessant quest led him to touch all bases rather than only one or two. In Lasswell's master orientation—I cannot think of a better expression to describe his intellectual style and stance—there is little room for exclusiveness. But there is ample room for a great variety of approaches to knowledge. Because, perhaps more than any other contemporary behavioral scientist, he disdained intellectual simplicity in a world of great practical complexity, he was not satisfied with occupying just one or two observational standpoints—a task that, for most of us, is a lifetime effort. He could not afford to be a "pure" theoretician, and he could not afford to be satisfied with doing empirical work alone; he could not afford to be a student only of the past or the present, but always had to occupy himself with the future; he could not limit himself merely to the analysis of values, but had to recommend their application in the crucible of public policy making; he could not sacrifice causal for functional analysis, just as he could not surrender an interest in details to an interest in wholes. The intellectual edifice he erected resembles a Gothic cathedral with its turrets and spires and arches and niches that, on close inspection, may evince flaws of one kind or another. But, like a Gothic cathedral, the edifice is built on firm foundations, and it is wondrous to behold in its total complexity and splendor.

10

The Informal Organization of

Small Decision-Making Groups

THERE ARE many reasons for studying "small" political groups—the family, the clique, the committee, the jury, the faction, and so on. Most politically active persons work in and through small groups, and they could probably not be active without such groups. Whether formal or informal, some small groups are tightly organized, like the military platoon; and some are very loosely knit, like the volunteer fund-raising committee. Many small political groups are parts of larger organizations, like the section of an administrative bureau; and many are more or less autonomous, like the jury or the city council. Some small political or politically relevant groups are highly salient to the political actor; others are very peripheral to his interests. But what all small political groups have in common is that they link the individual person to the larger society to which he belongs.

Small groups have long been studied in sociology and social psychology, and the literature on small groups is legion.[1] Political scientists have backed into this study almost inadvertently. Although role theory, reference group theory, and functional theory have been used in studying such groups as the family as a political unit, the legislative committee, the legislative delegation, the court, and so on, neither the "smallness" nor the "group-ishness" of the small group is treated as a critical property in these studies.[2] Certainly no effort has been made to develop small-group analysis as a specialization in its own right as has been the case in sociology and social psychology. A few exceptions may be noted,[3] but a book like Verba's *Small Groups and Political Behavior,* which could have opened up new lines of inquiry, is more often cited than read or used in political research.[4]

An important distinction must be made at the outset between two types of research on small groups. There have been, on the one hand, studies that seek to explain the functioning of the group by studying the individual behavior of members. In such research, the group is the object of analysis (the unit about which statements are to be made), and the individual person is the subject of analysis (the unit on which data are collected). There have been, on the other hand, studies that seek to explain the political behavior of the individual by studying some aspect of the group to which he belongs. In this research, the individual is the object of analysis and statements are made about his behavior; but the group is the subject of analysis: the research question is how the properties of the group affect the members.

The distinction between these two types of research is crucial. For if the group is to be the object of analysis, an assumption is clearly made that the group *as group* is a significant actor in the political arena. But even having come this far still presents difficulties. Studies that indeed do view the group as the actor have been dependent on evidence about the individual members. Thus statements about the structural or functional aspects of the group are in the nature of inferences from individual behavior rather than in the nature of propositions about the group as a unit of action. There are good reasons for this. Almost all small-group research in political science has been in the nature of case studies.[5] As long as an investigator deals with a single group, generalization is severely limited; we never know what the "case" is a case of. A large number of groups is needed before the group can be investigated as an action unit on its own level of analysis.

Put differently, what is needed is research in which the group is both object and subject of analysis. Data are collected about the group itself in order to make statements about the functioning of the group. If the group itself is to be both subject and object of analysis, then it must be understood as something more than the set of individuals composing it. It is the set of interpersonal relations or interactions that constitutes the group. A group, then, is not the sum total of its individual members, but the network of interindividual relationships that gives rise to the group's existence.

Of course, some properties of the group may be aggregative, as when we speak of the group's "median age" (as distinct from the group's longevity as a group—its collective age) or the group's "average opinion" (as against its "decision," which may well be different from any one member's individual choice). But the more "groupish" properties of the group cannot simply be aggregated. There are integral properties such as the group's size; emergent properties such as its consensus; structural properties such as its organization; or contextual properties such as its environment (as when we speak of a "rural council"). These latter types of properties are not simply attributes of individuals to be added up but inhere in the group as a group independently of the particular members who at any one moment compose the group (see Lazarsfeld and Menzel, 1965; Selvin and Hagstrom, 1966).

Of the various types of group properties important to group action, we are here most interested in those relational properties that make for the group's informal organization. Structure has been given little scientific shrift in recent years, partly because of the theoretical emptiness of formal institutional analysis. But structural analysis must remain a critical concern of political science, just as it is of continuing concern in biology, geology, chemistry, linguistics, and almost every other science. For *all* political activity, be it that of an individual or a group, or even that of an "amorphous" mob on the streets, is limited or constrained by the structure of the relationships that obtain in the group. Otherwise statements about group behavior are necessarily limited to surface forms studied from the outside and likely to be as inadequate as the formal institutional descriptions no longer adequate in the study of large and highly organized collectivities.

A group's "living structure" cannot be studied from the outside. Some method that will reveal the group's internal relationships and interactions must be applied. Sociometry—the measurement of interpersonal relations and interactions in the group—is one method of penetrating surface form.[6] Although many technical difficulties must be overcome, the "sociometric survey" is in fact a viable tool of structural analysis.[7] This essay seeks to show how sociometry can be used in identifying some of the relational properties of small decision-making groups—in this case eighty-two non-partisan city councils of the greater San Francisco Bay metropolitan region ranging from five to nine (and in one case thirteen) members[8]—and in formulating "laws of structure." The essay deals with the morphology and not the physiology of the councils. It is not concerned with such problems as "structural effects"—the consequences of group structure on individual behavior—or the parametric determinants of group properties. It is concerned with the "structure of properties"—how some of the group's multiple properties may be interrelated, how these relationships may be interreted, and how the legislative group as a subject of analysis may be used to make statements about legislative groups as objects of analysis.

Types of Decisional Structure

One of the legislative group's most obvious and critical properties is its "decisional structure." Legislatures are presented with issues under circumstances requiring collective choice. One of the most important structures of relationships among group members that emerges in the course of legislative activity is its decisional structure. The relationship between any two or more members who, by virtue of their individual stands on issues, are aligned with each other may be deliberate or circumstantial. If member A and member B over a long series of decisions always vote on the same side of an issue, they are evidently related to each other, although one does not know, without empirical inquiry, whether they deliberately "vote together," or whether they come to their decisions quite independently, without mutual awareness of their behavior or prior agreement. Bloc analysis of legislative decision making, long familiar in the study of legislative and judicial bodies, is based on overt behavior and makes no a priori assumptions about the genesis of the bloc (see Rice, 1927; Grumm, 1965; Sprague, 1968). Once a bloc has been identified, the posteriori assumption may be made that if A and B or more members vote together, they have similar attitudes. Or the further assumption may be made that in future votes on the same or similar issues the bloc will reappear, thus making for order and regularity in the decision-making group's behavior. By decisional structure, then, is meant the more or less stable voting pattern that emerges in legislative or judicial decision making.

In the case of nonpartisan city councils, conventional bloc analysis is impossible because in most councils votes are either not recorded or, if recorded, names are not reported in council minutes. As an alternative to roll-call data each respondent was asked a sociometric question about his own and others' voting behavior. With whom, the question asked, did the respondent vote on controversial issues, and with whom did others vote?[9]

Analysis of the sociometric data from the city councils revealed three types of voting pattern—unipolar, bipolar, and nonpolar. These voting patterns will conceptually be treated as decisional structures. A council with a *unipolar* structure is one in which all members nearly always vote together, although there may be an occasional deviant. A council with a *bipolar* structure is one in which there is a relatively permanent division between two factions, although there may be swing voters who from time to time shift between factions. A council with a *nonpolar* structure is one that does not exhibit any recurrent voting pattern; there may be minority cliques that vote together, but there is a sufficient degree of shifting around that no single pattern repeats itself from one vote to the next.

These three decisional structures, taken together, constitute an empirical classification constructed from responses to questions about voting patterns. The first, and in a sense most important, question the researcher must ask about an empirical classification is concerned with the theoretical dimension underlying it. This question is prior to analysis that would seek to explain why a given group has the decisional structure it does (dependent-variable analysis) or analysis that would seek to explain how different decisional structures affect the functioning of the group (independent-variable analysis). For unless the research has determined what dimension is masked by a classification, any attempt to relate that classification to other variables must end in theoretical confusion.

In speculating about the theoretical dimensions that might be inherent in the typology of decisional structures, it became clear that more than one order could reasonably be assigned to the classification. In fact, three orderings suggested themselves—a conflict to harmony ordering, a fragmentation to integration ordering, and a permissiveness to constraint ordering. Each order, as Figure 10.1 indicates, calls for a different arrangement of the decisional structure typology.

Figure 10.1 shows that the empirical classification is not a single scale that orders councils on some single "most-to-least" dimension, but rather is a multidimensional classification. If the research can ferret out the several dimensions of a classification, its theoretical richness is correspondingly enhanced. What is offered in the first part of this essay, then, is analysis designed to show that the three orderings noted in Figure 10.1 are empirically viable; and, second, analysis that shows the theoretical validity of ordering the typology differently depending on the research question of interest.

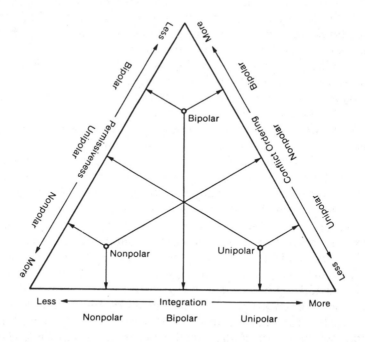

Figure 10.1   Ordinal dimensions of decisional structure typology

Dimensions of Decisional Structure

FIRST ORDERING: HARMONY AND CONFLICT

Any decisional structure should reflect the degree of harmony or conflict that obtains among its members. The unipolar council should be the most harmonious. It is a council in which voting splits rarely, if ever, occur. This is not to say that there are no disagreements; it is to say that prior to voting the group resolves any disagreements. At the other extreme of the harmony-conflict continuum is the bipolar council, the group that on important and controversial issues more often than not divides into two stable, permanent factions. Whatever its source, conflict pervades the group and becomes crystallized in the bipolar pattern. The majority faction usually prevails, although it may at times lose as one or another member "swings" over to the minority. The sources of conflict may be many and will vary from council to council—there may be lasting ideological differences, splits arising out of personal antagonisms, or commitments to different and hostile constituencies outside the council.

If the polarity typology contains a harmony-conflict dimension, nonpolar structures should be located between the two extreme poles. There are issues or personal difficulties that divide the council, but disagreements are neither so enduring nor so intense that councilmen cannot shift from issue to issue and form changing coalitions. As lines of cleavage are temporary, recurrent voting patterns as in the unipolar and bipolar situations do not develop. While nonpolar structures clearly contain conflictual elements, they also contain elements of harmony.

Any variable itself containing the harmony conflict dimension should therefore be ordered along a linear scale that locates the polarity structures from conflict (bipolarity) to harmony (unipolarity). A variable of this sort is the oppositional activity that may develop in a council. One would expect that where conflict is pronounced, oppositional activity as a group property should also be high; and where there is little conflict, opposition should be a rare occurrence. As Table 10.1 shows, this is in fact the case.[10]

SECOND ORDERING: INTEGRATION AND FRAGMENTATION

In addition to the harmony-conflict dimension, the decisional structure typology should contain a dimension that orders the structures from the most integrated to the least integrated or fragmented. Fragmentation must not be confused with conflict. Individuals in a group may be only loosely bonded to each other and have only minimal common interests. Yet such a group need not be a conflictual group. In fact, mutual avoidance may

Table 10.1 Conflict ordering and in-group oppositional activity, by percent

| | Conflict ordering | | |
| | Conflict←————————————→Harmony | | |
Oppositional activity	Bipolar (N = 20)	Nonpolar (N = 29)	Unipolar (N = 33)
High	45	31	12
Medium-high	10	21	30
Medium-low	20	34	12
Low	25	14	46
Total	100	100	100
Gamma = .30			

avert conflict. On the other hand, in a group where conflict is highly institutionalized, the structure may be well integrated—in Simmel's terms, the conflict may bind group members together.

Nonpolar councils, it has been noted, are less conflictual than bipolar councils, although they are more conflictual than unipolar ones. If our theoretical reasoning is valid, this is not surprising, because councils with nonpolar structures are poorly integrated—they consist of multiple factions, cliques, and/or isolates. The pattern of interpersonal relationships is fragmented but not necessarily conflictual. By way of contrast, bipolar structures, though conflictual, are more integrated as two stable factions confront each other. Unipolar structures, of course, are the most integrated. It seems reasonable, therefore, to order the polarity types from high to low integration—unipolar, bipolar, and nonpolar, in that order.

If nonpolar councils have the least-integrated or most-fragmented decisional structure, one may ask how a majority necessary for decision making comes about. Or, put in the language of functional analysis, one may ask how a nonpolar group solves the "problem" of integration.

One way, perhaps a necessary way, in which majorities in loosely knit groups can be formed is through joint sponsorship of proposals.[11] Individuals, cliques, or factions seek each other out as the group moves from issue to issue and form alliances that, even though temporary, make it possible to dispose of council business. One expects nonpolar councils to be characterized by more cosponsorship than bipolar councils. In the latter cosponsorship is less necessary to create a new alliance but more necessary to maintain a standing coalition, for unless the bipolar split is enduring and pervasive, there are always marginal members whose support either faction seeks to retain. In the unipolar structures, of course, cosponsorship is likely to be minimal, although even here the desire to maintain a united front may call for some coalition building. As Table 10.2 shows, the expected relationships do in fact occur. The more fragmented the decisional structure (nonpolarity), the more cosponsorship seems to occur; the more integrated the structure (unipolarity), the less is cosponsorship a council property.

In addition to cosponsorship, it seems that what has come to be called "opinion leadership" may serve as an integrating mechanism. Opinion leadership is conceived here as a group property. It may be recalled that opinion leadership was first discovered in connection with the study of mass communication (see Lazarsfeld, Berelson, and Gaudet, 1948; Katz and Lazarsfeld, 1955). The "mass" has, by definition, a highly fragmented and inchoate structure of interpersonal relations. It is through the emergence of opinion leadership that otherwise disjointed opinions and attitudes are collected into organized positions on political issues. The opinion leader serves as both catalyst of the mass mood and transmitter of elite messages. In playing the interstitial role of opinion leaders, strategically placed individuals exert interpersonal influence and transform a "mass" incapable of collective action into a "public" that can make decisions on controversial issues.

The fact that, as Table 10.3 shows, opinion leadership as an integrating force also emerges quite strongly in fragmented (nonpolar) small legislative groups attests to its importance in political life.[12] Only one of the twenty-nine nonpolar (3 percent) but thirteen of the thirty-three unipolar councils (40 percent) are "low" on the opinion leadership index. From the point of view pursued here, opinion leadership, like coalitional activity, seems to confirm the theoretical validity of the decisional structure typology as including an integration fragmentation dimension.

Table 10.2   Integration ordering and cosponsorship, by percent

	Integration ordering Fragmentation ⟵——————⟶ Integration		
Cosponsorship	Nonpolar (N = 29)	Bipolar (N = 20)	Unipolar (N = 33)
High	28	10	10
Medium-high	31	40	24
Medium-low	38	25	42
Low	3	25	24
Total	100	100	100
Gamma = .35			

Table 10.3   Integration ordering and opinion leadership, by percent

Opinion leadership	Fragmentation←————————→Integration		
	Nonpolar (N = 29)	Bipolar (N = 20)	Unipolar (N = 33)
High	28	30	12
Medium-high	31	25	21
Medium-low	38	20	27
Low	3	25	40
Total	100	100	100
Gamma = .37			

THIRD ORDERING: PERMISSIVENESS AND CONSTRAINT

The three decisional structures are also likely to differ in the degree to which conformity to expected voting behavior is rewarded and deviation is sanctioned. Where, as in the nonpolar pattern of voting, the individual member has much freedom of choice, a "live-and-let-live" atmosphere makes for a great deal of permissiveness in political conduct, and few constraints are imposed on the individual by the group as a whole, by factions, or by individuals. Voting behavior need not be and is not sanctioned. On the other hand, such "freedom of movement" is likely to be highly constrained in bipolar structures where more or less disciplined factions confront each other, where a high premium is set on loyalty to faction, and where deviation from the factional alliance is likely to be severely sanctioned. If there is, then, a third ordering of the decisional structures, from those where conduct is least constrained to those where it is most constrained, unipolar councils are probably located in the middle of the continuum. Although members of the group with a unipolar structure are generally expected to conform to the group's consensus, occasional deviation is permitted because it does not seriously affect the group's basic harmony and integration.

City councils, being essentially volunteer groups, do not have at their disposal all of the means to punish aberrant conduct as do more professionalized and partisan legislatures. One sanction available to them, however, is the awarding or withholding of respect. In small, face-to-face groups great value is likely to be placed on retaining the respect of one's peers. One would expect, therefore, that in a structure like the nonpolar one, where much permissiveness prevails, respect is more valued than in bipolar structures, where factional cleavage is maintained by granting respect to members of one's own faction and withholding it from members of the opposing faction. In bipolar structures, moreover, deviation from a factional alliance is likely to be punished by withdrawal or at least nonattribution of respect. It was found, for instance, on the individual level of analysis, that "swingers" in bipolar councils were less respected than those who stuck to their factions. In *bipolar* councils containing swingers, only 40 percent were accorded respect, while of the nonswingers—those who never crossed factional lines—64 percent were named as being respected.[13] As Table 10.4 shows, if the decisional structures are ordered along the permissiveness-constraint dimension, it appears that respect as a group property is more characteristic of the nonpolar, permissive councils than of the bipolar, nonpermissive councils.[14] The data suggest that level of permissiveness or constraint in voting conduct is a meaningful dimension of the decisional structure typology.

AN UNEXPECTED FINDING: THE PUZZLE OF AFFECT

Respect for one's peers, one might surmise, should be closely related to affect—the degree to which one values them as friends. This is in fact the case. The correlation coefficient for the respect and affect relationship is +.22. Yet, surprisingly, affect cannot be ordered by the decisional structure typology in the same way as respect. Nor can it be ordered, as one might expect, along the integration-fragmentation dimension. One might have supposed that affect or declarations of friendship would be most characteristic of unipolar structures and least characteristic of bipolar structures. But, as Table 10.5 shows, this is not the case. On the contrary, affect is actually ordered in a direction that one would least expect—along the conflict dimension. Affect, it appears, is positively related to conflict and

Table 10.4 Permissiveness ordering and respect, by percent

| | Permissiveness ←————————→ Constraint | | |
Respect	Nonpolar (N = 29)	Unipolar (N = 33)	Bipolar (N = 20)
High	34	28	15
Medium-high	28	24	20
Medium-low	17	21	30
Low	21	27	35
Total	100	100	100
Gamma = .23			

Table 10.5   Conflict ordering and affect, by percent

| Affect | Conflict ⟵ ——————————— ⟶ Harmony | | |
	Bipolar (N = 20)	Nonpolar (N = 29)	Unipolar (N = 33)
High	25	24	18
Medium-high	35	31	15
Medium-low	15	24	21
Low	25	21	46
Total	100	100	100

Gamma = .26

Table 10.6   Distribution of intrafactional and interfactional friendship nominations in bipolar decisional structures, by percent

Nominations given by—	Own faction	Other faction	Total
Members of majority (N = 72)	89	11	100
Members of minority (N = 30)	83	17	100

Source: Peter A. Lupsha, "Swingers, Isolates and Coalitions: Interpersonal Relations in Small Political Decision-Making Groups" (Ph.D. diss., Stanford University, August 1967), p. 189, table 8.7.

negatively related to harmony in the council's decisional structure.[15] How can one explain this apparently anomalous finding?

The hypothesis suggests itself that in a council permeated by conflict that makes for sharp factional differentiation and polarization, the members are inclined to emphasize and value whatever emotional ties of friendship bind them together in the otherwise hostile group context. On the other hand, in a politically harmonious group expressions of affect are not forthcoming as much because interpersonal relations are not strained and demonstrations of mutual affect are not needed to maintain the group's harmony. In the bipolar structures, the antagonistic atmosphere of the group as a whole seems to call out strong friendship relationships in the council's subgroups, but not across subgroup lines. Proof of this hypothesis cannot be pursued here because it requires a more detailed analysis of the bipolar councils, which has not as yet been completed. However, it can be reported that in an analysis based on *individual* respondents as the units of analysis, Peter Lupsha found that in bipolar councils overwhelming majorities of both majority and minority factions named members of their own subgroups as "friends" (Table 10.6)

A NEGATIVE FINDING: EXPERTISE

A final group property introduced into the analysis is the council's emphasis on expertise, but there was no reason to expect that this variable would in any theoretically meaningful way be related to the decisional structure typology.[16] We found no significant empirical relationship, whatever the ordering. In other words, expertise as a group attribute may be present or absent regardless of whether the decisional structure is conflictual or harmonious, integrated or fragmented, permissive or constraining. This does not mean that expertise is an unimportant group property. It may well be very relevant to other aspects of council behavior. It merely means that it is not related to the voting splits that, in the final stage of the legislative process, give the council its characteristic decisional structure.

Configurations of Properties

It has been shown that certain empirical types of decisional structure found in small legislative bodies can be ordered to make theoretical sense. Moreover, these orderings aid in gaining insight into various interpersonal relationships in the real world of legislative decision making. This world is complex and multidimensional. Its multidimensionality is a fact of political life. Varieties of order in political life are "troublesome" only if one mistakes the pure world of theory for the complex world of political relationships.

Because the purpose of the analysis so far has been to explore different dimensions of the legislative body's decisional structure, no assumptions have been made about causation. This severely limits the explanatory power of the analysis. It has the advantage of any heuristic method: in the real world of legislative groups, structural variables or collective properties may coexist, regardless of whether they are related to each other in a causal or even functional order. Coexistence may be mutually reinforcing and symmetrical. Causal analysis, on the other hand, must assume asymmetry: one variable is assumed to be "stronger" than the other and to have "power" to order the second variable.

How, then, does the decisional structure influence the pattern of the relationships among other properties of the council? To answer this question, one may initially assume that the various relational properties identified in the analysis—opinion leadership, cosponsorship, oppositional activity, affect, respect, and expertise—are themselves interrelated in a way that is consistent with their individual relationships to the decisional structure. Table 10.7 presents the correlation matrix for all possible pairwise relations

Table 10.7   Correlations between council relational properties

	Opinion leader- ship	Cosponsor- ship	Opposi- tional activity	Af- fect	Re- spect	Exper- tise
Opinion leader- ship	—	.54	.52	.49	.32	.26
Cosponsorship		—	.48	.35	.21	.30
Oppositional ac- tivity			—	.26	.36	.26
Affect				—	.22	.30
Respect					—	.20
Decisional struc- ture	.37	.35	.30	.26	.23	.00

among the council's relational properties. It should be noted that the properties have been ordered as variables on the basis of the strength of the correlation coefficient between each property and the decisional structure.

Two aspects of the matrix stand out. First, the matrix is highly symmetrical. With some exceptions in the respect and expertise columns, the gamma values of the pairwise relations decline in the same order as do the gamma values for the correlation of each property with the decisional structure. The greatest disorder occurs in the relationships between expertise and the other variables. Expertise, it will be recalled, does not seem related to the type of decisional structure encountered in a council. It now appears that although it is positively related to other properties, the relationship is rather indeterminate and generally weaker than that of the other associations (within a narrow range of .20 and .30). The respect variable shows an unexpectedly high relationship with oppositional activity (.36). But otherwise the pattern of the matrix is symmetrical, suggesting that the associations among the council properties are not altogether random. Evidently a council's multiple properties not only coexist, but they coexist in an orderly fashion.

Second, the correlations are strongest among those variables that are also most strongly related to the decisional structure—notably opinion leadership, cosponsorship, and oppositional activity. These are the intrinsically most "political" properties of the council's informal organization. They apparently contribute more to the variance of council legislative behavior than do the politically less-relevant affect, respect, and expertise variables.

However, it is not unreasonable to assume that both the apparent symmetry and strength of the relationships among council properties are artifacts of the multidimensional nature of the decisional structure typology. In other words, it is likely that some properties are more related to each other and other properties less related, depending on the particular dimension that is being tapped. In order to pursue this line of speculation, it is necessary to control the various relationships by holding decisional structure constant. How will the symmetry of the relationships be affected once the effect of multidimensionality in the decisional structure typology is removed? And how will the strength of the relationships be affected? Table 10.8 presents the correlations with the decisional structure variable controlled.

Two outcomes should be predicted. First, symmetry in the correlation matrices should disappear. A given decisional structure's mix of dimensions is likely to have different impacts on the relationships among the different variables. In the unipolar councils, the high level of harmony and integration in the decisional structure should have an impact different from that of the high level of conflict and constraint in the bipolar structure. Similarly, the high level of permissiveness and fragmentation in the decisional struc-

Table 10.8 Correlations between council relational properties, decisional structure constant

	Cosponsorship	Oppositional activity	Affect	Respect	Expertise
Unipolar					
Opinion leadership	.46	.49	.66	.18	.31
Cosponsorship		.63	.40	.32	.26
Oppositional activity			.42	.47	.29
Affect				.26	.51
Respect					.38
Bipolar					
Opinion leadership	.41	.64	.46	.63	.03
Cosponsorship		.39	.31	−.01	.11
Oppositional activity			−.03	.25	.20
Affect			.56	.13	
Respect					.00
Nonpolar					
Opinion leadership	.59	.33	.17	.22	.52
Cosponsorship		.35	.22	.11	.63
Oppositional activity			.12	.41	.36
Affect				−.02	.23
Respect					.25

ture of nonpolar councils should have its own characteristic effect on the associations among group properties.

Second, the values of the correlation coefficients should change in the controlled matrices from those observed in the original matrix, and they should change in a predictable way. For instance, in the unipolar councils the highly integrated and harmonious character of the decisional structure should make for correlations among the council's multiple properties that are generally higher than those in the original matrix. On the other hand, one might expect that in bipolar councils the constraints of the decisional structure and the conflict prevailing there will tend to reduce the strengths of the various relationships, although some might increase because of the possibly integrative functions of conflict in the bipolar situation. Finally, the strength of associations should be more unpredictable in the nonpolar councils. The high degree of permissiveness and low level of integration in the decisional structure of these councils should have relatively little impact, making the pattern less cohesive than the unipolar configurations and more factional than the bipolar ones.

In order to facilitate inspection of Table 10.8, the correlation coefficients indicating an increase over the original values have been italicized. The results are very much in line with our speculations. In the unipolar matrix, eleven of the fifteen coefficients are higher than those reported in Table 10.7, and two—for the relationships between opinion leadership, on the one hand, and cosponsorship and oppositional activity, on the other hand—remain relatively high. Unipolar councils evidently have not only a harmonious and integrative decisional structure, but the web of relationships among other properties is more tightly knit than is the case in nonpolar and bipolar settings. On the other hand, in the bipolar councils only three of the fifteen coefficients increase once decisional structure is held constant. The nonpolar councils present some difficulty in interpretation. For the most evident and least expected aspect of the nonpolar matrix is the spectacular increase of the coefficients for expertise in four of the five possible relationships. But only two of the other ten possible correlations have increased over the original correlations. Not surprisingly in groups highly dependent on constant realignment of working majorities, only one linkage— between opinion leadership and cosponsorship—is exceptionally strong.

Moreover, the original symmetry of the matrix in Table 10.7 has disappeared, as predicted. However, each of the controlled matrices of Table 10.8 has its own characteristic and by no means arbitrary pattern. These patterns evidently reflect the underlying dimensions of each polar type of the decisional structure and give meaning to the different relationships within each configuration. In exploring the meanings, I shall pinpoint and use mainly those relationships that are especially notable (where gamma

= .30 or more) and shall call attention to patterns in the table by broken lines representing clusters A, B, and C.

CLUSTER A

First of all, it may be noted that the politically most-revelant variables— opinion leadership, cosponsorship, and oppositional activity—remain highly interrelated in each matrix. Regardless of decisional structure, these variables constitute the core of each configuration. However, the highest correlations among the three variables change from one cluster to the next. In the unipolar matrix, it is oppositional activity and cosponsorship that are most closely associated; in the bipolar matrix, it is oppositional activity and opinion leadership; and in the nonpolar matrix, it is opinion leadership and cosponsorship.

How can these variations be explained? In the context of this analysis, they must be explained in terms of the dimensions implicit in a particular decisional structure. In other words, different assumptions consonant with what is known about the relationship between each variable and the decisional structure of each configuration need to be made. It may be recalled, for instance, that unipolar councils are especially low in oppositional activity (Table 10.1). It may be assumed, therefore, that oppositional activity, when it should emerge in these councils, is not tolerable, and that it will be countervailed by cosponsorship. This would seem to explain the strong correlation (.63) between these two variables in the unipolar configuration.

On the other hand, in the conflictual, bipolar councils, oppositional activity is a fact of political life—a "given" that almost defines the bipolar structure. In the bipolar situation, opinion leadership may serve to crystallize the lines of cleavage that characterize the decisional structure, on the one hand, but it may also serve to integrate either side of the division. If this is so, it may explain the strong correlation (.64) between oppositional activity and opinion leadership in the bipolar configuration.

Finally, as shown earlier (Table 10.2), cosponsorship is most closely associated with the fragmented, permissive nonpolar decisional structure. In a council with a nonpolar structure, the formation of a successful coalition is highly dependent on winning supporters for a proposal, and this can best be done, it seems, by searching for cosponsors among those whose voice counts the most—the opinion leaders. And, as has also been noted (Table 10.3), opinion leadership is an especially prominent property of councils with a nonpolar decisional structure. The high correlation (.59) between cosponsorship and opinion leadership in the nonpolar configuration seems to be consonant with this interpretation.

CLUSTER B

Although in cluster A only the highest correlation coefficients in each set of triple relationships have been singled out, the other coefficients are also substantial. But from here on, the character of each polar configuration changes. Most dramatic, perhaps, is the difference between the unipolar and nonpolar matrices in regard to the affect and expertise variables (cluster B). In the unipolar configuration, it appears, the core set of relationships—opinion leadership, cosponsorship, and oppositional activity—is sustained by fairly strong connections between each of the core variables with affect; in the nonpolar configuration, although there are positive if weak relationships between affect and each core variable, it is expertise that emerges as an important property with moderate to strong linkages to the core set of properties. Again, explanation of these outcomes requires the introduction of some assumptions.

Affect, it will be recalled, was negatively related to the harmonious end of the decisional structure typology. This should not lead to the assumption that affect cannot emerge as an important property in the kind of political situation represented by the unipolar configuration. The negative value placed on oppositional activity in the councils with a unipolar structure can be assumed to mobilize friendship as a means to reduce or avoid internal friction. Once mobilized, opinion leaders and cosponsors are sought out among those considered friends, making for the linkages observed in the unipolar matrix. By way of contrast, these linkages are much weaker in the nonpolar configuration. And in the bipolar matrix, affect and oppositional activity are not related. In the bipolar situation, we can assume, affect does not serve to unify the group as a whole but rather one or another of the two factions or both. Rather than serving as an integrative bond for the council as a whole, affect, as noted earlier, serves to sustain the basic division of the legislative body.

Expertise, it appears, is not a particularly salient property in the politicized bipolar configuration. The relationship between expertise and the configuration's core variables is low. In the unipolar matrix, although the relationships are somewhat stronger, expertise does not appear to be critical to council functioning. It is in the nonpolar configuration that expertise is strongly linked with the core variables. We may assume that in this configuration in which oppositional activity has only moderate connections with opinion leadership and cosponsorship, on the one hand, and weak linkages with affect, the nonpolitical and nonaffective property of expertise has much freedom to make itself felt. Although expertise in the nonpolar configuration is only moderately related to oppositional activity, it is strongly related to opinion leadership and cosponsorship. We can assume that in a situation of relatively low political and affective salience, opinion leaders and cosponsors are sought out among those who are considered most informed and knowledgeable. The highly fragmented and permissive and only moderately conflictual nature of the nonpolar decisional structure is conducive to the emergence of expertise as a property that is strongly related to the configuration's core variables.

CLUSTER C

A final cluster that may be noted in Table 10.8 involves some correlates of opinion leadership. In the unipolar matrix, opinion leadership is highly linked with affect (.66); in the bipolar matrix, with respect (.63); and in the nonpolar matrix, with expertise (.52). The differences are consonant with our interpretations of the three configurations. Of the "nonpolitical" properties, affect or bonds of friendship have high political salience in the basically harmonious and integrated context of unipolar councils; respect, a more impersonal evaluation of one's peers, facilitates communication and exchange in the otherwise conflictual context of bipolar councils; and expertise, as noted already, is most relevant in the fragmented, permissive context of nonpolar councils with their low interpersonal and political cohesion. That each of these properties is strongly linked with opinion leadership probably symptomizes the structural roots of such leadership. Whether it is rooted in affect, in respect, or in expertise would seem to depend on the basic nature of a given polar configuration—the degree to which it is harmonious or conflictual; the degree to which it is integrated or fragmented; and the degree to which it is permissive or constrained.

The significant finding of the first part of this analysis was that some of a legislative body's relational properties associated with a given dimension of its decisional structure are *not* associated with another dimension, as follows:

Legislative group properties	Decisional structure orderings		
	Integration	Conflict	Permissiveness
Opinion leadership	Yes	No	No
Cosponsorship	Yes	No	No
Oppositional activity	No	Yes	No
Affect relations	No	Yes	No
Respect relations	No	No	Yes
Expertise	No	No	No

Each dimension of the decisional structure, it was suggested in the second part, seems to give rise to a characteristic configuration among the council's several relational properties. Because each configuration is permeated by a dominant dimension once decisional structure is held constant, there are differences not only within a common core of properties that includes opinion leadership, cosponsorship, and oppositional activity, but there are also differences from configuration to configuration that are rooted in different "mixes" of the core properties with such other relational variables as affect, respect, and expertise.

The variables analyzed and linked in this study are "relational properties" of the total legislative structure. They are properties emerging from interpersonal relationships that make the legislative body a "living group." They are not, of course, its only properties. Role, status, and norm structures are also important properties. There are properties such as the legislature's governing style, atmosphere, or political practices. And there are such properties as its collective attitudes, perceptions, and decisions. The configuration of properties treated in this study may be regarded as constituting the legislative group's informal organization under different conditions of decisional structure.

11

Political Matrix and

Political Representation

SCHOLARS interested in theorizing about political representation in terms relevant to democratic governance in mid-twentieth-century America find themselves in a quandary. We are surrounded by functioning representative institutions, or at least by institutions formally described as representative. Individuals who presumably "represent" other citizens govern some 90,000 different political units—they sit on school and special-district boards, on township and city councils, on county directorates, on state and national assemblies, and so forth. But the flourishing activity of representation has not yet been matched by a sustained effort to explain what makes the representational process tick.

Despite the proliferation of representative governments over the past century, *theory* about representation has not moved much beyond the eighteenth-century formulation of Edmund Burke. Certainly most empirical research has been cast in the Burkean vocabulary (see Eulau et al., 1959; Miller and Stokes, 1963). But in order to think in novel ways about representative government in the twentieth century, we may have to admit that present conceptions guiding empirical research are obsolete. This in turn means that the spell of Burke's vocabulary over scientific work on representation must be broken (Eulau, 1967).

To look afresh at representation, it is necessary to be sensitive to the unresolved tension between the two main currents of contemporary thinking about representational relationships. On the one hand, representation is treated as a relationship between any one individual, the represented, and another individual, the representative—an *interindividual* relationship. On the other hand, representatives are treated as a group, brought together in the assembly, to represent the interest of the community as a whole—

Written with Kenneth Prewitt.

an *intergroup* relationship. Most theoretical formulations since Burke are cast in one or the other of these terms.

Current empirical studies of representation by and large make individualistic assumptions. Partly these presuppositions are rooted in the individualistic culture of democratic politics; but they are also eminently congenial to the methodology of survey research that takes the individual as the empirical unit of analysis. In concentrating on the individual, be he representative or represented, contemporary research has gained much insight into the ideology of representation and possibly into representational behavior. We know, for instance, that the representative may see himself as a "trustee" or "delegate" (or some mixture) and that such self-images serve the public official in defining political situations, in guiding his actions, or in justifying his decisions.[1] But research into the rationalizations of the representatives has not led to an adequate theory that would explain the functioning of contemporary representative government. Other investigations are less "individualistic" in their presuppositions. In particular the theoretical discussions of "public interest" or "general will" suggest an understanding of representation as a relationship between collectivities. These investigations, however, have not provided the empirically grounded theory of representation we feel is needed.

A viable theory of representation, it seems to us, cannot be constructed from individualistic assumptions alone. It must be constructed out of an understanding of representation as a relationship between two collectives— the representative assembly and the represented citizenry. However, neither can a viable theory be advanced in the absence of empirical investigation into the thinking and the acting of the individuals in the collectives. What we grope toward, then, is a theoretically adequate treatment of representation as a property of the political system, a treatment tutored by systematic data.

A Fresh Look at Representation

Our beginning point is a highly suggestive passage in Professor Pitkin's (1967, p. 224) explication of the concept of representation. She elaborates on representation as something that "must be understood at the public level":

The representative system must look after the public interest and be responsive to public opinion, except insofar as non-responsiveness can be justified in terms of the public interest. At both ends, the process is public and institutional. The individual legislator does not act alone, but as a member of a representative body.

By elevating representation from the level of individual relationships to the level of the political system, Pitkin (ibid., pp. 221–222) suggests that representation is, in her own words,

primarily a public institutional arrangement involving many people and groups, and operating in the complex ways of large-scale social arrangements. What makes it representation is not any single action by any one participant, but the over-all structure and functioning of the system, the patterns emerging from the multiple activities of many people.

Having pointed out that representation is a systemic phenomenon, Pitkin goes on to note that representation may or may not emerge from whatever is the relationship between citizens and public officials. "I am not suggesting," she writes, that representation "must emerge from any particular system; there is no guarantee that it will. But it may emerge, and to the extent that it does we consider that system as being a representative government" (ibid., p. 224).

If, as Pitkin suggests, representation is a collective and public phenomenon that may or may not emerge in a political community, and if emergence of a representative relationship is conditioned by the "over-all structure and functioning of the system," our attention should be directed to properties of the political system that either facilitate or impede representation. This we propose to do.

In describing representation as an emergent property of the political system, Pitkin anticipates a course of methodological inquiry that has engaged us for a number of years and that underlies the procedures adopted in present research on the governance of cities. First, our analysis assumes that representation as well as other variables we consider are group rather than individual properties; thus we make statements about governing bodies and not individual public officials. Second, although we study eighty-two governments formally defined as "representative," we see representation not as something existing by definition but as something that emerges in the relationship between governing assemblies and governed citizens. Third, whether the particular relationship we might call representation does emerge is affected by the political matrix within which representatives and represented act. Finally, the analysis is configurative, not causal; we want to determine how a particular configuration of system properties, including representation, is linked together.

Of course not all properties of the political community are likely to be equally relevant to the emergence of representation. Our reading of the theoretical literature about American politics directed us to four variables usually considered germane to representation: the degree of social pluralism, the effectiveness of elections as sanctioning mechanisms, the support available to the governing group, and the recruitment processes that select public officials. For present purposes, we consider these four variables— taken together—to constitute a political matrix. The configuration of the political matrix, then, should be critical to how the governing group responds to social pressures and political demands.

Two of these properties—degree of social pluralism and election effectiveness—are first-order system variables that can be directly measured with relevant indicators. The other two properties—recruitment and support—in addition to representation, are constructed into group properties from individual data. The data base for our measures of these three variables consists of interviews with 423 city councilmen in eighty-two cities of the San Francisco Bay metropolitan region. In order to make the relevant information appropriate for systemic analysis it was necessary to convert the responses of individuals into group properties. This we did in one of two ways. In the case of representation and support we treated the councilmen as informants. We read appropriate questions in the interview schedule for the council *as a whole* and assigned the council to a code category. Because in this analysis we use only one measure of representation, no further index construction was necessary. Our measure of support is constructed from five separate indicators that are sufficiently cumulative to permit a simple summation index. Recruitment as a systemic property, on the other hand, was measured by aggregating the codings of each individual councilman's recruitment pattern into a single council measure. We describe the procedures more fully as we introduce the measures in the analysis.

To employ these coding procedures, of course, is to take certain liberties. For example, although we sometimes speak of community support for the council, we actually are inferring level of support from responses of the councilmen themselves. This is not the place to engage in a complicated defense of whether "definitions of the situation" do indeed serve as the "reality" for those who see it as such. Our intent is to explore in a tentative fashion the relationship among several variables; level of community support being one of these variables, we sought the best measure possible within the confines of our data. A second methodological assumption is that single group measures can be constructed from the individual responses of those who belong to the group without doing violence to the data. Again, this is not the time to present an extended discussion of "group properties" and how to construct them. Our general strategy is to pursue certain theoretical questions as vigorously as possible, but to report specific findings in a tentative way, paying full heed to the data difficulties.

Representation as Response

Whether the relationship between the governing few and the governed many can be said to be a representative one depends, of course, on how the term is defined. "Representation" has been subject to a variety of definitions. Some studies have described a legislative assembly as representative when the social and economic characteristics of the constituency were fairly well mirrored in the assembly. Other studies, pursuing the logic of "mirror representation," have been less concerned with demographic representation and instead have examined whether in ideology or general values the assembly reflected the constituents. Yet other studies, dropping the mirror analogy, have defined representation in terms of equal access to the assembly by all members of the constituency.

The definition of representation that guides our theoretical endeavors differs from these formulations. In coding the interviews, we made what to us was a surprising discovery: of the eighty-two councils, as many as thirty-six did not in any discernible manner seem to act in response to any politically organized views in the public. These thirty-six councils seemed to rely on their own sense of what the community needs were. This finding alerted us to Pitkin's observation that representation is an emergent property whose appearance cannot be taken for granted. The finding further suggested the importance of looking at the representative relationship in terms of whether the elected assembly acts in response to public views, especially views as delivered in some identifiable manner.

Pitkin left no stone unturned in her effort to salvage the concept of representation as a viable tool for theorizing about problems of democratic governance. After reviewing and interpreting almost any conceivable formulation of the concept's meaning, she settles for this definition: "representing here means acting in the interest of the represented, in a manner responsive to them" (1967, p. 209). We find this definition useful because it seems to conceive of representation in two related ways: first, the representative assembly defines *what* it should do—"acting in the interest of the represented"; that is, it decides on the political agenda and, in so doing, formulates community goals. Second, the assembly does so in a manner *responsive* to the sentiments of the constituents.[2]

In studying the protocols from the councils, it became clear that, as they govern, councils can act in response to two types of politically organized and publicly voiced opinions. First, councils can consider the views and wishes of attentive publics, of fairly well defined and permanent interest clusters in the community. These attentive publics may have differing views of how the community should be governed, in which case the council must compromise and adjust. Or the attentive publics may be more or less of the same view, in which case the council need only determine what this view is and act upon it. In either case, we say that the council, by acting in response to the viewpoints and thinking of attentive publics, represents these publics. Second, the council may not concern itself with cohesive attentive publics but may, instead, act in response to ad hoc pressures and petitions. Neighborhood groups, for instance, may organize on a sporadic basis, make claim on the council for some service or benefit, and expect to be listened to by "their representatives." Under these conditions, councils placate or respond to specialized and transitory citizen groups. If in the first case the council represents attentive publics, in this case it represents issue-specific groups of citizens.

There is a third type of representative relationship with the public. As previously noted, some councils appear to be altogether immune to external pressures; no identifiable groups of citizens, permanently or sporadically organized, appear to intrude on council deliberations about community affairs. In such cases, councils may or may not be acting *in the interest* of the represented (an issue we do not explore here); they are not, however, acting *in response to* the represented. Rather, these councils entertain a self-defined image of what community needs are. It is in terms of its own image that the council tackles the problems that come to its attention.

The eighty-two councils divided into the three categories as follows:[3]

Councils responsive to attentive publics	20	24%
Councils responsive to ad hoc issue groups	26	32%
Councils entertaining self-defined image	36	44%

The distribution of the councils into this three-category classification essentially sets the question. For present analytic purposes, representation is taken to mean a relationship between governed and governors wherein the governing group responds to ("represents") politically organized viewpoints among citizens, that is, responds to something *other* than its own image of what the community needs. With representation so understood, we ask: under what political conditions is a representative relationship between governors and governed likely to emerge in a community? Our analysis examines both the patterns among the four variables that we have singled out as relevant for representation and the connections between the political matrix, as constructed from these four indicators, and the emergence of representation.

Representational Response Style and Social Pluralism

An assumption that frequently appears in discussions of representation and modern society might be stated as follows: increasing complexity and differentiation in modern societies makes it more and more difficult for representative bodies to respond to the variety of interests that constitute the political community. Persons who make such observations usually assume representation to be a relationship between individuals. We were interested to see if representation, treated at the systemic level, was indeed less likely to emerge in larger and more complex communities. Table 11.1 presents relevant data.

Using population size as an indicator of a community's social pluralism,[4] it is clear that responding to interests voiced from the community is *facilitated* in the more pluralistic communities. How are we to reconcile this finding with the assumption that social complexity impedes the exercise of the representational function? It may be correct that the larger and more complex a social system, the more difficult it is for any *one* citizen to make his wishes known or for any *one* representative to respond to individual constituents. The data in Table 11.1 emphasize why an individualistic conception of representation is obsolete. Representation as a relationship between too collectives—the represented and the representatives—appears to emerge more easily in the larger, more complex communities than in the smaller, more homogeneous communities. To understand representation as a systemic property we may have to rethink many of our conventional assumptions. Indeed, the responsiveness of the representative assembly is facilitated under just those conditions assumed to impede individual responsiveness.

The pattern in Table 11.1 makes considerable sense. It may well be that

Table 11.1   City size as indicator of social pluralism and council response style, by percent

Representational response style	City size		
	<10,000 (N = 32)	10,000–50,000 (N = 33)	>50,000 (N = 17)
To self-defined image	56	39	29
To ad hoc issue groups	31	36	24
To attentive publics	13	25	47
Total	100	100	100

$$\frac{\chi^2}{df} = \frac{8.10}{4} = 2.03$$

Gamma = .38

in the smaller and more homogeneous communities the social structure is such that there is simply little opportunity for the council to respond to stable, attentive publics or to ad hoc, spontaneous issue groups. Unlike in larger and heterogeneous cities, where various social groups are present and likely to make their demands known to the city council, in the smaller, more homogeneous settings, the group life is likely to be less developed and the public pressures brought on the council are probably less frequent or urgent. If this is so, councils in small cities are unable to identify groups to which they might wish to respond, if they only could, and will have to rely on their own images of what is in the best interest of the represented. As Table 11.1 shows, this is in fact the case: the smaller the city, the more councils act in their self-images; the larger the city, the more councils are responsive to groups that articulate interests.[5]

Representational Response Style and Electoral Tolerance

It is customary to entertain many assumptions, which often remain untested, about the consequences of elections for representation. Different nominating procedures (primaries versus conventions), voting rules (list versus transferable vote), electoral arrangements (at-large, multimember versus single-member constituencies), counting procedures (majority versus proportional), election types (partisan versus nonpartisan), and so on are said to produce very different types of elected representatives.

Even more to the point, assumptions about elections are very central in writings that consider such issues as "accountability" and "responsiveness." As Dahl (1956, p. 131) has written, elections "are crucial processes for insuring that political leaders will be somewhat *responsive to the preferences of some ordinary citizens.*"[6] The assumption made by Dahl and by many other writers on democratic politics is that public officials choose policies in anticipation of likely electorate response at the next election. Schlesinger (1966, p. 2) employs similar reasoning and states the point even more strongly: "The desire for election and, more important, for reelection becomes the electorate's restraint upon its public officials."[7] In democratic theory, then, elections are viewed as the sanction available to the public. In the absence of this sanction, officeholders would not be accountable. And if the governors are not accountable, it is difficult to imagine them being responsive. "The point of holding [the elected official] to account after he acts is to make him act in a certain way—look after his constituents, or do what they want" (Pitkin, 1967, p. 57).

The difficulty with these assumptions about representative democracy is that they, in turn, make the assumption that elections do indeed remove or threaten to remove men from public office. We have serious doubts that this is the case. For one thing, and a fact too often overlooked by theorists who emphasize elections as a sanction, a very sizable group of officeholders retire from office voluntarily. As Charles Hyneman sharply pointed out five decades ago, turnover in legislatures is due not to election defeats, or even to fear of same, but occurs because men simply decide to leave public office. The real task, Hyneman wrote in 1938 (p. 30), "is to find out why so many legislators, senators and representatives alike, choose not to run again."[8] In his analysis of eight states covering the period 1925–1933 he found that *more than 60 percent* of the retirements from both lower houses and senates were due to failure to seek reelection.[9]

Alerted by Hyneman to the question of voluntary retirement, we checked to see how frequently city councilmen retired from office for reasons other than election defeat. In eighty-two cities over a ten-year period (five elections per city), more than half of the councilmen retired voluntarily from office. Although a few leave the council to seek higher office, survey data indicate this number is not large. And although a few might retire out of threat of election defeat, survey data indicate that this occurs very infrequently.[10]

This high and persistent rate of voluntary retirement from elected office certainly should caution us against the easy assumption that "elections make public officials responsive" and thus guarantee representative government. For if the representative body plans to depart from office in any case, why should it be concerned with voter approval of its policies? To explore the relationship between elections and representative response style, we need to determine whether the voting public does indeed ever remove incumbents from office.

We constructed an index of "forced turnover" based on the number of incumbents who won, divided by the number of incumbents who sought reelection over a ten-year period (five elections). (The index does not include incumbents who were appointed to office in the expired term.)[11] In twenty-one cities no incumbent seeking reelection was defeated. On the other hand, in only four cities did as many as half of the incumbents suffer defeat. The distribution, therefore, is highly skewed toward success in being reelected. Nevertheless the spread of election defeats is sufficient to permit us to classify cities into three theoretically useful groups: those in which a bid for reelection never failed, those in which it sometimes failed but less often than 25 percent of the time, and those in which it failed for at least one of every four incumbents.

We derive from general democratic theory a simple hypothesis. Cities with the highest rate of forced turnover, where electoral tolerance is relatively low, should have councils tending to act in response to public pressures and petitions. Conversely, councils that govern in a milieu where elections never force anyone from office will act in response only to their own image of what the community needs. This, as Table 11.2 shows, is the case.

Thus, on the one hand, conventional democratic theory appears to be confirmed. The presence of an electorate that removes men from office leads to more acts of response by the representative body. On the other hand, conventional theory also holds that councils not responding to political groups would be ousted from office. If we read Table 11.2 in reverse, it is evident that this does not happen; elections do not necessarily remove councils that respond only to their own image of community needs. The inability of conventional theorizing about elections to help us explain Table 11.2 is due to an oversight in much of the contemporary literature about representative democracy. Nowhere that we could find have scholars systematically examined the implications for representation *if elections are not used to force turnover* on representative bodies. But the reluctance, or inability, of the electorate to remove public officials is something we must take into account if our theory of representation is not to make unfounded empirical assumptions. Just why nonresponsive councils are seldom removed from office is a question to which we turn momentarily, but first we take a quick look at the relationship between social pluralism and electoral tolerance.

We expect that the electorate uses its voting powers to force turnover more often in larger cities, where pressures on the governing bodies are diverse and frequent, than in the more homogeneous and politically quiet environment of the smaller community. Table 11.3 shows this to be the case. The medium-sized and larger cities are characterized by higher rates of forced turnover than are the smaller cities, although even in the latter

Table 11.2   Forced turnover and representational response style, by percent

Representational response style	Forced turnover		
	None (N = 21)	1–24% (N = 39)	25 + % (N = 22)
To self-defined image	71	41	23
To ad hoc issue groups	19	31	45
To attentive publics	10	28	32
Total	100	100	100

$$\frac{\chi^2}{df} = \frac{10.96}{4} = 2.74$$
Gamma = .44

Table 11.3   City size and forced turnover, by percent

Forced turnover	City size		
	<10,000 (N=32)	10,000–50,000 (N=33)	>50,000 (N=17)
None of incumbents	37	25	7
1–24%	41	45	64
25 or more %	22	30	29
Total	100	100	100

$$\frac{\chi^2}{df} = \frac{6.26}{4} = 1.57$$

Gamma = .28

election defeats are not uncommon. Interpreting Tables 11.2 and 11.3 together, it seems that electoral tolerance is negatively related to the degree of representational response. Where councils need not fear the vote of the people, they are also less likely to act in response to the voice of the people.

Representational Response Style and Community Support

For the purpose of our theoretical exploration, let us assume that the first three tables provide findings on which we can build. Governing bodies with self-defined images of the public interest are found in smaller communities and are less subject to electoral sanctions than councils that act in response to public pressures. This is a paradox for representaional theory. In order to solve the paradox, it is necessary to consider another aspect of the political matrix that may be related to a council's representational response style—a system property we characterize as "community support." We expect, for instance, that where a council is generally supported in what it does by the citizenry, it is relatively free to define the community interest in its own image. And if this is so, it helps explain why a council, though nonresponsive, faces little risk in being ousted from office.

In order to characterize the citizenry of the eighty-two cities as more or less supportive of the council, we assumed that support was forthcoming if, according to council reports, any one or all of the following conditions were met: (1) that the public held a favorable and respectful image of the council; (2) that the public was in general agreement with the council on its duties; (3) that the public did not include disruptive elements; and (4) that there were not many groups steadily critical of the council's policies. We combined these items into a single index of community support.[12]

The measure of community support allows us to investigate the paradox that councils acting on the basis of their own images are less exposed to electoral sanctioning than councils that placate ad hoc issue groups or are attentive to more stable interest groups. As Table 11.4 shows, communities in which the electorate does not force incumbents from office are seen as overwhelmingly supportive of their councils; in communities where some or relatively many incumbents are forced from office, the citizens are seen as almost evenly split in the support they are giving their councils.

In communities, then, in which the citizenry is on the whole satisfied with council operations and policies and is apparently giving the council its support, we can assume that citizens do feel "represented" by the council even though the council follows its own definition of what is in the best interests of the governed. If this inference is sound, it helps explain why councils that do not act in response to community groups are yet free of threats of election defeats. It is precisely because it does not hear from the public that the council is able to rely on its own judgment. As Table 11.5 indicates, there is a very significant difference in councils' representational response styles between the more and less supportive political milieux, and the relationship is exceptionally strong. The table and our analysis suggest that, in dealing with representation as a system property, we must at all times keep in mind that it is embedded, as Pitkin so well put it, "in the complex ways of large social arrangements." It remains, therefore, to ascertain in what type of community support is forthcoming. From all that we know about small, relatively homogeneous cities, we expect that they are more likely to have a supportive citizenry than will larger, more heterogeneous cities. Table 11.6 shows that our expectations are met: the relationship between support and social pluralism is as strong as the relationship between support and reponse style. Small communities, it appears, generate relatively high levels of political support that, in

Table 11.4 Forced turnover and community support, by percent

Level of community support	Forced turnover		
	None (N=21)	1–24% (N=39)	25+% (N=22)
Relatively high	81	49	45
Relatively low	19	51	55
Total	100	100	100

$$\frac{\chi^2}{df} = \frac{7.14}{2} = 3.57$$
Gamma = −.42

Table 11.5 Community support and representational response style, by percent

Representational response style	Community support	
	Relatively high ($N = 46$)	Relatively low ($N = 36$)
To self-defined image	63	19
To ad hoc issue groups	17	50
To attentive publics	20	31
Total	100	100

$$\frac{\chi^2}{df} = \frac{16.52}{2} = 8.26$$
Gamma = .54

Table 11.6 City size and community support, by percent

Level of community support	City size		
	<10,000 ($N = 32$)	10–50,000 ($N = 33$)	>50,000 ($N = 17$)
Relatively high	72	58	23
Relatively low	28	42	77
Total	100	100	100

$$\frac{\chi^2}{df} = \frac{10.59}{2} = 5.30$$
Gamma = − .53

turn, leave the governing body free to pursue community interests as it sees fit.

Recruitment and Representation

The study of political representation must, at some time, confront the naked fact that in any political community a handful of men are chosen to govern over a very large number of citizens. As Lord Bryce (1924, p. 542) observed:

In all assemblies and groups and organized bodies of men, from a nation down to a committee of a club, direction and decision rest in the hands of a small percentage, less and less in proportion to larger size of the body, till in a great population it becomes an infinitesimally small proportion of the whole number. This is and always has been true of all forms of government, though in different degrees.

The phenomenon that so impressed Bryce alerts us to the fascinating research problem of linking political recruitment and political representation. Since it is clear that a few men are chosen to govern the many and since, at least under democratic rules, the few are charged to "represent" the many, it is important for a theory of representation that we investigate how the few are chosen. This directs our attention to political recruitment—the process or set of processes by which in a city of, say, 30,000 inhabitants, the population is narrowed to only five men who, as councillors, assume formal authority to govern the remaining 29,995 citizens.

In spite of the obvious logical connection between how the governors are recruited from the people and how they represent the people, the linkage has received little attention in empirical political studies. Some years ago, one of us (see Wahlke et al., p. 269) had occasion to point out that "the relationship between the process of selection of legislators and the modes and consequences of legislative behavior . . . offer wide and fertile fields for empirical research," but the relevant questions were not pursued in *The Legislative System* or, as far as we can tell, in any other subsequent work.

One of the main reasons for this inattention to the link between recruitment and representation is the tendency of scholars to treat recruitment as an individual characteristic. There are studies of the political career, of the selective effect of personality on political success, of nominations of candidates, of the ascent and descent of political leaders, and so on.[13] Although these studies are productive in their own right, the preoccupation with recruitment at the individual level blocks theorizing and empirical research that could connect recruitment and representation. If the position taken here that representation is a systemic property be accepted, however, it is evident that recruitment must also be conceptualized at that level.

We should note that there are studies which treat recruitment and representation at least as aggregate variables. These are the studies that examine the socioeconomic attributes of elected officials and compare them with a demographic profile of their constituents.[14] The difficulty with this research design is that it locks the analyst into a very narrow definition of both recruitment and representation. As to recruitment, it means studying who is selected but not the processes by which this happens. For representation it means that the analysis is limited to a "mirror theory" wherein the very complex process of representation is reduced to a very simple formula of statistical "representativeness." This approach can yield only limited understanding.

Our own conception of recruitment centers in the problem of "sponsorship"—the degree to which the recruitment process is open or unsponsored and the degree to which it is closed or sponsored. Where sponsorship is highly developed, persons already in established political positions exercise considerable control over who will sit on the council. Sponsorship implies that there are fairly determined or even institutionalized pathways to office. The route to the council might be through an apprenticeship on the planning commission or by being an officer of the Chamber of Commerce or by being active in a local ethnic association. For a man to gain a council seat in a community where sponsorship dominates political recruitment, it is important and maybe even necessary for him first to join the inner circles. Sponsorship does not mean, however, that restrictive criteria are being applied, at least as we normally think of restriction in political recruitment. Our analysis is not concerned with whether persons with the "wrong" social traits are eliminated from consideration. In addition, sponsorship is not a notion that masks some conspiracy theory. A community can rely heavily on sponsorship as a means for recruiting political talent without there being manipulation by powerful persons behind the scene.

Sponsorship is an issue of considerable theoretical interest to students of political recruitment. A problem for most elected governing groups is how to maintain some policy continuity despite personnel turnover. This is an especially difficult problem for city councils, where, as we have seen, the rate of voluntary retirement is high and the average tenure is fairly low. (The average number of years of service is 6.5.) Continuity of policy viewpoint can be maintained despite turnover if control can be exercised over successive recruits. A procession of like-minded men through office is equally as effective in stabilizing city policies as is low turnover. If indeed sponsorship aids a governing group to maintain control over both its members and its policies, sponsorship should also relate to how the group defines its representational function. A reasonable hypothesis is that sponsored recruitment insulates the council from certain political experiences and that this insulation will in turn lead to a representational response style that minimizes the impact of organized demands from the public on council thinking.

The measure of sponsorship used here was derived by aggregating individual recruitment patterns at the council level. Just as any one councilman could, on the one extreme, be an "outside challenger" who initiated his own career and attained a council seat with minimum prior contact between himself and those already in office, so the council group as a whole could have followed this career line. At the other extreme, just as an individual might have been asked to run for office by current incumbents or even appointed to office, so the council as a group could have had this experience. Between these extremes more or less prior involvement with city affairs could be characteristic of individual councilmen or the council as a whole. Sponsorship is admittedly a highly multidimensional measure as it pertains to the council, but it undoubtedly captures at the group level something of the rich variety of recruitment patterns that are possible.[15]

Recruitment patterns, of course, are part of the political matrix and are likely to be related to other system properties. In communities where elections are not a sanctioning mechanism and where there is, as a result, little or no forced turnover, the recruitment pattern is likely to be characterized by considerable sponsorship, while in politically volatile systems relatively little sponsorship is likely to be practiced. As Table 11.7 reveals, these expectations are reasonably well substantiated by the data.

Similarly, we expect that sponsorship is more likely to appear in a supportive political environment than in a critical one. In a community seen as supportive, where the council is relatively free to do as it pleases precisely because what the council does pleases the citizenry, incumbents are likely to bring into the council men who have already had experience in local community affairs and who can be counted on to continue the policies that seem so satisfactory. On the other hand, and the relatively weaker relationships shown in Table 11.8 underline the point, a council more exposed to criticism and social pressures may *also* seek to perpetuate its policy views by bringing like-minded and trusted members into the council fold. On balance, then, either alternative is possible. Support as a system property and recruitment through sponsorship are moderately related.

Recruitment practices might also be related to the degree of social heterogeneity or homogeneity of a community. In small communities where men are more likely to share each other's characteristics, know each other better, and are more likely to be of similar mind, sponsorship should be

Table 11.7   Forced turnover and political recruitment, by percent

Amount of sponsorship	Forced turnover		
	None (N = 21)	1–24% (N = 39)	25 + % (N = 22)
Little	5	36	27
Some	38	51	59
Much	57	13	14
Total	100	100	100

$$\frac{\chi^2}{df} = \frac{18.59}{4} = 4.65$$
$$\text{Gamma} = -.44$$

Table 11.8 Community support and political recruitment, by percent

Amount of sponsorship	Community support	
	Relatively high (N = 46)	Relatively low (N = 36)
Little	19	33
Some	48	53
Much	33	14
Total	100	100

$$\frac{\chi^2}{df} = \frac{4.50}{2} = 2.25$$
Gamma = .38

Table 11.9 City size and political recruitment, by percent

Amount of sponsorship	City size		
	<10,000 (N = 32)	10,000–50,000 (N = 33)	>50,000 (N = 17)
Little	19	30	29
Some	37	61	53
Much	44	9	18
Total	100	100	100

$$\frac{\chi^2}{df} = \frac{11.14}{4} = 2.79$$
Gamma = − .34

practiced more frequently than in more pluralistic settings. Again the data suggest, as Table 11.9 shows, that this seems to be the case, although a good deal of sponsorship is evidently also practiced in the larger and medium-sized cities.

We noted in connection with Table 11.1 that the response style of a council depends in some important measure on the actual presence of groups or publics to which the representative group can respond. We assumed that the same reasoning would hold for recruitment practices: a socially diverse community would sustain a relatively open recruitment process. Although the reasoning is not incorrect, Table 11.9 indicates that recruitment practices may be less affected than response style by community characteristics. This being the case, the relationship between recruitment and representation is perhaps more problematical than our initial theoretical reasoning might suggest.

Where a council is free to recruit its own successors, with a view toward maintaining continuity in policy leadership by like-minded and trusted men, it should also be free from those public pressures that would force it to consider views other than its own when selecting policies. But, it seems, sponsorship is practiced to some degree in the larger, more pluralistic cities where councils are exposed to a politically more active environment. It is not surprising, therefore, that, as Table 11.10 shows, the relationship between recruitment and representation is relatively weak. Although the data point in the theoretically expected direction—councils practicing "much" sponsorship seem more likely to follow their own image of the community interest, while councils characterized by "little" sponsorship are more likely to respond in one way or another—the relationship between the two variables is lower than that between any other unveiled in the total configuration of the analysis.

Because of the small number of cases, we are generally reluctant to subject the data to a multivariate analysis that would permit us to untangle the relationship between recruitment and representation. However, since councils in the larger cities reported more sponsorship than expected, we decided to control the relationship between recruitment and representation by city size—collapsing, however, both the size and the representation variables. Table 11.11 reports the results.

It appears that where *much* sponsorship is practiced in a city's recruitment process, size does not have an independent effect on representational style. In large and small cities, councils practicing a great deal of sponsorship tend to follow their own image of community interests. But where sponsorship is less frequently practiced, councils in large cities are more responsive to issue groups or attentive publics than councils in the smaller cities. In the latter, one-half of the ten councils with open recruitment

Table 11.10   Political recruitment and representational response style, by percent

Representational response style	Amount of sponsorship		
	Little (N = 21)	Some (N = 41)	Much (N = 20)
To self-defined image	38	37	65
To ad hoc issue groups	33	36	20
To attentive publics	29	27	15
Total	100	100	100

$$\frac{\chi^2}{df} = \frac{4.85}{4} = 1.21$$

Gamma $= -.25$

Table 11.11   Political recruitment and representational response style, controlled by city size, by percent

	City size					
Sponsorship	<25,000			>25,000		
Representational response style	Little (N = 10)	Some (N = 27)	Much (N = 15)	Little (N = 11)	Some (N = 14)	Much (N = 5)
To self-defined image	50	41	67	27	29	60
To issue groups and publics	50	59	33	73	71	40
Total	100	100	100	100	100	100
		Gamma = − .25			Gamma = − .32	

practices yet are able to pursue their own conceptions of the community interest. This may be due, of course, to the fact, suggested in regard to Table 11.1, that in smaller cities there may just not be any groups or publics sufficiently active to be paid attention to by the council. In general, we can conclude that the uncontrolled results of Table 11.10 do not give too distorted a picture of the relationship between recruitment and representation.

Because community support seems strongly related to the kind of representation that emerges, whereas recruitment seems less critical, we controlled the recruitment-representation relationship by our support variable. Table 11.12 shows some interesting outcomes. Where the community is supportive, sponsorship has no effect at all on representational style. Regardless of whether much or little sponsorship occurs, councils in supportive communities are pursuing their own notions of the public interest. There is, of course, one very plausible interpretation of why sponsorship is so unrelated to response style in such communities. In small cities, recruitment processes need not be controlled to insure a succession of like-minded men through office. In the socially homogeneous and politically satisfied community, anyone who presents himself for office is acceptable. Selection of public leadership by some random method is as likely to produce men with roughly the same views as does selection by sponsorship. Thus the high-support but low-sponsorship communities do not present an anomaly at all.

However, in communities where support from the citizenry is relatively low, sponsorship has the expected consequences for representational behavior. Councils with little sponsorship are almost always those that respond to public pressures, while those with more sponsors apparently are

Table 11.12   Political recruitment and representation response style, controlled by community support, by percent

| Sponsorship
Representational
response style | Community support | | | | | |
| | Relatively high | | | Relatively low | | |
	Little (N = 9)	Some (N = 22)	Much (N = 15)	Little (N = 12)	(N = 19)	Much (N = 5)
To self-defined image	78	50	73	8	21	40
To issue groups and publics	22	50	27	92	79	60
Total	100	100	100	100	100	100
		Gamma = .00			Gamma = −.52	

Table 11.13   Forced turnover and representational response, controlled by community support, by percent

| Representational
response style
Forced turnover | Community support | | | | | |
| | Relatively high | | | Relatively low | | |
	None	1–24%	25 + %	None	1–24%	25 + %
To self-defined image	82	58	40	25	25	8
To issue groups and publics	18	42	60	75	75	92
Total	100	100	100	100	100	100
		Gamma = .55			Gamma = .42	

those less likely to respond (but the small number of cases does not permit us to be confident that this result is sufficiently stable to allow a firm inference). While recruitment does seem to play a role in representation, the degree of support that a community is willing to give is clearly a more important factor in shaping representational style.

Support, in turn, is attentuated by the political system's electoral tolerance. As Table 11.13 indicates, in a relatively supportive environment where retirement is forced upon incumbents by electoral defeat, councils tend to be attentive rather than self-sufficient in their representational behavior. In less supportive communities forced turnover accentuates the tendency for councils to act in response to community groups. Eleven of twelve councils with high forced-turnover rates indicated responsiveness to issue groups or attentive publics, 15 percent more than reported in the original Table 11.2. The fact that our measure of forced turnover is truly independent of our representational style and support measures makes this result all the more significant.

The analysis suggests that the four components of the political matrix—the complexity of the social environment, the impact of elections in forcing incumbents from office, the degree of public support perceived by the council, and the amount of sponsorship in political recruitment—may explain a great deal about whether a responsive relationship between governors and governed will emerge. Since the analysis has been configurative, on the assumption that representational "responding to" emerges, if it does, in the context of the "over-all structure and functioning of the system," we do not assess the relative impact of any given variable. Rather we stress two things: first, there seems to be a theoretically meaningful cluster of political phenomena that is strongly related to the response style adopted by the governing body; and second, under certain, very identifiable political conditions the governing body may remain indifferent to any views of the public good except its own and yet not suffer at the hands of an antagonistic electorate. What, then, do we make of these findings for a theory of representation?

In order to pursue a theory of representation, we have chosen a particular concept of representation. The concept with which we work stresses that political representation is a relationship between two collectivities—that is, representation occurs when the few who are chosen to govern respond to some organized demands or preferences of the many who permit themselves to be governed. The theory to which this concept directs us is one which emphasizes that a politically responsive relationship may or may not emerge, and that the type of community in which it does emerge is characterized by an identifiable matrix of properties.

The analysis led to some unexpected findings; we summarize them here. What we have attempted is to break new ground in theorizing about representation in modern society; the specific findings to which our theorizing activity give rise will undoubtedly be modified as additional empirical work along these lines takes place. The findings, then, are presented as suggestive of what we may expect from a rethinking of "representation" rather than as confirmed facts about the political world.

1. By the definition we introduced, an elected assembly is representative when it acts in response to publicly expressed and more or less organized

viewpoints from the citizenry. We found that the governing councils often act in response to interest groups or attentive publics in the larger, more diverse communities. In the smaller, homogeneous cities, councils tend to rely on their own image of what the community requires. Thus, as an initial observation, we suggest that as a systemic property representation is more likely to emerge under just those conditions often presumed to impede responsiveness at the individual level.

2. A theory of representation as an emergent property may have to be adjusted in the light of certain facts about elections too long ignored. We are not sure, as one author (Pennock, 1968, p. 8) has stated it, that "elections are thought of as providing the great sanction for assuring representative behavior." The patterns uncovered in our analysis suggest a considerably more complex relationship between elections and representative government. Where an aroused electorate does, from time to time, unseat incumbents, the governing groups do tend to be attentive. However, it does not follow that elected assemblies concerned only with their own definition of the political situation will be turned out of office, for such self-images may indeed coincide with public preferences.

3. A council tends not to be responsive, as we use the term, where the public is viewed as being most supportive. This finding suggests a major qualification to the assumption that "elections force representativeness." Representative government can function quite independently of elections, though only under certain conditions. A politically satisfied community is apparently unconcerned about whether the council acts in response. If the job is being done, the citizens would just as soon not be bothered. It appears then not to be the inattentive council that is thrown out of office but only the council whose performance is suspect.

4. A fourth finding is one that validates the observations just made: communities in which the council sees itself as generally supported tend to leave to the council itself the selection of its successors. The pattern of sponsored recruitment, in which candidates are insulated from the competitive struggle for a council seat, tends to be associated with a representational style also suggesting a certain insulation from public pressures.

Students of democratic politics are deeply interested in the processes available to the public for controlling and holding accountable the political leadership; the analysis presented here is closely related to an understanding of these processes. It appears that members of the public dissatisfied with their representative assembly can intrude into its deliberations and force attentiveness in two ways at least: (1) by playing a role in determining who is selected to the representative body and (2) by defeating incumbents when they stand for reelection. Put differently, when members of the public control the constituting of the representative assembly, they also influence how that assembly will define its representational role. When, however, citizens do not exercise that control, allowing the assembly more or less to determine its own members and seldom unseating an incumbent, they thereby permit the representative group the privilege of defining for itself the goals and programs of the community.

12

Life Space and Social Networks

as Political Contexts

THE SINGLE most important feature in any one person's social environments are other persons—an almost banal observation.[1] Uncannily, the facts behind this observation have never been systematically investigated in national studies of the mass public. In order to give it empirical grounding, a set of innovative survey questions was included in the September wave of the 1980 panel of the National Election Studies—the so-called social network questions. They were designed to probe the effects of a person's interactions with some other persons—in this case neighbors—on his or her political behavior.[2]

Theoretical Background

CONTEXT DISTINGUISHED FROM ENVIRONMENTS

That interpersonal relations affect political behavior is the warrant of "contextual analysis," which employs areal units like census tracts, cities, counties, or states (Putnam, 1966; Segal and Meyer, 1969; Wright, 1976, 1977; and especially Huckfeldt, 1979, 1980, 1983a,b, 1984). In fact, that "context" influences individual political behavior is now widely accepted. Partly, no doubt, because it has become a fashionable term, context is often used rather loosely and ambiguously. Other terms—like "situation," "condition," or "environment"—can sometimes be readily substituted. But a distinction should be made between context and environment.

As we understand it, underlying the use of "social context" as a scientific

---

Written with Lawrence S. Rothenberg.

term is the assumption that context emerges from and is created by a person's interactions with other individuals. It is therefore "compositional" in structure. As a compositional phenomenon, social context emerges out of interpersonal relations, interactions, and cognitions that are direct and immediate but also contingent on shifts in the configuration of the actors involved.

Context conceived as something that emerges out of interpersonal relations *at the level of the dyad* is difficult to observe empirically in research on the mass public. Not that observation is impossible; it is a matter of scarce resources. As a result, investigators who take social context seriously rely on aggregate demographic data or electoral statistics conveniently available for such areal units as census tracts or counties. These units are chosen, then, out of necessity. When individual-level survey data are used in contextual studies of political behavior, they are collected at respondents' places of residence.[3] The data on areal units thus serve as surrogates for direct, individual-level information about dyadic, triadic, or more complex social interactions.

Environments are more remote, more stable, and less contingent on changes in personnel than is context. Of all the environments within which the individual person copes—the international, the national, the natural or physical, and so on—social environments are particularly significant, for it is in these environments that the person becomes oriented to action. They may be experienced directly or indirectly, and social relations within them may also be direct or indirect.

The distinction between social environments and social context is diagrammed in Figure 12.1. In the diagram, some of a person's multiple social environments are depicted as a set of concentric circles with the individual at the center. Each circle thus represents an environment with which the individual may have to cope, but "linkage" to the various environments need not involve direct interpersonal relations.

However, as indicated in the diagram by the cone-shaped sector cutting across some or all of the concentric circles, one may also have more or less enduring, frequent, or intimate contacts with *particular* individuals in the various environments. These individuals constitute a person's "egocentric networks" or "action sets." They are, in another formulation, the "significant others" in a person's multiple environments (Mead, 1934). These significant others may themselves be directly related in face-to-face encounters, as they invariably are in primary groups, but they need to be. Social context, then, as we define it, emerges out of a person's egocentric networks or action sets and can be used to conduct contextual analysis of political behavior.

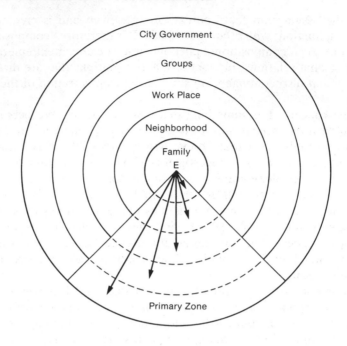

Figure 12.1   Ego's Environment and Primary Zone Context

INTERACTION AND COMPOSITION

All contextual analysis is based on the assumption that, as we have pointed out, interaction between an individual and other persons must have taken place. In order to operationalize such interactions, compositional measures are employed. These measures may tap group-level properties with regard either to independent variables (what Sprague terms the "social resonance" model) or to the dependent variable itself—the "behavioral contagion" model (see Sprague, 1982; also Huckfeldt, 1983b).[4]

Now, the difference between contextual analysis drawing on aggregate data, on the one hand, and on individual-level data, on the other hand, is as follows: while the former can only *assume* that interaction has taken place, the latter is in a position to "create" the context by composing the observations conducted on interacting individuals. To put it another way, at best analysts using aggregate data can hope that an individual has interacted with some of the other individuals who make up the aggregate; it is a virtual certainty that he or she does not interact with all of them. In contrast, in the research reported here the composite measures are based

on information about some of the persons with whom an individual interacts.

We are able to develop these composite measures because in the 1980
National Election Study an effort was made to obtain information about
one social environment—the neighborhood of respondents' place of residence; and about *one* social context—the particular neighbors with whom
they interact. The accounts respondents give of their own behavior *in* the
neighborhood and of their relations *with* particular neighbors are used to
construct a social context that we denote as the "neighborhood primary
zone" (NPZ).

SOCIAL CONTEXT AND SOCIAL PROCESS

Although contextual models differ in their specifications of social context
as an independent variable, all of them come to the same conclusions
concerning the effects of context on individual political behavior. But they
also share the theoretical dilemma that the mechanisms or processes producing contextual effects are elusive. There is now persuasive evidence
that social context, however measured, has effects on political behavior,
but *why* it does is a question whose answer remains largely conjectural.

Paradoxically, while contextual analyses introduce a truly *social* set of
independent variables, most explanations of contextual effects on political
behavior rely on one or another psychological theory that is geared to the
individual rather than to the mechanisms that intervene between the social
context as stimulus and behavioral responses. Let us illuminate this by an
example. Conversation about politics with friends may bring home to a
person that his or her views are not in agreement with those of the friends.
Contextual analysis would predict that bringing one's views in line with
those of the others is the most likely option to be followed, making for
what has been called "the political homogeneity of social groups" (Lazarsfeld, Berelson, and Gaudet, 1948, pp. 137–49). But how is the process
of bringing views in line to be explained?

Familiar answers to this question are of an individual-psychological sort.
The person simply conforms to avoid conflict, seeks social approval, learns
through experience, succumbs to social influence, strains for "cognitive
balance" (Heider, 1958), resolves felt dissonance through rational reas-
sessment (Festinger, 1957), and so on. But all of these explanations beg
the question of the social process that intervenes to make interpersonal
interactions effective stimuli for the behavior that is observed (Homans,
1961). At issue in contextual analysis is not why the individual person
responds as a result of his or her "own" motivations, predispositions,

preferences, perceptions, reference behavior, and so on—in short, what Sprague (1982, p. 115) calls a person's "susceptibility" to effects stemming from context. Rather, what is unsettled are the behavioral consequences of *contingent variations* in a person's social context. In applications of contextual analysis, therefore, as Sprague (1982, p. 116) rightly observes, "the problem is to produce hypotheses about the interaction-information system of the microenvironment."

Aggregate contextual analysis may produce the sought-for hypotheses about the mechanisms of social interaction and their effects on individual behavior; but only individual-level data on a person's interactions can really test an intuition about a social mechanism like reinforcement. For instance, if individual voting is to be explained contextually, the relevant equation calls for a contextual variable that is some composite measure of network partisanship (the resonance model) or of network voting (the contagion model). If interaction has an effect on voting behavior above and beyond any individual effects, the inference that the *social* process taking place is one of reinforcement may be sustained. A partisan voter in a dense or supportive partisan context should be expected to exhibit more relevant behavior (as in voting for party candidates) than a party identifier in a less dense and possibly conflictual context.

Contextual analysts show or try to show that interpersonal relations give rise to a politically relevant social context through the *composition* of individual-level attributes of the participants. Our goal in this analysis is to come closer to capturing the dynamics of interactions that presumably have an impact on individual behavior. The technique for measuring interaction employed in this study is a truncated version of social network analysis—truncated because it depends for information on only one side of the dyadic relationship, the survey respondent, without confirmation from the other side. As far as we know, most survey-based studies of social networks are of this order (Laumann, 1973; Fischer et al., 1977; Fischer, 1982). Ideally, one would like to have direct data on both "self" and "other" in the interaction (which may or may not be reciprocal), but the sampling frame of the National Election Study surveys does not make this possible. Nevertheless, this study is based on data considerably more extensive and satisfactory than have been previously available. It is the first *nationwide study* of its kind.[5]

Network analysis traces the "links" or "ties" that connect one person to another, either directly or indirectly. By tracing them, it seeks to identify, describe, and possibly explain the configuration of linkages that constitutes the network's structure. A person's egocentric network or action set, then, makes for a social context that, as we have suggested in Figure 12.1, may cut across a person's various environments. There is an extensive interdisciplinary literature on social network analysis that, in the last thirty years or so, has grown by leaps and bounds. We cannot review this literature here,[6] and we will not explicate all network concepts or hypotheses. We will define those we use as we proceed with the analysis. Suffice it to say that we will be concerned with the length, frequency, and intimacy of respondents' contacts with some of their neighbors, and with the politically salient content that their interactions may have. Although we cannot demonstrate this empirically, we believe that social networks as contexts have a more powerful effect on individual behavior than the effects observed in aggregate contextual analysis. As Sprague (1982, p. 117), a practitioner of the latter mode of analysis, candidly notes, "contextual effect will be more powerful the closer empirical measurement approaches the theoretical unit of the primary group and the closer measurement estimates true frequencies of interaction."

The networks we construct and use for analyzing their contextual effects are limited to "neighbors." This restriction was a purposive decision when the research was designed because we wanted to investigate whether "place of residence," as identified in aggregate contextual analysis, is in fact a politically salient context, and for whom. We do not deny that many politically relevant interpersonal relations take place where people reside and sleep. But we are less sanguine than some aggregate contextual analysts are that "impersonal encounters" or casual interactions in the neighborhood are politically manifest—and manifest enough to justify a reliance on the locality of residence as the sole source of contextual effects on *political* behavior (Huckfeldt, 1980, p. 250). We would emphasize, therefore, that many people spend their waking hours in social environments other than that delimited by their place of residence. Politically significant others may be encountered elsewhere—in places of work and worship, in shopping centers or recreational areas remote from the immediate neighborhood. In the next section we will explore a person's "life space"—the arenas where a person may be involved in various activities—and the influence that this life space may have on social and political interaction.

However, even if the neighborhood as an environment is not part of a person's life space and is not politically salient, it does not follow that an individual cannot or does not have socially or politically relevant contacts with *particular* neighbors. In a later section we therefore seek to validate what we call a person's neighborhood primary zone (NPZ). We shall subsequently specify a causal model of some of the NPZ's elements in order to show that it is cognitively structured, and thus justify the assumption that how a person cognitively relates to the NPZ is behaviorally salient. In turn, out of the NPZ's components or elements we shall construct a measure of the network's political "knit" in order to test the contextual hypothesis. Finally, we examine the NPZ's contextual effects on some aspects of the respondents' political judgments and behavior in the course of the 1980 electoral season. We must emphasize in advance the multiplicity of an individual's social networks as interpersonal contexts. Thus the NPZ model is necessarily underspecified because of limitations in measurement. If one had data on all of a person's social networks, the contextual effect should be considerably stronger than the effect that can be demonstrated in this study. (For study design and measurement tools, see the Appendix.)

Life Space: Of Day-Dwellers and Night-Dwellers

To discover whether place of residence is the *socially* significant environment in people's lives, and whether this environment influences political behavior, we adopted the conception of a person's life space (borrowed from but not as used by Lewin, 1951). For some people the residential neighborhood is the focal point of their daily lives—we dub them "day-dwellers." For other people the residential neighborhood is not the place where they spend the bulk of their waking hours—we dub them "night-dwellers." In order to obtain an operational measure for the day-dweller and night-dweller distinction and to validate the life-space concept, the respondents were asked where they engage in life's "normal" activities—working, shopping, relaxing, and worshipping. Table 12.1 presents the basic data. Shopping and the pursuit of leisure or recreation are predominantly neighborhood centered, although a substantial number of people do go "elsewhere." One-half of the respondents also attend a house of worship in their neighborhood, while the other half go elsewhere or do not attend church at all. In contrast, jobs draw people out of their localities. Of those who work, only a third do so in the neighborhood.

In order to speak of day-dwellers and night-dwellers, however, one must first establish that people remaining in the neighborhood for one activity tend to remain there for others, and that people going elsewhere for one

Table 12.1   Place of life-space activities, by percent

Place	Shopping (N = 759)	Working (N = 752)	Worshipping (N = 762)	Relaxing (N = 758)
Neighborhood	61	20	50	69
Elsewhere	39	41	32	31
No work/church	—	39	18	—
Total	100	100	100	100

activity tend to do so for others. Table 12.2 presents the intercorrelations among the four life-space measures. The coefficients are all statistically significant and confirm that the day-dweller and night-dweller or life-space concept has construct validity; but they are also low enough to suggest that life space is a continuum ranging from day-dwelling at one end to night-dwelling at the other.

To form a single continuous measure of day-dwelling and night-dwelling, an additive scale (the life-space scale) was formed. Its distribution (Table 12.3) shows that individuals vary considerably in how much they are involved in their neighborhood, although overall there are more day-dwellers than night-dwellers.

To test the behavioral implications of the day-dweller and night-dweller distinction (now measured as a continuum), we first examine in a simple, bivariate manner how a person's life space is related to involvement in the neighborhood and "nonpolitical," or "purely social," relations with particular neighbors. Part A of Table 12.4 presents the correlation coefficients for the relationships between the life-space measure and seven social (non-

Table 12.2   Intercorrelations among places of life-space activities (rho)

Activity	Working	Worshipping	Relaxing
Shopping	.122[a]	.264[a]	.076[b]
Working	—	.124[a]	.125[a]
Worshipping	—	—	.120[a]

N = 742–757

a. $p \leq .01$
b. $p \leq .05$

Table 12.3   Life-space scale: day-dwellers and night-dwellers

Life-space scale	Score	%	N
Night-dweller	4	3.7	27
	5	3.7	27
	6	12.3	90
	7	11.8	87
	8	15.8	116
	9	12.4	91
	10	18.0	132
	11	16.3	120
Day-dweller	12	6.0	44
Total		100.0	734

Table 12.4 Correlations between life space (day-dwelling versus night-dwelling) and neighborhood social/political aspects

Neighborhood aspects	r	N
A. Social		
Years of residence in neighborhood	.146[a]	732
Life commitment to neighborhood (rho)	.126[a]	734
Presence of "known" neighbors (rho)	.082[a]	733
Number of "known" neighbors	.103[a]	568
Length of contact with "known" neighbors	.126[a]	566
Intimacy of contact with "known" neighbors	.132[a]	566
Frequency of contact with "known" neighbors	− .051	554
B. Political		
Knowledge of neighborhood party (rho)	.032	732
Political conversation with neighbors	.030	567
Knowledge of neighbors' party affiliation	.036	564
Knowledge of neighbors' voting intentions	− .021	558
Political agreement with neighbors	.072	301

a. $p \leq .01$

political) variables. With one exception—frequency of contact—the coefficients are in the "right" direction and statistically significant. As one might expect, day-dwellers have lived in the neighborhood longer than night-dwellers; they are more committed to living in the neighborhood rather than moving out; they are more likely to have friends or acquaintances in the neighborhood as well as more of them; they have known their neighbors for more years; and they report being on more intimate terms with particular neighbors than do night-dwellers.

None of these findings is startling, but to assume, as practitioners of aggregate contextual analysis are forced to do, that a person's place of residence is the most relevant indicator of life space as a context for *political* behavior, is still an open question. To explore this assumption, a number of interview questions ascertained the respondents' perceptions of their neighborhood as a "political" (rather than purely social) context.

Part B of Table 12.4 shows that, in marked contrast to the previous findings on the social aspects of a person's life space, *none* of the relationships is statistically significant. This is a rather challenging finding because it seems to falsify the assumption that place of residence, presumably captured by aggregate demographics, can be considered a politically salient social context. Day-dwellers are no more able than night-dwellers to report on the existence of a local party organization; they are no more likely to talk about politics with particular neighbors; they are no more likely to be in political agreement with friends or acquaintances in their neighborhood, to know or be able to guess their neighbors' party affiliation or how their neighbors plan to vote in the forthcoming election.[7]

A person's life space is likely to be a function of individual attributes, such as gender, age, or education, which in turn may account for different attitudes toward or perceptions of the neighborhood and of neighbors. Both younger and more educated people are more likely to be night-dwellers (and the two groups overlap significantly). Women, on the other hand, many of whom are still housewives, are more likely than men to be day-dwellers. The life-space measure may therefore be tapping social-psychological differences related to these personal attributes rather than to day- or night-dwelling as such.

Regression and probit coefficients (the latter for three ordinal variables) were estimated for the impact of day- and night-dwelling on perceptions of the neighborhood or reported relations with neighbors, while controlling for age and education, as well as for education-related variables like "political interest" and sense of "personal efficacy." Table 12.5 presents the estimates. Not surprisingly, once age is controlled for, the number of years

Table 12.5 Regression and probit estimates for impact of life space on neighborhood social/political aspects

Dependent variables	Constant	Age	Education	Political interest	Personal efficacy	Life space
A. Social						
Years of residence	2.521	.426[a]	−.284[c]	−1.517[a]	.298	.255
Life commitment[d]	.137	.018[a]	.010	.069	−.003	.063[a]
"Known" neighbors[d]	−.626	.001	−.048	−.029	−1.355	−.074[a]
Number of neighbors	2.609[a]	.001[b]	.000	.015	.052[b]	.033[a]
Length of contact	9.123[a]	.296[a]	−.831[a]	−.147	.132	−.028
Intimacy of contact	3.991[a]	.001	−.110[a]	.005	.133[b]	.099[a]
Frequency of contact	1.621	−.033	−.216[a]	−.038	−.097	.061
B. Political						
Knowledge of local party[d]	.298[a]	−.009[a]	−.021	−.144[a]	−.075	.020
Political conversation	6.734[a]	.002	.058[a]	.358	.029	.027
Neighbors' party known	3.490[a]	.007[b]	.015	.143[b]	.126[b]	.021
Neighbors' vote known	3.078[a]	−.003	.018	.219[a]	.094[c]	−.007
Political agreement	3.745[a]	.005	−.012	.093	−.034	.026

a. $p \leq .01$
b. $.01 < p \leq .05$
c. $.05 < p \leq .10$
d. Probit estimates.

a person has lived in the neighborhood and the number of years he or she has known particular neighbors are no longer significantly related to the character of one's life space. But day-dwellers are still significantly more likely to be committed to their neighborhood, to have friends or acquaintances in the neighborhood as well as more of them, and to be on more intimate terms with them. On the other hand, a person's life space seems to have no direct effect on political behavior or perceptions of the neighborhood as a politically relevant arena. None of the life-space estimates in part B of Table 12.5 is statistically significant.

The life-space analysis leads to two conclusions. First, for many people the residential neighborhood is not the significant place where they spend their waking hours—the hours of the day when they interact with others and are presumably in a position to pick up politically salient information or cues from those with whom they directly interact. This is especially true of people in the work force. While the residential neighborhood may give rise to *one* important social context for many people, it is by no means the only context, and for many people the neighborhood is likely to be a less important environment than some other location where they pursue life's activities. Concentrating on the neighborhood alone provides only a very partial picture of people's interpersonal relations and interactions.

Second, while we found that day-dwellers differ from night-dwellers in the neighborhood as a social milieu, we also found that life-space conditions do not significantly affect political behavior or attitudes, or perceptions of the neighborhood as a political milieu. This finding should not be misunderstood or misinterpreted. It does not mean that people's *primary* relations with neighbors do not matter politically; it only means that their *life-space circumstances (or activity environments) do not matter.* Even those who are mainly night-dwellers may have some friends or acquaintances among their neighbors who are politically salient for them. The critical element in "neighborhood effects" may be the strength or weakness of personal ties with *particular* neighbors, the neighborhood primary zone, and not the neighborhood as an environment as such.

Given our findings and interpretation, we shall explore in more detail the NPZ, on the assumption that it is direct interpersonal (primary) ties *in* the neighborhood rather than the neighborhood "as a whole" that is politically salient. Put somewhat differently, as life space does not appear to have a direct effect on how people are related to their neighborhood or particular neighbors politically, any effect of the neighborhood is likely to be mediated by the NPZ.

The Structure of the Neighborhood Primary Zone

The concept of NPZ denotes that a person, in this study the respondent, is linked to neighbors in more or less characteristic ways, necessarily social and possibly political, and that these linkages are themselves systematically interwoven to constitute a single sociopolitical context. Insofar as the NPZ is an empirically specifiable entity, and insofar as its partisan character can be established, it should have contextual effects on individual political behavior.

The concept "primary zone" comes from social network analysis and should be distinguished from the older and more familiar concept "primary group" (Shils, 1951). In a primary group all the persons involved know each other and interact with each other in face-to-face situations. By way of contrast, a primary zone may, but need not, be a primary group. The term does not require or imply that the persons known to one individual know each other. It does not require or imply that the persons identified by an individual as friends, neighbors, colleagues, and so on will reciprocate the identification. And while the primary group is necessarily and invariably "small," a primary zone may be very "large" because it consists of all of an individual's dyadic relations in a multitude of social roles. The primary zone is an ego-centered network, with an individual at the core of a set of dyadic relations with persons directly known to him or her but which also connect that individual with others not directly known. This egocentric network is thus an action set, which means that the persons in the network may serve an individual (the network's "root" or "anchor") instrumentally in establishing new contacts, orienting belief and conduct, or performing some function (helping to cut a tree, informing on job opportunities, advising on how to vote, and so on).

A person's NPZ is not a collective unit with norms and decision rules of its own that would make it a group capable of joint action (like, say, a committee or a multiperson court). But it is not a random aggregate of the people in an individual's social environment either. Thus respondents' reports about their NPZ's "members" should fit together in more or less systematically structured and predictable ways, so that one can treat the NPZ's elements as a composite variable in the analysis of the respondents' political behavior.

Six NPZ elements are specified: (1) length of contact with neighbors, (2) frequency of contact, (3) intimacy of contact, (4) political conversation, (5) knowledge of NPZ partners' party affiliation, and (6) knowledge of NPZ partners' vote intentions. To test for the validity of the NPZ construct, we shall first examine the relationships among its elements after the individual-level data have been combined into composite variables. Subsequently, in order to examine in greater depth how the six elements fit together, we shall employ a causal model of their relationships.

Our expectations for the direct relationships among the NPZ's six components are straightforward—they should be positive. The longer NPZ partners have been known, the more frequent and intimate should be their connection with the respondent, and these social components of the NPZ should be positively related to its three political components. Table 12.6 presents the zero-order correlation coefficients among the six NPZ elements. All are in the hypothesized direction, but three—for the relationships between length of contact, on the one hand, and frequency of contact, political conversation, and vote knowledge, on the other hand—are not statistically significant, as is also the case for the relationship between frequency of contact and knowledge of the NPZ partners' party affiliation. Nevertheless, in view of the overall positive results, we accept the validity of the NPZ construct.

To deepen understanding of the NPZ's structure, we explore whether the six NPZ elements "hang together" by way of a causal model. Figure 12.2 presents a diagram of the model we propose to test. For this purpose we posit "vote knowledge" as the dependent variable. For the purpose of model specification we also include in the regression five individual-level, personal attributes of the respondent: age and education, political interest, sense of personal efficacy, and strength of party identification, measured by three dummy variables. In addition we include the life-space variable because we want to see whether NPZ interactions are related to a person's status as a day-dweller or night-dweller. Our hypothesis in this connection is that they are not, in light of our previous finding that life space has no direct impact on political behavior. Indeed, as the regression coefficients in Table 12.7 show, there is no statistically significant relationship between

Table 12.6   Correlations among neighborhood primary zone components

NPZ components	Intimacy	Frequency	Conversation	Party known	Vote known
Length of contact	.308[a]	.013	.041	.173[a]	.007
Intimacy of contact		.315[a]	.185[a]	.210[a]	.078[a]
Frequency of contact			.065[c]	.030	.073[b]
Political conversation				.412[a]	.355[a]
Neighbors' party known					.653[a]
N = 545–566					

a. $p \leq .01$
b. $.01 < p \leq .05$
c. $.05 < p \leq .10$

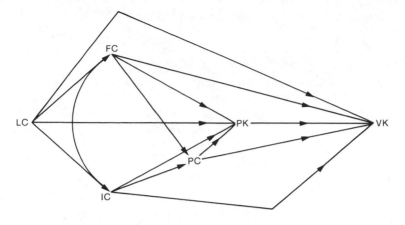

LC = Length of Contact with Primary Zone
FC = Frequency of Contact with Primary Zone
IC = Intimacy of Contact with Primary Zone
PC = Political Conversation in Primary Zone
PK = Knowledge of Primary Zone Party Identification
VK = Knowledge of Primary Zone Vote Intention

Figure 12.2   Model of Neighborhood Primary Zone
as Political Context

life space and five of the NPZ components. Only intimacy of contact is related. Day-dwellers are somewhat more likely than night-dwellers to have close friends in the neighborhood.

In general, the relationships observed in the original correlation analysis (Table 12.6) remain intact in the causal model of Table 12.7. But length of contact is not significantly related to knowing or being able to guess NPZ partners' vote intentions, and there is a negative relationship between intimacy and knowledge of the NPZ's vote intentions. Assuming that this result is correct, how can one explain the apparently anomalous finding that the more intimate one's social relations with NPZ partners, the less likely it is that one knows or can guess their vote intentions? The question is of interest in view of the finding that intimacy and talking about politics with one's NPZ partners are significantly associated. This, again, is something of a puzzle.

To cope with this puzzle, we suggest that intimacy may yet contribute indirectly to knowing the NPZ's vote intentions through other variables in the model: we know that intimacy promotes political conversation and an awareness of the NPZ's partisanship, and we know that intimates are more frequently in contact with their NPZ partners than those with less close ties. Also, the behavioral, attitudinal, and cognitive relationships among

Table 12.7   Causal model of neighborhood primary zone (OLS)

Independent variables	Dependent variables					
	Length of contact	Intimacy of contact	Frequency of contact	Conversation	Party known	Vote known
Constant	8.879[a]	4.102[a]	1.961[b]	5.934[a]	6.136[a]	1.363[a]
Age	.283[a]	−.014[a]	−.037[a]	.003	−.002	−.005[b]
Education	−.700[a]	−.056[b]	−.209[a]	.079[a]	.014	.004
Life space	.092	.091[a]	.095	.013	.010	−.018
Length		.053[a]	.015	−.003	.017[a]	−.005
Interest				.329[a]	−.053	.076[c]
Efficacy				.009	.083[b]	.022
Strong party identification				.088	.777[a]	.224[c]
Weak party identification				−.175	.516[a]	.096
Lean party identification				−.116	.512[a]	.091
Intimacy				.152[a]	.083[a]	−.052[c]
Frequency				.010	−.014	.032[b]
Conversation					.392[a]	.112[a]
Party known						.645[a]
R^2	.281[a]	.047[a]	.122[a]	.164[a]	.253	.465[a]
N = 496–561						

a. $p \leq .01$
b. $.01 < p \leq .05$
c. $.05 < p \leq .10$

the NPZ's elements may result in a higher level of knowledge of the NPZ's vote intentions among persons strongly tied to each other. In order to test for these speculations, the paths between intimacy of contact and vote knowledge were decomposed (a procedure whose results admittedly should be taken with some caution). We found that the *total* indirect impact of intimacy on knowledge of NPZ vote intentions is .178—twice as great as the original direct correlation of .078. Thus intimacy increases knowledge of the NPZ's prospective vote. The net effect, then, of intimacy on knowledge of the NPZ's vote prospects is in the originally expected and demonstrated direction.

We have shown that the NPZ is a structured "entity" that has construct validity. We now turn to one of its dimensions—its political "knit"—which is of great interest in social network analysis and should be expected to produce contextual effects. When speaking of the NPZ's political knit, we are referring to the degree of "tightness" (or "looseness") of the relationships among the NPZ's members, with particular emphasis given to the network's political aspects. The relevant measure was obtained by a principal-components factor analysis.[8] Extracting a score based on the first factor alone, the measure takes on this form:

NPZ political knit = − .04350 (average length of contact)
  + − .05103 (level of intimacy) + .01078 (degree of contact frequency)
  + .09115 (political conversation) + .60462 (knowledge of party affiliation) + .35986 (knowledge of voting intentions)

Each respondent's NPZ political knit is thus measured as the summation of the factor loadings multiplied by the individual's standardized scores for the NPZ's six separate components. Clearly, the measure basically taps whether members of the NPZ are closely knit politically or have only peripheral political ties. We shall use this measure, along with other compositional measures, to estimate the contextual effects of the NPZ on some aspects of the respondents' political behavior.

NPZ Effects on Political Behavior

Using familiar measures found in the National Election Studies—candidate and party placements on the "feeling thermometers," preelection vote intention, and postelection reported vote choice—we shall examine two possible contextual effects: differences in respondents' partisan or candidate evaluations and voting behavior. The relevant independent contextual variable is the partisan composition of the NPZ adjusted by its political knit. The partisan composition of the NPZ is a function of the party identifications of all its members—the respondent's and his or her NPZ partners. Optimally, the partisan composition of the NPZ would be constructed out of all its members' self-identifications as Democrats or Republicans. Because we do not have direct self-identification data for the respondents' NPZ partners, we must rely here on their characterizations of the partners as Democrats or Republicans.[9]

NPZ PARTISAN COMPOSITION

The partisan composition of the NPZ will be defined as "supportive" if it is consistent with the respondent's own party identification; it will be defined as "conflictual" when the partisan character of the NPZ differs from the respondent's own party identification. The "NPZ partisan composition scale" consists initially of five possible scores: (1) all NPZ members have the same party identification as the respondent; (2) a majority of the NPZ have the same partisanship as the respondent; (3) half of the NPZ identify with one party, half with the other party; (4) only a minority of the NPZ have the same party identification as the respondent; (5) no NPZ partner has the same party identification as the respondent (that is, all identify—or, rather, are said to identify—with the "other" party). The analysis is necessarily limited to the respondents identifying themselves and their NPZ partners as Democrats or Republicans, since only for these respondents can one speak of a partisan NPZ context that is supportive of or conflicts with their partisan predilections. In order to place both Democrats and Republicans on a single support–conflict continuum, Democratic respondents are scored from -5 (NPZ is fully supportive) to -1 (NPZ is fully conflictual), and Republican respondents are scored from $+1$ (NPZ is fully conflictual) to $+5$ (NPZ is fully supportive).

Table 12.8 reports the distribution of the respondents on the "NPZ partisan support index." While 40 percent of the respondents indicate that all of their NPZ partners have the same party identification as themselves (those scored -5 and $+5$), some 27 percent report NPZs whose partisanship they perceive as completely inconsistent with their own (those scored

Table 12.8   Relationship between neighborhood primary zone partisan support and respondent's strength of party identification

Character of neighborhood primary zone	Score	Strength of identification			N	Row%
		Strong	Weak	Leaning		
Supportive Democratic	-5	57%	47%	16%	99	25
	-4	12	15	5	26	6
	-3	5	13	5	18	5
	-2	7	9	11	19	5
Conflictual Democratic	-1	19	16	62	54	14
Total		100%	100%	100	216	55
N		84	95	37		
tau-$B = .263$; $p \leq .001$						
Conflictual Republican	$+1$	12%	33%	38%	50	13
	$+2$	4	5	28	19	5
	$+3$	12	11	11	20	5
	$+4$	27	14	4	27	7
Supportive Republican	$+5$	45	37	19	61	15
Total		100%	100%	100%	177	45
N		51	79	47		
tau-$B = .265$; $p \leq .001$						
Total N					393	100

-1 and $+1$). The remaining third of the NPZs are "mixed" in partisanship, that is, supportive or conflictual to varying degrees.

In the case of partisan support, context-induced variance in political behavior is especially difficult to observe and measure because of potential collinearity between partisan context and individual partisanship. Table 12.8 also shows that there is a relationship, though not an overwhelming one, between the *strength* of respondents' own party identification and the perceived partisanship of their NPZs (tau-B for Democrats = .263, for Republicans = .265). In general, and regardless of whether they are Democrats or Republicans, respondents with stronger identifications are more prone to report a supportive NPZ, and vice versa. Citizens with stronger identifications seem to be more inclined than those with weaker identifications to seek out particular neighbors with similar partisan dispositions and to be reinforced in their own partisan stance by these contacts; or they may project their own identification onto their NPZ partners. But we cannot shed further light on these individual-psychological mechanisms here.

However, when partisan *direction* is included in the measurement— combining Democratic and Republican responses to form the 10-point partisan-support index—a high level of multicollinearity ($r = .852$) between respondents' party identification and the partisan composition of their NPZs results.[10] Consequently, if one were to employ these two variables (that is, respondents' own party identification and NPZ partisan support) in contextual analysis of political behavior, precise enough estimates of either the individual-level or the contextual variable's effects would be difficult to come by.[11] In order to adjust for multicollinearity, we take account of the NPZ's political knit, on the assumption that it is interrelated with an NPZ's partisan context: tightly knit NPZs should be more supportive, and loosely knit NPZs should be more conflictual.[12] While the adjusted index is still relatively highly correlated with the respondent's individual-level party identification ($r = .575$, as against the prior $r = .852$), the correlation is sufficiently reduced to discern whether the NPZ as a partisan context has an effect on political behavior, independent of respondents' own party identification.

IMPACT ON PARTISAN AFFECT

Citizen affect for political parties and their candidates is frequently considered antecedent to the vote decision itself. Taking off from social reinforcement theory, our expectations are these: persons with politically supportive NPZs should be more favorably disposed, in a partisan manner, toward their own party and its candidate, all other things being equal; and, vice versa, persons with politically conflictual NPZs should be less favorably disposed in a partisan manner.[13]

For the purpose at hand, respondents' partisan affect is measured by four feeling thermometers concerning Jimmy Carter, Ronald Reagan, the Democratic party, and the Republican party. In addition, to obtain more reliable readings of candidate and party affect, the differences between the Carter-Reagan and Democratic-Republican thermometer values are employed. We proceed to estimate the simple model:

NPZ impact $= b_0 + b_1$ (direction and strength of R's party identification) $+ b_2$ (NPZ partisan support $\times$ relative knit) $+ e$

Table 12.9 presents the zero-order correlations between respondents' candidate and party affects, on the one hand, and their own party identification and NPZ partisan support, on the other hand. Respondents' own identifications are clearly more highly correlated with candidate and party affect than is NPZ partisan support, although all of the coefficients are statistically significant. Moreover, as the regression analysis of Table 12.10 shows, despite the greater effect of party identification, NPZ partisan contextual effects are also discernible in the respondents' candidate and party affect: specifically, the contextual measure of NPZ partisan support is significantly related to the affect for Ronald Reagan, the Carter-Reagan difference, the Republican party, and the Democratic-Republican difference on the thermometers. The coefficients of affect for Carter and the Democratic party alone are also in the hypothesized direction but fail to reach statistical significance. It was a "bad year" for the Democrats—only their presumably long-held party identification made respondents feel positively; the NPZ as a partisan context did relatively little to reinforce favorable affect for the Democratic party and its presidential candidate.

EXPLAINING THE VOTE

The simple act of voting is enormously complex, and sophisticated electoral research seeks to explain all of this complexity. Obviously, no single variable like the contextual variable NPZ can come close to penetrating the mystery of the vote, and doing this is not really our intent. Our purpose is to explore what we believe to be a new, politically salient contextual factor that, while not likely to explain much variance, should be expected to add to our understanding of the electoral process and voting behavior.

Two dependent measures are available for this purpose: the respondent's own *vote intention* in September when the network data were collected, and the respondent's *vote choice* as reported after the November election. As previously, we specify a model that includes the respondent's party

Table 12.9 Correlations between candidate/party affect, respondent's party identification, and NPZ partisan support

| | Affect | | | | | |
Party identification and NPZ support	Carter	Reagan	Carter-Reagan difference	Democratic party	Republican party	Democratic-Republican difference
Respondent party identification	-.541[a]	.439[a]	-.520[a]	-.660[a]	.545[a]	-.744[a]
NPZ support × NPZ knit	-.341[a]	.316[a]	-.415[a]	-.411[a]	.367[a]	-.479[a]

N = 360

a. $p \le .01$

Table 12.10 Regression estimates for candidate/party affect, respondent's party identification, and NPZ partisan support

| | Affect | | | | | |
Party identification and NPZ support	Carter	Reagan	Carter-Reagan difference	Democratic party	Republican party	Democratic-Republican difference
Constant	74.013[a]	46.078[a]	27.935[a]	78.462[a]	48.031[a]	30.430[a]
Respondent party identification	-8.167[a]	5.567[a]	-13.733[a]	-8.146[a]	5.561[a]	-13.707[a]
NPZ support × NPZ knit	-.045	.866[b]	-1.312[b]	-.376	.557[c]	-.932[b]
F	74.220[a]	44.252[a]	113.868[a]	275.994[a]	77.118[a]	224.881[a]
Estimated R^2	.294[a]	.199[a]	.389[a]	.435[a]	.302[a]	.557[a]
N = 360						

a. $p \le .01$
b. $.01 < p \le .05$
c. $.05 < p \le .10$

identification and the NPZ's partisan support structure as independent variables. Again, the question is whether the NPZ partisan context affects the respondent's intended or reported vote, net of party identification. Because both dependent variables are ordinal, we measure the effects by way of probit procedures.

Table 12.11 presents the frequencies for the two variables. What is immediately noticeable is the difference between the September vote intentions and the November voting, evidently due to movement away from Carter and Anderson to Reagan. We will be concerned only with the Carter and Reagan vote intentions and vote choices. The probit results indicated in Table 12.12 show that the NPZ as a partisan context seems to make no significant independent contribution in explaining vote intentions. The result for the reported vote is somewhat more ambiguous: the t-ratio significance level is just slightly above .10 (the critical point for a .10 level is 1.282). While by standard criteria one cannot dismiss the null hypothesis that NPZ partisan context is unimportant for explaining vote choice, there is at least a plausible hint that it has some effect.

One explanation for why NPZ partisan context does not seem to be very effective in affecting vote intention and vote choice lies in the nature of the construct itself. Specifically, the construct does not capture the respondent's September perception of the NPZ's vote intention. We could not use this variable in the same way as we used the respondent's perception of the NPZ's partisan composition because of simultaneity bias. Therefore, to employ the NPZ's vote intentions in a model that satisfies statistical assumptions, we focus on stability or change and resort to temporal precedence.

For this purpose, we develop a new variable that measures the respondent's vote change from September to November by assigning a score of -1 to respondents switching to Carter, $+1$ to those switching to Reagan, and 0 to those who remained stable (Key's, 1966, "standpatters") in their

Table 12.11 Distribution of respondents' intended (September) and reported (November) votes

Candidate	Score	Intended vote		Reported vote	
		%	N	%	N
Carter	1	43	142	39	117
Anderson	2	10	33	5	17
Reagan	3	47	155	56	169
Total		100	330	100	303

Table 12.12 Probit estimates for intended (September) and reported (November) votes, by respondent's party identification and NPZ party support[a]

Party identification and NPZ support	Intended vote		Reported vote	
	Beta	t-ratio	Beta	t-ratio
Constant	−1.171[b]	−7.083	−.853[b]	−5.306
Respondent party identification	.588[b]	9.020	.550[b]	8.334
NPZ Support × NPZ knit	.002	.041	.045	1.171
Estimated R^2		.547		.544
N		297		286

a. Not including Anderson voters.
b. $p \le .01$

Table 12.13 Distribution of respondents on vote change/stability index

Voting behavior	Score	%	N
Switch from Reagan to Carter	−1	8	43
No change from vote intention	0	78	437
Switch from Carter to Reagan	+1	14	81
Total		100	561

candidate preferences. While the overwhelming majority of respondents (78 percent) reported voting for the candidate for whom they had intended to vote in September, slightly more than a fifth did change their preferences—with almost twice as many of the switchers moving to Reagan as to Carter (Table 12.13). The simple bivariate relationship shows that those who switched to Carter or Reagan tend to have NPZs planning to vote for the candidate for whom they ultimately vote (rho = .079, $p \le .05$). For obvious reasons, we control the relationship between respondents' vote change or stability and the NPZ's intended vote by respondents' own party identification.

The probit results reported in Table 12.14 confirm the contextual hypothesis: Republicans with pro-Reagan NPZs in September were more likely to vote for Reagan in November, while Republicans with pro-Carter NPZs tended to switch to Carter; similarly, Democrats with pro-Carter NPZs in September remained stable in their vote preference, while Democrats with pro-Reagan NPZs tended to switch to Reagan. While the respondents' own party identification has a strong influence on whether they are likely to stay loyal or switch, in accounting for vote stability and change it appears that the NPZ exerts an independent contextual effect.

Table 12.14 Probit estimates for vote change/stability, by respondent's party identification and NPZ's vote intention

Party identification and NPZ vote intention	Beta	*t*-ratio
Constant	.831[a]	3.409
Respondent party identification	.085[a]	2.596
NPZ's vote intention	.076[b]	1.787
Estimated R^2	.036	
N = 435		

a. $p \leq .01$
b. $.01 < p \leq .05$

This study has presented two major findings: first, the neighborhood as a geographic unit does not appear to be a perceptually salient environment for political behavior; and second, *particular* neighbors, *individually linked* to a citizen, appear to constitute a social network that has an independent effect on partisan affect for the political parties and their candidates as well as on stability or change in vote preferences as the electoral season goes forward. While the neighborhood appears to be of minor importance as a political *environment,* social relations among particular neighbors make for an interpersonal *context* that has an impact on political behavior.

These findings seem to be at odds with those of contextual analysis, which finds a person's place of residence to have an influence on political behavior. In fact, the findings are not in conflict. As pointed out earlier, contextual analysis based on aggregate indicators invariably assumes that behind the demographic data loom interpersonal relations and social interactions. In other words, aggregate data serve as proxies for information on interpersonal contacts in the neighborhood. This set of contacts is captured directly by the kind of social network approach taken in this study. Moreover, the life-space analysis indicates that the neighborhood is not the only or, for that matter, the most significant environment in which people are exposed to political cues. We therefore agree with Sprague's (1982, p. 109) comment that "the social network perspective simply emphasizes that better information about the structure of social interaction should lead to more successful empirical work."

Sprague is also correct in pointing out that demographic contextual analysis and individual-based social network analysis pose "no contradiction at the level of theory" (ibid.). Both types share the assumption, as Sprague (ibid., p. 100) puts it, that "contextual effects on political behavior are substantial and that ignoring them, or, more usually, denying them, assures substantial misunderstanding in our knowledge of political behavior." The current status of theory in contextual analysis is, unfortunately, dictated by the availability of data and not, as it should be, the other way around. Contextual analysts are dependent on data where they can find them, and then they must make use of whatever theory appears to be germane. We were fortunate in having at our disposal data stemming from a study explicitly inspired by some of the theoretical concerns of social network analysis. The next step in the contextual analysis of political behavior is obviously to generate data that are guided by prior, hypothesis-specific theoretical considerations so that theory can speak to the data as much as the data now speak to the theory.

Appendix: Design, Sample, and Measurement

The data for this study come from the year-long Major Panel of the National Election Study (NES) conducted in 1980 by the Center for Political Studies, University of Michigan. The data are available from the Inter-University Consortium for Political and Social Research, P.O. Box 1248, Ann Arbor, Michigan 48106 (see ICPSR, 1983).

A random probability sample of the noninstitutionalized population was first interviewed in January 1980 and reinterviewed in June, September, and November, after the presidential election. The new questions on respondents' "life space" and "neighborhood primary zone" appeared in the panel's September wave after having been pretested in the NES 1979 Pilot Project (for analyses of the pilot data, see Eulau and Siegel, 1980, 1981; Weatherford, 1982). They were designed by the senior author of this study and formated by Maria Sanchez, Director of Studies for NES.

Of the 769 September respondents, 734 were available for life-space measurement, but only 587 of these reported knowing any of their neighbors. Therefore, only the latter were available for the neighborhood primary zone analysis. Comparison of NPZ respondents and nonrespondents shows that there are no statistically significant differences between them with regard to age and family income. There is a significant difference, however, in the educational attainment of the two sets, with NPZ respondents' educational level being on average an entire year higher (12.47 versus 11.50 for nonrespondents). Not surprisingly, NPZ respondents knowing some neighbors are slightly more likely to be female, with the difference of 6.7 percent being statistically significant ($p \leq .06$).

With regard to the four life-space variables, there are no statistically significant differences between those reporting that they shop or work in the neighborhood as against elsewhere. On the other hand, 14.6 percent more NPZ respondents than nonrespondents report attending worship services in the neighborhood, while 14.8 percent more nonrespondents than NPZ respondents report not going to church at all. Similarly, more NPZ respondents than nonrespondents indicate spending their leisure time in the neighborhood. Both of these differences are statistically significant. In general, then, the sample of NPZ respondents is better educated and has slightly more females than the nonrespondents; and while there are *not* any significant differences on *all* four life-space measures, the NPZ respondents are more likely than the nonrespondents to be day-dwellers rather than night-dwellers on the composite life-space index.

The composite life-space measure is a simple additive scale based on questions asking respondents where they engage in a specific activity—whether in the neighborhood or elsewhere. "Neighborhood" was defined for the respondent as "people who live wihin four or five blocks of you, or in whatever you think of as your neighborhood." For the purpose of building the composite life-space measure, those pursuing a given activity in the neighborhood were given a score of 3, and those engaged elsewhere were given a score of 1. Those not working and/or not attending a church were given a score of 2. The scale thus ranges from a possible total score of 12 (pure day-dwellers) to a score of 4 (pure night-dwellers), which allows us to treat it as a continuous variable.

The scoring of the composite measures for the NPZ is more complex because not all NPZ respondents acknowledged knowing as many as three neighbors (the maximum asked for). In fact, 439 respondents gave three names; 99 gave two names; and 49 gave only one name. Before composing the data on neighbors into single additive measures, therefore, and to give each measure the same range of values for those who gave fewer than three names, the raw scores were weighted by multiplying the scores for one name by 3 and those for two names by 1.5.

FOUR

Of Emergence

and Development

13

Developmental Analysis

and Constructs

CONCERN with methodology has not been a hallmark of political science. One seeks in vain in the vast literature of politics for the kind and degree of methodological awareness easily found in the work of economists, sociologists, or psychologists. Again, there has been some change in recent years. Younger scholars, under the influence of the neighboring social sciences, have increasingly paid serious attention to methodological matters.[1] But their efforts have remained random and noncumulative. The only persistent and consistent discussion of methodology can be found in the work of Harold D. Lasswell, and there it is scattered through numerous books and articles of three decades (see Easton, 1950; Lipsky, 1955).

The Nature of Decision: Facts, Values, and Expectations

In specifying decision-making behavior as its proper focus of attention, political science deals with a most complex series of human actions. Lasswell is acutely aware of this complexity. Rational decision making, he suggests in clarifying the concept, "depends on clear conception of goals, accurate calculation of probabilities, and adept application of knowledge of ways and means" (1948a, p. 30). In other words, a decision is an act, or a series of acts, involving the simultaneous manipulation of facts, values, and above all, expectations. The decision maker cannot do without expectations about the future—expectations relating, for instance, to the probability of a long or short war, rising or falling national income, the stability or instability of foreign governments. Being explicit about one's expectations necessitates their assessment in terms of values, goals, or objectives, on the one hand, and in terms of whatever factual knowledge may be available, on the other hand. While every decision "turns in part upon a picture of significant changes in the emerging future," it is the task of the decision maker "to think creatively about how to alter, deter, or accelerate probable trends in order to shape the future closer to his desire" (ibid., p. 32).

Each of these components of decision-making behavior is predicated on three different types of thought. Lasswell refers to these types as goal thinking, trend thinking, and scientific thinking. Goal thinking relates to the analysis and selection of values or objectives toward which decisions are directed. Trend thinking involves the analysis of past tendencies and future probabilities. And scientific thinking refers to the analysis of limiting conditions through the application of appropriate skills. In other words, each of the three aspects of decision-making behavior has "built in," so to speak, three quite different, and possibly even conflicting, modes of thought or universes of discourse.

It seems to me that at the base of the difficulties characteristic of political science as a scientific discipline lies the problem of clarifying the three forms of symbolic behavior outlined by Lasswell, to keep them distinct in the analysis of decision-making activity, and yet to see their interrelations in the process of actual decision making. The methodological problem is nothing less than to connect statements of value or preference, statements of fact, and statements of expectation. All three types of statement are essential in decision making and in thinking about decision-making behavior.

It is not possible here to examine the problem of just how these patterns of thought are interrelated or can be interrelated, and whether Lasswell succeeds in doing so. As a matter of fact, it seems to me that Lasswell sidesteps the issue—perhaps because it cannot be resolved. The following is typical of the kind of statement he makes in this respect:

For maximum rationality it is necessary to use each tool, with no excessive reliance upon one. Each tool is part of the total process by which the mind can seek and perhaps find correct orientation in the entire manifold of events . . . The thinker can rely first upon one line of attack upon his problem, then another. By moving back and forth from one "lead in" to the next, he can increase the likelihood of arriving at policies that facilitate democracy. (1948b, pp. 203–204, 208)

Lasswell's concern with the problems of expectation has, however, successfully culminated in the conception of "developmental analysis" and of "developmental constructs." And it is with this phase alone of Lasswell's formulations that I want to deal. For here, it seems to me, Lasswell's work is especially suggestive. That this should be the case is not surprising. Preoccupation with decision making necessarily leads to developmental notions. For decision making is predominantly future oriented. It is, Lasswell points out, "forward-looking, formulating alternative courses of action extending into the future, and selecting among the alternatives by expectations of how things will turn out" (Lasswell and Kaplan, 1950, p. xvi). The accent is clearly on "expectations of how things will turn out." In fact, one may say that the other ingredients of decision making, to be successful, are predicated on correct expectations of how things will turn out.

It follows, too, that a theory of the political process or, at least, a conceptual schema that has decision-making behavior as its empirical referent is predicated on the availability of constructs that are descriptive of the emerging future. Such constructs presumably make possible "the planned observation of the emerging future [which] is one of the tasks of science" (1948a, p. 219). The name Lasswell gives such planned observation is "developmental analysis." A "developmental construct," the tool of developmental analysis, is a statement of expectations concerning the future expressed in certain core concepts. In the study of international relations, for instance, Lasswell advances "interdetermination," "bipolarization," "militarization," or "totalitarianization" as developmental constructs (1951a, pp. 29–39). Thinking in developmental terms is to be explicit about one's anticipations of the shape of things to come.

One may ask how developmental analysis differs from other procedures designed to deal with the problem of uncertainty as far as the future is concerned. Formal methods of decision making rely on the rules of probability in making rational choices. A probability prediction means that one possibility in a given range of possibilities is more likely to occur than another—on the assumption that extraneous factors are randomly distributed so that an outcome is unlikely to occur by chance alone and is therefore to be attributed to nonchance events. Lasswell is not altogether happy with probability models as far as policy making is concerned—for the reason that it is not easy for the decision maker to enumerate in advance the range of possibilities that will be open to him (1955, p. 392).

Lasswell therefore proposes developmental analysis as "another method of estimating the future. It does not throw away the available stock of trend information or of scientific knowledge." But, he continues,

it does not attempt to limit the mind of the decision-maker (or advisor) to precisely ordered trend or scientific information. On the contrary, the accent is upon scrutinizing the whole context in which the precise data and relationships have been obtained and established. The result may be to direct attention to the unrepresentative character of some of the information at hand. (Ibid.)

Elsewhere Lasswell has described developmental analysis as an effort to achieve "productive insight into the structure of the whole manifold of events which includes the future as well as the past" (1948a, p. 147). In order to approximate this objective, developmental analysis requires configurative methods. It utilizes

several interrelated and mutually facilitating patterns of thought, which we may abbreviate as the clarification of goal *values*, the assessment of *trends*, the review of scientific knowledge of conditioning *factors*, the *projection* of developmental constructs of the future, and the invention and estimating of policy *alternatives* designed to increase the probability of the realization of the goal values. (1951b, p. 473)

Society as a Continuum of Social Change

Developmental analysis proceeds from the assumption that societies are constantly changing. It follows, as a postulate, that "any given society, at any given period of time, can be conceived as an interval on some continuum of social change" (Lasswell, Lerner, and Pool, 1952, p. 27). A developmental construct specifies the terminal phases of the continuum—"the 'from what' and 'toward what' of developmental sequences" (Lasswell and Kaplan, 1950, p. xv). It represents a provisional pattern of the from what–toward what relationship, with one set of terms referring to selected features of the past, another to the future. Or, as Lasswell puts it elsewhere, "a developmental construct characterizes a possible sequence of events running from a selected cross-section of the past to a cross-section of the future" (1951a, p. 4).

A developmental construct, these definitions suggest, is tentative and hypothetical. In view of its futuristic component it can be nothing else. For this reason Lasswell also refers to developmental constructs as "speculative models of the principal social changes of our epoch . . . They specify the institutional pattern from which we are moving and the pattern toward which we are going" (1951c, p. 11).

Although developmental analysis selects different points at which to observe, in cross-section, the characteristics of a given epoch, it is concerned not with "stages" of development but with "patterns of succession of events" (Lasswell and Kaplan, p. xv). In its full stress on time, developmental analysis differs from those approaches that seek to subject the future to inner logical restriction by thinking in terms of stages. Developmental analysis makes use of the conception of stages, but it does not allow itself to be subordinated to this method. Rather than emphasizing stages as significant aspects of social change, developmental analysis "throws the time axis—the 'from what, toward what'—into relief" (1951a, p. 5).

Developmental analysis must not be confused with trend analysis. Extrapolation is a necessary part of developmental analysis, but building expectations about the future on extrapolation alone is, in Lasswell's terms, an essentially "itemistic procedure" (1948a, p. 147). Extrapolation, he suggests, is only "a prelude to the use of creative imagination" (ibid., pp. 32–33). For a trend "is not a cause of social change; it is a register of the relative strength of the variables that produce it" (ibid., p. 32). Nevertheless, because trend curves summarize many features of the past, they must be carefully considered in the formulation of developmental constructs. But a developmental construct, in contrast to a trend curve, "is frankly imaginative though disciplined by careful consideration of the past" (ibid., p. 147). In other words, trends derive their significance from being imbedded in developmental constructions.

Developmental constructs, like most models in the social sciences, "are actuarial rather than purely theoretical" (Lasswell, Lerner, and Pool, 1952, p. 64). Most of the constructs of social science are based on estimates of the parameters from the statistics derived from observation. It is inspection of the data that suggests the main variables and their relative weights in prediction. The process yields an empirical model that can then be tested against new data.

Finally, it requires emphasis that developmental constructs are not scientific propositions. This may be seen if they are compared with equilibrium models. Equilibrium analysis is concerned with the systematic interaction of variables that constitute a system in that they tend toward the maintenance of a particular pattern of relationships. Equilibrium analysis seeks to isolate such systems and investigate the conditions of their maintenance. Developmental analysis has an equilibrium component—"laws of change in addition to characterizations of the process of change." But, Lasswell warns, "confusion between these components may interfere with sound appraisal of both" (Lasswell and Kaplan, 1950, p. xv, n. 5). Contrasting examples are the Darwinian and Marxian conceptualizations of development. Darwin's developmental analysis of the evolutionary process can be clearly distinguished from statements of those conditions and mechanisms that are supposedly operative in the process of evolution. But Marxian laws of social change, so-called, are seldom explicitly distinguished from the description of a specific historical process—"data confirming the account of that process is often mistakenly construed as evidence for the supposed laws according to which the changes occur, and conversely" (ibid., p. xv). Moreover, the Marxist construct of the emerging classless society involves a claim of inevitability that cannot be accepted, for "events in the future are not knowable with absolute certainty in advance: they are partly probable and partly chance" (1951c, p. 11). Conceptions like the Marxist construct of the classless society, or the liberal notion of continued progress, are not developmental constructs, Lasswell points out, "since it was usually assumed by the forecaster that he was making a deduction about the future from a valid scientific law" (Lasswell, Lerner, and Pool, 1952, pp. 7–8).

Developmental Constructs and Knowledge

Developmental constructs are not to be considered predictions, even when confirmed by future events. Yet developmental constructs are anticipatory in nature. But if they refer to the future, then, why are they not predictions? A prediction, Lasswell suggests, not only "refers to a category of events rather than a unique occurrence," but also "puts the stress upon an estimate of probability (or randomness)," and it "is made contingent upon the occurrence of conditions which, on the basis of past observations, have controlled the phenomenon being considered" (ibid., p. 6).

If this is the meaning of prediction, it is evident why developmental constructs are not predictive statements. For, Lasswell maintains, "we cannot depend upon the future to conform to the ordinary postulates of probability theory, such as that a series of uniform events is in prospect (as in the tossing of the same penny to show 'heads' or 'tails')." It is necessary, therefore, "to appraise the degree to which the more familiar probability postulates will apply" (1951a, p. 5). For instance, it might have been reasoned in 1900 that the non-European world was likely to increase its power in the next fifty years, and that this development would be accompanied by a tendency of European nations to unite in the face of the non-European threat. This prediction would have miscarried. For it would have been based on the erroneous inference that Europeans are sufficiently identified with each other and sufficiently alert to change to feel jointly threatened rather than individually advantaged by the growth of non-European states. In other words, had the prediction been based on an inference from conditions, it could be said that "a scientific proposition is being deductively applied." But in 1900, as Lasswell points out, "it would not have been clear what conditions were to be assumed to hold before the proposition might have been supposed to apply" (Lasswell, Lerner, and Pool, 1952, p. 7).

The task of prediction, then, is more complicated than simply extrapolating a trend or applying relevant scientific laws and hypotheses. It is precisely the task of developmental constructions to help surmount the difficulties involved in anticipating the future. But are developmental constructs wholly arbitrary? The answer is no. For it can be tested "whether the stated conditions actually hold—whether the trends in the past and present have been, in fact, toward" the state of affairs anticipated by the given construct (ibid., p. 66).

As speculative models, then, developmental constructs are of value in suggesting significant hypotheses that can be tested. Insofar as these hypotheses derive their significance from their origin in a developmental framework, their utility in research is guaranteed, for "in research, as elsewhere, activity directed by an explicit and important purpose is bound to be more relevant, economical, and lucid than activity which is routinized" (ibid., p. 75). Or, as Lasswell writes elsewhere, a developmental construct "can at any given moment be taken as the point of departure for gathering and appraising data about trends and conditions on a global scale" (1948b, p. 207). This discussion clarifies the meaning of developmental constructs further. Rather than being a direct statement concerning the future, it appears that a developmental construct primarily serves as "a means of improving judgments of the future" (1951a, p. 4). As a tool of analysis it may be particularly valuable in situations in which extrapolations of trends and extrapolations of conditions collide. For it may help "to estimate which factors are likely to resolve the conflict" (Lasswell, Lerner, and Pool, 1952, p. 7).

But as developmental constructs are not statements of fact, and because they are statements of expectations, their hypothetical quality raises certain questions of knowledge. If the term "knowledge" is reserved to statements of fact, that is, statements concerning what is actually observed, Lasswell suggests that it "does not properly apply to statements about future events." But one may ask whether there are criteria of knowledge relevant to choosing among different developmental constructs, particularly if interpretations of trends seem to be conflicting. Lasswell takes the position that "under certain restrictions it is reasonable to extend our knowledge of the past into the future" (1951a, pp. 3–4). By "restrictions" Lasswell means the available knowledge of conditioning relationships that have held true in the past. For instance, available knowledge may suggest that population growth is affected by pessimistic expectations about world politics. On the further assumption, therefore, that in a prolonged crisis of insecurity the factor of pessimism will have to be taken into account, it seems reasonable to modify the population curve in accordance with such knowledge.

In other words, as projections of trends into the future, developmental constructs do not have the status of knowledge. But they may be appraised in a scientific frame of reference. For any future trend will register and interact with the equilibrium of those factors that condition each other. A developmental construct such as Lasswell's famous concept of the "garrison state," he asserts, is "neither a dogmatic forecast, nor, methodologically, a simplistic extrapolation of past trends into the future" (Lasswell, Lerner, and Pool, 1952, p. 66).

Of course, developmental constructs are less generalized than the concepts used in equilibrium analysis. For instance, if we speak of the world as moving from a multipolar toward a bipolar state system, the constructs employed here lack the generality of a concept like "political system." But, Lasswell points out, "the lesser generality of the developmental standpoint gives it a correspondingly more direct purport for action" (Lasswell and Kaplan, 1950, p. xv).

Developmental Analysis and Policy Science

We may ask how developmental constructs are elaborated and how their relevance is assessed. Lasswell's reply is crisp and, on the face of it, scandalizingly simple: "Select according to goal values." As grounds for his position Lasswell mentions "the characteristics of rational thought." For, he points out, "rational thinking takes the consequences of its own exercise into account." Moreover, he continues, "among the factors moulding the future are interpretations of the future." And since expectations of the future have an impact on action, notably policy decisions, "we proceed rationally when we operate with a clear conception of our possible effect upon the shape of things to come" (1951a, p. 5). Since it is the particular function of policy to achieve goal values, a first step in the creation of developmental constructs is the clarification of the values presumably to be realized by decision making.

This is not the place to discuss the particular values in terms of which Lasswell creates his developmental constructs. While he specifies "human dignity" as a central value, he maintains that "the relative significance of values for persons and groups is to be discovered by inquiry and not settled by definition" (ibid., p. 6).

In pleading for the inclusion of values in the construction and selection of developmental constructs, Lasswell deviates from the positivistic bias of much of social science. "In some ways," he writes, "the thinking in the United States about human relations has been unnecessarily one-sided in the amount of emphasis put upon derivation [justification] and upon science. This has meant a relative de-emphasis upon the *clarifying* of goals, the projection of future developments, including especially the *invention* of future lines of policy" (1948b, p. 204).

Lasswell has increasingly come to speak, therefore, of "policy science" as a convenient term that distinguishes positivistic social or political science from an approach where "knowledge is mustered for clear-cut objectives, and is fully related to the most likely contingencies to appear in the un-folding processes of history" (ibid.). One of the distinctive functions of policy science is "to facilitate the modification of trends by making explicit what the trends in fact have been and whither they lead with respect to social goals" (Lasswell, Lerner, and Pool, 1952, p. 74). In this task developmental analysis and projective thinking have a central role:

> This mode of thinking is indispensable for responsible action, which invariably consists in selecting programs in the light of expectations about future contingencies. No one plans a military campaign, a party program or business enterprise without modifying his conceptions of policy in the light of estimates of what will happen under various circumstances. (1948b, p. 204)

In other words, because developmental analysis implies a picture of the future—"a picture of the alternatives by which goals are likely to be affected by what we, or anyone else, will probably do"—it also "includes the evaluation of new *invented* ways of moving toward the goal, and embraces the products of creative imagination about the ways and means of policy" (ibid., p. 203).

Developmental constructs, evidently, are the products of a mutual cross-fertilization of goal thinking, trend thinking, scientific thinking, projective thinking, and probability thinking. The five types are clearly discernible in what is probably Lasswell's most complete description of what he means by a developmental construct:

> A "developmental construct" is a speculative model in which the present is characterized as a transition between a selected pattern of events located in the past and a pattern imputed to the future. No claim of scientific validity is made for the model, although the present state of knowledge is taken into account in setting up the hypothesis. The developmental construct is not a simple extrapolation of recent trends, but a critical weighing of future outcomes considered as an interacting whole. By highlighting some major possibilities we may be led to revise our previous estimates of the situation, and to guide research and policy activities with a view to taking advantage of emerging opportunities for analysis, insight, and perhaps control. (1954, p. 360)

In short, a given developmental construct, such as that of bipolarization, is nothing less than an "ideal-type" concept of a social process symbolized in its nomenclature. It represents an ideal-type exaggeration of the relationship between empirical and hypothetical (or past and future) situations.

But why did Lasswell seek to fashion developmental constructs as tools of analysis? Indeed, what purpose does it serve to seek to comprehend complex patterns of human behavior in terms of such relatively simple constructs as bipolarization or garrison state? Do these constructs not oversimplify complicated processes of action? Needless to say, perhaps, these constructs do oversimplify the problems implicit in their construction. But all scientific constructs oversimplify. And in simplifying problems they presumably aid in the understanding of reality.

Developmental Analysis and the Self

One of the most recurring themes in Lasswell's writings is the idea that political analysis is "nothing less than correct orientation in the continuum which embraces the past, present, and future" (1935, p. 4). By such orientation Lasswell means self-orientation in the context of time. Such orientation, he writes, "can be expedited by the self-conscious consideration of details," and both developmental and equilibrium patterns of thinking may be helpful (1935, p. 16). Otherwise "details will be incorrectly located" (ibid., p. 4). Developmental constructs, then, are deliberately created "for the purpose of orienting ourselves in the succession of significant events, past and future" (1948a, p. 136).

But developmental constructs serve not only the task of correct self-orientation. They also serve that of self-stimulation. The developmental standpoint, Lasswell writes, is designed to bring "the process of inquiry into closer accord with the needs of policy, when this standpoint is deliberately taken as a technique of self-stimulation in the envisioning of alternative futures" (Lasswell and Kaplan, 1950, p. xvi, n. 10). As a technique of self-stimulation, developmental analysis will serve the policy maker as well as the social scientist. Once he has clarified his goals, Lasswell suggests, the policy maker "must orient himself correctly in contemporary trends and future probabilities. Concerned with specific features of the future as they are ever emerging from the past, he needs to be especially sensitive to time, and to forecast with reasonable accuracy passage from one configuration of events to the next" (1948a, p. 32). Similarly, discussing the utility of the garrison state construct for the social scientist, Lasswell emphasizes that "it is to stimulate the individual specialist to clarify for himself his expectations about the future, as a guide to the timing of scientific work. Side by side with this 'construct' of a garrison state there may be other constructs; the rational person will assign exponents of probability to every alternative picture" (ibid., pp. 146–147).

Lasswell's concern with correct self-orientation of the policy maker or the social scientist has its source in his long-term interest in the psychology of politics and the application of psychiatric techniques in the study of political behavior (see Lasswell, 1930). The central task of psychoanalysis or psychiatry is to help the disturbed patient to orient himself correctly vis-à-vis his social environment. In aiding his patient, the therapist is essentially future oriented. It is not accidental, therefore, that as Lasswell's interests turned from the pathology of political behavior to its creative possibilities, he was to make use of the notion of correct self-orientation. He explicitly states that the ways and thoughts of the therapist and those of the policy maker are very much similar:

The therapist is always oriented toward the future since he must guide his intervention in the life of the patient according to an estimate of contingent outcome . . . It is well known to every policy maker who influences or estimates the future that systematic knowledge is always insufficient for his purposes. Hence he becomes accustomed to employ whatever information is at hand that will provide a basis of inference about the future . . . Some of the available information is unsystematic, yet helps in imagining and assessing a "developmental construct" of the sequence of future events . . . With a clearer image of order the pertinence of scientific knowledge can be better appraised. The therapist goes further. He may invent courses of action designed to increase the likelihood that desired outcomes will in fact occur. (1956, p. 114)

A second task of analysis is to create insight and understanding in the total context. Both patient and therapist are modifiable by exposure to information about the patient's conduct in past situations. "The great and creative insistence by Freud on the efficacy of insight," Lasswell continues,

carries with it a challenging and dynamic implication for the future of man in society. It puts into a special category the data obtained by scientific procedure and the generalizations on hand at any given cross-section in time, when they relate to human interactions . . . But knowledge of interaction may produce insight and in this way modify future events in ways that result in changing the scientifically established relationships themselves. It is not that scientific laws are unverified; it is simply that they are always to be taken as historical summaries of event relations, and the assessment of the likelihood that they will obtain in the future is a special problem. (Ibid., pp. 114–115)

The special problem to which Lasswell refers is, of course, the central problem of the analysis of decision making and, for that matter, of all social action. It is more generally known as the problem of the "self-fulfilling" or "self-denying" prophecy. It is this problem that developmental analysis seeks to surmount by incorporating in the developmental constructs of the future those very predictions of the future that, by becoming known, may affect the future. In other words, developmental analysis makes a virtue of the fact—which gives social science in general a great deal of trouble—that a prediction, by becoming itself a factor in the definition of the situation, guarantees or prevents the emergence of anticipated results. But because once a prediction becomes known the individual can change his behavior in such a way as to confirm or deny the validity of a social law, Lasswell emphasizes that "an element of free choice is thereby introduced which reduces our reliance upon prediction" (1951a, p. 4).

Lasswell touches here upon a theme that has occupied him for many years. As he pointed out in *World Politics and Personal Insecurity,* published in 1934:

Now it is impossible to abolish uncertainty by the refinement of retrospective observations, by the accumulation of historical detail, by the application of precision methods to elapsed events; the crucial test of adequate analysis is nothing less than the future verification of the insight into the nature of the master configuration against which details are construed. Each specific interpretation is subject to re-definition as the structural potentialities of the future become actualized in the past and present of participant observers. The analyst moves between the contemplation of detail and of configuration, knowing that the soundness of the result is an act of creative orientation rather than of automatic projection. The search for precision in the routines of the past must be constantly chastened and given relevance and direction by reference to the task of self-orientation which is the goal of analysis. (1935, p. 17)

Developmental constructs, then, are acts of the creative imagination. As imaginative estimates of the future they enable policy makers or social scientists to orient themselves in the pursuit of their activities. For, as Lasswell puts it in another publication, "even in an automatizing world some top-level choices must be made. In that sense at least discretion is here to stay" (1955, p. 399).

It was not my purpose to criticize Lasswell's notion of developmental analysis, but rather to piece together in reasonably orderly fashion his widely dispersed references on the subject. Ultimately, of course, the test of a method's usefulness in scientific inquiry is its application in empirical research.

On the positive side, it seems to me, Lasswell has successfully come to grips with two problems: first, he has dealt with the implications for political science of the fact that political behavior is value oriented or goal seeking, by pointing out that values or goals are not independently existing onto-logical entities but are shaped in and by the very processes of behavior of which they are a part; and, second, Lasswell has brought into sharp focus the fact that political behavior is oriented toward the future and antici-patory, as well as related to the past and retrospective.

On the negative side, it seems to me, Lasswell's undisciplined ways of presentation have tended to make his total work seem disjointed. His dependence on readily available examples or analogies rather than on meticulous research have made his work suggestive but hardly evidential. This is quite clear in his discussion of the relationship between developmental and equilibrium models of analysis. His treatment of the problem is not satisfactory. The relationship between the two methods of analysis is probably the central methodological problem on which he touches, and Lasswell gives the impression of having solved it without actually having done so. He seems aware of the fact that equilibrium models in social science, in rejecting or avoiding the possibility of entropy, do not cope with the problem of change. Developmental analysis, on the other hand, though specifying initial and terminal states, does not say anything about the character of these states in the pattern of change. One should expect, therefore, an attempt at the integration of developmental and equilibrium models. Lasswell's discussion in this respect is suggestive, but there appears to be a failure of theoretical nerve at the most crucial point of his methodological work. Instead, Lasswell is satisfied with stating that both models may be strategically employed when needed. The question remains, it seems to me, whether it is possible to say, without taking account of developmental sequences as elaborated by developmental analysis, that any given system is in equilibrium or not. Talcott Parsons (1951, p. 483), in discussing the relationship between equilibrium theory and processes of change in the social system, sticks his neck out in asserting that equilibrium analysis is necessarily prior to an analysis of change: "The essential point is that for there to be a theory of change of pattern . . . there must be an initial and a terminal pattern to be used as points of reference." These initial and terminal points are assumed to be in equilibrium, of course. If Lasswell were to carry developmental analysis to its logical conclusion, he would have to assert the opposite—that it is impossible to know whether the points are in fact in equilibrium, or entering or departing from an equilibrium condition, without a prior analysis of the developmental se quences that would reveal past changes of the system or suggest possible future changes. But this Lasswell does not do, and in not doing it he seems to miss a methodological opportunity.

Policy Maps and Policy Outcomes:

A Developmental Analysis

IN SPITE OF common challenges stemming from the common environment shared by all cities in a metropolitan region, continued and even increasing social and economic differentiation among and within cities rather than homogenization and integration are the most significant features of the contemporary metropolitan scene (Williams et al., 1965).[1] Cities within the same metropolitan region are not only maintaining but also developing distinct and unique "public life styles." Urban sociology and urban geography have raised a multitude of questions and given a multitude of answers in seeking to account for the fact that cities facing basically similar challenges from the environment react so differently to these challenges. Most relevant research deals with the problem of differentiation and its effects on the development of cities in terms of historical settlement patterns, economic location and growth, or geographic space distribution (Chapin and Weiss, 1962; Thompson, 1965).

But differences in municipal life styles may also be the result of differences in public policies deliberately pursued by local governments in the metropolitan area. If this is so, the common pressures from the environment are evidently interpreted differently in the process of public decision making that seeks to cope with them. It would seem, then, that metropolitan cities are in different stages of policy development. Leaving aside momentarily the meaning of "stages of policy development," we can ask a number of questions that may shed light on the relationship between environmental pressures and public policies designed to meet these pressures. If cities are in different stages of policy development, how can the stages be identified? Is policy development linear and "progressive," or is it reversible? Do the stages of policy development in fact correspond to

Written with Robert Eyestone.

relevant conditions of the environment? But if there are no differences in environmental challenges, what makes for arrested development in one city, while a similarly challenged city takes off or another is highly developed? On the other hand, if cities are in different stages of development, is it due to their possessing uneven resource capabilities by which environmental problems can be solved? But how can one explain why cities with equal resources adopt quite different public policies? What is the character of the policies designed to meet environmental challenges? Are they attempts to adjust the city to the changing environment, or are they attempts to control the environment, or both?

Questions like these in turn direct our attention to the need for exploring the policy perspectives of urban decision makers. How do municipal policy makers perceive their community's environment and problems stemming from environmental conditions? What are their short-term policy positions, and what are their long-range policy images of the future? Are their perceptions of problems, policy orientations, and expectations related to the city's stage of policy development? And if this is the case, what are we to make of the relationship from a theoretical point of view? Although we do not propose to deal with all of these questions, it seems to us that they provide the cutting edge of an empirical theory of urban public policy.

This study of the policy maps of city councils in relationship to city policy development is part of a much larger project on municipal legislative bodies conducted in the ninety-odd cities of the San Francisco Bay metropolitan region since 1964 (see the Appendix).

The Model

The model guiding the analysis is a partial one, and we shall not be dealing in the analysis with all of its relevant empirical components. The model predicts city policy development as a response to external and internal features of the urban environment. The model assumes that city size, density, and growth as well as resources are antecedent variables; that individual or group demands and decision makers' policy orientations are intervening variables; and that policy outcomes and resultant stages of policy development are consequent variables. Of course, in empirical reality neither city size, density, or growth nor city resources are truly independent precisely because public policies may be designed to control the city's environment or increase its resources. But for the purpose of short-term analysis we can assume these variables to be independent.

Policy outcomes are assumed to follow each other in a characteristic sequence that constitutes the city's policy development. These outcomes are responses to environmental challenges, such as those occasioned by high population density or a high growth rate. Moreover, they are indicative of policy makers' willingness to utilize city resources. Changes in city size or density due to growth as well as in resource capability bring about changes in policy outcomes that move the city along from one stage to another in the developmental process. The process of policy development need not be unidirectional; at least temporary reversals are possible.

Environmental challenges may or may not be perceived by policy makers as "problems" requiring action. Even if problems are not perceived and no action is taken, there is a policy that is reflected in policy outcomes. Policy makers' sensitivity to environmental challenges is influenced by the demands that are made on them as well as by their own policy preferences and policy images. Therefore, city policy development is not only due to changes in the environment but is mediated by policy makers' orientations to action. For instance, whether or not resources are mobilized for development depends to a large extent on demands made on government as well as on the policy preferences of policy makers.

However, policy makers' perceptions of problems, policy positions, and policy images—their "policy maps," so to speak—are themselves not independent of policy development. Because policy development is cumulative in that past policy outcomes constrain current policy proposals— what is feasible and what is not—policy maps are likely to be formulated, consciously or unconsciously, within the restrictive context of the stage of development in which a city is momentarily located. In other words, policy makers cannot do as they please. The model assumes, therefore, that decision makers' policy maps reflect as well as shape policy development.

The Concepts and Measures

POLICY AND POLICY OUTCOMES

"Policy" is defined as the relationship of a governmental unit to its environment. It finds expression in general programs and specific decisions, or in policy declarations of decision makers. But because a policy need not be declared to be a policy, analysis cannot rely on manifest statements or overt decisions alone but must concern itself with policy outcomes. By policy outcomes we mean the concrete manifestations of policy—revenues, expenditures, regulations, court decisions, the exertion of police power, and so on. Policy outcomes, then, reflect the orientations of policy makers, regardless of whether or not a conscious decision has been made. On the other hand, because policy outcomes may at times represent unanticipated results not intended by policy makers, policy analysis cannot altogether ignore policy declarations. In fact, the relationship between policy intentions and policy outcomes challenges the analyst of public policy.

To develop our concept of policy further, we conceive of public policy as a response of government to challenges or pressures from the physical and social environment. Changes in public policy either adjust or adapt the political system to environmental changes, or they bring about changes in the environment. Which course of action is chosen depends on a multitude of factors—the structure of the political system; its human and physical capabilities; the degree of mass or elite involvement in the political process; the vitality of private associations making public demands; and, last but not least, the perceptions, preferences, and orientations of policy makers.

The problematics of policy making arise out of the relationship between changes in the environment that require some response, the ways in which these changes are experienced as challenges by decision makers, and the values that decision makers may seek in formulating policy. Policy, then, is a response to environmental pressures, both physical and social, as well as anticipation of a future state of affairs. If this is the case, a change in policy is both causal and purposive: it is "caused" by environmental challenges, but it is also directed toward a goal and shaped by a purpose. The tension arising out of the simultaneous impact of causal and purposive "forcings" is a basic dilemma in the scientific study of politics.

Analysis of policy outcomes through time requires a classification of policies.[2] We distinguish between "adaptive" and "control" policies. The measure used as an indicator of an adaptive policy is the percentage of *total* government expenses spent for health, libraries, parks, and recreation.[3] These major accounting categories used to report expenditures presumably include the major amenities offered by cities. A "high-amenities" city differs from a city with a traditional services orientation in that it spends less of city income for fire and police services or public works.[4]

The measure used to indicate a city's control policy is the percentage of all *general* government expenses spent by the planning commission. *General* government expenses include essentially all administrative expenses and salaries *not* included under fire, police, or recreation categories, and so on.[5]

POLICY DEVELOPMENT AND ITS MEASUREMENT

Policy outcomes are responses to changes and challenges in the environment. Policy development refers to a set of policy outcomes that follow each other sequentially through time. If the annual outcomes are similar, we speak of the resulting profile as a *stage* of policy development. Three stages will be identified: *retarded, transitional,* and *advanced.*[6] The median of medians for all cities with respect to planning and amenities expenditures over a period of eight years serves as the criterion of similar or dissimilar outcomes.

The definition of a set of sequential and similar outcomes as a stage presupposes continuity and stability. But the conception of development implies that one stage may, sooner or later, be followed by a new stage. It is unlikely that one stage will suddenly yield to another. Not only may development revert; even if development is "progressive," the transformation from one stage to the next may involve a series of dissimilar outcomes—some outcomes characteristic of an earlier stage, others characteristic of a later stage. If this occurs, an eight-year profile cannot easily be assigned to one stage or another. Put differently, we cannot easily predict whether the system will remain in the earlier stage or move into a later stage.

To cope with this possibility, we define a set of sequential but dissimilar policy outcomes as a *phase* of development. The notion of phase suggests that the sequence is less clearly bounded and, perhaps, of shorter duration than a stage. As we are constructing three stages of development, we must provide for two phases—an *emergent* phase that indicates movement from the retarded to the transitional stage, and a *maturing* phase that is located between the transitional and advanced stages.

Figure 14.1 illustrates how annual policy outcomes are assigned to a stage or phase of policy development. If planning and amenities expenditures fall below the grand medians in every year of the eight-year sequence,

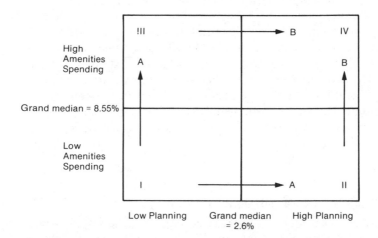

Figure 14.1   Categories of policy outcomes over eight-year period

the profile is classified as *retarded* (cell I); if one or the other type of expenditure falls above the grand medians, the profile is designated as transitional (cells II and III); and if both planning and amenities expenditures are above the medians in all eight years, the profile is assigned to the *advanced* stage of development (cell IV). If during the eight-year sequence expenditures move across the median lines, the profiles represent phases of development: outcomes moving from cell I to cells II or III (arrows A) are classified as *emergent;* those moving from cells I, II, or III into cell IV (arrows B) are designated as *maturing.*

Cases of "reversals" for which the model does not provide are assigned to stages or phases of development in such a way that "reversal errors" are reduced as much as possible. This involves informed but, we hope, not arbitrary assignment decisions.[7] We are satisfied that the reversals are not sufficient to invalidate the typology of policy development. As Table 14.1 shows, for the eighty-two cities whose policy profiles can be identified over an eight-year period, there were 572 opportunities for change in annual outcomes.[8] Of these opportunities eighty, or 14 percent, represented reversals from one year to the next. In the other 86 percent of opportunities, there either was no change—that is, all outcomes remained in the same stage over all eight years—or change occurred in the hypothesized ("progressive") direction. Reversals in stable-stage cities are due, of course, to the assignment of some "impure" cases where reversals seem to be only temporary deviations from the regular pattern.

A validity test. In order to test the validity of the typological constructs and the underlying assumptions, we can divide the eight-year period into two four-year periods and assign each period's profile to either a stage or a phase of policy development. Cross-tabulation permits us to inspect the internal movement of the policy profiles from one period to the next. If our assumptions and assignments are reasonably valid, we should be able

Table 14.1 Developmental typology of city policy profiles with opportunities for change and reversals

Development type	Cities N	Opportunities N	Number of reversals				Reversals	
			1	2	3	4	N	%
Retarded	11	76	7	2	0	0	11	14
Emergent	14	98	5	5	1	0	18	18
Transitional	26	182	9	6	0	1	25	14
Maturing	15	104	5	6	1	0	20	19
Advanced	16	112	4	1	0	0	6	5
Total	82	572	30	20	2	1	80	14

to predict, from knowledge of a profile's location on the development scale in the first four-year period, where it will be located in the second four-year period. We predict that cities in a stage of development are less likely to move than cities in a phase of development. We also predict that when there is movement, it is more likely to be in the hypothesized "progressive" direction than in a reversed direction. Table 14.2 presents the results.

It is readily evident that, with some exceptions, both predictions are supported by the data. Of the fifty cities in stages of development during the 1958–1961 period, thirty, or 60 percent, remained in the same stage during the following 1962–1965 period; but of the thirty-two cities in a phase of development during the earlier period, only nine, or 28 percent, remained there in the later period. If we consider the direction of movements, it appears that of the twenty cities in stages during the earlier period that did move, sixteen, or 80 percent, advanced in the expected direction. But this result is, of course, largely a function of the boundaries set to the typology: retarded cities can only move forward and advanced cities can only move backward. More significant, therefore, is the fact that none of the advanced cities reverted, suggesting that once this plateau is reached, institutionalization of policies makes reversal unlikely; and the further fact that of the ten transitional cities that did move, six moved forward and four backward. Similarly, of the fourteen emergent cities that moved, ten, or 71 percent, moved forward as expected and only four returned to the retarded stage in the later period; but of the nine moving maturing cities, a bare majority of five reverted to the transitional stage. Of course, these results, whether "favorable" or not from the developmental standpoint, may be influenced by the original data. Some policy outcomes as measured are in some cases very close to the median-of-medians cutting point that serves as the criterion for assignment, so that we may be dealing here with errors over which we have no control. Nevertheless, we believe that the

Table 14.2 Policy development of cities in developmental sequence from 1958–1961 to 1962–1965

State of development in 1958–61	State of development in 1962–1965				
	Retarded (N = 11)	Emergent (N = 14)	Transitional (N = 26)	Maturing (N = 15)	Advanced (N = 16)
Retarded (N = 16)	6	9	0	0	1
Emergent (N = 16)	4	2	7	3	0
Transitional (N = 24)	1	3	14	5	1
Maturing (N = 16)	0	0	5	7	4
Advanced (N = 10)	0	0	0	0	10

weight of the evidence is sufficient to warrant our interpretation of Table 14.2. It is also noteworthy that few of the movements, either forward or backward, exceed one step at a time. Of the twenty-six cities moving forward and having an opportunity to do so by *more* than one step (that is, those retarded, emergent, and transitional in the first period), twenty-one, or 81 percent, moved one step only; and of the nine cities moving backward and having an opportunity for more moves (that is, those transitional and maturing in the first period), all but one reverted only one step.

Reversed development is an empirical fact of life. While stages of development as conceived by historians are inevitably consecutive and irreversible, policy development is in fact reversible. Although we assume that in general stages and phases follow each other in "progressive" order, an assumption that the results of Table 14.2 certainly do not falsify, no rigid assumptions need or should be made about the direction of change. Policy is the creation of men and can be changed by men, within certain constraints imposed by environmental necessities, in whatever direction they prefer. Otherwise the concept of policy would make little sense.

RESOURCE CAPABILITY

A city's resource capabilities can be measured in a variety of ways. Ideally, we would like to think of resource capability as the maximum amount of income a city can expect annually when serious efforts are made to tap all possible income sources, including current revenues from taxes, borrowed funds, grants in aid, income from utilities, and so on. However, we have no way to determine whether such efforts have been made. Moreover, were we to use the readily available city income figures as a measure of resource capability, the measure would contravene our assumption that some cities are more pressed for revenue than others. Nor can we use a measure equivalent to per capita gross national product that is used in the comparative study of nations.[9] For a high proportion of the production of any city crosses city boundaries and is not available to support local government expenditures. Needed is a measure of the wealth remaining wholly within city limits and available to local taxation or such state taxation as is refundable to the city.

The measure we are using is, therefore, total assessed valuation per capita subject to local taxation for fiscal 1965–66, as determined by the California State Board of Equalization. In using this measure we assume that wealth in the form of private, commercial, and industrial property will be a potential source of revenue, and that per capita assessed valuation is a rough indicator of a city's resource capability.[10] A city will hesitate to institute new programs or expand old ones if it has a low level of assessed valuation per capita but may be more inclined to do so if it has a high level of valuation.

POLICY MAPS

Policy is a theoretical concept imposed on observed reality. Regardless of whether specific decisions have been deliberately made or not, what we observe are policy outcomes from which city policy is inferred. If, as we shall suggest, policy outcomes are positively related to environmental challenges, the presumption that the policy was intended to meet the pressures of the environment is strong, but it is only a presumption. And because it is only a presumption, the investigation of policy makers' "policy maps" becomes an important component of policy analysis.

What do we mean by "policy map"? In the first place, we assume that if policy is a response to environmental challenges, these challenges will have been perceived by policy makers. They may choose, consciously or unconsciously, not to act, but such nonaction is also a response that will be reflected in policy outcomes. By being perceived, the environmental challenges become "problems" or "policy issues." In order to tap this facet of the policy map, we asked this question:

Mr. Councilman, before talking about your work as a councilman and the work of the council itself, we would like to ask you about some of the problems facing this community. In your opinion, what are the two most pressing problems here in (city)?

The policy map consists, secondly, of the policy maker's recommendations for action, or "policy positions"—those preferences that he either brings into the policy-making situation or evolves in the course of decision making. Again, his not consciously entertaining a policy position on an issue is yet to be considered a policy orientation and a component of his policy map. We therefore asked this question:[11]

Now, looking toward the future, what one communitywide improvement, in your opinion, does this city "need most" to be attractive to its citizens?

Finally, we assume that the policy map includes the policy maker's "ends-in-view" or values—those hopes and expectations concerning the future that policy decisions are to bring about. The following question was designed to yield what one may think of as the "policy image":

Now, taking the broadest view possible, how do you see (city) in the future? I mean, what kind of a city would you personally like (city) to be in the next twenty-five years?

Whether these three components of the policy map constitute a consistent whole, a "perspective" as Harold Lasswell (Lasswell and Kaplan, 1950, p. 25) would call it, is an empirical question not central to the present study, but one we shall speculate about in the conclusion. Needless to say, perhaps, knowledge of the policy map does not permit prediction about the outcome of decision making on any particular policy issue. But we proceed on the assumption that policy maps represent important linkages between environmental challenges and public policies.

UNITS OF ANALYSIS AND INTERPRETATION

Although the data on policy maps come from interviews with individuals, our analysis uses councils as the units of analysis. Decision making by legislative bodies is a collective act. Not the individual councilman but the council, as a whole or under the majority rule, is the effective policy maker. Because policy outcomes as measured by budget data are due to collective decisions (or nondecisions), the legislative group rather than the individual legislator is the more viable unit of analysis. Council perceptions, positions, or images are therefore constructed or reconstructed from data about individuals or provided by individuals, permitting us to make statements about city councils and not about city councilmen. We shall report the rules followed in this procedure in the text or notes.[12] This type of analysis is, of course, made possible by the relatively large (though for satisfactory statistical purposes still all too small) number of legislative groups being investigated. As far as we know, no similar type of analysis using as many as eighty or so units has ever been undertaken in the comparative study of legislative bodies.

In reading and interpreting the tables, a number of methodological considerations must be kept in mind. In the first place, we are dealing with data that come from truly independent sources—the federal census reporting population characteristics, city budgets reporting financial allocations, and interviews with city councilmen. These different kinds of data are used to construct quite different properties of the units—city councils—that we are observing. The census yields data that are best interpreted as representing the council's "contextual" properties; the budget data are representative, in a very direct sense, of the council's "emergent" properties; and the interview data provide the basis for "aggregate" properties.[13] To relate properties as diverse as these is extraordinarily difficult. But for this reason one cannot simply write off even modest relationships between variables as not significant.

Second, the typology of policy development that serves as our major device for ordering the data is not a simple continuum. While the five types constitute an ordinal ranking on a scale from "more developed" to "less developed," they also represent qualitative differences associated with different levels of development. In other words, a city's movement from one stage into another may be due to structural changes in causal factors rather than simple gradual increases. This means that variables related to city policy development may well exhibit sharp changes at certain points in the developmental sequence rather than incremental changes from one stage to another. For instance, a council's orientation to action may change radically after it has left the retarded stage and entered the emergent phase and then not change at all. Also, variables need not change monotonically across the five developmental types. Development may be related, for instance, to city growth in the early stages or phases but may decline in the advanced cities. Or cities at the three intermediate levels of policy development may show characteristics not shared by the least- and most-developed cities. Or cities in the two phases of development may be more similar to each other than to cities in the immediate neighboring stages.

Analysis

ENVIRONMENTAL CHALLENGES AND POLICY DEVELOPMENT

City size, density, and growth rate are direct indicators of challenges from the environment that every city faces. They bring in their wake problems that the city council may seek to solve through policies that adapt the city to the environment or that control environmental pressures. As the typology of city policy development is built on outcomes that reflect such policies, it follows:

Hypothesis 1a: The larger a city's size, the more developed is city policy likely to be.

Hypothesis 1b: The greater a city's density, the more developed is city policy likely to be.

Hypothesis 1c: The greater a city's growth, the more developed is city policy likely to be.

Table 14.3 shows that the three hypotheses are not falsified by the data. Moreover, the data show a pattern of policy development that, with two exceptions, is highly linear. We have no explanation for the deviation from the pattern of the transitional cities in the low-density category. With regard to growth we note, as we perhaps might have expected, a leveling off of the effect of growth in the advanced stage, the terminus of development. Apparently, once policy development has reached the advanced stage, growth is likely to be marginal in its effect on city policy.

Table 14.3   Relationships between city size, density, and growth and policy development by percent

	Policy development				
	Retarded (N = 11)	Emergent (N = 14)	Transitional (N = 26)	Maturing (N = 15)	Advanced (N = 16)
Population size[a]					
<10,000	82	79	35	13	0
10,000–50,000	18	21	46	67	44
>50,000	0	0	19	20	56
Total	100	100	100	100	100
Density[a]					
<2,000	73	58	19	41	0
2,000–4,000	18	28	50	26	44
>4,000	9	14	31	33	56
Total	100	100	100	100	100
Growth Rate[b]					
<10%	54	36	43	13	19
10–50%	46	49	39	47	62
>50%	0	14	19	40	19
Total	100	100	100	100	100

a. Size and density data for 1965.
b. Growth rate for 1960–1965.

RESOURCE CAPABILITY AND POLICY DEVELOPMENT

The resources available to a city government are an important constraint on the expenditures it can make and the policies it can follow. Resource capability is largely an objectively limiting factor, but it is also subjective in that its limiting effect is interpreted by the city council before it becomes a factor in the policy-making process. For instance, the council estimates how high a tax rate city residents are willing to approve. High resource capability is necessary for policy development, but it is not sufficient. Nevertheless, we hypothesize:

Hypothesis 2: The higher a city's resource capability, the more developed is city policy likely to be.

Table 14.4, part A, shows that there is no support for the hypothesis. In fact, more of the retarded cities seem to have high resource capability than any of the other cities in various stages or phases of development. However, the distributions may be misleading. As we suggested, policy development is dependent on policy makers' willingness to mobilize re-

Table 14.4   Relationship between city resource capability and policy development, by percent

Assessed valuation per capita	Policy development				
	Retarded (N = 11)	Emergent (N = 14)	Transitional (N = 26)	Maturing (N = 15)	Adva (N =
Part A					
>$2,600	54	28	38	33	4
$1,700–$2,600	18	44	24	47	2
<$1,700	27	28	38	20	3
Total	100	100	100	100	10
Part B					
Size <25,000					
<$1,700	27	28	24	13	
>$1,700	73	72	39	54	
Size >25,000					
<$1,700	—	—	15	7	2
>$1,700	—	—	23	27	6
Total	100	100	100	100	10
Density					
<2,000					
<$1,700	9	14	0	7	
>$1,700	63	44	19	33	
>2,000					
<$1,700	19	14	38	13	3
>$1,700	9	28	43	47	6
Total	100	100	100	100	10
Growth					
<10%					
<$1,700	9	0	19	0	
>$1,700	46	36	23	13	1
>10%					
<$1,700	18	28	19	20	2
>$1,700	27	36	39	67	5
Total	100	100	100	100	10

sources, and their willingness to do so may depend on the intensity of pressures from the environment *regardless* of available resources. Therefore, one must control the relationship between resource capability and policy development by such indicators of environmental challenges as size, density, or growth rate. Table 14.4, part B, reports the findings.

In the smaller cities, presumably less subject to environmental challenges, fewer of the more-developed than of the less-developed cities are low in resource capability, just as hypothesized; but development also declines in cities of the same size with high capability, counter to the hypothesis. In the larger cities, on the other hand, resource capability is highly related to policy development in the advanced stage.

Controls for density reveal the same pattern even more distinctly, In the low-density, high-capability cities policy development declines, counter to the hypothesis; but in the densely populated cities high resource capability is related to policy development across the continuum in linear order.

Finally, if resource capability is controlled by growth rate, the developmental process clearly follows the hypothesized pattern only in the high-growth cities with high assessed valuation (and again in linear fashion except for leveling off in the advanced stage). The data do not permit us to say anything about the slow-growing, low-capability cities; but in the slow-growth, high-capability and the high-growth, low-capability cities Hypothesis 2 is clearly falsified.

Policy makers evidently respond to environmental pressures less in terms of the resources that are available than in terms of their willingness to mobilize these resources. It is for this reason that inquiry into policy makers' perceptions of city problems, policy positions, and policy images becomes an important part of policy analysis.

PROBLEM PERCEPTIONS AND POLICY DEVELOPMENT

Environmental challenges are not self-evident. They become evident only if and when they give rise to "problems" that come to the attention of policy makers. The perception of a problem means that traditional ways of doing things—policies—are inadequate or at the very least that their adequacy is in question. It is through the perception of problems, then, that the policy process is set in motion. But if policy makers do not respond to problems generated by environmental challenges, either by not perceiving them or not acting upon them, this does not mean that there is no policy. It simply means that prevailing policy continues.

In collegial bodies like legislatures or councils a problem is a problem if the members *between them* are aware of the problem, but it is not necessary for all or even most of the members to perceive it. Different members have access to different aspects of the environment. Because of varied membership, elected collegial bodies can be more sensitive to the environment than are administrative hierarchical organizations. "Problem diversity," therefore, refers to the absolute number of different problems articulated by a council, adjusted for comparison across councils by the total number of mentions in each council.[14] Because, as we have seen, the more-developed cities face more severe environmental challenges, we formulate:

Hypothesis 3: The more diverse the problems perceived by a council, the more developed is city policy likely to be.

Table 14.5 shows that this hypothesis is falsified by the data. In fact, problem diversity is greatest among the councils of the retarded cities where one might least expect it and declines almost linearly in the following stages and phases, though there is some leveling off at the more-developed end of the development continuum.

How can one interpret this finding? One plausible answer is that policy develops in response to few but intensively felt problems, while a multitude of minor problems that are not critical do not stimulate the policy process. If this is so, we should expect that problems are more "visible" to the council as a whole in the more-developed than in the less-developed cities. A measure of "problem visibility" must take account not only of the absolute number of problems that are articulated, but also of the number of councilmen who articulate any one problem.[15] We postulate:

Hypothesis 4: The more visible problems are to the council, the more developed is city policy likely to be.

Table 14.6 tends to support the hypothesis, although there is some dropping off at the advanced stage. One might expect this because, as the very

Table 14.5 Relationship between problem diversity and policy development, by percent

| Diversity score quartile | Policy development | | | | |
	Retarded (N = 9)	Emergent (N = 12)	Transitional (N = 25)	Maturing (N = 15)	Advanced (N = 16)
I. (Most)	45	33	20	27	6
II.	22	17	28	20	44
III.	22	33	28	13	31
IV. (Least)	11	17	24	40	19
Total	100	100	100	100	100
Index	+34	+16	−4	−13	−13

Table 14.6 Relationship between problem visibility and policy development, by percent

Visibility score quartile	Policy development				
	Retarded (N = 9)	Emergent (N = 12)	Transitional (N = 25)	Maturing (N = 15)	Advanced (N = 16)
I. (High)	22	17	28	40	12
II.	11	33	24	13	45
III.	0	25	36	20	31
IV. (Low)	67	25	12	27	12
Total	100	100	100	100	100
Index	− 45	− 8	+ 16	+ 13	0

concept "advanced" suggests, a council in this stage of policy development is likely to have the challenges stemming from the environment well in hand. As a result, not only are fewer problems perceived in this stage, but the few problems are so self-evident that, though of great urgency, they fail to stand out as particularly visible.

Problem visibility may be thought of as setting the council's legislative agenda. The more visible a problem, the more likely it is to be considered by the council. But the visibility is at most a necessary and not a sufficient condition for legislative action. In order to act, the council must in fact be agreed that the problem is a problem. We therefore measure the degree of council agreement on the single most visible problem as well as council agreement on the general policy area that seems most problematic.[16] We propose:

Hypothesis 5: The more agreement on the single most visible problem, the more developed is city policy likely to be.

Hypothesis 6: The more agreement on the most visible problem area, the more developed is city policy likely to be.

Table 14.7 tends to support these hypotheses, but we note an interesting deviation from the expected patterns in the cities of the emergent phase. While on the single-problem measure more councils in the emergent phase reveal high agreement, these councils are least agreed on the general area of problems facing their cities. We can only speculate on these results. It may be that being in the emergent phase is, on the one hand, a disorienting condition that makes it difficult to achieve agreement on the general area of problems that require action; but that, precisely because of this condition, high agreement can be reached on the single most urgent problem. However, we also note that all councils, regardless of level of policy de-

Table 14.7 Relationship between agreement on specific problem and general problem area and policy development, by percent

Single problem agreement	Policy development				
	Retarded (N = 9)	Emergent (N = 12)	Transitional (N = 25)	Maturing (N = 15)	Advanced (N = 16)
67–100%	22	50	36	47	46
51–66	45	25	32	20	41
50–50	33	25	32	33	13
Total	100	100	100	100	100
Index	− 11	+ 25	+ 4	+ 14	+ 33
Problem area agreement					
67–100%	33	17	32	13	37
51–66	0	8	16	54	13
0–50	67	75	52	33	50
Total	100	100	100	100	100
Index	− 34	− 58	− 20	− 20	− 13

velopment, can evidently reach agreement more readily on a specific problem than on a general area of related problems.

What kinds of problems or problem areas are most salient to city councils? And is such salience related to policy development? As Table 14.8 shows, no three councilmen in any council, whatever the city's stage or phase of development, articulated problems relating to amenities; and only a few councils on various levels of development mustered enough members who considered planning or zoning as especially pressing problems. Amenities clearly do not rank high on the agenda of problems considered pressing. Put differently, amenities appear to be luxuries that councils are willing to indulge in only after other urban problems, notably sewerage and drainage, financing of services, and transportation, have been solved. But planning and zoning also do not stand out as pressing problems. Either these matters are being satisfactorily handled already, so that they are perceived as problems by only a few councils, or they are not recognized as viable means for coping with environmental challenges.[17]

When asked why they considered a problem to be a problem, a variety of reasons were given by councilmen that could be coded into three categories—operational and financial, political, and inevitable or uncontrollable. Councils were characterized in terms of the dominant set of reasons

Table 14.8 Problems and problem areas perceived as pressing by city councils

	Policy development					
Types of problems perceived	Retarded (N = 9)	Emergent (N = 12)	Transitional (N = 25)	Maturing (N = 15)	Advanced (N = 16)	Total (N = 77)
Services and utilities						
Sewerage and drainage	1	1	5	2	—	9
Sanitation and disposal	—	1	—	—	—	1
Water sources	1	—	1	—	1	3
Financing services	—	1	2	4	3	10
Total in area	2	3	8	6	4	23
Percent in area	22%	25%	32%	40%	25%	30%
Amenities						
Total in area	—	—	—	—	—	—
Promotion and development						
Planning, master plan	—	1	—	—	3	4
Zoning and maintenance	2	1	4	—	—	7
Transportation and traffic	—	1	5	2	3	11
Attract business and industry	—	1	2	—	—	3
Urban renewal and development	—	1	—	—	3	4
Assessment and taxes	—	—	—	2	—	2
Total in area	2	5	11	4	9	31
Percent in area	22%	42%	44%	27%	57%	40%
Social and remedial						
Water pollution	—	—	—	—	1	1
Race and ethnic problems	—	—	—	—	1	1
Educational problems	—	—	—	1	—	1
Housing	1	—	—	—	—	1
Total in area	1	—	—	1	2	4
Percent in area	11%	0%	0%	7%	12%	5%
Governmental and intergovernmental						
Annexation	1	—	—	—	—	1
Local government personnel	—	1	—	—	—	1
Citizen participation	—	—	—	—	1	1
Total in area	1	1	—	—	1	3
Percent in area	11	8	0	0	6	4
Not classifiable	3	3	6	4	0	16
Percent in area	34	25	24	26	0	21
Grand total	100%	100%	100%	100%	100%	100%

that were given.[18] We do not entertain any particular hypothesis about how councils on various levels of development are likely to rationalize their city's problems. But we note two results in Table 14.9. First, great majorities of councils in all cities, regardless of level of policy development, attribute community problems to circumstances beyond their control. This is to say that a substantial number of problems, as we have speculated all along, have their roots in environmental conditions. But we also note that "political" reasons are given by more councils as we move from the retarded to the advanced stage of development. The linearity of the data suggests that politicization of the decision-making milieu in these cities may well be related to policy development. The more politicized the social environment, the more likely it seems to be that policy development takes place.

POLICY POSITIONS AND POLICY DEVELOPMENT

Once problems have been identified and agreed on as agenda items, the legislature or council will seek to evolve a policy position. A policy position by the council, whether held by all members or only a majority, is of course an emergent property of the council following upon interaction, deliberation, and possibly compromise, and it is not simply the addition of individual members' policy preferences. What we are tapping, then, when we ask individual councilmen to suggest the "most-needed" communitywide improvement and then aggregate these recommendations, is not the council's policy as it emerges in the voting situation, but rather the initial state of a council position before the legislative process has had an opportunity to affect the decisional outcome.[19] But as actual council policy is reflected in the policy outcomes out of which the typology of policy development is constructed, inquiry into the hypothetical initial state of the policy process

Table 14.9 Reasons given for problems and policy development, by percent

| Type of reasons | Policy development[a] | | | | |
	Retarded (N = 9)	Emergent (N = 12)	Transitional (N = 25)	Maturing (N = 15)	Advanced (N = 16)
Operational-financial	22	8	36	20	25
Inevitable-uncontrollable	78	92	84	73	62
Political	11	17	12	27	38

a. Percentages total more than 100 because any one council could give sets of reasons that are numerically tied.

can shed light on the dynamics of policy making. We shall first explore the diversity and visibility of improvement recommendations made by councils in varying stages and phases of policy development. Again we stipulate:

Hypothesis 7: The more diverse improvements recommended in a council, the more developed is city policy likely to be.

And again, as with problem perceptions, we find the diversity hypothesis falsified by the data.[20] As Table 14.10 shows, highly diverse improvement proposals are just as likely to be made in the less-developed as in the most-developed cities. However, although problem and improvement proposal diversity is low in the more-developed cities, and perhaps because of it, we expect that the improvement recommendations that are made are highly visible in these cities. Hence:

Hypothesis 8: The more visible the improvements recommended in a council, the more developed is city policy likely to be.

Table 14.11 supports the hypothesis.[21] Recommendations for improvements are more visible in the more-developed than in the less-developed cities, and only in maturing and advanced cities do a majority of councils fall into the two upper visibility quartiles.

We expect on the basis of this finding that councils in the more-developed cities are more agreed on what specific improvements or what general improvement areas are needed than councils in the less-developed cities:

Hypothesis 9: The more agreement there is in a council on the single most needed improvement, the more developed is city policy likely to be.

Hypothesis 10: The more agreement there is in a council on a general improvement area, the more developed is city policy likely to be.

Table 14.10   Relationship between improvement diversity and policy development, by percent

Improvement score quartile	Policy development				
	Retarded (N = 9)	Emergent (N = 12)	Transitional (N = 25)	Maturing (N = 15)	Advanced (N = 16)
I. (Most)	33	50	20	13	31
II.	33	17	36	33	0
III.	11	8	16	27	57
IV. (Least)	22	25	28	27	12
Total	100	100	100	100	100
Index	+11	+25	−8	−14	+19

Table 14.11   Relationship between improvement visibility and policy development, by percent

	Policy development				
Improvement score quartile	Retarded (N = 9)	Emergent (N = 12)	Transitional (N = 25)	Maturing (N = 15)	Advanced (N = 16)
I. (High)	11	25	28	7	31
II.	22	17	16	46	31
III.	33	25	24	40	13
IV. (Low)	33	33	32	7	25
Total	100	100	100	100	100
Index	−22	−8	−4	0	+6

Table 14.12   Relationship between agreement on specific improvement and general improvement area and policy development, by percent

	Policy development				
Single-improvement agreement	Retarded (N = 9)	Emergent (N = 11)[a]	Transitional (N = 25)	Maturing (N = 15)	Advanced (N = 16)
67–100%	11	0	12	7	6
51–66	0	36	20	33	19
0–50	89	64	68	60	75
Total	100	100	100	100	100
Index	−78	−64	−56	−53	−69
Improvement area agreement					
67–100%	22	45	40	60	37
51–66	45	45	28	33	44
0–50	33	10	32	7	19
Total	100	100	100	100	100
Index	−11	+35	+8	+53	+18

a. One council of this type could not be properly measured and had to be dropped from the tabulation.

Table 14.12 presents the data.[22] They represent some interesting findings. In the first place, with respect to agreement on the single most visible improvement proposal made, there is a very low level of agreement regardless of a city's location on the policy development continuum. Only few councils are highly agreed, and only a few more manage to achieve better than simple-majority agreement. In all types of city policy development, majorities of the councils fall below the majority criterion needed for agreement. Interestingly, and although the percentage differences are small, fewer councils in both types of "phase" cities are in the nonagreement category than councils in the "stage" cities. But, in general, we must consider Hypothesis 9 as being falsified by the data.

If we turn to the less-demanding Hypothesis 10—less demanding because agreement is needed only on a general area rather than on a specific case of improvement—the data give only weak support to the hypothesis. Although few of the retarded councils are high on improvement area agreement and the more-developed councils tend in the expected direction, the significant aspect of the table is that only one council in each of the two types of "phase" cities is unable to achieve a minimal level of agreement.

What are we to make of these unexpected findings? Are they merely due to random fluctuations in the data, or are they of theoretical significance? We must seek an explanation in the nature of the emergent and maturing phases of policy development as these were defined. Cities in these phases undergo sudden bursts of activity, reflected in policy outcomes, that move them from one stage into another. It would seem that this unfolding of policy-making "energy" is greatly aided by *predecisional* agreement or at least by relatively little disagreement in councils as to what improvements or areas of improvement are most needed. This finding and our interpretation suggest that we are tapping a very real component of the policy process by aggregating individual responses into a group response.[23]

What types of improvement were recommended by the councils that are agreed? Because of the dispersion of single-improvement recommendations, we shall present only the data on improvement areas.[24] What is of interest in the data presented in Table 14.13 is, first of all, that the improvement areas are quite different from the comparable problem areas of Table 14.8. Only one council in a maturing city suggested services and utilities as an area needing improvements. But while no council had perceived amenities as a *problem,* a fourth of the councils in each of the developmental types, except the retarded, reported that amenities constitute an area where improvements are needed.

This discontinuity in council policy maps from problem perceptions to policy positions requires explanation. Does it mean that councils do not behave rationally? One might be inclined to think so, but discontinuity is not necessarily the same thing as inconsistency. Because amenities are not recognized as "problems," it does not follow that councils may not wish to pursue policies to obtain amenities for their cities. For policies, we

Table 14.13 Relationship between needed improvement areas and policy development, by percent

	Policy development				
Improvement area	Retarded (N = 9)	Emergent (N = 11)	Transitional (N = 25)	Maturing (N = 15)	Advanced (N = 16)
Services and utilities	0	0	0	7	0
Promotion and development	0	8	4	14	25
Amenities	11	25	28	26	25
Less than three informants	89	67	68	53	50
Total	100	100	100	100	100

argued, are not simple conditioned responses to environmental challenges; they are also the products of those ends-in-view, values, or images of the future that policy makers carry with them into the policy-making situation. While the policy positions articulated in response to the question about needed improvements may not be relevant to the problems that councils perceived and articulated, they are certainly not inconsistent with them. The results suggest that policy images are important components of the council's policy map as a whole.

POLICY IMAGES AND POLICY DEVELOPMENT

What kind of future a legislative body envisages is likely to color its perceptions of environmental challenges and its current policy preferences. But images of the future are also likely to be projections of current trends in a city's policy development. They tend to orient the council toward the future and may influence future development, but they are not independent of present tendencies. Moreover, the more limited the legislature's jurisdiction, the better defined its image is likely to be. In the case of municipal councils whose tasks are well set by statutory requirements and limitations we can expect that long-range goals are well defined.

Because we know that policy development varies with demographic indicators of environmental challenges such as size, density, and growth, and because we also can assume that these indicators are highly related to ecological factors such as residential patterns or level of industrialization, we hypothesize:

Hypothesis 11a: The more developed a city's policy, the more will councils tend to envisage the city's future as "balanced" or industrial.

Hypothesis 11b: The less developed a city's policy, the more will councils tend to envisage the city's future as residential and/or recreational.

The ease with which it was possible to classify responses into the categories of "residential" or "recreational," on the one hand, and of "balanced" or "industrial," on the other hand, supports our speculation that long-range images or goals are likely to be well defined in legislative bodies with limited scopes of action.[25] As Table 14.14 shows, the reciprocal Hypotheses 11a and 11b are well supported by the data.

Because policy images are well defined, we hypothesize that there is a great deal of agreement within the councils on policy goals. But as, by definition, the less-developed cities are engaged in a more-limited range of activities than the more-developed ones, we can expect the difference to be reflected in the level of agreement:

Hypothesis 12: The less developed a city's policy, the greater the proportion of councils reaching high agreement on the image of city future.

Table 14.15 supports the hypothesis. It not only supports it but reveals an extraordinarily high level of agreement, especially in the retarded and emergent cities where two-thirds and more of the councils are unanimously agreed on the policy image. But in the transitional, maturing, and advanced cities, too, most councils agree on long-range goals by overwhelming majorities. We are dealing here, it seems, with that substantive consensus on values that facilitates the democratic process of bargaining, compromise, and adjustment It is within this consensus that disagreements over particular policies can be resolved and lasting community conflicts be reduced to manageable format. However, the fact that agreement on future goals is inversely related to policy development represents a profound dilemma for democratic theory.

Table 14.14 Relationship between policy image and policy development, by percent

	Policy development				
Content of image	Retarded (N = 9)	Emergent (N = 12)	Transitional (N = 25)	Maturing (N = 15)	Advanced (N = 16)
Residential-recreational	56	50	52	27	13
Split or nonclassifiable	22	8	12	7	19
Balanced and/or industrial	22	42	36	66	68
Total	100	100	100	100	100

Table 14.15 Relationship between agreement on policy image and policy development, by percent

Policy image agreement	Policy development				
	Retarded (N = 9)	Emergent (N = 12)	Transitional (N = 25)	Maturing (N = 15)	Advanced (N = 16)
100%	78	67	52	53	50
67–99	0	25	32	27	31
51–66	0	0	4	13	0
Split or nonclassifiable	22	8	12	7	19
Total	100	100	100	100	100

A metropolitan city's development toward distinct and differentiated styles of social life is powerfully shaped by policies that are responses to challenges from the metropolitan environment. Whether a city stands still, moves forward to reach a new level of development, or reverts to an earlier state depends on the strength of such challenges as can be measured by city size, density, or growth rate. In general, development involves the adoption of policies that either adapt the city to the changing environment or control the environment. In this process of adjustment and control through appropriate policies, the city's resource capabilities seem to play only a limited part. It appears that policy makers' willingness to tap city resources in order to adopt appropriate policies is a critical component of the policy development process.

Policy makers' willingness to set their city on a course of development depends on the content of their policy maps—how they perceive the problems facing the city, what preferences they entertain with regard to policy alternatives, and how they envisage the city's future. In general, it seems that municipal decision makers' policy maps constitute a consistent whole, although there may be discontinuities and deviations. It also appears, in general, that the various components of the policy map are meaningfully related to the stage or phase of city policy development. There is in the councils of a metropolitan region such as that around the San Francisco Bay a satisfactory level of agreement on what the problems are that cities in different stages of development face, and there is very high agreement on what the city's future should be like. There is less agreement, as one might expect, on the specific policies that should be adopted to obtain the goals that are envisaged, but there is sufficient agreement on the general area of issues that needs attention.

It has been the burden of our argument that the systematic study of public policy cannot be content with correlating indicators of environmental challenges or indicators of resource capability to policy outcomes. Rather, it was our assumption that policy development is greatly influenced by the predilections, preferences, orientations, and expectations of policy makers—in short, by the political process itself. The data presented in the analysis, though limited, confirm the validity of this assumption. Yet, as we noted, the fact that level of agreement on policy goals seems to be inversely related to policy development raises many problems for the policy maker. Not the least important is the question of how a developed community can maintain a sufficient consensus on public goals. In the city councils of the San Francisco Bay metropolitan region a high level of agreement on policy goals still exists. Whether it will continue to exist in the face of increasing differentiation of areas within the city challenges the urban political process.

Appendix

The data used in this report come from the following sources: (1) city size, density, and growth data from the 1960 and 1965 Censuses of Population; (2) city per capita assessed valuation data and expenditure data for planning and amenities from the *Annual Report of Financial Transactions concerning Cities of California,* for the fiscal years 1958–59 to 1965–66, published by the state controller; and (3) data concerning council policy maps from interviews with city councilmen conducted in 1966 and 1967.

The interviews, using both open-ended and closed questions, averaged about three hours in length. In addition, councilmen were asked, at the end of each interview, to fill out a written questionnaire. Interviews were held, as Table 14.16 shows, in eighty-nine cities located in eight counties around the San Francisco Bay. Two councils refused to cooperate altogether, and in four others not enough councilmen were interviewed to permit analysis at the council level. Inadequate budget data in the case of six cities incorporated after 1959 further reduced the number of councils available for this analysis to seventy-seven. One city, incorporated after interviewing had begun, has been excluded from the study as has been the city-county of San Francisco because its Board of Supervisors is a much more professionalized legislative body than the other councils of the region.

Table 14.16 Interview targets and missing data

Results	Number of councils	Number of councilmen
Interview targets	89	488
Access refused	− 2	− 10
Total	87	478
Deficient council data	− 4	− 12
Total	83 (93%)	466
Interview refusals		− 31
Total		435 (89%)
No budget data avail-able for analysis	− 6	
Total	77 (87%)	

15

A Quasi-Longitudinal, Quasi-Experimental

Design for Comparative Policy Analysis

IN RECENT YEARS several efforts have been made to explain public policies by the use of a study design that treats the outputs of policy as dependent variables, usually by relating them to such independent variables as a polity's socioeconomic or political-structural characteristics. One of the weaknesses of this research has been that it does not include data on the political attitudes and orientations of policy makers themselves, for one might expect that their positions on public issues make a difference in policy outputs. Hence conclusions reached about the importance of "politics" in the formation of policies are incomplete at best.

But this weakness, partly remedied in the research reported here, is not my major concern. Rather, what interests me is the attempt to explain public policy by way of causal models, for this strikes me as something of an anomaly. At issue, therefore, is the question of whether the design of research involved in causal modeling of public policy is sufficiently isomorphic with policy as a behavioral process in the real world to warrant confidence in the inferences that are made about the emergence of policy.

The plausibility of causal modeling being an appropriate technique for explaining public policy is largely predicated on acceptance of the familiar conception of the political system that deals in inputs and outputs. This conception is congenial to causal modeling because it permits a quick and easy step from treating inputs as "causes" to treating outputs as "effects." In other words, policy outcomes are assumed to be the ultimate dependent variable to be accounted for,[1] and the research question is whether exogenous variables (environmental, economic, social, and so on) or endogenous variables (political structures and processes) account for variance in policy. The prior question—whether the input-output system model corresponds to what goes on in the real world of policy—is largely ignored. Also ignored is Easton's (1965b, p. 89) caveat that this "approach to the analysis of political systems will not help us to understand why any specific policies are adopted by the politically relevant members in a system."

The problem of whether causal modeling is the proper technique for explaining public policy is exacerbated by the perplexing and discomforting findings that political variables seem to account for little or none of the variance in policy outputs.[2] "This, I submit," comments Salisbury (1968, p. 164) after reviewing the relevant research, "is a devastating set of findings and cannot be dismissed as not meaning what it plainly says—that analysis of political systems will not explain policy decisions made by those systems."

In spite of Easton's caveat and Salisbury's blunt conclusion, policy research continues causal modeling. Instead of raising questions about the conception of policy implicit in causal modeling, the failure to find relationships between political variables and policy outputs is attributed to the inadequacy of input or output indicators or to errors in measurement. Much effort, perhaps misspent, is devoted to the search for more valid indicators of both independent political variables and dependent policy variables, and to the correction of measurement errors.

If modeling is to be used in the analysis of public policy, it should follow rather than precede an empirically viable conception of policy. Such a conception is not likely to emerge, in *deus ex machine* fashion, from causal modeling all kinds of indicators of presumed inputs and outputs that may or may not be germane. Of critical importance are not the indicators but the designs for their analysis. An analytical design is a way to produce the readings of the empirical indicators. Like a definition, it may be willful, but it must not be arbitrary. Thoughtlessly imposing a causal model on the policy process is not likely to yield valid knowledge.

This chapter describes alternative ways of exploring, if not explaining, public policy. Following Stouffer's (1962, p. 297) injunction that "exploratory research is of necessity fumbling, but . . . the waste motion can be reduced by the self-denying ordinance of deliberately limiting ourselves to a few variables at a time," it initially presents a rather simplistic causal model of policy that employs only five variables. It also presents a rather intricate post facto quasi-longitudinal design for observing variations in components of the causal model. This design seeks to make the best of empirical data that are basically static, but it is inspired by another Stouffer (ibid.) comment that we need "many more descriptive studies involving random ratlike movements on the part of the researcher before we can even begin to state our problems so that they are in decent shape for fitting into an ideal design." Before proceeding, it is necessary to explain the conception of policy that is employed and introduce the variables that are being manipulated in the analyses.

A Conception of Policy

Policy is a strictly theoretical construct that is inferred from the patterns of choice behavior by political actors and the consequences of choice behavior. Choice behavior is manifest in actual decisions, such as the vote counts in legislative bodies, budgetary allocations, or the assignment of personnel to specified tasks. The consequences of choice behavior are manifest in the behavior that follows upon choice, especially compliance or noncompliance. If the behavioral patterns are consistent and regular, the existence of policy is inferred and identified. But behavioral patterns themselves, whether intended or not, are not policy but manifestations from which the nature or direction of policy is inferred.

So defined, policy is distinguished from the intentions, goals, or preferences that political actors may entertain in making choices. Although intentions, goals, or preferences may influence choice, policy cannot be inferred from them. Policy may be consonant with intentions, goals, or preferences, but this can only mean that they have been realized in practice. This conception of policy differs from the conventional usage, when we say, for instance, that it is the policy of government to end discrimination in housing. It may be the intention of the government to end discrimination, but behavior in pursuit of this intention may or may not occur. Because something is intended, it does not follow that it is in fact the policy.

As a process, policy is the collectivity's response to conditions of the physical and social environment. A policy is operative as long as it is successful, that is, as long as the response that it represents proves rewarding. In fact, it is the rewarding of the response that makes policy what it is—a set of consistent and regular behavioral patterns through which governing units cope with environmental conditions. Changes in policy, that is, changes in response, presumably occur when there are changes in environmental conditions. If there is no appropriate response, and if the old response pattern or policy continues, no reward is likely to be forthcoming. As the policy no longer proffers rewards, it may actually become dysfunctional, if insisted upon, or it may simply be obsolete. In responding to environmental conditions, the characteristics of the governing unit may affect the form of response—its political structure; its human and physical resources; the degree of mass or elite involvement in governance; the vitality of private interests making public demands; and, last but not least, the perceptions, orientations, and preferences of policy makers themselves.

The problems of policy making arise out of the relationship between changes in the environment that call for some response, the ways in which these changes are experienced as problems requiring solutions, and the values that policy makers may seek in responding to changes. Policy, then, functions as a response to environmental conditions, both physical and social, that has built into it an anticipation of a future state of affairs. If this is the case, a change in policy is both causal and purposive: it is "caused" by environmental stimuli, but it is also directed toward a goal and shaped by a purpose. The tension arising out of the simultaneity of causal and purposive "forcings" is a basic property of policy.

The problem of causal modeling policy is congruent with the nature of policy in the real world. Policy as a response to environmental challenges inferred from behavioral patterns manifest in outputs or outcomes of choice processes is truly "caused." However, as the response is also in pursuit of a goal, value, or end-in-view, it is purposive. But behavior in pursuit of a goal, or purposive behavior, is "caused" in a sense quite different from what we have in mind when we say that a change in environmental conditions brings about or causes policy as a response. When we say, therefore, that a purpose "informs" or "orients" a response, we do not mean that the response is caused by a purpose in the same sense that it is caused by an environmental stimulus. If this is so, grave doubts may be raised about the applicability of causal assumptions to policy analysis.

The problem is confounded by the fact that the relationship between environment and policy is probably symmetrical. In the sense that policy is a response, it is caused by environmental conditions; but as policy is itself a sequence of behavioral patterns through time, it has a reactive effect on the environment. Put differently, it is best to assume that policy and environment are interdetermined. As policies cumulate through time, they come to constitute an environment of their own that persists because, insofar as policy proves rewarding, the behavioral patterns involved in responding to environmental challenges have proved rewarding and therefore are continued. But it is just for this reason that the values or goals that policy makers pursue in responding to the environment are not independent of the interdetermined relationship between environment and policy. If this is so, it goes a long way in explaining what has been called "incremental decision making," although this formulation places the explanatory accent elsewhere (see Wildavsky, 1964; Lindblom, 1965). Empirically, it means that current policies do not deviate widely from the goals implicit in policy as a response to the environment—hence the finding that past expenditure patterns are the best predictors of future expenditures, apparently leaving little room for other variables to affect policy (Sharkansky, 1969, pp. 113–125). Psychologically, it means that policy is inert, unless environmental challenges are so overwhelming that innovative behavioral responses are called out. Given the fact that goals are implied in ongoing policy, it is simply "easier" or "cheaper" to behave incrementally than to act otherwise.

The model of the policy process that emerges from these considerations consists of three major variables: the physical-natural environment, the policy environment (that is, the configuration of relevant policies that emerges through time), and what may be called the "policy map"of policy makers. The policy map, in turn, consists of three components: first, policy makers' perceptions of the environmental challenges or problems they are called to act upon; second, the goals or images of the future they have in mind as they respond or fail to respond to the environment; and third, the positions they take in making choices in regard to the problems confronting them.

The propositions that can be derived from this conception of policy and that constitute a theoretical model of the policy process are as follows:

1. The physical-social environment and the policy environment are interdetermined. For instance, there is a reciprocal relationship between urbanization as an environmental stimulus and policy as a response. But policy can also influence the course of urbanization, as when land is set aside for industrial or commercial growth or when taxing policies favor urbanization. As an interdeterminate relationship, it is subject to the conditions of a moving equilibrium: a change in environmental stimuli engenders a change in policy, and a change in policy alters the environment.

2. An environmental challenge calling for a policy response has the expected effect only if it is perceived by policy makers as constituting a problem situation. Unless environmental challenges are experienced as problems, policy responses are not likely to be forthcoming.

3. Environmental challenges may be, but need not be, directly related to policy makers' images of the future. They need not be related because goals or images refer to the future and can be independent of past or present conditions. But images may be related indirectly to environmental conditions if the latter are perceived as problems and suggest a reformulation of images.

4. Environmental challenges are not directly related to policy positions, for positions need only be taken if the challenges are seen as problems and become issues to be settled.

5. The policy environment, that is, the set of ongoing policies that has emerged through time, may be, but need not be, related to the perception of challenges from the environment as problems. Policy environment will not be related to problem perceptions if the relationship between it and the environmental challenge is in equilibrium; it will be related if the latter relationship is disturbed. Put differently, if ongoing policies successfully cope with environmental challenges, the latter are unlikely to be perceived as problems.

6. The policy environment is related to policy makers' images of, or

goals for, the future. The policy environment is, by definition, rewarding. And if the policy environment is rewarding, images and goals are not likely to deviate widely from the images and goals that are implicit in ongoing policies and, in fact, are likely to be congruent with them.

7. The policy environment is not directly related to policy positions. For positions are at best intentions that may or may not be consonant with ongoing policies.

8. The relationship between the perception of problems and policy images is highly problematic. On the one hand, one can assume that images as views of the future are totally independent of perceptions of current problems. On the other hand, one can also assume that the perception of strong challenges from the environment leads to a reformulation of images or that the perception of problems, even if rooted in the reality of environmental challenges, is "colored" by preferences or expectations inherent in images. Put differently, what policy makers perceive as problems and what they envisage for the future may be at loggerheads; but perceptions of problems may reshape images, or images may shape the perception of problems. As a result, the relationship between problem perceptions and policy images as such is indeterminate and depends largely on antecedent conditions.

9. Policy images are directly related to policy positions. Because positions are policy makers' declarations of how they intend to cope with environmental challenges, they are likely to be tutored by their images or ends-in-view.

10. Perceptions of problems, stimulated by environmental challenges, are directly related to policy positions. For if no problems stemming from environmental conditions are perceived, there is no need to adopt policy positions.

Alternative Designs for Policy Research

The task at hand is to ascertain just what kind of analytic design represents the "best fit" with the theoretical model of the policy process. Moreover, the design should be appropriate for the data that are available. The causal designs implicit in most policy research have in fact been dictated by available data, and to admit this is the better part of wisdom (but a wisdom rarely articulated in policy studies). However, even if data collection precedes rather than follows the formulation of the design, it should specify its criteria of proof in advance.

Causal modeling recommends itself as an analytic design in manipulating nonexperimental data, and the more explicit the assumptions associated with different causal models, the more trustworthy are the inferences that can be drawn. On the other hand, this should not lead to a situation where alternative designs making use of the same data are ruled out. There has been a strong tendency to do this, largely because of failure to recognize that the design implicit in causal modeling is, at best, just one truncated design derivative of the classical experimental design. In fact, causal models are only one alternative in adaptations of the classical experimental design to real-world policy analysis.

There are several truncated designs, but only one will be reviewed here because it is relevant to the design to be employed later in this discussion. In this design, let us call it the random panel design (as distinct from the longitudinal panel design in which the same unit is observed at two points in time),[3] two different units or sets of unit are compared at different times. As shown in Figure 15.1, the assumption is made that if the unit observed at $time_0$ had also been observed at $time_{0+1,}$ it would have the characteristics of the second unit actually observed at that time. Vice versa, the assumption is made, of course, that if the unit actually observed at $time_{0+1}$ had been observed "before" at $time_{0,}$ it would have been identical in properties with the unit actually observed at that time.

The juxtaposition of truncated or quasi-experimental designs and the classical experimental design serves to sensitize the analyst to the truth value of the proof involved in his design. None of the quasi-experimental designs satisfies the theoretical assumptions and technical requirements of the classical design. However, because they are not satisfactory from the perfectionist's perspective, it does not follow that they are not creditable; it only follows that the proof of any hypothesis tested by the design is at best partial.

The validity of the propositions advanced earlier cannot, therefore, be proved in any strict sense. The best proof can be harnessed by subjecting

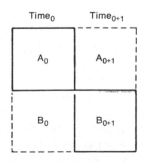

Figure 15.1   Random panel design

the propositions to alternative designs in order to determine whether they predict observations. Two designs are possible with the kind of data that is available. Both designs are predicated on the initial empirical observation of a close and strong relationship between urbanization as the environmental challenge and policy environment as the response. The strength of the relationship alerts us to two observations. First, it is important to keep in mind that the data used to measure level of urbanization and degree of policy development refer to a time period clearly prior to the time period in which the data for the policy map components were collected. In other words, the possibility that any one of the policy components has an antecedent effect on either urbanization or policy development, or both, can be ruled out, and the relationship between urbanization and policy development need not be subjected to "control" in order to determine whether it is spurious. And second, the strength of the relationship suggests that there may be a strong "interaction effect" on observed relationships between each of the two variables and the components of the policy map, and among the latter themselves.

Because so much current policy research is cast in the postcorrelational design, I shall first examine the fit between the theoretical model derived from the conception of policy described above and the empirical causal model that can be constructed from the data. I shall then present an alternative design that, by introducing further assumptions about the nature of quasi-experimental designs, may represent a stronger test for the propositions of the theoretical model.

The Causal Model

For the purpose of modeling the relationships among the variables of the theoretical model, I shall treat level of urbanization and state of policy environment as independent variables, and policy positions as the dependent variable.

My first task is to determine the independence of the relationships between the two independent variables and the dependent variable (propositions 4 and 7), for only if these relationships are zero, as hypothesized, can it be assumed that problem perceptions and policy images are truly intervening variables. To test the null hypothesis, I control the relationships by both problem perceptions and policy images. The resulting second-order partial correlation coefficients are .07 for the urbanization-position relationship, and $-.03$ for the policy environment–position relationship. Clearly, I cannot reject the null hypothesis of no direct relationship between the two independent variables and the dependent variable. Problem perceptions and policy images can be assumed to function as intervening variables.

I shall deal next with the bothersome question of the relationship between the two intervening variables (proposition 8). Recall that the relationship was characterized as indeterminate. Because this relationship has important implications for all the model's linkages, I shall present it as a zero-order relationship and as a partial relationship controlling successively for the other three variables individually and jointly.

It appears from Table 15.1 that, if uncontrolled, the relationship between problem perception and policy image is quite weak. In other words, there is only a very slight tendency for policy makers with a balanced (rather than residential) image to perceive growth problems (rather than service-related matters). When the possible reactive effect of policy position on the relationship is partialed out, the relationship becomes somewhat stronger. However, it declines when controlled for the possible effect of policy environment, and it altogether vanishes when controlled for level of urbanization. To explore the relationship further, it was controlled for the possible simultaneous effect of urbanization and policy environment. The result, as Table 15.1 shows, is highly instructive. The relationship continues to remain weak, but it significantly changes in direction. Apparently now it is policy makers with a residential (rather than balanced) image who perceive problems of growth confronting them, while those with a balanced image now perceive service-connected matters as problems. However, the weakness of the relationship confirms my initial proposition that the direction of the relationship is quite indeterminate.

The implications of this indeterminacy require elaboration. One way of doing this is to examine the relationship between problem perception and policy position. If this relationship is controlled for the possible effect of policy image, it appears to be quite strong ($g = .61$), as expected (proposition 10). But its direction is confounding. One might have expected that policy makers perceiving growth problems would advocate further devel-

Table 15.1 Zero-order and partial relationships among components of policy map

$g_{PI,PP}$	=	.24	$g_{PP,PoP}$	= $-.43$	$g_{PI,PoP}$	= .54
$g_{PI,PP}/PoP$	=	.50	$g_{PP,PoP}/PI$	= $-.61$	$g_{PP,PoP}/PP$	= .54
$g_{PI,PP}/PoEn$	=	.32	$g_{PP,PoP}/PoEn$	= $-.35$	$g_{PI,PoP}/PoEn$	= .54
$g_{PI,PP}/Urb$	=	.04	$g_{PP,PoP}/Urb$	= $-.51$	$g_{PI,PoP}/Urb$	= .52
$g_{PI,PP}/PoEn, Urb$	= $-.32$		$g_{PP,PoP}/PoEn, Urb$	= $-.62$	$g_{PI,PoP}/PoEn, Urb$	= .57
$g_{PI,PP}/PoP, PoEn, Urb$	= $-.26$		$g_{PP,PoP}/PI, PoEn, Urb$	= $-.90$	$g_{PI,PoP}/PP, PoEn, Urb$	= .66

Key: PI = policy image; PP = problem perception; PoP = policy position; PoEn = policy environment; Urb = urbanization.

opment. This is clearly not the case. Instead, those perceiving growth as a problem take an amenities position, and those perceiving service problems favor further development (hence the negative sign of the coefficient).

I can also shed at least some light on the indeterminate relationship between problem perception and policy image by examining the relationship between policy image and policy position. The relationship is moderately strong ($g = .54$) and reveals that those with a residential image take a position favoring amenities, while those with a balanced image favor further development.

If I juxtapose the findings concerning the relationship between problem perception and policy position, on the one hand, and between policy image and policy position, on the other hand, the indeterminacy of the problem perception–image relationship becomes explicable. It appears that policy makers with a residential image perceive problems of growth because these problems probably jeopardize the residential image of the future that they prefer. They therefore take an amenities position that is congenial to their image of the future. Vice versa, those seeing or preferring a balanced city do not perceive problems of growth as threatening and, seeing service problems, favor further development as their position, presumably because further development will maximize the city's resources needed for the effective provision of services. It would seem, therefore, that policy positions are "doubled caused" by problem perceptions and policy images. This seems to be a true double-causation relationship and explains, therefore, the weak relationship between problem perceptions and policy images, for this relationship does not need to exist in a model of this kind at all.

However, it would be unduly hasty to accept this interpretation. As both policy images and problem perceptions were assumed to be related to policy environment (propositions 5 and 6), a third-order partial test controlling for policy environment, for level of urbanization, and successively for each component of the policy map seemed indicated. Table 15.1 shows the outcome. Not only is the relationship between policy image and problem perceptions further weakened ($g = -.26$), but the relationships among the policy map's other components are strengthened ($g = -.90$ and $.66$, respectively). I infer that the major pathway of environmental conditions and ongoing policies moves, in fact, through the cognitive screen of problem perceptions, although the effect of policy images on policy positions is also strong. The relationship between policy image and problem perceptions is not a crucial link in the chain of causation.

I shall turn now to the independent variables of the model. I have noted already that levels of urbanization and policy environment are not directly related to policy positions. However, both independent variables, being highly related to each other and interdeterminate (proposition 1), are likely to be stimuli for problem perceptions (propositions 3 and 6). The question of causal ordering the effect of the independent variables on the intervening variables is hardly at issue because the time order of the variables is unambiguous.

Of interest, therefore, is largely the question of which of the two independent variables contributes more to the variance in problem perceptions and policy images. Table 15.2 presents the zero-order correlation coefficients, the first-order partials (controlling for one of the independent and one of the intervening variables). Some of the consequences of the sequentially introduced controls are noteworthy. In the first place (see Table 15.2, A) a fairly strong positive relationship links level of urbanization and problem perceptions and withstands all controls (in support of proposition 2). The more urbanized the environment, that is, the more intense the environmental challenges, the more likely will policy makers perceive problems connected with growth. Second (see Table 15.2, B), the relationship between urbanization and policy image, weak in the first place, almost vanishes when it is controlled (in support of part of proposition 3). Third (see Table 15.2, D), the state of the policy environment has a strong effect on the formulation of policy images and withstands successive controls (in support of proposition 6). In other words, the more mature or advanced the policy environment, the more do policy makers hold a balanced image of the city's future. In entertaining policy goals, it seems, policy makers do not entertain "far-out" views. Finally (see Table 15.2, C), and this is perhaps the most interesting finding, the relationship between policy environment and problem perceptions, evidently nonexistent when uncontrolled, grows increasingly stronger as it is controlled by urbanization and policy image. As suggested in proposition 7, this relationship is likely to vary with the degree of equilibrium in the relationship between environmental challenges and policy environment. The negative

Table 15.2   Zero-order and partial relationships among urbanization, policy environment, and components of policy map

A	$g_{Urb,PP}$	= .57	C	$g_{PoEn,PP}$	= .08
	$g_{Urb,PP}/PoEn$	= .73		$g_{PoEn,PP}/Urb$	= −.32
	$g_{Urb,PP}/PoEn, PI$	= .64		$g_{PoEn,PP}/Urb, PI$	= −.53
B	$g_{Urb,PI}$	= .58	D	$g_{PoEn,PI}$	= .81
	$g_{Urb,PI}/PoEn$	= .30		$g_{PoEn,PI}/Urb$	= .75
	$g_{Urb,PI}/PoEn, PP$	= .10		$g_{PoEn,PI}/Urb, PP$	= .80

coefficients show that the less mature or the less advanced the policy environment, the more are policy makers likely to perceive problems related to growth.

This result, however, pinpoints a problem that the causal model cannot successfully tackle. I can best state the problem in the form of a syllogism that reflects the data, as follows:

The more urbanized the environment, the more developed is the policy environment ($g = .80$).

The more urbanized the environment, the more are problems related to growth perceived ($g = .64$).

The more developed the policy environment, the more are problems related to growth perceived.

The data, however, show that the logical conclusion derived from the premises is not empirically viable. In fact, the opposite is true: the less developed the policy environment, the more are problems of growth at policy makers' focus of attention ($g = -.53$). It would seem, therefore, that there is a condition present in the relationship between urbanization and policy environment that eludes the causal model. Proposition 7 suggested that this condition may be the degree of equilibrium in the relationship. The equilibrium condition is concealed in the causal model and can only be ascertained by a design that manipulates the data in a different way. As we shall see later, there are a number of cities that are, in fact, in disequilibrium—those that are highly urbanized but whose policy environment is less developed than one should expect from an equilibrium point of view.

Figure 15.2 summarizes all the relationships obtained by partial correlation analysis. It is of the utmost importance to emphasize the tentative nature of the results because "all other things" are probably not equal, and relevant error terms are probably not uncorrelated. Determining causal directions under these conditions is likely to be controversial. While in the present model there is no doubt as to the true independence and priority of the urbanization and policy environment variables, and while direct relationships between them and the dependent variable—policy position— probably would not exist even if additional variables were introduced, the flow of causation through the two intervening variables is not self-evident. For instance, are the effects of urbanization or policy environment on the taking of policy positions mediated more through policy images or through problem perceptions? To answer this question, I can compare the predictions that are possible with the actual results that were obtained for the intermediate links of the causal sequence.

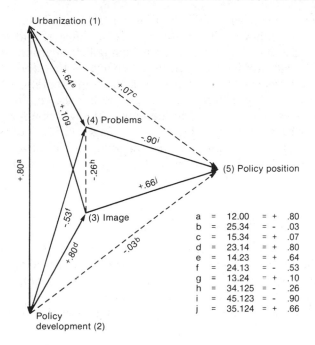

Urbanization (1)

+.64e

+.07c

+.109

(4) Problems

-.90i

+.80a

-.26h

(5) Policy position

+.66j

-.53f

(3) Image

+.80d

-.03b

Policy
development (2)

a	=	12.00	= +	.80
b	=	25.34	= -	.03
c	=	15.34	= +	.07
d	=	23.14	= +	.80
e	=	14.23	= +	.64
f	=	24.13	= -	.53
g	=	13.24	= +	.10
h	=	34.125	= -	.26
i	=	45.123	= -	.90
j	=	35.124	= +	.66

Code for interpreting direction of coefficients:

Image—problem perception:
(+) = Balance-growth or residential-service
(-) = Balance-service or residential-growth

Image—policy position:
(+) = Balance-development or residential-amenities
(-) = Balance-amenities or residential-development

Problem perception—policy position:
(+) = Growth-development or service-amenities
(-) = Growth-amenities or service-development

Figure 15.2   Causal model of policy process

If problem perceptions or policy images are truly intervening between the independent and the dependent variables, I should predict that the relationship between the independent variable x and the dependent variable y equals the product of the correlations between each and the intervening variable z. In other words, I predict that $r_{xy} = (r_{xz}) \cdot (r_{zy})$. Table 15.3 presents the calculations.

Comparison of the predicted and actual outcomes shows that, while far from perfect, the fit is excellent for the chain in which urbanization and policy positions are linked by problem perceptions and good for the chain that runs through policy images. The fit is fair for the chain that links policy environment to policy positions through policy images, and so we need not reject it. But it is poor for the chain from policy environment to policy positions through problem perceptions. I conclude, therefore, that policy positions are primarily taken in response to the perceptions of problems that stem from environmental challenges and are secondarily influenced by policy images weakly related to the nature of environmental challenges (urbanization) but strongly related to ongoing policies (policy environment). I can reject the assumption that ongoing policies have an effect on policy positions through the intervention of problem perceptions.

A Hypothetical Longitudinal Design

Although the causal model, if cautiously interpreted, fits the theoretical model of the policy process quite well and may be accepted as constituting some explanation, it lacks longitudinal depth. Assumptions were made about the time ordering of the relationships between each of the two independent variables and the two intervening variables, but not about

Table 15.3 Test of models of policy process

	Relationships	Predicted[a]	Actual	Fit
1	Urbanization x ↓ .57 Problem perception z ↓ .42 Policy position y	$r_{xy} = .24$	$= .25$	Excellent
2	Urbanization x ↓ .58 Policy image z ↓ .54 Policy position y	$r_{xy} = .31$	$= .25$	Good
3	Policy environment x ↓ .08 Problem perception z ↓ .42 Policy position y	$r_{xy} = .03$	$= .29$	Poor
4	Policy environment x ↓ .81 Policy image z ↓ .54 Policy position y	$r_{xy} = .44$	$= .29$	Fair

a. Predictions are based on uncontrolled correlations between variables.

any time ordering between the two independent variables alone. They were treated as synchronic, although it was suggested that the reciprocal relationship between them could alternatively be one of equilibrium and disequilibrium. But if this assumption is made, it follows that the relationship at any one point in time is only a special case of "alternating asymmetries" at different points in time (see Rosenberg, 1968, pp. 8–9). Is there a design, then, appropriate to treating the data in such a way that inferences can be made from the observed relationship between the independent variables that is synchronic to hypothetical relationships that are diachronic?

One of the drawbacks of the causal model cast in the postcorrelational design is that it disguises original relationships in the data among the variables of the model. For instance, the relationship between level of urbanization (measured by city size) and the state of the policy environment is so strong from the correlational perspective that we are prone to ignore the cases that deviate from the regression line. In order to pinpoint these deviant cases more sharply, Table 15.4 presents the cross-tabulation of the data in bivariate form. It shows that we are dealing with two kinds of deviant situations. First, in cell *C* we note six cases of cities that are "more developed" in spite of limited environmental challenges. These cases are "truly deviant." They cannot be accounted for by the contingent relationship between urbanization and policy environment. In other words, the observed outcome can be attributed to policy makers' purposes, preferences, and efforts.

But this is not possible with the seventeen cases in cell *B*. Although they are statistically deviant, they could be considered truly deviant only if one were to assume that the relationship between urbanization and policy environment is invariably in equilibrium. But this is a quite unrealistic assumption. If we conceive of a reciprocal relationship as a succession of "alternating asymmetries," it is much more realistic to assume that there is likely to be a lag between stimulus and response, that as urbanization

Table 15.4 Policy environment and urbanization (size), variables dichotomized

	Size dichotomized	
Development dichotomized	Less urban <17,000 (N = 41)	More urban >17,000 (N = 41)
Retarded, emergent, progressed Less (N = 52)	A = 35	B = 17
Mature, advanced More (N = 30)	C = 6	D = 24

proceeds and challenges the policy maker, an appropriate response is not immediately forthcoming. This reasonable assumption allows me to construct a dynamic model of the policy process. (1) As long as environmental challenges are weak (the city is small, less urbanized), the policy environment is "less developed"—challenge and response are, indeed, in equilibrium. (2) As the city grows and environmental challenges become urgent (the city is now large, more urbanized), there is an initial lag in policy response—the policy environment remains "less developed" so that challenge and response are in disequilibrium. (3) As the challenges from the environment are not likely to abate, and as ongoing policies are not appropriate, policy makers as purposive actors will, sooner or later, adopt positions that reestablish the equilibrium between urbanization and policy environment.

This transformation of the static into a dynamic model of the relationship between environmental conditions and the policy environment suggests that the seventeen cases in cell *B* cannot be considered truly deviant. They represent situations that can be expected to occur "normally" in the sequence of events that link past and future. In searching for a design appropriate to the analysis of data that are synchronic but nonetheless should be interpreted diachronically, it is clearly advantageous to make a number of assumptions that combine familiar assumptions made for the postcorrelational design with assumptions made for the random panel design, as follows:

As in the panel design, the less-urbanized, less-developed cities are assumed to be "control groups." Having not been exposed to the stimulus of urbanization, they have no opportunity to respond. The two sets of cities that are more urbanized (whether less or more developed) are assumed to be experimental groups. Both have been exposed to the stimulus of urbanization.

As in the panel design, it is assumed that if both experimental-group cities had been observed at an earlier time, they would have looked like the control-group cities; or the second experimental group of cities (more urbanized, more developed) would have looked like the first experimental group (more urbanized, less developed) at an earlier time. A corollary assumption is that if it were possible to observe the control-group cities at a later time, after more urbanization had taken place, they would in sequence look like the two experimental-group cities.

As in the postcorrelational design, it is assumed that the two experimental-group cities are similar in all respects except for the differences in policy environment; the control group and the first experimental-group cities are assumed to be similar in all respects except for the difference in level of urbanization.

As in the postcorrelational design, the difference in outcome (policy environment) between the two experimental-group cities is assumed to be due to a third factor (or several other factors), which is the test variable—in our case the components of the policy map, and especially the relationships among these components themselves.

Although the set of assumptions made in constructing the design is complex, it merely combines a number of assumptions now routinely made in quasi-experimental designs for the analysis of real-world data. What the design shows is that once latent assumptions are made explicit, comparison of evidently static situations can be used to test hypotheses about change in the real world for which direct data are not available. Although the three sets of cities being compared are actually observed at the same point in historical time, longitudinal assumptions derived from adaptations of the classical experimental design serve to infuse an element of dynamic interpretation into comparative analysis—a recognition of the fact that comparative statics is, indeed, a special case of dynamics.

As Figure 15.3 shows, the design permits three kinds of comparison by way of test variables: (1) comparison of A_0 and B_{0+1}, (2) comparison of A_0 and C_{0+2}, and (3) comparison of B_{0+1} and C_{0+2}. As I postulate that urbanization is a necessary but not sufficient condition for policy change, the comparison between A_0 and C_{0+2} is not enlightening; for, while the two situations can be expected to differ significantly on test variables, I cannot say whether the difference in the policy environment is due to the test factors or to change in urbanization. Moreover, both situations are in equilibrium. Of the other two comparisons that are possible, that between A_0 and B_{0+1} serves as a control test. As no change in policy environment

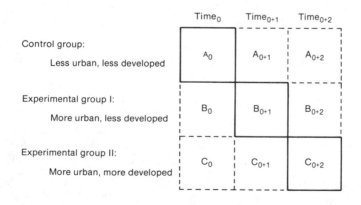

Figure 15.3   Quasi-longitudinal design of policy process

is observed, yet there is a change in urbanization, it follows that increased urbanization is not sufficient to bring about a change in policies. The comparison between B_{0+1} and C_{0+2} is the most relevant because it is the appropriate test for rejecting the null hypothesis that a change in the policy environment is not due to purposive action.

The research question asked is: why in situation B_{0+1} has the policy environment not changed in spite of a change in the necessary condition for such change, that is, increased urbanization? My hypothesis is, of course, that policy change has not taken place because of policy positions taken by policy makers that impede it.

Quasi-Longitudinal Analysis

The data will be analyzed within the constraints of the quasi-longitudinal design in three ways: first, as marginal distributions; second, as conjunctive patterns; and third, as correlations.

MARGINAL ANALYSIS

Table 15.5 shows the marginal distributions of the councils on the three components of the policy map. They will be treated as if the data were genuinely longitudinal. From this perspective, Table 15.5 is highly informative.

First, growth is experienced as a problem by majorities of the councils in all three periods, but it is most felt in $time_{0+1}$, when the "ecopolicy system" (as we shall call the relationship between urbanization and policy environment) is in disequilibrium. In the third period, when there has been an appropriate policy response to restore the equilibrium, the urgency of

Table 15.5   Distribution of councils on policy map components by states of ecopolicy system, by percent

Components of policy map	$Time_0$ Less urban, less developed (N = 27)	$Time_{0+1}$ More urban, less developed (N = 14)	$Time_{0+2}$ More urban, more developed (N = 18)
Growth is problem	56	93	78
Development is position	37	36	56
Balance is image	33	50	89
Problem-position differential	19	57	22

problems connected with growth is somewhat reduced, but these problems continue to concern policy makers.

Second, in view of the prominence of growth problems at $time_{0+1}$, it is revealing that so few councils (36 percent) at that time take policy positions in favor of development. In fact, they do not differ at all from $time_0$. Only in the third period, when the ecopolicy system is again in equilibrium, do a majority of councils take positions that are presumably capable of coping with the problems of growth. It may be noted that a discrepancy between perceiving growth as a problem and taking prodevelopment positions also occurs in the equilibrium situations at $time_0$ and $time_{0+2}$, but it is considerably less than in the disequilibrium state at $time_{0+1}$ (19 and 22 percent respectively, versus 57 percent). The need for services and not growth-related problems, the earlier causal analysis has shown, makes for policy positions favoring development. But as service problems are not seen as critical at $time_{0+1}$, it becomes understandable why positions preferring amenities are more widely held in this period by comparison with the third period.

Third, as Table 15.5 shows, policy images change dramatically and systematically through time. While at $time_0$ only 33 percent of the councils envisage a balanced future for their cities, 89 percent do so at $time_{0+2}$. Of particular interest, however, is the fact that at $time_{0+1}$, when the ecopolicy system is in disequilibrium, the councils are exactly split, with half holding an image of a balanced future and another half holding an image of a residential future. In the disequilibrium situation, councils tend to behave quite randomly. For instance, councils do not unequivocally adopt policy positions in favor of development, in spite of the fact that they are keenly aware of problems connected with growth. These problems, it would seem, are looked upon as nuisances that can be wished away by pursuing amenities policies, and if problems connected with service are not perceived, further development is an option that does not enter the policy map.

Although I cannot prove, with the data at hand, that the policy environment as a response to the challenge of urbanization is facilitated or impeded by the policy map, I can look at the data as if they could be used as tests, provided they are read cautiously. In treating the same data in this hypothetical manner (as if the policy map components were the independent variables and the ecopolicy system the dependent variable), Table 15.6 should be read as follows: for instance, while of the councils with a residential image 67 percent are "found" at $time_0$ (in the less-urbanized, less-developed state of the ecopolicy system), of those holding a balanced image 50 percent are "found" at $time_{0+2}$ (when the system is more urban, more developed), and so on. If the data are read in this way, it is evident that the image component of the policy map discriminates

Table 15.6   Distribution of councils on states of ecopolicy system by policy map components, by percen‸

Ecopolicy system	Policy map components					
	Image		Problem		Position	
	Balanced (N = 32)	Residential (N = 27)	Growth (N = 42)	Services (N = 17)	Developed (N = 25)	Amenitie‸ (N = 34)‸
$Time_0$	28	67	36	71	40	50
$Time_{0+1}$	22	26	31	5	20	26
$Time_{0+2}$	50	7	33	24	40	24
	Gamma = −.69		Gamma = −.45		Gamma = −.24	

most strongly among the three states or periods of the ecopolicy system ($g = -.69$), that problem perceptions discriminate moderately ($g = -.45$), and that policy positions discriminate very little ($g = -.24$). This is not surprising; as I noted in the causal model (Figure 15.2), neither urbanization nor policy environment as a separate variable has a direct effect on policy positions. As the causal model demonstrated, perceptions of problems and policy images are critical intervening variables that link reality to policy positions. But the marginal distributions also suggest that the topography of the policy map may be quite different at different periods or in different states of the ecopolicy system.

CONJUNCTIVE PATTERNS

The data can be looked at in terms of the particular combinations formed by the components of the policy map. These conjunctive patterns probably constitute the most "realistic" representations of the policy maps as "wholes." Eight such patterns are possible, and my interest is in the frequency of particular patterns at different points in time or in different states of the ecopolicy system. Table 15.7 presents the data.

It appears from Table 15.7 that some conjunctive patterns occur only at $time_0$, that some occur mainly at $time_0$ and $time_{0+1}$, and that some occur in all three periods, although dominantly at $time_{0+2}$. One pattern (BSA) does not occur at all. Councils with a residential image that perceive service problems are exclusively found at $time_0$, regardless of their positions on policy. However, when councils with a residential image experience growth problems, they are found not only at $time_0$ but also at $time_{0+1}$, when the ecopolicy system is in disequilibrium. Again, policy positions seem to make little difference. As a balanced image is adopted but problems of growth continue to be experienced, councils are now more often found at $time_{0+1}$ and $time_{0+2}$, but especially in the later period. When a balanced image is combined with a recognition of service as a problem and a prodevelopment position is taken, the majority of councils have reached the state of the ecopolicy system that is characteristic of the last time period, although some remain in the earlier states as well. While the configuration of patterns is by no means monotonic, it is far from random (yielding a gamma coefficient of .56). Above all it gives more detailed insight than do the marginal distributions into why it is that some councils experience disequilibrium in their ecopolicy system, that is, why it is that the policy environment is not in step with the challenges of the urbanizing environment and all that urbanization implies. These are evidently councils in which, because residential images prevail, growth is experienced not as a problem to be handled by appropriate policies, but as a problem that is unwelcome. However, when a balanced image comes to be accepted, policies to cope with growth problems are adopted and, in due time, the ecopolicy system regains equilibrium.

CORRELATION ANALYSIS

It remains to look at the transformation through time of the relationships among the components of the policy map. It is likely that at different times one or the other component is more relevant to the adoption of a particular policy position. Moreover, as the relationships among policy map components are more or less interdependent, it is desirable to observe the flow of the effects of one component on the other. Figure 15.4 presents the models using the phi coefficient.[4]

Table 15.7 Distribution of councils by conjunctive patterns of policy map components in three states of ecopolicy system, by percent

Conjunctive patterns	$Time_0$	$Time_{0+1}$	$Time_{0+2}$
RSD ($N = 3$)	100	0	0
RSA ($N = 7$)	100	0	0
RGD ($N = 4$)	50	25	25
RGA ($N = 13$)	46	46	8
BGD ($N = 11$)	27	27	46
BGA ($N = 14$)	29	21	50
BSD ($N = 7$)	14	29	57
BSA ($N = 0$)	0	0	0

Key: R = residential image; S = service problems; A = amenities position; B = balanced image; G = growth problems; D = development position.

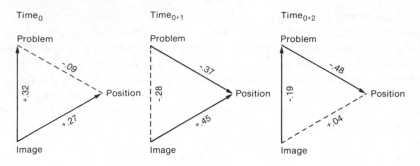

Figure 15.4   Structure of policy map in three states of ecopolicy system

The diagrams suggest not only that the relationships among map components assume different values at different times, but that the map itself seems to undergo structural change. At $time_0$, when the challenges of urbanization are weak and the policy environment is relatively little developed, councils perceiving growth as a problem tend to entertain a balanced image of their city's future and favor development, while councils perceiving service-connected problems tend to hold a residential image and favor amenities as their policy positions (phi = .32). The perception of problems is unrelated to policy positions (phi = $-$.09). In fact, of course, and whatever the internal structure of the policy map, we know that the policy environment is little developed—ongoing policies, compared with those at later periods, do not particularly stress either development or amenities. Available resources are invested in meeting the minimal service needs of these communities. The policy environment is static and in equilibrium with the urban condition.

At $time_{0+1}$, as the challenges of urbanization come to be felt, the structure of the map changes drastically. Councils perceiving problems of growth now tend to hold a residential image (phi = $-$.28), a rather anomalous behavior, and they tend to favor amenities policies. This is, of course, the *RGA* pattern observed in Table 15.7 that seems to be so characteristic of this period. The anomaly may be due to the effect that policy images seem to have in $time_{0+1}$. Although problems are seen quite realistically, policy images tend to have a fairly strong effect on the policy positions that are taken (phi = .45). On the other hand, councils perceiving service problems now have a balanced image. But, more significantly, there is now a linkage between problem perceptions and policy positions. Councils seeing growth problems still favor amenities positions, while councils perceiving service problems advocate further development (phi = $-$.37).

An anomalous situation is unlikely to persist. Sooner or later the policy map will be restructured to fit the exigencies of urbanization. Our quasi-longitudinal design permits us to observe how the policy map is restructured. Most notable at $time_{0+2}$ is the fact that the relationship between policy images and policy positions vanishes (phi = .04), while the relationship between problem perceptions and policy positions becomes stronger (phi = −.48). Moreover, the relationship between problem perceptions and images is also almost vanishing (phi = −.19). The fact that two of the relationships among map components more or less disappear is due, of course, to the emergence of balanced images in council policy maps in this state of the ecopolicy system. As we saw in Table 15.5, sixteen of the eighteen councils (89 percent) entertain an image of balance at $time_{0+2}$. As a result, there is little room for images to discriminate among policy positions or problem perceptions. And, as a further result, it is the perception of problems that now almost alone influences the policy positions that are taken. Councils seeing service-connected problems favor development policies, presumably to mobilize the resources needed to pay for swelling demands for such services in the wake of increased urbanization; councils experiencing the pangs of growth tend to favor amenities, presumably to offset the unpleasantness of growing urbanization. The policy environment at this time is, not unexpectedly, in congruence with the policy map. By operational definition, it is in an environment in which ongoing policies are geared to both development and amenities policies. In any case, the policy map no longer blocks, as it did at $time_{0+1}$, the taking of positions congenial to the emergence of a policy environment that is in equilibrium with the challenges stemming from heightened urbanization.

If I say that not only the values in the relationships among policy map components change but that the structure of the map itself changes, I mean, of course, that different models define the linkages between the map's points. To determine the adequacy of alternate models, Table 15.8 presents predicted and actual results for the following three models of three-variable relationships (Figure 15.5).

Table 15.8 shows that the dual-effect model best characterizes the policy map structure at $time_0$. Policy images, it seems, have a pervasive effect on the structure of the map, influencing both the perception of problems and the positions that are taken. The fit of prediction and result is only fair, but it is adequate enough to retain the model. At $time_{0+1}$, the effect of the policy image on policy positions is complemented by a relatively independent effect of problem perceptions, as predicted in the dual-cause model. In the last period, insofar as policy images are still relevant, their effect is totally mediated through the intervention of problem perceptions. They

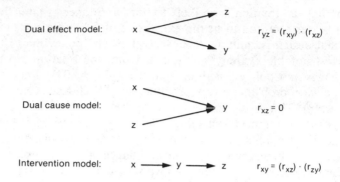

Figure 15.5   Three models of three-variable relationships

Table 15.8   Predicted and actual relationships between policy map components in alternate models during three states of ecopolicy system

Types of model	Predicted	Actual	Fit
Dual effect model at time			
0	.08	−.09	Fair
0 + 1	−.13	−.37	Poor
0 + 2	−.00	−.48	Poor
Dual cause model at time			
0	−.02	.32	Poor
0 + 1	−.17	−.28	Good
0 + 2	−.02	−.19	Fair
Intervention model at time			
0	−.03	.27	Poor
0 + 1	−.10	.45	Poor
0 + 2	.09	.04	Very good

have no independent effect on policy positions that are strongly determined by problem perceptions. The fit of the intervention model at $time_{0+2}$ is very good.

Although it has been repeatedly pointed out that the data cannot be used to test the validity of the inferences made about the course of policy through historical time, it appears that comparative cross-sectional data can be analyzed by way of a post facto, quasi-longitudinal design, and that this analysis yields a model of policy that not only is plausible but is in principle testable in a genuine natural-state experiment if appropriate data are collected at the proper time. I can summarize the model as in Table 15.9.

Policy as a response to challenges from the physical and social environment is an emergent property of politics contingent on political behavior that is, in part, purposive but not unrelated to changing environmental conditions. Because political behavior is imbued with purposes that are its goals or ends-in-view, policy inferred from behavioral patterns may, at times, be at odds with environmental requirements for appropriate responses. The resultant disequilibrium in the relationship between environment and policy is resolved as the configuration of relevant orientations—what I have termed the policy map—undergoes structural change. This change, it appears, is largely due to cognitive adjustments to environmental pressures. It serves to ease behavioral rigidities in the relationship between policy and environment so that a satisfactory equilibrium can be reestablished. Put differently, "what is" and "what ought to be" are dimensions of political behavior that constitute an interlocking series of events through time. In this moving manifold of events, policy emerges as a resultant of causal and purposive forcings that are themselves interrelated in ways that seem commensurate with ongoing policies—what I have termed the policy environment.

Table 15.9 Predictive model of policy development

Model variables	Observations on police map at—		
	$Time_0$	$Time_{u+1}$	$Time_{0+2}$
Policy image	Residential	Ambivalent	Balanced
Problem perception	Services	Growth	Services and growth
Policy position	Amenities	Amenities	Development and amenities
Predicted ecopolicy state	Less urban, less developed	More urban, less developed	More urban, more developed

16

Representation as an Emergent:

A Situational Analysis

CONTEMPORARY RESEARCH on political representation follows essentially itemistic procedures. Individual actors—representatives and/or represented—serve as the units of analysis, and their attributes or conduct are subjected to modes of treatment establishing relationships that range from simple bivariate to complex multivariate. With very few exceptions, research has not heeded Pitkin's (1967, p. 224) conception of representation as a property of the political system that may or may not emerge out of the individual-level relationships between legislators and voters.[1]

Although theorizing about representation involves assertions about the relations that exist, under specified conditions, between the represented and their representatives, empirical research that would treat these linkages in emergent and systemic terms has been elusive because the data needed for this purpose have not been available; or, if available, as in the Miller-Stokes American Representation Study of some twenty-five years ago, have been treated by the itemistic procedures of correlational analysis.[2]

This chapter explores the feasibility of using the extraordinarily complex data sets of the 1956–1958–1960 Miller-Stokes study for the purpose of validating a dynamic model of representation as an emergent system of policy responsiveness.[3]

Most remarkable about the unusual data sets assembled by Miller and Stokes, used only very partially in their influential article (1963), is that they have never been widely exploited. As Miller (personal communication, June 17, 1977) has informed us, "given the fact that the data have been in the public domain as long as they have, I am at a loss to explain why others didn't stumble upon at least some of the nuggets that seem to be so accessible." Yet, it seems to us, there is an explanation. Miller and Stokes had presented their model in terms of behavioral patterns at the

---

Written with Paul D. Karps.

individual level of analysis—the representative's conduct on roll calls being the behavior of an object unit (the unit whose behavior is to be explained), while the subject unit (the unit whose behavior is used to explain the conduct of the object unit) was a transformed property of a macrounit—the district or constituency.[4] What Miller and Stokes did was something largely unfamiliar at the time to political scientists mostly schooled to deal *either* with individual-level survey data *or* with aggregate, census-type data. The congressional district as a macrounit was difficult to conceive as a unit useful to explain individual behavior in a multilevel analysis because of prevailing methodological preconceptions stemming from individualistic behavioralism. Moreover, Miller and Stokes themselves as well as those following them and adopting the policy congruence model of representation interpreted it in individualistic terms. There is nothing "wrong" with this usage of the data except that it obscures the multilevel character of the model. Actually, by aggregating citizen preferences at the district level and using the district as a unit of analysis, Miller and Stokes (unwittingly) anticipated in part the procedures that would be required to operationalize Pitkin's systemic conception of representation.

Our use of the Miller-Stokes data sets differs from the itemistic procedure of correlational analysis. In correlational or path-analytic models, *each item,* such as constituency preference, representative's attitude, or representative's roll-call score, is separately linked to every other item, either directly or indirectly by treating some variables as intervening. Each pair of items is expressed in terms of a correlation coefficient or a regression coefficient, and the product of all relationships is expressed by some summary statistic like Multiple R, compound-path coefficient, or a simultaneous equation. Because in the Miller-Stokes model representation is defined as "congruence" or "agreement" between the individual components of the model or as the "sum" of congruences expressed in a summary statistic, a high coefficient is interpreted as evidence of representation being present and a vanishing coefficient as evidence of representation being absent. As a result, and because the temporal priority of the model components in "real time" is not captured by the summary statistic even if the variables were introduced into a regression in temporal order (rather than in terms of computer estimates of the original correlation coefficients), the itemistic approach cannot construct representational situations as emergent systems in different stages of development.

The Concept of Representational Situation

That it is feasible and, in fact, necessary to think of representation in terms of "situations" really follows from Pitkin's postulate of representation being an emergent property of the political system. Emergence is a process in time.[5] A process in time is constituted by a series of events that are sequential and may be "objective" (as legislative roll calls are) or "subjective" (as policy preferences are). Our intention here is to deal with representation as a process in time, even if, like a snapshot, it has to be treated as a "moment,"[6] rather than as a timeless institution or political pattern. If the events are differentially linked, they produce different situations. A situation may thus be described in terms of the structural relationships existing between "event-variables" observed at different points in time. A situation, then, is a temporally bounded set of event-variables, with a beginning and an ending to the sequence of events being observed. The duration of a situation may be relatively long or short, depending on the "life expectancy" of the event-variables. Life expectancy of the event-variables, in turn, is largely determined by the periodicity of situations as wholes. In the case of the representational situations to be constructed out of relevant event-variables, the situations are of about two years' duration as a function of the biennial periodicity of congressional elections and congressional terms.[7]

Another way to conceive of a situation, especially in regard to representational situations, is as a "context in transition." It is not fortuitous that, etymologically, "situation" derives from the Latin noun *situs*, which can be variously translated as "position" or "station," that is, in spatial terms; or as "situation" or "condition," that is, in temporal terms. A situation is thus both a configuration and a sequence of event-variables that constitute a context within which other events occur and that presumably has an impact on the shape of these events. A "situation politics" is a model of politics in which political acts or events are treated within structurally defined and temporally bounded contexts.

To make this abstract explication of the concept of situation concrete, let us draw on the variables available from the Miller-Stokes American Representation Study. (For description of the measures, see the Appendix.) These variables are "events" because they were collected at different points in time—constituency preferences in connection with the 1956, 1958, and 1960 elections; congressional roll-call votes for the eighty-fifth (1957–1958) and the eighty-sixth (1959–1960) terms; and congressmen's preferences about the time of the 1958 elections. Now, what is significant for the construction of representational situations is the fact that the variables can be temporally ordered and that they are periodicitous in being bounded by the length of the two congressional terms at the focus of research attention. Figure 16.1 describes the flow of events observed for the two periods under consideration.

The three event-variables to be linked for the purpose of constructing

Representational Period	Event Variables		
	Constituency Preferences	Roll–call Votes	Congressman's Preferences
1956-1958 (85th Congress)	1956 ———→	1957-1958 ———→	1958
1958-1960 (86th Congress)	1960 ←———	1959-1960 ←———	1958

Figure 16.1   Component event-variables of representational situations

representational situations do not follow each other in the same sequence in the two periods. This is due to the fact that there is only one measurement of congressmen's preferences.[8] While the situations to be constructed will be composed of generically identical event-variables and will constitute the same configuration, the different, in fact symmetrically reversed, sequencing of the events probably has theoretically significant implications for the interpretation of the representational situations in the two time periods. However, as a situation is conceived as a "moment," as a single configuration of events, the representational situations are directly comparable across the two time periods and not affected in this regard by the temporal order of the variables.

Nevertheless, situations are dynamic properties of the political system in the sense of being contexts in transition. Just as contexts are stable states that impinge on actors and their actions, so situations are creations of actors and the resultants of their actions. Situations, then, are brought about by the interactions and relationships among actors over time. Just what situations "look like" and how they come about depends on the nature of the relationships that occur among the "enacted" events that constitute situations. In the case of the representational situations, the events have certain valences; roll calls, constituents' preferences, and representatives' preferences are either in favor of or opposed to given objects of contention (here civil rights, social welfare, foreign involvement) that are given different valuations.

As all three event-variables are positively or negatively valenced, it follows that when brought into structural relationships with each other, the linkages themselves will be positively or negatively valenced. For example, if a constituency favors civil rights and has a representative who also favors it as well as acts on his own and his district's preferences, the emerging representational situation is itself fully valenced in favor of civil rights; or there may be disharmonies in the representational situation, as when, for instance, the constituency is opposed to civil rights, yet the representative is favorable. When he then votes with his constituents, the emerging situation will be different from when he votes against them in accord with his own preferences.

Our concern is not with the positively or negatively valenced policy direction of an emergent representational situation but with congruence regardless of valences. In other words, a situation in which all or some of the component event-variables are negatively valenced is treated in the same manner as when all or some of them are positively valenced. This will become more clear as we proceed with the actual construction of the four representational situations. Suffice it to say here that by constructing representational situations in terms of congruence and incongruence among the variables regardless of policy valence, pro or con, we are seeking to establish continuity with Miller and Stokes' causal model of representation rather than celebrate discontinuity. However, while the procedure used by Miller and Stokes was itemistic and analytic in relying on correlational analysis, our procedure is configurational and synthetic.

Finally, something must be said about the "perception of constituency attitudes" variable that served Miller and Stokes as an important intervening component of their model. Miller and Stokes certainly demonstrated the significance of representatives' perceptions of constituencies' policy preferences as an important facet of representation. Our definition of representational situation as a configuration and sequence of valenced policy positions, behavioral or attitudinal, does not require the use of the cognitive component. In fact, rather than treating perceptions of constituency preferences as intervening variables, we are interested in the contextual effect of different representational situations on the accuracy of the perceptions and the relationship between perceptions and other aspects of representation within representational situations.

Construction and Explication of Representational Situations

Dualistic theories of representation provide for two alternatives in the conduct of the representative: either he can, should, or will act in such a way that his legislative conduct reflects the preferences of his constituents; or he can, should, or will act in such a way that his legislative behavior corresponds to his own preferences. We can diagram these alternatives as in Figure 16.2, where CP = constituency preference, RP = representative's preference, and RC = roll-call votes. The diagrams show that these alternatives constrain the relationship between the constituency's and the representative's own preferences: it has to be negative. But there is nothing in the real world that limits representation at the individual level to these

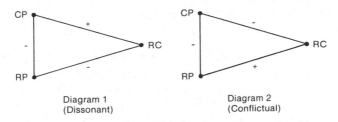

Figure 16.2   Models of representational situations

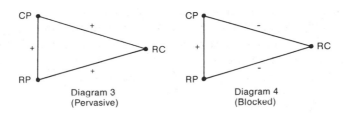

Figure 16.3   Models of representational situations

alternatives. First, the representative may act in such a way that his conduct satisfies both his own preferences and those of his constituency. In this case, of course, the representative's preferences and those of his constituency will also be congruent. But, second, there is the possibility of the representative's legislative conduct not being in agreement with either his own or his constituency's preferences; rather, it is in agreement with the preferences of political actors not directly involved in the relationship between himself and his constituency, such as executive or administrative officials, special interest–group spokesmen, national (nonlegislative or legislative) party leaders, and so on. In this case, the representative's and the constituency's preferences are also congruent, but so strong is the "external" pressure that neither can prevail in his roll-call behavior. These two possibilities can be diagrammed as in Figure 16.3.

Each of the four possibilities presented in Diagrams 1 to 4 (Figures 16.2 and 16.3) constitutes a type of representational situation. By stipulating that the relationship between the representative's and the constituency's preferences is necessarily and invariably constrained by the other two relationships in any given situation, it is also possible to stipulate that each of the four types of situation is dominated by the other two linkages—between the constituency's preference and the representative's roll-call conduct, on the one hand, and between the representative's own preferences and his roll-call behavior, on the other hand. Emerging from these stipulations is a typology of representational situations, as follows:

1. Both $CP \leftrightarrow RC$ and $RP \leftrightarrow RC$ are positive (in which case $CP \leftrightarrow RP$ also will be positive): a situation called *pervasive* because it is permeated by congruent relationships throughout (Diagram 3).
2. Both $CP \leftrightarrow RC$ and $RP \leftrightarrow RC$ are negative (in which case $CP \leftrightarrow RP$ will be positive): a situation called *blocked* because the effect of both constituency and representative's preferences on legislative conduct are obstructed (Diagram 4).
3. The $CP \leftrightarrow RC$ relationship is positive, but the $RP \leftrightarrow RC$ linkage is negative (in which case the $CP \leftrightarrow RP$ connection is also negative): a situation called *dissonant* because the representative may feel uncomfortable in having to act counter to his own preferences (Diagram 1).
4. The $CP \leftrightarrow RC$ relationship is negative, but the $RP \leftrightarrow RC$ bonding is positive (in which case the $CP \leftrightarrow RP$ linkage is negative): a situation called *conflictual* because the representative is in disagreement with his constituency (Diagram 2).

To construct the situations empirically, crude classificatory combinations of the originally scaled variables were thought to yield more robust syntheses than would more refined techniques.[9] For this purpose, the three original scale or index scores were dichotomized at the median of the range, and all cases were placed in an eight-cell cross-tabulation matrix made possible by the dichotomization (Figure 16.4). Because our concern is in the congruence of preferences and roll calls regardless of their valences, the eight individual cells of Figure 16.4 can be collapsed into the four paired cells conceptualized in connection with Figure 16.5.

This construction of representational situations is not unrelated to the

Congressman's Preferences	Constituency Preferences			
	Pro		Con	
Congressman's Roll Calls	Pro	Con	Pro	Con
Pro	Pervasive	Dissonant	Conflictual	Blocked
Con	Blocked	Conflictual	Dissonant	Pervasive

Figure 16.4 Empirical construction of representational typology

Relationship Between Representative's Preferences and Representative's Legislative Conduct	Relationship Between Constituency Preferences and Representative's Legislative Conduct	
	Congruent	Incongruent
Congruent	Pervasive (Diagram 3)	Conflictual (Diagram 2)
Incongruent	Dissonant (Diagram 1)	Blocked (Diagram 4)

Figure 16.5   Theoretical construction of representational typology

tradition in theorizing about representation that centers in the presumed antinomy of mandate and trusteeship as basic principles of representation. Although the typology developed here rejects the classical antinomy as false and obsolete, it incorporates some potentially valid aspects of each of the opposed principles. On one side of the antinomy is the assumption that the represented alone can know what is in their best interest; that they can state this interest in the form of preferences; and that they can, will, and perhaps should express these preferences by way of instructions to their representatives. By implication, only the representative following instructions is responsive to the interests of the represented, and the representative refusing to accept instructions cannot possibly be responsive in this sense. It is the validity of this implication of the mandate theory that is denied by the conception of representation as trusteeship. In this conception, the representative, following his own judgment, decides by himself alone whether the wishes of his constituents are in fact in their best interest.

No representative will ever concede that his or her views, preferences, or positions would or could be counter to the "best interest" of the represented. This is the reason why Pitkin's (1967, p. 209) definition of political representation as "acting in the interest of the represented, in a manner responsive to them," creates many operational problems and produces propositions that are not empirically falsifiable; that is, they are tautological. It may also explain why "policy congruence" between representative and represented has been so attractive as a definition of representation, as if no other considerations need be applied in formulating what representation is about. For is not policy congruence presumptive evidence of responsiveness *regardless* of whether the representative has followed instructions or his own judgment in taking positions on public issues in legislative roll calls? And is this presumptive evidence not all the more persuasive when policy agreement exists not only between the preferences of constituents and the representative's roll-call positions but also between both of these and the representative's own declared preferences?

The answer to these questions has to be positive, but it requires the most emphatic proviso that *under no condition must policy congruence of any kind be taken as a direct or even surrogate indicator of responsiveness in the interest of the represented.* All that congruence permits one to assume (and this is a great deal) is that when it occurs, in one or another of the four situational modes of representation developed here (see Figure 16.5), it may affect other behavior that is perhaps "responsive" in one way or another, or that it is indirectly conducive to responsiveness in Pitkin's sense of "acting in the interest of the represented, in a manner responsive to them." Policy congruence, then, as Miller and Stokes (1963, p. 49) recognized but as their descendants have failed to do, is only "a starting point for a wide range of analyses" and not an end point.

Ordering the Typology by Frequency Distributions

If expectations are to be entertained about the influence that any one type of representational situation will have on the behavior of representatives as they go about the business of representation other than making legislative decisions, a first step is to specify the ordering potential of the typology. It is not unreasonable to deduce from the construction of the four types in terms of the two critical relationships ($CP \leftrightarrow RC$ and $RP \leftrightarrow RC$) that the pervasive situation is the least stressful in both a sociological and a psychological sense because it is permeated by positive relationships among the three event-variables; and that the blocked situation is the most stressful because it is dominated by negative relationships. There is no difficulty, then, in locating these two situations at opposite ends of the typology.

The other two types emerging from the confluence of the component event-variables are fungible. They cannot be ordered intrinsically because their stress potential, though probably more than that of the pervasive and less than that of the blocked situations, is likely to vary with the salience of the positive and negative relationships for the political actors in one or the other situation. In one situation, the fact that the representative votes against district preferences, while acting on his own, may be the affectively or cognitively most salient aspect; in the other situation, the fact that the representative disregards his own preferences in deference to his constituency's wishes may be most salient.

Ordering the typology is of course also complicated because any pair of situations shares some but not other congruent or incongruent linkages, as follows:

1. Pervasive and blocked situations share $CP\overset{\pm}{\leftrightarrow}RP$.
2. Pervasive and dissonant situations share $CP\overset{\pm}{\leftrightarrow}RC$.
3. Pervasive and conflictual situations share $RP\overset{\pm}{\leftrightarrow}RC$.
4. Conflictual and blocked situations share $CP\leftrightarrow RC$.
5. Conflictual and dissonant situations share $CP\leftrightarrow RP$.
6. Dissonant and blocked situations share $RP\leftrightarrow RC$.

These conditions in the typology prevent it from being fully ordinal.

What our interpretation of the representational situations points to is making the frequency distributions of the cases in each situation the ordering criterion. If the situations are characterized by more or less stress in a social-psychological sense, and if one asumes that there is a tendency for less stressful situations to prevail over more stressful ones, ordering the typology by the frequency distributions of the cases in the four types over the three issue areas in the two time periods is not an unreasonable procedure. Using the criterion of descending proportionality, we order the typology as reported in Table 16.1. Because we assume that civil rights but also the social welfare issue would be differently experienced and interpreted in North and South, the data are presented by region as well. Table 16.1 reveals:

1. With some notable exceptions, pervasive situations include pluralities of cases in nine out of twelve opportunities (including two ties); in two opportunities the pervasive situation ranks second. Overall, the pervasive situation stands first in the typology on the basis of the frequency criterion.
2. By way of contrast, blocked situations include the smallest proportions of cases in eight out of the twelve opportunities, and they are in third place three times. By the frequency criterion, the blocked situation is located at the end of the typology opposite the pervasive situation.
3. Conflictual situations are in first place (including two ties) in five of the twelve opportunities and in second place seven times. All conflictual situations include larger proportions of cases than the dissonant and blocked ones. The conflictual situation clearly ranks second in the typology by the frequency criterion.
4. Dissonant situations are in third place in eight out of the twelve opportunities and in fourth place four times. The dissonant situation is located in the third position of the typology.

Table 16.1 Distributions of cases in representational situations, by region, period, and issue area, by percent

	Pervasive	Conflictual	Dissonant	Blocked	N =	No. errors
North, 1956–1958						
Civil rights	49	26	17	8	1,470	0
Social welfare	48	36	10	6	1,591	0
Foreign involvement	27	41	24	8	1,182	1
North, 1958–1960						
Civil rights	54	24	22	0	1,657	0
Social welfare	50	39	9	2	1,700	0
Foreign involvement	40	34	19	7	1,273	0
South, 1956–1958						
Civil rights	80	17	3	0	688	0
Social welfare	15	51	10	24	723	3
Foreign involvement	31	42	0	27	723	3
South, 1958–1960						
Civil rights	48	48	4	0	655	0
Social welfare	64	20	0	16	612	1
Foreign involvement	39	39	1	21	655	1
Times ranking first	9 (2 ties)	5 (2 ties)	0	0		
Times ranking second	2	7	0	1		
Times ranking third	1	0	8	3		
Times ranking fourth	0	0	4	8		

By the frequency criterion, then, it is fairly easy to order the representational situations in the typology. As Table 16.1 shows, there are nine "errors" in the seventy-two pairwise comparisons involving the order of frequencies in the distributions of the cases, or an error ratio of 12 percent. The order of the typology so established by the frequency criterion is informative in regard to the assumption made about the stress potential of each representational situation. If stress avoidance is to be considered evidence of situational rationality, one should indeed expect more cases to fall in the pervasive than in the other situations and the fewest in the blocked situations. By the frequency criterion, then, the conflictual situation would seem to be less stressful than the dissonant. It should be recalled that in the conflictual situation the representative votes against the preferences of his constituents and in line with his own preferences. It appears that the conflictual is more tolerable than the dissonant situation where the representative pleases his constituents but displeases himself.

Nevertheless, one must ask why so many cases do fall into the conflictual type of representational situation. We offer two, more or less speculative, hypotheses. First, a great deal of research has shown that, except on issues of great salience to their districts, legislative representatives are not particularly inclined to take cues from their constituents (see Wahlke, 1971). Moreover, as constituents are generally ill informed about the particulars of their representatives' legislative conduct, the situation here called conflictual seems to be "easier to live with" social-psychologically than the dissonant and blocked situations.

Second, no assumptions are made about the degree of responsiveness to be found in the different representational situations; although the representative does not appear to be responsive to the policy preferences of his constituency in conflictual situations, he may well be responsive in other aspects, such as being the provider of services, obtaining budget allocations for his district, or being his constituency's symbolic agent (see Chapter 19). Because the representative may serve these other needs of his constituents, a conflictual representational situation is not necessarily a politically, and especially electorally, precarious one.

There are some other observations to be made about the order of the representational typology created by the application of the frequency criterion. First, the order is maintained in all four civil rights possibilities, regardless of period and region. Civil rights was, in the middle and late fifties, an issue domain in which the avoidance of stress, or at least its reduction, was crucial for political survival, especially in the South. As Table 16.1 shows, four-fifths of the southern cases in the first period are in the pervasive situation in which the representative votes both his own and the constituency's preferences. There are other aspects in connection with the civil rights issue that will be dealt with later.

Second, as Table 16.1 also shows, eight out of the nine errors in the frequency distributions occur in the South in connection with the social welfare and foreign involvement issues. What is there in southern situations, assuming that the data are reliable,[10] that makes for these results, especially if compared with the results in the North? The clue comes from the fact that so comparatively many of the southern cases are found in the blocked situation where the representative, though sharing his constituents' preferences, votes against both his own and his constituents' predilections (and, presumably, in favor of the preferences of "third" parties). Having paid their dues to the constituency and having followed their own preferences on civil rights,[11] southern congressmen in the fifties had considerably more freedom than their northern colleagues on other issues of relatively less interest to their constituents. This made southern representatives eminently "available" for the kind of bargaining and compromising that is the spice of legislative politics. Being in harmony with their constituents on the central issue that mattered, having come through the crucible of primary elections, being unopposed or weakly opposed in general elections, and having accumulated seniority in the Congress, some southern congressmen were evidently free to vote in ways independent of constituency preferences and counter even to their own predilections. Although the data in Table 16.1 are merely suggestive, one may assume that the cases in blocked situations involved southern congressmen who, being Democrats, voted along with their Republican colleagues as part of the conservative coalition in the social welfare area; or who, in the foreign involvement domain, supported other interests. The potential flexibility of southern congressmen and their independence from their constituencies in the social welfare and foreign involvement areas are also evident in the high proportion of cases falling into conflictual situations.

Validation through Turnover Analysis

The ways in which the component event-variables of representational situations are put together may be arbitrary; but the results must not be whimsical. That is, as the typology is intended to be serviceable as a research instrument beyond the time and place-specific circumstances that yielded the data from which the representational situations are constructed, it must have some universal properties to be valid as a theoretical structure in its own right. As representational situations are configurations that involve sequences of events, stability and change are properties that transcend time and place, and that can serve as explanatory concepts to validate the typology apart from immediately observable data. One may then ask two questions. First, are the representational situations as conceptualized sufficiently stable from one period to another to warrant being considered theoretical and not merely empirical constructs? And second, if there is situational change, is the direction, if not determined by laws of change, at least theoretically plausible? To answer these questions, we proceed in two ways: first, by inspecting the *patterns* and *distributions* that appear in the turnover matrices (Tables 16.2 and 16.3); and second, by pinpointing particular circumstances where the patterns seem to be broken and a "deviant" condition seems to confirm the overall pattern.

THE STABILITY-CHANGE CRITERION

All things being equal (issue area, region, and unknown externalities), one might expect the pervasive situation to be the most stable and the blocked situation to be the least stable, with degree of stability or change in the conflictual and dissonant situations difficult to anticipate. As situational

Table 16.2 Stability and change in representational situations, 1956–1958 to 1958–1960, in North, by issue area, by percent

	Situation, 1958–1960				
	Pervasive	Conflictual	Dissonant	Blocked	N
Civil rights, 1956–1958					
Pervasive	83	13	(4)[a]	0	714
Conflictual	40	60	0	0	380
Dissonant	2	11	87[b]	0	255
Blocked	11	36	47	6	121
Social welfare, 1956–1958					
Pervasive	68	32	0	0	778
Conflictual	44	41	(15)	0	566
Dissonant	0	64	36	0	156
Blocked	28	(42)	4	26	91
Foreign involvement, 1956–1958					
Pervasive	55	45	0	0	319
Conflictual	41	51	0	(8)	471
Dissonant	(28)	5	52	(15)	289
Blocked	0	33	55	12	90

a. ( ) = turnover errors.
b. Exception to hypothesized diagonal pattern.

Table 16.3 Stability and change in representational situations, 1956–1958 to 1958–1960, in South, by issue area, by percent

	Situation, 1958–1960				
	Pervasive	Conflictual	Dissonant	Blocked	N
Civil rights, 1956–1958					
Pervasive	40	60	0	0	479
Conflictual	75	25	0	0	118
Dissonant	0	0	100	0	23
Blocked	0	0	0	0	0
Social welfare, 1956–1958					
Pervasive	82	18	0	0	110
Conflictual	80	20	0	0	260
Dissonant	33	67	0	0	70
Blocked	(42)	0	0	58[b]	172
Foreign involvement, 1956–1958					
Pervasive	51	49	0	0	155
Conflictual	41	59	0	0	304
Dissonant	0	0	0	0	0
Blocked	(26)	0	5	69[b]	196

a. ( ) = turnover errors.
b. Calls attention to unusually high percentage.

transformations are due to changes at the level of the individual person, stressful situations are more likely to turn over than situations of low stress. Therefore, and as our measure of stability or change is the proportion of cases that remain in the same situational category from one period to another or the proportion that move, we would expect least turnover in the pervasive and most in the blocked situations of the first period.

The proportions reported in the main diagonal of Table 16.2 reporting the turnovers in the North indicate that, with one exception (marked "b"), there is most stability in the pervasive-pervasive and least stability in the blocked-blocked circumstances, with varying results in the conflictual-conflictual and dissonant-dissonant conditions—the variations being a function of the issue domains. The patterns are somewhat less pronounced in the South (Table 16.3), but vanishing numbers of cases, especially in the dissonant cells, reduce confidence in the reliability of the results. The expected difference between pervasive-pervasive and blocked-blocked circumstances occurs in only two of the turnover tables for the South (in the civil rights and social welfare domains), but there are surprisingly high percentages of cases in the blocked-blocked cells for social welfare and foreign involvement (marked "b"). One is being informed here about an evidently "deviant" condition in the South already foreshadowed by the unusually large proportion of cases in the blocked situations for both periods noted in Table 16.1. The suggestion was made that this was due to the availability of southern politicians in the game of legislative exchange in the social welfare and foreign involvement domains. The relatively high proportions of cases in the blocked-blocked cells of the turnover matrix of Table 16.3 suggests that, in this respect at least, there was little change; or, to put it differently in the perspective of validation, the blocked situation remained blocked in many cases where one should expect it to remain blocked. Politically speaking, there was simply no incentive in the South for situational change under conditions at the microlevel that, in the North, would have been found "impossible," and that, as Table 16.2 shows, were in fact highly unstable. The deviant situation in the South would seem to confirm rather than falsify the proposition that blocked situations are the least stable in the typology.

Just why, in the North, so relatively many dissonant situations remained stable is more of a puzzle, especially in connection with civil rights. The commonsensical interpretation would be this: inasmuch as the representative in a first-period dissonant situation deferred, on the strongly constituency-salient issue of civil rights, to his district, presumably in a pro direction in the North and a con direction in the South, he would have no reason to change his conduct on civil rights roll calls if his constituency did not change. But as other components of the situation can also change, the matter requires more detailed examination at the microlevel of analysis.

In general, to judge by the stability-change criterion, the different situations are quite sensitive to pressures for stability or change in expected ways. Even deviant results would seem to confirm rather than negate the theoretically expected patterns.

THE DIRECTION-OF-CHANGE CRITERION

Turnover analysis to validate the representational typology can be guided by a second criterion that postulates two requirements: first, changes will be away from the more stressful toward the less stressful situations among the available alternatives, or, if in the "false" direction, will be toward the least stressful among the available alternatives; and second, changes will be "one step at a time" or only between adjoining cells in the turnover matrix. If these requirements were met, the following changes would be observed in the movement of cases from one situation in the earlier period to another situation in the later period:

1. *Blocked* situations will change primarily into dissonant situations and secondarily into conflictual and pervasive, in that order.
2. *Dissonant* situations will change primarily into conflictual and secondarily into pervasive situations, in that order; if the change is false, it can only be to the blocked situation.
3. *Conflictual* situations will change into pervasive ones; if in the false direction, more will turn into dissonant than into blocked situations.
4. *Pervasive* situations can change only in a false direction, but will turn more into conflictual than into dissonant or blocked situations, in that order.

Tables 16.2 and 16.3 show that these requirements are met in most of the test opportunities, both North and South. There are, altogether, sixty-six opportunities for change (three per four situations in three issue areas in two regions—$3 \times 4 \times 3 \times 2 = 72$—but six altogether empty cells in the South, due to absence of cases in two situations, reduce the number to sixty-six change opportunities). As the parenthesized figures in Tables 16.2 and 16.3 indicate, there are eight errors of direction, an error ratio of 12 percent. Four of these errors are for cases moving in the right direction and four for cases moving in a false direction. The figures also show that the proportions of cases moving in the false direction are never more than 15 percent of all cases in the situation of origin. Of the errors in the right direction, three involve "jumps" of cases from blocked situations of origin.[12]

Turnover analysis lends considerable credence to the validity of the representational typology. There is relative stability of situation where it makes sense to expect most stability, and there is relative change where it makes sense to expect most change. Moreover, the changes are in theoretically viable directions and involve surprisingly few errors. There are deviations from what a perfect turnover structure might look like; but as we are dealing with empirical structures in six existentially very different circumstances involving three different issue areas quite differently experienced in two regions of the country, the results of the turnover analysis are highly supportive of the theoretical validity of the representational typology and of the four representational situations as such.

Validation through Dependent-Variable Test

If representational situations are at all valid constructs of the political reality in which representatives orient themselves to action, they should be of predictive or explanatory use. In the Miller-Stokes model, congressmen's ability or success in accurately perceiving their constituents' preferences served as a critical intervening variable mediating between constituency preferences and congressional roll-call behavior. Because we do not include perceptual accuracy as a component property of representational situations, we can use it to test the validity of the representational typology.

Other things being equal, one should find more representatives with accurate perceptions in situations in which they vote *with* their constituencies—pervasive and dissonant—than in situations in which they vote *against* constituency preferences—conflictual and blocked. If this were not the case, if representatives were voting in accord with their constituents' preferences "blind," any relationship between constituency preferences and legislative conduct on issues would have to be considered a matter of pure chance. But it can be assumed that the structures emerging from linking various event-variables are not fortuitous occurrences. In particular, if representatives vote their constituencies' preferences, they presumably do so in reasonably accurate knowledge of what these preferences are. This would be especially compelling in the dissonant situation in which the representative votes with the constituency against his own preferences. Being willing to subordinate one's own preferences to those of constituents is something the representative would not want to do unless convinced that he has a fairly accurate understanding of what constituents' preferences really are.

By way of contrast, in conflictual situations in which the representative fails to vote with his constituency, the political stress involved, due to value conflicts, is likely to make for affective ambiguity and, as a result, for cognitive distortion. Misperception, in turn, inadvertently confirms the representative's belief that, by voting his own preferences, he is in fact voting those of his constituency. In this situation, then, inaccurate perceptions serve to make an otherwise politically difficult set of circumstances a viable alternative to the dissonant situation in which accurate perceptions incline the representative to sacrifice his own preferences.

It is difficult to speculate about the effect of blocked situations on the perception of constituency preferences. On the one hand, in these situations the representative presumably takes his cues from external actors or conditions; so it does not matter whether he perceives his constituency's preferences accurately or not. On the other hand, as his own preferences and those of the constituency are identical, yet he votes against both (see Diagram 4, Figure 16.3), he may well know what he is doing and have very accurate perceptions of constituency wishes. It is difficult to say, therefore, whether one should expect many or few representatives with accurate perceptions in the blocked situation. Unfortunately, an answer will remain empirically moot because an insufficient number of cases precludes analysis.

Table 16.4 presents the findings. In addition to whatever situational effects there may be, there are both issue-domain and regional effects. As the marginal totals show, in each region and in each period, the proportions of representatives with accurate perceptions decrease systematically (with the exception of the welfare area in the South) from the civil rights through the social welfare to the foreign involvement areas. This result is what one would expect from knowledge about the salience of the three issue areas during the two periods and, as a bonus, confirms the validity of the accuracy measure (which is also confirmed by the ascending proportions of "missing cases" as one moves from civil rights to foreign involvement). The regional effect is most noticeable in the civil rights area where more southern than northern congressmen have accurate perceptions, and in the social welfare area where southern congressmen, in contrast to their northern colleagues, seem extraordinarily inept (in both periods) in appraising their constituents' preferences.[13] Finally, in the foreign involvement domain (where accuracy in perceptions is probably most difficult to come by), the proportions of congressmen with accurate cognitions are strikingly similar in North and South.

What of the effect of the representational situations? Leaving out the blocked situations because of the small numerical bases for percentaging, the data generally confirm the hypotheses. In situations in which the representative votes with his constituents, the pervasive and dissonant, there are more accurate perceptions (see cells with double underlining in Table 16.4) than in conflictual situations where comparatively fewer accurate perceptions are found (see cells with single underlining). There is a slight tendency for the dissonant situations to produce more accurate perceptions than do the pervasive situations, as was anticipated. Of eleven possible comparisons, 63 percent show more representatives with accurate perceptions in the dissonant than in the pervasive situations, but the differences are often very small. However, the pervasive situations, with a falsification ratio (see Table 16.4 for explanation of ratio) of 75 percent, are evidently more conducive to accuracy in perceptions than the dissonant situations with a falsification ratio of only 58 percent. (But the latter ratio may not be fully reliable because of data limitations in the southern sample.)

An additional test is possible by examining the relationship between representational situations and perceptual accuracy under conditions of stability and change. If our original hypothesis is correct, the proportions of accurate perceptions should remain relatively larger in stable pervasive and dissonant than in stable conflictual situations, while they might decline

Table 16.4 Proportions of representatives with accurate perceptions of constituency preferences, by representational situations, issue areas, region, and period

	Pervasive	Conflictual	Dissonant	Blocked	Total	Missing cases
North, 1956–1958						
Civil rights	72%	32%	74%	91%	62%	
	(714)	(373)	(227)	(42)	(1356)	114 = 7%
Social welfare	59%	25%	15%	54%	43%	
	(687)	(475)	(156)	(91)	(1409)	182 = 11%
Foreign involvement	40%	11%	56%	0%	28%	
	(267)	(437)	(235)	(90)	(1029)	153 = 12%
North, 1958–1960						
Civil rights	63%	39%	69%	0%	59%	
	(858)	(329)	(316)	(0)	(1503)	154 = 9%
Social welfare	49%	37%	50%	46%	44%	
	(676)	(624)	(144)	(24)	(1468)	232 = 13%
Foreign involvement	24%	21%	37%	34%	26%	
	(443)	(384)	(204)	(94)	(1125)	148 = 13%
South, 1956–1958						
Civil rights	76%	49%	100%	0%	73%	
	(475)	(78)	(23)	(0)	(576)	112 = 16%
Social welfare	18%	0%	0%	0%	4%	
	(110)	(299)	(79)	(94)	(573)	150 = 20%
Foreign involvement	21%	29%	0%	45%	31%	
	(96)	(260)	(0)	(115)	(471)	252 = 34%
South, 1958–1960						
Civil rights	93%	58%	100%	0%	75%	
	(273)	(315)	(23)	(0)	(611)	44 = 6%
Social welfare	0%	17%	0%	0%	4%	
	(355)	(116)	(0)	(59)	(530)	82 = 13%
Foreign involvement	72%	14%	0%	0%	31%	
	(153)	(255)	(9)	(54)	(471)	184 = 28%
Falsification ratio[a]	75%	83%	58%			

a. Falsification ratio is, in pervasive and dissonant columns, the percentage of cells out of all cells in which proportions of representatives with accurate perceptions are *above* proportions recorded in corresponding cells of total column; in conflictual column, the ratio refers to cells where proportions are *below* proportions in corresponding cells of total column.

in changed circumstances. To examine this proposition, we use a turnover table for the representational situations in the North (but omit northern blocked and all southern data because of possible unreliability). As the cells in the main diagonal of Table 16.5 show, stable pervasive and dissonant situations continue to include more congressmen with accurate perceptions than do the stable conflictual situations. But the table shows another interesting and serendipitous result. As representatives find themselves in circumstances where 1956–1958 pervasive situations have changed into conflictual ones in 1958–1960, more of them have accurate perceptions than those who have remained in stable conflictual situations; the proportional numbers of the latter remain about the same as they had been in the earlier period. The proportions of those with accurate perceptions whose situations changed from pervasive to conflictual are considerably higher for all three issue areas, as follows:

	Accurate perceivers in conflictual situations		
	1956–1958	1958–1960 Stables	1958–1960 Changers
Civil rights	32%	33%	50%
Social welfare	25	20	59
Foreign involvement	11	12	52

Table 16.5 Proportions of congressmen in stable and changed representative circumstances with accurate perceptions of constituency preferences in three issue areas, North

	Situation, 1958–1960		
	Pervasive	Conflictual	Dissonant
Civil rights, 1956–1958			
Pervasive	79% (588)	50% (96)[a]	0% (30)
Conflictual	31% (144)	33% (229)	— —
Dissonant	0% (4)	— —	75% (223)
Social welfare, 1956–1958			
Pervasive	59% (436)	59% (251)[a]	— —
Conflictual	33% (174)	20% (218)	24% (83)
Dissonant	— —	0% (99)	42% (57)
Foreign involvement, 1956–1958			
Pervasive	25% (123)	52% (144)[a]	— —
Conflictual	14% (185)	12% (200)	— —
Dissonant	31% (82)	— —	68% (110)

a. Exception to hypothesized diagonal pattern.

Overall, then, the dependent-variable test shows the representational typology to have considerable predictive and explanatory potential in both synchronic and diachronic treatment. It seems to measure with reasonable validity and reliability outcomes of behavior at the microlevel in at least three of the four representational situations. If the test has not validated the blocked situation, it is because of the instability and possible unreliability of the data in this category of the representational typology.

Appendix: The Miller-Stokes American Representation Study Measures

The dependent variables of the Miller-Stokes model were the roll-call votes of congressmen during the Eighty-fifth (1957–58) Congress in three issue areas designated as "civil rights," "social welfare," and "foreign involvement." These roll calls—six on civil rights issues, eight on social welfare issues, and ten on foreign involvement issues—were Guttman scaled, with very highly reproducibility coefficients. Similar scales of roll calls in the same three issues are available for the Eighty-sixth (1959–60) Congress. (For a description of the scale components and scale procedures, see ICPR, 1971, pp. 619–624.)

The independent variables of the Miller-Stokes model were citizens' attitudes on matters of civil rights, social welfare, and foreign involvement obtained from interviews with a national probability sample conducted in connection with the 1958 congressional elections. Responses to particular questions were initially combined into indices, and scores were assigned to the individual respondents in the sample. However, in order to correlate the political attitudes of the respondents, in each congressional district where they were interviewed, with the attitudes and roll-call votes of their respective congressmen, the individual-level index scores were transformed into district attitude scores by way of aggregation—the district measure being the arithmetic mean of the individual-level scores. Similar district-level measures of citizen attitudes in the three issue areas are also available for the 1956 and 1960 national elections. Indeed, the bulk of the respondents for the three elections constitute a panel, and it is the panel data that are used in the present analysis. (For a full description of the mass-public attitudes and the procedures used in constructing the indices and aggregating the individual-level data, see ICPR, 1971: inserted note 8, dated January 21, 1972.)[14]

The intervening variables in the congruence model were, first, the congressmen's own attitudes in the three issue areas of civil rights, social welfare, and foreign involvement; and second, their perceptions of their constituents' attitudes in the same three areas. The attitude measures were derived from relevant items in the interviews with congressmen and congressional candidates and constituted Guttman-type scales. (For a description of the scales, see ICPR, 1971, p. 611.) Congressmen's perceptions of constituent attitudes were elicited by the following question that was asked concerning each of the three issue areas: "How do the people in your district feel about . . . ? Would you say that: more of them are in favor; they are evenly divided or not much opinion on this in the district; or more of them oppose it." For detailed wording of the questions, see ICPR, 1971, pp. 173–174).

In order to develop our own measure of perceptual accuracy, we cross-tabulate congressmen's perceptions of district opinions with the actual (aggregated) district attitudes in each of the three issue domains. As the perception variable was measured on a three-point scale, we also trichotomize the originally continuous district attitude scores by partitioning the range of the scores so that the pro, neutral, and con categories of the trichotomized measure stand in a 2:1:2 relationship. Cross-tabulation of the two trichotomized measures yields a nine-cell table. Cases falling into the main diagonal (pro-pro, neutral-neutral, con-con), are characterized as being "accurate"; all other combinations as "inaccurate."

To correspond to the two time periods, 1956–1958 and 1958–1960, and to be consistent with the arrangement of the Miller-Stokes data into preelection files and postelection files, we construct the accuracy measure for both Eighty-fifth Congress incumbents and those elected to the Eighty-sixth Congress (15 percent of the congressmen in the "new" Eighty-sixth Congress were themselves new members). In both cases 1958 constituency preferences serve as bases for determining the accuracy of representatives' perceptions. The 1958 (rather than 1956 or 1960) district preferences are used because they are temporally most proximate to representatives' perceptions and, therefore, probably provide the most reliable measure of accuracy.

FIVE

Of Choice and Decision

Logics of Rationality in Unanimous

Decision Making

MY STARTING POINT is an empirical observation: the tendency of much democratic decision making to terminate in unanimous or near-unanimous voting.[1] My problem is elusive: does unanimity in democratic decision making satisfy criteria of rationality?[2]

A Problematic Situation

Democratic decision making is most readily observable in legislative bodies.[3] The great amount of unanimous or near-unanimous decision making in the final stage of the legislative process is a matter of record (see Key, 1958, pp. 727–731; Leiserson, 1958, pp. 339–344). Many of these decisions are made, of course, by the formal rule of "unanimous consent" or on private-bill calendars that prohibit passage for further consideration.[4] Most of these actions lie outside the arena of political warfare or any other lines of cleavage. But others involve subjects of real importance for individuals or groups.[5] Some of these have the endorsement of all interested parties, thus making for unanimity or near-unanimity, but others do not. This set of decisions—where one should expect division on substantive grounds of divided interests, but where it does not occur—makes unanimity a puzzling affair. For there is no overt evidence as to why it should occur—no log-rolling, no leadership instructions, no purposive "engineering of consent." There has been, as I shall point out, some empirical speculation about the possible dynamics of the legislative process when it culminates in this kind of unanticipated unanimity, but real empirical evidence is scarce.[6]

Unanimity or near-unanimity may occur, then, in vital as well as minor policy matters. However, in democratic political systems differences over issues of public policy between political actors and conflicts between them are generally expected. The democratic system is, by definition, a contrivance designed to institutionalize conflicts and facilitate the clarification, crystallization, and resolution of political differences. A democratic legislature is an institution composed of opposed sides, and, the more the lines of division follow predictable lines, the more rational would the legislative process seem to be. If predicted divisions do not occur, the rationality of legislative decision making becomes problematical. Regardless, therefore, of whether issues of high policy significance are involved or not, the fact that many legislative actions where controversy might be expected are consummated by unanimity poses a problem for political theory. This is not to imply that in every case of legislative action division is thought desirable. In crisis situations, notably war and economic emergencies threatening community survival, unanimity rather than division is the preferred decision norm and celebrated as a political achievement.[7]

Unanimity as Formal Rule

In order to come to grips with the problem, I shall briefly turn to the institutional arrangements, where unanimity is a formal, constitutional requirement of decision making, for two reasons—one theoretical, the other methodological. In the first place, there has been a good deal of explicit theoretical concern with the constitutional unanimity rule from the standpoint of its rationality. And second, it would seem that constitutional unanimity, with its imputed rationality, may serve as a kind of "ideal type" (see Parsons, 1949, pp. 604–605). Treated as an ideal-type model, rational constitutional unanimity provides a criterion for appraising the rationality of the several situations where unanimity emerges as an empirical phenomenon. As Weber (1947, p. 92) puts it,

by comparison with this [ideal type] it is possible to understand the ways in which actual action is influenced by irrational factors of all sorts, such as affects and errors, in that they account for the deviation from the line of conduct which would be expected on the hypothesis that the action were purely rational.

The most familiar case of constitutional unanimity is found today in an international decision-making body such as the Security Council of the United Nations. Here unanimity among the permanent members is a requirement for any substantive decision to be made. The empirical reasons for the rule are well known: on the one hand, the area of potential disagreement between nations is so large and, on the other hand, its "interests" are considered so "vital" by each participating nation that, in order to win support for and acceptance of a decision, unanimity rather than another voting rule is made the formal and effective requirement.[8]

Unanimity as a voting requirement is a rule of long standing. Indeed, unanimity did not give way to majority voting until certain conditions—just as those characteristic of international decision making today—had given way to other conditions. Gierke (1972, pp. 312–335) reports that in the political life of the early Germanic tribes unanimous consent was sought for decisions precisely because a strong feeling of individuality made for the recognition that what could not be done unanimously would not be done at all. In other words, unanimity appeared as the only decision rule that, if each participant was to be guaranteed membership in the decisive group, facilitated the replacement of private by collective action.

On the other hand, unanimity may serve to prevent collective action. Simmel (1950, pp. 240–241) discusses the dysfunctional consequences of the unanimity rule in the Polish Diet and the Aragonese Cortes, but of interest here are the conditions that made for maintaining the rule—among them the inequality in status and power of the participants, insufficient rules for deliberation, resistance of the constituent members to a feeble executive authority, and others. If, in the case of the Germanic tribes, each participant was to be guaranteed membership in the decisive group because all participants were deemed equal, in the cases described by Simmel, membership in the decisive group was to be guaranteed because the participants were unequal in status and power.

Unanimity, it seems, can be the preferred decision rule in two quite different, indeed polar, situations. On the one hand, it may facilitate the transition from private to collective action among equals who recognize that the advantages to be gained from collective action for each participant will be greater than the advantages to be gained from private action. The unanimity rule, then, is the only decision rule capable of resolving deadlock—which means that neither collective nor private action is possible.[9] For under any other rule—majority voting or dictatorship, for instance—each partner would not have a guarantee of being in the decisive group and, therefore, would prefer deadlock. But precisely because each participant is thought to be equal to every other participant and because the advantages to be derived from collective action are greater than those from private action, unanimity must be considered the rational decision rule in this situation.

This explication does not take account, of course, of the costs of decision making that may be involved in unanimity. It is concerned only with the utilities for each actor that he may anticipate from collective as against private action. But as, in this case of collective action by equals, the costs of unanimity can be assumed to be less than the costs of deadlock, rational actors who are equal will be willing to pay the costs of unanimity.[10]

On the other hand, unanimity may be preferred as the constitutional decision rule in situations where it is the objective of unequal participants to block collective action, not because private action is preferred, but because deadlock is preferred to both private and collective action. Again, unanimity alone guarantees each participant to be in the decisive group, but unanimity is the chosen decision rule not because it resolves deadlock, but because it institutionalizes it. The costs involved may be considerable and, in the long run, as has often been pointed out, dysfunctional for the individual participants as well as for the collectivity because it makes for constitutional anarchy. Unanimity rational in the short run may contain, therefore, the seeds of irrationality in the long run.

The discussion suggests that, under specified conditions, unanimity may be more rational than other formal decision rules. This may come as a startling conclusion, for common sense and experience would seem to prove otherwise. But it is startling only if one fails to specify the conditions. Let me repeat them as a paradigm:

1. Each participant in the decisional situation is equal in status and power to every other participant.
2. Each participant in the decisional situation is guaranteed membership in the decisive group.
3. Each participant expects greater advantages for himself from collective than from private action.
4. The costs of unanimous decision making for collective action are less than the costs of deadlock.

The explication suggests that, under the conditions specified, the constitutional unanimity rule appears as the "ideal-rational" decision rule, whereas other decision rules appear as variants that become relevant only if the conditions for unanimity are not met.[11] The conditions are, of course, extremely strict and not likely to be found in the real world of politics. This is precisely the reason why the constitutional unanimity rule, however rational it may be, has to yield to behaviorally more viable rules like majority voting or dictatorship.

Implicit in the model of constitutional unanimity is the assumption that unanimity is rational if, upon their merits, all possible alternatives among decision rules—such as exceptional majority voting, bare majority voting, plurality voting, decisional dictatorship (arbitration), or even anarchy— have been considered. The availability of alternative rules, then, is a necessary condition of rationality in the choice of a rule, but it is not a sufficient condition. A second condition is that the decision of how to make decisions involve conscious selection of the rule to be followed in preference to other rules. In other words, if unanimity occurs in a voting situation without alternative decisional possibilities having been consciously contemplated, the unanimous decision cannot be considered as prima facie rational. Now, it is evident that the rationality criterion, so interpreted, pertains to constitutional unanimity, for it is the only situation in which unanimity as a decision rule is consciously selected and institutionalized as against other rules.

But what of situations where unanimity occurs but is not a constitutional rule of decision making? For instance, if a city council unanimously adopts a measure, even though individual members may be reluctant at first to support it, because it believes that a split decision would undermine its authority in the community, and if the alternatives of unanimous versus split decision have been consciously considered, the decision is rational, given the group's values. On the other hand, if the relationship between the group's perception of its authority in the community and its voting pattern is not consciously invoked, and if it has consequences that were not consciously anticipated, then the unanimous decision must be explained on another than its rational basis. Consciousness, then, has to be postulated as an important ingredient of rationality, for otherwise the behavior involved in a unanimous decision where unanimity is not a formal rule would have to be accepted, ex post facto, as rational.

Whether unanimity in situations where it is not a formal voting requirement is rational or not is, therefore, a matter of empirical determination. I shall come back to various possibilities later on.

Ways of Decision Handling

As already mentioned, the defense of the formal, constitutional unanimity rule must be predicated on certain behavioral assumptions that, however, are not empirically tenable. The rule seems to assume that human beings are invariably rationally calculating, in the sense that they seek to maximize personal benefits by some hedonistic calculus and make choices, including the decision of how to make decisions, in terms of least cost. And it seems to be assumed that men live in some kind of state of nature, very much as that of the social-contract theories. In these theories one individual is related to any other individual in some private way that is assumed to be prior to social bonds of family, friendship, or any other interpersonal link, and that the individual enters only if it suits his own interests.

These assumptions cannot be made if one wishes to develop an empirically relevant typology of situations in the real world, where unanimity is not a formal decision rule but an existential phenomenon. In the first place, decisions in the real world are not made as if they were the decisions of an individual alone. An individual may take the initiative in seeking to achieve his own interests through collective action. But a great deal of collective decision making is designed to achieve public as well as individual interests. The behavioral assumption must be made that man is, indeed, a social animal, that he always lives in a group and is part of a group. The notion implicit in the individualistic model of rationally calculating man that only individual but not public interests are "natural" cannot be maintained as behaviorally adequate. The conception of the solitary, individual man unrelated to others but by ties of self-interested calculation does not provide a viable model.

It would seem that when unanimity occurs spontaneously in democratic decision making, it stems from a confluence of two behavioral dimensions— the ways in which decisions are generally handled and the ways in which interests are articulated. I shall deal with the latter in the next section.

Constitutional unanimity has been called a formal decision rule. Taking this as a clue, I would like to suggest that decisions, whatever the constitutional rule for decision making, may be handled informally as well as formally and that both informal and formal patterns may characterize decisional behavior. In fact, the combination of formal and informal processes seems to be characteristic of the kind of behavior conventionally called "political." Though the range from informal to formal patterns is best thought of as a continuum of decision handling, I shall, for conceptual brevity, present a trichotomous classification.

Informal-consensual decision handling. Here the emphasis is on the spontaneously consensual and informal character of the decision process. Because there is much customary consensus on the prerogatives of the actors, decision making is likely to be characterized by little conflict. Decisions are handled through traditional, interpersonal arrangements that are only weakly institutionalized in the governmental sense, but they are highly stable nevertheless. Not only are the relations of the members of the collectivity easygoing, face to face, and permanent, but the group itself is likely to be held together by strong bonds of solidarity. Conflict, if it occurs, is likely to be settled through the intervention of mediators. The situation here stylized is probably characteristic of primary groups, but it can probably be extended both to modern committees in a generic sense and to larger communal groups that are fairly homogenous in composition, culturally isolated, and relatively static in development.

Formal-ministerial decision handling. At the opposite pole of the decision-handling continuum, behavior is thought to be formal-ministerial. As the concept "ministerial" conveys, decisions are handled ex officio, that is, by persons who do what they do by virtue of the official position they occupy in the group. Rather than being spontaneous, decision handling is routinized and bureaucratized. There is relatively little room for personal intervention. Decisions are made by rules that are highly institutionalized, either by constitution or convention. Maximum value is placed on consistency in decision handling. Decisions are likely to be functionally specialized, with great attention being paid to impersonal authority rather than to personal opinions. Favoritism is improper. The participants in the decision process are not held together by ties of friendship, but rather by formal arrangements that, if removed, would spell the end of the relationship. Conflicts will be resolved by appeal to higher jurisdiction. The formal-ministerial pattern would seem to be characteristic of courts of law or administrative organizations where the personal attributes of the decision makers are considered irrelevant, and where the group is likely to be heterogeneous in background and pluralistic in composition.

Political decision handling. This type of decision handling may be located somewhere in the middle between consensual and ministerial ways of making decisions. In other words, it partakes of both formal and informal, personal and impersonal patterns. On the one hand, there is likely to be some agreement, more or less, on the "rules of the game" that is as deeply ingrained as are the norms of consensual decision handling.[12] On the other hand, the relations among decision makers are also regulated by formal constraints as in the ministerial pattern. On the one hand, a good deal of the behavior involved in political decision handling is personal—there is room for bargaining and trades that, unlike the ministerial process, give the actor fair latitude in negotiations before the decision is made. On the other hand, limits are set to decision handling, not only by formal rules, but by the whole network of interpersonal relations outside of the decision-making group itself (the political environment). The political decision-handling pattern seeks to cope with conflict not through mediation or other pacifying techniques, as the informal-consensual pattern, or through appeal to jurisdictional authority, routine, or precedent, as the formal-ministerial pattern, but through clarifying and crystallizing the conflict in debate or negotiation in order to arrive at a point where the decision will represent a compromise that is acceptable to both sides. Unlike the consensual pattern, the composition of the group is more heterogeneous, although it is held together by some shared characteristics, such as language, historical background, or common fate.

While I have referred, for illustrative purposes, to some particular types of human group, such as the primary group or the administrative organization, as being representative of one or another way of decision handling, the three patterns should be clearly understood as analytic categories and not as concrete processes that can be identified in crystalline purity with particular decision-making structures.[13] Any one pattern of decision handling can probably be found, with more or less impact, in any one concrete decision-making structure. Whether it will or not is an empirical research question, not a conceptual or definitional problem.[14]

Ways of Interest Articulation

It seems reasonable to assume, for the purposes of this discussion, that men engage in collective political action to advance both their individual interests and those of the group to which they belong. If the group's decision is unanimous, furthermore, it may be assumed that different types of unanimity will result, depending on the ways in which individual and group interests are articulated within the group, as well as depending on the ways of decision handling that are practiced. These assumptions would seem to be more tenable than individualistic assumptions, for they derive directly from the social nature of man. We can assume that, precisely because every man is inevitably and invariably a member of a group, he will want to realize his group's as well as his own individual interests.[15] It is in the interchange of individual and group articulation of interests that the particular format of decision making emerges.

It is necessary to explain here why I am using, in a discussion that is to deal with the rationality of unanimous decision making, the concept of "interest" rather than the concepts of "goal" and "utility" that are usually employed in connection with treatments of rational action. I do so partly in order to disengage the discussion from models of rationality that make individualistic assumptions, as those of economic choice, or from models that make assumptions about the relationship between means and ends, as those of organizational behavior. But there is a positive reason as well for introducing the notion of "interest" as a critical dimension. It is a term more appropriate in models of *political* decision making. Unlike organizational or economic behavior, political behavior rarely centers in the search for or the achievement of a single goal or a single value. The multivalued "ends" and the equally diverse "means" of politics are often difficult to disentangle. The objects of political activity are more or less coherent complexes of individual and group demands and their supporting expectations. To these complexes we give the name of "interests."[16] Any particular decision, even though it may relate to a particular end or means of collective action, is invariably embedded in a more or less well-articulated configuration of propinquitous demands, expectations, and evaluations that influences not only the content of decisions but also their format. The ways in which interests, so defined, are articulated may help to account for particular voting patterns—whether unanimous, majoritarian, or plural.

Moreover, speaking of interests is advantageous in a discussion of political decision making for another reason. Interests are likely to be characterized by an intrinsic reciprocity precisely because they refer to both public and private spheres. Academic excellence, for instance, is an interest of the university (the group) as a whole because it concerns the university's standing among all universities. But the university's academic excellence is also an interest that affects every individual member of the university— students, faculty, and administration alike. The more specifically academic excellence as an interest is articulated by the group as a whole as well as by its individual members, the more agreement can undoubtedly be achieved in connection with any particular decision that may have to be made.

I have spoken of "interest articulation" without defining it. I mean by it the ways in which individual or group interests are structured in the perceptions and verbalizations of the decision makers. In order to deal with this structuring most efficiently, I shall dichotomize interests into those that are "specific" and those that are "diffuse." These articulations represent forms of orientations to action that decision makers bring into the choice situation.[17] From this perspective, both individual interests and group or public interests may be described as being specifically or diffusely articulated.

Interest diffuseness. Interests may be said to be diffusely articulated if the demands that are made, either by an individual or by a group, do not constitute a hierarchy of preferences that would give priority in decision making to one demand over another. In other words, the decision maker will promote any demand that is compatible with other demands, whether public or private, without, at least initially, ordering these demands in terms of the values that may be involved. By not committing himself to one demand over another in advance, the decision maker is likely to be guided in the choices he makes by the exigencies of the decisional situation, and he is likely to respond to the situation in terms of his predispositions at the time of decision making and the nature of the problem at hand. For instance, a city council is intent on making the city "a better place to live in." It does not quite know what it means by this or how to achieve it. Its interest is diffusely articulated. A proposal to build a community ball park is made, seconded, and, in due time, voted on, without much attention being given to alternatives.

Interest specificity. Interests may be said to be specifically articulated if the different demands that are made, either by an individual or by a group, can be readily located within some hierarchy of preferences so that the relevance of a demand in regard to other demands, and to the choice problem at hand, can be specifically determined. In other words, the decision maker will give priority to that one of his demands over all other demands that is immediately relevant to the problematic situation. To put this somewhat differently, the decision maker confronts the problematic situation in terms of specifically articulated interests and the requirements for their achievement, but this behavior will be compatible with the exclusion, temporary or permanent, of other interests. For instance, a political group decides to support X, who is running for office. The group proceeds to collect money, distribute leaflets, and arrange coffee hours for the candidate. The group's interest in seeing X win is specifically articulated, for in ordering its preferences it presumably concluded that support of this candidate will not preclude advancing and attaining other interests.

It is possible now to suggest ways of collective interest articulation that result when individual and group interests are either specifically or diffusely articulated. The following matrix shows the possibilities:

		Articulation of member	
		Specific	Diffuse
	Specific	(1)	(2)
Articulation of group		Pluralism	Monism
	Diffuse	(3)	(4)
		Dictatorship	Anarchy

In cell (1) of the matrix, as the interests of every individual in the group as well as of the group itself are specifically articulated, the decisional problem is one of dealing with specific demands of a rather plural character by setting priorities through bargaining. Because of the probably very great number of specific demands that are made, the setting of priorities is never likely to be completed. Decisions are likely to be made through majority voting by shifting coalitions. Collective articulation is essentially plural and democratic.

In cell (4), on the other hand, inaction is the likely result, for the diffuseness of interest articulation, by all the members as individuals and by the group as a whole, prevents collective articulation. In fact, the situation has so little empirical viability that the group is likely to disintegrate in view of its inability to articulate individual or group interests. Insofar as there is articulation, it is best conceptualized as anarchic.

The outcome of cell-(2) articulation is quite different. In a situation in which the group's interest articulation is specific but the individual's articulation is diffuse, there is likely to be strong pressure to accede to group demands. Unlike the situation in cell (1), the individual with diffuse interest articulation will not order his own individual preferences in view of the group's specifically articulated interests. The situation points toward a monistic articulation of group interests with unanimous decision making as a strong possibility.

Finally, the situation that emerges in cell (3) suggests dictatorship as the form of interest articulation in decision making. Because the interest articulation of the group as a whole is diffuse, so that there is no predecisional ordering of group preferences, and because at least some individuals have specifically articulated interests, there is a strong strain, initially, toward conflict. But because, unlike in the plural order, group articulation is diffuse, the conflict is likely to be resolved through dictatorship—that is, one person (or a subgroup like a triumvirate) comes to dictate the terms of collective interest articulation. In some respects, this situation, if reinforced by structural constraints of coercion, points to the kind of pseudounanimity that, as Friedrich and Brzezinski (1965, p. 132) suggest, "makes the totalitarians insist on the complete agreement of the entire population under their control to the measures the regime is launching." But even without coercion, group-diffuse, individual-specific interest articulation is likely to make for some form of dictatorial collective articulation.[18]

My concern in the following will be only with the articulation outcomes suggested by cells (2) and (3), for in these situations some form of unanimity appears as a likely decisional result. The process represented by cell (1) is of no further interest because, if a unanimous decision emerges at all, we can assume that we are dealing with the genuine article that is eminently rational. Presumably, there has been free choice among alternatives and conscious selection, after specific individual or group demands have been deliberated upon and negotiated. But unanimity is not likely in a situation in which individual and group articulation is specific. Majority voting is sufficient to reach decisions. The process represented by cell (4) will also be ignored in the following discussion. It refers to a situation in which deadlock seems to be preferred. Neither private nor collective action would be possible.

A Typology of Unanimity

A typology of unanimity has the immediate purpose of locating empirical situations of or hypotheses concerning unanimous decision making in a consistent schema. A typology of this kind can be constructed out of the two dimensions that have been discussed—ways of decision handling and ways of interest articulation.

The behavioral assumption is made, to repeat, that the relationship between individual and group is such that individual and group interests need not conflict but are both attainable simultaneously through collective action. Unanimity in decisional patterns would then be evidence of the validity of the behavioral assumption. This does not mean that unanimity is the inevitable decisional outcome whenever a certain way of decision handling and a certain constellation of interest articulation intersect. However, there is a strong presumption that one or another type of unanimity, when it occurs, is ascertainable in terms of the intersection or confluence of the two dimensions.

We can construct a six-cell unanimity matrix. In interpreting the types represented by the cells, it will be assumed that the three ways of decision handling will intersect with the two critical ways of interest articulation (group-specific/individual-diffuse and group-diffuse/individual-specific) in characteristic fashion. The tendency toward unanimity is assumed to be present, then, when group and individual ways of interest articulation are asymmetrical, and when they are molded by the prevailing ways of decision handling so that the particular type of unanimity is clearly distinct from every other type. The following matrix represents the typology:

Ways of interest articulation	Ways of decision handling		
	Consensual	*Political*	*Ministerial*
Group-specific	(1)	(3)	(5)
Individual-diffuse	Ancestral	Bargained	Functional
Group-diffuse	(2)	(4)	(6)
Individual-specific	False	Projected	Injunctive

Ancestral unanimity. If the group's interests are specific, but individual interests are diffuse, and if, at the same time, decisions are handled consensually, there is likely to be a very strong commitment to make unanimous decisions, partly because there is long-standing agreement on what, under certain circumstances, should be done, and partly because the maintenance of group solidarity requires that it should be done unanimously. Individual interests, being diffuse, are submerged in group interests, and there is, therefore, little opportunity for individual interests to be sufficiently crystallized to affect the decisional situation and to occasion division. Alternatives facing the group are decided by traditionally ordered priorities, with little likelihood that group agreement will be disturbed by the intrusion of specific individual interests. Whatever private interests an individual may have are fulfilled in the achievement of the group's interests. Unanimity may be said to be ancestral.

This type of ancestral unanimity seems to be implicit in Keefe's (1956,

p. 311) hypothesis concerning unanimous decisions in American state legislatures:

The area of agreement on legislative questions is so large in some two-party states that significant divisions along discernible lines (e.g., party, rural-urban, sectional, conservative-liberal, etc.) must necessarily be something less than frequent. It may not be so much a matter of "leadership" as simply a case of like-minded legislators moving from bill to bill in the broad fields of state public policy where consensus rather than conflict obtains.

The hypothesis implies that even in modern, functionally highly differentiated political systems there remain vestiges of traditional, customary understandings of what things should or should not be done by the polity. These group preferences are so firmly established and so widely shared that they preclude the emergence of specific individual interests that might be at odds with group interests.

False unanimity. An altogether different configuration characterizes the decisional situation in which the interests of the group are diffuse but those of the individual members are specific, yet where decision handling is essentially consensual. The group's inability to order its interests preferentially, but the existence of specific individual interests, creates a situation that is potentially full of tension and conflict. Yet the habit of handling decisions consensually and the need to maintain group solidarity, although group interest articulation is diffuse, makes for superficial agreement that prohibits the airing of individual interests inimical to group solidarity. As a result, individual interests, though specific, are suppressed or concealed in the name of the group. Mediators or conciliators cannot function because they have no way of identifying the sources and parties of conflicts. As group interest articulation is diffuse, decisions, even though unanimous, are not genuine expressions of group consensus. Unanimity may be said to be false.

An illustration of false unanimity is the detailed description of the "politics of unanimity" by Vidich and Bensman (1960, p. 176) in their study of the village and school boards of a small, rural community. The school board, for instance,

reaches its decisions through a process of discussion which results in an inchoately arrived-at unanimous decision in which no vote, or only a perfunctory one, is taken . . . It becomes central to the psychology of the members of the board to attempt to minimize or avoid crises, and this leads to further demands for unanimity and concealment.

As a hypothesis, the notion of concealment or "false unanimity" is probably more viable in small legislative bodies, such as city councils or committees, than in large institutionalized groups, like state legislatures or the Congress, where a façade of unity is practically impossible in normal conflictual situations, and where partisanship rather than friendly agreement is the public expectation.

Bargained unanimity. Where the task of decision making is to integrate diffuse individual interests in terms of specific group interests in a decision-handling structure that is "political," unanimity, if it occurs, probably stems from successful trading and bargaining among the individual members. The bargaining process is facilitated, on the one hand, by the diffuseness of the individual interests: no intransigent positions are likely to be taken, and the spirit of compromise prevails. Moreover, the specificity of group interests sets limits to the bargaining process—not everything goes, for if everything goes, bargaining will not lead to compromise. In this situation, then, conflicts are resolved through compromise in terms of specific group interests. Unanimity may be said to be bargained.

Bargained unanimity is implicit in Truman's (1951, p. 392) explanation of unanimous decisions in larger legislative bodies. He suggests that

even where virtual unanimity prevails in the legislature, the process of reconciling conflicting interests must have taken place—though perhaps at an earlier stage wholly or partly outside the legislature and the formal institutions of government. When this happens, the legislature merely registers the decision.

There is the assumption, then, first, that conflict has in fact occurred, but second, that the conflict has been so successfully resolved that it culminates in unanimity.[19]

Projected unanimity. If, on the other hand, group interests are diffuse yet individual interests are specific, the political bargaining process encounters difficulties. The absence of an articulated group interest makes the political game appear to be fragmented and kaleidoscopic. Conflict is not suppressed as it is in the case of false unanimity, and the game is played as in the case of bargained unanimity. But as political decision handling is not altogether formal and contains informal patterns, there is likely to be a tendency to go along with a somewhat fictitious group consensus. The consensus is fictitious because the group interest is not really articulated. How can unanimity be explained in this situation? I shall suggest a hypothesis.

Because group interests are poorly articulated and diffuse, the decisional situation will appear ambiguous to the decision makers. Yet, as there is a pressure for decision—individual specific interests are promoted—some perceptual structuring of the ambiguous situation is needed. Therefore, the individual decision maker will tend to project his own preferred interests on the group as a whole. Not knowing where others stand, such projection provides the individual with a perceptual anchorage point. He expects others to decide in the way in which he himself decides. This psychological ordering of the ambiguous situation involves a great deal of perceptual distortion.[20] But it may have the effect of creating a cognitive environment in which psychological pressure toward a unanimous decision becomes very great. If it is believed that everybody agrees with everybody else, the image of unanimity can serve as a kind of protective screen from responsibility for failure to resolve an issue in those terms in which it was originally defined by the individual with specific interests himself. Unanimity may be said to be projected.

Projected unanimity seems to be implicit in an interesting finding by Crane concerning party cohesion in the Wisconsin legislature. One might surmise that the absence of division in a legislative party is simply a function of legislators' indifference concerning a piece of legislation. Party cohesion, for instance, should occur only in policy matters where the group's interest is specific enough for legislators to feel strongly about the stakes at issue. Yet, Crane (1960, pp. 246–247) reports, "party cohesion was most easily maintained on those issues about which legislators were least concerned and apparently regarded as least important." In other words, cohesion within the parties occurred on unimportant rather than, as one might expect, on important issues. Although we are dealing here with a subgroup rather than the full group, it would seem that in the situation described by Crane we encounter a case of projected unanimity for the subgroups in question. Individually specific interests seem to be surrendered in favor of a psychologically satisfying, if unreal, unanimity.

Functional unanimity. The impact of ministerial decision handling on a situation in which individual interests are diffuse but group interests are specific is likely to produce a kind of unanimity that is compelling because alternatives are drastically reduced. Decision makers, whether themselves in a ministerial position, as judges are, or whether acting on the advice of persons in ministerial positions, as legislators do on recommendations from administrative experts, appeal to and accept "authority" precisely because individual interests, being diffuse, do not intrude strongly on the decision process. At the same time, the specificity of group interests provides an evaluative reference point for what action must be taken. This does not mean that disagreements over group interests do not exist. But they are clarified and resolved in terms of rather impersonal criteria, such as routine, precedent, or specialized knowledge. Unanimity may be said to be functional.

To illustrate functional unanimity, let us shift to judicial decision making. For instance, speaking of the "powerful factors normally operating to achieve unanimity in the decisions of the Supreme Court," Prichett (1948, p. 24) attributes unanimous decisions, among other reasons, to "the generally settled character of the American legal system, fairly strict adherence to the principle of stare decisis, and the broad similarities in training and background which tend to characterize Supreme Court justices . . ." Pritchett also points out that "the influence of a strong and skillful Chief Justice is of great importance in leading to the discovery of solutions satisfactory to all members of the Court."[21] In other words, an issue is resolved by appeal to the authority of precedent.

Analogous to the authority of precedent in judicial decision making is probably the authority of routine in legislative action. In city councils, for instance, routine handling of issues serves as an impersonal criterion for deciding what should or should not be done. Or a legislative group may accept the recommendations of an administrative specialist—an engineer who advises on the location of a bridge, or a city manager. Acceptance of an expert's judgment is presumably based on his professional disinterestedness that stems from his specialized know-how rather than from his personal relations with his clients.

Injunctive unanimity. This is, of course, the behavioral situation that underlies the constitutional unanimity rule. The constitution itself becomes a ministeriallike reference point. Individual interests are so specific and group interests so diffuse that unanimity is the only way of protecting individual interests from each other or preventing the emergence of a collective decision to which individual members cannot subscribe. As suggested earlier, unanimity in this situation may either create deadlock or serve to resolve it. The formal rule of unanimity enjoins the individual members from imposing their specific interests upon each other. Unanimity may be said to be injunctive.

But unanimity of this kind can be present without being constitutionally required. The consensus of the Quaker meeting seems to be of this order. Although formal voting is eschewed, an issue is discussed until a solution emerges to which all individuals can agree or, at least, from which any one individual will not dissent. In the case of the Quaker meeting, the appeal to "conscience" serves as the impersonal criterion for giving or withholding consent. This procedure is functionally equivalent to the constitutional unanimity rule. It is because the process involved is costly and time-consuming that democracy is willing to deviate from the unanimity rule and accept that degree of coercion which majority voting, in the Quaker view, implies.

The typology of unanimity here outlined is probably not exhaustive, for it is necessarily an artifact of the dimensions that were used in constructing it. However, it suggests that unanimity is a multifaceted behavioral phenomenon that cannot be treated as a monomorphic structure. Moreover, the typology seems to be sufficiently comprehensive to accommodate various empirical descriptions of or hypotheses about unanimous voting. We are now in a position to examine the kind of rationality that may be involved in the various types of unanimous decision making.

Criteria of Rationality

As mentioned earlier, one need not start off from the behavioral assumptions of the individualistic theory of rationality in order to use the conditions of constitutional unanimity as criteria in appraising the rationality of unanimous decisions in real-life situations that are not controlled by the formal rule. Let me restate both the assumptions and the conditions for "spontaneous unanimity" (unanimity not constitutionally required) as they have emerged from the discussion, so that they can be referred to in the following appraisal.

Behavioral assumption: There is no necessary conflict between individual and group interests (though there may be), and both individual and group interests can be attained through collective action. Because each participant decision maker expects to attain his individual interests and the interests of the group through collective action, he will accept the costs of unanimity as being less than the costs of deadlock. Unanimity has the effect of making each participant in the decision equal in status and power to every other participant, and it assures him membership in the decisive group.

First condition: A unanimous decision is rational if it is made in a situation that has the potential for free choice among alternative decisional patterns (such as majority voting or dictatorship). This condition states essentially a requirement made of the environment of choice.

Second condition: A unanimous decision is rational if it is consciously chosen from among alternative decisional patterns. This condition states essentially a requirement made of the individual actor.

To what extent, then, do the types of unanimity developed in the previous section conform to the behavioral assumptions and meet the conditions of rationality here specified?

Ancestral unanimity: prerationality. Ancestral unanimity does not seem to invalidate the behavioral assumptions, but it does not satisfy the first condition. The decision-handling structure is such that alternative decisional patterns are not contemplated. The behavioral style of ancestral unanimity seems to be prerational, in the sense that long-standing agreement on unanimity as a way of making collective decisions precludes the availability of alternatives. The consensus is genuine enough, but as there is no potential for free choice among alternative patterns of decision making, it is prerational rather than rational.

False unanimity: counterrationality. In the case of false unanimity, the behavioral assumptions seem to be falsified. There is no guarantee in this situation that individual interests can be achieved through collective action, for they are suppressed in the name of group solidarity. On the other hand, unanimity is chosen as a preferred decisional pattern over alternative patterns, and consciously so. The rationality involved, if it can so be called, is a kind of counterrationality of fear that deters individuals from pursuing certain of their interests and that leads them to act counter to these interests in order to achieve a group interest that is poorly articulated. The consensus of false unanimity is counterrational rather than prerational, as is the consensus of ancestral unanimity.

Bargained unanimity: satisfying rationality. The process that culminates in bargained unanimity seems to meet all the behavioral assumptions as well as the conditions of rationality. However, as the ways of decision handling call for trading, bargaining, and compromise among diffuse individual interests in terms of group-specific interests, the latter are themselves subject to negotiation. The rationality involved is more likely to be of the kind that Simon (1957a, pp. 204–205) calls "satisficing." Therefore, unanimity is by no means the "best" decisional pattern under the circumstances, but it is "good enough" for the attainment of the individual interests at stake. Majority voting might well be a better alternative, but it seems to be consciously ruled out if the participants in the decision-making situation can arrive at a satisfying solution through unanimity. This kind of bargained unanimity, then, is satisficingly rational.

Projected unanimity: irrationality. Projected unanimity fails to meet both conditions of rationality. It gives the participants the impression of being able to attain individual and group interests through collective action without really doing so. The decisional process of projected unanimity seems to stymie the ways of decision handling that one should expect. Because group interests are diffusely articulated, the individual decision maker is left without a stable point of reference for trading, bargaining, and compromising—a situation in which alternative decisional patterns cannot be consciously chosen. The decisional impasse is resolved through unconscious projection of individual upon group interests—a process that violates the behavioral assumptions and is unlikely to attain individual or group interests. Insofar as a decision is unanimously reached in this way, it is irrational in the sense of being accidental or essentially random. Any other decisional pattern is equally plausible.

Functional unanimity: procedural rationality. In situations where the group's interests are specifically articulated and decision handling is largely ministerial, reliance on authority or precedent would seem to make for a kind of rationality that is procedural in appraising the relevance of alternative decisional patterns, given the group's specific and individuals' diffuse interests. Although the process of cumulatively procedural-rational decision making might ultimately tend to reduce alternatives in contravention of the first condition, there is little probability that decisional alternatives in the final stages of decision making will ever be exhausted. Unanimity itself is almost self-evident proof of the procedural rationality involved in the process, for it is likely to occur only after alternative decisional patterns have been consciously eliminated as a result of convincing argument that the choice to be made cannot be anything but unanimous.

Injunctive unanimity: maximizing rationality. Injunctive unanimity presents the situation in which the individual participant with his specifically articulated interests uses his dissent whenever collective action seems to threaten his interests. The rationality involved is essentially maximizing from the individual's point of view. However, injunctive unanimity would seem to falsify our behavioral assumptions. If carried to its ultimate logical conclusion, the attempt to maximize one's individual interests at the expense of the group's interests through unanimity would be self-defeating by creating deadlock, a situation that the rationally maximizing actor does not prefer. Insofar as he prefers some action to deadlock, he will continue to debate an issue until unanimity is reached. Insistence on unanimity in this sense meets both conditions of rationality, for alternative decisional patterns are consciously rejected.

What general observations can be made about the logic of rationality in different unanimous decision-making situations? First of all, only one type—injunctive unanimity—meets the requirements of rationality derived from the classical individualistic conception of the maximizing individual. Because the requirements of maximizing rationality are severe, we should expect that only very few of the spontaneous unanimous decisions reached in the real world of politics would be of the injunctive type. Indeed, the sparse use of the formal unanimity rule in modern circumstances suggests that injunctive unanimity does not recommend itself to rational men except in the most extreme cases where they feel their "vital interests" to be at stake.

Second, only one type of unanimity—projected unanimity—is clearly irrational. It is irrational because unanimity emerges as the outcome of unconscious psychological mechanisms in a situation where one should expect division. Little is known about this type of irrationally projected unanimity, but it should be of considerable empirical research interest. For there is reason to believe that this type of unanimity is not uncommon in large political systems where neither consensual nor ministerial ways of decision handling provide feasible behavioral alternatives.

Third, a distinction must be made between the irrational behavior involved in projected unanimity and the counterrational behavior of false unanimity. The difference is largely due to the two different ways of decision handling, but whereas in projected unanimity the process of decision making remains altogether obscure, in false unanimity it is all too evident. Here decisions are made in self-conscious, if not widely shared, awareness of the consequences that would ensue if the decision makers were to promote their specifically articulated interests. Yet they act purposefully counter to their individual interests in the name of a unity that is largely fictitious. Counterrationality might be thought of as a kind of mixture of prerationality and irrationality, perhaps as a kind of pseudorationality. It approximates both kinds but is precluded from being completely prerational or irrational by virtue of its consciousness of alternatives of decisional patterns.

Fourth, the notion that decisions can be made unanimously in the sense of prerationality, as the concept is used here, should not strike one as particularly novel. That a group's consensually validated ways of doing things have an influence on current behavioral patterns has been widely observed in simple societies, and it has been hypostatized into principle by conservative ideologues who distrust the maxims of utilitarian rationality. That this type of prerational, ancestral unanimity is also found in modern decision-making situations should surprise only those who write off as irrelevant the pertinacity of informal, personal ways of decision handling in complex collectivities.

Fifth, the typology certainly supports the notion that there is a point where the achievement of group interests is halted and circumscribed by the free play of individual interest seeking through trading, bargaining, and compromise. This point is not likely to be the optimal point for either the attainment of group interests or the attainment of individual interests. But it is likely to satisfy the requirements of rational men. The point is reached not through maximizing but through "satisficing" rational conduct. The extent to which the "satisficing"-rational type of bargained unanimity is characteristic of unanimous decision making in real-life politics is unknown. In all probability it is rather rare, for "satisficing" rationality does not require unanimity as a decisional pattern that is preferable to others. Satisfaction of interests can be more readily achieved through plurality or majority decisions.

Finally, the typology identifies procedural rationality as a companion of the kind of unanimity that has been called functional. A great deal of unanimity found in modern legislative bodies, as in judicial and administrative institutions, is procedurally rational. It is a kind of rationality that is "built in," so to speak, the kind of situations where the attainment of interests is sought by reliance on available resources. This has long been recognized in judicial and administrative settings, but the presence of procedural-rational unanimity in more immediately political situations, as those of legislative bodies, would seem to defy the conventional categories of institutional analysis. However, recent research on legislative processes and legislative behavior shows that specialization and reliance on expertise are not alien to primarily political decision making (see Wahlke et al., 1962, pp. 193–215). The notion of procedural-rational unanimity is likely to be fruitful in explaining much of the unanimous decisional outcomes in democratic institutions such as legislatures and other deliberative bodies where, in general, majority voting is the norm.

Unanimity and Democracy

We may return now to the starting point of this inquiry: why unanimity in democratic decision making? Is such unanimity rational? The typology of unanimity suggests that unanimous decisions may be stimulated by the confluence of diverse types of interest articulation and decision handling. From the perspective of interest articulation, the typology intimates that there may be some pressure toward unanimity whenever either group interests are specifically articulated yet individual interests are diffusely articulated, or vice versa. The incidence of these occurrences is an empirical research question. At the same time, different ways of decision handling give unanimity, when it occurs under one or another condition of interest articulation, a characteristic style or format. The task of research is to locate and classify unanimous decisions in terms of the critical ways in which decisions are generally handled in choice-making situations.

What of the rational character of unanimity? Quite clearly, great caution is called for in assessing the kind of rational conduct involved in the various types of unanimity that have been identified. One result of the argument is beyond doubt: the assumption that unanimity in democratic decision making is necessarily irrational does not seem to be warranted. Only one type—projected unanimity—could be called irrational. Other types of unanimity seem to meet various criteria of rationality, while other types are prerational or what I have called counterrational. Even if one were to combine the latter with the irrational type, it would seem that unanimity is not inevitably a deviation from some norm that requires majority voting (or some other decision rule) as the only legitimate form of democratic decision making. Moreover, what was called bargained unanimity is eminently rational in the "satisficing" sense. Unanimity appears to be a legitimate form of democratic decision making, although the kind of rationality involved always requires specification. One might well argue that it is perhaps more difficult to get men in responsible decision-making posts to disagree than to agree, just as in the world of business it seems more difficult to provide for competition that must often be "enforced" in the face of a "natural" inclination toward monopoly. But the central point to be made is that unanimity is not necessarily dysfunctional and symptomatic of a breakdown of the democratic process.

18

Decisional Models

---

in Political Contexts

POLITICAL SCIENCE suffers from a chronic disciplinary malaise. In spite of the advances *we* have made in the last thirty years or so, we are still possessed by some kind of collective sense of timidity—almost a complex, but not quite. We still think we must go (hat in hand) to the social psychologists, sociologists, or economists and, as I have heard so often, "borrow" their theories and methods.

Isn't it about time that—instead of only asking what political scientists can learn *from* the other behavioral sciences, as we have done for so long and continue to do—we should assert what we can significantly contribute *to* the other disciplines? The answer, obviously, must be yes. But this requires that political scientists shed some of their timidity vis-à-vis the other disciplines. A good example is a somewhat forgotten, provocative article by Leoni (1957)—forgotten perhaps because of its unduly polemical (but to me enjoyable) character. The issue here is not whether Leoni is right or wrong but his candor. Among other things, Leoni asked whether "consistency" in decision making is sufficient for specifying rationality if the premises of an action are absurd, illogical, or blind; and he dared to suggest that real-world decision makers do not assign numbers to utilities in the way of the rational choice models of economics. "I suspect," Leoni (1957, pp. 229–230) wrote, "that a certain inferiority felt by non-mathematicians has prevented them from objecting more openly and courageously to some of the procedures and theories adopted by mathematicians (such as Neumann and Morgenstern, 1947) in order to 'describe' or to 'improve' decision-making." The theories of the subjective probability theorists, he acrimoniously continued, "seem to have been invented for their own personal enjoyment." My point is that if we make ourselves more forcefully heard in interdisciplinary circles, perhaps some of the theories and hypotheses of the other behavioral sciences will take a structure and content more immediately germane to the real-world interests of political science than is now the case. To put it in a nutshell: interdisciplinary travel cannot take place on a one-way street.

"Decision making," as used in the literature, is an excellent example to illustrate what I have in mind. Leaving aside for the moment some of the problematic aspects of the concept and its potential utility in the study of politics, one element that political science must contribute to an interdisciplinary understanding of decisional processes is an awareness of the coercive quality of decisions when they are politicized. Lasswell (1955, p. 381), always our teacher when it comes to being perceptive, put it this way:

All decisions are interactions in the social process; and they involve community coercion. The role of coercion is obvious in the case of victory or defeat, in war or revolution. It is less evident in the case of legislation or court decision; however, it is usually assumed that community coercion will be applied against the violator of a statute . . . When speaking technically we may reserve the word "decision" for the choices made in the political process. They involve sanctions (that is, severe actual or potential deprivations).

Now, any social-psychological model of *political* decision making that does not calibrate into its equations degrees of coercion present in both political processes and political outcomes strikes me as utterly useless. Yet I miss references to the coercive aspects of decision making in the relevant literature. Clearly, doing research on the coercive element of decision making would be one of the particular contributions that political science should be expected to make to a generic theory. By bringing this concern and relevant research to the attention of the other behavioral sciences, political science can have some influence on the shape and directions of decision-making analysis in general.

A second example from another perceptive student of politics, pointing in the opposite direction, suggests when decision-making models may *not* be appropriate in studying what may yet appear to be decisional situations. Reviewing the tantalizing findings that the "policy outputs" of American state legislatures seem to be largely determined by socioeconomic or environmental variables, Wahlke (1970, pp. 79–80) draws the implications for the decisional process or, rather, its absence:

One major implication . . . would seem to be that "policy output" is not determined by "legislative decisions" at all. Whatever legislative bodies are doing when they debate and vote on proposals to spend more or less money on this or that program, it is no longer easy to think of them as "deciding" or "choosing" to do so. If their collective action is predictable ultimately from key features of the socioeconomic environment within which the legislature operates—whether or not it is somewhat predictable proximately from elements of the political structure underlying the legislative and other institutions in its particular political system—their individual behavior hardly can be the product of free, voluntary choice among competing demands. Or, at the very least, the linkage between policy demands and policy output is much more complex and circuitous than we have taken it to be hitherto.

In this case, then, bringing "decision making" as a conceptual tool to bear on the analysis would be ill conceived and inappropriate. I shall come back to the question of how one can know (decide?) when a decision is a decision so that it can be subjected to an analysis that makes use of decisional models. Here I want to demur lest I be misunderstood. I am not objecting to studying decision making as an empirical phenomenon where it is appropriate.

However, in advancing the need for a generic approach, I certainly do not want to deny contextual specificities in particular institutional arenas where "decisions" may appear as what they are not or, for that matter, the opposite. I certainly do not mean to imply that all politics is decision making or that, if decision making is absent, there is no politics. The intellectual process involved is reciprocal: just as the formulation of a generic concept like decision making requires derivation from specific decisional events, the latter are dependent for conceptual significance on the former. The generic concept cannot (and must not) be imposed when not contextually appropriate. Again, it seems to me that political scientists interested in the decisional process must bring their knowledge of context to the attention of those other behavioral scientists who may wish to study decision-making processes by experiment or simulation so that they will introduce more realistic parametric constraints than seems to be commonly the practice.

The Problem of Definition

There are different ways of defining things. One method is to say what a thing is not. Before doing this, however, I shall introduce a number of concepts that, most people would agree, belong to a family of terms both similar to and yet sufficiently different from "decision" to facilitate specification. In addition to decision, it seems to me, one tends to think of problem, choice, conclusion, division, judgment, option, preference, resolution, selection, and undoubtedly others. Now, intuitively, these concepts all imply some behavioral situation in which a unit (individual, group, collectivity, and so forth) orders a set of alternatives in some way and acts on this ordering. The act may affect the unit itself or some other unit. Miraculously, perhaps, I have described a behavioral situation that seems to be covered by the family of concepts and that seems to point to an empirical referent without using any of the reference concepts. The question one can ask, therefore, is how decision differs from, say, problem solving, judgment, choice, or conclusion, and so on. I do not propose to make all possible pairwise comparisons, but adduce only a few for the purpose of tentative specification.

Another preliminary step is called for. It seems advantageous to see, at least intuitively, how decision fits into the family of related concepts in terms of an element that is immanent in the concept of decisional decisiveness. The question one asks, then, is how decisive the behavior referred to by the various concepts is likely to be. Using this criterion, I would rank the concepts as follows (without insisting that this is necessarily the most accurate ranking if one were to employ more careful procedures than intuition): problem, preference, option, choice, division, judgment, selection, conclusion, vote, decision. In terms of the decisiveness criterion, the rank order is intended to convey a range that varies from least to most decisive, from broad to narrow, from tentative to final, from open to closed, from abstention to commitment, from least to most sanctioning and sanctioned behavior. I shall leave these words as primitive, undefined terms, trusting common usage to provide their meaning in context.

Now it is quite clear that, despite the very different attributes that can be assigned to the members of our conceptual family, they are often used interchangeably. Space limitations do not permit me to demonstrate it, but few would probably dissent. That the interchange occurs is no longer inexplicable: after all, the concepts do belong to the same family; the usual complaint about the multimeaning nature of social science terms and their ambiguity is evidently rooted, in the present case, in the rich, undifferentiating character of our language. Rather than complaining about this ambiguity, one should take advantage of it or, to put it as Gertrude Stein might have said, "Decision is what you make it." The concepts assigned to the family of which decision is a member mean many different things to many people who, more often than not, do not mean what they seem to say or do not say what they seem to mean.

For the present purpose, I shall limit myself to only a few examples of the use of decision by reference to some of the related concepts. Let me emphasize that I am examining here not the analytic utility of the concept of decision but how it is, in fact, used. In terms of the concept's attributes, it may be interpreted or used as a synonym of problem solving—that is, it may be given very broad meaning. This very broad usage is well articulated by Simon (1966, p. 15). He does not insist on "decision" as a critical keyword in his "decision-making framework":

If I had used the labels "action theory," "game theory," "economic theory," or "influence theory" for what I am about to say, my comments would not be much altered . . . In talking about decision-making, I am dealing not with some highly special aspect of the political process, but with its central core. Voting, legislating, adjudicating, and administering have always been conceived of as decision-making processes.

Simon may get away with so sweeping a gesture, for the world is his oyster, but lesser minds do not so get away. If decision equals action, game, economic, or influence and presumably other labels, it is not a very useful analytic concept in either finding, explaining, or predicting anything. What March (1966, p. 70) concluded about the concept of power—that it "gives us surprisingly little purchase in reasonable models of complex systems of social choice"—might just as well be applied to other, at one time or another fashionable, concepts like system, action, communication, exchange, or decision. The trouble with the frameworks built on and around these concepts is their unboundedness. They are so broad, soft, tentative, open, and noncommital that one must soon ask, indeed, what influence, system, exchange, power, communication, and decision are *not*. In the end, it is true that all social relations partake of the properties to which such generic concepts refer. Not only do the concepts in our family of concepts imply decision, but so do patterns of behavior like loving ("she loves me, she loves me not"), buying, voting, and so on. But if the concept of decision can be applied to so vast a range of social phenomena, it has little analytic utility in understanding any one particular phenomenon. Admittedly, broad generic concepts stimulate theorizing that, to a large extent, depends on metaphors and analogues (and that goes also for the uses of differential equations now so prominent in our computer-sophisticated age). But it makes operationalization of concepts in what presumably interests us—politics and political behavior—extraordinarily difficult.

As one turns to the other end of the continuum that represents our family of concepts—voting—one encounters the opposite difficulty. Here is a concept that refers to a highly identifiable, specific act of behavior about which there appears to be little ambiguity. The concept of voting seems to refer to something hard and narrow, providing finality and closure, commitment and decisiveness. Indeed, it is not unusual to read about "voting decision"—a rather redundant term. But, as we have learned in the last forty years of research on voting (in elections), the apparently simple act of voting is much more complicated than the concept's common meaning implies. Long ago, in their famous study of Erie County, Lazarsfeld and his associates (1944) concluded that the vote is a function of what they called "crystallization," a process over time rather than a "decision" (in the ordinary sense) reached on election day in the voting booth—that it may not be a decisional act at all. Later, the Michigan election researchers (Campbell et al., 1960) came to locate the vote in a "funnel of causality" that threatens to be infinite at one end (more about this later). There are attempts to treat the vote as "decision" in a very narrow sense, and positive theorists, much influenced by either economic theories of rationality or statistical decision theory, find in voting the beginning and end of politics. However, as an early statistical decision theorist (Bross, 1953, p. 263) has pointed out,

the ballot box works well when decisions are relatively non-technical and when the group loyalty is strong enough so that minority voters are willing to stay with the group and accept the majority decision. When the decision is complex and confused, the action of the voters tends to be based on irrelevant issues rather than upon the data relevant to the decision at hand.

This is the reason, the author continues, why one has representative government.

A narrow and finalistic view of voting as decision excludes too much of possible relevance from the field of observation, and it tends to reduce decision to the trivial. In a very interesting book on the behavior of congressmen at the roll-call stage of the legislative process, Matthews and Stimson (1975) seek to justify their use of roll calls as indicators of something they call "normal decision making." They go to great lengths in anticipating the objections of critics who would argue that roll-call analysis deals in trivialities because the "important" decisions are made in different stages and places of the legislative process. In fact, Matthews and Stimson largely persuade me of the correctness of the critics' position, for although their theory of roll-call behavior as involving "cue taking" is not only plausible but well demonstrated, subsuming it under the label of "normal decision making" is something of a lingual trick that does not really say what it says and hides what it does not say. Although there is a good deal of voting on important matters on the floor of the House, there is not much decision making—unless one calls "cue taking" decision making, normal or otherwise. But, again, cue taking takes place in all aspects of life, from buying a piece of soap to what is permissible conduct at a cocktail party to voting. In concentrating on the narrow and evidently decisive end of conceptualization in the context of our family of decision-related concepts, one evidently ends up in the same diffuse state in which one ends up if one begins with an intuitively broad and tentative conceptualization.

I do not wish to be misunderstood in regard to the research by Matthews and Stimson. I think it is well done and significant. I merely want to be explicit about what they are doing. They clearly restrict what they call "normal decision making" to a very limited span of time in the total legislative process—basically, the period from when the bell sounds and congressmen rush to the floor to the moment they cast the vote. It is then when, most often, cue taking evidently occurs (although there may be a late-evening or early-morning telephone call). For all practical purposes, Matthews and Stimson eliminate what is often referred to, as in Holsti's (1976) contribution, as the "predecisional" and "postdecisional" phases of the decision-making process. These terms are suggestive because they seem to give credence to and reinforce the reality of something called "decision." If there is a predecisional phase and a postdecisional phase, there surely must be a decision-making phase and a decision, and it must be possible to identify the temporal boundaries of just when the process moves from the predecisional to the decisional phase and from the latter to the postdecisional phase. I am not familiar enough with the literature to know whether and just how these boundaries have been specified in studies, referred to by Holsti (ibid.), that presume to examine the "entire decision-making process." However, it would seem to me that the broader one's conception of the process assumed to take place, the more ill defined will the boundaries be; and the narrower the conception, the better defined will they be, until one reaches the point in the process where Matthews and Stimson locate, both physically and temporally, "normal decision making."

This explication would seem to clarify why it is that "decision" is so congenial a term to many political and other social scientists. Even though the research using the concept is beset by many operational difficulties, regardless of whether one thinks of decision making as something broad like problem solving or something narrow like voting, there is something so decisive about the concept of "decision" that it almost inevitably imposes itself on the political consciousness. It has the aura of irreversibility and finality (even though decisions can be reversed, and though reversing decisions is more difficult even than making them). Decisions seem to represent the "ultimate" in the political process. In some respects, the concept of decision shares the quality of being a "point of no return" with the concept of power (if it could ever be nailed down for operational use) and even with the classical concept of sovereignty with its emphasis on will and supremacy. There is evidently (but only evidently) something in the political situation that calls out a kind of monistic response and the effort to reduce the great complexity of political life to a single, final act and event. All this is very palpable but, on reflection, full of difficulties that cannot be easily coped with by invoking an intuitively attractive concept. I shall, in the following, briefly touch on some other, but by no means all, of these difficulties.

The Problem of Context

The capacity of the scientific mind to construct the most imaginative models of the real world is both its glory and despair—glory because it permits breaking through what were previously thought to be impenetrable barriers; despair because, by leaving the world of the senses in search of directly unobservables, it all too often loses touch with just the reality it seeks to explain. So it is with decisions and decision making. We are treated to the most intricate mathematical or statistical models that the human mind can invent; we are trained in the manipulation of logically unassailable economic models based on premises of rationality; and we are invited to apply the most minute psychological models of human consciousness in the kinds of situation to which concepts such as problem solving, choice behavior, or decision making can be applied.

Yet, there is the difficulty of determining the relevance of these formulations to the situations or contexts that we conventionally call "political." In fact, the problem of definition is immediately dependent on this difficulty. A definition refers to *what* is to be studied under some conceptual tent, regardless of *how* it is to be used and where. In the case of decision and related concepts, the definitional problem is highly dependent on situation and context, and this is at least one of the reasons why the analytic utility of decision-related constructs is problematic. The sweep of events and contexts of concern to the political scientist are so enormous that it is difficult to see how a unitary conception will ever emerge that would satisfy, say, both the rational choice model builder and the student of electoral or legislative voting. Much of what the latter is concerned with as decision is likely to be circumscribed by such specific parameters that one may well ask what the armory of conceptual tools from statistics, economics, or psychology can contribute to either discovery or explanation. One encounters in this connection the paradox of decisions being treated as nondecisions or nondecisions being treated as decisions (see Bachrach and Baratz, 1963; Wolfinger, 1971; Frey, 1971). Yet, whatever the ontological status of "decisions as nondecisions" or "nondecisions as decisions," one would not want to exclude possibly relevant empirical observations from the domain of political science.

If one moves from modest concerns—such as the behavior of very small institutionalized "decision-making groups" like city councils or even larger groups like state and federal legislatures ("modest," of course, only in the scale of the domain, not theoretical significance)—to the behavior of nations in the world system of international politics, the situational and contextual differences in degrees of freedom and constraints relevant to the application of the concept of decision loom even larger. On first reading Holsti's (1976) informative contribution, I found it rather astounding (and appalling) that in the field of international politics today's research situation in the use of cognitive variables seems to be where the field of voting behavior was when the behavioral revolution, so-called, of thirty-five years ago got under way. On second thought, I am not really very much surprised, given not only the discontinuity in the development of theory and research as well as the fragmentation of the discipline of political science, but also the great range of different contexts in which the discipline works. Having said this, however, let me add that I find it incredible how our colleagues in some of the discipline's subfields are still arguing about things that can surely be subjected to empirical exploration and testing, such as whether the behavior of decision makers is determined by structural features of the context or by ideological considerations, whether the behavior involved is conflictual or bargaining, and so on.

For understandable reasons, Kirkpatrick (1975) does not indicate, in his otherwise extraordinarily exhaustive reviews of the psychological literature relevant to the study of decision making at the individual level, just which theories and models may be most appropriate in what situations or contexts. I am not sufficiently expert in these matters to do anything but raise the question. But I would think that the social-psychological formulations one harnesses—unless one adopts, as some people do, whatever happens to be the latest fashion—will depend on circumstances. Choice behavior (if I may be permitted to change the term, for variety's sake) is surely likely to be determined by different psychological mechanisms or processes in crisis and noncrisis situations, in favorable and unfavorable political conditions, or in small and large collectivities. And if decisions have different semantic and ontological status in elections, legislatures, bureaus, courts, voluntary associations—each constituting quite different institutional contexts—then one would expect different fits for different models in these quite different institutional settings. Certainly, Simon's (1957b) path-breaking work on administrative decision making has had great impact—for better or worse—on the study of political behavior in arenas other than the context of large bureaucratic organizations that he had in mind. For many years the overwhelming numbers of studies of decision processes, whatever the locale of research, were cast in the image of Simon's organizational model wherein goals are assumed to be given and decision making refers to the process of implementation to achieve these goals. I had to discover the problems involved many years ago when first confronting them in the legislative setting. My colleagues and I (Wahlke et al., 1962, pp. 378–379) later wrote:

Indeed, the decisional model, at least as borrowed from organization theory, does not really seem applicable to the legislative process, even if the latter calls for decision making. In organizational theory a decision involves a choice of a preferred project from among a number of clearly specified and numerically limited alternative projects. But in the legislative process it is often by no means clear what the alternatives are. In fact, it is one of the objectives of the legislative process to evolve and identify alternatives, and the whole process is much less rational than the organizational decision-making model assumes. The legislative process is political precisely because the choices facing legislators may be ill defined.

Having had this insight, it seemed to us that "the notion of the legislature as a decisional system tends to limit the focus of inquiry more than seems appropriate . . . The decisional approach ignores the fact that a good deal of legislative behavior does not involve decision making at all," and so on.

I would insist, therefore, that the application of social-psychological models should vary from context to context—a role-taking model may be most appropriate in the legislative context, a memory model in the judicial setting, a problem-solving model in the administrative situation, an attitudinal model in electoral voting, a cognitive perception model in international affairs, and so on. In short, and especially in response to rational decision-making models, the usefulness of decision-related sociological concepts and psychological theories cannot be determined by analytic or deductive logic. Their utility can be ascertained only in contexts where synthetic propositions referring to empirical reality can be verified or falsified. Specifying the appropriateness of particular psychological models to particular events or contexts clearly remains on the agenda of conceptual inventory making.

The Problems of Unit and Level

The demand for contextual treatment of decision-relevant concepts and models calls attention to the problems of unit and level of analysis. As I have written about this elsewhere (see Chapters 2–4), I shall be brief. That the unit of decision-making analysis has to be either an individual person or a more or less large group of persons can be taken for granted; what cannot be taken for granted is whether the logical or psychological processes characterizing the individual decision maker are transferable to group-decisional situations. This is, of course, not much of a problem for the rational choice decision-making models derived from economics. Group decisions are largely aggregated results of individually rational persons, although there are complicating results, like the Arrow paradox (1951), that keep rational choice modelers both funded and busy.

However, there is trouble in this connection, occasioned not so much by methodological assumptions about the individual person as by the inferences made from the individualistic model to collective decision making. Riker and Ordeshook (1973, pp. 33–34), for instance, make this reasonable statement:

Individual preferences and the choices that reveal them have social consequences. Indeed, these consequences together make up the social environment and are in fact social institutions. As such they stand behind all individual action. Hence individual choice is not independent of prior social choice, which itself originated in individual choice. Certain selected and enforced social choices are, therefore, the causes as well as the effects of individual persons' acts.

But from this premise, with which no empirical contextualist would disagree, they come to the amazing conclusion that "this inexorable relationship between individual and social choice dispels any possibility of a satisfactory distinction between individual and collective decision-making." In one fell swoop Riker and Ordeshook deny that organizations, institutions, or macrostructures generally have properties that cannot be reduced to the level of individuals. They have no level-of-analysis problem because they recognize no autonomous units other than individual persons. What they do, in fact, is to assume a conceptual isomorphism between individual and group decision making. But the existence of such an isomorphism is yet to be proved and cannot simply be assumed. *Political* decision-making processes at the level of collectivities are not just economic markets, and whatever may be true (in theory) of markets is not necessarily true of political situations and contexts.

There is a stimulating discussion by Holsti (1976, p. 16) where he refers to the argument that analysis of "international behavior" at the level of the individual decision maker is uneconomical because more of the variance can be accounted for at other, presumably "higher," levels of social organization. Apart from role, institutional, and other constraints limiting the individual's cognitive possibilities, there is the argument that "there is little variance among leaders with respect to their decision-making behavior in any given circumstances." Alas, if the latter were, in fact, true (something that can be empirically demonstrated), the argument would indeed favor macrolevel analysis, but only *after* it has been conducted at the microlevel of the individual. For if there is no or little variance at the microlevel, it legitimizes and facilitates the aggregation of cognitions at the collective level of a decision-making group. The argument about variance here creates a false dualism. Macroanalysis is, in fact, strengthened and not weakened by microanalysis if there is little variance at the microlevel. If there were a great deal of variance at the microlevel, it would threaten the whole enterprise of treating collectivities as autonomous units at their own level of analysis. I suspect that opponents of microanalysis indeed expect more variance at the microlevel than they are willing to admit; and if this is true, it requires more cautious analysis than has been traditionally undertaken at the macrolevel, especially in a field like international politics. Holsti is, of course, dubious about the homogeneity-of-belief hypothesis that macroanalysts seem to cherish about behavior at the microlevel. The study of political behavior, on whatever level it is conducted, must be *meaningful* to the political science observer who is not simply some randomly picked person or a psychologist or an economist. For the political scientist, political behavior, including decisional behavior, takes place in a context that is invariably macro in character, for the political process or governance begins when two persons stand in a relationship to each other, and that relationship is macro. If one can construct this context out of observations made about the individual participants' behavior at the microlevel, one is all the better off analytically when one wants to establish micro-macro linkages. Without some macroconstruct meaningful to the scientific observer, the microperspective on decision making or any other form of political conduct is theoretically rootless. At this point, I do miss in the quest for cognitive approaches to decision making an explicit statement of just how work at the microlevel comes to be relevant to the macroconcerns of political science, and how these macroconcerns can serve as guides in specifying microvariables that presumably explain the decision process in given contexts and decision outcomes in given situations.

The feasibility of using microanalytic data about the voting patterns of individuals, in order to construct decisional structures and processes at the macrolevel, has been demonstrated by Eulau and Prewitt (1973). The concept of "decisional structure" formulated and operationalized by these researchers for the purpose of comparing the behavior of groups as integral units is yet to be applied to units larger than the small groups they studied. However, it is a good example of how microlevel data relevant to decision making can be meaningfully used at the macrolevel of inquiry into decision making. Such macrolevel construction can go a long way in making microanalytic, psychology-based models of decision-making behavior relevant to political institutions and processes.

The burden of this essay has been that the concept of "decision" and the family of words associated with it are, on the one hand, not specific enough to have much analytic utility and, on the other hand, not generic enough to permit building a more general conceptual framework sufficiently different from other frameworks (like system, action, or merely governance) to warrant excessive investment of definitional effort. However, if the concept and derivative models *are* used, they ought to be contextually relevant and sensitive to the level-of-analysis problem. To these caveats I want to add a final one: given the concept's ambiguity (which really does not bother me much, if caution is used), one should not burden it with more interpretative ballast than it can carry. This seems to happen when research in political science is exposed to interdisciplinary fertilization. Because our own work can be greatly enriched by steeping ourselves in other disciplines, it does not follow, as Kirkpatrick (1975) seems to assume, that there will be movement from general bodies of theory to specific operationalization. For one thing, I do not believe that this is what actually happens in research. Rather, one finds oneself confronted with very specific operational tasks and then desperately looks for a body of theory.

Is what one thinks to be a decision, in fact, a decision; and how can one find out? How does one know that what appears to be the outcome of a decision is, in fact, such an outcome and not simply the outcome of antecedent or contemporary events? What theory should one apply? It is quite easy to call on Bayesian statistics where the concept of decision serves to test the null hypothesis. But rejecting the null hypothesis at some theoretically specified level of confidence is different from applying a similar notion to the real world of decision making. Moreover, as I must often tell my students, statistical significance is not theoretical significance, which depends on the tradition and development of political theory and not on statistics. This mode of thinking does not help us determine when a decision is a decision or when an outcome is a *decisional* outcome.

The reason why I hesitate to accept decision as a master concept is my suspicion that it will not help us circumvent the pitfall of infinite regression, which is also characteristic of concepts like power or conflict and many others *when they are used in attempts to create single, comprehensive organizing frameworks*. Defining politics as "authoritative allocation of values" or as involving "binding decisions" and then putting all of politics into some input-output "system model" gets us back to exactly where the analysis of power left us. At least I know of no persuasive empirical evidence that decision-related hypotheses would escape the fact of infinite regression. As soon as we ask about the premises of decisions or the premises underlying particular decision rules and so on, we are, in fact, stepping backward into infinity because the premises we are looking for are themselves the products of decisions in some more distant logical or temporal past. And those decisions have their premises ad infinitum.

19

Components of Representational

Responsiveness

WITH THE PUBLICATION in 1963 of "Constituency Influence in Congress" by Miller and Stokes, the direction was set for a novel approach to the study of political representation.[1] The virtue of this original study notwithstanding, the approach had some quite unexpected consequences for subsequent theoretical development and empirical research. Much of this development and research was due less to the impact of Miller and Stokes's innovative approach as such than to its vulgarization. The questions addressed here are two: first, we propose to unravel the continuing puzzle of representation, which was probably made even more puzzling by the thoughtless use of the concept of "congruence" that Miller and Stokes had introduced into discourse about representation; and second, we propose to explicate the concept of "responsiveness" by decomposing it into four components that seem to correspond to four targets of representation.

The Miller-Stokes Model

Miller and Stokes themselves were well aware of the broader context of theory and research on representation,[2] but the focus of their particular analysis was a more limited one than "representation." They were interested in the degree to which "constituency control," rather than "party voting," determined congressional roll-call behavior: "The fact that our House of Representatives . . . has irregular party voting does not of itself indicate that Congressmen deviate from party in response to local pressures" (1963, p. 45). The analysis addressed an old question: which factor, party or constituency, contributes more to variance in roll-call voting (all

---

Written with Paul D. Karps.

other things being equal)? The question had been previously asked in numerous studies relying, of necessity, on aggregate surrogate indicators of presumed district predispositions, most of them demographic or ecological.[3]

Miller and Stokes's research was a giant stride in the study of representation because it freed analysis from dependence on surrogate variables as indicators of constituency attitudes or predispositions. Miller and Stokes interviewed a sample of congressional constituents (voters and nonvoters) and their respective congressmen (as well as nonincumbent candidates), whose attitudes in three broad issue domains they compared with each other, with congressmen's perceptions of constituency attitudes, and with corresponding roll-call votes. Their tool of analysis was the product moment correlation coefficient, and their mode of treatment was "causal analysis," which was then being introduced into political science. Miller and Stokes found the relationships among the variables of their model to vary a good deal from issue area to issue area, being strongest in the case of civil rights, weaker in the case of social welfare, and weakest in the case of foreign involvement. They concluded:

The findings of this analysis heavily underscore the fact that no single tradition of representation fully accords with the realities of American legislative politics. The American system *is* a mixture, to which the Burkean, instructed-delegate, and responsible-party models all can be said to have contributed elements. Moreover, variations in the representative relation are most likely to occur as we move from one policy domain to another. (Ibid., p. 56)

We have no quarrel with this general conclusion concerning the American system. We are bothered by the definition of what Miller and Stokes call "the representative relation" and its operational expression. This "relation" is the similarity or, as it is also called, the "congruence" among the four variables of the causal model that serves the purposes of analysis.[4] This specification of congruence as the expression of the representative relation has had great influence on later researchers, both those working in the tradition of, or with the data made available by, the Michigan group and those working independently with fresh data of their own.[5] The concern here is not this influence as such but rather the gradual erosion of alternative theoretical assumptions about representation, of which Miller and Stokes themselves are fully cognizant. As a result of this erosion, what for Miller and Stokes (ibid., p. 49) was only "a starting point for a wide range of analyses" became an exclusive definition of representation: high congruence was interpreted as evidence of the presence of representation, and low congruence was taken as proof of its absence.

Whatever congruence may be symbolizing, it is not a self-evident measure of representation. Later researchers, poorly tutored in theories and practices of representation, tended to ignore this. Miller and Stokes, in order to use congruence as a measure, had stipulated three conditions for constituency influence or control. First, control in the representational relationship can be exercised through recruitment—constituents choose that representative who shares their views so that, by following his "own convictions," the representative "does his constituents' will." Second, control can be obtained through depriving the representative of his office—the representative follows "his (at least tolerably accurate) perceptions of district attitude in order to win re-election." And third, "the constituency must in some measure take the policy views of candidates into account in choosing a Representative" (ibid., pp. 50–51).

The electoral connection is, of course, only one of the links between representative and represented. And it should by no means be taken for granted that it is the most critical, the most important, or the most effective means to ensure constituency influence on or control over public policies and the conduct of representatives. It is so only if one or all of the conditions for constituency control specified by Miller and Stokes are satisfied. This is also precisely the reason why attitudinal or perceptual congruence is not an exclusive measure of representation; it is simply the "starting point," as Miller and Stokes knew, in the puzzle of representation. Anyone who has the least sensitivity to the representative process recognizes that representatives are influenced in their conduct by many forces or pressures or linkages other than those arising out of the electoral connection and should realize that restricting the study of representation to the electoral connection produces a very limited vision of the representational process. Miller and Stokes themselves were eminently aware of this, as their conclusion indicated. Yet, only three years after publication of their analysis, when two other analysts (Cnudde and McCrone, 1966), subjecting the Miller and Stokes data to an alternative causal analysis, found no support for recruitment as a condition of representation, constituency control was reduced to a purely psychological function in the representative's mind, and the danger of limiting the "representative relation" to attitudinal and perceptual congruence was demonstrated. Moreover, these analysts altogether ignored Miller and Stokes's important third condition for constituency influence through the electoral connection: constituents' taking account of the candidate's policy views in choosing the representative.

Indeed, Miller and Stokes themselves had the most trouble with this last condition. The overwhelming evidence of their research and that of others denies the condition: most citizens are not competent to perform the function that the model assumes—that elections are in fact effective sanctioning mechanisms in the representational relationship. Miller and Stokes gave a number of "reasons" for why representatives seem to be so sensitive about their voting records—for if voters do not know the record, this sensitivity is surely puzzling. They suggested that the voting record may be known to the few voters who, in close contests, make the difference between victory or defeat, and that the congressman is "a dealer in increments and margins." They also speculated that the voting record may be known to opinion leaders in the district who serve as gatekeepers and conveyors of evaluation in a two-step flow of communication. But there is no evidence for this in their own research.[6]

The Crisis in Representational Theory

It would not yield further theoretical dividends to review in any detail the empirical studies of representation that, in one way or another, are predicated on the attitudinal-perceptual formulation of congruence that had served Miller and Stokes as a starting point but that, for most of their successors, became a terminal point. Most of these studies are distinguished by lack of historical-theoretical knowledge of representation and of independent theoretical creativity. In particular, they are cavalier in regard to a number of dilemmas that, by the middle sixties, had forced themselves on the attention of scholars interested in theoretical understanding of the problem of representation. That these dilemmas were articulated by different scholars at about the same time was probably coincidental, but the coincidence is important because it emphasized the possibility of alternative research directions.

First, representational theory made assumptions about citizen behavior that were negated by the empirical evidence. Wahlke, examining the role of the represented in the representational relationship, concluded that the evidence did not justify treating citizens as significant sources of policy demands, positions, or even broad orientations that could be somehow "represented" in the policy-making process. Citizens simply lack the necessary information for effective policy choices to be communicated to their representatives, even if they were to make the effort to communicate. This being the case, Wahlke concluded that the "simple demand-input model" of representation was deficient. This is, of course, precisely the model that Miller and Stokes had in fact constructed in order to organize and explain their data. Wahlke (1971) suggested that a "support-input model" might be more appropriate.[7]

Second, given the limited capacity of the represented to formulate policy, a viable theory could no longer ignore the asymmetry of the representational relationship. Eulau suggested, therefore, that research should proceed from the structural assumption of a built-in status difference between representative and represented in which the former rather than the latter give direction to the relationship. Representational theory would have to deal with the tensions arising out of status differentiation rather than deny their existence (Eulau, 1967). Once status is introduced as a variable into the representational equation, the model of the representational relationship can be recursive, and the causal ordering of the relevant variables is likely to be reversed.

Finally, in a linguistic study of the concept of representation, Pitkin (1967) found the traditional theories of representation flawed. She advanced the proposition that representation, referring to a social relationship rather than to an attribute of the individual person, could be meaningfully conceptualized only as a systemic property. Representation might or might not emerge at the level of the collectivity, the criterion of emergence being the collectivity's potential for "responsiveness." Political representation "is primarily a public, institutionalized arrangement involving many people and groups, and operating in the complex ways of large-scale social arrangements. What makes it representation is not any single action by any one participant, but the over-all structure and functioning of the system, the patterns emerging from the multiple activities of many people" (ibid., pp. 221–222). Moreover, after considering every conceivable definition, Pitkin concluded that political representation means "acting in the interest of the represented, in a manner responsive to them" (ibid., p. 209). However, there is also the stipulation that the representative "must not be found persistently at odds with the wishes of the represented without good reason in terms of their interest, without a good explanation of why their views are not in accord with their interests" (ibid., pp. 209–210).

Pitkin's formulation creates many measurement problems for empirical research. Concepts like "wishes," "good reason," "interest," or "views" are difficult to operationalize. She provides no clues as to how "responsiveness" as a systemic property of the political collectivity can be ascertained and how, indeed, it can be measured in ways enabling the scientific observer to conclude that representation has in fact emerged at the level of the political system. Pitkin's treatment seems to stress the condition in which the representative stands ready to be responsive when the constituents do have something to say. A legislature may, therefore, be responsive whether or not there are specific instances of response. In other words, Pitkin emphasized a potential for response rather than an act of response. There are considerable difficulties in empirically working with a concept stressing the possibility of an act rather than the act itself. Moreover, the formulation ignores Wahlke's injunction to jettison the demand-input model. Nevertheless, Pitkin's work had an almost immediate and profound effect on subsequent empirical research (see Prewitt and Eulau, 1969; Muller, 1970; Peterson, 1970).

Research on representation following the watershed year of 1967 has taken two major innovative routes. First, taking their cue from Wahlke's critique of the demand-input model that makes fewer requirements on the capacity of the represented to play a role in the representational process. However, their model continues to be based on congruence assumptions. Their analysis, conducted at the level of the individual, largely consists of comparison of the represented and representational elites in terms of relevant attitudes, perceptions, and behavior patterns.

Second, taking a cue from Pitkin, Eulau and Prewitt (1973) transformed data collected at the level of individuals into grouped data and conducted their analysis of representation at the macrolevel of small decision-making groups (city councils). In contrast to Patterson and his associates, Eulau and Prewitt stressed actual rather than potential response to constituent inputs, whether of the demand or support variety. In retrospect, it appears, they were harnessing "reactive" behavior rather than responsive behavior in Pitkin's sense, for they ignored the direction of the response—whether it was in fact "in the interest of" the constituents at the focus of representation. But these retrospective musings only suggest that the problem of conceptualizing representation in terms of responsiveness remains on the agenda of theory and research. As Loewenberg (1972, p. 12) summed up the situation:

Representation . . . is an ill-defined concept that has acquired conflicting meanings through long use. It may be employed to denote any relationship between rulers and ruled or it may connote responsiveness, authorization, legitimation, or accountability. It may be used so broadly that any political institution performs representative functions or so narrowly that only an elected legislature can do so. To a surprising extent, the Burkean conceptualization of the representative function is still in use, and Eulau's call for a concept adequate to modern concerns about the relationship between legislators and their constituencies has not been answered.

Responsiveness as Congruence

Although the expectations or behavioral patterns to which the term "responsiveness" refers were implicit in the concept of "representative government,"[8] the term as such had not been used by Miller and Stokes or others as the defining characteristics of representation. By 1967, when Pitkin's work was published, the term struck an attractive chord as the ideals of "participatory democracy" were once more being revived in neopopulist movements that had intellectual spokesmen in the social sciences.

Even though one should not expect a close affinity between the vocabulary of participation and the vocabulary of representation on logical-theoretical grounds, a term like "responsiveness" stemming from considerations of representative democracy could easily blend in with considerations of participatory democracy. When analysts of political participation like Verba and Nie came to pay attention to empirical work on representation, they had little trouble in linking, by way of an adaptation of the assumption of congruence, the concept of responsiveness to their work on participation. Interestingly, although they did not cite or refer to Pitkin's linguistic analysis, Verba and Nie found, on the one hand, that "responsiveness, as far as we can tell, rarely has been defined precisely, almost never has been measured, and never has been related to participation" (1972, p. 300). On the other hand, they acknowledged Miller and Stokes, who had not used the term: "Miller and Stokes in their analysis of the relationship between constituency attitudes and Congressmen, do deal with responsiveness in ways similar to ours" (ibid., p. 300n3).

Indeed, in examining and seeking to explain the effects of different degrees of citizen participation on the responsiveness of community leaders, Verba and Nie (ibid., p. 302) present a rechristened version of the congruence assumption of representation, which they call "concurrence":

Our measure of congruence depends on how well the priorities of the citizens and the leaders match. Several types of concurrence are possible . . . our measure of the concurrence between citizens and community leaders measures the extent to which citizens and leaders in the community choose the same "agenda" of community priorities.

But they immediately raise the critical problem of causality: "whether we have the warrant to consider our measure of *concurrence* to be a measure of responsiveness. Just because leaders agree with citizens and that agreement increases as citizens become more active, can we be sure that it is citizen activity that is causing leaders to *respond* by adopting the priorities of the citizen?" (ibid., p. 304).

In order to test for the causal relationship, Verba and Nie compared the correlation coefficients obtained for the relationship between "citizen activeness" and concurrence, on the one hand, and between "leader activeness" and concurrence, on the other hand. Finding that the correlation for citizens are "much stronger" than those for leaders, Verba and Nie concluded that their measure of concurrence "seems to be a valid measure of responsiveness to leaders" (ibid., pp. 331–332). But this mechanical comparison is not a test of causality at all in regard to the direction of responsiveness. In fact, it amounts to a false interpretation of the data. The correlations for citizens simply mean that more active citizens see things (priorities to be done in the community) more as leaders do than is the case with less active citizens; the correlations for leaders simply mean that the more active leaders see things more as citizens do than is the case with less active leaders. The strength of the coefficients, all of which are positive for both citizens and leaders, does not prove anything about the direction of causality—whether citizens influence leaders or leaders influence citizens, or whether citizens are responsive to leaders or leaders to citizens. It cannot be otherwise because Verba and Nie's measure of concurrence, like Miller and Stokes's measure of congruence, is neutral as to direction and requires that the direction of the relationships involved in the model be theoretically stipulated. There is no such stipulation in the Verba and Nie application of the concurrence measure to the question of linkage between leaders and led.

Causal analysis, then, does not free the analyst from defining his terms— be they power and influence, or responsiveness—in advance and stipulating the direction of expected relationships in advance.[9] The mechanical application of statistical tests of a possible causal structure does not necessarily model real-world relationships if the operational definitions of the model's components make no theoretical sense. Verba and Nie's two-edged use of responsiveness, operationalized in terms of the directionless concept of concurrence, is intrinsically characterized by ambiguity. If concurrence is a measure of responsiveness of leaders to citizens, it cannot be a measure of responsiveness of citizens to leaders. If one were to take their comparison of the correlations between participation and concurrence for citizens and leaders as an indication of anything, it would have to be that leaders are responsive to citizens and citizens are responsive to leaders, varying in degree with degree of participation.

Pitkin, it was noted, had raised the importance of responsiveness as the critical characteristic of representation, but she had left the term undefined. Representatives, in order to represent, were to be responsive to their constituents, but Pitkin did not specify the content or target of responsiveness. Verba and Nie had taken a step forward by specifying public policy issues as the target of responsiveness. In focusing exclusively on congruence or concurrence in regard to policy attitudes or preferences, they ignored other possible targets in the relationship between representatives and represented that may also give content to the notion of responsiveness. By emphasizing only one component of responsiveness as a substantive concept, they reduced a complex phenomenon like representation to one of its components and substituted the component for the whole. But if responsiveness is limited to one component, it cannot capture the complexities of the real world of politics. It is necessary, therefore, to view responsiveness as a complex, compositional phenomenon that entails a variety of possible targets in the relationship between representatives and represented. How else could one explain that representatives manage to stay in office in spite of the fact that they are *not* necessarily or always responsive to the represented as the conception of representation as congruence or concurrence of policy preferences requires?

It deserves mention that Miller and Stokes had themselves realized that there are possible targets of responsiveness other than policy issues. They emphasized the "necessity of specifying the acts *with respect to which* one actor has power or influence or control over another" (1963, p. 48). Their target, they conceded, was only the set of issues lying within the three policy areas of civil rights, social welfare, and foreign involvement. But significantly they added, "We are not able to say how much control the local constituency may or may not have over *all* actions of its Representative, and there may well be pork-barrel issues or other public matters of peculiar relevance to the district on which the relation of Congressman to constituency is quite distinctive" (ibid., p. 48). Miller and Stokes did not specify what they referred to as "other public matters." It is the task of the rest of this discussion to suggest what some of these other targets of responsiveness might be.

Components of Responsiveness

There are four possible components of responsiveness that, as a whole, constitute representation. While each component can be treated as an independent target of responsiveness, all four must be considered together in the configurative type of analysis that, it seems to us, the complexity of the representational nexus requires. The first component is, of course, *policy responsiveness,* where the target is the great public issues that agitate the political process. Second, there is *service responsiveness,* which involves the efforts of the representative to secure particularized benefits for individuals or groups in his constituency. Third, there is *allocation responsiveness,* which refers to the representative's efforts to obtain benefits for his constituency through pork-barrel exchanges in the appropriations process or through administrative interventions. Finally, there is what we shall call *symbolic responsiveness,* which involves public gestures of a sort that create a sense of trust and support in the relationship between representative and represented. It is possible that there are other targets of responsive conduct that, in composition with the four here tapped, constitute the matrix of representational relationships. But the main point we are trying to make is this: responsiveness refers not just to "this" or "that" target of political activity on the part of the representative but to a number of targets.

Only when responsiveness is viewed as a compositional phenomenon can the approach to representation-as-responsiveness recommended by Pitkin be useful. It is the configuration of the component aspects of responsiveness that might yield a viable theory of representative government under modern conditions of societal complexity.

POLICY RESPONSIVENESS

How the representative and the represented interact with respect to the making of public policy lies at the heart of most discussions of responsiveness. Responsiveness in this sense refers to the structure in which district positions on policy issues, specified as some measure of central tendency or dispersion, are related to the policy orientation of the representative—attitudinal or perceptual—and to his subsequent decision-making conduct in a given field of policy.

The premise underlying the specification of policy responsiveness is the presence of a meaningful connection between constituent policy preferences or demands and the representative's official behavior. This is what Miller and Stokes called "congruence" and what Verba and Nie called "concurrence." Whatever the term, the operational definition is the same: if the representative and his constituency agree on a particular policy, no matter how the agreement has come about, then the representative is responsive. There are, as has been noted, several problems with the model of representation built on the operationalization of responsiveness as congruence, notably the problem that congruence is neither a necessary nor a sufficient condition for responsiveness. The representative may react to constituency opinion and hence evince congruent attitudes or behavior, yet not act in what is in the best interest of the constituency as he might wish to define that interest, thereby being in fact unresponsive. Further, the representative may make policy in response to groups and interests other than his constituents, including executive and bureaucratic agencies. Whether such conduct is also in the interest of his district as he sees it is an empirical question. But whatever the formulation and findings, it cannot be denied that policy responsiveness is an important component of representation.

The notion of policy responsiveness is implicit in some of the classical theories of representation. First of all, the controversy over mandate versus independence, whether the representative is a delegate or a trustee, though considered obsolete by Eulau (1967, pp. 78–79) and in many respects resolved by Pitkin (1967, pp. 144–167), is still intriguing and relevant to the present discussion. For the debate is over whether the representative should act according to what *he* thinks is in the "best interest" of the constituency, regardless of constituency "wants," or whether he should follow the "expressed wishes" of the district, regardless of how he personally feels. The debate really turns on the competence of the citizenry in matters of public policy. For while the citizenry may know what it wants, it may not know what it needs. Second, therefore, an appropriate definition of policy responsiveness will be related to the classical issue of "district interest" as against "district will." There is no denying that the notion of policy responsiveness pervades empirical research on legislative decision making, even when the issue of representation as a theoretical one is not raised. (For recent research, see Turner and Schneier, 1970; Kingdon, 1973; Clausen, 1973; Jackson, 1974; Matthews and Stimson, 1975.) However, precisely because this is the case, it is important not to ignore other components of responsiveness in the representational relationship. Exclusive emphasis on the policy aspects of responsiveness may give a one-sided view and may not help in solving the puzzle of representation.

SERVICE RESPONSIVENESS

A second target for responsiveness to define the representational relationship concerns the nonlegislative services that a representative actually performs for individuals or groups in his district. Service responsiveness, then, refers to the advantages and benefits that the representative is able to obtain for particular constituents. There are a number of services that constituents may expect and that the representative considers an intrinsic part of his role. Some of them involve only modest, if time-consuming, requests, such as responding to written inquiries involving constituents' personal concerns or facilitating meetings and tours for visitors from the home district. Newsletters or columns in local newspapers may be used to inform constituents of legislation that may be of interest and use to them. Much of this work is routine and carried out in regular fashion.

Another link in the chain of service responsiveness is often referred to as case work (see Clapp, 1963). Given his official position and presumed influence, the representative is in a position to solve particular problems for members of his constituency. The representative intervenes between constituents and bureaucrats in such matters as difficulties with a tax agency, delays in welfare payments, securing a job in government, and so on. Providing constituent services and doing case work constitute for many representatives more significant aspects of their representational role than does legislative work like bill drafting or attending committee hearings. These "errand boy" functions deserve more theoretical attention than they have been given in contemporary research. In some important situations the representative may actually serve as an advocate and even lobbyist for special interests in his district vis-à-vis the legislature, departmental bureaucracies, or regulatory agencies. This type of responsiveness is indeed crucial in trying to understand modern representative government.

This notion of service responsiveness seemed to underlie Eulau and Prewitt's (1973, pp. 424–427, 649–650) operational definition of responsiveness. In their study of San Francisco Bay Area city councils, they initially divided these small representative bodies into those that seemed to be somehow responsive to constituent needs or wants and those that did not seem to be responsive. They then distinguished among the former councils those that were responsive to important standing interests in the community or attentive publics, and those that more often were responsive only to temporary alliances having a particular grievance or request. This conception of responsiveness, then, is based on the kind of group or individuals whom the representative perceives as being primarily served by his activities. Zeigler and Jennings (1974, pp. 77–94), in a study of school boards, present a similar conception of responsiveness, conceptually distinguishing more sharply between "group responsiveness" and "individualized responsiveness." Both of these research teams, then, defined responsiveness in terms of the significant recipients of representational services.

That service responsiveness is an important element in representation should be apparent. Moreover, there is every reason to believe that it is increasing rather than declining. Until the middle sixties, it was generally assumed that case work and the advocacy of special interests bring advantages and benefits only to those who take the initiative in soliciting the representative's help. But as Fiorina (1977, p. 180) has pointed out, at least with reference to the federal level, increased bureaucratic activity in the wake of increased federal largesse to all kinds of population groups has also motivated congressmen to "undoubtedly stimulate the demand for their bureaucratic fixit services." The representative does not just respond to demands for his good offices and services; he has become a kind of hustler who advertises and offers them on his own initiative.[10]

This explication of service responsiveness has been entirely focused on the relationship between the representative and particular constituents. The representative can also be responsive in his unique role as a middleman in the allocation of more generalized benefits. We refer here to what has been traditionally called "pork-barrel politics" and to what we shall refer, for lack of a better term, as "allocation responsiveness." Both service responsiveness, whether initiated by the representative or not, and allocation responsiveness, which is always initiated by him, are important elements of representational behavior and important pillars in the representational relationship.

ALLOCATION RESPONSIVENESS

It has long been recognized that pork-barrel politics in legislative allocations of public projects involves advantages and benefits presumably ac-
cruing to a representative's district as a whole. Although traditionally these
allocations were seen as "public goods," with the expansion of the government's role in all sectors of society—industry, agriculture, commerce,
health, education, welfare, internal security, and so on—the distinction
between public and private benefits is difficult to maintain. Again, as Fiorina (1977, p. 180) has felicitously put it in connection with federal politics,
"The pork-barreler need not limit himself to dams and post offices. There
is LEAA money for the local police; urban renewal and housing money
for local officials; and educational program grants for the local education
bureaucracy. The congressman can stimulate applications for federal assistance, put in a good word during consideration, and announce favorable
decisions amid great fanfare." Such allocations may benefit the district as
a whole, or they may benefit some constituents more than others because
they make more use of the benefits. The critical point to be made is that
in being responsive as an "allocator," whether in the legislative or the
bureaucratic processes, the representative seeks to anticipate the needs of
his clients and, in fact, can stimulate their wants.

Legislators' committee memberships sometimes serve as indicators of
allocation responsiveness, as revealed in Fenno's (1973) studies of legislative conduct in committees of the U.S. House of Representatives. A
representative from a district that has a particular stake in a committee's
jurisdiction will often seek a post on a parent committee but also on a
particularly suitable subcommittee; such membership presumably enables
him to act in a manner responsive to the best interests of his district and
some or all of his constituents.

However, one cannot automatically assume that a legislator serving on
a committee "not relevant" to his district is necessarily unresponsive and
not interested in securing allocations. Legislators often seek preferment
on important committees like Rules, Appropriations, or Ways and Means
not because these committees are directly "relevant" to the interests of
their constituents, but because they place members in positions of power
and influence vis-à-vis administrative agencies that distribute benefits, such
as the Army Corps of Engineers, the Park Service, or the Veterans Administration. These secondary bonds are probably as critical in securing benefits
for the district as are the primary bonds resulting from "relevant" committee assignments. However, the secondary bonds have less symbolic
value than do the primary bonds. And symbolic payoffs, we shall see, are
an important fourth component of representational responsiveness.

SYMBOLIC RESPONSIVENESS

The fourth component of responsiveness is more psychologically based than the others. The first three components all somehow tap a behavioral aspect of representation: policy responsiveness is oriented toward the decision-making behavior of the representative in matters of public controversy, while service and allocation responsiveness are oriented toward particularized or collective benefits obtained through the acts of the representative. The representational relationship is, however, not only one of such concrete transactions but also one that is built on trust and confidence expressed in the support that the represented give to the representative and to which he responds by symbolic, significant gestures in order to, in turn, generate and maintain continuing support.

The notion of symbolic responsiveness has been alluded to by Wahlke (1971) in examining the role of the constituency in the representational relationship. He found little evidence for presuming that a district makes specific policy demands on its representative. Rather, he suggested the relevance of Easton's concept of diffuse support (1965a, pp. 247–340) as a key component in the relationship between the represented and their representative. He states that the "symbolic satisfaction with the process of government is probably more important than specific, instrumental satisfaction with the policy output of the process" (Wahlke, 1971, p. 288). The important question then becomes, "how do representative bodies contribute to the generation and maintenance of support?" (ibid., p. 290).

In an era of cynicism about the functioning of representative institutions, the ways in which representatives manipulate political symbols in order to generate and maintain trust or support become critical aspects of responsiveness. Edelman (1964, 1971), following the earlier work of Lasswell, Merriam, and Smith (1950), has emphasized the importance of symbolic action in politics. The need for giving symbolic reassurance is being demonstrated by the "reach out" efforts of one president of the United States—walking down Pennsylvania Avenue after his inauguration, fireside chats, telephonic call-a-thons, visits to economically stricken areas, being "Jimmy" Carter, and so on. The purpose of all of these symbolic acts is to project an image that the president is truly the people's representative and ready to be responsive to them. By mobilizing trust and confidence, it is presumably easier to go about the job of representation than would otherwise be the case.

Fenno (1975), in a paper titled "Congressmen in their Constituencies," emphasizes the importance of political support in the representational relationship. The representative's "home style"—how he behaves *in* his constituency—is designed not just to secure constituent support and reelection but also to give the representative more freedom in his legislative activities when he is away from home. Symbolic politics has the purpose of building up credit to be drawn on in future contingencies. Although Fenno does not cite Wahlke at all, it is significant that his analysis approximates the "support-input model":

> congressmen seek and voters may give support on a non-policy basis. They may support a "good man" on the basis of his presentation "as a person" and trust him to be a good representative. So, we might consider the possibility that constituent trust, together with electoral accountability, may also provide a measure of good representation. The point is not that policy preferences are not a crucial basis for the representational relationship. They are. The point is that we should not start our studies of representation by assuming that they are the only basis for a representational relationship. They are not. (1975, p. 51)

Fenno's comments are all the more germane to the argument of this chapter because it is interesting to note that this most eminent of legislative scholars deflates the prevailing obsession with policy responsiveness as the sine qua non of representation. In fact, much of what may appear to be policy responsiveness is largely symbolic responsiveness. From session to session, legislators on all levels of government—federal, state, and local— introduce thousands of bills that have not the slightest chance of ever being passed and, more often than not, are not intended to be passed. Yet representatives introduce these bills to please some constituents and to demonstrate their own responsiveness.[11]

Responsiveness and Focus of Representation

Once the concept of representation-as-responsiveness is decomposed, policy responsiveness appears as only one component of representation and, perhaps, as by no means the dominant link between representative and represented. There is no intrinsic reason why responsiveness in one component of representation cannot go together with unresponsiveness in another. An individual or group may disagree with the representative's position and behavior on an issue of public policy and, as a result, may be unrepresented in this sense; yet the same individual or group may be well represented by a person who is responsive by attending to their particular requests for some type of service. Similarly, it is possible for a representative to be responsive with regard to securing public goods for his constituency while simultaneously being quite unresponsive with respect to issues of public policy. Finally, what matters in symbolic responsiveness is that the constituents feel represented, quite regardless of whether the representative is responsive in his policy stands or in the services or public goods he provides for his constituency.

Moreover, even if attention is given only to policy responsiveness, research cannot simply neglect some of the classical questions of representational theory, such as the issue of representing the district's will as against its interest, or the issue of the focus of representation. It is easily conceivable that being responsive to a district's will—the wants of its people— may involve being unresponsive to a district's interest—the needs of its people. With regard to the focus of representation, being responsive to the electoral district may produce unresponsive behavior in the larger unit of which the district is a part and, of course, vice versa.[12]

In fact, a closer look at the question of representational focus will reveal further the potentially multidimensional character of the phenomenon of responsiveness. The representative can perceive his "constituency" in a multitude of ways,[13] thereby making the number of foci quite large. One might organize these possible foci into three categories. The first category entails a geographic focus; the representative may perceive his constituency in terms of nation, region, state, district, or any other territorial level of society. The second category would include particular solidary or functional groupings like ethnic, religious, economic, and ideological groups, whether organized or not. Finally, the representational relationship may have as foci individual persons ranging from distinguished notables to unknown clients in need of help and to personal friends.

Representational focus, then, can differ a great deal in each of these three ways. The crucial point, however, is that the focus of representation might vary with each of the four components of responsiveness. While one might find particular foci, according to the three categories, for policy responsiveness, one might find altogether different foci in regard to any of the other components of responsiveness. Any empirical combination is possible within relevant logical constraints. Empirical research has yet to address the relationship between modes of responsiveness and foci of representation and to untangle the web of complexity created by the relationship.

Responsiveness versus Response

The generally confused and confusing use of "responsiveness," especially when linked to notions of "concurrence," is only symptomatic of a malaise that has come to characterize the "scientific" study of politics. The malaise is to substitute "theory construction" as a technique for substantive theory or theorizing. Fiorina (1974, p. 24), after reviewing the empirical research on representation of recent vintage, has come to a similar conclusion. We quote him precisely because he is not ignorant of or inimical to the new technological dispensations of our time:

Too often it seems that the increasing availability of electronic computing facilities, data banks, and canned statistical packages has encouraged a concomitant decline in the use of our own capabilities. Rather than hypothesize we factor analyze, regress, or causal model. We speak of empirical theory as if it miraculously grows out of a cumulation of empirical findings, rather than as a logical structure one must carefully construct to explain those findings.

When Fiorina identifies "data banks" as one of the villains, he presumably implies that the user of these facilities has grown increasingly remote from his subjects of observation and lost touch with the humanity he is supposed to understand. Indeed, there are today users of survey research who have never interviewed a single person in their lives. Not surprisingly, therefore, causal models are being reified as if they described reality rather than being abstractions from reality. In the case of representational responsiveness, for instance, the causal direction has been assumed to point from the represented to the representative; the latter has been assumed to be the object of stimuli to which he responds (or does not respond) in the fashion of Pavlov's famous dog. But such a model, even if one provides for intervening attitudinal or perceptual processes, does not approximate representational relationships that are, above all, transactions not necessarily structured in the ways of the S-O-R paradigm.

To appreciate the complexity of representational relationships as transactions, it is simply erroneous to assume that responsiveness—whatever component may be involved—is somehow the dependent variable in a causal structure. "Responsiveness" and "response" are not the same thing. On the contrary, a representative whose behavior is purely *reactive*—a condition that is hard to conceive on reflection but one that the "concurrence model" postulates—is the very opposite of a politically responsive person in Pitkin's sense. As that person has been chosen, elected, or selected from the multitude or mass to be a representative, that is, as he occupies a superior position in the relationship by virtue of his "elevation," one should expect him not merely to be reactive but to take the initiative. Whether he does or not is, of course, an empirical question; but the question cannot be answered by simply substituting an inappropriate model of causation for empirical observation and a viable theory of representation that would guide both observation and analysis.

As already suggested, the attractiveness of the notion of responsiveness in the most recent period has been due in part to the fusion of participatory and representational ideas about democracy. But in the participatory theory of democracy the leader—insofar as the model admits of leadership at all—is largely a reactive agent guided by the collective wisdom of the group. He is at best the executor of the group's will, indeed a human facsimile of Pavlov's dog. He reacts, presumably, but he is not responsive. One is, in fact, back to the "instructed-delegate" model in which there is no room for discretion in the conduct of the representative. A causal model of representation that draws its arrows only in recursive fashion from the represented to the representative cannot capture, therefore, the meaning of responsiveness in Pitkin's sense. It excludes *ab initio* what is yet to be concluded.

It is a grievous error, against which Fiorina warned, to assume and to act as if the assumption were valid, that "causal analysis" will automatically yield "theory," or that by simple inversion of causal assumptions something meaningful will come out of a causal analysis. Theorizing involves something more than arbitrarily inverting the causal directions on the assumption that the resultant statistical structure will somehow reflect reality. It involves *giving reasons* and *justifying* the assumptions one brings into the causal analysis. It involves "going out on a limb," as it were, and saying something substantive about the phenomena being investigated, rather than hiding behind the artifactual "findings" of a causal analysis that may be inappropriate in the first place.

A next step in the study of representation as responsiveness must take off from the compositional nature of the phenomenon. This step cannot be limited to simplistic measures like congruence or concurrence in connection with one component of a complex set of transactional relationships. Any inferences one may make about the functions of any one component of responsiveness in "representative government" must be related to inferences one may make about the functions of other components. Otherwise the puzzle of representation—having representative government but not knowing what it is about—will continue to bewilder the political imagination.

20

Skill Revolution and

Consultative Commonwealth

MY VISION is a commonwealth in which human needs are discovered, human purposes formulated, and human problems handled by political processes better adapted to the requirements of a rapidly changing technological society[1] than are participative, representational, or bureaucratic processes alone. I am not saying that this commonwealth is one in which human needs are satisfied, human purposes achieved, and human problems solved. There is a world of difference between discovering and satisfying needs, between formulating and achieving purposes, between handling and solving problems. The vocabulary is experiential rather than existential, processual rather than programmatic.

My argument is that the "consultative commonwealth"[2] is at least one probable outcome of the relationship between the skill revolution of modern times and some of the socially problematic consequences of modern technology. The consultative commonwealth is not an inevitable outcome of contemporary trends. It is, however, a plausible construct—more optimistic than Lasswell's (1948a, pp. 146–157) construct of the "garrison state," and more pessimistic than Bennis's construct of the "temporary society."[3] My task is to explore some of the logical and empirical linkages between the skill revolution, an empirical phenomenon, and the consultative commonwealth, a developmental conception of the future (see Chapter 13).

Skill Revolution

The skill revolution of the last hundred years is one of the significant factors in the development of industrial and technological society. Many occupations, and especially the oldest and still most prestigious among them—

the professions of law, of the clergy, the academy, and medicine—have their roots in a distant past.[4] What is new, and what not even Emile Durkheim (1960) envisaged when he sought to explain the consequences of the division of labor for society, is the incredible specialization in and proliferation of occupations that have accompanied industrial and technological developments. Harold Lasswell (1948a, p. 135) refers to this set of events as skill revolution and sees it as the basis for an observational standpoint in the study of politics "which cuts across the conventional categories of class and nation."

The emphasis on skill is to provide not an alternative but a complementary frame of reference for the observation of social and political situations. An integrative view of society and politics cannot neglect nation and class as both significant social realities and analytic categories. But cutting across these realities and categories is skill specialization that, it is clear, does not stop at national boundaries or class barriers. It is as much a part of social change in the United States as in the Soviet Union (Black, 1960; De Witt, 1961; Fischer, 1968; Lodge, 1969), and in the white-collar middle class as in the blue-collar working class (Blau and Duncan, 1967; Hall, 1969).

Skill specialization is probably the best directly available indicator of social and technological changes as behavioral dimensions. It has the virtue of empirical concreteness and relatively easy operational specification at the level of individual behavior. It therefore facilitates predictions about the future of political organization and processes in technological societies, regardless of their formal constitutional regimes.

Research on the political implications of the skill revolution has varying scholarly objectives. Lasswell (see Lasswell, Lerner, and Rothwell, 1952) was primarily interested in the rise and decline of skill elites for an explanation of the distribution of political values and the political transformation of societies (Burnham, 1941; Young, 1961; Galbraith, 1967). Because scientific or other knowledge, higher education, and rational intelligence are important values, some analysts use similar notions to predict the emergence of societies in which owners, workers, or consumers have lost, and managers, scientists, or technologists have gained control of the means of political power. They do so by rather fanciful leaps of the imagination, not to mention neglect of intervening or contravening social processes. Changes in the composition of social and political elites will not be suspended in the future. But these changes rarely bring with them the one-tailed transformations that are so resolutely predicted.

The permeation of society's public and private spheres by the old professions and many new skill groups is likely to continue in the foreseeable future. Yet it is premature to speak, as Frederick C. Mosher does, of "the professional state,"[5] at least in the sense that the professions will, in Daniel Bell's terms, constitute "the leadership of the new society."[6] It is a fragile presupposition that the possessors of new skills or specialized old skills will necessarily be dominant, if not exclusive, holders of political power. Tendencies contrary to the skill revolution evoked in response to social malfunctionings of technological society may attenuate or dissipate the concentration of power in the hands of those who have the new skills and specialized knowledge.

Imaginative extrapolations of trends in the structure and distribution of skills are conducive to the creation of benevolent or malevolent utopias; but constructs of the future are useful only to the extent that they permit us to orient ourselves meaningfully and correctly in the present. Apocalyptic visions of the future have just the opposite effect. They disorient the beholder and make it impossible for him to observe and explain the world as a prelude to predicting what it is likely to be or changing it in a preferred direction. What is needed to make research on the political implications of the skill revolution significant is a construct of the future that breaks with the familiar linear extrapolations of the effect of the skill revolution on the transformation and distribution of political power. The concept of the consultative commonwealth is such an alternative construct.

Research guided by the construct of the consultative commonwealth does not focus simply on the appearance of new elites whose influence is grounded in the possession of socially, economically, or politically useful skills and esoteric knowledge. Rather, it concentrates on the attitudes, orientations, and, especially, modes of conduct in their relationships with others that skill specialists bring to the task of governance. If skill specialists are asked to help in the manipulation of social problems and in the delivery of human services, not their positions in the hierarchies of power but their ways of doing things deserve our close research attention. This focus does not preclude other types of investigation into the political implications of the skill revolution. However, with a few exceptions, political scientists have not been much concerned with the political behavior of individual professionals,[7] or with professional associations as what Corinne L. Gilb (1966; see also Mayer, 1968; Freidson, 1970b) calls "private governments," or with professional organizations as conventional pressure groups.[8] There is, then, a gap in our knowledge of the political implications of the skill revolution at the microlevel of the individual as well as at the macrolevel of society.

Research on the professions promises to be a fascinating entry point into some problematic aspects of social structure and social change. The demographic and biographical approaches to the study of elites have not yielded the hoped-for results in contributing to an understanding of social and political change: the demographic approach is too aggregative and conceals more than it reveals at the level of the individual (Matthews, 1954; Marvick, 1961; Dogan and Rokkan, 1969); the biographical approach is too molecular and reveals more than is needed at the level of society (Edinger, 1964; Greenstein, 1969). Because politics is an emergent coefficient of the skill revolution, the professions are important topics of investigation (Nagel, 1961, pp. 366–380). For specializing professions are critical interstitial structures between the individual person and society.

If the emphasis is on those occupations conventionally called professions, it is not because there is a sharp dividing line between them and other vocations, or because the professions may in fact occupy positions of power and prestige in social and political systems (Reiss, 1961; Ben-David, 1963–64; Robinson, 1967). It is because the consultative processes stemming from professionalization in the wake of the skill revolution and the modes of conduct normally associated with professionalism have crystallized more fully in the professions and paraprofessions (Etzioni, 1969). The strenuous efforts made by many occupations to achieve professional status, whatever such status may mean to them, are further indications of the political implications of the continuing revolution in skills for the governance and servicing of modern societies (Mitchell, 1959).

Future-in-Coming: Emergencies

The consultative commonwealth is only a tentative construct, but among alternative models of the shape of political things to come it is more persuasive than most others. It is more persuasive because its emergence can be observed at the microlevel of individual professional behavior. This is not to accept the convenient and comfortable assumption that present trends or countertrends will continue indefinitely into the future. Far from it. The weakness of futuristic extrapolation of trends is its neglect of the puzzling problem of how past, present, and future are connected in human action (Bell, 1969).

Scenarios of the future are never played out as expected. There are two methodological points to be made about the construct of the consultative commonwealth. First, though a construct of the future, it is tutored by theory and empirical research. Its utility is to be judged not by its predictive power, for the future is not known and can therefore not be used to test derivative hypotheses. Rather, its utility must be judged by its ability to give rise to research and thought in the present that may be relevant to the future.

Second, not only is the future unknown but the laws of social development leading to the future are unknown. Every construct of the future therefore makes assumptions about the developmental process. The developmental model underlying the construct of the consultative commonwealth assumes oscillations between the polar ends of a temporal continuum. It assumes that there is no action without reaction, no force without resistance, no unity without plurality, no identity without difference, no growth without decay. The polar principle assumes that contradictory social processes are mutually entailed through time.[9]

The skill revolution and notably its vanguards, the professions, provide a suggestive point of departure. The professional is not a man who creates knowledge but a specialist who translates knowledge into action. The man of knowledge is a "longhair," and a longhair is by definition an impractical person. The professional is not a longhair, for he applies knowledge to practical concerns.[10] Unlike the man of knowledge, the professional "does something" that is oriented to the future in terms of goal values to be realized. The physician seeks to make the sick person healthy; the lawyer tries to recover a victimized person's rights; the professor as teacher strives to lead the student out of ignorance to understanding; the minister hopes to ease the penitent's road to salvation. This is not all that physicians, lawyers, professors, or ministers do, but their main task is to use their knowledge or experience in helping people meet problems that they cannot handle themselves;[11] and they do so by forming images of a desired future for their patients, children, students, or parishioners.

Much of what the professional does is routine. It is routine because the problem at hand has usually been encountered before, or because the solution has been codified in a work of reference. But sometimes the professional confronts a genuinely new problem for which there is no ready-made solution. He then faces a situation of uncertainty that is, in effect, an emergent future because he must "do something" about it and cannot avoid the problem or postpone action (Fox, 1959, 1967). In an emergency the professional will deal with the problem as best he can, relying on his general skill, ingenuity, and what is called "intuition"—an estimate of the future. When the professional is involved in an emergency, the future is in the making. The future is simply the present-in-transition, and the present is the future-in-coming.

At the macrolevel of analysis, attention turns to the professions as collectivities and how they orient themselves to action in problematic social situations.[12] There is no lack of situations in contemporary society that call for professional intervention and the application of professional skills. How the professions relate themselves to problematic social and technological situations is therefore a matter of great significance for the future.

The relationship between the behavior of the professions as prototypical carriers of the skill revolution in a rapidly changing world and a viable construct of governing processes in the future is directly pertinent to many critical social problems—for instance, the formulation of public policies concerning, and the adequate provision of those human services in, fields like health, education, welfare, and safety that are the domain of the highly skilled occupations. These are not the only fields in which the skill revolution has consequences for the problems of society; but the provision of professional services, from medical care to legal aid, education, welfare, and protection—services on which modern society heavily depends for successful functioning—is inadequate in both distribution and quality.[13] Access to these services has come to be claimed as a common right of citzenship;[14] it is a right in conflict with differential privilege inherent in a segmented and stratified social structure. The realization of the right of access to professional services cannot be left, therefore, to the spontaneous working of the economic market.[15] Indeed, if there were no maldistribution and inadequacy in delivery, professional services in health, education, welfare, or protection would hardly be regarded as urgent matters of public concern.

The professions, paraprofessions, and subprofessions are sufficiently diverse, and their circumstances sufficiently different, that it is dangerous to generalize about matters as complex and intricate as the provision of a multitude of services. This is why a developmental construct like the consultative commonwealth is useful, indeed necessary, for research. For it should demonstrate that the problems involved in the provision of human services are not soluble simply by recourse to facile policy panaceas, faith in benign administrative palliatives, or dependence on political mobilization of inadequately served groups of clients.

This is not to say that these means are unimportant political change mechanisms or that their consequences, whichever, are unimportant. On the contrary, they are themselves issues in the relationship between skill revolution and consultative commonwealth (Edelman, 1971). For they are symptomatic of the strains and tensions between changing social expectations concerning the delivery of human services on the one hand, and difficulties facing the professionalization of these services, on the other hand.

Polarity: Professionalization and Deprofessionalization

Skill revolution is not to be equated with professionalization; it does not in itself generate either the process of professionalization or the ideology of professionalism.[16] Because the most highly developed skills are in short supply, the skill structure will remain stratified; and those most highly placed in the skill structure, the professions, will be responsible for the delivery of human services and decision making concerning these services. The shape of the skill structure, however, will not remain the same.[17] Internal differentiation among those at the top of the skill hierarchy and the addition of new skill specialists are likely to broaden the structure and to increase the pool of trained personnel available for service, potentially enabling both the public and the private sectors to respond more adequately to the novel problems created by high technology—either those that are foreseeable by-products of scientifically grounded technology or those that are the unanticipated and socially harmful consequences of technological change.[18]

Although defining "profession" is important, it may become a passion, as it understandably is for those occupations that are striving for professional status.[19] In opting for a definition, one should let the problem at hand serve as the guide. The problem in this instance is to build a construct of the future commonwealth that pays attention not only to the professionalization of social or technical services and policy making, but also to a variety of countertendencies that are indicative of deprofessionalization.

On the one hand, the increasing application of scientific knowledge, technical skill, and rational intelligence will professionalize the delivery of human services and bring professionals into the policy-making process, in both the public and private sectors (Wilensky, 1967; Price, 1965). Moreover, if present trends continue, the provision of a great variety of services to all citizens will be high on the agenda of politics. The availability of a basic body of abstract knowledge with connected skills, and the performance of services, then, are the defining properties of what is meant by profession, and the patterns of behavior or conduct associated with these properties are the building blocks of the consultative commonwealth.[20] In this perspective, the internal transformation of the older professions and the appearance of some new professions, responding to changes in scientific or technical knowledge and the demand for new services, are significant social and political processes.

On the other hand, professional skill and expertise are being challenged in these fields by countercurrents to professional approaches released in the name of consumerism, community power, and open access for previously excluded groups, especially women and ethnic minorities (Epstein, 1970a; Bowles and DeCosta, 1971; Curtis, 1971). First, because professionalism is a *political* ideology, it motivates not only those who use it to protect their social status and those who aspire to higher social status, but also those who see in professionalism a defense of the status quo (Thoenes,

1966). And second, professionalization—the transformation of an occupation into a profession—is a *political* process because it involves, among other things, a quest for statutory legitimacy and related publicly sanctioned privileges as well as for public acceptance. It is therefore always exposed to the vagaries of politics.

Ironically, both professionalizing and deprofessionalizing tendencies derive from two major changes in the classical relationship between professional and client. First, professionals increasingly work in and for organizations with clients who are not their employers but rather the consumers of their services. And second, professional dominance in the professional's relationship with clients is contained by the appearance of client organizations that presume to speak for individual or collective clients.

A number of derivative consequences follow: As professionals come to work in political milieux, politicization of the professional-client relationship tends to undermine professional autonomy. The challenges encountered from clientele organizations, with their own ideas about the provision of services and performance, tend to undercut professional authority. The need of professionals to protect their own interests may lead to unionization, which, in the view of some, endangers the professional norm of commitment to the public interest. The location of professionals in bureaucratic organizations with their tendency to inertia and ritualistic behavior can easily thwart experimentation, innovation, and discretion.[21] Finally, the built-in obsolescence of professional skills in a rapidly changing scientific and technological culture makes for tensions within and between the professions that weaken professional credibility and legitimacy.

At the same time, society will also be much more demanding in its expectations concerning the delivery of services. The demand for more and better services, combined with tendencies toward the deprofessionalization of services, represents a paradox. Rather than improving service, deprofessionalization would have just the opposite effect. This is so because it would involve an altogether irrational reversal of normal expectations. The normal chain follows a sequence in which a client in need of help seeks out a competent specialist whose professional authority he accepts and to whom he grants decisional autonomy. Deprofessionalization reverses this chain, because its main effect is to reduce professional autonomy. But reduced autonomy weakens professional authority; weakened authority devalues professional competence; and devalued professional skill will impoverish the quality of the service that is rendered.

In the perspective of contemporary countertendencies to professionalization, then, the consultative commonwealth would seem to breed the seeds of its own destruction and negate the promises of the skill revolution.

Before accepting this dismal prospect, however, some other considerations are in order. One need not be a dialectitian to recognize that deprofessionalizing tendencies in turn generate their own countervailing forces. The professions do not passively accept deprofessionalizing challenges, be they internal to a profession or external. They develop adaptive techniques and coping strategies that blunt the impact of deprofessionalization and, in fact, strengthen a profession's authority and autonomy.

The consultative commonwealth, in taking account of deprofessionalizing pressures in its consultative arrangements, also contains within itself the seeds of renewal.[22] It differs, then, from those constructs of the future society that are based on one-sided extrapolations of either tendencies alone, or countertendencies alone, in the formation and circulation of skill elites. These models are deficient in two respects. First, they fail to recognize the dynamics of the polarity principle in the development of societies, especially those in the stage of advanced technology. And second, they neglect the normative capabilities of politics. However, even if deprofessionalizing tendencies are accounted for, it is more probable than not that the future commonwealth will be highly dependent on professional services.

Because increasing demand for services will continue to exceed available supply, the power of skill specialists is always balanced by new demands coming fron dissatisfied clienteles. If all of this were only a matter of supply and demand in the economic sense, political science would not have much of a contribution to make to its understanding. But the problem of professional services is not just an economic question; it is also an eminently political question, for it involves relationships of authority and autonomy between those who provide and those who demand the services.

To appreciate the political issue, I take a clue from an insightful passage by that wise student of the occupations, Everett C. Hughes. Investigation of the challenges facing the professions and of their responses, Hughes (1958, p. 85) suggested, "is study of politics in the very fundamental sense of studying constitutions. For constitutions are the fundamental relations between the effective estates which make up the body politic." Professionals are involved in four constitutional relationships—with clients, with organizations, with their own colleagues, and with the larger society. The structures and functions of these relationships and the norms of professional conduct in a particular relationship, for the professional and his significant others, create political issues that differ a good deal from profession to profession, from one institutional setting to another, and from one set of relationships to the next. They should therefore be expected to have different consequences as one projects the consultative commonwealth of the future.

Relationship with Clients

Of all the professional's relationships, that with clients is of fundamental constitutional importance for the evolution of social institutions and public policies. The classical relationship between professional practitioner and client is contractual and in the nature of an exchange. The client takes the initiative in seeking out the professional and, by paying a fee, employs him to perform the desired service. Professions differ in their responses to client initiatives; but, in general, the relationship is assumed to be reciprocal.

As the interaction proceeds, however, the relationship is transformed. Once having "placed himself in the hands" of the professional, the client becomes a dependent. The client is still free to reject the professional's advice and help, but he does so at his own risk and, for all practical purposes, does not do it. Client behavior is important, then, in defining the professional's role. As long as the relationship is built on trust, which, in turn, derives from the client's recognition of his own ignorance and the professional's competence, the client is willing to accept the practitioner's decisions concerning his needs. In effect, then, what was initially a functional relationship is transformed into an intrinsically hierarchical relationship. This transformation is overlooked by those who take a benign view of professional expertise as purely functional and who expect the infusion of expertise into the creation and delivery of human services to have ipso facto salubrious consequences for society (Lane, 1966).

Because the relationship between professional and client is one of authority, in a generally democratic culture it is likely to be ambivalent, if not conflictual. Although, in essence, the client surrenders himself to the professional, neither party is fully comfortable. If the resulting ambivalence or conflict remains contained and does not seriously interfere with the service, it is because there also remains in an open market, the possibility for the client to terminate the consultation or for the professional to withdraw his service. But if the market is restricted or state-controlled, and if free choice of services is impossible, tension and even hostility will characterize the professional-client relationship. Although maldistribution or substantive inadequacy of medical, legal, welfare, or protective services is the manifest target of current discontent, some of the dissatisfaction, especially among those who depend on state-provided and state-controlled services, stems from the tension built into the authority relationship.

Ambivalence and conflict may also rise because the client's perspective of professional service and what is brought to that perspective may differ from the professional's perspective in the first place. Because of this difference, as Hughes (1958, p. 54) has noted, professionals, although "convinced that they themselves are the best judges, not merely of their own competence but also of what is best for the people for whom they perform services, are required in some measure to yield judgment of what is wanted to these amatuers who receive the services." Professionals are understandably reluctant to do this. If, therefore, the professional wishes to insist on the correctness of his own judgment, it is incumbent on him to mold client expectations of what constitutes proper service. More often than not, however, in order to make clients accept their authority, professionals rely for persuasion on institutional means, notably the doctrine of "free choice,"[23] rather than on professional ways.

Reliance on the authority of status exacerbates the professional-client relationship in the contemporary democratizing environment. In the classical model, the environment in which professional-client interaction was played out did not consciously enter the relationship because professional and client could be assumed to share the same environment. Professionals, of middle-class status by definition, either served those above them in the class structure or those on their own level; and if they served the lower classes, their institutional authority was not questioned. Because of social class barriers, professionals found it difficult to empathize with the lower orders of society, even if they served them occasionally in charitable ways. It was the great genius of the Roman Catholic Church that by replicating in its own hierarchy the class structure of society, and by recruiting its servants from among all social classes to serve all social classes, it did not lose contact with its lower-class clienteles, even as democratization of the hierarchy provided for mobility within the ranks of the clergy (Able, 1968). Such rootedness in the total environment was never the case with physicians, lawyers, or professors, even after the social recruitment base was widened, precisely because institutional professionalization caused these professionals to consider themselves, and to be considered, middle class in status. Identification with the middle class alienated professionals from the lower-class environment.

As a result of the extension of professional services to the working and lower classes, professionals now encounter clients whose perspective is very different from their own. The shock of recognizing the difference in environment is more or less shared in the different professions, and it has led to the belief that in at least some cases and situations not the individual client but his entire social environment requires professional treatment. Credit for discovering the salience of the environment in professional practice must be given to social work, but the discovery has now considerable influence in law, medicine, and university teaching. In the academy, retreating into the "ivory tower" is no longer an appropriate professional posture, as it is recognized that an environment favorable to the pursuit of knowledge cannot be taken for granted.

The discovery of the environment and the movement toward professional intervention in the environment have created a profound crisis in the professions. If the environment must be changed before the client's problems can be treated, the role of the client in the relationship with the professional comes to be redefined. This is so because clients are themselves a part of the environment and, as a result, are seen as important components in shaping the environment. The client perspective intrudes into the professional-client relationship more than it ever has. Much of the current crisis in professional services turns on the nature of client participation in decisions concerning these services. The professional schools, sensitive to this, increasingly try to give instruction not only in subjects that relate to the environment in which the prospective professional will work, but also in subjects that provide him with skills in organization, negotiation, human relations, and so on (Schein, 1972).

If the professionals fail to persuade clients of what constitutes proper service, they leave themselves open to client demands of what proper service should be. They allow themselves to be pressured into conformity with client expectations, even if it violates professional criteria of service. As Hughes (1958, p. 83) noted, this is especially likely in periods of social unrest: "In time of crisis, there may arise a general demand for more complete conformity to lay modes of thought, discourse and action."

The pressure for conformity to lay perspectives comes from people who occupy higher- or lower-status positions in society than does the professional himself. The legal profession, itself highly stratified, is especially exposed to client perspectives (Carlin, 1962; Ladinsky, 1963; Smigel, 1964). In the academy some professors yield to student pressures for conformity to their interpretations of what learning and knowledge are all about by lowering standards and "being with it," sometimes assuming student styles and demeanor. Deprofessionalization has become a burning issue in social work. As one critic (Specht, 1972, p. 6) writes,

the new activist spirit in social work downgrades professional practice, which is ineffective in dealing with social problems. In place of professionalism the activists offer the idea that revolution will create change more rapidly than social work practice, which may be correct. But this is not what the profession prepares one to do, nor should it.

Professional consultants at the highest levels of policy making often conform to policy makers' wishes and predilections, permitting their knowledge to be used for societal objectives that from a professional perspective may be undesirable.[24]

Perhaps the problem of differing perspectives between professional and client is insoluble. If so, there will always be an element of conflict in the relationship. If the professional only relies on his authority without further efforts at persuasion, the client is in no position to evaluate the grounds of the professional's advice. Under these conditions professionals will jealously guard their monopoly on expert knowledge and status, but clients will not comply with professional advice and, in some cases, they will revolt against the prescriptions of the experts. Most recently there has been a trend toward reducing professional autonomy and enabling clients to enforce professional responsibility in the provision of services that has hitherto been the professions' own prerogative. Professionals in turn resent lay interference, especially when, as in teaching or librarianship, clients can bring pressure on policy-making elected boards. In this context, present trends toward unionization of professionals takes on an aspect that goes beyond the bread-and-butter unionism of old, for it is as much a matter of politics as of economics. If professionals feel that laymen make undue demands in areas of competence they consider their own, the collective withdrawal of services—traditionally frowned upon "as unprofessional conduct"—is a very real possibility (Moskow and McLennan, 1970).

All of these developments could have possibly disastrous consequences for professional service. If the client cannot distinguish between the professional's authority that is based on expertise and his authority that is based on status or power, the basic trust on which the professional-client relationship is founded becomes eroded. In revolting against the professional's status and power, however, the client also revolts, if inadvertently, against professional knowledge and competence.

Relationship with Organizations

The professional increasingly encounters the client not in private but in organizational settings.[25] The original professions—clergy, law, academy, and medicine—had been characterized as *freie Berufe* or "free callings." Freedom referred to independence from organizational constraints. Although clergymen and academics depended for support on church and university, the professions were assumed to be free in two senses: first, the professional's behavior was guided by norms created by himself and designed to protect him against external pressures—the professions enjoyed autonomy; and second, the professional worked alone with individuals by applying his best professional judgment and was unencumbered by responsibility to an employing organization—the professions had authority.

The professional's work today is likely to take place in organizational and institutional settings that restrict his freedom more than was the case before the skill revolution reached its apogee.[26] The professional in these settings is subject to two modes of authority—organizational-hierarchical authority in the hands of administrative officials, and the authority of skill and competence exercised by professional colleagues, both inside and outside the organization (Peabody, 1964). The two forms of authority are conflictual and make for stress and strain in professional conduct vis-à-vis administrators, colleagues, and clients.[27] As a result, "disjunctive processes" are widespread.[28] Speaking of the academy, for instance, Logan Wilson (1963, p. 293) notes:

Even though academicians are professional men and women enjoying a high degree of independence as specialists per se, they function within an institutional framework which evaluates, ranks, and rewards them in terms of their presumed value to the organization. The whole process is so complex that it is inevitably a source of misunderstanding, and the results are unavoidably a further source of real or alleged grievance to some individuals.

If this is true in the highly permissive context of the university, it is surely even truer in the highly organized contexts of public or private bureaucracies.

If the professional's identification and commitment are stronger than his organizational loyalty (Marvick, 1954; see also Gouldner, 1958), rather than being threatened by bureaucracy, it may be professionalism that disturbs administrative ways of doing things. Hierarchical authority in administrative decision making is being undermined, Francis E. Rourke (1969, p. 105) suggests, by "the growing power of skilled professions in the work of public bureaucracy . . . Professionalism is rapidly succeeding politics as the principal source of decentralization of authority in American bureaucracy. A subordinate who is master of esoteric skills is no easier to dominate than one backed by a strongly entrenched group of political supporters."[29]

This transformation is by no means self-evident, because the problem of coordinating specialized expertise in organizations was long obscured by the ready availability of what Max Weber (1947, pp. 329–341) called "legal-rational authority" or bureaucracy. The most obvious answer to the question of how best to coordinate specializations leads to the bureaucratic model that stresses rationalization, routinization, and standardization. Despite wide variations in practice, the organizational settings in which professionals work—hospitals, law firms, government bureaus, research laboratories, corporation offices, labor unions, religious organizations, universities, engineering firms, and so on—remain basically bureaucratic. What is happening, however, is an interpenetration of bureaucratization and professionalization—"the culture of bureaucracy invades the professions; the culture of professionalism invades organizations" (Wilensky, 1964, p. 150).[30]

In the broadest historical perspective, skill revolution, professionalization, and bureaucracy are symptoms of the same secular trend in Western
society that Talcott Parsons (1954) describes as making for rationality,
impersonality, functional specificity, and universalism.

If bureaucratic means of coordination had not been as well developed
as they were when the skill revolution reached the professions, consultative
modes of coordination as immanent properties of professionality might
have emerged sooner than they did. However, bureaucratization and professionalization are possibly isomorphic in structure and characterized by
convergent tendencies with respect to authority—"professional authority
is more similar to bureaucratic authority than is generally recognized"
(Freidson, 1970a, p. 211).[31] While it is difficult empirically to disentangle
the two phenomena because of their interdetermination,[32] the isomorphism
between bureaucratic and professional authority, if true, casts doubt on
some romantic notions that organization theorists have about the superi-
ority of functional over hierarchical forms of coordination. If only professional or functional criteria were dominant in organizations, bureaucratic
pathologies like arbitrariness, unimaginativeness, authoritarianism, rigidity, and so forth, would miraculously yield to creativity, flexibility, involvement, and so on (see Blau, 1959; Thompson, 1961). That the professions
themselves may be tainted by bureaucratic tendencies is, therefore, a so-
bering thought.

In addition, the organizational context of professional practice is a source
of deprofessionalizing tendencies that are as yet little understood. Deprofessionalization, in this connection, means loss of professional identity.
There are two contradictory possibilities. On the one hand, loss of professional identity may be due to initial overidentification with and subsequent
overreaction against the organization. This makes it difficult to separate
out the alleged evils of bureaucracy from the alleged evils of professionalism. Attacks within the professions on "professionalism," which is sometimes seen, probably rightly, as a conservative force, are easily misplaced.
At least it is not at all clear whether they are directed at the bureaucratic
or at the professional component of the organization that is seen as requiring change if policy formulation and human services are to be im-
proved.

Deprofessionalization in this sense has become a very real issue, although
it varies a good deal from profession to profession, depending to a large
degree on a profession's involvement in public policy as a condition for
the realization of its professional goals. For instance, a profession like
social work, which is directly affected by public policy, has a strong stake
in welfare policies and public financial support. Attacks on professionalism
have become an almost endemic feature of discourse in social work. In

teaching at the primary and secondary levels, the long quest for professional status seems to have abated in recent years as teachers turn to unionization rather than professionalization as a means to improve their working conditions, raise their social status, and influence public policy (Zeigler, 1967; Gambino, 1972). By contrast, however, technical professionals are reported to evince "a complete lack of consensus on what needs to be done," with unionizers in one camp and "professional purists" in the other (Shapley, 1972, p. 618).

On the other hand, loss of professional identity may be due to an inability to discover a specific client in organizational settings. A person's sense of identity is in no small part determined for him by the significant others with whom he interacts. Loss of professional identity is inevitable if the professional cannot identify the clients whom he is supposed to serve.

In the classical model of the profession, the professional was expected to serve a particular client, usually in a face-to-face encounter, and by serving the client to serve, in a vague way, society. As long as client interests and societal interests could be assumed to be the same, there seemed to be no problem. Again, this consonance varied from profession to profession. Physicians, for instance, had little trouble in this respect, at least until recently. Health was a value on which a social consensus existed, and in treating his patient, the physician was serving society. Today the conflict over abortion and the disagreement about the artificial prolongation of life have created considerable affective dissonance about the value of life. Similarly, while justice is presumably the consensual aim of the legal profession, it has long been recognized that what may be good for the lawyer's client may not advance the best interests of society.

The complexity of modern social and technological problems defies the simplicity of the traditional model. "Client uncertainty" is so pervasive that it not only makes for deprofessionalization but prevents some aspiring occupations from becoming professionalized. Who, for instance, is the client of the corporate manager who so desperately seeks professional status? Is it the employing corporation, the stockholders, the consumers, or society at large (see Whyte, 1956; Lewis and Stewart, 1961; Ewing, 1964)? University professors are highly sensitive to client uncertainty. Who are their clients? The students whom they teach, the colleagues who benefit from their research, the governing board who pays their salaries, the publishers for whom they write texts, the government agency or business with whom they consult, or society at large? Client uncertainty obscures what providing a service means, and it suggests the great potential for conflict in the provision of services.

In some circumstances, the professional serving various clients is under enormous pressure to help some but not other clients. University professors have been subjected to much pressure, if not force, to refuse service to some clients whose policies or goals other clients disapprove (see Lipset, 1970; Kadish, 1972). This type of pressure for *selective* service undermines professional autonomy, and without autonomy—the right to decide whom to serve—the very concept of profession is meaningless.

Relationship with Colleagues

The professional's best defense against client uncertainty caused by organizational complexity is his identification with colleagues. Strong collegial ties are an important requisite of professional autonomy. Yet the professional's relationship with colleagues is by no means always simple. It is *relatively* simple if two professional colleagues enter a reciprocally advantageous consultative relationship, for it is mutually deferential and consensual in the sense that both partners share a common perspective. As a result, control problems like those arising in the professional-client relationship because of the confusion between the authority of expertise and the authority of status do not occur. The ideally limiting case seems to be the kind of relationship that exists when one scientist consults another. Indeed, Hughes (1952) and Parsons (1959) suggest that there is a basic structural difference between science and profession that makes for differing authority relationships between scientific colleagues, on the one hand, and professional colleagues, on the other. It seems preferable to make this role differentiation less sharp. The university-based scholar in his role as teacher stands in a professional relationship to his colleagues because they share a student clientele; the practicing attorney sometimes stands in a scholarly relationship to his colleagues at the bar or on the bench.

Nevertheless, as an analytic distinction the differentiation between the scholar-scientist and the professional with clients is suggestive; it calls attention to different control mechanisms and consultative relationships. Scientists control each other directly and publicly. They do so by frank and open reporting of the assumptions that go into the gathering of evidence, of the methods used in analyzing the evidence, and of the evidence itself.[33] Scientific associations are primarily learned societies whose principal goals are to publish journals and hold meetings in order to faciliate scientific communication and exchange.[34] Although there are standards as to what is good or bad scientific work, there is no such thing as a code of ethics for scientists in their role as scientists. Of course, when scientists become policy advisers or perform services for public or private organizations, they take on the professional role and come to be concerned about "proper professional conduct."

In contrast to pure scientific knowledge, much professional knowledge is a kind of tacit know-how that cannot be readily communicated and evaluated and that may even be secret or confidential.[35] Only extraordinary cases of abuse in professional behavior generally come within the purview of collegial control. Because direct control as in relationships among scientists is not available, the professions seek to maintain professional standards through their organizations, codes of ethics, and government-sanctioned licensing. Yet the professional control mechanisms are weak. Although holding a professional license implies professional authenticity, codes of ethics are poorly enforced,[36] and membership in professional associations, being voluntary, is far from universal.[37]

A profession as a whole, then, is by no means a community of like-minded equals or an *imperium in imperio* as is sometimes claimed. It is a complex aggregate of skill specialists working in a great variety of settings and differentiated not only in function but also in esteem, status, authority, and influence (Moore, 1963). Specialization and subspecialization in the wake of the skill revolution accentuate these tendencies.

Stratification within and between the professions, as in all status systems, restricts vertical communication. As a result, although interprofessional collaboration may be needed—as in the modern hospital where physicians depend on nurses, technicians, pharmacists, and other specialists—professionals of higher status may not get the cooperation they need from lower-status professionals (see Freidson, 1963; Perrow, 1965; Glaser, 1970). Stratification reduces society's potential for consultation even if there is growing professionalization of human services.

Whether efforts to democratize the professions will improve the delivery of services is an open question. It is probably true, as Cynthia F. Epstein (1970b, p. 981) observes in discussing the entry of women into the professions, that

many of today's gifted young professionals are no longer eager to enter the traditional inner corps of the professions . . . This seems to be particularly so in law and medicine where there are signs of a breakdown in the collegial structure and an increasing challenge to the traditional insistence on recruits of particular types.

But this may actually reinforce already existing oligarchical tendencies in the professions. If the professional associations are to be the guardians of professional standards and interests, those best qualified in terms of professional rather than extraneous criteria will continue to emerge as professional leaders. This will mean, as Roberto Michels would predict, that associational oligarchs will continue to rule, although their ideological blinders may be different from those worn by their predecessors. If the leadership of the professions is to constitute an influential elite of merit, however, it will emerge not from the application of plebiscitary techniques to professional control but from consultative understandings and arrangements. As Wilbert E. Moore (1970, p. 167) has put it well, "the criteria in organizational advancement tend to be mixed, and, as in all representational systems, the very attributes that distinguish a man from his colleagues may set him apart from their interests, rather than representing them with exceptional skill."

Relationship with Society

Society's dependence on specialized and skilled professional services is balanced, in a constitutional sense, by the professions' dependence on society for accreditation. Accreditation, a profession's success in having "license" to perform its services, is contingent on society's satisfaction with professional performance. Involved is not just the legal permission to practice a trade, with its complementary prohibition to others who do not have the requisite skills; also involved is the profession's legitimacy to carry out a "mandate" for society. This means that only the profession, and no one else, can collectively presume "to tell society what is good and right for the individual and for society at large in some aspect of life" (Hughes, 1958, p. 79).

The relationship between profession and society is in a deepening crisis. At issue is the profession's authority within its area of competence. Authority is a precondition for the exercise of the profession's mandate to determine what is in the best interests of society as a kind of collective client. At issue also is the profession's autonomy from societal constraints, which, in this connection, means that professional performance can be judged only by the profession itself, for only the profession is qualified to do so (Goode, 1969, p. 291). Professional authority and autonomy are threatened by a number of developments over which a profession has little control. One development, it was noted, is the organizational context in which professionals work, and in which the profession's functional and the organization's hierarchical authority come into conflict. Another development is a generally more competitive environment. An old profession may encounter competition from new professions or semiprofessions whose work is adjacent or overlapping. In the case of the legal profession, for instance, "tax accountants, marital counselors, labor arbitrators, and a host of others are engaged in matters that are in part legal" (Moore, 1970,

p. 112). What is challenged is the profession's claim to exclusive mastery of a body of unique knowledge and related skills.

Finally, professional services come to be seen not as purchasable private goods but as public goods with accessibility to all as a matter of right. Clients have come to the realization that professionals not only do things *for* them but also *to* them (Hughes, 1958, pp. 69–70). This varies of course considerably from client to client. While the big Wall Street law firm can do little to its corporate client but give it bad advice, the social welfare worker has almost absolute control over the poor welfare mother on relief (see Lipsky, 1972, pp. 205–212). While the corporation has effective sanctions over the law firm, the solitary welfare recipient has practically none. Like corporate clients, organizations of individual clients (for example, welfare rights organizations) have come to demand a voice in the professional decisions affecting them.

This demand jeopardizes one of the professions' most cherished prerogatives—the authority to determine client needs. To protect this prerogative, the professions have always sought to justify themselves in terms of the mandate given them by society. Indeed, the mandate of service in the public interest more than authoritative expertise has been the justification for insisting on autonomy. Yet a profession's mandate is always probationary, in very much the same sense in which an elected representative's term of office is probationary.

A profession's persistence as a "community within a community" is contingent, as any mandate is contingent, on continued ability to satisfy the public trust placed in it as the custodian of esoteric competences (Goode, 1967). At least until recently, the professions were given this public trust. The legal profession was expected to be directly concerned with the administration of justice and relevant legislation; and the medical profession was expected to concern itself with the organization, distribution, and remuneration of medical services.

Their public roles expose the professions to public criticism, and their public mandate has come to be questioned. The professions are accused of not meeting societal expectations of proper policy or service, and their role as agents of the public interest in particular areas of policy or service is being attacked on the ground that they have been more self-serving than other-serving.[38] This criticism, Parsons suggests, tends to confuse private motivation with the institutional setting that differentiates professionals from those who, like businessmen, pursue private gain.[39] But the professions organize themselves as interest-group associations in the same way as do labor unions or business organizations. And although one should not confuse a profession as such with its associational instruments, the professions have been no less "selfish," whatever this means, than other interest groups (Gilb, 1966; Truman, 1951, pp. 93–98, 168–169, 249–250, 452–453). Public sensitivity to the professions' political involvement in favor of their own rather than public interests is widespread.

That they are in trouble as trustees of the public interest has not gone unnoticed in the professions themselves. How to respond to societal distrust of their integrity proves to be perplexing. Investigations conducted at Stanford over the last few years concerning the political behavior and attitudes of professionals in particular institutional settings or with respect to particular public issues, indicate much political ambivalance within the professions themselves.[40] In the ministry a "new breed" of activist clergymen feel that the churches should give forceful leadership on public issues (Quinley, 1972). City planners have come to realize that they "must be able to persuade, bargain and compromise, lest decision-makers listen to those who are better able to persuade, bargain and compromise" (Buck, 1972). Law students evidently continue to prefer careers in the private sector, but extracurricular experience may be an increasingly important factor in determining their choice (Lochner, 1971). Countergroups in law and medicine organize law communes and people's clinics that challenge the traditional priorities of these professions (Becker, 1975). Policy-oriented scientists "go public" and expand the scope of conflict over issues of public policy (O'Connor, 1974). Journalists seem to be quite sensitive to the problem of how their reporting the news affects the success or failure of protest groups in different fields of welfare (Goldenberg, 1975). Black professionals are concerned about the effect of their work environment, whether predominantly black or white, on their leadership potential in home communities (Levine, 1973). All of these studies reveal tensions that arise out of the relationship between the professions' presumed obligations to the public interest, their investment with a public trust, and the increasing criticism of their work both inside and outside the professions.

The Stanford studies show that ritualistic invocation of the professions' mandate to serve the public interest is not sufficient to help them out of their quandary. For it is the definition of the public interest that *is* the quandary. The problem of definition is of course not unique to the professions.[41] In the absence of an accepted formal definition, contextual treatment seems most appropriate.

The context in which most professionals worked was long pervaded, and to a large extent still is pervaded, by the ethos of social and economic individualism. This ethos set limits to the services that professionals sought to render and were expected to render. In effect, service in the public interest was defined in terms of those who could afford professional services. This meant that the professions largely served the interests of the affluent society rather than the interests of what Michael Harrington (1962) has called "the other America." The professions were satisfied that they were serving the public interest if their services met "effective demand," that is, the demand of those who could purchase their services.

The definition of professional service in the public interest is changing, from an essentially economic to a social-moral content. The new definition refers to "unmet needs" rather than to effective demand. It is an open question whether the new definition will help the professions overcome the crisis in their relationship with society. On the one hand, if the professions succeed, by their own practices and the policies they are able to influence, in broadening the range and improving the quality of the services they provide for society, their claim to autonomy is strengthened rather than weakened. This is perhaps something that the American Bar Association and the American Medical Association have yet to learn.

On the other hand, the notion of unmet needs is sufficiently ambiguous to create new troubles. The substitution of unmet needs for effective demand gives the impression that one is somehow dealing with a self-evident, readily usable standard for judging professional performance. In fact, just the opposite is the case. Effective demand is an economic market phenomenon that, within its defined parameters, can be measured; unmet need is a moral criterion that is by no means easy to operationalize. In general, unmet needs become visible only when those whose needs are not met rise to the occasion, as happened in the sixties. Insofar, however, as the professions accept unmet needs as a criterion by which to judge the adequacy of human services, they also seem to admit that clients have a right to participate in the making of policies that had previously been their own professional mandate (see Kaufman, 1969).

Protest and Response

In fact, what clients articulate are not unmet needs but unmet wants. Client participation in decisions appropriately within the province of the professions violates the constitutional basis of the professional-client relationship. This basis cannot be democratic if professional service is to have any meaning. As T. H. Marshall (1965, p. 164) has pointed out, "authority passes to the professional, who must give [the client] what he needs, rather than what he wants. The client, unlike the customer, is not always right." If the protest movement of recent years is not to be a mere "revolution for the hell of it," its influence on the delivery of human services depends, as Michael Lipsky (1968; also Wilson, 1961) has persuasively shown, on increasing the bargaining ability of powerless groups in the arena of politics by building viable organizations and harnessing stable political resources.

Protest as such is symptomatic of unmet needs, but it can only articulate demands. It therefore does not absolve the professions from their responsibility to determine needs. Whatever other functions are served by protest, demands for community control and client participation in *professional* decision making are probably more a distraction than a remedy (Beck, 1969).[42] Community power as a panacea for solving the problems of professional service is at best ironic, for local sovereignty—whether in the name of the feudal prince or the common people—has always been a shibboleth of conservatism and reaction. As Wilbert Moore (1970, p. 169) remarks, "decentralization does not end oligarchy; it only dissipates and therefore in a sense extends it."[43]

In the perspective of professionalism, the protest movement attacks something endemic in professional service. Hughes (1958, p. 54) has pointed out that "in many occupations, the workers or practitioners (to use both a lower and a higher status term) deal routinely with what are emergencies to the people who receive their services."[44] If this is true of normal situations, it is even truer when service must be rendered to mass publics under bureaucratic conditions in times of crisis. The client's feeling of being neglected is not something easily dealt with. Although consultative forms of interaction between spokesmen for professional services and organized clienteles may be conducive to mutual understanding of this dilemma, it would be utopian under modern organizational conditions to expect an easy solution of the routine-versus-emergency problem.

Very much the same can be said of another problem to which Hughes has called attention—the problem of mistakes and failure. Sensitivity to the possibility of mistakes and failure is common to both the social worker in a local welfare agency and the economist on the president's Council of Economic Advisers. Mistakes harm both the professional and his client; the absence of clear-cut criteria of success or failure makes the problem all the more perplexing. Clients tend to confuse the successful conclusion of the service with good professional work. For this reason professionals insist on peer judgment of their performance. The medical quack, the shyster lawyer, and the grandstanding professor will please their customers but not their colleagues. To protect themselves against mistakes, the professions place great emphasis on routine, ritual, etiquette, and approved ways of doing things. Referral to and consultation among colleagues serve the same function of minimizing risk. In this connection, the division of labor is not just technical but also psychological.

The volatility and sometimes violence of what has been called "the revolt of the client" are for some professionals traumatic experiences. Their consequences are difficult to foresee because it is impossible to separate out long-term secular changes in the professions from changes in response to

immediate social pressures. For a time it appeared that the protest movement, as two sociologists concluded in 1969, "attacks the basic legitimacy
of the occupational and institutional claims to power of the professional"
on a number of grounds: "(1) the expertise of the practioners is inadequate,
(2) their claims to altruism are unfounded, (3) the organizational delivery
system supporting their authority is defective and insufficient, and (4) this
system is too efficient and exceeds the appropriate bounds of its power"
(Haug and Sussman, 1969, p. 156). Although this funeral oration was
probably premature, the paradox of the last two points calls attention to
at least one important problematic aspect of the skill revolution's impact
on the provision of professional services in modern technological society.

Self-criticism within the professions has long been directed toward the
growing fragmentation of services due to specialization and subspecialization.[45] The fragmentation of service is seen as a source of client discontent
because it seems to depersonalize and standardize the professional-client
relationship, making the client feel that he is merely an assembly of parts
rather than a whole person with interrelated problems requiring an integrative solution. At least some professionals have therefore called for holistic treatment of the client that would restore his dignity as a whole person
(see Lynd, 1958).

Precisely the opposite argument has also been made. The protest movement is seen as opposed to restoring the client as a whole person through
institutional coordinating mechanisms. "The client seems to be rejecting
what he considers institutionalized meddling under the cover of professional concern," write Haug and Sussman (1969, pp. 157–158); and they
continue:

Outreach programs from the client perspective have become out-grab. Students
want to organize their own courses and call in the professional as a consultant.
The "whole man" approach in medicine infringes on areas of social relations where
clients consider themselves competent; patients want to turn to the doctor when
in trouble, but not be bothered otherwise. This suggests that the client is demanding
the right to define the problem, and then call upon the professional only as a
specialist in a narrow domain.

Although their evidence is flimsy, Haug and Sussman (ibid., p. 159)
present a rather ingenious theory about the consequences of the client
revolt as they describe it:

since the major thrust of the client revolt has been against the institutional con-
comitants of professionalism, including the tendency of the professional to extend
his authority beyond the limits of his legitimate special expertise, one might predict
a narrowing of professional authority to the most limited and esoteric elements of
his knowledge base. This is unlikely to mean, despite client-revolt rhetoric, that

the professional will fully lose the core of his autonomy, the right to define the nature of the client's problem. Even if the client exercised his right to pick and choose the time and place of his use of the professional's expertise, once the client enters the interaction, the expert's knowledge of cause-effect will permit him to diagnose and respecify the original complaint or need into his terms.

These analysts conclude, therefore, that the tension between professional and society can lead to deprofessionalization, but that "what the client demands—the professional as a limited consultant—may be less a curse than a blessing in disguise" (ibid., p. 160).

There is something comforting in this theory. On the one hand, it does not contradict the skill revolution hypothesis of progressive specialization; on the other hand, it anticipates changes in the professional-client relationship that, on close inspection, seem to be radical without really being so. The theory may well be true.

Despite antiprofessional tendencies in the protest movement, a new balance in organized professional-client relations seems to be emerging. On the one hand, the protest movement comes to realize that it needs professional assistance. As Lipsky (1970, p. 168) points out,

the need for skilled professionals is not restricted to lawyers . . . Protest groups may need architects and city planners to present a viable alternative to urban renewal proposals. They may need consultant assistance to present testimony concerning the inadequacy of governmental programs. They may need grantsmen to compete for federal and private philanthropic funds.

On the other hand, new developments within the professions in response to changing social values appear as reassertions of professional authority. Representation of client interests and their satisfaction through new professional roles rather than through direct client participation is the most noteworthy of these developments (see Michaelson, 1969; Bazell, 1971).

The new "advocacy role" is available at both the level of individual service and societal policy making. In this role, the professional does not just respond to client demands and, by responding, serve society; rather, his task is to anticipate needs, initiate services, and improve society.

There are some real difficulties with the advocacy role. In the enthusiasm accompanying its discovery, it was easy enough to mistake advocacy as a *professional response* to presumably unmet social needs, with activism as a *political* response. Clearly and intentionally identifying advocacy with political action, a professor of social work has defined the advocate as "the professional who identifies with the victims of social problems and who pursues modification in social conditions"; and he has argued that the advocate "will need to have the professional dedication to take the risk and be political" (Brager, 1968, p. 15). Needless to say, this interpretation has not gone unchallenged, and there is no indication that this is the meaning given it by most members of the legal profession, where it originated in the first place (Du Cann, 1964).

Paradoxically, its radical appearance notwithstanding, advocacy implies an essentially paternalistic attitude. Although he does not give it this interpretation, Edgar H. Schein (1972, p. 51), speaking of "role innovators," has this to say:

These members of the profession accept its central or pivotal norms but try to redefine where, how, and on whom the profession is to be practiced. A strong theme in this group has been the concern for the ultimate client, who is the actual receiver of professional services but who may have little or no voice in the design of those services—the consumer, the low-income tenant, the welfare recipient, the nonpaying charity case in the local hospital, the ghetto dweller. Thus, advocacy law and advocacy architecture are efforts by some lawyers and architects to provide services to clients who never saw themselves as clients, who did not realize that they were entitled to any voice in their own affairs, and who could not pay professional fees.

The professional as advocate not only knows what is best for people but also has the advantage over political representatives of not being responsible to his clients as elected officials are responsible to their constituents. So the professional as advocate must fall back on the collective mandate given his profession by society. But in taking the generalized mandate theory seriously, advocate professionals should answer some serious questions. What will happen if things go wrong? To whom will the advocate professional be accountable? His clients, his peers, his employers, or only his own conscience? What would accountability imply? Would it imply restitution? Risking censure or suspension of license? Dismissal from the job? Most of these questions have yet to be answered.

Advocacy as a professional response to unmet social needs and not as a substitute, in professional guise, for social action, has come to be accepted in the planning professions. This profession has understandably long been of interest to political science, for two reasons—first, because its clientele is never an individual person, and second, because its activities are clearly and intimately implicated in the public interest (see Meyerson and Banfield, 1955; Altshuler, 1965; Rabinovitz, 1969). The plight of people displaced by urban renewal projects became a source of protest, but protest alone would never have brought about a solution in the public interest (Rossi and Dentler, 1961). What makes possible a broadening of the meaning of public interest is the intervention of advocacy planners who bring the interests of the deprived groups into the planning process by giving them expert advice. The relationship between the expert-advocate, individual or firm, and the client organization has taken a variety of forms. Blecher

(1971), in an analysis of six demonstration programs, found that when the relationship followed the classical model of a strictly formal contract between professional and client, relations of the client group with public authorities were less conflictual than when the client organization tried to influence directly the technical aspects of the planning process.

The most significant contribution of the advocacy role, or what the lawyers interestingly call "public interest work," is perhaps not its immediate payoffs to clients in need, but its bringing the profession's idealized model of public service somewhat closer to reality than it has been in the past. Nevertheless, the present extent and future promises of the advocacy role should not be overestimated. As a very thorough recent study of the legal profession (Marks, 1972, p. 250) concludes,

The level of public interest work by those parts of the private bar that we observed was low; the delivered efforts of private firms represent only a small part of the available energies of those firms. For the bar as a whole the response appears to be even smaller; indeed it appears to be infinitesimal. Certainly one cannot say that the bar as a whole has fashioned a public interest response unless some of the institutional definitions of professional responsibility are being affected by its efforts.

Because it is dependent on government or foundation support that may be withdrawn, or because clients themselves may reject an advocate's help, the role is difficult to sustain. Nevertheless, as a new form of professional conduct, and if it is not misused, professional advocacy is quite in line with the realities of technological society. However, it should not be considered an alternative to either conventional or unconventional politics. Although in articulating and advocating client needs the professional puts them on a firmer knowledge base then would otherwise be the case, interest-group formation and pressure politics will continue to be primary ways to influence policy making and administration.

To predict the outcome of the contemporary ferment in the relationship between the professions and society is imprudent. There is only a thin line between politicization that leads to deprofessionalization of human services, on the one hand, and responsible involvement in those public issues that are the legitimate concern of the professions, on the other hand. Political awareness will make the professions perhaps more responsive to societal needs; but professionals must bring to the treatment of public issues professionally pertinent criteria of substance and conduct that warrant their being respected for their knowledge and skills rather than for the particular ideological predilections that may be the fashion of the moment. The winds of politics are moody and have a way of changing faster than professional responses to these winds.

The Consultative Commonwealth

Rooted in the social and technological changes occasioned by the modern skill revolution, the consultative commonwealth does not denote a revolutionary state. On the contrary, the construct assumes that as a result of the prominence of old and new professions in policy making and the delivery of human services, consultative modes of interaction will be a pervasive feature of governance in the future society. Consultation is the most characteristic aspect of the relationships among professional skill specialists and between them and their clients. Consultation will not be the dominant process but will complement, supplement, and implement other governmental processes like democratic participation, bureaucratic organization, pluralistic bargaining, or oligarchic decision making.

It is because professionalization and deprofessionalization are mutually entailed that professionalization will not usher in the bureaucratic state of rulership through professional expertise, and deprofessionalization will not bring in the democratic state of governance through client participation. There will be both more bureaucratization and more democratization, but the skill revolution will inject professional ways of doing things into the emerging commonwealth. Although they are necessary, neither bureaucratic nor democratic techniques are sufficient to cope with the extraordinarily complex social and technological problems of the future. Consultation will be a necessary but also not sufficient condition of the future commonwealth.

In the real world of politics, consultation is contaminated by other social processes so that it can never occur in pure form. The consultative commonwealth is therefore not a political system in which men of knowledge or skill specialists have uncontested power to constitute a new ruling class. Rather, it is a system of government in which professional norms and modes of conduct are acknowledged components of individual and collective choice making, at the level both of policy and of administration. The construct assumes that insofar as familiar bureaucratic-hierarchical and participative-representational patterns continue, they will be permeated by consultative patterns. This is so because in the technological society, the ways of consultation are, on balance, well suited to the formulation and delivery of professionally based services. For consultation infuses professional expertise as well as client perspective into the policy process and the delivery of services.

Consultation as a form of interaction does not assume equality among all participants. It takes for granted that the participants are unequal precisely because the professional whose advice or service is sought is superior to the client in his area of competence. Were it otherwise, the whole notion of expertise and skill specialization would be meaningless. The inequality taken for granted is of course based on an authority of competence and not of position. The client may be superior or equal to the consultant in social status or organizational position, but for the purpose of consultation he is dependent on the consultant. But a political milieu reduces the status advantage that the professional normally has in his client relationships. Professionals cannot simply depend on their authority but may have to persuade their clients, especially if the clients are highly placed executive or legislative policy makers. Policy makers as clients do not stand in awe of professionals.

There are also limits to professional dominance at the humble end of government where the low-level bureaucratic professional encounters his clients. One of the paradoxes of professional practice is that the professional's reputation partly depends on his being evaluated, whether he likes it or not, by clients—that is, precisely by those persons least qualified technically to judge professional performance. The more that human services are extended to larger classes of people and become professionalized, the less are clients willing to be passive recipients of service, and the greater is their demand for high performance (Gilb, 1966, p. 89). The professional's need for at least some client approval has always been a source of client control.[46]

It is the nature of pluralistic processes to multiply channels of consultation, thereby introducing competition into the advisory function. As expert encounters expert, alternative solutions become political compromises that safeguard the commonwealth against the professional or personal biases of skill specialists.[47] What Rourke (1969, p. 45) says of bureaucrats is equally applicable to professionals in political milieux: "In the case of advice, the power of bureaucrats is indirect, resting as it does upon their ability to persuade political officials that a certain course of action should be taken. Bureaucrats have influence only if politicians accept their advice."

Constitutionally speaking, then, the consultative commonwealth is characterized by status ambiguity. In the classical professional-client model, the professional is in a superior and the client in a subordinate position. In the professional-colleague relationship, the actors appear to be in equal positions. And in the professional-organization relationship, the professional's position appears to be subordinate to that of the organizational supervisor. But in reality these constitutional relationships vary a good deal and may actually be reversed. Clients do have ways of controlling the professional; status jealousies among professionals interfere with mutual deference; and professionals in organizations have ways of gaining the upper hand. Especially in organizational settings in which the professional interacts simultaneously with clients, colleagues, and supervisors, ambi-guities inherent in any one relationship will be confounded by the com-plexity of the total network in which all the actors are enmeshed.

The need to integrate specializations and subspecializations into a co-herent professional service is best met through consultation. Neither mar-ket-type exchange mechanisms nor hierarchical modes are sufficient to coordinate diverse specialties. Status differences within and among the professions make nonconsultative ways of coordination problematical, for they ignore ambiguities in status relationships. On the one hand, the "su-perior" professional is expected to "direct" the work of subordinate per-sonnel; but on the other hand, for some purposes the higher-skill specialist "depends" or "relies" on the lower-skill specialist, as physicians depend on nurses or university professors rely on librarians (see Pelz, 1960).

Traditional solutions to the coordination of specialized services have been, first, to have professionals run their own affairs, as professors do in some universities; second, to turn coordination over to lay boards, as in primary or secondary education; and third, to create altogether new ad-ministrative professions, like the city manager or hospital administrator. All of these modes of coordination make implicit assumptions about status differentiation. By transcending formal social or bureaucratic status lines and organizational barriers, consultation facilitates the utilization of diverse knowledge and intelligence that otherwise would not be brought to bear on policy making or administration, including knowledge of what is polit-ically feasible and attainable.

Consultation will not erase ambiguities in professional relationships be-cause status differentiation is immanent in skill differentiation. Therefore, interprofessional bargaining and negotiations concerning jurisdictional matters will continue in the consultative commonwealth (Gilb, 1966, pp. 162–164), as will hierarchical forms of conflict resolution. This is likely to be so because, as Moore (1970, p. 73) puts it, "authenticated professionals are scarcely more prone to rational and sensible compromises and reason-able innovations than others who occupy a privileged position."

The consultative commonwealth will be circumscribed by political and economic processes that may, but need not, involve consultation. Many human services will continue to be rendered by occupations whose pro-fessionalization is more a distant aspiration than an early prospect. To expect that in the foreseeable future the two largest and most powerful institutional sectors of society—government and business—will be fully professionalized would be to burden the construct of the consultative com-monwealth beyond its heuristic capability.[48] Government, in particular, will be guided by the politics of elections, group processes, and bureaucratic inertia. The continuing skill revolution will accentuate the professionalization of advice and services *in* government, which is something different from the professionalization *of* government. Increased sensitivity of professionals to their own position in society and to the nature of their relationships with clients as diverse as slum dwellers and high-policy makers will make for more rather than less politics in the consultative commonwealth,[49] but technological developments and the delivery of human services become increasingly dependent on consultation as the linkage mechanism between democracy and bureaucracy.[50]

Notes

References

Credits

Index

Notes

Introduction

1. The best and still most authoritative review of these developments is to be found in Dahl (1961b).

2. See, especially, Truman (1955), who, as chairman of the Committee on Political Behavior of the Social Science Research Council, was in an excellent position to observe the impact of "the revolution in the behavioral sciences" on political science. In other fields the interdisciplinary orientation led to new or freshly strengthened subfields like "culture and personality" in anthropology, political psychology within social psychology, political sociology, economic geography, political economy, and so on. Most of these developments can be traced back to the 1920s, but it was only in the 1950s that the behavior-oriented interdisciplinary approaches became pervasive (see Eulau, 1963c).

3. In psychology the interdisciplinary orientation meant just the opposite: having long stressed the isolated individual, psychologists discovered culture and interpersonal relations as contexts of individual behavior. Newcomb's text (1950) was particularly influential. There even was the formulation of an "ecological psychology" (Barker, 1968).

4. Questions concerning self-identification in terms of social class had been asked in earlier surveys, but the Michigan surveys also asked questions on "class awareness," of the class with which the respondent identified himself and the "other" class (with which the respondent did not identify).

5. Ego psychology suggested the concept of "class identification"; for a leading user, see Centers (1949). Social determinism was explicit in the work of Lazarsfeld and associates (1948).

6. For reasons I can no longer recall, the project failed to deal, as it should have done, with the relationship between the legislature and the governor or executive bureaucracy, by all odds the most "significant others" in the legislature's external environment.

7. Falter's (1982) book is by far the best and most disinterested review of the impact of the behavioral sciences on political science. Falter only errs, it seems to

me, in his assessment of Lasswell's contribution to the behavioral movement by giving too much attention to Lasswell's early Freudian view of psychopathology and too little to the rest of his work.

8. I called the book an "essay," as defined by the dictionary: "a literary composition, analytical or interpretative, dealing with its subject from a more or less limited or personal standpoint." And I continued: "It does not pretend to be wise or erudite, nor to be systematic, comprehensive, or exhaustive. I have not reviewed the literature nor consulted my own voluminous files, though I occasionally reread my earlier comments on the subject. I wrote this book as a personal document, off the cuff, setting down what came to mind as it derived from my experiences in political life, in reading, in teaching, and in research" (Eulau, 1963a, pp. vi–vii).

Ironically, my "failure" to link what I wrote with the literature was faulted by Robert E. Lane (1964) in his review of the book. Lane felt that I should have done what I intentionally did not want to do—get into arguments. "It seems to me," Lane wrote, "that the way to advance the argument over the fruitfulness of one way of looking at the field, compared to another, is to come to grips with what others have said about it. An argument with a vague generalized other is not really an argument at all." Lane was both right and wrong. I did not want to make an "argument" precisely because there had been enough argumentation, and if I had entered the fray here, as I did on other occasions, I would surely not have come to write the book that I wanted to write. And I am still convinced that an "argument" does not advance a science, though it might advance argumentation.

9. I note with interest that this was not recognized by most of my colleagues of the behavioral persuasion but by a "classical" political theorist. Referring to *The Behavioral Persuasion in Politics,* Dante Germino (1967, pp. 190–191n5) wrote that it "is a remarkably moderate exposition. Some of his statements are unexceptionable . . . , and it is clear that the author strives for disinterested political inquiry. His definition of behavioralism . . . is general and undogmatic . . . [h]e is not without respect and sympathy for 'the classical tradition in political science.' For Eulau, behavioralism is not a revolt against that tradition . . . Eulau dedicated this book to Harold Lasswell, but many observations in it, as well as its general tone, are so far removed from Lasswell's teaching that we may possibly already be with Eulau on the road to a revisionist behavioralism." There follow some critical comments on my presumed technological fix, followed by the familiar distortion that neither I nor any other behavioralist ever asserted: "It is rather difficult to see how any computer could ever answer the question of the *summum bonum* for man." Germino concludes: "The misplaced emphasis on technology in Eulau's book is regrettable, but he is far more cautious in his claims and more aware of the difficulties than are most behavioralist political scientists."

10. For individual-level studies of the city council project, see Prewitt, 1970; Black, 1970, 1972; Cronin, 1970; Eyestone, 1971; Loveridge, 1971; Zisk, 1973.

11. And I continued in this admittedly polemical vein: "As in the old public administration, it seems to me, there is in the new public policy the same simplistic quest for the technological fix, the same whimsical choice of topical issues, the same self-deception about influence on governmental decision making, the same

emphasis on an innocuous reformist theory, the same untrustworthy trust in the 'case' as a source of insight and, above all, the same anti-intellectual attitude toward basic or theoretical research" (Eulau, 1977a, pp. 419–420).

12. Most remarkable about the unusual data sets assembled by Miller and Stokes, used only very partially in their own work, is that they have not been widely exploited by others. As Miller informed me in a private communication (June 17, 1977), "given the fact that the data have been in the public domain as long as they have, I am at a loss to explain why others didn't stumble upon at least some of the nuggets that seem to be so accessible."

13. Particularly germane are Lasswell's (1948a) essays "Skill Politics and Skill Revolution," "The Garrison State and Specialists on Violence," and "The Rise of the Propagandist."

14. I dealt with the tensions between "civility" and "technology" in a number of essays prepared at a time when these tensions were particularly observable, in the era of the "counterculture" of the late 1960s and early 1970s. Both the new technocrats and the counterculturists, it seemed to me, were trampling on the liberal temper of civility that is a necessary condition for a pluralistic and tolerant politics. See Eulau (1977b).

1. The Behavioral Persuasion in Politics

1. I am using "group" in the most generic sense of the term as referring to a society, a nation, a region, a community, a tribe, an organization, a social class, a committee—any collectivity whose members are in more or less direct and permanent contact with each other.

2. Units and Levels of Analysis

1. For linguistic convenience, I shall use the term "group" in referring to any collective of two or more individuals that is an "action unit," that is, any unit, from the dyad to a nation, that can make a collective decision committing all the members of the unit to a course of action. An action unit is to be distinguished from an "aggregate unit." Like an action unit, an aggregate unit or, simply, an aggregate is an empirical phenomenon whose behavior can be observed. But an aggregate differs from a group in that its "unit character" is an artifact of quantification and not the result of interactions or relationships between its components. Interaction is not a necessary condition of an aggregate's existence. This does not mean that the behavior of an aggregate may not have consequences for the behavior of an action unit. A change of government as a result of changes in the behavior of the electorate (an aggregate) is an obvious example. An aggregate is composed of action units—individuals or groups—with identical or similar properties. We can speak of an aggregate of individuals or of an aggregate of groups.

2. Apropos the behavioral-versus-institutional controversy, Donald E. Stokes (1966, p. 1) has made this comment: "It is in a way remarkable that the antithesis between institutions and behavior should ever have seemed plausible to political scientists. Perhaps it never did to the keenest observers."

3. For a highly perceptive discussion of the "ecological fallacy" and some of the relevant literature, see Price (1968).

4. As far as I can tell, Oliver Garceau (1951) was the first political scientist to call attention to the task of linking different units of analysis.

5. For a persuasive recent statement, see Lynd (1958). For other aspects of the "part-whole" problem, see Lerner (1963).

6. See, for instance, Rokkan (1962, p. 48), where "micropolitics" is defined as "the analysis of individual citizens' reactions to the political events and alternatives in their communities."

3. Closing the Micro-Macro Gap

1. The two most useful references to the "Lazarsfeld school" and micro-macro analysis are Lazarsfeld and Menzel (1965) and Selvin and Hagstrom (1966).

4. Multilevel Methods and Comparative Analysis

1. This aspect is ignored, for instance, in a very important study by Kasarda (1974). He compares the implications of size for comparison between these units: 178 school systems (which he calls "institutions") in Colorado; 207 local "communities" *(sic)* in Wisconsin; and 43 nonagriculturally based nations (called "societies"). While Kasarda uses size (treated as an independent variable), he does not deal with the possible contextual effects.

2. For a critique on this ground, see Scheuch (1969, p. 141): "Almond and Verba asked cross-sections of the population of various nations about what one is proud of in one's own country, and the between-nation differences in responses were used as expressing stability of political institutions; certainly such answers are mainly reflections of collective properties in the minds of respondents."

5. Class and Party as Interactive Role Systems

1. The minor parties, so-called, are minor precisely because they find it difficult to survive in the institutional context formed by the operation of the two major parties.

2. Extraneous data suggest that it was a temporary deviation, as do the data reported here. Poll data from 1947–1948 show Eisenhower able to win the presidential office under the label of either party. See Hyman and Sheatsley (1953).

3. Much has been made in recent years of the fact that Charles A. Beard's economic interpretation of the making and ratification of the Constitution may be faulty because his research was incomplete and his classifications were in many cases wrong. But one who reads the critics is impressed by the fact that while Beard's classification of economic divisions and resulting interpretation may be wrong in detail, the politics of the period was clearly a politics of social class. If it were otherwise, one should indeed wonder why James Madison ever wrote Number 10 of *The Federalist*. For a study of Beard, see McDonald (1958).

4. The study was made by Philip Converse of the Survey Research Center, University of Michigan, and the findings are reported in Miller (1958).

5. This is, of course, an "ideal-type" construct of the system. In empirical reality, American voters do have other choices: they may abstain from voting, as very many do, or they may vote for "third" parties, as very few do.

6. The multiparty system is more likely to be characterized by class politics or other special-interest politics. But this need not mean that it is, therefore, any less "stable" than a two-party system—as the experience of the Scandinavian states shows.

7. Since these ideas about the mutual functions performed by the class and party systems were first formulated, a somewhat similar formulation has been made by Ranney and Kendall (1956, pp. 506–509). These authors stress the function of the parties in reducing what they call the "civil-war potential" of American society and do not really mention the integrating effect of the class system on the political parties.

8. For the distinction between concrete and analytical structures, see Levy (1958).

9. Cited by Gross (1953, p. 60). Gross rejects this conception.

10. Income was dropped as a component of the 1956 index because between 1952 and 1956 it proved so variable as an indicator that it seriously undermined the stability of the index and interfered with the comparability of results. Of the original 1952 sample of 1,614 respondents, 414 cases, including farmers, housewives, and other occupational groupings, were dropped because they could not be properly classified. Of the 1956 sample of 1,772 respondents, 463 cases were dropped for the same reason.

In the case of the 1952 data, forty-five different combinations of occupational, income, and educational categories were placed in a cross-tabulated "property space" that permitted each respondent to occupy a single position in the resulting class structure. In the case of the 1956 data, the property space consisted of fifteen cells. Using the method of arbitrary numerical reduction, this procedure yielded scores for every possible combination—9 in the 1952 matrix and 7 in the 1956 matrix. The score categories were then cut into four "classes" and finally dichotomized into two.

11. In 1952, of the 1,200 respondents located on the *objective* index of social class, 35 percent identified themselves as middle class, 60 percent as working class, 2 percent as lower class, and another 1 percent as upper class, while 2 percent did not know or their view could not be ascertained. Somewhat different questions and coding procedures used in 1956 do not provide exactly similar data for that year. However, of the total of 1,772 respondents in 1956, 64 percent acknowledged thinking of themselves as being either middle class or working class, and 97 percent were prepared to assign themselves to one of these classes—61 percent working class and 36 percent middle class.

12. Of the 1,200 objectively classified respondents in 1952, another sixty-eight cases were lost because they did not identify themselves as either working class or middle class. In 1956, of the 1,309 objectively classified respondents, fifty-one cases had to be eliminated for the same reason.

6. Conflict and the Network of Legislative Roles

1. At the time when this was written, in the late 1950s, we noted the following: "Indicative of the state of affairs [in the field of legislative research] is the fact that organizational theorists have a specialized medium of communication in the *Administrative Science Quarterly*. No equivalent journal is devoted to the study of legislative behavior and processes" (Wahlke et al., 1962, p. 377n2). Since then, with the growth of legislative research from the early 1960s on, the situation has drastically changed. But it was not until February 1976 that the first issue of the *Legislative Studies Quarterly,* published at the Comparative Legislative Research Center, University of Iowa, appeared.

2. The most notable works in this genre are Truman (1951), Latham (1952), and Gross (1953).

3. Garceau and Silverman's (1954) study of the Vermont legislature represents a definite shift in conceptualization from the conventional "group-influence model" to a more complex model of interaction between a legislature and its clientele.

4. Keefe (1956) summarizes relevant formulations and critically appraises the deficiencies of this approach.

5. It can be argued that the conflict hypothesis does not account for significant and numerically frequent patterns of behavior in state legislatures. Keefe (1956, p. 734), for instance, points out that unanimity and consensus in many cases "may not be so much a matter of 'leadership' as simply a case of like-minded legislators moving from bill to bill in the broad fields of state public policy where consensus rather than conflict obtains." But this interpretation is possibly deceptive. As Truman (1951, p. 392) points out, "even a temporarily viable legislative decision usually must involve the adjustment and compromise of interests. Even where virtual unanimity prevails in the legislature, the process of reconciling conflicting interests must have taken place—though perhaps at an earlier stage wholly or partly outside the legislature and the formal institutions of government. When this happens, the legislature merely registers the decision."

6. For an interpretation of role as setting "premises" in decision making, see Simon (1957a, p. 201).

7. For an excellent historical analysis of the relationship between legislation and representation, see Akzin (1936).

8. For a convenient and comprehensive summary of definitions, see Fairlie (1940).

9. See Beer (1957, p. 613), who points out how little general legislation was proposed or enacted in those days.

10. For the conception of "bounded rationality" as well as the notion that roles constitute some of the premises of decision-making behavior, we are indebted to Simon (1957a).

11. For a perspicacious discussion of ambiguities in representation, see Gosnell (1948, pp. 124–142).

12. That organized interest groups and group activity occur in all developed Western systems is now widely accepted. See, for example, the comments of G. Heckscher in Ehrmann (1958, p. 170), and LaPalombara (1960, pp. 29–30).

This is *not* to say, however, that the *legitimacy* of pressure-group activity is universally admitted, even in Western systems.

13. See Eldersveld (1958) and Garceau (1958). For discussion of the general problems of research, theory, and conception, see also Mackenzie (1955), Almond (1958), and de Grazia (1958).

14. See, for example, Gross (1953, p. 143); Truman (1951, pp. 159–167) lists these and similar group characteristics, adding to the list of "group cohesion."

15. "Accommodation" does not necessarily mean "accession," although that is, of course, one form that accommodation may take. Accommodation here means conscious consideration, of the sort implied in Stewart's (1958, pp. 3–27) discussion of "consultation."

16. These two dimensions are suggested not only in numerous general social-psychological discussions of role concepts and self concepts, but also by two of the very few empirical and analytical studies of group politics. Garceau and Silverman (1954) suggest that differences in legislative behavior toward groups, as well as legislators' ideas about appropriate behavior toward them, are associated with different levels of information about groups. Samuel H. Beer (1957), in his analysis of operative theories of interest representation in Britain, suggests a number of respects in which legislators' different conceptions of the appropriate place of interest groups (described as old Tory, old Whig, liberal, radical, and collectivist theories) imply different conceptions of how legislators should behave toward such groups or their agents. Beer singles out for special attention one facet of the legislator-group role relationship—that involving the activity of the legislator as agent of a group (the "interested M.P.").

7. Law and Politics

1. In the National Opinion Research Center survey of occupations (Reiss, 1961, p. 54, Table II–9), state governor ranked second; federal cabinet member, fourth; mayor of large city, sixth; congressman, seventh; and head of department in state government, twelfth.

2. See Landis (1955) for a discussion of codes of ethics in such professions as accounting, architecture, medicine, law, engineering, ministry, teaching, and public administration.

8. Polarity in Representational Federalism

1. Italics added. All of the following references are to the Beloff (1948) edition of *The Federalist*.

2. The passage continues: "Before the sentiments impressed on their minds by the mode of their elevation, can be effaced by the exercise of power, they will be compelled to anticipate the moment when their power is to cease, when their exercise of it is to be reviewed, and when they must descend to the level from which they were raised; there for ever to remain unless a faithful discharge of their trust shall have established their title to a renewal of it" (No. 57, pp. 293–294).

3. These are the words of Chief Justice Taney in *Ableman* v. *Booth,* 21 How. 506 (1859).

4. In the gamma statistic, for instance, the measure of association is simply the cross-product of these pulls. The bivariate case can be generalized to more complex multivariate situations. See Galtung (1969, pp. 195–196).

5. I have stressed this elsewhere; see Chapter 9.

6. See Cohen (1949, p. 14): "The opposition between contrary categories is neither absorbed nor in any way transcended by their unity, any more than abstract unity can be generated by abstract difference."

7. See Cohen (1931, p. 166): "Thus physical science employs this principle when it eliminates the vagueness and indetermination of popular categories like *high* and *low, hot* and *cold, large* and *small, far* and *near,* etc. It does so by substituting a definite determination such as a deteminate number of yards or degrees of temperature. The indetermination and consequent inconclusiveness of metaphysical and of a good deal of sociological discussion results from uncritically adhering to simple alternatives instead of resorting to the laborious process of integrating opposite assertions by finding the proper distinctions and qualifications."

8. For an empirical test of representation as systemic responsiveness, see Chapter 11.

9. Sundquist (1969, p. 242) points out that today "added to the traditional federal-state-local or federal-state-county-town structure of federalism are new bodies with jurisdiction over new areas—multicounty bodies interposed between the states and their local governments, and neighborhood bodies acting as a link between the people and their local governments within the larger cities."

9. Configurative Analysis

1. David Easton (1950) is wrong, I think, in dating Lasswell's commitment to democratic values as of the beginning of World War II.

2. I do not think Lasswell would give this example of a widely distributed individual event today. With air pollution a physical problem of collective survival, the interpersonal importance of breathing is evident.

3. For a discussion of the distinction between emergence as part of an evolutionary cosmogeny and as a thesis about hierarchical organization, see Nagel (1961, pp. 366–380). Nagel argues that the evolutionary version of the emergence doctrine is not entailed by the conception of emergence as irreducible hierarchical organization.

10. The Informal Organization of Small Decision-Making Groups

1. It would be silly even to attempt a relevant bibliography here. I shall list three books that have had some effect on my own thinking on small groups; three "readers" that contain some of the best research that has been done; two small paperbacks that may be useful as introduction; and a handbook. The books: Ho-

mans (1950); Thibaut and Kelley (1959); and Collins and Guetzkow (1964). The readers: Cartwright and Zander (1953); Hare, Borgatta, and Bales (1955); and Hyman and Singer (1968). The paperbacks: Olmstead (1959) and Shepherd (1964). The handbook: Hare (1962).

2.   For a "small-group" political study based on interaction theory, see March (1953); for an application of reference group notions, see Fiellin (1962); for a "structural-functional" study, see Fenno (1962).

3.   The most significant exception is Barber (1966). See also McClosky and Dahlgren (1959); C. O. Jones (1962); and Schubert (1964).

4.   Verba (1961) summarized and assessed much of the sociological and social-psychological literature in order to suggest its relevance for political science. The same was true of a book by a political scientist published the following year (Golembiewski, 1962). See Eulau, 1962b.

5.   The great exception is Barber (1966), whose study includes twelve local boards of finance in Connecticut.

6.   See Moreno (1960). Another method is "interaction analysis"; see Bales (1950). A third method is "participant observation," as in Whyte (1955).

7.   The feasibility of using sociometric questions for comparative purposes in survey research on institutional units was first explored by the State Legislative Research Project in 1957. See Buchanan, "Subject Matter Experts" and "The Bonds of Friendship" in Wahlke et al. (1962). Samuel C. Patterson (1959) was the first political scientist to use the "sociogram" as an analytical tool. Group indices based on sociometric choices were used by Eulau (1962a). See also Francis (1962). A pilot analysis based on some of the sociometric data collected by the City Council Research Project was reported in Eulau and Lupsha (1966).

8.   Interviews were conducted in 1966 and 1967 in eighty-seven of the ninety San Francisco Bay area cities then in existence. The city of San Francisco was omitted because its county-city type of council—called Board of Supervisors—was more professional than and very different from the councils in the other cities. In two cities the whole council refused to be interviewed (for reasons well known to us: both cities were at the time involved in controversies with the state and/or county). In five cities analysis at the group level could not be performed because only three or fewer councilmen were interviewed. That is, group analysis was attempted only if, for instance, four out of five persons had been interviewed. Of the eighty-two councils in this analysis, sixty-seven had five members, eleven had seven members, three had nine members, and one, Palo Alto, had thirteen members.

9.   The question: "When the Council is in disagreement on an issue, would you say there is more or less the same line-up of votes here in (city)? I mean, do some members seem to vote together on controversial issues? IF YES: With whom do *you* usually vote on controversial matters? Now, what about the others? are they united or split? IF SPLIT: Who would you say votes most often together when the others are split?"

Implicit in the question was, of course, the assumption that councilmen line up with each other more or less regularly *regardless* of the content of specific issues.

If one were to ask this question of legislators or judges on other levels of government, it would be absurd or ridiculous. But at the local level and in the case of small groups, it is neither absurd nor ridiculous.

In the first place, the issues with which a city council deals are considerably less diverse than those facing state or federal legislative bodies or courts. The probability that the same members line up with each other over many issues is therefore much greater than in legislatures dealing with more complex and diverse matters. Second, in small groups in which interpersonal relations are face-to-face and often intimate, stable factionalism, in spite of varying issues, is quite likely to result from group pressures to conform to the norms, attitudes, and behavior of those whose affect, respect, or help one values. Third, where different issues do make for shifting coalitions or blocs in the council, one would have reason to expect that councilmen will articulate irregular voting patterns if they occur. And this, in fact, was the case in twenty-nine out of the eighty-two councils. Finally, as the analysis will show, the decisional structures identified by the sociometric question do in fact yield empirical relationships that are clearly not due to chance.

10. The question: "If there is disagreement on the Council in regard to some key problem, which member's opposition would you be most concerned about?"

All of the measures of the council's "relational properties" introduced represent what sociometry calls "expansiveness" indices. The expansiveness index permits group members to choose as many other persons as they wish. It is an index that measures the "pervasiveness" of the phenomenon—such as coalitional or oppositional activity, opinion leadership, expertise, respect, and affect—in the group as a whole. It is labeled "expansiveness" by Proctor and Loomis (1951). The formula: $E = N/M$, where E = expansiveness, N = number of all nominations made in the group, and M = number of all members (size of group).

Although the index appears to be very simple, it actually hides other properties. It takes account of the number of individuals named, regardless of the number of individual choices they received, and the average choices made in the group: $N/M = P/M \times N/P$, where P = number of individual persons named.

Because rank ordering of the councils in terms of the individual scores obtained by the expansiveness index yielded many ties, the scores were used to divide the councils into quartile distributions (or terciles, if quartiles were impossible). The analysis relies chiefly on comparison of the "high" and "low" quartiles.

Gamma is used as a measure of relationships because it seems especially suited to data ordered by ordinal assumptions. Gamma has the virtue of being a symmetric measure that is responsive to one-way associaton; it varies between -1 and $+1$; and it has a clear conceptual meaning: the proportion of positive pairs in the crosstabulation less the proportion of negative pairs. See Weiss (1968, pp. 198–201).

11. The question: "On a key problem as we just talked about, is there any council member you would especially like to have join you as a cosponsor of a proposal you might have?"

12. The question: "Who among the present council members would you say are the most likely to have their opinions accepted by the other council members?"

13. This information comes fom research conducted by Peter A. Lupsha for the City Council Research Project. See Lupsha (1967, p. 137).

14. The question: "Who, among the present councilmen, would you say is the most respected? I mean the kind of man a new member would look up to when he's just learning about the Council and how it works?"

15. The question: "Whom among all the councilmen do you *personally* like the best?"

16. The question: "I would like to ask you about the other councilmen in this connection. Is there another councilman, or several, who is especially expert in some aspects of Council work?"

11. Political Matrix and Political Representation

1. We note, in making this statement, that of 474 state legislators interviewed in the late fifties, 38 percent failed to articulate any kind of representational role in response to an open question about how they would describe the job of being a legislator (see Wahlke et al., 1962, p. 281). Ten years later, of the 435 city councilmen interviewed in connection with this study, as many as 59 percent failed to make any spontaneous mention of their putative representational role in response to the same question. As far as we know, no student of representational behavior has as yet examined the implications of the evidently low salience of thinking about representation among political practitioners.

2. Pitkin's treatment of responsiveness appears to stress the condition in which the representative assembly stands ready to be responsive when the constituents do have something to say. An assembly may, therefore, be responsive whether or not there are specific instances of response. Our analysis stresses the actual act of response rather than simply the potential for it. The difficulties of empirically working with a concept stressing the possibility of an act rather than the act itself dictated our decision to modify Pitkin's theoretically suggestive definition.

3. The coding procedure used was as follows: two investigators, reading jointly, read through all parts of the interview schedules pertinent to how councilmen defined their relations with the public for all members of any given council. If the councilmen seldom mentioned any groups or groupings in the public, or if they failed to describe an actual case where they had been responsive to public pressures, or if they simply asserted (a not unusual occurrence) that they knew what was best for the community and acted upon it, the council was placed in the "self-defined image" code. If the councilmen made references to neighborhood groups or to transitory groups wanting, say, a stoplight at a given corner or to election groups, and if the councilmen indicated that they responded to pressures from such groups and attempted to placate them, then the council was coded in the "responsive-to-issue-groups" category. If the councilmen defined for us a fairly well organized public, attentive to what the council was doing, and if the councilmen indicated (usually by citing an illustrative case) that they were responsive to these attentive publics, the council was placed in the "responsive-to-attentive-publics" code. The procedure, then, used the councilmen as individual informants about the response style of the council. It is quite possible, though not a frequent occurrence, for a given individual councilman not to feel responsive to, say, attentive publics but to describe the council as acting in that way.

4. That size is an adequate indicator of "social pluralism" may not be self-evident. We refer the reader to Hadden and Borgatta (1965) for evidence of the correlative power of size as an indicator of a city's demographic and ecological diversity and pluralism.

5. In Table 11.1 and all following tables our interpretation of the data is largely based on comparison of the distributions in "high" and "low" categories of the independent (column) variable. However, we are attaching to each table two statistics: the raw chi-square score adjusted for degree of freedom, which can tell us something about the relative order of the data; that is, by dividing chi-square by the table's degree of freedom, it is possible to compare tables of different numbers of cells as long as the "N" remains the same or nearly so. Because we are not essentially dealing with a sample but with a universe (eighty-two out of ninety cases in the defined universe), we are not concerned with the sampling problem of whether the distribution in any table is due to chance or not at some set level of confidence. Gamma is introduced as a measure of relationship because it seems especially suitable to data ordered by ordinal or weak ordinal scales.

6. Emphasis added. At another point Dahl (1956, p. 72) argues: "The effective political elites, then, operate within limits often vague and broad, although occasionally narrow and well defined, set by their expectations as to the reactions of the group of politically active citizens who go to the polls."

7. Schlesinger's (1966) study is a very careful and ingenious examination of how the political opportunity structure in the United States might facilitate or impede political ambitions and thus affect the working of democracy. He does not, however, consider the consequences for democratic politics if men in public office are not ambitious.

8. Hyneman (1938, pp. 25–27) also remarks that his finding "completely knocks out the supposition that the transiency of legislative personnel is due to the fickleness of the voter at the polls. . . . Only 16.2 per cent of the 1,965 House members and 14.7 per cent of the 511 senators who quit service during this period were eliminated by defeat in the general election."

9. Possibly one of the reasons Hyneman's findings have had such little impact on theories about elections is that he was concerned with the implications of turnover for questions of legislative experience. Students who followed Hyneman's lead also addressed themselves to this question. As far as we have discovered, no political scientist has yet considered how the high rates of voluntary retirement might affect the attention of lawmakers to voter preferences. For a later treatment of this question, see Prewitt (1970).

10. The mean percent of voluntary retirements is 53; the standard deviation is 18. The rate of voluntary retirement is not related to any major demographic characteristic of the city, not to size, population density, percent of the working force in manufacturing occupations, nor to median income. The stability of this rate across all types of cities suggests that it is a very permanent, even institutionalized, feature of nonpartisan city politics in the San Francisco Bay area. By the way, only three of the eighty-two cities studied have limitations on tenure. The survey data that help us understand the reasons for the high rates of voluntary retirement are presented and analyzed in Prewitt (1970).

11.   Appointed incumbents were excluded because of the high rate of appointment to the councils—24 percent for all cities averaged over the ten-year period. Appointment can be a strategy designed, in this context, to assure election. Omitting these appointed incumbents therefore strengthens the index of forced turnover. The aggregate election data that were used in constructing these analyses were initially collected by Gordon Black, then a member of the City Council Research Project, and Willis D. Hawley, then at the Institute of Governmental Studies, University of California at Berkeley.

12.   Four of the five items used in the support index were coded by using the informant procedure described in note 3. Councils were classified according to whether they reported (1) the public to have a respectful view toward councilmen, (2) the public to be in agreement with the council's definition of its duties, (3) the public to include disruptive and unfriendly elements, and (4) the public to be generally supportive in its behavior toward the council. The fifth item, whether there are critical groups in the community, was initially an aggregate measure of individual responses to a question about the number of critical groups. Councils were ranked in terms of this aggregate measure, and those above the median were said to have supportive publics; those below, to be operating in a nonsupportive publics; those below, to be operating in a nonsupportive environment. Each council was given a score of 1 for each plus on the five items. The support scores were then dischotomized to provide the "relatively high" and "relatively low" classes used in the analysis.

13.   The literature, of course, is quite large. Representative studies are reviewed in Prewitt (1965).

14.   See, for instance, Matthews (1954); the collection of articles in Marvick (1961); and the chapter by Dye in Jacob and Vines (1965). This issue is explored with the city council data in Prewitt (1970, chap. 2).

15.   The measure of sponsorship is particularly problematic since we are summing not just individual experiences to get a group score but individual experiences that took place over a considerable span of time in some cases. It may be that the aggregation of individual career experiences into a council recruitment measure disguises more variance in the original data than the index should be burdened with. Councilmen enter the council at very different points in time, and recruitment, as a system property, may have undergone major changes since the entry experiences of the older members. For the present, however, we are trapped by our own data; when we began the study we still were thinking of recruitment as an individual attribute and thus mainly collected data about individual careers. Despite the relatively weaker nature of our sponsorship measure, we are reluctant to give up our theoretical posture. We simply note, then, that the weaker relationships in tables using the sponsorship measure may be traced to these methodological difficulties. A council was given a sponsorship measure by computing the mean of six alternative paths to office. The "sponsorship continuum" ranged from the case in which an outside challenger initiates his own career and attains a council seat with minimum contact between himself and those already in established positions, to the case in which a councilman was deliberately selected—either asked to run or appointed to the council by those already in office. The means were then ranked

and, for present purposes, the lowest quartile in the rank order constitutes the low-sponsorship councils; the highest quartile constitutes the high-sponsorship councils; the remainder we assigned to the middle group.

12. Life Space and Social Networks as Political Contexts

1. It is, of course, a pregnant observation, at least from the "level-of-analysis perspective" (Eulau, 1969a; Chapter 2, this book). Harold D. Lasswell anticipated many of the concerns involved in the observation when he wrote, in an essay that deserves contemporary attention: "The significant feature in the environment of any personality is another personality, and the significant feature in the environment of any culture is another culture" (Lasswell, 1948c, p. 203).

2. How one person politically "influences" another has long been of theoretical interest to social scientists (Katz and Lazarsfeld, 1955); and the impact on individual behavior of "primary groups"—family, friendship circle, work team, and so on— has been well documented (Berelson, Lazarsfeld, and McPhee, 1954; Campbell, Gurin, and Miller, 1954; McClosky and Dahlgren, 1959; Finifter, 1974). But difficulties in securing pertinent data have obstructed research on politically salient *dyadic* interactions as the building blocks for a sociological (rather than a psychological) understanding of individual-on-individual (interpersonal rather than group-on-individual) political effects. After a promising start made in the 1940s and 1950s by a group of investigators at Columbia University, relevant research has languished (Sheingold, 1973; Eulau, 1980), although there have been intermittent revivals of interest, especially concerning the influence of neighborhoods and neighbors (Foladare, 1968; Fitton, 1973; Crenson, 1978, 1983).

3. See the pioneering contextual study of individual political behavior by Warren E. Miller (1956, p. 708): "The counties to be studied, 72 in number, are further defined for us by the availability of relevant and crucial data. They are the counties included in the Survey Research Center sample of the adult citizens of the United States."

4. The present research principally tests the social resonance model. Examining the behavioral contagion model requires the specification of a simultaneous equation. The NES data are not sufficiently rich to allow such a model to be estimated. The authors, in collaboration with Professor James H. Kuklinski, University of Illinois, are now engaged in a project that, by way of a snowball sampling design, has collected data of this kind (see Eulau, 1984b). Since this project will make available more data on each member in a person's social network (that is, education, social class, policy preferences, ideology, and so on), it will be feasible also to operationalize the behavioral contagion model.

5. What gives methodological warrant to using one person's reports of his or her own behavior and perceptions of the behavior of others, instead of direct observation, is the high probability, demonstrated in many empirical and experimental studies (Nisbett and Ross, 1980), that cognition itself has patterns stemming from the interactions of individuals in emergent social contexts. The patterns and substance of cognitions, of course, change over time in response to the dynamics of social interaction or as a function of a person's individual growth and devel-

opment. In this connection it is of the utmost importance *not* to assume that cognitions are simply epiphenomena totally determined by social structure (whether microinterpersonal or macroenvironmental); and it is equally important *not* to assume that cognition and its patterns are exclusively innate to the individual person as a result of biological-evolutionary development. As Piaget (1970) has taught, cognition and its patterns develop in the course of the individual's active and purposive exploration of the environment, the social processes in that environment, and the social contexts brought about by interactions with others. Cognitions of self and other may therefore stand as surrogates for direct observations and can be used, with proper caution because of ambiguities in the data, as valid and reliable proxies for information about the structure of social networks.

6. For a selective overview, see Weatherford, 1982; for a brief technical overview, see Knoke and Kuklinski, 1982. There exists now an interdisciplinary association called International Network for Social Network Analysis (INSNA) that, since August 1978, has sponsored a lively scholarly journal, *Social Networks*. INSNA also publishes an informative bulletin, *Connections*.

7. This conclusion differs from that offered by one of us in an earlier analysis of the 1979 NES Pilot Project data. The difference is due to two facts: first, the earlier conclusion was based on a comparison of only "pure" day- and night-dwellers as well as on exceptionally small numbers of cases (ranging from twenty-seven to forty-two; and second, no statistical tests of significance were performed because of the obvious unrepresentativeness of that purposive subsample (see Eulau and Siegel, 1980).

8. Ideally, we would employ a multiple-indicator approach to measure NPZ political knit, such as that developed by Joreskog and his associates (Joreskog and Sorbom, 1981). However, since this procedure is not yet feasible when one is dealing with limited dependent variables, we employ the factor-analytic method instead.

9. This creates interpretative difficulties because we can only guess about the psychological processes involved in this characterization. The designation of another person as a Democratic or Republican identifier may be due to a respondent's *projecting* his or her own party identification onto the NPZ; or the respondent's party identification may be due to his or her *introjecting* the identification of NPZ partners (Eulau and Siegel, 1981). We must treat this issue as moot. Rather, we adopt without further justification the assumption that respondents' descriptions of their NPZ's partisan composition are accurate and reliable cognitions or "definitions of the situation."

10. This multicollinearity is due to (1) an artifact of scale construction: all Democrats were given negative scores and all Republicans positive ones; and (2) the initially observed positive relationship between respondents' strength of party identification and their perceptions of the NPZ's partisan composition, as reported in the text.

11. Performing the analysis separately for Democrats and Republicans would result in too large a reduction in the number of cases for meaningful estimation.

12. As the partisan support index is curvilinear on the partisan homogeneity-heterogeneity dimension, introducing political knit into a revised index should have a moderating effect on the relationship between the NPZ's partisan composition

and respondents' party identification. We computed the revised partisan support index by multiplying the original partisan support scores by the value of the NPZ's political knit.

13. Because these expectations are so strong, all of the significance levels in this section reflect one-tailed tests.

13. Developmental Analysis and Constructs

1. See, for instance, Garceau (1951); Eldersveld (1951); Leiserson (1953). All of these articles are reprinted in Eulau, Eldersveld, and Janowitz (1956).

14. Policy Maps and Policy Outcomes

1. Oliver P. Williams (1966) has argued that metropolitan regions are collections of small groups of residents and the economic superstructure necessary to sustain them. Each group is characterized by the choice of a distinctive life style; and because members of the various groups wish to live in congenial environments, they tend to be found in similar locations throughout the region. Precisely where they are located is a matter of economics and the remnants of past land uses in the region, but the fact of congeniality is a major cause of similarity in location choice.

2. Much classificatory activity, in the field of public policy analysis as elsewhere, is a game. Either the inventors of classifications and typologies do not make it clear just what analytical purpose the classification is to serve, or they may even imply that by having a classification they have explained something. We make this point to have it understood that we are interested not in justifying or defending the particular typology of policy development that we have constructed, but in examining its utility in the analysis at hand.

3. Since education and public welfare policies are not made at the city level in California, we cannot use expenditures in these areas as measures of policy outcomes.

4. The amenities measure is an attempt to tap Williams and Adrian's (1963, pp. 198–225) concept of amenities.

5. Expenses by the planning commission include both expenses and outlays, therefore encompassing the range of items from paper supplies to salaries of full-time city planners to special outside studies commissioned by the city planning commission. California State law requires every city to have a planning commission, but this body may be, and frequently is, a standing committee of citizens appointed by the city council and incurring no expenses charged against the city. Therefore, the actual dollar amount spent by the planning commission would seem to be a good indicator of the extent of a city's commitment to the idea of planning as a way to control the environment. General government expenses rather than total government expenses are used as the percentage base in order to make planning definitially independent of amenity expenditures.

6. It is important to keep in mind that, while we are using categories reminiscent of such concepts as "traditional," "transitional," and "modern" used in

the literature of comparative politics, our observations cover only a small segment of that part of the historical developmental process usually called "modern." It is all the more significant that, even within this small part, we can locate cities in clearly different stages of policy development. This suggests that a concept like "modern" disguises a great deal of the variance that more microscopic analysis can reveal. The point is that our stages "correspond" only analytically to similarly conceived stages used in the long-term analysis of national development.

7.   For a more detailed discussion of how the development typology was constructed and cities assigned to a stage or phase of policy development, see Eyestone and Eulau (1968).

8.   This calculation is made as follows: over eight years, each city's annual outcomes could change seven times. This would make for 82 × 7, or 574, opportunities for all cities. However, as we missed data for the first fiscal year in two cities, we must deduct two opportunities, giving us the 572 figure.

9.   For a discussion of system capabilities, see Almond (1965).

10.   Assessed valuation includes private houses and property, commercial property, and industrial property. From private property a city derives personal property revenues and a portion of state income tax revenues; from commercial property it receives property and sales tax revenues; and from industrial property it gets property tax revenues.

11.   This is not the only question we asked in this connection. For instance, we also asked a great many closed "agree-disagree" questions, some of which we used in our earlier analysis (Eyestone and Eulau, 1968).

12.   This is not the place to discuss the methodological problems and procedures involved in "stepping up" the data from the level of the individual (microanalysis) to the level of the group (macroanalysis). Suffice it to say that our empirical results justify the viability of the procedures, although we would be the first to admit that many technical problems remain to be solved.

13.   Paul F. Lazarsfeld has written in many places about the variety of "group properties" that need to be distinguished in analysis lest errors of inference be made. See, for instance, Lazarsfeld (1959) or Lazarsfeld and Menzel (1965). We are not dealing with the global, structural, or relational properties of councils here.

14.   That is, the absolute number of individual problems named was divided by all problem responses made in a council. The resulting scores, which could range from 0 to 1, were rank ordered and divided into the quartile ranges used in the analysis.

15.   That is, the number of problems named was multiplied by the number of respondents and divided by all responses squared. The resulting score was subtracted from 1 to rank order the councils from high to low. The formula then is $1 - NP \times NR/r^2$, where NP = number of problems, NR = number of respondents, and r = number of total responses.

16.   The measure of agreement on a single problem is simply the proportion of councilmen among all respondents who mentioned the most frequent problem. For the measure of problem-area agreement, the number of responses in the area receiving the most responses was divided by the number of responses in all areas. Five "problem areas" were provided for classification of individual problems: ser-

vices and utilities, amenities, promotion and development, social and remedial problems, and governmental and intergovernmental problems.

17. Our measure of salience, as mentioned in the text, was whether a problem or problem area was mentioned by at least three respondents. We shall not try to interpret the proportions obtained for the services and utilities as well as promotion and development areas across the developmental continuum because the results may be an artifact of council size. As five councils in the transitional stage, three in the maturing phase, and seven in the advanced stage had more than five members (usually seven), and as no retarded or emergent council had more than five members, clearly any one problem had more of a chance to be named by at least three respondents in the more-developed cities. But as, for instance, nine of the advanced councils had only five members, yet all advanced councils are accounted for in naming at least one problem, the council-size factor does not seem to have too much of a distorting effect. But we note it as interesting that the more developed a city's policy, the more councils tend to mention problems related to utilities and services and to promotion and development.

18. The dominant set of reasons was simply defined as that set which included the most responses among all sets, regardless of absolute number.

19. We could argue our case more liberally on statistical grounds and possibly test it if we had more and numerically more diverse legislative bodies available for analysis: the larger a legislative body, the more likely it is that averaged individual preferences will approximate, if not correspond to, the preference of the collectivity.

20. The improvement diversity measure was constructed in the same way as the problem diversity measure. See note 14 above.

21. The improvement visibility measure was constructed in the same manner as the problem visibility measure. See note 15 above.

22. The improvement agreement measures are the same as those used in connection with problem agreement. See note 16 above.

23. We would like to point out here that we had very similar results in the earlier study (Eyestone and Eulau, 1968) in which we used a *closed* agree-disagree scale measuring attitudes concerning the scope of government activity and in which we used *individual* councilmen as our units of analysis.

24. An improvement area was assumed to be salient in council preferences if at least three respondents articulated problems in the area.

25. Because an "industrial" future was envisaged in only a handful of councils, we combined this category with the "balanced" category, which implies that the council envisages a balance in residential, commercial, and industrial development.

15. A Quasi-Longitudinal, Quasi-Experimental Design for Comparative Policy Analysis

1. See, for instance, Dye (1966, pp. 3–4). The nomenclature of policy research is ambiguous. Output and outcome are sometimes treated as synonyms, sometimes as antonyms, as when outcome is conceived as a consequence of output. Our own use of policy-related concepts will be explained in the text.

2. The output of relevant studies is considerable. See especially the work of Thomas R. Dye, Richard I. Hofferbert, Richard E. Dawson, and James A. Robinson, and others. For a critical evaluation, see Jacob and Lipsky (1968).

3. This is the design usually employed by the University of Michigan's Survey Research Center in its famous election studies. A national random sample of respondents is interviewed prior to the election, and the same sample is interviewed after the election. Changes in response to the same question are assumed to be due to events, including the election itself, in the intervening period. See Campbell et al. (1960, pp. 16–17).

4. We opt here for the phi measure because it is not subject to a difficulty arising in gamma for a 2-by-2 table, also known as Yule's Q. For, in the case of the latter, if one of the cells vanishes, the measure appears as unity ($+1$ or -1) in spite of an imperfect relationship between the variables. Phi, like Q, is a symmetric measure and may be interpreted as the Pearson r. Its values are likely to be less than those of Q. Hence the phi and gamma values are not directly comparable.

16. Representation as an Emergent

1. For critical treatment of the prevailing research traditions, see Chapter 19. Although many studies often cite Pitkin's work in a footnote, they do not follow her instructions. Neither do they adopt her definition of representation as responsiveness, nor do they raise analysis to the systemic level. Exceptions are Prewitt and Eulau (1969; see Chapter 11); Jennings and Zeigler (1971); and Eulau and Prewitt (1973).

2. The main reason for the poverty of appropriate data in the study of representation has been the cost of data collection. Although Wahlke et al. (1962) had proposed interviewing both constituents and lobbyists as "significant others" in an original research design, they had to be satisfied with interviewing legislators alone because of the cost factor (but, perhaps, also because the sponsoring Political Behavior Committee of the Social Science Research Council did not, at the time— 1955–56—appreciate the importance of the proposal to interview representatives as well as represented). The Miller-Stokes 1958 data sets are therefore unique.

3. The data used in this research were made available through the Inter-University Consortium for Political and Social Research.

4. For an introduction to the language of multilevel analysis, see Chapters 2 and 3; on data transformation across levels of observation and analysis, see Chapter 4.

5. Connoisseurs of social science terminology (which is not unrelated to one's thought processes and products) are probably aware of our indebtedness, in adopting the concepts of "event" and "emergence" as well as "process," to the political theories of Harold D. Lasswell. See, especially, Lasswell (1948c); Lasswell and Kaplan (1950, pp. ix–xxiv); Marvick (1977); and Chapters 9 and 13 in this book.

6. Although "moment" is usually (and correctly) defined as a point or instant in time, it should be noted that it derives from the Latin verb *movere*, which is at the base of the noun *momentum*, "movement." Just what a moment "is" depends,

therefore, on the total time perspective in which it is calibrated. It may refer to a "stage" in historical development, that is, a relatively protracted period. The point to be made is that "moment" does not necessarily have the static implications that it seems to have in ordinary usage. It is an event in a series of moving events.

7. The concept of "situation" has not been given serious attention in political science or social science generally. The formulation presented here is indebted to a number of writers who, over the years, have influenced our thinking. But see, especially, Parsons (1951); Volkart (1951).

8. It will be noted that we are not using 1958 constituency preferences in constructing the representational situations. We do not do so for two reasons: first, because the timing of the 1958 constituency preferences and representatives' preferences is coincidental—data concerning them being collected almost simultaneously; and second, because it would be impossible properly to sequence the roll calls, that is, it would make no sense to use the 1957–58 roll calls that preceded the expression of preferences, but it would be difficult to use the 1958 constituency and representatives' preferences as not sequentially linked variables. Yet, our concept of situation requires clear sequencing of all the component event-variables.

9. There is another important reason for crude classification. Although the various measures of constituency preferences, congressmen's preferences, and their roll-call scores in the three issue domains sought to achieve *conceptual* equivalence, there is much differentiation in the *empirical* data to caution against the impression that all three scales in a given issue area or across issue areas are identically calibrated. If one ignores this limitation in the data, one may place undue confidence into the more refined measures originally created. The procedure, though crude and yielding crude results, prevents one from misconceiving the nature of the original instruments and what they measure in reality.

10. We insert this cautionary note because it should not be forgotten that we are dealing with weighted data. While the percentages for the southern cases in Table 16.1 are based here on the full complement of the weighted data, it is evident that especially in some of the dissonant and blocked situations the percentages are quite small and, "in reality," stand for only one or two districts-cum-representative. In later tables the dissonant and blocked situations yield many "missing-data" cells, despite the fact that the weighted cases for the South are about 600. But it takes only one or two nonresponses to an interview question in the real world to drop the cases out of the cells of a cross-tabulation.

11. Internal analysis of the data shows that in both the Eighty-fifth and the Eighty-sixth Congresses fully 100 percent of the southern congressmen in the weighted sample ($N = 655$) voted *against* civil rights. Of the 80 percent *southern* pervasive-situation civil rights cases in 1957–58, all (100 percent) were *against* civil rights (con-con-con). By way of contrast, of the 49 percent *northern* pervasive-situation civil rights cases in the same period, 94 percent were *for* civil rights (pro-pro-pro) and only 6 percent were against (con-con-con). The fact of course is that, in the fifties, civil rights was a much more salient, constituency-based issue in the South than in the North.

12. One can express the error ratio obtained for the six turnover tables also in terms of the actual changes at the level of each unique case. There were, altogether,

2,771 changes over all issue areas in both regions; of these 437, or 15 percent, were in directions not meeting the stipulated requirements for change.

13. In fact, the proportions here are so much "out of line" that one must suspect the reliability of the data more than the perceptual ineptness of southern congressmen; our apologies in advance.

14. The aggregation of individual-level index scores at the district level has been criticized because, in the case of some districts, the responses of at best a handful of interviewees were used to obtain the district measure. As a result, one can entertain reservations about the reliability of the measures thus obtained. Miller and Stokes (1963, pp. 46–47n3; see also ICPR, 1971: memorandum of January 21, 1972, p. 11) have defended the use of the aggregated data in terms of the weighting of the sample of districts into which the individual respondents were distributed. We are not in a position to assess the validity and reliability of the Miller-Stokes weighting procedures, but we are most cautious when, in using the weighted data, we encounter cells where the size of N strikes us as being so small as to make the distributions highly labile, even if we obtain acceptable confidence levels.

17. Logics of Rationality in Unanimous Decision Making

1. "Democratic" here simply means that there must not be in the decision-making situation external structural constraints that make free choice impossible, as in dictatorship (where only the dictator has free choice). There may be, of course, constraints—and I shall mention some of them later on. But whatever other conditions may be specified for democratic decision making, I require of the situation only that it contain a *potential* for free choice. I shall leave the adjective "near-unanimous" operationally undefined and, subsequently, absorb it into the unanimous category. For, conceptually, it makes little difference whether unanimity is fully achieved or not. Where unanimity is not a constitutional decision rule, there is always the bitter-end intransigent or the unpredictable maverick whose behavior defies the tendency toward unanimity. This may be an empirically interesting phenomenon. But the quantitative deviations from the norm that are permissible in order to speak of "near-unanimous" decisions need not be defined for the theoretical purposes of this discussion.

2. There are numerous models of rational behavior. Most prominent are the "means-ends" model often encountered in theories of formal organization, the "maximization" model of economic theories, the "minimax" model of game theory, and the "adaptive behavior" models found in psychology. All of these models make behavioral assumptions that present advantages and difficulties. My discussion of rationality in unanimous decision making does not require that I systematically explicate various models or choose between them. I shall invoke one or the other as the discussion of one or another type of unanimity may suggest. For my purposes the only requirements of rationality that must be met, whatever assumptions are made or whatever other conditions are specified, are that there be a free choice among alternatives and that the choice be consciously made. Nevertheless, I should acknowledge that my thinking in the matter has been greatly influenced by Herbert A. Simon's discussions of rationality (see Simon, 1954, 1957a).

3. The emphasis here is on "observable." Although, for certain theoretical purposes, the electorate can be conceived as a "committee," the secrecy of the electoral process and its aggregate character make observation impossible. Similarly, the decision-making process in juries escapes direct observation. It is for this reason that I shall deal, at least initially, with decision making in legislative bodies, although here, too, much of what occurs remains hidden.

4. These constraints are external to the decision-making process, as are dictatorial constraints, and therefore not within the purview of this discussion, which assumes the potential for free choice among alternatives.

5. William J. Keefe, in a study of the 1951 Pennsylvania legislature, found many unanimous or near-unanimous votes on such matters as mental health, the training of the physically handicapped, increased aid to the blind, the local department of health operations, stream clearance, control over narcotics, absentee voting for military electors, sabotage control, retirement systems, school-district and school-board elections, merit-system extensions, and improvement of state institutions (see Keefe, 1954, pp. 452, 461–462).

6. In part, this lack of evidence is probably due to prevailing research strategies. Studies of legislative decision making by way of roll-call votes are usually limited to the relatively few situations in which legislatures are divided. The criteria used to determine whether a roll call is to be considered controversial vary, and different research methods employed by different students have led to divergent findings about the importance of one or another factor that is assumed to make for division.

7. In other words, crisis situations may be considered as introducing constraints of an environmental character that make for self-imposed structural constraints. Again, the potential for free choice is severely restricted. Actually, the choice in these situations has already been made elsewhere, and the final decision is not really a matter of choice but rather of promulgation.

8. For a mathematical formulation of the constitutional unanimity rule in international bodies, see Black (1958, pp. 140–155).

9. This definition of deadlock differs from that of Robert A. Dahl (1956, p. 41) when he writes that "if the deadlock solution is followed, then no governmental action is taken; but if no governmental action is taken, then in fact x is government policy." The situation to which Dahl's statement refers, and quite accurately, is one where the choice is between one collective action as against another, not, as is the situation here, where the choice is between collective action and private action, but where private action will also not be taken.

10. It seems to me that this aspect of the cost problem involved in unanimous decision making has been neglected by those who only compare the decision costs of unanimity with the decision costs of majority voting or dictatorship. The fact that, among equals, deadlock in a situation that calls for collective action (because private action is not the alternative) may be more expensive than unanimity that makes collective action possible has been neglected (see, for instance, Buchanan and Tullock, 1962, pp. 85–116).

11. Buchanan and Tullock (1962, p. 96) come to the same conclusion, if by a very different theoretical route.

12. For an enlightening discussion of the slippery concept of consensus and the

extent of consensus on decision rules in American politics, see Prothro and Grigg (1960).

13. For the distinction between analytic and concrete structures, see Levy (1958).

14. See below, note 21, where I point out that the Supreme Court's ways of decision handling have been quite different from time to time. It seems that all three ways of decision handling here described have been variously employed.

15. This is not to deny that, in reality, there will occur pathological deviations from the norm. Criminals, certainly, seek to maximize their personal utilities without regard to the utilities of others or the public costs that are involved. But even within the criminal community there are "public interests" that the individual criminal can disregard only at great risk for himself.

16. This definition is indebted to Lasswell and Kaplan (1950, p. 23): "An interest is a pattern of demands and its supporting expectations." "Interest" is admittedly an ambiguous term. Although widely used in political science, it has not been really explicated or operationalized. Truman's (1951, p. 34) definition—"The shared attitudes . . . constitute the interests"—does not seem useful for my purposes.

17. The notion that interest articulation may be specific or diffuse is indebted to Talcott Parsons' (1951, p. 77) conception of "pattern variables," defined as "a dichotomy one side of which must be chosen by an actor before the meaning of a situation is determinate for him, and thus before he can act with respect to that situation." However, my own usage, it should be noted, deviates somewhat from the Parsonian explication of the specificity-diffuseness "dilemma." For similar formulations, see Almond and Coleman (1960, pp. 33–38).

18. We may well speak of the "arbitrator" as a dictator in the sense that his decision in a dispute is unanimously accepted, by prearrangement, by both sides to a dispute, as in labor-management relations.

19. Unfortunately, Truman then gives what seems to me a rather dubious example. The last sentence quoted here continues: "as the Congress did in its declaration of war after Pearl Harbor." I am not clear what conflict Truman had in mind that was resolved prior to the declaration of war. If he means the battle between internationalists or interventionists and isolationists, it is inaccurate to say that it had been solved prior to Pearl Harbor. It would be more appropriate to say that it was "tabled." Moreover, as I suggested in note 7, the unanimity accompanying the declaration of war is not likely to be one that can be considered due to a process of free choice.

20. For other examples of the projection hypothesis in politics and some proof, especially in electoral voting, see Thomsen (1941) and Lazarsfeld, Berelson, and Gaudet (1948).

21. Pritchett names other factors as well, such as "the discussion which goes on around the judicial conference table, out of which consensus can often be achieved." This suggests that judicial unanimity can also be explained as "bargained unanimity." And "false unanimity" through concealment seems to be relevant in explaining the Court's behavior under Chief Justice Marshall. See Schmidhauser (1960, p. 114): "The price of maintaining the fiction of judicial certainty, decisiveness, and unity was the camouflaging of real doubt, and occasionally, the acceptance by individual justices of positions which they personally knew to be

erroneous. Justice Story was, without doubt, the most careful legal scholar on the Supreme Court during this period. Yet he was persuaded, on several occasions, to accept erroneous decisions silently for the sake of the Court's reputation and unity." In other words, one should not confuse a given type of unanimity with a particular institution.

19. Components of Representational Responsiveness

1. Miller and Stokes (1963). A revised version is included in Campbell et al. (1966, pp. 351–372). We shall be citing the original article because we are interested here only in the theoretical aspects of the analysis that remained unaffected by the revision. The particular analysis was part of a much larger study of representation conducted in connection with the 1958 congressional elections.

2. In note 2 of their original article Miller and Stokes refer to Eulau et al. (1959); Hanna F. Pitkin's then unpublished Ph.D. dissertation, which presumably led to her later *Concept of Representation* (1967); de Grazia (1951); and Fairlie (1940).

3. The two most significant studies of the fifties in this genre were Turner (1951) and MacRae (1958).

4. The operational definition was expressed as follows: "In each policy domain, crossing the rankings of Congressmen and their constituencies gives an empirical measure of the extent of policy agreement between legislator and district." The measure itself was expressed as follows: "To summarize the degree of congruence between legislators and voters, a measure of correlation is introduced" (Miller and Stokes, 1963, p. 49n10).

5. See, for example, Stone (1976, p. 8) where one finds the bland statement: "Representation is conceived as congruence or agreement between the behavior of the legislator and the opinion of the constituency on comparable policy dimensions." Compare this also with Clausen (1973, p. 128): "Given the principal orientation of this book, the policy orientation, representation is further defined as the congruence of the policy requirements of the constituency with the policy decisions of the representative."

6. Instead, to illustrate the constituency's sanctioning power through elections, Miller and Stokes relied on data for a single congressional district in a case that is both inappropriate and deviant, involving the defeat of Congressman Brook Hays in the Fifth Arkansas District where all *voters* in the sample ($N = 13$) had read or heard "something" about Hays and his write-in opponent. But, as Miller and Stokes admit, the case was inappropriate: the voters probably knew little about Hays's legislative record in the previous Congress but punished him for his nonlegislative role in the Little Rock school crisis. The Hays case indicates the power of an aroused electorate in an unusual situation; but even if they know the legislative records of their representatives, electorates are rarely so aroused over any one of the many legislative issues with which representatives deal.

7. The core ideas of this article were first presented by Wahlke in a 1967 paper before the Seventh World Congress of the International Political Science Association in Brussels, Belgium.

8. We could cite here, of course, an extensive "institutional" literature that has come to be neglected by "behavioral" students of representation. For a particularly useful recent introduction that paints a broad canvas, see Birch (1971).

9. The problem with causal analyses of phenomena like influence or responsiveness is that the direction of the relationship to which they presumably refer cannot be inferred from the causal structure of the statistical model that may be applied. The statistical model assumes the existence of a conceptual isomorphism between its ordering of the variables and their real-world ordering. The existence of a *possible* isomorphism between the direction of a political relationship and a causal relation between two variables in a statistical model was brought to the attention of political scientists in a series of papers by Herbert A. Simon (1957a). Attempting to define political power, Simon found that "the difficulty appeared to reside in a very specific technical point; influence, power, and authority are all intended as asymmetrical relations." It seemed to him that "the mathematical counterpart of this asymmetrical relation appeared to be the distinction between independent and dependent variables—the independent variable determines the dependent, and not the converse." But, he pointed out in a significant passage that causal analysts seem at times to overlook, "in algebra, the distinction between independent and dependent variable is purely conventional—we can always rewrite our equations without altering their content in such a way as to reverse their roles." The problem, then, is one of giving operational meaning to the asymmetry that is implied in the definition of influence or power: "That is to say, for the assertion, 'A has power over B,' we can substitute the assertion, 'A's behavior causes B's behavior.' If we can define the causal relation, we can define influence, power, or authority, and *vice versa*" (Simon, 1957a, p. 5). The most significant term in Simon's explication of the causal relation is "vice versa." It suggests that the definition of the "causal relation" and the definition of the phenomenon to be causally treated (here influence) are interdependent events. In other words: "If we can define influence, we can define the causal relation."

10. Unfortunately Fiorina then characterizes the new-style congressman as an "ombudsman." This attribution is inappropriate because an ombudsman, though presumably available for the settlement of grievances, is not the kind of "hustler" whom Fiorina sees as coming on the stage of representation. Of course, both roles seem to be involved—that of the ombudsman and that of the hustler.

11. For example, Froman (1967, p. 36) found that in the Eighty-eighth Congress (1963–64) 15,299 bills and resolutions were introduced in the House of Representatives, whereas only 1,742, or a little over 11 percent, were reported by committee.

12. For the distinction between "style" and "focus" of representation, see Eulau et al. (1959) and Chapter 6 in this book.

13. Fenno (1978, pp. 1–30) has also seen the need to decompose the concept of constituency. He suggests that congressmen perceive several distinct types of constituency to which they respond in different ways—the geographical constituency (district), the reelection constituency (supporters), the primary constituency (strongest supporters), and the personal constituency (intimates).

20. Skill Revolution and Consultative Commonwealth

1. By "technological society" I mean a society in which not only agricultural and industrial production have been automated, computerized, and otherwise rationalized, but one in which also the provision of human services is increasingly subject to technological innovation. I prefer this expression to "postindustrial society" because the latter does not really convey a meaning of the direction of change. A technological society need not be "technocratic." The construct of "consultative commonwealth" assumes the technologization (and professionalization) of human services, but not rule by the technologists. See Ferkiss (1969) or Brzezinski (1970).

2. "Consultative" is related to consult and consultation. These words derive from the Latin *consultare,* which has at least three behavior-relevant meanings. All of these meanings define, etymologically, the consultative commonwealth. First, depending on the context in which it is used, *consultare* can be translated as consider, deliberate, cogitate, reflect, think over, advise with, take advice from, and so on. The variety of these meanings is less helpful, however, than the meanings of the more primitive Latin verb *consulere,* which directly calls attention to the reciprocal character of the consulting relationship. On the one hand, *consulere* means to ask, question, or examine; on the other hand, it means to give counsel. The reciprocity appears even more strongly in the German translation of *consulere,* where it simultaneously means to ask someone *(jemanden befragen)* and to advise someone *(jemanden beraten).*

To seek, give, or take advice is hardly the only property of professional behavior. Interestingly, *consultare* refers to a second family of meanings that define the consulting relationship. In some contexts, *consultare* is used as a synonym for *curare*—to care for or worry about—and for *prospicere*—to provide for. In this usage, then, both an empathetic and a providential aspect of consultation are emphasized.

Third, the related adjective *consultus*—one who is consulted—may be used as a synonym for *intellegens, peritus,* or *eruditus*—intelligent, expert, or learned; and the process to which *consultus* applies is supposed to be *diligens* or *accuratus*—careful or accurate.

In combination, the different meanings and uses of *consultare* yield a comprehensive profile of the consultative relationship. The relationship is entered voluntarily for the purpose of deliberation or consideration because one party, the seeker of advice, is ignorant or in need of help, while the other party, the consultant, is a skilled or learned person who gives advice diligently and intelligently. But the consultant is not just an expert but also a compassionate person who cares for and worries about the matter brought to him for counsel, and he has the gift of accurate diagnosis and wise prognosis.

3. See Bennis and Slater (1969). In this utopia, problem solving by strangers with diverse professional skills is expected to occur through organic rather than mechanical means of interaction; the executive becomes a coordinator who mediates among task forces; and "people will be evaluated not according to rank but according to skill and professional training. . . . Adaptive, problem-solving tem-

porary systems of diverse specialists, linked together by coordinating and task-evaluating specialists in an organic flux—this is the organization form that will gradually replace bureaucracy as we know it" (p. 74). Bennis's view of democracy, although he does not seem to know it, is anarchosyndicalist: "democracy seeks no new stability, no end point; it is purposeless, save that it purports to ensure per-petual transition, constant alteration, ceaseless instability. . . . Democracy and our new professional men identify primarily with the adaptive process, not the estab-lishment" (p. 12).

4. The classical work on the professions remains Carr-Saunders and Wilson (1933). See also Carr-Saunders and Wilson (1934). For a contemporary overview, see Lynn (1965).

5. This is not to say that I disagree with Mosher's appraisal that "the emergence of the professions [has] revolutionized the precepts and practices of public em-ployment" (1968, p. 123). By turning over the recruitment, training, and accred-itation of skilled employees to the professions and the universities, current practices "are challenging, modifying, or overturning the most central—and most cher-ished—principles associated with civil service reform" (p. 124). It is unlikely, Mosher concludes, "that the trend toward professionalism in or outside government will soon be reversed or even slowed" (pp. 132–133).

6. "The leadership of the new society will rest," writes Daniel Bell (1967, p. 27), "not with businessmen or corporations as we know them . . . but with the research corporations, the industrial laboratories, the experimental stations, and the universities."

7. Among the few exceptions are Kaufman (1960); Cohen (1963); Eulau and Sprague (1964); Wood (1964); Zeigler (1966); Rogow (1970); Janowitz (1971); Ladd and Lipset (1972).

8. The pioneering study is Garceau (1941); see also Kelley (1956); Huntington (1957); Eckstein (1960); Grossman (1965); Mayer (1968); Freidson (1970b).

9. The polarity principle is explicated in the writings of the philosopher Morris R. Cohen. See, for instance, Cohen (1949, pp. 11–13): "The principle of polarity is suggested by the phenomena of magnetism where north and south pole are always distinct, opposed, yet inseparable. We can see it in general physics where there is no action without reaction, no force or cause of change without inertia or resistance. In biology the life of every organism involves action and reaction with an envi-ronment. There is no growth without decay . . . This suggests a supplement to the principle of causality. Not only must every natural event have a cause which de-termines that it should happen, but the cause must be opposed by some factor which prevents it from producing any greater effect than it actually does . . . The principle of polarity, of necessary opposition in all determinate effects, thus be-comes a heuristic principle directing our inquiry . . . Yet the principle of polarity is not the same as that of the Hegelian dialectic."

10. Boguslaw (1965, p. 43) puts it nicely: "An applied scientist is a scientist who has had his hair cut." For further aspects of the problem, see Barber and Hirsch (1962), as against Gouldner and Miller (1965).

11. "The client," writes Hughes (1958, p. 141), "comes to the professional because he has met a problem which he cannot himself handle."

12. The best discussion of what is meant by a "problematic situation" is still Dewey (1938).

13. The literature on America's "unsolved problems" is legion, but few works treat the matter from the perspective of the professions. But see Wilensky and Lebeaux (1965); Wilson (1968); Ginzberg (1969); Eulau and Quinley (1970); Stevens (1971); Marks (1972).

14. An early and still one of the best arguments in this regard is Marshall (1965, pp. 159–179). The essay was first published in 1939.

15. Market regulation of human services is proposed by Friedman (1962, pp. 137–160).

16. As Wilensky (1964, p. 141) points out, "while there may be a general tendency for occupations to seek professional status, remarkably few of the thousands of occupations in modern society attain it."

17. As Goode (1969, p. 267) observes, "the occupational structure of industrial society is not becoming generally more professionalized, even though a higher percentage of the labor force is in occupations that enjoy higher prestige rankings and income and that call themselves 'professions.' "

18. There is a large literature on the consequences of technological change. Some of this literature is highly sensational; but see Brown (1954); Brickman and Lehrer (1966); Ewald (1968); Report of the Study of Critical Environmental Problems (1970); Teich (1972).

19. Vollmer and Mills (1966, p. viii) differentiate between professionalism and professionalization as follows: "Professionalism as an ideology may induce members of many occupational groups to strive to become professional, but at the same time we can see that many occupational groups that express the ideology of professionalism in reality may not be very advanced in regard to professionalization. Professionalism may be a necessary constituent of professionalization, but professionalism is not a sufficient cause for the entire professionalization process."

20. Wilensky (1964, p. 138) comes to a similar minimal set of criteria: "(1) The job of the professional is *technical*—based on systematic knowledge or doctrine acquired only through long prescribed training. (2) The professional man adheres to a set of professional norms."

21. For a balanced view, see Thompson (1969).

22. For similar optimistic estimates of the future, see Etzioni (1968) and Breed (1971).

23. This is reinforced by monopolistic practice, the prestige of the profession as a whole, and the imputation of competence to the individual consultant. As Freidson (1970a, pp. 120–121) points out, this doctrine is unsatisfactory because it allows the consultant "to rest on the authority of his professional status without having to try to present persuasive evidence to the client that his findings and advice are correct."

24. Although this theme has much agitated the academic professions in recent years, it is not especially new. Leighton (1949, p. 128) reports a Washington saying that "the administrator uses social science the way a drunk uses a lamppost, for support rather than illumination." See especially Lyons (1969).

25. For a variety of perspectives, see Glaser (1968). See also Howton (1969).

26. By 1962, it was possible to speak of a "knowledge industry," so pervasive had knowledge making become in the American economy. See Machlup (1962). Also Chorafas (1968).

27. See Wilensky (1956); Kornhauser (1962); Glaser (1964); Hagstrom (1965); Klaw (1968); Hirsch (1968).

28. The president-elect of the American Chemical Society has complained recently that the first loyalty of chemists, 70 percent of whom are employed in industry, is to their employers. He feels that for the chemist to discharge his responsibility to society, he must have a "professional atmosphere where [he] will identify with his profession rather than his employer" (in Science 175: 501, February 4, 1972).

29. Because he sees professionalism in government as a political force, yet insists that "the importance of preserving the independence and integrity of certain kinds of expertise in government is thus very great," Rourke (1969, p. 110) concludes that "the need for professional autonomy begins to assert itself in all phases of bureaucratic policy-making." Rourke concedes that professionals are no more immune from political pressure than other public officials and suggests that public policy making in bureaucratic settings "becomes in effect a mixed system of politics and professionalism" (p. 111).

30. Marshall (1965, p. 171) articulated the same idea as early as 1939 when he wrote that in modern democratic societies "State and professions are being assimilated to one another. This is not happening through the absorption of the professions by the State, but by both of them moving from opposite directions to meet in a middle position."

31. This is Freidson's central argument in analyzing professional dominance and the ordering of the health services; see, especially, Freidson (1970b, pp. 127–164).

32. There may be more than meets the eye in all this, for it has also been suggested that professional authority, in addition to being based on knowledge and competence, "does rest to some extent on tradition," and "to some degree the professional's authority is charismatic" (Toren, 1969, p. 152).

33. Freidson (1968, p. 26) points out that if this is so, it suggests an "unemphasized point, namely, that the type of influence or authority exerted by the professional on his clients must be quite different from that exerted by the scientist on his colleagues—that professional and scientific 'authority' are different even though profession and science are both characterized by special technical competence."

34. Of course, professional associations like the American Bar Association or the American Medical Association are also devoted to the promotion of knowledge by way of learned meetings and journals. In turn, purely scientific societies share some of the characteristics of the professional associations. This is precisely the reason why the distinction between science and profession is at best of limited analytic value.

35. Wilensky (1964, p. 149) also remarks that "the tacit component of their knowledge base is a seldom-recognized cause of the tenacious conservatism of the established professions."

36. Carlin (1966, p. 170) estimates that "only about 2 percent of the lawyers

who violate generally accepted ethical norms are processed, and fewer than 0.2 percent are officially sanctioned." If lawyers are so reluctant to enforce their ethics, other professions are likely to be even more lax.

37. Gilb reports that in 1960 less than half of attorneys belonged to the American Bar Association, and only 42 percent of the teachers to the National Education Association. Only 45 percent of America's 344,823 doctors were reported to be dues-paying members of the American Medical Association in June 1972 (see *San Francisco Chronicle,* June 17, 1972, p. 5).

38. Marshall (1965, p. 165) has argued that the professions "have not always struck a true balance between loyalty to the client and loyalty to the community, and they have sometimes treated loyalty to the profession as an end rather than as a means to the fulfillment of other loyalties. They are often accused of neglecting the public welfare."

39. Parsons (1954, p. 36) writes: "Perhaps even it is not mainly a difference of typical motives at all, but one of the different situations in which much the same commonly human motives operate. Perhaps the acquisitiveness of modern business is institutional rather than motivational."

40. These investigations were made possible in part by a training grant from the National Institute of Mental Health; in part by support for dissertation research from the National Science Foundation; and in part by fellowship support from the Social Science Research Council, the Danforth Foundation, and the Mabelle McLeod Lewis Research Fund.

41. See Schubert (1960, p. 11): "Most of the literature characteristically tends either to define the public interest as a universal, in terms so broad that it encompasses almost any type of specific decision, or else to particularize the concept, by identifying it with the most specific and discrete of policy norms and actions, to the extent that it has no general significance."

42. For an opposite point of view, see Gittell (1967). See also Levin (1970).

43. See Lowi (1971, p. 80): "Decentralization through delegation of power merely meant conversion from government control to a far more irresponsible, enigmatic, unpredictable group control."

44. As Hughes continued: the professional's "very competence comes from having dealt with a thousand cases of what the client likes to consider his unique trouble."

45. Carr-Saunders (1955, p. 283) writes: "As a consequence of the trend toward specialization, the professional man no longer takes a comprehensive interest in his client. He feels that he has no general responsibility for those who come under his care, and the personal relationship between practitioner and client is weakened."

46. Client control, however, may be frustrated by what Kerr (1954, p. 93) calls "institutional markets" in which the boundaries of service are not set by the participants in the consultative relationship but by institutional rules.

47. Multiple advocacy as a conscious decision-making strategy is recommended by George (1972).

48. "There are professional ethics for the priest, the soldier, the lawyer, the magistrate, and so on," Durkheim (1958, pp. 29–30) observed in lectures given

three-quarters of a century ago, and then asked: "Why should there not be one for trade and industry?" No answer has yet been forthcoming, but see Barber (1963). The English socialist R. H. Tawney (1920, chap. 7) argued that nationalization of industry was a necessary condition of its professionalization.

49.   Bell (1968, p. 238) comes to the same conclusion, if by a different route: "It is more likely, however, that the postindustrial society will involve *more* politics than ever before for the very reason that choice becomes conscious and the decision-centers more visible."

50.   On contemporary institutional trends, see Moynihan (1965); National Research Council (1968); National Science Board (1969); Cronin and Greenberg (1969); National Research Council (1972).

References

Abell, P. 1971. *Model building in sociology*. London: Weidenfeld & Nicolson.

Able, A. I., ed. 1968. *American Catholic thought on social questions*. Indianapolis: Bobbs-Merrill.

Akzin, B. 1936. The concept of legislation. *Iowa Law Review* 21:713–750. Reprinted in *Legislative behavior: a reader in theory and research*, ed. J. C. Wahlke and H. Eulau. Glencoe, Ill.: Free Press.

Almond, G. A. 1958. A comparative study of interest groups and the political process. *American Political Science Review* 52:270–282.

—— 1965. A developmental approach to political systems. *World Politics* 17:195–203.

Almond, G. A., and J. S. Coleman, eds. 1960. *The politics of the developing areas*. Princeton, N.J.: Princeton University Press.

Almond, G. A., and S. Verba. 1963. *The civic culture: political attitudes and democracy in five nations*. Princeton, N.J.: Princeton University Press.

Altshuler, A. 1965. *The city planning process: a political analysis*. Ithaca, N.Y.: Cornell University Press.

Arrow, K. J. 1951. *Social choice and individual values*. New York: Wiley.

Bachrach, P., and M. S. Baratz. 1963. Decisions and nondecisions: an analytic framework. *American Political Science Review* 57:632–642.

Bailey, S. K. 1950. *Congress makes a law*. New York: Columbia University Press.

Bales, R. F. 1950. *Interaction process analysis*. Cambridge, Mass.: Addison-Wesley.

Banks, A. S., and R. B. Textor. 1963. *A cross-polity survey*. Cambridge, Mass.: M.I.T. Press.

Barber, B. 1957. *Social stratification*. New York: Harcourt Brace.

—— 1963. Is American business becoming professionalized? In *Sociological theory, values, and sociocultural change*, ed. E. A. Tiryakian. New York: Free Press.

Barber, B., and W. Hirsch, eds. 1962. *The sociology of science*. New York: Free Press.

Barber, J. D. 1966. *Power in committees: an experiment in the governmental process.* Chicago: Rand, McNally.

Barker, R. G. 1968. *Ecological psychology: concepts and methods for studying the environment of human behavior.* Stanford, Calif.: Stanford University Press.

Bazell, R. J. 1971. Health radicals: crusade to shift medical power to the people. *Science* 173:506–509.

Beck, B. M. 1969. Community control: a distraction, not an answer. *Social Work* 14:14–20.

Becker, R. A. 1975. *Potential groups: an exploration of the conditions and processes of group formation among doctors and lawyers.* Ph.D diss., Stanford University.

Beer, S. H. 1957. The representation of interests in British government. *American Political Science Review* 51:613–650.

Bell, D. 1967. Notes on the post-industrial society. *Public Interest* 6:24–35, 102–118.

——— 1968. The measurement of knowledge and technology. In *Indicators of social change: concepts and measurements,* ed. E. B. Sheldon and W. E. Moore.New York: Russell Sage Foundation.

——— ed. 1969. *Toward the year 2000: work in progress.* Boston: Beacon.

Beloff, M., ed. 1948. *The Federalist or, the new constitution.* Oxford: Basil Blackwell.

Ben-David, J. 1963–64. Professions in the class system of present-day societies: a trend report and bibliography. *Current Sociology* 12:247–330.

Bendix, R. 1960. *Max Weber: an intellectual portrait.* Garden City, N.Y.: Doubleday.

Bennis, W. G., and P. E. Slater. 1969. *The temporary society.* New York: Harper & Row.

Berelson, B. F., P. F. Lazarsfeld, and W. N. McPhee. 1954. *Voting: a study of opinion formation in a presidential campaign.* Chicago: University of Chicago Press.

Biddle, B. J., and E. J. Thomas, eds. 1966. *Role theory: concepts and research.* New York: Wiley.

Binkley, W. E. 1947. *President and congress.* New York: Knopf.

Birch, A. H. 1971. *Representation.* London: St. Martin's Press.

Black, C. E., ed. 1960. *The transformation of Russian society.* Cambridge, Mass.: Harvard University Press.

Black, D. 1958. *The theory of committees and elections.* Cambridge: Cambridge University Press.

Black, G. S. 1970. A theory of professionalization in politics. *American Political Science Review* 64:865–878.

——— 1972. A theory of political ambition: career choices and the role of structural incentives. *American Political Science Review* 66:144–159.

Blalock, H. M. 1964. *Causal inferences in nonexperimental research.* Chapel Hill: University of North Carolina Press.

——— 1970. *Toward a theory of minority-group relations.* New York: Capricorn.

Blau, P. 1959. *The dynamics of bureaucracy.* Chicago: University of Chicago Press.

536   REFERENCES

————— 1960. Structural effects. *American Sociological Review* 25:178–193.

————— 1969. Objectives of sociology. In *A design for sociology: scope, objectives, and methods,* ed. R. Bierstedt. Philadelphia: American Academy of Political and Social Science.

Blau, P. M., and O. D. Duncan. 1967. *The American occupational structure.* New York: Wiley.

Blaustein, A. P., and C. O. Porter. 1954. *The American lawyer: a summary of the survey of the legal profession.* Chicago: University of Chicago Press.

Blecher, E. M. 1971. *Advocacy planning for urban development: with analysis of six demonstration programs.* New York: Praeger.

Boguslaw, R. 1965. *The new utopians: a study of system design and social change.* Englewood Cliffs, N.J.: Prentice-Hall.

Bowles, F., and F. A. DeCosta. 1971. *Between two worlds: a profile of negro higher education.* New York: McGraw-Hill.

Brager, G. A. 1968. Advocacy and political behavior. *Social Work* 13:5–15.

Breed, W. 1971. *The self-guiding society.* New York: Free Press.

Brickman, W. W., and S. Lehrer, eds. 1966. *Automation, education and human values.* New York: Crowell.

Brodbeck, M. 1959. Models, meaning, and theories. In *Symposium on sociological theory,* ed. L. Gross. Evanston, Ill.: Row, Peterson.

Bross, I. D. J. 1953. *Design for decision.* New York: Wiley.

Brown, H. 1954. *The challenge of man's future.* New York: Viking.

Bryce, J. 1924. *Modern democracies.* New York: Macmillan.

Brzezinski, Z. 1970. *Between two ages: America's role in the technetronic era.* New York: Viking.

Buchanan, J. M., and G. Tullock. 1962. *The calculus of consent: logical foundations of constitutional democracy.* Ann Arbor: University of Michigan Press.

Buck, J. V. 1972. *City planners: the dilemma of professionals in a political milieu.* Ph.D. diss., Stanford University.

Burke, E. 1949. Speech to the Electors of Bristol. In *Burke's politics,* ed. R. J. S. Hoffman and P. Levack. New York: Knopf. Speech dated 1774.

Burnham, J. 1941. *The managerial revolution.* New York: John Day.

Campbell, A., and H. C. Cooper. 1956. *Group differences in attitudes and votes.* Ann Arbor, Mich.: Survey Research Center, Institute for Social Research.

Campbell, A., G. Gurin, and W. E. Miller. 1954. *The voter decides.* Evanston, Ill.: Row, Peterson.

Campbell, A., P. E. Converse, W. E. Miller, and D. E. Stokes, 1960. *The American voter.* New York: Wiley.

Campbell, D. T. 1958. Common fate, similarity and other indices of the status of aggregates of persons as social entities. *Behavioral Science* 3:14–25.

Carlin, J. E. 1962. *Lawyers on their own.* New Brunswick, N.J.: Rutgers University Press.

————— 1966. *Lawyer's ethics: a survey of the New York bar.* New York: Russell Sage Foundation.

Carr-Saunders, A. M. 1955. Metropolitan conditions and traditional professional relationships. In *The metropolis in modern life,* ed. R. M. Fisher. Garden City, N.Y.: Doubleday.

Carr-Saunders, A. M., and P. A. Wilson. 1933. *The professions.* Oxford: Clarendon Press.

———— 1934. Professions. In *Encyclopaedia of the Social Sciences* 12:476–480. New York: Macmillan.

Cartwright, D. S. 1969. Ecological variables. In *Sociological Methodology,* ed. E. F. Borgatta. San Francisco: Jossey-Bass.

Cartwright, D., and A. Zander, eds. 1953. *Group dynamics: research and theory.* Evanston, Ill.: Row, Peterson.

Centers, R. 1949. *The psychology of social classes.* Princeton, N.J.: Princeton University Press.

Chapin, F. S., Jr., and S. F. Weiss, eds. 1962. *Urban growth dynamics.* New York: Wiley.

Chorafas, D. N. 1968. *The knowledge revolution: an analysis of the international brain market.* New York: McGraw-Hill.

Clapp, C. 1963. *The congressman: his job as he sees it.* Washington, D.C.: Brookings Institution.

Clausen, A. R. 1973. *How congressmen decide.* New York: St. Martin's Press.

Cnudde, C. F., and D. J. McCrone. 1966. The linkage between constituency attitudes and congressional voting: a causal model. *American Political Science Review* 60: 66–72.

Cohen, B. C. 1957. *The political process and foreign policy.* Princeton, N.J.: Princeton University Press.

———— 1963. *The press and foreign policy.* Princeton, N.J.: Princeton University Press.

Cohen, M. R. 1931. *Reason and nature.* New York: Harcourt, Brace.

———— 1933. *Law and the social order.* New York: Harcourt, Brace.

———— 1949. *Studies in philosophy and science.* New York: Holt.

Cohen, M. R., and E. Nagel. 1934. *An introducton to logic and scientific method.* New York: Harcourt, Brace.

Collins, B. E., and H. Guetzkow. 1964. *A social psychology of group processes for decision-making.* New York: Wiley.

Cooper, J. 1977. Congress in organizational perspective. In *Congress reconsidered,* ed. L. C. Dodd and B. I. Oppenheimer. New York: Praeger.

Cooper, J., and G. C. Mackenzie. 1981. *The house at work.* Austin: University of Texas Press.

Crane, W., Jr. 1960. A caveat on roll-call studies of party voting. *Midwest Journal of Political Science* 4:237–249.

Crenson, M. A. 1978. Social networks and political processes in urban neighborhoods. *American Journal of Political Science* 22:578–594.

———— 1983. *Neighborhoods in politics.* Cambridge, Mass.: Harvard University Press.

Cronin, T. E. 1970. Metropolity models and city hall. *Journal of the American Institute of Planners* 36:189–197.

538   REFERENCES

Cronin, T. E., and S. D. Greenberg, eds. 1969. *The presidential advisory system.* New York: Harper & Row.

Curtis, J. L. 1971. *Blacks, medical schools, and society.* Ann Arbor: University of Michigan Press.

Dahl, R. A. 1956. *A preface to democratic theory.* Chicago: University of Chicago Press.

———— 1961a. *Who governs? democracy and power in an American city.* New Haven: Yale University Press.

———— 1961b. The behavioral approach in political science: epitaph for a monument to a successful protest. *American Political Science Review* 55:763–772.

Dahl, R. A., and C. E. Lindblom. 1953. *Politics, economics, and welfare.* New York: Harper.

Dahl, R. A., and E. R. Tufte. 1973. *Size and democracy.* Stanford, Calif.: Stanford University Press.

Davis, J. A. 1961a. A technique for analyzing the effects of group composition. *American Sociological Review* 26:215–225.

———— 1961b. Problem and method: compositional effects and the survival of small social systems. In *Great books and small groups.* New York: Free Press.

De Grazia, A. 1951. *Public and republic: political representation in America.* New York: Knopf.

———— 1958. The nature and prospects of political interest groups. *Annals of the American Academy of Political and Social Science* 319:113–122.

Dewey, J. 1938. *Logic: the theory of inquiry.* New York: Holt.

De Witt, N. 1961. *Education and professional employment in the U.S.S.R.* Washington, D.C.: National Science Foundation.

Dogan, M., and S. Rokkan, eds. 1969. *Quantitative ecological analysis in the social sciences.* Cambridge, Mass.: M.I.T. Press.

Drinker, H. S. 1955. Legal ethics. *Annals of the American Academy of Political and Social Science* 297:37–45.

Driscoll, J. M. 1955. Some analytic concepts for the comparative study of state legislatures. Paper presented at the annual meeting of the American Political Science Association, Boulder, Colo., September 7–9, 1955.

DuCann, R. 1964. *The art of advocacy.* London: Penguin Books.

Durkheim, E. 1958. *Professional ethics and civic morals.* Glencoe, Ill.: Free Press. First published in French in 1950. Durkheim delivered these lectures between 1890 and 1912.

———— 1960. *The division of labor in society.* Glencoe, Ill.: Free Press. First published in 1893.

Dye, T. R. 1966. *Politics, economics and the public: policy outcomes in the American states.* Chicago: Rand McNally.

Easton, D. 1950. Harold Lasswell: policy scientist for a democratic society. *Journal of Politics* 12:450–477.

———— 1953. *The political system: an inquiry into the state of political science.* New York: Knopf.

———— 1965a. *A system analysis of political life.* New York: Wiley.

—— 1965b. *A framework for political analysis.* Englewood Cliffs, N.J.: Prentice-Hall.

Eckstein, H. 1960. *Pressure group politics: the case of the British medical association.* Stanford, Calif.: Stanford University Press.

Edelman, M. 1964. *The symbolic uses of politics.* Urbana: University of Illinois Press.

—— 1971. *Politics as symbolic action: mass arousal and quiescence.* Chicago: Markham.

Edinger, L. J. 1964. Political science and political biography: reflections on the study of leadership. *Journal of Politics* 26:423–439, 648–676.

Ehrman, H. W. ed. 1958. *Interest groups on four continents.* Pittsburgh: University of Pittsburgh Press.

Elazar, D. J. 1962. *The American partnership.* Chicago: University of Chicago Press.

—— 1966. *American federalism: a view from the states.* New York: Crowell.

Eldersveld, S. J. 1951. Theory and method in voting behavior research. *Journal of Politics* 13:70–87.

—— 1958. American interest groups: a survey of research and some implications for theory and method. In *Interest groups on four continents,* ed. H. W. Ehrmann. Pittsburgh: University of Pittsburgh Press.

Ellul, J. 1967. *The technological society.* New York: Knopf.

Epstein, C. F. 1970a. *Woman's place: options and limits of professional careers.* Berkeley: University of California Press.

—— 1970b. Encountering the male establishment: sex-status limits on women's careers in the professions. *American Journal of Sociology* 75:968–982.

Etzioni, A. 1968. *The active society.* New York: Free Press.

—— ed. 1969. *The semi-professions and their organization: teachers, nurses, social workers.* New York: Free Press.

Eulau, H. 1941. Theories of federalism under the Holy Roman Empire. *American Political Science Review* 35:643–664.

—— 1962a. Bases of authority in legislative bodies: a comparative analysis. *Administrative Science Quarterly* 7:309–321.

—— 1962b. Small groups, big organizations, and mass society. *Public Administration Review* 22:230–235.

—— 1962c. Comparative political analysis: a methodological note. *Midwest Journal of Political Science* 6:397–407.

—— 1963a. *The behavioral persuasion in politics.* New York: Random House.

—— 1963b. Dreamer's journey: Morris R. Cohen. In *Journeys in politics.* Indianapolis: Bobbs-Merrill. First published in 1949 in *Antioch Review* 9:414–419.

—— 1963c. Social science at the crossroads. In *Journeys in politics.* Indianapolis: Bobbs-Merrill. First published in 1951 in *Antioch Review* 11:117–128.

—— 1967. Changing views of representation. In *Contemporary political science: toward empirical theory,* ed. I. de S. Pool. New York: McGraw-Hill.

—— 1969a. *Mirco-macro political analysis: accents of inquiry.* Chicago: Aldine.

—— 1969b. *Behavioralism in political science.* New York: Atherton.

—— 1977a. The place of policy analysis in political science: the interventionist synthesis. *American Journal of Political Science* 21:419–423.

—— 1977b. *Technology and civility: the skill revolution in politics.* Stanford, Calif.: Hoover Institution Press.

—— 1980. The Columbia studies of personal influence: social network analysis. *Social Science History* 4:207–228.

—— 1984a. Legislative committee assignments. *Legislative Studies Quarterly* 9:587–633.

—— 1984b. The redwood network project: small-scale research at the local level. *ICPSR Bulletin* 4:2:1–2.

Eulau, H., and P. A. Lupsha. 1966. Decisional structures and coalition formation in small legislative bodies. *In Lawmakers in a changing world,* ed. E. Frank. Englewood Cliffs, N.J.: Prentice-Hall.

Eulau, H., and V. McCluggage. 1984. Standing committees in legislatures: three decades of research. *Legislative Studies Quarterly* 9:195–270.

Eulau, H., and K. Prewitt. 1973. *Labyrinths of democracy: adaptations, linkages, representation, and policies in urban politics.* Indianapolis: Bobbs-Merrill.

Eulau, H., and H. Quinley. 1970. *State officials and higher education.* New York: McGraw-Hill.

Eulau, H., and J. W. Siegel. 1980. A post-facto experiment in contextual analysis: of day- and night-dwellers. *Experimental Study of Politics* 7:1–26.

—— 1981. Social network analysis and political behavior: a feasibility study. *Western Political Quarterly* 34:499–509.

Eulau, H., and J. D. Sprague. 1964. *Lawyers in politics: a study in professional convergence.* Indianapolis: Bobbs-Merrill.

Eulau, H., S. J. Eldersveld, and M. Janowitz, eds. 1956. *Political behavior: a reader in theory and research.* Glencoe, Ill.: Free Press.

Eulau, H., J. C. Wahlke, W. Buchanan, and L. C. Ferguson. 1959. The role of the representative: some empirical observations on the theory of Edmund Burke. *American Political Science Review* 53:742–756.

Ewald, W. E., Jr., ed. 1968. *Environment and change: the next fifty years.* Bloomington: Indiana University Press.

Ewing, D. W. 1964. *The managerial mind.* New York: Free Press.

Eyestone, R. 1971. *The threads of public policy: a study in policy leadership.* Indianapolis: Bobbs-Merrill.

Eyestone, R., and H. Eulau. 1968. City councils and policy outcomes: developmental profiles. In *City politics and public policy,* ed. J. Q. Wilson. New York: Wiley.

Fairlie, J. A. 1940. The nature of political representation. *American Political Science Review* 34:236–248, 456–466.

Falter, J. W. 1982. *Der "positivismusstreit" in der Amerikanischen politikwissenschaft.* Opladen: Westdeutscher Verlag.

Feierabend, I. K., and R. L. Feierabend. 1966. Aggressive behaviors within polities, 1948–1962: a cross-national study. *Journal of Conflict Resolution* 10:249–271.

Fenno, R. F., Jr. 1962. The house appropriations committee as a political system: the problem of integration. *American Political Science Review* 56:310–324.

—— 1966. *The power of the purse: appropriations politics in Congress.* Boston: Little, Brown.

—— 1973. *Congressmen in committees.* Boston: Little, Brown.

—— 1975. If, as Ralph Nader says, Congress is "the broken branch," how come we love our congressmen so much? In *Congress in change: evolution and reform,* ed. N. J. Ornstein. New York: Praeger.

—— 1978. *Home style: House members in their districts.* Boston: Little, Brown.

Ferkiss, V. C. 1969. *Technological man: the myth and the reality.* New York: Braziller.

Festinger, L. 1957. *A theory of cognitive dissonance.* Evanston, Ill.: Row, Peterson.

Fiellin, A. 1962. The functions of informal groups in legislative institutions. *Journal of Politics* 24:72–91.

Finifter, A. W. 1974. The friendship group as a protective environment for political deviants. *American Political Science Review* 68:607–625.

Fiorina, M. P. 1974. *Representatives, roll calls, and constituencies.* Lexington, Mass.: D. C. Heath.

—— 1977. The case of the vanishing marginals: the bureaucracy did it. *American Political Science Review* 71:177–181.

Fischer, C. S. 1982. *To dwell among friends: personal networks in town and city.* Chicago: University of Chicago Press.

Fischer, C. S., R. M. Stueve, et al. 1977. *Networks and places: social relations in the urban setting.* New York: Free Press.

Fischer, G. 1968. *The Soviet system and modern society.* New York: Atherton.

Fitton, M. 1973. Neighborhood and voting: a sociometric examination. *British Journal of Political Science* 3:445–472.

Foladare, I. S. 1968. The effect of neighborhood on voting behavior. *Political Science Quarterly* 83:516–529.

Fox, R. C. 1959. *Experiment perilous.* Glencoe, Ill.: Free Press.

—— 1967. Training for uncertainty. In *The professional in the organization,* ed. M. Abrahamson. Chicago: Rand McNally.

Francis, W. L. 1962. Influence and interaction in a state legislative body. *American Political Science Review* 56:953–960.

Freidson, E., ed. 1963. *The hospital in modern society.* New York: Free Press.

Freidson, E. 1968. The impurity of professional authority. In *Institutions and the person,* ed. H. S. Becker et al. Chicago: Aldine.

—— 1970a. *Professional dominance: the social structure of medical care.* New York: Atherton.

—— 1970b. *Profession of medicine.* New York: Dodd.

Freud, S. 1949. *Group psychology and the analysis of the ego.* London: Hogarth Press.

Frey, F. W. 1970. Cross-cultural survey research in political science. In *The methodology of comparative research,* ed. R. T. Holt and J. E. Turner. New York: Free Press.

———— 1971. On issues and nonissues in the study of power. *American Political Science Review* 65:1081–1101.

Friedman, M. 1962. *Capitalism and freedom.* Chicago: University of Chicago Press.

Friedrich, C. J. 1946. *Constitutional government and democracy.* Boston: Ginn & Company.

Friedrich, C. J., and Z. K. Brzezinski. 1965. *Totalitarian dictatorship and autocracy.* New ed. Cambridge, Mass.: Harvard University Press.

Froman, L. A., Jr. 1967. *The congressional process: strategies, rules, and procedures.* Boston: Little, Brown.

Galbraith, J. K. 1967. *The new industrial state.* Boston: Houghton Mifflin.

Galtung, J. 1969. *Theory and methods of social research.* New York: Columbia University Press.

Gambino, J. W. 1972. Faculty unionism: from theory to practice. *Industrial Relations* 11:1–17.

Garceau, O. 1941. *The political life of the American medical association.* Cambridge, Mass.: Harvard University Press.

———— 1951. Research in the political process. *American Political Science Review* 45:69–85.

———— 1958. Interest group theory in political research. *Annals of the American Academy of Political and Social Science* 319:104–112.

Garceau, O., and C. Silverman. 1954. A pressure group and the pressured: a case report. *American Political Science Review* 48:672–691.

Geertz, C. 1973. *The interpretation of cultures.* New York: Basic Books.

George, A. L. 1972. The case for multiple advocacy in making foreign policy. *American Political Science Review* 66:751–785.

Germino, D. 1967. *Beyond ideology: the revival of political theory.* New York: Harper & Row.

Gerth, H., and C. W. Mills. 1953. *Character and social structure.* New York: Harcourt, Brace.

Gierke, O. 1972. Ueber die geschichte des majoritaetsprinzips. In *Essays in legal history,* ed. P. Vinogradoff. Nendeln, Liechtenstein: Kraus. First published in 1913.

Gilb, C. L. 1966. *Hidden hierarchies: the professions and government.* New York: Harper & Row.

Ginzberg, E., with M. Ostow. 1969. *Men, money, and medicine.* New York: Columbia University Press.

Gittell, M. 1967. Professionalism and public participation in educational policy making: New York City, a case study. *Public Administration Review* 27:237–251.

Glaser, B. G. 1964. *Organizational scientists: their professional careers.* Indianapolis: Bobbs-Merrill.

———— ed. 1968. *Organizational career: a sourcebook for theory.* Chicago: Aldine.

Glaser, W. 1970. *Social settings and medical organization: a cross-national study of the hospital.* New York: Atherton.

Gold, D. 1961. Lawyers in politics: an empirical exploration of biographical data on state legislators. *Pacific Sociological Review* 4:84–86.

Goldenberg, E. 1975. *Making the papers.* Lexington, Mass.: Lexington Books.

Golembiewski, R. T. 1962. *The small group: an analysis of concepts and operations.* Chicago: University of Chicago Press.

Goode, W. J. 1967. Community within community: the professions. *American Sociological Review* 22:194–200.

―――― 1969. The theoretical limits of professionalization. In *The semi-professions and their organization,* ed. A. Etzioni. New York: Free Press.

Goodman, L. 1959. Some alternatives to ecological correlation. *American Journal of Sociology* 65:610–625.

Gordon, M. M. 1949. Social class in American sociology. *American Journal of Sociology* 55:262–268.

Gosnell, H. F. 1948. *Democracy—the threshold of freedom.* New York: Ronald.

Gouldner, A. W. 1958. Cosmopolitans and locals: toward an analysis of latent social roles. *Administrative Science Quarterly* 2:281–306, 444–480.

Gouldner, A. W., and S. M. Miller, eds. 1965. *Applied sociology: opportunities and problems.* New York: Free Press.

Greenstein, F. I. 1969. *Personality and politics.* Chicago: Markham.

Grodzins, M. 1966. *The American system: a new view of government in the United States.* Chicago: Rand McNally.

Gross, B. M. 1953. *The legislative struggle.* New York: McGraw-Hill.

Grossman, J. B. 1965. *Lawyers and judges: the ABA and the politics of judicial selection.* New York: Wiley.

Grumm, J. C. 1965. A systematic analysis of blocs in the study of legislative behavior. *Western Political Quarterly* 18:350–362.

Hadden, J. K., and E. F. Borgatta. 1965. *American cities: their social characteristics.* Chicago: Rand McNally.

Hagstrom, W. O. 1965. *The scientific community.* New York: Basic Books.

Hall, R. H. 1969. *Occupations and the social structure.* Englewood Cliffs, N.J.: Prentice-Hall.

Hare, A. P., ed. 1962. *Handbook of small group research.* New York: Free Press.

Hare, A. P., E. F. Borgatta, and R. F. Bales, eds. 1955. *Small groups: studies in social interaction.* New York: Knopf.

Harrington, M. 1962. *The other America.* New York: Macmillan.

Haug, M. R., and M. B. Sussman. 1969. Professional autonomy and the revolt of the client. *Social Problems* 17:153–161.

Hedlund, R. D. 1984. Organizational attributes of legislatures: structure, rules, norms, resources. *Legislative Studies Quarterly* 9:51–121.

Heider, F. 1958. *The psychology of interpersonal relations.* New York: Wiley.

Hilgard, E. R., and D. Lerner. 1951. The person: subject and object of science and policy. In *The policy sciences: recent developments in scope and method,* ed. D. Lerner and H. D. Lasswell. Stanford, Calif.: Stanford University Press.

Hirsch, W. 1968. *Scientists in American society.* New York: Random House.

Hofstadter, R. 1955. *The age of reform.* New York: Knopf.

Holsti, O. R. 1976. Cognitive process approaches to decision-making. *American Behavioral Scientist* 20:11–32.

Homans, G. C. 1950. *The human group.* New York: Harcourt, Brace.

—— 1961. *Social behavior: its elementary forms.* New York: Harcourt, Brace.

Howton, F. W. 1969. *Functionaries.* Chicago: Quadrangle Books.

Huckfeldt, R. R. 1979. Political participation in the neighborhood social context. *American Journal of Political Science* 23:579–592.

—— 1980. Variable responses to neighborhood social contexts: assimilation, conflict, and tipping points. *Political Behavior* 2:231–257.

—— 1983a. The social context of ethnic politics. *American Politics Quarterly* 11:91–112.

—— 1983b. The social context of political change: durability, volatility, and social influence. *American Political Science Review* 77:929–944.

—— 1984. Political loyalties and social class ties: the mechanisms of contextual influence. *American Journal of Political Science* 28:399–417.

Hughes, E. C. 1952. Psychology: science and/or profession. *The American Psychologist* 7:441–443.

—— 1958. *Men and their work.* Glencoe, Ill.: Free Press.

Huntington, S. P. 1957. *The soldier and the state.* Cambridge, Mass.: Harvard University Press.

Hyman, H. H., and P. B. Sheatsley. 1951. The current status of American public opinion. In *The teaching of contemporary affairs,* ed. J. C. Payne. Menasha, Wis.: Banta.

—— 1953. The political appeal of President Eisenhower. *Public Opinion Quarterly* 17:443–460.

Hyman, H. H., and E. Singer, eds. 1968. *Readings in reference group theory and research.* New York: Free Press.

Hyneman, C. S. 1938. Tenure and turnover of legislative personnel. *Annals of the American Academy of Political and Social Science* 195:21–31.

—— 1940. Who makes our laws? *Political Science Quarterly* 55:556–581.

Inter-University Consortium for Political Research. 1971. *The 1958 American representation study: congressmen and constituents.* Ann Arbor, Mich.: ICPR.

Inter-University Consortium for Political and Social Research. 1983. *American national election study: major panel file III.* Ann Arbor, Mich.: ICPSR.

Jackson, J. E. 1974. *Constituencies and leaders in Congress.* Cambridge, Mass.: Harvard University Press.

Jacob, H., and M. Lipsky. 1968. Outputs, structure, and power: an assessment of changes in the study of state and local politics. In *Advance of the discipline,* ed. M. D. Irish. Englewood Cliffs, N.J.: Prentice-Hall.

Jacob, H., and K. N. Vines, eds. 1965. *Politics in the American states.* Boston: Little, Brown.

Janowitz, M. 1971. *The professional soldier: a social and political portrait.* New York: Free Press.

Jennings, M. K., and R. G. Niemi. 1981. *Generations and politics: a panel study of young adults and their parents.* Princeton, N.J.: Princeton University Press.

Jennings, M. K., and H. Zeigler. 1971. Response styles and politics: the case of school boards. *Midwest Journal of Political Science* 15:290–321.

Jones, C. O. 1962. The role of the congressional subcommittee. *Midwest Journal of Political Science* 6:327–344.

Jones, H. W. 1962. Political behavior and the problem of sanctions. In *The ethics of power: the interplay of religion, philosophy, and politics,* ed. H. D. Lasswell and H. Cleveland. New York: Harper.

Joreskog, K. G., and D. Sorbom. 1981. *Lisrel V: analysis of linear structural relationships in maximum likelihood and least square methods.* Uppsala, Sweden: University of Uppsala, Department of Statistics.

Kadish, S. H. 1972. The theory of the profession and its predicament. *AAUP Bulletin* 58:120–125.

Kasarda, J. D. 1974. The structural implications of social system size: a three-level analysis. *American Sociological Review* 39:19–28.

Katz, E., and P. F. Lazarsfeld. 1955. *Personal influence.* Glencoe, Ill.: Free Press.

Kaufman, H. 1960. *The forest ranger: a study in administrative behavior.* Baltimore: Johns Hopkins University Press.

——— 1969. Administrative decentralization and political power. *Public Administration Review* 29:3–14.

Keefe, W. J. 1954. Parties, partisanship, and public policy in the Pennsylvania legislature. *American Political Science Review* 48:450–464.

——— 1956. Comparative study of the role of political parties in state legislatures. *Western Political Quarterly* 9:726–742.

Kelley, S., Jr. 1956. *Professional public relations and political power.* Baltimore: Johns Hopkins University Press.

Kerr, C. 1954. The Balkanization of labor markets. In *Labor mobility and economic opportunity,* ed. E. W. Bakke et al. New York: Wiley.

Key, V. O., Jr. 1952. *Politics, parties, and pressure groups.* 3rd ed. New York: Crowell.

——— 1958. *Politics, parties, and pressure groups.* 4th ed. New York: Crowell.

——— 1966. *The responsible electorate: rationality in presidential voting, 1936–1960.* Cambridge, Mass.: Harvard University Press.

Key, V. O., Jr., and F. Munger. 1959. Social determinism and electoral decision: the case of Indiana. In *American voting behavior,* ed. E. Burdick and A. J. Brodbeck. Glencoe, Ill.: Free Press.

Kingdon, J. W. 1973. *Congressmen's voting decisions.* New York: Harper & Row.

Kirchheimer, O. 1961. *Political justice: the use of legal procedure for political ends.* Princeton, N.J.: Princeton University Press.

Kirkpatrick, S. A. 1975. Psychological views of decision-making. In *Political Science Annual 6,* ed. C. P. Cotter. Indianapolis: Bobbs-Merrill.

Klain, M. 1955. Politics—still a dirty word. *Antioch Review* 15:457–466.

Klausner, S. Z. 1967. *The study of total societies.* Garden City, N.Y.: Doubleday-Anchor.

Klaw, S. 1968. *The new Brahmins: scientific life in America.* New York: Morrow.

Knoke, D., and J. H. Kuklinski. 1982. *Network analysis.* Beverly Hills, Calif.: Sage Publications.

Kornhauser, W. 1962. *Scientists in industry: conflict and accommodation.* Berkeley: University of California Press.

Ladd, E. C., and S. M. Lipset. 1972. Politics of academic natural scientists and engineers. *Science* 176:1091–1100.

Ladinsky, J. 1963. Careers of lawyers, law practice, and legal institutions. *American Sociological Review* 28:47–54.

Landau, M. 1972. *Political theory and political science: studies in the methodology of political inquiry.* New York: Macmillan.

Landis, B. Y., ed. 1955. *Ethical standards and professional conduct.* Philadelphia: American Academy of Political and Social Science.

Lane, R. E. 1964. Review of "The behavioral persuasion in politics" by Heinz Eulau. *American Political Science Review* 58:105–106.

———— 1966. The decline of politics and ideology in a knowledgeable society. *American Sociological Review* 31:649–662.

LaPalombara, J. 1960. The utility and limitations of interest group theory in non-American field situations. *Journal of Politics* 22:29–49.

———— 1970. Parsimony and empiricism in comparative politics: an anti-scholastic view. In *The methodology of comparative research,* ed. R. T. Holt and J. E. Turner. New York: Free Press.

Larsen, J. A. O. 1955. *Representative government in Greek and Roman history.* Berkeley: University of California Press.

Laski, H. J. 1939. The obsolescence of federalism. *New Republic* 98:367–369.

Lasswell, H. D. 1930. *Psychopathology and politics.* Chicago: University of Chicago Press.

———— 1935. *World politics and personal insecurity.* New York: McGraw-Hill.

———— 1936. *Politics: who gets what, when, how.* New York: McGraw-Hill.

———— 1948a. *The analysis of political behavior.* New York: Oxford University Press.

———— 1948b. *Power and personality.* New York: Norton.

———— 1948c. General framework: person, personality, group, culture. In *The analysis of political behavior.* New York: Oxford University Press. First published in 1939 in *Psychiatry* 2:533–561.

———— 1951a. *The world revolution of our time.* Stanford, Calif.: Stanford University Press.

———— 1951b. *The political writings of Harold D. Lasswell.* Glencoe, Ill.: Free Press.

———— 1951c. The policy orientation. In *The policy sciences,* ed. D. Lerner and H. D. Lasswell. Stanford, Calif.: Stanford University Press.

———— 1954. The world revolutionary situation. In *Totalitarianism,* ed. C. J. Friedrich. Cambridge, Mass.: Harvard University Press.

———— 1955. Current studies in the decision process: automation versus creativity. *Western Political Quarterly* 8:381–399.

———— 1956. Impact of psychoanalytic thinking on the social sciences. In *The state of the social sciences,* ed. L. D. White. Chicago: University of Chicago Press.

———— 1963. *The future of political science.* New York: Atherton.

Lasswell, H. D., and A. Kaplan. 1950. *Power and society: a framework for political inquiry.* New Haven: Yale University Press.

Lasswell, H. D., D. Lerner, and C. E. Rothwell, 1952. *The comparative study of elites.* Stanford, Calif.: Stanford University Press.

Lasswell, H. D., D. Lerner, and I. de Sola Pool. 1952. *The comparative study of symbols.* Stanford, Calif.: Stanford University Press.

Lasswell, H. D., C. E. Merriam, and T. V. Smith. 1950. *A study of power.* Glencoe, Ill.: Free Press.

Lasswell, H. D., N. Leites, et al. 1949. *Language of politics.* New York: Stewart.

Latham, E. 1952. *The group basis of politics.* Ithaca, N.Y.: Cornell University Press.

Laumann, E. O. 1973. *Bonds of pluralism.* New York: Wiley.

Lazarsfeld, P. F. 1959. Evidence and inference in social research. In *Evidence and inference,* ed. D. Lerner. New York: Free Press.

Lazarsfeld, P. F., and H. Menzel. 1965. On the relation between individual and collective properties. In *Complex organizations,* ed. A. Etzioni. New York: Holt, Rinehart.

Lazarsfeld, P. F., B. Berelson, and H. Gaudet. 1948. *The people's choice.* New York: Columbia University Press.

Leighton, A. H. 1949. *Human relations in a changing world.* New York: Dutton.

Leiserson, A. 1953. Problems of methodology in political research. *Political Science Quarterly* 68:558–584.

——— 1958. *Parties and politics: an institutional and behavioral approach.* New York: Knopf.

Leoni, B. 1957. The meaning of "political" in political decisions. *Political Studies* 5:225–239.

Lerner, D., ed. 1963. *Parts and wholes.* New York: Free Press.

Levin, H. M., ed. 1970. *Community control of schools.* Washington, D.C.: Brookings Institution.

Levine, E. B. 1973. *Role conflicts among black businessmen.* Ph.D. diss., Stanford University.

Levy, M. J., Jr. 1958. Some aspects of "structural-functional" analysis and political science. In *Approaches to the study of politics,* ed. R. Young. Evanston, Ill.: Northwestern University Press.

Lewin, K. 1948. *Resolving social conflicts.* New York: Harper.

——— 1951. *Field theory in social science.* New York: Harper.

Lewis, R., and R. Stewart. 1961. *The managers: a new examination of the English, German and American executive.* New York: Mentor.

Leys, W. A. R. 1962. A comparative investigation of the norms of official conduct. In *Ethics and bigness: scientific, academic, religious, political, and military,* ed. H. Cleveland and H. D. Lasswell. New York: Harper.

Lindblom, C. E. 1965. *The intelligence of democracy.* New York: Free Press.

Linz, J. J. 1969. Ecological analysis and survey research. In *Quantitative ecological analysis in the social sciences,* ed. M. Dogan and S. Rokkan. Cambridge, Mass.: M.I.T. Press.

Lipset, S. M. 1970. The politics of academia. In *Perspectives on campus tensions,* ed. D. C. Nichols. Washington, D.C.: American Council on Education.

Lipset, S. M., P. F. Lazarsfeld, A. H. Barton, and J. Linz. 1954. The psychology of voting: an analysis of political behavior. In *Handbook of social psychology,* vol. 2, ed. G. Lindzey. Reading, Mass.: Addison-Wesley.

Lipsky, G. A. 1955. The theory of international relations of Harold D. Lasswell. *Journal of Politics* 17:43–58.

Lipsky, M. 1968. Protest as a political resource. *American Political Science Review* 62:1144–58.

——— 1970. *Protest in city politics: rent strikes, housing and the power of the poor.* Chicago: Rand McNally.

——— 1972. Toward a theory of street-level bureaucracy. In *State, schools, and politics,* ed. M. W. Kirst. Lexington, Mass.: D. C. Heath.

Lochner, P. R. 1971. *Learning to be a lawyer: homogenization and differentiation into public and private sector professional roles.* Ph.D. diss., Stanford University.

Lodge, M. C. 1969. *Soviet elite attitudes since Stalin.* Columbus, Ohio: Merrill.

Loewenberg, G. 1972. Comparative legislative research. In *Comparative legislative behavior: frontiers of research,* ed. S. C. Patterson and J. C. Wahlke. New York: Wiley.

Loveridge, R. O. 1971. *City managers in legislative politics.* Indianapolis: Bobbs-Merrill.

Lowi, T. J. 1971. *The politics of disorder.* New York: Basic Books.

Lupsha, P. A. 1967. *Swingers, isolates and coalitions: interpersonal relations in small political decision-making groups.* Ph.D. diss., Stanford University.

Lynd, H. M. 1958. *On shame and the search for identity.* New York: Harcourt, Brace.

Lynn, K. S., ed. 1965. *The professions in America.* Boston: Beacon.

Lyons, G. M. 1969. *The uneasy partnership: social science and the federal government in the twentieth century.* New York: Russell Sage Foundation.

Machlup, F. 1962. *The production and distribution of knowledge in the United States.* Princeton, N.J.: Princeton University Press.

MacIver, R. M. 1947. *The web of government.* New York: Macmillan.

Mackenzie, W. J. M. 1955. Pressure groups: the "conceptual framework." *Political Studies* 3:247–257.

MacRae, D., Jr. 1958. *Dimensions of congressional voting.* Berkeley: University of California Press.

Macridis, R. C. 1955. *The study of comparative government.* Garden City, N.Y.: Doubleday.

Malinowski, B. 1939. The group and the individual in functional analysis. *American Journal of Sociology* 44:938–964.

Mannheim, K. 1948. *Man and society in an age of reconstruction.* New York: Harcourt, Brace.

March, J. G. 1953–54. Husband-wife interaction over political issues. *Public Opinion Quarterly* 17:461–470.

——— 1966. The power of power. In *Varieties of political theory,* ed. D. Easton. Englewood Cliffs, N.J.: Prentice-Hall.

March, J. G., and H. A. Simon. 1958. *Organizations.* New York: Wiley.

Marks, F. R., with K. Leswing and B. A. Fortinsky. 1972. *The lawyers, the public, and professional responsibility.* Chicago: American Bar Foundation.

Marshall, T. H. 1965. *Class, citizenship, and social development.* Garden City, N.Y.: Doubleday-Anchor. First published in 1939.

Marvick, D. 1954. *Career perspectives in a bureaucratic setting.* Ann Arbor: University of Michigan Press.

——— ed. 1961. *Political decision-makers: recruitment and performance.* Glencoe, Ill.: Free Press.

——— ed. 1977. *Harold Lasswell on political sociology.* Chicago: University of Chicago Press.

Matthews, D. R. 1954. *The social background of political decision-makers.* Garden City, N.Y.: Doubleday.

——— 1960. *U.S. senators and their world.* Chapel Hill: University of North Carolina Press.

Matthews, D. R., and J. A. Stimson. 1975. *Yeas and nays: normal decision-making in the U.S. House of Representatives.* New York: Wiley.

Mayer, M. 1968. *The lawyers.* New York: Harper & Row.

McClosky, H., and H. E. Dahlgren. 1959. Primary group influence and party loyalty. *American Political Science Review* 53:757–775.

McDonald, F. 1958. *We, the people—the economic origins of the Constitution.* Chicago: University of Chicago Press.

Mead, G. H. 1934. *Mind, self and society.* Chicago: University of Chicago Press.

Merritt, R. L., and S. Rokkan, eds. 1966. *Comparing nations: the use of qualitative data in cross-national research.* New Haven: Yale University Press.

Meyerson, M., and E. C. Banfield. 1955. *Politics, planning, and the public interest.* Glencoe, Ill.: Free press.

Michaelson, M. G. 1969. Medical students: healers become activists. *Saturday Review* August 16: 41–43, 53–54.

Miller, W. E. 1956. One-party politics and the voter. *American Political Science Review* 50:707–725.

——— 1958. The socio-economic analysis of political behavior. *Midwest Journal of Political Science* 2:239–255.

Miller, W. E., and D. E. Stokes. 1963. Constituency influence in Congress. *American Political Science Review* 57:45–56.

——— 1966. Constituency influence in Congress. In *Elections and the political order,* ed. A. Campbell, P. E. Converse, W. E. Miller, and D. E. Stokes. New York: Wiley.

Mills, C. W. 1951. *The American middle classes.* New York: Oxford University Press.

Mitchell, W. 1959. The ambivalent social status of the American politician. *Western Political Quarterly* 12:683–698.

Moore, W. E. 1963. But some are more equal than others. *American Sociological Review* 28:13–18.

——— 1970. *The professions: roles and rules.* New York: Russell Sage Foundation.

Moreno, J. L., ed. 1960. *The sociometry reader.* New York: Free Press.

Mosher, F. C. 1968. *Democracy and the public service.* New York: Oxford University Press.

Moskow, M. H., and K. McLennan. 1970. Teacher negotiations and school decentralization. In *Community control of schools,* ed. H. M. Levin. Washington, D.C.: Brookings Institution.

Moynihan, D. P. 1965. The professionalization of reform. *The Public Interest* 1:6–16.

Muller, E. N. 1970. The representation of citizens by political authorities: consequences for regime support. *American Political Science Review* 64:1149–66.

Nagel, E. 1961. *The structure of science.* New York: Harcourt, Brace.

National Research Council, Advisory Committee on Government Programs in the Behavioral Sciences. 1968. *The behavioral sciences and the federal government.* Washington, D.C.: National Academy of Sciences.

National Research Council, Committee on the Utilization of Young Scientists and Engineers in Advisory Services to Government, Office of Scientific Personnel. 1972. *The science committee.* Washington, D.C.: National Academy of Science.

National Science Board, Special Commission on the Social Sciences. 1969. *Knowledge into action: improving the nation's use of the social sciences.* Washington, D.C.: National Science Foundation.

Neumann, J., and O. Morgenstern. 1947. *Theory of games and economic behavior.* 2nd ed. Princeton, N.J.: Princeton University Press.

Newcomb, T. M. 1950. *Social psychology.* New York: Dryden.

Nisbett, R., and L. Ross. 1980. *Human inference: strategies and shortcomings of social judgment.* Englewood Cliffs, N.J.: Prentice-Hall.

O'Connor, R. 1974. *Scientists in politics: a study in political participation.* Ph.D. diss., Stanford University.

Odegard, P. 1958. A group basis of politics: a new name for an ancient myth. *Western Political Quarterly* 11:689–702.

Olmsted, M. S. 1959. *The small group.* New York: Random House.

Parsons, T. 1949. *The structure of social action.* Glencoe, Ill.: Free Press. First published in 1937.

––––––– 1951. *The social system.* Glencoe, Ill.: Free Press.

––––––– 1954. *Essays in sociological theory.* Glencoe, Ill.: Free Press.

––––––– 1959. Some problems confronting sociology as a profession. *American Sociological Review* 24:547–559.

––––––– 1960. The distribution of power in American society. In *Structure and process in modern societies.* Glencoe, Ill.: Free Press.

Parsons, T., and E. A. Shils, eds. 1951. *Toward a general theory of action.* Cambridge, Mass.: Harvard University Press.

Patterson, S. C. 1959. Patterns of interpersonal relations in a state legislative group. *Public Opinion Quarterly* 23:101–109.

Patterson, S. C., R. D. Hedlund, and G. R. Boynton. 1975. *Representatives and represented: bases of public support for the American legislatures.* New York: Wiley.

Peabody, R. L. 1964. *Organizational authority.* New York: Atherton.

Pelz, D. C. 1960. Interaction and attitudes between scientists and the auxiliary staff. *Administrative Science Quarterly* 4:321–336, 410–425.

Pennock, J. R. 1968. Political representation: an overview. In *Representation: Nomos X,* ed. J. R. Pennock and J. W. Chapman. New York: Atherton.

Perrow, C. 1965. Hospitals: technology, structure, and goals. In *Handbook of organizations,* ed. J. G. March. Chicago: Rand McNally.

Peterson, P. E. 1970. Forms of representation: participation of the poor in the community action program. *American Political Science Review* 64:491–507.

Piaget, J. 1970. *Structuralism.* New York: Harper & Row.

Pitkin, H. F. 1967. *The concept of representation.* Berkeley: University of California Press.

Prewitt, K. 1965. Political socialization and leadership selection. *Annals of the American Academy of Political and Social Science* 361:96–111.

——— 1970. *The recruitment of political leaders: a study of citizen-politicians.* Indianapolis: Bobbs-Merrill.

Prewitt, K., and H. Eulau. 1969. Political matrix and political representation: prolegomenon to a new departure from an old problem. *American Political Science Review* 63:427–441.

Price, D. K. 1965. *The scientific estate.* New York: Oxford University Press.

Price, H. D. 1968. Micro- and macro-politics: notes on research strategy. In *Political research and political theory,* ed. O. Garceau. Cambridge, Mass.: Harvard University Press.

Pritchett, C. H. 1948. *The Roosevelt court.* New York: Macmillan.

Proctor, C. H., and C. P. Loomis. 1951. Analysis of sociometric data. In *Research methods in social relations,* ed. M. Jahoda, M. Deutsch, and S. W. Cook. New York: Dryden.

Prothro, J. W., and C. M. Grigg. 1960. Fundamental principles of democracy: bases of agreement and disagreement. *Journal of Politics* 22:276–294.

Przeworski, A., and H. Teune. 1970. *The logic of comparative social inquiry.* New York: Wiley Interscience.

Putnam, R. D. 1966. Political attitudes and the local community. *American Political Science Review* 60:640–654.

Quinley, H. E. 1972. *The prophetic clergy: social activism among Protestant ministers.* Berkeley: University of California Press.

Rabinovitz, F. F. 1969. *City politics and planning.* New York: Atherton.

Ranney, A. 1962. The utility and limitations of aggregate data in the study of electoral behavior. In *Essays on the behavioral study of politics,* ed. A. Ranney. Urbana: University of Illinois Press.

Ranney, A., and W. Kendall. 1956. *Democracy and the American party system.* New York: Harcourt, Brace.

Reiss, A. J., Jr. 1961. *Occupations and social status.* New York: Free Press.

Report of the Study of Critical Environmental Problems. 1970. *Man's impact on the global environment.* Cambridge, Mass.: M.I.T. Press.

Rice, S. A. 1927. The identification of blocs in small political bodies. *American Political Science Review* 21:619–627.

Riesman, D. 1950. *The lonely crowd.* New Haven: Yale University Press.

Riker, W. H. 1962. *The theory of political coalitions.* New Haven: Yale University Press.

Riker, W. H., and P. C. Ordeshook. 1973. *An introduction to positive political theory.* Englewood Cliffs, N.J.: Prentice-Hall.

Riley, M. W. 1964. Sources and types of sociological data. In *Handbook of modern sociology,* ed. E. L. Faris. Chicago: Rand McNally.

Robinson, J. P. 1967. *Measures of occupational attitudes and occupational characteristics.* Ann Arbor, Mich.: Survey Research Center, Institute for Social Research.

Rogow, A. A. 1970. *The psychiatrists.* New York: Putnam.

Rokkan, S. 1962. The comparative study of political participation. In *Essays in the behavioral study of politics,* ed. A. Ranney. Urbana: University of Illinois Press.

Rosenberg, M. 1968. *The logic of survey research.* New York: Basic Books.

Rossi, P. H., and R. A. Dentler. 1961. *The politics of urban planning.* Glencoe, Ill.: Free Press.

Rourke, F. E. 1969. *Bureaucracy, politics, and public policy.* Boston: Little, Brown.

Salisbury, R. H. 1968. The analysis of public policy: a search for theories and roles. In *Political science and public policy,* ed. A. Ranney. Chicago: Markham.

Scarrow, H. A. 1969. *Comparative political analysis.* New York: Harper & Row.

Schattschneider, E. E. 1942. *Party government.* New York: Farrar and Strauss.

Schein, E. H. 1972. *Professional education: some new directions.* New York: McGraw-Hill.

Scheuch, E. K. 1969. Social context and individual behavior. In *Quantitative ecological analysis in the social sciences,* ed. M. Dogan and S. Rokkan. Cambridge, Mass.: M.I.T. Press.

Schlesinger, J. 1966. *Ambition and politics.* Chicago: Rand McNally.

Schmidhauser, J. R. 1960. *The Supreme Court.* New York: Holt.

Schubert, G. 1960. *The public interest.* Glencoe, Ill.: Free Press.

―――― 1964. The power of organized minorities in a small group. *Administrative Science Quarterly* 9:133–153.

Segal, D. R., and M. W. Meyer. 1969. The social context of political partisanship. In *Quantitative ecological analysis in the social sciences,* ed. M. Dogan and S. Rokkan. Cambridge, Mass.: M.I.T. Press.

Selvin, H. C., and W. O. Hagstrom. 1966. The empirical classification of formal groups. In *College peer groups,* ed. T. M. Newcomb and E. K. Wilson. Chicago: Aldine.

Shapley, D. 1972. Unionization: scientists, engineers mull over one alternative. *Science* 176:618–621.

Sharkansky, I. 1969. *The politics of taxing and spending.* Indianapolis: Bobbs-Merrill.

Sheingold, C. A. 1973. Social networks and voting: the resurrection of a research agenda. *American Sociological Review* 39:712–720.

Shepherd, C. R. 1964. *Small groups: some sociological perspectives.* San Francisco: Chandler.

Shepsle, K. A. 1978. *The giant jigsaw puzzle.* Chicago: University of Chicago Press.

Shils, E. A. 1951. The study of the primary group. In *The policy sciences,* ed. D. Lerner and H. D. Lasswell. Stanford, Calif.: Stanford University Press.

Shively, W. P. 1969. "Ecological" inference: the use of aggregate data to study individuals. *American Political Science Review* 63:1183–96.

Simmel, G. 1950. The phenomenon of outvoting. In *The sociology of Georg Simmel,* ed. K. H. Wolff. Glencoe, Ill.: Free Press.

Simon, H. A. 1954. Some strategic considerations in the construction of social science models. In *Mathematical thinking in the social sciences,* ed. P. F. Lazarsfeld. Glencoe, Ill.: Free Press.

———— 1957a. *Models of man.* New York: Wiley.

———— 1957b. *Administrative behavior: a study of decision-making processes in administrative organization.* New York: Macmillan. First published in 1947.

———— 1966. Political research: the decision-making framework. In *Varieties of political theory,* ed. D. Easton. Englewood Cliffs, N.J.: Prentice-Hall.

Singer, J. D. 1961. The level of analysis problem in international relations. *World Politics* 14:77–92.

———— ed. 1968. *Quantitative international politics: insights and evidence.* New York: Free Press.

Smigel, E. O. 1964. *The Wall Street lawyer.* New York: Free Press.

Specht, H. 1972. The deprofessionalization of social work. *Social work* 17:3–15.

Sprague, J. D. 1968. *Voting patterns of the United States Supreme Court.* Indianapolis: Bobbs-Merrill.

———— 1982. Is there a micro theory consistent with contextual analysis? In *Strategies of political inquiry,* ed. E. Ostrom. Beverly Hills, Calif.: Sage Publications.

Stevens, R. 1971. *American medicine and the public interest.* New Haven: Yale University Press.

Stewart, J. D. 1958. *British pressure groups.* Oxford: Oxford University Press.

Stoke, S. M. 1950. An inquiry into the concept of identification. *Journal of Genetic Psychology* 76:163–189.

Stokes, D. E. 1966. Analytic reduction in the study of institutions. Paper presented at the annual meeting of the American Political Science Association, New York, September 7–10, 1966.

Stone, W. J. 1976. *Representation in the United States House of Representatives.* Ph.D. diss., University of Michigan.

Stouffer, S. A. 1962. Some observations on study design. In *Social research to test ideas.* New York: Free Press.

Sundquist, J. L. 1969. *Making federalism work: a study of program coordination at the community level.* Washington, D.C.: Brookings Institution.

Tawney, R. H. 1920. *The acquisitive society.* New York: Harcourt, Brace.

———— 1929. *Equality.* New York: Harcourt, Brace.

Teich, A., ed. 1972. *Technology and man's future.* New York: St. Martin's Press.

Thibaut, J. W., and H. H. Kelley. 1959. *The social psychology of groups.* New York: Wiley.

Thoenes, P. 1966. *The elite in the welfare state.* New York: Free Press.

Thompson, V. A. 1961. *Modern organization.* New York: Knopf.

———— 1969. *Bureaucracy and innovation.* University: University of Alabama Press.

Thompson, W. R. 1965. *A preface to urban economics*. Baltimore: Johns Hopkins University Press.

Thomsen, A. 1941. Psychological projection and election. *Journal of Psychology* 2:115–117.

Tolman, E. C. 1951. A psychological model. In *Toward a general theory of action*, ed. T. Parsons and E. A. Shils. Cambridge, Mass.: Harvard University Press.

Toren, N. 1969. Semi-professionalism and social work. In *The semi-professions and their organization*, ed. A. Etzioni. New York: Free Press.

Truman, D. B. 1951. *The governmental process*. New York: Knopf.

——— 1955. The impact on political science of the revolution in the behavioral sciences. In *Research frontiers in politics and government*. Washington, D.C.: Brookings Institution.

Turner, J. 1951. *Party and constituency: pressures on Congress*. Baltimore: Johns Hopkins University Press.

Turner, J., and E. V. Schneier, Jr. 1970. *Party and constituency: pressures on Congress*. Rev. ed. Baltimore: Johns Hopkins University Press.

Vallier, I. 1971. Empirical comparisons of social structure: leads and lags. In *Comparative methods in sociology*, ed. I. Vallier. Berkeley: University of California Press.

Veblen, T. 1921. *The engineers and the price system*. New York: Viking.

Verba, S. 1961. *Small groups and political behavior—a study of leadership*. Princeton, N.J.: Princeton University Press.

——— 1971. Cross-national survey research: the problem of credibility. In *Comparative methods in sociology*, ed. I. Vallier. Berkeley: University of California Press.

Verba, S., and N. H. Nie. 1972. *Participation in America: political democracy and social equality*. New York: Harper & Row.

Vidich, A. J., and J. Bensman. 1960. *Small town in mass society*. Princeton, N.J.: Princeton University Press.

Volkart, E., ed. 1951. *Social behavior and personality: contributions of W. I. Thomas to theory and social research*. New York: Social Science Research Council.

Vollmer, H. M., and D. L. Mills. 1966. *Professionalization*. Englewood Cliffs, N.J.: Prentice-Hall.

Wahlke, J. C. 1970. Policy determinants and legislative decisions. In *Political decision-making*, ed. S. Ulmer. New York: Van Nostrand-Reinhold.

——— 1971. Policy demands and systems support: the role of the represented. *British Journal of Political Science* 1:271–290.

Wahlke, J. C., H. Eulau, W. Buchanan, and L. C. Ferguson. 1962. *The legislative system: explorations in legislative behavior*. New York: Wiley.

Weatherford, M. S. 1982. Interpersonal networks and political behavior. *American Journal of Political Science* 26:117–143.

Weber, M. 1946a. Politics as a vocation. In *From Max Weber: essays in sociology*, ed. H. H. Gerth and C. W. Mills. New York: Oxford University Press.

——— 1946b. Science as a vocation. In *From Max Weber: essays in sociology*, ed. H. H. Gerth and C. W. Mills. New York: Oxford University Press.

———— 1947. *The theory of social and economic organization.* New York: Oxford University Press.

Weinstein, F., and G. M. Platt. 1973. *Psychoanalytic sociology.* Baltimore: Johns Hopkins University Press.

Weiss, R. S. 1968. *Statistics in social research.* New York: Wiley.

Whyte, W. F. 1955. *Street corner society.* 2nd ed. Chicago: University of Chicago Press.

Whyte, W. H., Jr. 1956. *The organization man.* Garden City, N.Y.: Doubleday Anchor.

Wildavsky, A. 1964. *The politics of the budgetary process.* Boston: Little, Brown.

Wilensky, H. L. 1956. *Intellectuals in labor unions: organizational pressures on professional roles.* Glencoe, Ill.: Free Press.

———— 1964. The professionalization of everyone? *American Journal of Sociology* 70:142–146.

———— 1967. *Organizational intelligence: knowledge and policy in government and industry.* New York: Basic Books.

Wilensky, H. L., and C. N. Lebeaux. 1965. *Industrial society and social welfare.* New York: Free Press.

Williams, O. P. 1966. A framework for metropolitan political analysis. Paper presented at the Conference on Comparative Research in Community Politics, in Athens, Ga., November 16–19, 1966.

Williams, O. P., and C. R. Adrian. 1963. *Four cities: a study in comparative policy making.* Philadelphia: University of Pennsylvania Press.

Williams, O. P., H. Herman, C. S. Liebman, and T. R. Dye. 1965. *Suburban differences and metropolitan policies: a Philadelphia story.* Philadelphia: University of Pennsylvania Press.

Wilson, J. Q. 1961. The strategy of protest: problems of negro civic action. *Journal of Conflict Resolution* 3:291–303.

———— 1968. *Varieties of police behavior.* Cambridge, Mass.: Harvard University Press.

Wilson, L. 1963. Disjunctive processes in an academic milieu. In *Sociological theory, values, and sociocultural change,* ed. E. A. Tiryakian, New York: Free Press.

Wolfinger, R. E. 1971. Nondecisions and the study of local politics. *American Political Science Review* 65:1063–80.

Wood, R. C. 1964. Scientists and politics: the rise of an apolitical elite. In *Scientists and national policy-making,* ed. R. Gilpin and C. Wright. New York: Columbia University Press.

Wright, G. C. 1976. Community structure and voting in the south. *Public Opinion Quarterly* 40:201–215.

———— 1977. Contextual models of electoral behavior: the southern Wallace vote. *American Political Science Review* 71:497–508.

Young, M. 1961. *The rise of the meritocracy, 1870–2033.* London: Penguin Books.

Zeigler, H. 1966. *The political world of the high school teacher.* Eugene, Oreg.: Center for Advanced Study of Educational Administration.

———— 1967. *The political life of American teachers.* Englewood Cliffs, N.J.: Prentice-Hall.

Zeigler, L. H., M. K. Jennings, with G. W. Peak. 1974. *Governing American schools.* No. Scituate, Mass.: Duxbury Press.

Zisk, B. H. 1973. *Local interest politics: a one-way street.* Indianapolis: Bobbs-Merrill.

Credits

Chapter 1 is abridged from *The Behavioral Persuasion in Politics* (New York: Random House, 1963). Dedicated to "Harold D. Lasswell, Persuader," the book reflected the contents of three undergraduate courses offered annually at Stanford University between 1958 and 1961. Copyright held by Heinz Eulau.

Chapter 2 was first published in my *Micro-Macro Political Analysis: Accents of Inquiry* (Chicago: Aldine Publishing Company, 1969). The book was dedicated to Samuel J. Eldersveld, Robert E. Lane, Dwaine Marvick, Herbert McClosky, Warren E. Miller, and John C. Wahlke, "workmen all who within a standard deviation or two traveled the same road." Copyright held by Heinz Eulau.

Chapter 3 was written for a symposium, *Political Scientists at Work*, edited by Oliver Walter (No. Scituate, Mass.: Duxbury Press, 1971), where it appeared under the title "The Legislative System and After: On Closing the Micro-Macro Gap." It is reprinted here by permission of the editor and copyright holder, Oliver Walter.

Chapter 4 appeared in *American Behavioral Scientist*, vol. 21, pp. 39–62 (September–October, 1977). It is reprinted here, in somewhat abridged form, by permission of Sage Publications, Inc., the copyright holder (© 1977). The essay was excerpted from a much longer paper, "Some Aspects of Analysis, Measurement and Sampling in the Transformation of Micro- and Macro-level Unit Properties," prepared for a National Science Foundation conference held at Lake Lawn Lodge, Delevan, Wis., May 13–15, 1974.

Chapter 5 is abridged from my *Class and Party in the Eisenhower Years* (New York: Free Press, 1962). It is reprinted by permission of Free Press. Dedicated to my friend Everett K. Wilson, sociologist at the University of North Carolina, the book made use of data from the 1952 and 1956 national election studies of the Survey Research Center, University of Michigan. The analysis was begun in the summer of 1954, in connection with the Seminar on Political Behavior sponsored by the Committee on Political Behavior of the Social Science Research Council. Robert E. Agger, Robert E. Lane, and Warren E. Miller were particularly stimulating colleagues in the seminar. The writing of the monograph was much aided by a fellowship at the Center for Advanced Studies in the Behavioral Sciences during 1957–58. For review of the final manuscript I was indebted, as put at the time, "to my good friends Samuel J. Eldersveld and Morris Janowitz for reading parts of the manuscript and making valuable suggestions—for which, counter to etiquette, I am perfectly willing to hold them responsible."

Chapter 6 draws on sections of *The Legislative System: Explorations in Legislative Behavior* (New York: John Wiley and Sons, 1962), written with John C. Wahlke, William Buchanan, and Leroy C. Ferguson. The material reprinted here is by permission of the copyright holder, John C. Wahlke. The sections abridged here were all originally drafted by me, as indicated in the book, except for the section on pressure-group roles that was drafted by Wahlke, who kindly permitted me to use it in this chapter. The book was the final product of the State Legislative Research Project, sponsored and supported by the Social Science Research Council's Committee on Political Behavior. Many persons and institutions were helpful in the project, begun in 1955. I cannot possibly acknowledge them all here. My own particular and direct thanks are to Stanley Newman (now an anthropologist), Peter Orleans (now a sociologist), and Suzanne Berger (now a political scientist), who, as undergraduate students at Antioch College, conducted many interviews in the Ohio legislature.

Chapter 7 is drawn from *Lawyers in Politics: A Study in Professional Convergence*, written with John D. Sprague (Indianapolis: Bobbs-Merrill, 1964). The chapter is reprinted by permission of the publisher and copyright holder, Bobbs-Merrill Educational Publishing, Indianapolis. The original manuscript benefited from careful criticism and useful comment by Robert E. Agger, William Buchanan, Richard Fagen, Howard Sachs, Martin Shapiro, Joseph A. Schlesinger, John C. Wahlke, and Everett K. Wilson. My main debt is, of course, to John Sprague, who, in this enterprise as in several others through the years, proved to be an indefatigable and exciting colleague.

Chapter 8 was first published in *Publius: The Journal of Federalism*, vol. 3, pp. 153–171 (Fall 1973). It is reprinted by permission of the Center for the Study of Federalism, Temple University. A prior version of the essay was presented at the Sugarloaf Conference, Temple University, April 23–25, 1972.

Chapter 9 is reprinted, by permission of the publisher, from the *Journal of Politics*, vol. 30, pp. 3–24 (February 1968), where it appeared under the title "The Maddening Methods of Harold D. Lasswell: Some Philosophical Underpinnings." The original article has been slightly cut. I am indebted to Arnold A. Rogow, who stimulated the essay and subsequently included it in his *Politics, Personality, and Social Science in the Twentieth Century: Essays in Honor of Harold D. Lasswell* (Chicago: University of Chicago Press, 1969).

Chapter 10 was first published in the *Midwest Journal of Political Science*, vol. 13, pp. 341–366 (August 1969) and is reprinted by permission of the University of Texas Press. The larger project from which the data were drawn was known as the City Council Research Project, which I directed between 1962 and 1972 at the Institute of Political Studies, Stanford University, and which was funded by the National Science Foundation. Malcolm E. Jewell, then editor of the *MJPS*, made valuable suggestions for revision of the original manuscript, for which I remain grateful.

Chapter 11 is reprinted, by permission of the American Political Science Association, from the *American Political Science Review,* vol. 63, pp. 427–441 (June 1969). It was written with Kenneth Prewitt, who, as associate director, was for many years the "most significant other" in the City Council Research Project. Gabriel A. Almond, then director of the Stanford Institute of Political Studies, gave the project sympathetic support throughout.

Chapter 12 was written with Lawrence S. Rothenberg. It has not been previously published. The study was made possible by the inclusion of relevant survey questions in the September wave of the 1980 National Election Study, conducted by the Center for Political Studies, University of Michigan, and funded by the National Science Foundation. The data were obtained through the Inter-University Consortium for Political and Social Research. I am indebted to the Board of Overseers of NES and the study's director, Warren E. Miller, for making it possible to include the questions in the survey instrument.

Chapter 13 first appeared under the title "Harold D. Lasswell's Developmental Analysis" in the *Western Political Quarterly,* vol. 11, pp. 229–242 (June 1958). It is reprinted by permission of the journal.

Chapter 14 was written with Robert Eyestone, then an associate of the City Council Research Project. It is reprinted here in slightly changed form, by permission of the American Political Science Association, from the *American Political Science Review,* vol. 62, pp. 124–143 (March 1968).

Chapter 15 is reprinted, with the publisher's permission, from J. A. Laponce and P. Smoker, eds., *Experimentation and Simulation in Political Science* (Toronto: University of Toronto Press, 1972), where it appeared under the title "Policymaking in American Cities: Comparisons in a Quasi-longitudinal, Quasi-experimental Design." The study was prepared for the Roundtable Conference on Experimentation and Simulation, sponsored by the International Political Science Association and held in Vancouver, Canada, in March 1970.

Chapter 16 was written with Paul D. Karps. It first appeared in H. Eulau and J. C. Wahlke, eds., *The Politics of Representation* (Beverly Hills, Calif.: Sage Publications, 1978). It is reprinted by permission of Sage Publications, Inc. (© 1978). The study was initially presented at the annual meeting of the American Political Science Association in Washington, D.C., in September 1977. The data used in the study, collected in 1956, 1958, and 1960 by the Survey Research Center, University of Michigan, were made available through the Inter-University Consortium for Political and Social Research.

Chapter 17 is reprinted by permission of the publishers, Lieber-Atherton, Inc., from C. J. Friedrich, ed., *Rational Decision* (New York; Atherton, 1964). My gratitude is to Martin Shapiro, Richard A. Brody, Kenneth Prewitt, and John D. Sprague for comment that cleared up several confusions.

Chapter 18 was written for a symposium, "Political Decision-Making: Interdisciplinary Developments from a Microanalytic Perspective," organized by Samuel A. Kirkpatrick. The original title was "Problematics of Decisional Models in Political Contexts." The essay was published in *American Behavioral Scientist,* vol. 20, pp. 127–144 (September–October 1976). It is reprinted, in part, by permission of Sage Publications, Inc., the copyright holder (© 1976).

Chapter 19 was written with Paul D. Karps. It is reprinted, with permission, from *Legislative Studies Quarterly,* vol. 2, pp. 233–254 (August 1977). The original title was "The Puzzle of Representation: Specifying Components of Responsiveness." A previous version of the essay was presented at the annual meeting of the Western Political Science Association, March 31–April 2, 1977.

Chapter 20 was my presidential address before the annual meeting of the American Political Science Association in Washington, D.C., September 7, 1972. It is reprinted, with the permission of the association, from the *American Political Science Review,* vol. 67, pp. 169–191 (March 1973). The research for the studies on which the address was based was made possible by several grants from the National Institute of Mental Health.

Index

Abell, P., 124
Accountability, 284
Action sets, 301
Action units, 6, 13, 109–111
Activity environment, 310
Adaptive policies, 343
Affect, 50–51, 267–268, 274–275, 317–318
Aggregate data, 12, 69–70, 107–108, 259, 280, 290, 301, 304, 322, 457
Aggregates and wholes, 247–251
Allocation responsiveness, 15, 460, 463–464
Almond, G. A., 78, 112, 123, 124
Analogy, reasoning by, 78–79
Ancestral unanimity, 428–429, 433, 436
Attitudes and opinions, 54–57, 157, 165, 169; legislators' perceptions of constituency's, 399–400, 403–404, 409–410, 412, 453, 454
Authority relations, 58, 207–208

Bailey, S. K., 179
Barber, B., 137
Bargained unanimity, 430, 434
Behavior, 2–3, 6, 81, 94, 253, 370; political, 19–75, 152–153; legislative, 24, 38, 179–204; reference group behavior, 40; social, 49; and personality, 60; individual and collective, 77–78, 80; national behavior, 92–93; and class, 129–130, 135, 150, 152, 158–175; and party, 135, 152–153; perceptual aspects of, 142–157; role behavior, 142–175; and neighborhood primary zone, 315–323
Belief systems, 50–51

Bell, D., 472
Beloff, M., 223
Binkley, W. E., 182
Blalock, H. M., 108, 120–121
Blau, P., 108
Blecher, E. M., 495–496
Blocked situations, 401–413
Broker role orientation, 183
Bureaucracy, 13, 15, 27, 60, 483, 484
Burke, E., 134, 184, 185, 277

Career perspective, 9
Cartwright, D. S., 124
Case work, 462–463
Causal analysis, 5, 12, 367–391, 453, 458–459, 468
Centers, R., 139
Choices, political, 14, 26
City councils, 7, 11; decisional structure of, 260–276; as political matrix, 280–299; policy maps and outcomes of, 349–365
Class, 3–4, 41, 43, 45, 480; and party, 129–178; polarization between classes, 131, 133, 157; as role system, 136–137; index of, 138–139; identification, 139–158, 176; and attention to mass media, 153; awareness, 158–175, 177–178
Clique-dominated groups, 102
Cohen, M. R., 8, 9, 233
Cohesion, 100
Collective action, 77–78
Collectivists, 2
Collectivities, 4, 23, 24, 93, 109, 110, 115

Committees and subcommittees, 89, 91, 119, 464
Community support of governing body, 280, 287–289, 295–298
Comparative analysis, 107–125
Competition, 28
Complexity, 59, 64, 114–115, 283
Concurrence, 458, 459, 461
Configurative analysis, 9, 241–257
Conflict, 263, 268, 271, 272, 401–413, 417–418; and legislative role structure, 179–181, 201–204
Congruence, 59–61, 399–400, 453–454, 457–461
Constraint, 266–267, 271
Construction, 86–89, 93–94, 97
Consultative commonwealth, 15, 470–500
Contextual analysis, 9–10, 45–53, 103–104, 105, 109–110, 253–256, 300–323, 393–394, 446
Control policies, 343
Convergence, 5, 207–221
Correlational analysis, 393
Cosponsorship, 270–276
Crane, W., Jr., 431
Cross-pressure, 39–40
Cross-sectional studies, 70–71
Cultural analysis, 26, 34–35, 45–46, 253; patterns, 46–48; orientations, 48–51; political culture, 51–53; subcultures, 52–53

Dahl, R. A., 78–79, 114, 284
Darwin, C., 331
Data transformation, 95–96, 103–106, 111–113, 116, 118, 120–125
De Grazia, A., 183
Decision-making, 11–15, 25, 80, 98, 327–330; by small groups, 6, 258–276; unanimity in, 14, 417–438; and class, 136; by legislatures, 180–181, 260–261; by city councils, 260–276; informal-consensual, 422, 428; formal-ministerial, 422–423, 428; political, 423–424, 428, 439–451; predecisional and postdecisional phases, 445; nondecisions, 446
Decision units, 109, 110
Decisional structures, 7, 260–276
Delegate role orientation, 186–187
Demands, 142–143, 145, 147, 159, 176, 424
Depth analysis, 55

Descriptive attributes, 98
Developmental analysis, 9, 11, 71–72, 254, 329–339; of policy maps and outcomes, 340–365
Developmental constructs, 11, 15, 72, 329–339
Discrete data, 69
Dissonant situations, 401–413
Distributive properties, 99–100, 103–105
Dogan, M., 117
Drinker, H. S., 219
Dual federalism, 224, 227, 235
Dualism, 2, 3, 5, 8–9, 95, 242–246; false, 2, 4, 7, 109, 450
Durkheim, E., 471
Dyads, 8, 82, 301

Easton, D., 1, 132, 367, 368, 465
Ecological correlations, 122
Ecological fallacy, 80
Economic theory, 30–31, 90
Edelman, M., 465
Elazar, D. J., 224–225
Elections, as sanctioning mechanism, 279–280, 284–288, 296–297, 454
Emergence, 11, 244–256, 281, 298; representation as emergent property, 392–414
Empirical research, 3, 8, 22, 29–32, 67, 91, 111–112, 185, 331
Environment, 110, 300–301, 342–343, 350, 362, 369–372, 382; social, 10, 103–104, 301, 305–306, 310, 369, 371; physical, 103, 104, 371; activity, 310; policy environment, 371–372, 376–378, 381–385, 388–389
Epstein, C. F., 487
Equilibrium analysis, 331, 334, 339
Ethics, 73, 216–218
Ethnic groups, 131
Ethos, 101
Eulau, H., 112, 450, 455–457, 461, 463
Event manifold, 242–244, 248, 250, 256
Expectations, 35–36, 49, 58, 143, 147, 149–150, 158–159, 176, 327–328, 424
Experimental replication, 65–66
Expertise, 269–270, 274
External relations, 98

Facilitator role orientation, 190
False dualism, 2, 4, 7, 109, 450

False unanimity, 429–430, 434
Federalism, representational, 7, 8, 10, 222–237
Federalist, The, 222–224, 226–237
Feierabend, I. K., 112
Feierabend, R. L., 112
Fenno, R. F., Jr., 14–15, 88, 464–466
Field theory, 8
Fiorina, M. P., 463, 464, 467, 468, 469
Formal-ministerial decision-handling, 422–423, 428
Fragmentation, 263–265, 271, 273
Freud, S., 139
Frey, F. W., 111–114
Friedrich, C. J., 232
Function, 5, 13
Functional rationality, 14
Functional unanimity, 431–432, 434–435

Game, politics as, 46–47, 218
Geertz, C., 16
Generalized other, 9
Geographic areas, 188–189, 198, 300–301
Gerth, H., 137
Gierke, O., 419
Gilb, C. L., 472
Goal formulation, 281–282, 299, 327–328, 334, 369, 372
Goal thinking, 335
Gold, D., 205
Gordon, M. M., 136
Government expenses, 343, 351, 353, 388
Grodzins, M., 8, 224, 225
Group analysis, 6, 37–41, 52, 76–77, 80–83
Group-influence model, 179–180
Group interest, 14
Group norms, 101

Harmony, 263, 268, 271–272, 274
Harrington, M., 490–491
Haug, M. R., 493–494
Hegelian dialectic, 8, 233
Higher-order units, 110–111, 246–247, 253
Hofstadter, R., 214
Holsti, O. R., 445, 447, 449
House of Representatives, 226–231, 233; role structures, 193–198, 201–203
Hughes, E. C., 9, 16, 479, 481, 486, 492
Hyman, 217
Hyneman, C. S., 285

Hypothetical longitudinal analysis, 380–384

Idealism, 245
Identification, 57–58
Image, 49
Imputation, 88–89
Independence of professionals, 214–216
Individual analysis, 2–4, 6, 23–24, 81, 83, 93, 109, 115
Individual interest, 14
Individual-level data, 12, 107, 108, 301, 304, 457
Individual-society dualism, 242–246
Inference, 79–82, 116–117, 124–125
Informal-consensual decision-handling, 422, 428
Informant data, 97, 105
Injunctive unanimity, 432, 435
Institutional analysis, 3, 5, 24–25, 76–77, 80
Integral properties, 98–99, 101, 103–105, 118, 120
Integration, 263–265, 271–273
Interest, 14, 44
Interest articulation, 424–433
Interest groups, 189–190, 196
Interest orientation, 165, 169, 171, 172, 173, 175
Interpersonal relations, 24, 100–101, 301, 304, 322
Inventor role orientation, 183
Isomorphic analysis, 207, 208, 209, 211, 213, 220

Jennings, M. K., 463

Key, V. O., Jr., 131
Kirchheimer, O., 219
Kirkpatrick, S. A., 447, 451
Knowledge, 333–334
Kuklinski, J. H., 10

Laski, H. J., 225
Lasswell, H. D., 1, 8–9, 11, 15, 142–143, 241–257, 327–339, 440, 465, 471
Lawyers, 5, 205–221
Lazarsfeld, P. F., 6, 115, 122, 443, 444
Legislative behavior, 24, 38, 179–204
Legislators, 4, 13, 110; relationship with constituency, 15, 215–216, 279, 281–289,

Legislators (*cont.*)
293, 296–298, 392, 399–400, 403–404,
409–410, 412, 452–461; role orientations
of, 181–204; as professionals, 213–221;
perceptions of constituency attitudes,
396, 409–410, 412, 413–414, 453, 454
Legislatures, 91, 97; decision-making by,
13–14, 180–181, 260–261, 417–438; policy-making by, 179–204, 369–372; collateral, 229–230; decisional structures, 260–
261
Leoni, B., 439
Levels of analysis, 6, 8, 25–28, 76–91, 94–
95, 248–250, 254–255, 448–450; multilevel analysis, 84–89, 96, 107–125, 252–
253
Levels of organization, 246–247
Lewin, K., 9
Life space, 9–10, 300–323
Linguistic analysis, 456, 458
Lipsky, M., 491, 494
Loewenberg, G., 457
Longitudinal analysis, 12, 70–71
Lower-order units, 110, 111, 246, 247, 253
Lupsha, P., 268

MacIver, R. M., 132
Macridis, R. C., 180
Madison, J., 130, 132, 224
Manifold of events, 242–244, 248, 250, 256
Mannheim, K., 14
March, J. G., 443
Marshall, T. H., 491
Marx, K., 8, 129, 331
Mass media, 153
Materialism, 245
Matrix, political, 277–299
Matthews, D. R., 444–445
Mead, G. H., 8–9, 158–159
Meanings, 49, 64
Menzel, H., 115, 122
Merriam, C. E., 465
Merton, R., 109
Michels, R., 487–488
Micro-macro analysis, 3, 5, 11, 67–69, 89–
91, 94, 106, 113–117, 119, 249–252, 450
Miller, W. E., 12
Miller-Stokes American Representation
Study, 392–414, 452–455, 458, 460
Mills, C. W., 137, 214

Mirror representation, 281
Mitchell, W. C., 217
Moore, W. E., 488, 492, 499
Mosher, F. C., 471–472
Municipal policy-makers, 340–365

National behavior, 92–93
National character, 58
National Election Study, 10, 300–324
Neighborhood primary zone, 10, 301, 305–
324
Network analysis, 4, 8–10, 300–323; of rep-
resentational federalism, 7, 8, 10, 222–
237; of legislative roles, 179–198
Neutral role orientation, 190
Nie, N. H., 458–459
Normative expectations, 35–36
Normative orientations, 50

Observational standpoint, 64–65, 68, 336–
338
Opinion leadership, 265, 270–276
Opinions and attitudes, 54–57, 157, 165,
169; legislators' perceptions of constituency's, 399–400, 403–404, 409–410, 412,
453, 454
Oppositional activity, 270–276
Ordeshook, P. C., 449
Organizational analysis, 13, 98, 102, 246–
247, 258–276; professionals' relationship
with organizations, 214, 482–486

Panel studies, 11, 70–71
Parsons, T., 4, 8–9, 113, 152, 157, 208,
212, 214, 219, 339, 484, 486, 489
Participation in politics, 150, 152–153
Party, 3–4; and social network, 9–10, 300–
323; and class, 129–178; as role system,
134–135; identification, 138, 143, 145,
147, 315–317; perception of, 142–157,
160, 161–165, 169, 172–173, 175, 177–
178; and class identification, 153, 157,
176; and role taking, 159; and class
awareness, 160–161, 164–165, 169, 171–
173, 175, 177–178; cohesion, 431
Pattern variables, 9
Patterson, S. C., 457
Perceptions: of problems and policy, 66–
67, 353–358, 372, 376, 378, 385–386,
388–389; of political parties, 142–157,

Perceptions (*cont.*)
    160, 161–165, 169, 172–173, 175, 177–
    178; of class, 160–161, 164–165, 169,
    171–173, 175, 177–178; of constituency
    attitudes, 396, 409–410, 412, 413–414,
    453, 454
Permissiveness, 266–267, 271–273
Personality, 26–28, 34, 53–67; and values,
    57–59; and role, 59–67
Perspective, political, 142–143, 147, 150,
    157, 176
Pervasive situations, 401–413
Physical environment, 103, 104, 371
Pitkin, H. F., 12, 277, 279, 281, 399, 456–
    459, 461
Polar federalism, 235
Polarity principle, 8–9, 233–236
Policy analysis, 11, 98, 342; design for com-
    parative, 367–391
Policy congruence, 399–400
Policy development model, 11–12, 343–347
Policy environment, 371–372, 376–378,
    381–385, 388–389
Policy-making, 179–204, 369–372
Policy maps and outcomes, 11–12, 340–
    365, 367, 371, 385
Policy responsiveness, 15, 460–462
Policy science, 74, 334–336
Political decision-handling, 423–424, 428,
    439–451
Politico role orientation, 187–188
Power, 31, 136
Pragmaticism, 8
Prediction, 5, 12, 223, 255–257, 332, 337,
    473
Pressure politics, 189–190, 196, 282, 298
Prewitt, K., 112, 450, 457, 463
Primary group, 311
Pritchett, C. H., 431–432
Private occupation, 5
Probability models, 66, 329, 332
Probability thinking, 335
Problem-solving approach, 256
Professions, 5, 15–16, 205–221, 470–500;
    convergence of, 207–221; public service
    as, 213, 218–220, 488–496, 498; politi-
    cians as professionals, 213–221; relation-
    ship with organizations, 214, 482–486;
    independence of, 214–216; relationship
    with clients, 214–216, 479–482, 485–486,

491–496, 498–499; code of ethics, 216–
    218; professionalization and deprofes-
    sionalization, 475–478, 484–485; relation-
    ship with colleagues, 486–488, 492;
    relationship with society, 488–491, 496
Projected unanimity, 430–431, 434–435
Projective thinking, 332–335, 337
Propositions, testing of, 92–94
Przeworski, A., 111–112, 120
Psychological variables, 6, 40, 55, 99, 122,
    241, 245–246, 301, 336–337; of identifica-
    tion, 139–140, 158
Public profession, 5
Public service, 213, 218–220

Quasi-experimental analysis, 12
Quasi-longitudinal analysis, 12, 384–391

Random panel design, 373
Rational choice analysis, 6, 14–15, 30–31,
    417–438
Recruitment of public officials, 280, 289–
    297, 454
Reduction, 28, 85–89, 92–95, 97, 111–112,
    123–124, 252
Reference group, 40–41, 80
Relational properties, 96, 100–101, 104,
    105, 260
Relationships: social network analysis of,
    9–10, 300–323; of legislators with constit-
    uency, 15, 215–216, 279, 281–289, 293,
    296–298, 392, 399–400, 403 404, 409–
    410, 412, 452–461; among legislators,
    260–261; representation as, 277–279,
    281–283, 455–456; of professionals with
    clients, 479–482, 485–486, 491–496, 498–
    499; of professionals with organizations,
    482–486; among professionals, 486–488,
    492; of professionals with society, 488–
    491, 496
Religious groups, 131
Representation, 15, 184–185, 277–299,
    466–467; as relationship, 277–279, 281–
    283, 455–456; as response, 281–289; as
    emergent property, 392–414; Miller-
    Stokes American Representation Study,
    392–414, 452–455, 458, 460
Representational federalism, 7–8, 10, 222–
    237
Representational roles, 183–188

Representational situations, 12, 393–400
Resister role orientation, 190
Resource capabilities, 347–348, 351, 353
Respect, 267–268, 275
Respondent data, 97
Responsiveness, 15, 281, 282–289, 293, 296–298, 400, 403; components of, 452, 460–469; as congruence, 457–461
Retirement, from elected office, 285, 291
Riesman, D., 133
Riker, W. H., 449
Riley, M. W., 122
Ritualist role orientation, 182
Rokkan, S., 117
Role analysis, 4–6, 8, 33–37, 68, 80; and group analysis, 38, 39–40; and personality, 59–67; ideal-type network of legislative roles, 191–193, 196–198
Role behavior: and class identification, 142–157; and class awareness, 158–175
Role conflict, 36–37, 39–40, 61
Role orientations, 157; and class identification, 153; legislative, 181–204; ritualist, 182; tribune, 182; broker, 183; inventor, 183; representational, 183–188; trustee, 185–187; delegate, 186–187; politico, 187–188; and geographic areas, 188–189, 198; and pressure groups, 190; facilitators, 190; neutrals, 190; resisters, 190; typology of structures, 193–204; of lawyers, 207
Role potential, identification as, 138–142
Role system, 3–4; party as, 134–135; class as, 136–137
Rourke, F. E., 483

Salisbury, R. H., 368
Sampling, 66, 71, 78
Scarrow, H. A., 114
Schattschneider, E. E., 134
Schein, E. H., 495
Scheuch, E. K., 109, 115
Schlesinger, J., 284
Scientific knowledge, 471, 476
Scientific thinking, 328, 331, 335
Self-consciousness, 44, 336–338
Senate, 226–227, 231; role structures, 198–203
Service responsiveness, 15, 460, 462–463
Sheatsley, P. B., 217

Shepsle, K. A., 14
Shils, E. A., 152, 157
Simmel, G., 8, 419
Simon, H. A., 13, 434, 442, 447
Simultaneity, of individual and collective behavior, 77–78, 80
Singer, J. D., 6, 84
Situational analysis, 12, 254
Situations, representational, 393–404
Skill revolution, 470–500
Smith, T. V., 465
Social context, 9–10, 103–104, 110, 300–323, 446
Social environment, 10, 103–104, 301, 305–306, 310, 369, 371
Social mobility, 45, 131
Social networks, 4, 8–10, 300–323
Social pluralism, 279–280, 283–284, 297
Social process, 303–306
Social relations, 26–27, 33–45, 158–159
Socialization, 58, 206
Socioeconomic status. See Class
Sociometry, 7, 10, 101, 260
Spencer, H., 2
Sponsorship, 290–294, 295, 297–298
Sprague, J. D., 304–305, 322
Status, 41–43, 456, 480
Stimson, J. A., 444–445
Stoke, S. M., 152
Stokes, D. E., 2–3, 12, 123
Stouffer, S. A., 368
Stratification, 41–45, 137, 487
Structural properties, 94, 96, 101–105, 108, 118, 260
Sundquist, J. L., 225
Survey analysis, 55, 56, 66, 93, 108, 277, 301, 304
Sussman, M. B., 493–494
Symbolic responsiveness, 460, 465, 466
System analysis, 68, 251

Tawney, R. H., 158
Tension, 100
Teune, H., 111–112, 120
Theorizing activity, 28–32, 71
Thomas, W. I., 159
Time-series analysis, 11–12, 69–72
Tolman, E. C., 140
Topological psychology, 140

Transformation of unit data, 95–96, 103–106, 111–113, 116, 118, 120–125
Trend analysis, 330, 331
Trend thinking, 328, 335
Tribune role orientation, 182
Truman, D. B., 430
Trustee role orientation, 185–187
Tufte, E. R., 114

Unanimity, 14, 417–438; ancestral, 428–429, 433, 436; false, 429–430, 434; bargained, 430, 434; projected, 430–431, 434–435; functional, 431–432, 434–435; injunctive, 432, 435
Unit properties, 96–104, 115, 117
Units of analysis, 10, 23–25, 70, 76–95, 109–110, 117–118, 448–450; object and subject, 83–84, 87–89, 120–121, 259–260, 393; in policy outcomes, 349–350

Urbanization, 131, 340, 376–378, 381–385, 388–389

Vallier, I., 107–108, 116
Values, 73–74, 132–133, 136, 327–328, 334; and personality, 57–59; internationalization of, 152, 157
Vector analysis, 179
Verba, S., 6, 78, 112–113, 123–124, 258, 458–459
Vote intention and vote choice, 318–323, 443–444

Wahlke, J. C., 77, 440, 455–457, 465–466
Weber, M., 15, 206, 219, 418, 483
Whitehead, A. N., 242, 244, 256
Whole system analysis, 107–109
Wholes and aggregates, 247–251

Zeigler, H., 463